Language

THE SOCIAL MIRROR

FOURTH EDITION

Elaine Chaika

HEINLE
CENGAGE Learning™

Australia • Brazil • Japan • Korea • Mexico • Singapore • Spain • United Kingdom • United States

HEINLE
CENGAGE Learning

Language: The Social Mirror, Fourth Edition
Elaine Chaika

Editorial Director: Joe Dougherty

Publisher: Sherrise Roehr

VP, Director of Content Development: Anita Raducanu

Acquisitions Editor: Tom Jefferies

Executive Marketing Manager: Jim McDonough

Senior Field Marketing Manager: Donna Lee Kennedy

Product Marketing Manager: Katie Kelley

Senior Print Buyer: Betsey Donaghey

Design and Production Management: Steven Siebert

For product information and technology assistance, contact us at **Cengage Learning Customer & Sales Support, 1-800-354-9706**

For permission to use material from this text or product, submit all requests online at **www.cengage.com/permissions** Further permissions questions can be emailed to **permissionrequest@cengage.com**

ISBN-13: 978-1-4240-0432-4

ISBN-10: 1-4240-0432-2

Heinle
20 Channel Center Street
Boston, MA 02210
USA

Cengage Learning is a leading provider of customized learning solutions with office locations around the globe, including Singapore, the United Kingdom, Australia, Mexico, Brazil, and Japan. Locate your local office at **www.cengage.com/global**

Cengage Learning products are represented in Canada by Nelson Education, Ltd.

Visit Heinle online at **elt.heinle.com**

Visit our corporate website at **www.cengage.com**

Printed in the United States of America
3 4 5 6 7   25 24 23 22 21

To Bill, Skeezix, and Scamp

Table of Contents

TABLE OF CONTENTS

TABLE OF CONTENTS

TABLE OF CONTENTS

Disclaimer

This book is about the ways people use language in their social lives. Unfortunately, this can entail their use of taboo words, words which make many people feel disgusted, annoyed, and angry. Where such words have been elicited in solid studies of language use, and where they illuminate human behavior, I have included them here. I do not advocate their usage, nor do I think they are funny, titillating, or even interesting beyond what they reveal about certain speakers. Such words were unavoidable in Chapters 6 and 10. I am sorry about that, but they are part of the sociology of language.

Acknowledgments

Thanks are due to Janice Schuster, Norman Desmairis, Maureen Zeman, Ed Bailey, and the entire staff of the Providence College Library staff. Without their generous help, this book couldn't have been completed within four months, nor would it have been so rich in current scholarship. Thanks are also due to Teresia R. Ostrach, whose careful reading and pointed comments improved the entire. Without Steven Siebert's attention to detail and unflagging efforts in creating camera-ready copy, this would have been a far worse manuscript. The technical support persons at Nota Bene must also be lauded for their prompt help with the delightful intricacies of the program. Steven and Jeff and everybody else who created Nota Bene deserve thanks from all scholars everywhere.

Introduction

In a sense, every discipline asks and tries to answer questions. The sociology of language asks questions about our most basic human behavior, talking.

Have you ever wanted desperately to voice an opinion but had the words "stick in your throat"? Have you ever had the opposite experience of being compelled to speak when you didn't want to? Do you sometimes find yourself forcing "small talk" with someone you either don't know or don't much care for? Are there people who never seem to leave you room to "put your two cents in"? And others whom you feel you have to drag every word out of? Do members of some ethnic groups seem pushy to you, and others seem cold?

Has anyone ever accused you of having an accent? Do you notice that other people have accents? Is there one correct accent? What makes some grammar bad and other grammar good? How come there are different accents at all, especially since we all watch the same TV shows and go to the same movies? Are accents disappearing as more and more Americans migrate from their home states?

Why have some immigrant groups lost the languages that their forebears spoke, whereas others have retained the languages of theirs? Should English be made the official language of the United States?

Do you ever feel uncomfortable talking to people from cultures different from your own? Do they seem to stare too much or, conversely, never to look you in the eye? Have you ever noticed how some people smile too much, and others are stony-faced? Why is it that you always seem to be talking at cross-purposes with some people, whereas with others you find yourself right "in tune"? Do women and men really speak different languages?

These are the kinds of questions that interest people who study the sociology of language, the field also known as **sociolinguistics**. The reason that these are answerable in terms of sociology is that differences in speaking practices can most often be correlated with the practices of socially defined groups within a society or across societies. There are regional, ethnic, social class, occupational, and even age differences in modes of speaking, and there is no way to understand members of any society without understanding these differences. In fact, we find that every social

INTRODUCTION

division within a society relates to some facet of speech, or, to put it another way, when people identify with each other socially, their speech will reflect that identification.

Speech here refers to the entire complex of language: regional and social accents, social conditions under which one feels one can speak or even that one must. In contrast, under different conditions, one feels one must be silent. Every aspect of the speech situation is pertinent, affecting body motion, facial expression, tone of voice, the amount of personal space one maintains, one's choice of vocabulary items, even the grammar one chooses.

There is another side to communication as well. Not only do we use sociolinguistic rules to produce speech, but we also use them to make judgments about other people, and they, of course, judge us by the way we speak. In fact, much of what we understand people to be saying, the actual meaning that we retrieve, is governed by our sociolinguistic rules and the social situation itself. Comprehension is not just a matter of understanding the words a speaker uses.

It is not too much to say that without an understanding of ordinary speech practices, we cannot understand any society. Teachers, psychiatrists, social workers, lawyers, physicians all need to understand the variation in communication practices among the people they deal with. Much of this book will show that without such knowledge, these professionals are hampered in doing their work effectively.

This book will demonstrate that language structure and language use at any given time, and language change over time, reflect the social conditions within a society. Language and society are so intertwined that it is impossible to understand one without the other.

There is no human society that does not depend upon, is not shaped by, and does not itself shape language. Every social institution is maintained by language. Law, religion, government, education, and the family are all set in place and carried out with language. We use language to reveal or conceal our personal identities, our characters, and our background, often wholly unconscious that we are doing so. Almost all of our contact with family and friends and much of our contact with strangers involves speaking. And, much of that speaking is strongly governed by rules, rules that dictate not only what we should say but also how we say it. We manipulate others with language, and they manipulate us, often without either party being at all aware of the manipulation.

The sociolinguist is concerned with the stuff of everyday life: how people talk with their friends, families, and teachers as well as storekeepers, doctors, and enemies. Sociolinguistics is concerned with apparently trivial matters, with the talk on street corners and in bars as well as in the classroom or on the stage. Such seemingly trivial behaviors actually are the most ubiquitous and powerful regulators of society. The most rebellious of people obey the language dicta of their societies or risk being deemed insane or incorrigible. We don't think about how our speech is regulated. Nor do we think about who regulates it. As we shall see, to a large degree we regulate our own speech in accordance with how we wish to be perceived by others, but we regulate it in terms of what we know about the speech behaviors expected by the social group we belong to. Yet, we are typically unaware that we have such knowledge or that it affects our behavior in countless interactions every hour, every day, every lifetime. Think of how often and when you say "so anyway" or "well" before you make a statement, how often you pause and say "like," or whether or not you look people "in the eye" as they talk, or if it's true that you talk a lot if you're a woman and talk less if you're a man. Sociolinguists even study matters such as where people choose to sit in a cafeteria or at a meeting, or the amount of space they want between themselves and someone else while they are talking.

Such everyday matters are highly revealing, showing how a given society is stratified. People tend to think of social stratification as a matter of money, but it actually entails any kind of identity grouping in society. Money or lack of it can cut across social stratification. By **stratification** I mean the different groups that make up the society, those who are considered upper class or lower, those who consider themselves as belonging to one ethnic or racial group rather than another, and even those who feel it is worthwhile to work hard in school and those who do not. As we shall see, this is often not a matter of laziness or stupidity, but of different child-rearing practices, unconscious loyalty to one group, or alienation from another.

Moreover, such apparently diverse matters as politeness rules in society, the way we ordinarily converse, and the words that newspapers use to report incidents are all effective ways of maintaining power relations within society. Even the selection of a standard accent, dialect, or language is a strong force in determining who will and who will not have power in any modern nation.

Accordingly, most people find that an academic course in the sociology of language is both interesting and exciting, a true consciousness-raising experience. Students become more aware of their own behaviors, how they are responding to other people, and how others behave and respond. My readers have told me time and again how much more sensitive they have become to the way people act and what people really mean when they say something. Readers and students find themselves analyzing social interactions with heightened awareness.

INTRODUCTION

Typically, everyday language behaviors are ignored in education at all levels. Despite the intense interdependence of language and society and language and knowledge, it is still possible for students to study such fields as politics, sociology, and psychology without ever examining the daily, unself-conscious language through which all of these are mediated. Yet, it has become increasingly evident that, without such examination, there can be no social or political emancipation.

Inquiry into the social uses of language heightens one's sensitivity not only to one's own speech behavior but also to the speech of others, to sources of misunderstanding, to deeper understanding, to the sharpening of one's "intuitions" about people, and even to matters like how rock songs are sung and why and the dialogue in soap operas, novels, and movies. Sociolinguists increasingly have found that serious misunderstandings occur between members of different groups simply because they do not share the same rules for politeness, or because their ideas of what is permissible to joke about differ.

Examining the speech activities of different social groups also casts light on the conditions, values, and beliefs that have helped shape the groups. Conversely, it also shows how speech changes in every generation to meet social needs. Looking at changing speech practices shows us how society is changing.

Students of sociolinguistics should gain new respect for all peoples, more than any number of lectures on brotherhood or sisterhood could ever give them. This is because the sociology of language shows the true genius involved in all language activities. This genius can often be seen even when people use language considered incorrect or vulgar or when it is spoken by people whom we might otherwise view as primitive or technologically backward.

Chapter 1

What Is Language?

We take language very much for granted. It is just something that we use without thinking much about. Children are not taught their native language. They figure it out for themselves from social interaction. Language is multilayered and does not show a one-to-one correspondence between message and meaning as animal languages do. For this reason, every meaning can be expressed in more than one way and there are many ways to express any meaning. Languages differ from each other, but all seem suited for the tasks they are used for. Languages change with changing social conditions.

THE COMPLEXITY OF LANGUAGE

We so take our ability to speak and understand for granted that we usually don't stop to consider what is involved when we say even the simplest things. We certainly cannot articulate the complex sets of rules we use for pronunciation, for sentence construction, and for discourse production. Nor can we explain what we actually do when we understand another speaker. In fact, this knowledge lies below the level of conscious awareness. If it did not, if we were conscious of everything that goes into speaking, oral communication would be considerably slowed down as we'd have to be thinking of every move we have to make when speaking.

Stop one second. Pretend you are telling a friend what you did last night. How did you decide what words to use? There is almost always more than one word or phrase to express a message. There is always more than one grammatical form that can be used to express the same thought. How and why did you choose the one you did? There are even different ways of pronouncing the same words. Did you say something like "wont-cha" rather than "won't you"? Why would you expect your friend to know that "wontcha" really stands for 'won't you'? Or that "meetcha" means 'meet you'? And why did you choose one pronunciation over another?

Such questions are far from trivial, for the answers to them tell us not only about our society but, as we shall see, they also tell us vital things about what it is to be human, what it means to be able to utilize language to give and receive messages. Since we use language to learn and to remember, there isn't really any way to understand how the human mind functions without understanding language. Since all human societies are run by language, there is no way to understand societies without understanding how language is used to organize them and keep social behaviors orderly. In short, there is no way to understand humans without understanding language, its structure, and its use.

It is essential, then, to learn what all human languages have in common as well as how they differ. Understanding what they have in common helps us to define what a human being is, as does understanding how they may differ. We find that languages vary, but they don't vary randomly. They vary in certain respects only. In others, they are alike. However, most of this book will be concerned with the variations, for these are what constitute the sociology of language. This chapter will attempt to delimit what language itself is, how it is constructed, and how it is learned. Certainly, this does not substitute for an in-depth study of language, as in an introductory linguistics course, but it should give the reader a glimmering at least of the incredible complexity of language, of some of the issues that are at stake in sociology that are not so evident if one doesn't appreciate how language is constructed. For instance, we can iterate the proposition that all dialects are equally complex, and we will, but if the reader doesn't perceive the true complexity of even the most nonstandard of speech, this will appear to be merely an idealistic proposition.

Linguistics is the academic discipline that deals with the structure of human language and its varieties. Throughout most of this book, dialects rather than language as a whole will concern us. **Dialects** are varieties of a language, usually but not always mutually intelligible to their speakers. Dialects show a direct connection to an individual's social status, gender, and identity. The number of dialects in a community is a direct reflection of the complexity of that community's social makeup. Laypersons often call dialects **accents**. Strictly speaking, however, accents refers only to differences in the way words are pronounced, whereas dialects encompass differences in grammar as well as word choice. Here we talk about language itself, and whatever we say about it also pertains to dialects.

THE LEVELS OF LANGUAGE

Human language is multilayered. It is composed of a system of meaningless elements that combine by rules into meaningful structures. Sounds, meaningless in themselves, form meaningful words or parts of words. These words combine by rules into sentences, and the sentences combine into discourses, which include conversation, books, speeches, essays, and other connected sentences. Each level has its own elements and rules for use and each also relates to the other levels, also by rule. For instance, there are rules for putting together sounds in one's language, rules which allow you to place certain sounds next to each other but forbid you to place certain other sounds next to each other. There are also rules for which variants of sounds you may use when you are forming words and yet other rules for putting words into sentences.

As a consequence of being multilayered, human language is not **isomorphic** with its message. This means that there is no necessary one-to-one correspondence between message and meaning at any level.

In contrast, animal communication systems, so far as we can tell, are isomorphic in message and meaning, and there is no breakdown into separate layers of sound, words, or syntax. Both the multilayered character of language and its lack of isomorphism create its potential complexity in message production and in sociological significance.

Human language seems to be the only communication system that combines meaningless elements into meaningful structures. For most speakers, but not all, the meaningless elements are sounds. Languages of the hearing-impaired such as Ameslan (American Sign Language) substitute elements of gesture that are combined into larger units (Bellugi and Fischer 1972).

As far as we know, other animal communication systems are not multilayered and use only meaningful elements. That is, every sound, gesture, scent, or posture used in a nonhuman communication system means something in and of itself. Furthermore, the order in which the sounds and movements of nonhuman communication appear does not affect their meaning. If a monkey emits a call for 'food' and one for 'follow me,' it will mean 'follow me food' no matter which comes first. In nonhuman communication systems, the sum of the message always equals its parts.

In contrast, in human language, the message does not necessarily equal its parts. *A Venetian blind* is not the same as *a blind Venetian*, nor does *count the savings* mean the same thing as *the savings count*. Meaning in language can be more than the sum of its parts, as in *Gwen ordered pizza; Fred, chop suey; and Alex, a hot dog*. We know that Fred ordered chop suey and that Alex ordered a hot dog, even though the verb *ordered* is not repeated.

Meaning may as easily be less than the sum of its parts, as in *Max is a good kid*. There is no referential meaning to *is*. Many languages, like Russian and Chinese, leave the *is* out, saying the equivalent to 'Max a good kid.' Even to an English speaker, 'Max a good kid' has the same referential meaning as 'Max is a good kid.' Because there are some American speakers who do leave out the *is* in this kind of sentence, however, a distinctly social message is conveyed about the speaker's ethnicity and social class if he or she omits the *is*. Saying "Max is a good kid" and "Max a good kid" will convey the same message about Max but quite different messages about the speakers of each utterance in English. Thus, any utterance might convey both referential and social meanings, and these are not necessarily equal to the sum of the parts used.

Those languages—and dialects—which require the insertion of *is* do so because of arbitrary rules of language, not because of its meaning. That is, *is* and its counterparts *am, are, was, were, be, being,* and *been* do not refer to any action or emotion, nor even to a state, as do verbs like *run, hate,* and *live.* One cannot define *is* as one can such other verbs. In sentences like *Max is a good kid, is* has the major function of filling the slot reserved for verbs in the English sentence. Therefore, the use of *is* belongs to the level of **syntax,** the technical term for *grammar.*

Because elements of language, notably individual sounds, have no meaning in and of themselves, they can be divorced from meaning. Thus, human languages can multiply meanings far beyond those of other communication systems. The essentially meaningless elements of sound and syntax can be combined by rules into a multitude of words, sentences, and discourses. Humans are not confined to a repertoire of inborn messages, as are, for instance, birds, dogs, or elephants. Instead, humans can take the elements of their languages and use them to create new sentences, sentences that they have never heard before, sentences that can be understood by others who know the same language. For instance, look back to the beginning of this chapter, and see how many of the sentences (if any) you have either heard or read before, sentences which you, nevertheless, had no difficulty understanding.

In contrast, every other creature that we know of is limited to messages that are inextricably tied to meaning, so for them meaning can never be changed. This means that they can never express a new thought or convey a new message of any kind. To a dog, for instance, a growl is a growl. True, it can be used for play, but then it is still a growl, as when a dog is pretending to kill by worrying an old rag. The growl, even in play, cannot mean 'I love you' or 'I want to go with you.' The dog does have ways of "saying" those things, but he cannot make a growl carry those messages.[1]

A human, on the other hand, can say "I love you" sarcastically so that it conveys the meaning 'You really are a pest.' Then, too, the human can use the individual sounds in *I love you* in very different messages. For instance, the *l* and *v* in *love* can also be used in *villify,* a word that has quite a different meaning from *love.* Humans can even take sounds of their languages and combine them to make up new words, as long as they follow the rules of their particular language for combining sounds correctly. In English, for instance, one could use the *l* and the *v* to make up the word *cluvy* if there was a need for a new word to designate a thing, a quality, or an action for which there was no existing word. Alternatively, one could take an existing word, say *silly*, and make it mean something new. In fact, English *silly* once meant 'holy.' Apparently because people used it ironically often enough, it eventually took on its present meaning. Thus old elements, be they sounds, words, or sentences, can be used in new ways. This allows human languages to change over time, even within the lifespan of individuals, and these changes are sensitive to societal conditions.

Although there are built-in rules for word and sentence formation in human language, these rules are constructed so that an infinite number of new words and sentences can be created in any human language (Chomsky 1959, 1965, 1972). So far as we know, no other animal, no matter how intelligent, has such versatile options in its communication system. Therefore, other animals are not able to change their communications to fit new circumstances as humans can and do.

Most important is that all human languages can express things that have happened before, or have not happened but might. Language is not limited to the here and now or to the visible or the real. It seems to me that language is what has made humans so intelligent, not that our intelligence has made us create language. All that was necessary to start building a higher intelligence was the ability to convey a message to another about something that occurred or was seen by the speaker but not by the hearer. This could have been simply at first being able to say the equivalent of 'there is a dead carcass by the river.' Once human communication was freed from the here and now and the visible, then it became possible for people to know many things without ever experiencing them themselves. This called for a larger memory, of course; hence, the development of a large brain. Most importantly, humans now could consider the experiences of others and learn from them; things didn't have to be discovered anew in each generation and by each individual. Knowledge could be passed along to the next generation without its being built into the organism as instinct. That way, knowledge could be updated when conditions changed. Humans weren't limited by their ancestors' experiences. They could therefore take advantage of many ecological niches. No other animal has had this advantage because no other animal has developed language.

At this point you might be objecting. How about all those chimpanzees and gorillas and birds who have been taught human language? The answer is that they haven't. They have been taught to use certain symbols or signs which in their entirety, represent one meaning of a given word, but they can't use the "words" in a new way. For instance, Lana the chimp learned to push a key on a computer that had squiggles that represented *green*. She could press that key to mean the color green, but she couldn't extend its usage to mean 'young, naive' or 'unripe.' Moreover, there is no evidence that any of these animals could handle grammar rules of even the simplest sort (Terrace 1979). The following is a typical long string, one made by Nim Chimpsky, trained by Herbert Terrace and his assistants: *give orange me give eat orange me eat orange give me eat orange give me you.* This is not structured grammatically. All Nim could do was repeat words over and over in different orders. This string is representative of what all the trained animals did with language. All they did was request things they wanted. They never used their "languages" to tell their trainers how they spent their day, what interesting new thought they had that day, or anything that was not in the immediate, visible environment. It took years of intensive training to get these animals to learn at the most 250 or so words. Any toddler does that with no help at all from anyone, and the toddler learns early to put words together in a grammatical order. It seems to me that all the animal training did was give the chimps a new outlet for what they were already capable of communicating.

The Sounds of Language

The actual sounds that any language uses to form words have no referential meaning in and of themselves. The *b*'s in *baby, but, bad, bill,* or any other word in English—or any other language—have no inherent meaning. Words representing those meanings do not have to have *b*'s in them at all. In French, for instance, *baby* is *enfant* and *bad* is *mal*. So far as we know, the fact that English and French use different sounds in words meaning approximately the same thing makes no difference whatsoever. The sounds that a language uses are arbitrary. Out of the whole universe of sounds that humans can make, no language uses more than a small subset, and one subset of sounds is as good as another for "doing" language.

However, because individual sounds have no referential meaning in and of themselves, this doesn't mean that some of them can't have sociological meaning. That is, one pronunciation of a word might mark a speaker as being educated or hip or an outsider and another will mark him or her as being uneducated, nerdy, or very much part of a given group. The person who says "cayunt" [k^{h}eyənt] for *can't* is giving social and regional information quite different from that of the person who says "cahn't" [k^{h}ant] for *can't*. Similarly, saying "pinny" for *penny* may signal either regional or racial feelings of identity or both.

In terms of evolution of language, there must have come a time when sound was divorced from meaning for hominids, and that, in itself, must have been a major breakthrough. Once individual sounds were no longer inherently attached to meaning as in animal languages, then they could be combined and recombined into innumerable meaningful words, thus increasing the possible messages exponentially. It is linguistically more economical to have *b, m, a, d* mean nothing in and of themselves individually than if *b* always had to mean one thing, *a* another, and *d* still another. By meaning nothing in themselves, they are then available to create a plethora of words like *ad, am, ma, bam, bad, mad, dam,* and *dab,* as well as potentially *bamd, mbad, mab, ab, ba, damb, amb, amd, dma,* and so on.

Each language uses only some of the hundreds of possible sounds that human beings can hear and utter. Then, each has its own rules for combining these sounds into syllables. Even if two languages use the same sounds, the rules may not allow them to be combined in the same ways. For instance, both English and Swahili use the sounds [ŋ] "ng," [g], [w], and [e] "ay." However, Swahili allows the [ŋ] to appear at the start of words, whereas English can use it only at the end, as in *sing.*[2] Therefore, Swahili has a word [ŋgwe], which means 'strings,' but English does not. And, of course, there are combinations of sounds that English allows but Swahili does not, such as the combination of [gd] in *bagged.*[3]

Phonemes

Not only does each language use its own subset of sounds, but what is even heard as a different sound differs from language to language. We are all familiar with the fact that the Japanese have difficulty with the sounds [r] and [l] in English, so they may pronounce *baseball* as "basabaru." The reason for the final [u] is that in Japanese, words must end in a vowel, and the reason that [r] replaces English [l] is because [r] and [l] are one **phoneme** in Japanese. That is, the Japanese have both sounds, but they do not hear the difference between them because, in Japanese, an [l] automatically becomes an [r] in between vowels.

The fact that *Sally* is an old diminutive of *Sarah* and *Molly* was originally a form of *Mary* shows that even English speakers do process the similarity of [l] and [r], but in English, these are considered separate phonemes. Hence, we hear the difference between *rice* and *lice*. Languages like Japanese which automatically convert [l] to [r] in between vowels[4] are using these sounds as **allophones** of each other. That is, speakers don't even hear that they are using what to us are different sounds. They perceive [l] and [r] as one sound composed of the allophones [l] and [r]. Did you see the movie *Lost in Translation*? If so, you may recall the scene in which the Japanese woman orders Bill Murray to "lip my stockings." She was trying to say *rip*. The humor lies in the American's not being able to figure out what she meant. She herself didn't hear the American /r/ as an /l/.

Sometimes it is English which perceives two sounds as one. For instance, if you hold your finger to your lips and say "pit" and "spit," you will feel a strong puff of air when you make the first [p], but not when you make the [p] after [s]. This puff of air is called **aspiration**. In many languages, the aspirated [p] and the unaspirated one are two distinctly different sounds. For instance, in both Korean and Hindi, a [p] and a [pʰ] are heard as being as two clearly separate sounds, so [pal] and [pʰal] are two different words. In English, since we do not consciously distinguish between these sounds, we hear [pal] as a funny way of saying [pʰal]. Think of how a French, Spanish, or Italian speaker pronounces *pill*, for instance. That is the unaspirated [p] in [pal], but in English, the phoneme /p/ consists of two sounds with the aspirated one always occurring before a stressed vowel. In French, there is no aspirated [p] at all; hence, the French fail to put that puff of air in English words. English speakers automatically and erroneously do put the puff on words like French *peau*. When trying to speak a language which has both the aspirated and unaspirated [p]'s as separate phonemes, English speakers do the equivalent of what the Japanese do with [l]'s and [r]'s. That is, they treat them as one sound, and simply use each as an allophone according to the rules of English. A foreign accent is partially a matter of using the wrong allophones of a phoneme or not even distinguishing between phonemes in the foreign language.

No two languages divide up the phonetic universe into the same sounds. Each language uses a subset of all the possible sounds humans can produce, as noted above, but each language groups several sounds into one sound. The sound we think we hear is the phoneme. The several sounds that we hear as that one sound is the allophone. Apparently, the reason for this complexity is that we subconsciously notice the allophone and this tells us where the sound is in the word. For instance, when we hear the [p] in *spit*, even if we missed the [s], the very fact that there is no aspiration tells us an [s] probably occurred before it. By the same token, when we hear the [pʰ] in *pit*, we know that the sound occurred at the start of the word.

Because languages group their sounds into phonemes composed of allophones which occur in specific positions in words, this means that humans need only hear about 50% of every message and can still decode it reasonably accurately. This enables spoken language to be produced at a much greater rate than if each and every sound in the stream of speech had to be heard distinctly. When the Japanese speaker hears the /r/, it tells him or her that the sound came in between two vowels. When the English speaker hears the /pʰ/, it tells him or her that a new word has started. One reason that foreign accents can be difficult to understand is that we are not hearing the allophones, which are so important in decoding.

Morphemes

Technically, some whole words as well as the parts of words are called **morphemes**.[5] The word *renewed*, for instance, is composed of three morphemes: *re-*, *new*, and *-ed*. These are considered morphemes in English because we recognize the *re-* as a prefix that is attached to many words to convey the meaning 'again.' *New* is a morpheme that is also a word in itself. That is, it can stand alone with no other morphemes attached to it. The ending *-ed* is an English morpheme for past tense. This is required by the grammar of English in certain contexts. The word *renewed* thus illustrates the different kinds of morphemes that appear in languages: those used to add meaning to a given word; words in themselves; and affixes required by the grammar of a language. **Affixes** are morphemes that appear at the beginning or end of words, and, in a few languages, are inserted in the middle of them. Morphemes can be defined as the smallest unit in a language which gives meaning or has a grammatical function.

We are so used to what our language does in regards to word formation that we don't think of the many other ways there are to "do" a language. What we are used to seems natural and inevitable, but languages may achieve the same ends quite differently. This is readily seen in the use of morphemes. In English and other European languages, typically, morphemes required by grammar are put at the end of words as **suffixes**, but other languages have them at the beginning. That is, the grammatical information occurs in the **prefix**. We see this in Swahili:

faw 'break'	nfaw 'is breaking'
law 'go'	nlaw 'is going'
sun 'sleep'	nsun 'is sleeping'
ǰo 'fight'	nǰo 'is fighting'

What English does by the combining of the word *be*[6] and the morpheme *-ing* as a suffix, Swahili does by adding an *n* before the root word itself. This *n* is not merely a sound in Swahili. It is an entire morpheme and gives the Swahili speaker similar meaning to the English speaker's "is X-ing." Whether it is a single sound with meaning used as a prefix, as in Swahili, or a combination of a word with a suffix on the next word, as in English, the same effect is achieved, and one way of doing the verb is as efficient and sensible as the other.

To give an idea of how varied languages may be in how they convey messages, consider the plural in Samoan, a Polynesian language. It seems evident to English speakers that to indicate that one person has done something, one adds an *-s* at the end of the verb, as in *he goes* as opposed to *they* *go*. Samoan does this quite differently. It repeats the next to the last syllable of the verb to indicate plural. This is an example of an **infix** rather than a prefix or suffix.

manao 'he wishes'	mana**na**o 'they wish'
matua 'he is old'	matu**tu**a 'they are old'
malosi 'he is strong'	malo**lo**si 'they are strong'
punou 'he bends'	puno**no**u 'they bend'

(data from Gleason 1955)

Notice also that words that would be considered adjectives in European languages are verbs in Samoan. Again, different languages have different ways of conveying the same messages; even parts of speech are not inviolable across languages. This matter will arise again when we consider different dialects of English. No one way of forming plurals (or any other grammatical category) is inherently better than another, nor is one "part of speech" necessarily superior to another for conveying ideas. Different languages do different things for the same purposes with no apparent difference in communicability.

The actual intricacies of morphemes can be a course in itself, but this discussion should give some notion of the kinds of variety one may expect from language to language—or even from dialect to dialect.

Words

We think of words as being basic to language, but, as the foregoing shows, words themselves are created from phonemes and morphemes. We also think of words as containing a specific meaning, but, in fact, most words carry many meanings. For instance, the word *energy* in English refers to a human being's physical or mental energy or electrical or fossil fuel power, but it doesn't refer to the power of a machine. That is, it seems odd to say, "My new car has a lot of energy." Yet, in other languages, English *energy* would refer both to humans and machines but not fuels, or it would refer to physical energy but not mental, or to humans and not animals, so that one would need three separate words for the separate notions. Every word subsumes a different complex of meanings in different languages—or even different dialects of one language.

Syntax and Discourse

Words themselves combine by rules of syntax into **sentences**. Sentences, in turn, combine into **discourse**. This can be either oral, as in conversation, or written, as in texts. Although we usually think of sentences as having rules of grammar, we shall see that discourse also has rules. These determine the order in which sentences may be arranged, as well as what can be left out of a sentence and what must be included. Even the forms sentences take are often determined by their position in a discourse. For instance, whether one can make a noun like *children* into the corresponding pronoun *they* depends on where in the discourse *children* appears. For instance:

The children had dirty faces. They were eating candy.

versus:

The children were eating candy. They had dirty faces.

There is no way to consider the syntax of a sentence without considering the larger discourse, for the grammar rules we apply at the sentence level are, to some degree, dependent upon the surrounding sentences.

Notice that even what we consider a sentence depends on what rules of syntax we have chosen to use. For instance, the above can also be conveyed by the following:

Eating candy, the children got dirty faces.
The dirty faces resulted from the children's eating candy.

Here, not only have different rules of syntax been applied, but also different words meaning the same things in this context have been used in each paraphrase. There is always more than one way to say anything in any language.

The essence of language lies in the fact that elements must be combined to create messages. Such combining is what makes languages capable of expressing so many meanings. Also, because every part of every utterance does not have to have a specific meaning in human languages, humans are free to change meanings of words and phrases and to make up new ones. Thus, language changes as society changes. What people actually say and what they mean may be quite different. "There is no spaghetti sauce" may mean "Go out and buy some spaghetti sauce" or "I can't make supper" or even "You idiot. You forgot the spaghetti sauce again." As we shall see, much of what we call politeness depends on such disjunction between meaning and the actual words used.

Syntax and Grammar

The term **syntax** is used to refer to the rules for combining words into sentences. The more commonly used term for putting words together into sentences is **grammar**. Unfortunately, as commonly used, *grammar* is an evaluative term, so that people think of good or bad grammar. *Syntax* is a neutral term, therefore preferable in a study of social behavior. When discussing different social groups, it is often necessary to speak of differences in rules between their dialects. This is of great importance, both in understanding members of groups other than our own and in teaching.

If a syntax rule is not part of a dialect, we say it is **ungrammatical** for that dialect. The usual word **ungrammatical** will be used in this book, but with a meaning somewhat different from the one that the reader may be used to. Here it will always mean, 'the speakers of a given dialect do not use a particular form or word order.'

This never implies that using or not using a form or word order is good or bad. For instance, "I am wanting to know that" is ungrammatical for many Americans, but it is often heard from the British. In dialects of English spoken by urban educated Americans today, "he don't" is ungrammatical, but it is grammatical for most people who have little formal education. Ironically, "he don't" used to be grammatical for all English speakers, educated or not. This shows how arbitrary judgments are about what is proper in language.

Often, ungrammatical constructions are readily understandable. Our judgment of whether a construction is grammatical is not determined on the basis of comprehensibility alone. The rules of grammar in human languages constitute a system in themselves and do not have a one-to-one correspondence with meaning. One result of this is that we can understand little children and foreign speakers who do not have all the rules of grammar of our language down pat. We can also understand speakers of other dialects who use rules of grammar somewhat different from our own. Poets often make poetry by deliberately changing some grammar rules for artistic purposes. The human ability for poetry rests on our ability to deal with grammars not exactly like our everyday ones.

Another exceedingly important result of our being able to understand those whose grammar differs from our own is that members of different social groups within the same community can understand one another's speech despite dialect differences between them. Therefore, dialect can be an important marker of social divisions within a community without affecting communication.

Above all is the curious fact that using new or different grammar rules does not cause language to decay. Meaning can still be preserved. Only in the speech of victims of severe mental pathologies, such as those occurring from brain damage, is meaning usually lost. In such instances, few or no words may be recognizable, or syntax may be so faulty that it is impossible to figure out the relationship of words to each other.

The grammatical mistakes that most people call "bad grammar" really are social markers. They do not necessarily reflect poor intelligence or faulty knowledge on the part of the speakers. As much as one might deplore *ain't got none* or *him and me went*, they are regular productions in some dialects of English. Their speakers often know the "proper" *haven't got any*, but choose not to use because of the social messages they wish to convey.

The fact that two dialects or two languages have different rules does not make one inherently better than another. One may be socially preferred, but that is another matter. Today, for instance, using certain kinds of double negatives is considered incorrect in English. Certainly, no one has any trouble understanding that "I didn't do nothin'" means 'I didn't do anything.' No one ever takes it to mean 'I did something' just because, in mathematics, two negatives make a positive. In fact, double negatives are still used by the prissiest of English speakers in sentences like "I was not unhappy." Many languages habitually use double negatives. Italian, for instance, allows *Non ho fatto niente*, and French allows *Je n'ai rien fait*, both of which mean literally 'I haven't done nothing.'

To show how arbitrary the double negative rule is even in English, we can point to older stages of English. Shakespeare used double negatives frequently, especially for emphasis, as in "No sonne were he never so olde of years might not marry" (Abbott 1870, 295). Today, the same emphatic use of double and even triple negatives heard in English is considered nonstandard, as in "Ain't no cat can't get into no [pigeon] coop" (Labov 1972, 130). The rule forbidding double negatives is arbitrary. Languages work perfectly well with or without double negation. In English today, however, certain double negatives are socially wrong in certain circumstances. That is, although there is nothing inherently wrong with double negatives, there can be something socially wrong with some of them, but not necessarily all, at this time in history.

THE ARBITRARY NATURE OF LANGUAGE

The reader should always bear in mind the difference between the inherent worth of particular kinds of speech as opposed to their social worth. The two are not the same. The particular grammar rules of a language at a particular moment in history are frequently arbitrary. By *arbitrary*, we mean that they don't have to be the way they are, and different languages and dialects have different but equally good rules for such matters. This is in contrast to those features which all languages have in common, such as nouns and verbs. It has been taken as a given that the things all languages have in common are reflections of the human mind and are, therefore, not arbitrary (Chomsky 1972).

CHAPTER 1

Languages are also arbitrary in the sounds they use and in their word choice. Just because the English say "tree" for what the French and German call *arbre* and *Baum*, respectively, we can't draw any conclusions about their respective national characters. The words themselves and the sounds making them up are arbitrary choices, explicable only in terms of the history of each language. One word does as well as another to designate 'trees' so long as listeners understand what is meant.

Linguists have not been able to find any primitive languages, even among the so-called primitive peoples. All languages spoken in the world as far back as we have any records for are equally complex and can potentially do pretty much the same things. For example, every language has some way of indicating whether someone did the action or received it, as a sentence like "The boy bit the dog." English does it by word order. Russian does it by endings on each noun. Swahili does it by prefixes on each noun. Each way is as logical and intelligent as the other. The difference between languages and dialects is not what they can do, but how they do it (Gleason 1961, 232).

In their vocabulary and discourse rules, languages may differ in accordance with the values of their societies. Indeed, that is what this book is about. However, no language is fixed at any point. Language is not static. Any language can change in any way its speakers want it to, or need it to, and it can change as soon as speakers wish it to.

Every language has built into its very structure the mechanisms of change. All normal speakers of all languages have the ability to:

- Make up new words.
- Use old words in new ways.
- Compose sentences they have never heard before.
- Combine sentences into wholly new discourses.

Speakers, in short, can say new things in their old language. The corollary is that speakers of a language can understand:

- New words used in a context, often without the speaker's having to define them.
- Old words used in new ways.
- New sentences.
- New discourses.

Noam Chomsky calls the twin abilities of saying and understanding new things the creative aspect of language. He believes there is no way to understand the human mind without understanding its ability to handle creativity in language use. This book will show that there is no way to understand human society without considering this creativity. At the very least, it means that neither individuals nor their societies are wholly bound by the past.

LANGUAGE AND THOUGHT

The very fact that language can be made to take on new meanings shows that language and thought are not necessarily one and the same. So far as we know today, there is no one-to-one correspondence between language and thought.

Any thought can be expressed in many ways. That is, all languages allow paraphrase. For instance, if one wishes to inform someone that Jack and Ellen got married after a long courtship, one can express that in at least the following ways:

Jack and Ellen got married after a long courtship.
Jack is finally married to Ellen.
Jack and Ellen are finally married.
Jack and Ellen finally tied the knot.
At long last, Jack got married to Ellen.

Any native speaker of English could easily find yet other ways to indicate Jack and Ellen's state of matrimony. Note that the paraphrases are on different levels of the language. Some utilize different **lexical items**. That is, different words or different phrases are used to express the same idea. Notice that individual words may be paraphrased by phrases, as in the alternation between *married* and *tied the knot*, and *finally* and *at long last*. Other paraphrases work by changing **word order**. This last determines whether a preposition has to be used, so "Jack and Ellen" may be paraphrased by "Jack . . . to Ellen."

Furthermore, language also allows ambiguity, so that a word or a sentence can have more than one meaning. *Story* can mean either 'narrative' or 'level of a building.'[7] *Visiting relatives can be boring* can mean either 'relatives who visit can be boring,' or 'it can be boring to visit relatives.' Words and sentences can change meaning according to their contexts.

Not only are utterances potentially ambiguous, but the same words or sentences may be perceived as having very different intentions or forces in different contexts. For instance, "It's cold in here" on the surface means 'The temperature in this place is lacking in warmth.' However, given the right context, such as a hot summer's day in an air-conditioned room, it could mean 'Boy, that air conditioner works well.' Under somewhat different social conditions, it could also mean 'I can see I'm not wanted here.'

CHAPTER 1

The same sentence could also have the force of a command. If the person speaking has a right to command the person addressed, either because of social status or just because the person addressed is closer to the switch, then "it's cold in here" could be interpreted as 'turn the air conditioner off.' If the air conditioner had been reported to be malfunctioning, then the meaning could be construed as 'this thing is working just fine.'

So important is context to meaning and force of language that to quote someone out of context can constitute an actual lie. The enraged protests of politicians and other often quoted and misquoted newsworthy folks show us how easy it is to twist someone's meaning just by omitting sufficient context.

Later chapters will demonstrate that the context that determines meaning includes among other things:

- The social status of speakers.
- The speech event and the social conventions governing it.
- The social-cultural and physical environment.
- Previous discourse between the speakers or those known to them.
- The perceived intent of the speaker.

Meaning, in other words, has a social base. Words do not just mean. They mean in social interaction in a particular society and a particular context.

FIRST-LANGUAGE ACQUISITION

Acquiring language is very much a socially determined phenomenon. No child can learn an oral language without hearing one spoken. If a baby is exposed to more than one language, it will select for learning only those which it perceives have some social function. In many immigrant homes in the United States, therefore, children never learned the language of their grandparents—or barely learned that of their parents—although they heard it all the time, unless the family insisted that English not be used within the home or for certain social functions.

One very important consequence of the fact that language is always changing is that it cannot be learned solely by mimicking. The very fact that the same utterance may mean very different things in different contexts shows that people use active decoding strategies in order to understand. They have to match the sentence to the context in order to get the meaning.

Recent studies of how children learn to use language strongly suggest that no one teaches them how to understand. Even little toddlers extract meaning from what they hear by matching it to the context. Toddlers seem to expect that adults will use such a strategy (Baron 1977). The toddler who says, "Mommy sock" will use it to mean 'This is Mommy's sock,' 'Mommy put on my sock,' or even, 'I'm putting Mommy's sock on my doll' (Bloom 1970). One wonders how one could explain to fifteen-month-olds that they can utter the same words in the same order to give different meanings in different contexts. Again and again while examining the speech of young children, one finds that they are doing such things with words and sentences, things that no one could have taught them.

A simple, apparently trivial example demonstrates this assertion: toddlers habitually make errors in the past tense of irregular verbs, such as saying "comed" for *come*, "goed" for *went*, and "breaked" for *broke*. Interestingly, babies first use *went*, *came*, and other correct forms of irregular verbs as their parents do (Ervin 1964). However, as soon as they perceive that there is a regular past tense ending *-ed*, as in *played* and *cooked*, they apply it to all verbs to indicate 'past time.' Bowerman (1985, 88) shows that on all levels of language, initially, the child uses many words or other forms separately to give different meanings. Then he or she comes to recognize that several of these can be put together into one class. This is the point at which overregularizing occurs.

Furthermore, even babies growing up in educated homes prove very resistant to correction, continuing in these errors for years, despite the fact that the verbs involved are among the most common in the language and they constantly hear the correct forms from their parents, on television, and in the streets. Paradoxically, this shows how intelligent children are, not how stupid. For a baby to figure out a form like "goed" when all he or she has probably ever heard is "went" means that the baby is actively figuring out how the language is working. The baby has somehow categorized words into at least nouns and verbs, although, of course, without calling them that (Berko 1958; Menyuk 1971). The toddler acts as if he or she has categorized words into different parts of speech, some of which take tense endings and some of which do not. Not surprisingly, at the same stage, toddlers are using plural endings on nouns and, again, generalizing them to all nouns, making mistakes like "foots" and "mouses."

What makes the baby's performance all the more amazing is that many languages of the world, such as Chinese, do not use tense markers on verbs or plurals on nouns. Rather, they use words meaning 'before,' 'in the future,' 'next month,' and the like, if it is necessary to note the time. Similarly, if the amount of something talked about is relevant, then a quantifying word is used with the noun without added plural endings. This means that babies cannot be born expecting grammatical markers of any particular kind, as they have to be able to learn whatever language they will be exposed to in infancy.

Babies must be born knowing how to go about learning language, or else they would not be able to figure out the grammatical rules as they apparently do. English-speaking babies notice that there are tense and plural markers. Russian babies have an even more complicated task in learning word endings, for Russian has six different endings on nouns to indicate how they are being used in particular sentences, whether as the subject or the object or in some other function. Furthermore, there are three different genders in Russian, masculine, feminine, and neuter, and each uses a different set of endings. Still, before the age of two, Russian babies have begun to experiment with endings. Typically they are already using at least one to indicate direct objects. Like English-speaking babies, the Russian babies start out by generalizing one ending for a function. Just as the English speaker starts out putting *-ed* on a verb like *go*, the Russian baby puts the feminine direct object ending *-u* on all nouns, even masculine or neuter ones. Similar phenomena have been reported for babies who have to learn Turkish, Finnish, or Serbo-Croation, all languages that use many endings (Slobin 1979).

Babies who are exposed to languages that do not make use of endings, such as Chinese, have to make different kinds of analyses. For instance, Chinese makes use of an intricate set of noun classifiers, each of which is used with a different set of nouns, such as is marginally seen in English in expressions like a *gaggle of geese* or *a pride of lions.*

Although the specifics of the task vary from language to language, apparently the task itself is the same for all babies everywhere. They must figure out for themselves how the language around them works. Babies exposed to more than one language have to do this for each, often concurrently. We do not know how conscious babies are of what they are doing, only that their utterances show the result of analyzing language.

Why don't babies just mimic their parents' language? That would seem more efficient than the active analyses just discussed. As mentioned earlier, in order to use language creatively, which is the essence of language use, children cannot just mimic. If that were all they did to learn language, then children would be able to say only what they had already heard. Instead, they have to learn the unspoken rules that will enable them to express new thoughts or describe new situations so that others can understand them. From the start, human beings are not limited to the utterances they have heard.[8] This, of course, argues that there is free will, as Noam Chomsky pointed out.

There may also be a social reason for active analysis in the language-learning process. When they are grown up, children do not necessarily talk like their parents. They talk according to the social conditions facing them, not those facing their parents. Parental speech provides a springboard for children, not a template. From the start, human beings learn language for themselves so that they can adapt it to whatever situations they find themselves in.

Another reason babies do not just imitate may be that sheer imitation is not a very efficient way to learn. For instance, the irregular words in English today are chaotic. They no longer form regular classes (although once they did). There is no rule to tell which should be irregular, or if they are irregular, in what way. For example, there is an alternation of *i*, *a*, and *u* in a few irregular verbs, as in *sing, sang, sung, ring, rang, rung*. However, there are verbs that rhyme with these in the present tense, such as *bring, sting, cling*, and *think*, that do not follow the same pattern, although they, too, are irregular. Even if there is some discernible pattern in a few of the irregular verbs, there is no single applicable rule that excludes some verbs and includes others. One can only memorize which verbs change and how. Some of them, the most common irregular verbs, such as *eat* and *go*, have no analogs at all; that is, no other verbs change in the past tense as they do.

In terms of communicative efficiency, saying "eated" and "goed" works as well as "ate" and "went." By applying the -*ed* to all verbs and ignoring the exceptions, babies lose nothing in communicability and free themselves for other learning. When they learn more grammar and basic vocabulary, they can go back and sort out irregular forms.

The actual adult form of many of these verbs varies according to social and regional dialects. Often, the use of one rather than another marks the speaker as a member of a particular group. Saying *knew* instead of *knowed* or *brought* instead of *brang* gives an essentially social message about a person's identity. Such changes in form do not affect the actual meaning of the verb. Therefore, the fine points, so to speak, of verb forms can be deferred until an age when social identity is more important than it is to a toddler.

Another learning strategy that many young children employ is practice drills, repeating a word over and over, altering the context each time. For example, here are two such drills:

1. Stoly
    Stoly here
    Want a stoly
    Dave, stoly

Story, story
Story's de hat
Story's de big hat
Story's a hat

2. Turn of de water
   turn de water
   I turn de water
   I turn [th]is water
   I turn off de water
   Here Mommy now
   de bottle
                    (Weir 1962)

Readers who have studied a foreign language may note the similarity of these to oral practice drills. Yet nobody teaches children to create such drills. They do it on their own. They even select the items they choose to practice, here the difference between /l/ and /r/, and /d/ and /ð/'th'.[9] Weir claimed that this is evidence that children are somehow born knowing how to go about learning language.

Kuczaj (1983, 12) points out that crib speech may be the first time children use speech that is not tied to the here and now. As we've seen, this is a defining difference between human language and animal communication systems. He also notes that children practice because they are in control of the situation. Children usually play at what they are learning at the time. Given the enormous task of learning a language, it is not surprising that young children practice talk constantly, while playing with toys or by simply talking to themselves, often in imaginary situations that they have set up for themselves. One could say that the predilection for engaging in such activities is also proof that children have their own inborn strategies for learning.

Even when a young child can be made to imitate, his or her free productions are not necessarily affected. For instance:

3. *Child*:   Want other one spoon, Daddy.
   Father: You mean, you want the other spoon?
   Child: Yes, I want other one spoon, please, Daddy
   Father: Can you say "the other spoon"?
   Child: Other . . . one . . . spoon
   Father: Say . . . other
   Child: Other
   Father: Spoon
   Child: Spoon

Father: Other . . . spoon
Child: Other . . . spoon. Now give me other one spoon?
            (Fromkin and Rodman 1983, 333)

This toddler is not being stubborn or naughty. He shows every sign of trying to cooperate. Although the task clearly makes no sense to him, he dutifully repeats his father's words. The repetition does not make him see his error, however. He has made up a rule, one that works for him, and for the time being at least, he sticks to it. This is the same sort of behavior as continuing to say "goed" in the face of everyone else's "went." It has its analog in the child who has been drilled in school for years in the use of standard English, but never uses it.

It is not only words and sentence patterns that children do not imitate well. They may fail at simply repeating a sound, even one that they can use under some circumstances. In the following example, the little boy, then thirty-three months old, did regularly pronounce /p/ in *party* and *piggy*. However, he had misanalyzed the word *pool* as being *cool*.

4. *Mother*:   Say "pool."
    Child: Cool.
    Mother: No, say "pool."
    Child: Cool.
    Mother: No, listen, "puh-ool."
    Child: [watching intently, with great effort]: Cuh-ool.
    Mother: No! "Puh-puh-ool."
    Child: Oh! Puh-cool.

Even when they are corrected, children clearly have difficulty in locating the source of their errors. They don't seem to know what they are being corrected for. Data like those above caused researchers in the sixties to think that children don't learn to speak by imitating their caregivers,[10] that language unfolds naturally as children, on their own, listen to the speech around them and make up their own rules for producing that language. This view was reinforced by the above data that showed that children cannot and do not merely imitate what they hear around them.

Before then, it was assumed that people spoke as they did because of what they heard around them. Thus, it was thought that variation such as regional accents was caused by the density of communication networks (Bloomfield 1933, 328), because (as it was thought then) people mimicked what they heard. In a somewhat different context, this idea has been recently revived, not as a matter of behavioral stimulation but because people who interact together talk like each other as a way of bonding.

CHAPTER 1

Behavioral psychologists such as Skinner believed that children learn to speak the way they do because they receive positive reinforcement from their parents for speaking correctly. However, if children can't pinpoint their errors so that they can correct them, how could they know what part of the speech code they are being rewarded for? Their speech typically is a combination of correct and incorrect forms (from an adult point of view). The ramifications of one's beliefs about language learning are great for child-rearing practices and programs for children with pathologies, such as the deaf, the autistic, and the aphasic. Finding out how children actually do learn language is far from a trivial pursuit.

Landau and Gleitman (1986) and Gleitman (1985) discuss the reasons for believing that children are born with biological equipment that tells them how to go about learning a language. Landau and Gleitman cite reasons such as:

- 90% of the time, children hear contractions like "we'll" for *we will*, but early in the learning period they use the uncontracted form (7).
- Deaf children who are isolated in a hearing family make up their own sign language and follow the same developmental steps at the same ages as hearing children. For instance, the hearing-impaired child makes up signs composed of one gesture at the same age as hearing children use single words (16–17).
- Children create a full language from a Pidgin[11] language on their own when there is no one language for them to learn (17–18; Bickerton 1981).
- Despite the fact that blind children cannot see any of the stimuli that seeing children do, the blind learn language at the same rate and in the same ways as seeing children. On their own, they reinterpret words like *see* and *look* and relational words like *on* and *in* (19–22).
- Downs syndrome children go through the same stages of learning to speak as healthy children. The Downs children just start later and stop earlier, accounting for their diminished speech capacities (22–23).
- Children raised in bilingual language acquisition and bilingualism homes learn two or more languages at the same time and at the same rates as children learning only one, and they keep the different languages separate. They could not do this merely by imitating both languages (24–25).

Thus, the child is a born grammarian. According to this view, there is little caregivers can do to teach children to speak. Noam Chomsky, on the basis of taped recordings of academicians at scholarly meetings, claimed that speech input to children is faulty and fragmented, but miraculously, children are able to construct the grammars of any language to which they are exposed. Of course, the language at an academic meeting is loaded with slips of the tongue, hesitations, and false starts because people are thinking out loud and trying to encode new and difficult thought. This is not the usual input to young children.

Subsequent research (Snow 1986; Yamamoto 1990; Huttenlocher et al. 1992) has modified Chomsky's idea that children construct grammars out of fragmented adult speech. Rather, social interaction is required. For instance, hearing children of deaf parents don't learn to speak by being placed in front of a TV. From the time a baby learns to wave and say "bye-bye," language learning takes place through social interaction. Even neonates carry on "babbling dialogues" with their caregivers. The baby is encouraged to vocalize if the caregiver responds.

Huttenlocher et al. (1992) found conclusively that the amount of time that different mothers spoke to their children was related to their vocabulary growth, and that this was a mother-initiated effect. Interestingly, Yamamoto (1990) found that gender did not have a significant effect on language development although birth order did, but only in comprehension, not production. First-born children developed earlier than did later siblings. This was seen as the result of greater attention paid to first-born children. This finding is consonant with Huttenlocher et al. in that parental input to first-born children is probably much higher than with later children. Simply put, mothers have more time to speak with the first and only child than they do with their siblings.

Actually, many researchers have asserted that the one factor which does seem to accelerate language learning in older babies is parental imitation. Typically, this is done by expanding on the child's utterances, as when a child says, "dat car" and the caregiver expands it to "That is a red car" (deVilliers and deVilliers 1978, 203–09; Kuczaj 1983, 159–62). Others have found that children who imitate the most are those whose parents imitate them by expanding their utterances (Kuczaj 1983). Speech is ultimately social, so we expect that it will best be learned by social contact, especially if the child feels his or her speech is important to the parent or caregiver. The child feels that his or her speech is important to the caregiver when it is expanded this way. This constitutes an early dialogue between caregivers and children.

It occurs to me that there is another reason for expansions' facilitating language learning. Part of being able to learn anything is feeling that one can learn it. The parent who expands on children's utterances is, in effect, not only saying to the child, "What you say is important to me," but also, "I think you can learn to speak like me, and I will help you by providing you with models."

Even so, not all cultures encourage children this way, yet the children belonging to these cultures grow up to be linguistically very able. Shirley Brice Heath (1983, 75) describes in detail how African American children in a Piedmont town acquire language. In this community, caregivers do not expand on a baby's utterances, nor do they use baby talk. In fact, they talk about, but not to, the baby. They are aware of the way white middle-class mothers talk to their babies, however. One grandmother explains that she thinks it's silly the way white folks keep asking their children questions like "What's this? What's that?" She says that a child has to learn by keeping his (her grandson's) eyes open. She asks:

5. You think I kin tell Teegie all he gotta know to get along? He just gotta be keen, keep his eyes open, don't he be sorry. Gotta watch hisself by watchin' other folks. Ain't no use me tellin' 'im: 'Learn dis, learn dat. What's dis? What's dat?' He just gotta learn, gotta know; he see one thing one place one time, he know how it go, see sump'n like it again, maybe it be de same, maybe it won't. He hafta try it out . . . Gotta keep yo' eyes open, gotta feel to know. (Heath 1983, 84)

This sounds like basic training for verbal and mental agility, which it is. Heath says that preschoolers, especially boys, are always being presented with situations and then asked, "Now what you gonna do?" In Chapter 6, we will see the outcome of this kind of socialization in the clever rapping and other oral performances of African American males. Girls, in line with their adult roles, are taught to "fuss," directing complaints about someone or about an incident. Being a good "fusser" is considered an important part of the female role, including being a good mother. Girls, therefore, are encouraged to fuss at others (Heath 1983, 97–99).

In this community, babies are constantly around adults, playing at their feet as the adults talk. Although the adults don't direct words at them, babies and toddlers hear discourse constantly, and can be observed repeating the ends of adult utterances (Heath 1983, 86). This is a different kind of learning through social interaction, one very much in line with the idea that children have to learn for themselves as well as one in line with the expected behavior of adults, male and female.

The question naturally arises of the consequences of such different child-rearing practices. The schools are predicated on middle-class folkways. Clearly some children enter school with an advantage conferred on them by their upbringing. In England, class differences in how children are socialized have been directly blamed for the poor showing of the working class in school (Bernstein 1971; Martin 1983). Later chapters will discuss the relationship between school success and language socialization in greater detail.

CHAPTER 1

Notes

[1] Note that this does not mean that other creatures don't think. Nor does it mean that other animals aren't able to solve problems, even come up with new solutions. For instance, a dog I had was forbidden to sleep on the sofa. Every day when I came home from work, she would crawl out from under the sofa as I entered the apartment. She even made a show of stretching and yawning. Of course, she didn't know that I knew she had been sleeping on it until she heard my step. I could feel the spot still warm from her body, as well as observe the telltale shedding. However, her ploy, pretending to have been asleep under the sofa, showed creative thinking in her quest to circumvent my ban. Both ethological and laboratory evidence have shown that animals do think despite their lack of language.

[2] Note that when you say this, you don't actually pronounce a *g* at the end of the word. Nor do you pronounce an *n*. Try saying "nnnnnn" and then switch to the "ng" at the end of *sing*. See? The *ng* is not only one sound; it is a different sound from *n*, made in a different part of the mouth.

[3] The pronunciation of *bagged* doesn't have a sound for the *e*, so the *gd* are said together. In English, the spelling is a poor fit to the pronunciation, which is why we need a phonetic alphabet to represent actual sounds.

[4] This is not the only way [l]'s and [r]'s can be treated in different languages. In some, an [r] is used at the beginning and end of words and an [l] in between vowels. In others, [l] is always used before consonants and [r]'s are used everywhere else. Still others, like English, use [l] and [r] as two separate sounds. Yet others may lack one or the other sound completely, if not both.

[5] In actuality, this entire account of morphemes is woefully simplified. Not only can it be difficult to determine whether certain repeated elements are morphemes in a language, it is often not even possible to come up with a blanket definition of what a word is in a given language. Literate people usually consider a word to be whatever would be bounded by space in print, but as a definition, this doesn't work since many languages are not written, and even those that are do not consistently write individual words with spaces between them. For instance, for no reason apparent to me, in American English, *hairdresser* is written with no space between *hair* and *dresser*, but *hair net* is written with the space.

[6] This is true of any of its forms, such as *am, is, are, was, were, been.*

7   The British sometimes spell the word for level of a building as *storey* in order to distinguish it from the first meaning. Interestingly, despite the very different meanings attached to *story*, both derive from the same word, *historia*.

8   Nor are they later limited by the things they have read.

9   Weir's data were collected from her son's presleep monologues. Although many babies and young children do practice speech while alone in their cribs, it is not certain that all do. However, children also practice speech while playing with dolls, playing "house" or "school" with other children, and during related activities. Even much of the mindless chatter of toddlers and young children as they go around pointing to everything and naming it may well be a kind of self-instructional practice.

10   The term *caregiver* is used for "child care" rather than *caretaker* because the latter implies cold, impersonal institutional care rather than the nurturing, loving care which we hope children are receiving in their homes, at daycare centers, or at schools. *Caretaker* can also be used for inanimate structures, whereas *caregiver* is used only for children.

11   A Pidgin is a partial language that is used between people who must interact with each other, but neither side is able or willing to learn the other's language. It is a highly simplified, limited language form.

CHAPTER 1

Exercises

1. Find at least two examples in speech or print of new words or old ones used in new ways. Using *The Random House Dictionary, 2nd ed.* and/or *The Oxford English Dictionary*, verify that these are new.

2. Observe a young child talking. Tape-record or write down exactly what he or she says. Explain what rule(s) you think he or she has formed that lead to error.

3. Try to correct a young child's speech error. Do your results conform to those noted in the book?

4. Listen for slips of the tongue. Explain them in terms of what you know about the organization of language.

5. Listen to a foreign person speak English, and write down every word for which the English word sounds foreign because the wrong allophone was used. (That is, the sound is close to the way an English speaker would pronounce it, but is a little "off.") Try to figure out what the rule for that allophone is in English and how it must differ from the foreign language. Alternatively, if you know someone who speaks another language, ask them to say a word or two to you that has a sound that is not in English. Then try to pronounce the word, asking the speaker to correct you. How many times do you have to make the sound before the speaker verifies that you have made it correctly? Can you make it correctly at all? Ask the speaker if other English speakers pronounce that sound the way you did. Alternatively, ask the person how he or she knows someone is not a native speaker of his or her language by telling you which sound or sounds they mispronounce.

Chapter 2
Field Methods

Conclusions are only as good as the field methods they are based on. Field methods include laboratory experiments as well as observations recorded in the field, in the natural surroundings of the people whose speech is being studied. Sociolinguistic testing can be especially troublesome because one has to control very carefully to ensure that subjects are not responding to a factor other than the one being investigated. Measuring results statistically is often crucial to proving that results of an experiment did not occur by chance. Statistics show if there is a 95% chance that the outcome occurred because of the specific factors used to elicit responses. Behavior can be studied by careful observation or participant observation as well as through experiments, but the observations must be under controlled conditions, with the researcher carefully noting all of the factors in the context that could have influenced the results. People often think that they can make pronouncements on language and its use just by randomly observing those they come in contact with, but such observations are rarely valid. One must know many things about a person before one can validly interpret his or her speech behaviors.

RECIPES FOR DISCOVERY

The lot of a social scientist would be considerably eased—and the literature on the social sciences considerably reduced—if it were easy to devise investigative techniques to find out what one wants to know and be sure that one is getting the information one is seeking. However, humans are nothing if not complex, not to mention perverse, and they will react to the wrong thing, or misunderstand your question, or try to second-guess you and so not give a truthful response, or find ambiguities you never intended in the task you set up. A good deal of the time spent studying the social sciences, especially psychology, sociology, and linguistics, all of which are part and parcel of sociolinguistics, is spent trying to determine the flaws in the studies which are giving the conclusions.

Part of being a good researcher is being an inventive, ingenious designer of foolproof experiments. Unfortunately, nobody manages that all of the time, especially on a first try. All researchers have had the disheartening experience of carrying out what they think is a brilliant study and then having a commentator point out the fatal flaws in it which invalidate all the conclusions. There is no way to avoid this. It is not possible to give recipes for foolproof experiments. Well, perhaps, one could write a manual with a bunch of set techniques, but this would hardly advance knowledge, for the essence of study is to find out new things, and in order to find out new things, one must do new things, create new protocols, think of new and different ways to get at an understanding of how and why people act and react as they do.

What we can do is to give some general information about the different kinds of studies possible and what they are good for. We can point out some common pitfalls. We can discuss studies which have been done and show how their results may be interpreted differently from the way the researcher did. We can raise questions about what was done, who was chosen to participate in the studies, whether enough people were tested, even whether the conditions of the testing might have inhibited the subjects.

We can even ask if the researchers themselves knew enough about their topic to research it accurately. Can we trust their conclusions just because they hold a doctorate or have written a book? Unfortunately, not always. Some pronouncements about language behavior are highly flawed because the researchers have never looked at language objectively or have never learned what people actually do when they speak. Then there are those who have never studied linguistics but who apparently think that a mere holding of a doctorate in another field of study is sufficient for judgments on speech behavior. They don't bother with the nitty-gritty of getting representative samples, observing carefully the conditions which elicit different responses, or even getting others to corroborate their judgments.

Studying Language Problems

While still in graduate school, I was introduced to the strange speech of some schizophrenics by a resident in psychiatry. She asked me to listen to a tape of one of her patients to see if I could tell her why the woman talked that way. Naturally, I first looked into the psychiatric literature on schizophrenia to see what explanations had been offered. I found that psychiatrists and psychologists had consistently misinterpreted schizophrenic speech through the prism of their own disciplines, but without considering what is at stake when analyzing speech. They were using abnormal speech behavior as evidence for their theories about schizophrenia, but they didn't take into account what makes speech normal and then compare that to the deviant speech produced by schizophrenics. That is, if one wants to explain an abnormality, one must first describe how it differs from normality (Chaika 1990; McKenna and Oh 2005, 84–86, 123, 132, 137).

The psychiatric and psychological literature did at least give samples of such speech. Briefly, schizophrenics may start rhyming words for no apparent reason or produce chains of associated words which are irrelevant to the topic at hand. For instance, the aforementioned patient said, "My mother's name was Bill and coo. St. Valentine's Day is the start of the breedin' season of the birds. I like birds. . . ." Another, asked to identify a color, said, "Looks like clay. Sounds like gray. Take you for a roll in the hay. Heyday. May Day. Help. I need help."

In the 1970's when I started investigating these oddities, psychologists, noting its associational character, had been studying word associations in schizophrenics. That is, they ran tests designed to show that schizophrenics had weaker or stronger associations to words than non-schizophrenics did. However, the problem isn't what kind of word associations they had. It is why they produce speech on the basis of word associations at all. Normally, we ignore the associations to words we use in speech. We choose words on the basis of the topic we're on and what it is we want to convey. The deviance in psychotic speech is that the patients express word associations at all! Other psychologists, those who were behaviorists, believed that to cure schizophrenics, one must punish them for using strange speech and reward them for using normal speech. They were interested neither in the precise nature of their deviant speech nor in what might cause it. So far as I know, this was never a widespread practice. I came across it in one ward of one hospital.

Next, I looked at psychiatric explanations. I found two major theories. One was that schizophrenics wanted to give voice to unacceptable ideas, so they used incomprehensible speech to express those ideas. Well, if they didn't want others to know what their unacceptable ideas were, all they had to do is what we all do: say one thing when we mean another.

The other psychiatric interpretation was that schizophrenics' mothers didn't love them, but when they were children and said to their mothers "You don't love me," the mothers punished them for telling the truth. Thus, the children were put into a double-bind situation and never learned to communicate correctly. Actually, this theory had been advanced by an anthropologist named Bateson (1972), not a psychiatrist, although many psychiatrists embraced it. I have never been able to find any case history evidence that schizophrenics had been put into double-bind situations, or for that matter that normals hadn't been. Furthermore, through all my years of working with psychiatrists on this issue, none has ever verified such a scenario. Worse yet for the double-bind theory is that, typically,

31

CHAPTER 2

schizophrenics talk normally when they're not ill. In fact, often family members know that their son or daughter is having a schizophrenic episode because he or she is "talking that way again."

As a linguist, I, of course, first examined psychotic speech carefully, analyzing its structure. I also devised an experimental protocol to elicit discourse from both ill and normal subjects, comparing the features of both so as to better define what constituted psychotic speech. Over the years, psychiatrists listened and read, hooked up with linguists to make their own analyses of speech, and replicated my experiments. No longer do they talk of double-bind situations or deliberately obscure speech. They treat psychotic speech as evidence of an actual disturbance in brain function and have been identifying what parts of the brain are disturbed in these patients. It is not unusual for a psychiatrist to work with at least one linguist on their team and, I am happy to report, they largely agree with my findings. One need only look at the differences in the psychiatric literature before and after my first publication to see what a difference field methods make in solving problems (Chaika 1974). Since virtually every aspect of human behavior—its ills, woes and joys—is dependent upon language, it is very important to understand the requirements of good field methods when taking into account the findings of linguistics.

Anecdotal Evidence

Field methods impinge more directly on daily life. For instance, many people are influenced by pop books on what body motion means, or on the supposedly different languages men and women speak, or on how to speak to be a success. Some of these are insightful and worthwhile, but many suffer from being mere recitals of anecdotes, not based on formal studies. This chapter, indeed, this book, aims to lay out some guidelines for coming to valid conclusions about what you read.

Throughout this book, when discussing what speech behaviors indicate about a culture or a person, the research methods which have yielded insights are presented. Sometimes studies seem well-constructed, but other scholars can't replicate them. That is, a different researcher using the same methods got different results. Such situations are also included in this book. The problem then becomes one of trying to reconcile the differences in results.

This chapter gives an overview of some considerations in field methods, and throughout the text I cite scholarly studies which back up conclusions. The one thing that I always find unacceptable is a conclusion based solely on anecdotes. The fact that three of my friends say that their little girls talk more than their little boys does not suffice to prove that girls talk more than boys. The fact that Nancy's husband buries his head in a paper when he comes home from work and refuses to talk doesn't mean that all husbands do. Anecdotes might provide the springboard for a formal study of an issue, but they never are proof in their own right. They may be used as examples to illustrate a point, but there has to be independently gathered corroborating evidence. People often have a great many "commonsensical" notions about human behavior which, when investigated, turn out to be wrong. It is just such notions that lead to stereotyping and misunderstandings.

You Have a Funny Accent

Investigating the dialects spoken in any locale demands painstaking field work. One not only has to know how to scientifically analyze speech sounds (phonetics), one must also know how to analyze the rules people are using to construct sentences (syntax). Most important, one must also know how to elicit speech so that one finds out how people actually talk, not how they think they should be talking. As we shall see in Chapter 7, dialect investigation is painstaking, highly skilled research.

Still, almost everybody thinks they can analyze the language they hear around them. They make pronouncements about what is the proper way to speak and what not, whose speech is bad and whose is good, all with no objectivity and less knowledge. It has been found that people are quite unaware of how they really sound and what linguistic forms they actually use. Still, they assume that what they are used to is correct, and what people in another region say is not.

Actually, finding out how speech varies within a community or within a country gives us valuable sociological information, as we shall see in Chapter 9. People don't talk randomly. They don't use pronunciations for no reason at all or by random chance. Pronunciations, word choice, even grammatical forms all are linked to the social structure of the community the speaker belongs to. When a dialect investigator goes into a locale, he or she can't just listen randomly to people, because the background of speakers is relevant. One must know, at the very least, if the speaker is a native of the region under investigation. One also has to know what ethnic group, what level of education, what age, and what gender speakers are, as all of these are pertinent to the dialect variation in any community. Attitudes are also a factor in people's choice of speech forms.

Even armed with background information, one can't just ask people how they pronounce certain words or if they use certain expressions. We know that people will tell you that they speak the way they think they are supposed to speak. If, for example, one wants to find out if vowel sounds have merged[1] in an area, one can't give people a list of words to read. If one gives them a list with *don* and *dawn* on it, they will try not to pronounce them alike because Americans think that words that are spelled differently should be pronounced differently. So, informants have told dialect field workers that they pronounce *hole* and *whole* differently, or that *cough* and *rough* rhyme, although, so far as I know, all dialects of Canadian and American English pronounce the first pair alike and the second differently. Gordon (2006, 63) found that, in Missouri, 19% of his respondents marked *hole* and *whole* as being pronounced differently. And I've had students in a phonetics class tell me that *cough* and *rough* should be transcribed with the same vowel.

In order to get at actual pronunciation differences and similarities, one does things like ask informants to choose a word that has the same sound as, for instance, *bought*. If the informants aren't looking at the words in print, they'll come up with *lot* (or a similar word) if they actually don't distinguish between the vowels in these two words. Historically, these two words used different vowels, but, all over America, these are merging, and, as we shall see, this is sociologically important.

Other ways to get at someone's actual pronunciation is to ask them a question like, "If a mother deer is called a doe, what's the name of a baby deer?" /FAWN/. "What's another word for sunrise, or the first part of the day when the sun's coming up?" /DAWN/. "Do those words rhyme?" "Can you think of any boy's names that rhyme with those words?" (Labov, Ash, and Boberg 2006, 32–33). For those whose vowels have merged in *dawn* and *Don*, the field worker will elicit *John* or *Sean* or a similar name. If the informant can't provide a rhyming name, the vowels probably haven't merged. The field worker can prompt the informant to make sure it's not just that she or he can't think of a name. For instance, the field worker can ask, "If we talk about the average American, we can call him BLANK Doe. What name fills in the blank?" The informant's pronunciation of *John* will either rhyme with *dawn* or won't, thus giving evidence about the merger. In some dialects, the field worker will find that *John* rhymes with *dawn* because the vowel sound /a/ "ah" is used in both. In another dialect that also has merged, the vowel in both will be /ɔ/"aw." In yet others, the vowels in these two words are different and they don't rhyme. Each situation is diagnostic of different social and historical changes. Furthermore, one needs training in phonetics to learn how to hear fine-grained differences in pronunciation of vowels. Even trained dialect workers may find it hard to distinguish between certain sounds. They may disagree on what was said or how to represent it phonetically in print. To show how unreliable and useless random observations of a dialect are, I will cite the case of two men, a professor and a newspaper columnist, who habitually make fun of what they perceive as the Rhode Island accent. They have each claimed to me that Rhode Islanders say "beeyud" for *bad*. Actually, both men come from regions in which this pronunciation has become regular in the past few decades, but the one thing no Rhode Islander would ever say is "beeyud." To the contrary, natives of that state use a very conservative, even old-fashioned /æ/ sound in that word. Both men, independently of each other, have simply taken a pronunciation from their home regions, Chicago and Portland, Oregon, and ascribed it to Rhode Islanders. They dislike that pronunciation, and they, with justification, find the local accent unusual, so, in trying to mimic it, they use the disvalued pronunciation of their home regions.

Dialect studies are very precise and very time-consuming, but ultimately very revealing. They are only as good as the field methods used to collect data. Random observations of strangers' speech is not likely to yield valid information. This is true of all studies of speech. It must be elicited correctly and analyzed scientifically by people who have been trained to do that.

SOCIOLINGUISTICS AND FIELD METHODS

Field methods constitute the various ways we can collect information about members of society: individuals or groups. They include laboratory experiments, naturalistic observations of both daily and unusual activities, questions put to people, surveys of the research of others to glean new or more exhaustive information, and analysis of a culture's output: newspapers, TV shows, movies, music, and art.

In sociolinguistics, as in all scholarly research, what you get depends on how you go about getting it. That is, one's results are dependent upon the field methods one uses. In turn, one's methods must conform to what we have discovered about the normal speaking practices of those being investigated. For those groups for which no data or only outdated data are available, any research must be preceded by periods of careful observation to learn the politeness routines, the conditions under which people speak, what their body motions mean, and so on.

Given the incredible complexity of language and its ubiquitousness, devising valid field methods is especially difficult when one delves into language use and its import for society. All too often, language is the one variable that is ignored in all nonlinguistic research, despite the fact that virtually all investigation in the social sciences depends on language use, both by the researchers and by those being researched. That is, language use is almost always a variable which must be accounted for in one's results, but, unless the object of the investigation is language use itself, it is often ignored.

CHAPTER 2

Almost any social variable can affect the kinds of linguistic output one can get. For instance, an investigator cannot use the same methods in a bilingual community as in a monolingual one. As we will see, typically, bilinguals select which of their languages to use according to the social situation. Some will use one language only in the home, or only if relatives are present, finding it impossible to speak it to strangers. Others will find it impossible to speak anything but English unless they are speaking to someone of their own ethnic group. Others are insulted that the researcher makes no effort to speak their language, resenting having to speak English for tests or interviews. Still others will not use one of their languages if the researcher speaks it with a strong accent. To some degree, Americans find this when they go abroad. Even if they do speak the language of the country they are visiting, they may find that natives will slip into English as soon as they hear an American accent.

All of this is complicated by **diglossia** situations, in which members of a culture use different languages for different social purposes. Then the researcher must first ascertain what the proper language for a formal interview is, or the usual language selected for more casual interactions. If testing is to be administered in schools, then the language associated with formal schooling must be chosen. If an investigator uses the wrong language for the situation, the data gathered will be inaccurate.

Among monolinguals, close attention must be paid to the dialect or register selected in the testing situation. Monolinguals are as constrained in their speech output by the demands of the social situation as bilinguals are in their selection of language. For both groups, moreover, the social situation itself must be one conducive to eliciting speech. If a child is plucked out of a classroom and taken into a cubicle with a formally dressed adult who then picks up a toy and asks, "What's this?" the result may well be that the child feels intimidated, afraid that there's a catch somewhere, and so refuses to answer. After all, why would an adult ask such a silly question in such a foreboding atmosphere? William Labov pointed this out in his critiques of studies of inner-city children done in the 1950's by researchers like Bereiter and Englemann (1966). They claimed, on the basis of such interviewing techniques, that African American children were 'nonverbal.' In contrast, William Labov had an assistant dress in casual clothes, sit on the floor with a group of such children, and start playing verbal games with them, games they were well-practiced in. Under these circumstances, the same children who mumbled and stumbled with Bereiter and Englemann's testing proved themselves to have excellent verbal facility.

By carefully investigating the speech behaviors of African Americans, Labov noted that their verbal interactions consisted of a great deal of verbal jousting, and that the way to elicit speech data from this population was to allow them to compete with each other. Of course, this technique wouldn't work so well with children of other cultures who, for instance, have been trained not to interrupt each other, or taught that it is impolite to contradict someone. Since speaking practices vary so greatly among different cultural groups, these must always be accounted for in any investigation.

To get valid data from interviews, one must conduct them so that subjects are put at ease, unless one is specifically investigating behaviors associated with nervousness or hostility. If subjects are to be at ease, then the investigator must conform to their culture. If members of the culture are most comfortable talking in competition with peers, then there must be group interviews. If the subjects are children, and their culture does not allow easy conversation between adults and children, then the adult must dress informally, use the children's usual dialect, and even get down on the floor, ready to play. If not, the children may well respond to all questions with silence or an "I don't know" even if they do know. If members of a culture are uncomfortable talking to someone who is wearing a shirt or tie, then no shirt and tie should be worn. One cannot just go out and interview or test people. One must first find out something about the way they interact and the conditions under which they are likely to talk or to carry out the assigned task.

The equipment used is important in the results one gets. I find it best not to use hand-held microphones at all. Many speakers clutch them, face them directly, and earnestly talk into them. Others become flustered by them, hemming, hawing, and stuttering. One doesn't get good measures of speaker's fluency this way, and casual, everyday speech is virtually impossible to elicit and record under such circumstances.

The results are equally poor if the interviewer keeps shoving the microphone in the subject's face, TV-newsman-style. Even those who are at ease with microphones can cause problems with a hand mike. They forget themselves, start their usual gestures while talking, waving the mike back and forth to the detriment of the recording. A microphone that attaches around the neck is better.

The newer digital voice recorders are excellent replacements for tape recorders and microphones. The researcher can just lay one on a table. It is small and not intrusive. These recorders have sensitive pickup so you get good quality recordings, and subjects aren't nervous or self-conscious as you're recording them. I've used them in several situations with great success. Some studies now are conducted over the telephone! The new *Atlas of North American Pronunciation* (Labov, Ash et al. 2006) was based upon telephone interviews, which then were analyzed acoustically with a computerized speech program for capturing fine distinctions in pronunciations.

Finding Out What You Want to Know

The biggest problem with field methods is devising a test or experiment that tells you what you want to know. Often, despite the most careful planning, once a study is completed, results can be interpreted quite differently from what was originally intended. Experimental subjects may not have reacted as expected; they may have reacted to the wrong cue or been influenced by a speech feature other than the one being studied.

For instance, having subjects evaluate tape recordings of other speakers is a common methodology used for many purposes. If it is important to know how Americans feel about the pronunciation "uh" /ə/[2] instead of "er" /r/ in words like *other* and *teacher*, a tape of someone who uses the /ə/ a great deal would be played and then a tape of a strong /r/ pronouncer. Subjects can be asked to rank each speaker on personal qualities such as intelligence, confidence, sincerity, educational traits, and any other traits pertinent to the particular investigation.

The investigator could not record just any two speakers. Special care has to be taken to ensure that the only difference between the two speakers was the use of /ə/ instead of /r/. If one speaker pronounced the *th* in *other* as /d/ and a second pronounced it as /ð/, the subject might rate the speakers on the difference between those sounds, not on the way /r/ was pronounced. Or, if one of the taped speakers used an /ɔ/ "aw" in *talk* and the other used an /a/ "ah," those might be the crucial sounds in the evaluations.

This does not mean that evaluations of voices are not good. They are exceedingly valuable sources of information if they are set up correctly, as shown in the next section. The importance of good field methods cannot be overstressed, for what is found depends on how it was sought. The results that get analyzed depend wholly on the field methods used to collect them. Because of the richness of language data, triviality in testing is always a problem.

It is easy to devise careful experiments that elicit speech because speech can be elicited in so many ways, but one still can end up with trivial or fragmented data with little, if any, relation to normal functioning. For instance, one can ask subjects to memorize lists of words and recite them backward. Undoubtedly, people will differ in their ability to perform this task, but the relation of such performance to actual speech and memory is obscure. Word association tests, for another example, may tell us a lot about people's associations to given words, but they do not tell us how people select words in a sentence. Normal discourse is not produced by uttering words that are associated with each other. It is produced by selecting words that fit the intended meaning.

Unfortunately, it is not always immediately apparent that a given procedure is going to yield trivial results. The best that can be done is to ask questions like:

- What aspect of behavior am I testing for?
- Does this task tap the skills needed for that behavior?
- What could my subjects be responding to besides what I want them to?
- What factors could be influencing my results besides those I intended?

If an experiment does not work out as hoped or an investigation yields nothing of interest, that, too, is part of the process of discovery. It happens to just about everyone at one time or another.

Matched Guise Testing. In sociolinguistic studies, one often intends to test for one thing but ends up getting a reaction to another. For instance, if one wants to find out how prestigious a certain speech variety is, one might play tapes of people speaking that way and have test subjects fill out a rating questionnaire asking how educated, brave, honest, sincere, or whatever the speaker is. One would always include samples of speakers with other dialects. If one uses both male and female voices, however, the responses on the questionnaire may reflect the subject's feelings about men and women, not the speech variety itself. One can avoid this by having only people of the same sex on the tape. Even here, a problem arises. Perhaps the subject is responding not to the speech variety per se, but to the voice quality of the speaker. That is, a speaker might be downgraded because a subject found his or her voice grating, or a subject might be upgraded because he or she has such a mellifluous voice. In either event, we still haven't found out if the speaker's dialect itself is favored or not.

Wallace Lambert and his cohorts (Lambert, Giles, and Picard 1975) avoided the problem of reactions to taped voices by using the **matched guise** technique. They found people who could command two languages or dialects[3] equally well, and had them read passages in each guise. Subjects, not realizing that they were evaluating the same person, rated each. Their reaction, then, could be safely taken to be to the given language or dialect, not to other aspects of voice quality. Matched guise testing has proven fruitful in a variety of experimental procedures.

It is not always possible to find a bilingual or bidialectal speaker equally proficient in both varieties under consideration. Actors and actresses can be used, but with extreme caution. Although they fancy that they are giving accurate renditions of dialects or accents, usually they are using stylized stage dialects that do not conform to the genuine one. Every Bostonian knew that the mailman Cliff on the TV comedy *Cheers* didn't have a true Boston accent. And a native Rhode Islander finds the supposed Providence accents on Showtime's series *Brotherhood* laughable.

Testing for Voice Quality. Sometimes one wants to test voice quality itself. For instance, it is useful to find out if members of a society find high-pitched voices weak, graceful, charming, honest, or whatever, or if they find raspy voices commanding, irritating, sexy, masculine, convincing, or dishonest. Again, tapes can be used with subjects' filling out questionnaires, but now one deliberately wants speakers with different voice quality. Here, again, the sex of the speaker is important. A high voice might be attractive in a woman, but not in a man. Conversely, a deep voice in a woman might be downgraded but valued highly in a man, especially if the deep voice is associated with power or authority. Notice that in this kind of testing, one can ask questions designed to find out how weak, strong, dominant, submissive, honest, or dishonest the voice quality is, and that these judgments will differ according to the gender of the speaker. It is probably better not to ask directly, "Is this the voice of an honest person?" Rather, one could ask questions like, "Would you choose this speaker as a member of a team?" "What occupation would you find this person suitable for: manager, sales . . .?" One can also ask subjects to choose speakers for different tasks from an array of speakers on a tape.

One problem in determining reaction to voice quality (or to dialect features, for that matter) is that the meaning (semantic content) of what is being said might affect the subject's judgment. One obvious way to control for this is to have several speakers read an identical passage. Unfortunately, this bores listeners so much that they may start to tune out the readers. Another is to have each read paraphrases of one passage or to have each read successive paragraphs from one article or speech. That way, at least style and topic are limited. Another technique is to mask words by passing recorded speech through an acoustic filter that obliterates the higher frequencies of sound necessary for word recognition but leaves voice qualities like nasality, deepness, tremulousness, or breathiness (Kramer 1963; Laver 1968; Abercrombie 1967). Nowadays, computerized speech programs can be used to simulate voice qualities in experiments.

Observation and Participant Observation. In the social sciences, there is always a temptation to rely on haphazard personal observations. Some scholars do this a great deal, citing their intuitions about various matters. Others criticize insights offered from intuition. Actually, everyone uses hunches. It is a hunch that makes one want to investigate some aspect of behavior. Even a pioneer like Labov (1963, 1966) who insisted upon intricate methodologies, had hunches about what to test for. Moreover, analysis of data, no matter how those data are gathered, depends to a great extent on a scholar's intuition and insight. Especially when examining broad aspects of human behavior, it is rare that data inexorably lead just to one conclusion. Interpretation is important. Without it data are just a random collection of facts. For example, in a study of African American street gangs in Harlem, a research team headed by Labov (Labov et al. 1968) found that the boys within a gang all spoke somewhat differently. While that was true, it certainly was not interesting in itself. Indeed, linguists had long spoken of individual **idiolects**, as opposed to **dialects**. The latter are speech patterns shared by people within a regional or social group, whereas features of idiolects are not so shared. They are idiosyncratic, individual variations in speech.

What made Labov et al.'s study so valuable was that they had charted the friendship network of their subjects on graphs called **sociograms**. When the speech features of the boys were correlated with the sociograms, the variation in speech among the gang was seen to mirror social position within the group. It must have been a hunch that led them to use sociograms in the first place, a hunch based upon Labov's earlier correlations of speech with social facts. Some of the most interesting and valuable works about human behavior have had their impetus from intuition. The works of scholars like Erving Goffman and Harvey Sacks come immediately to mind. There is nothing wrong with hunches or intuitions, so long as a careful attempt is made to verify them. Intuition is no substitute for careful study, nor is it an excuse for sloppy, anecdotal conclusions.

Observation, both participant and nonparticipant, is vital to the social scientist. A participant observation is one in which the researcher takes part in the action, saying or doing something and then observing the reactions. An excellent example of this is Tannen's analyses of a Thanksgiving dinner with some friends (Tannen 1984). Nonparticipant observation is just looking, noting, and analyzing what is seen and heard in a situation.

Because speech behavior is so complex and inextricably dependent on context for its meaning, much behavior can be understood only through skilled observation. Researchers like Goffman, Sacks, and Birdwhistell, all concerned with discourse and/or body motion in natural circumstances, rely heavily on nonparticipant observation. However, they know how to correlate observations with known facts about human behavior, facts that often are based upon experiments. Valid observations also depend upon collecting data systematically, controlling for environmental factors, and using statistical measurements to validate results.

CHAPTER 2

Just going out into the streets and listening randomly is not likely to yield verifiable insights. First, the researcher has to define a problem, the object of the investigation. Then, likely spots for observation must be determined. Not only must one choose locales that have the right people doing the right things, but one also must consider such ordinary matters as where one is going to sit or stand. Will there be a place for unobtrusive listening and looking? In a participant observation, is there a place to start the interactions naturally so that subjects do not get suspicious? One must also make sure there is not so much noise or movement that confusion could result.

Sometimes the researcher can manipulate a situation under observation without actually participating in it. A student who wished to investigate whether the presence of women affected male speech invited friends to his house to watch a football game. While viewing the game, they commented loudly with a great deal of profanity, as was usual. The investigator had invited two females to drop in at the start of the game before there had been too much beer drinking. As the girls walked in, although the viewers did not acknowledge their presence, the comments instantly became devoid of offensive words. The following week, the experiment was repeated, but with the girls showing up after the viewers had drunk a great deal of beer. This time the profanity did not cease in the presence of the females. In essence, this was an observation, but one done in which conditions were controlled. The investigator did not actually participate, for he did not interact with the viewers beyond greeting them and saying good-bye. What he demonstrated was that, even in these liberated days, men feel inhibited about swearing in front of women, an inhibition, like so many others, lessened by alcohol.

A classic participant observation is Labov's (1966, 63–89) famous department store survey. Checking on his intuition that r-full pronunciation was becoming a sign of middle- and upper class-speech in New York City, Labov visited three department stores: Saks Fifth Avenue, Macy's, and the now-defunct Klein's. Saks caters to the wealthy, Macy's is a solid middle-class store, and Klein's, in an unfashionable neighborhood, was a low-priced store aimed at the blue-collar and lower classes, although, like Macy's, people of all classes shopped there.

Starting on the first floor of each store, Labov asked a sales clerk to direct him to a department he knew to be on the fourth floor. He called this the **casual** style. He then asked the question a second time to obtain a careful repetition. He called this the **emphatic** style. When he reached the fourth floor, he asked, "Excuse me, what floor is this?" On both floors, sales clerks had to answer, "Fourth floor." These words have the /r/ in two of the positions that it is not pronounced in so-called r-less speech: before a consonant and at the end of words when no other word follows.[4] That is, the /r/ isn't pronounced if a word ending in /r/ is said in isolation.

As he had predicted, Labov found almost no preconsonantal /r/'s in Klein's, somewhat more in Macy's, and the most in Saks. In the exclusive upstairs salons of Saks, there was even more incidence of /r/'s than on the first floor, which looks more like any other department store and has somewhat less-expensive goods. This study yielded a great deal of significant data in a short time. It had the advantage that the speech of the employees being analyzed was wholly unself-conscious and natural.

This survey is an example of an ingenious investigation, but it also illustrates some real dangers of observation. Since he did not ask any of the salesclerks where they came from, it might be that those who were /r/-full were not native New York City speakers. New York has long been a mecca for people around the country. Also, there is no check on what Labov actually heard. We have to take his word for the fact that he heard what he said he did. Yet, linguists, especially, know all too well that people hear what they expect to hear. There are various degrees of sharpness in pronouncing /r/, as Labov himself noted. Often, listeners fail to hear a lightly constricted /r/.

The greatest pitfall in all science is that an investigator finds what he or she sets out to find. There is simply an all-too-human tendency not to notice what is not relevant to one's purpose and to think that one has seen or heard what is. Labov himself admits this problem with the department store survey, and he did follow it up with other experiments that studied the same feature of speech, using careful and highly innovative methodologies.

Verifying Results

One can lessen the problem of personal bias in a study such as Labov's department store study in two ways. First, get a partner. At least there will be one other pair of ears or set of eyes to verify what is going on. Second, in these days of tiny recorders, tapings are possible if one adheres to ethical standards, as noted below.

Audio and video recordings of your studies certainly enhance verifiability. The advent of good audio recorders has made the dialect worker's lot simpler than the older method of transcription as the consultant spoke, but they are not panaceas. For one thing, recordings made in the field, as opposed to a lab, may prove to be fuzzy when played back. Environmental noises, hissing, and buzzing may intrude. One finds that the subject's voice fades in and out, or comes out as an indistinct mumble, often in crucial places. Also, even experienced phoneticians may have problems determining exactly which sounds were uttered. Certain sounds come through as almost identical on tape. For instance, it is sometimes difficult to distinguish between /f/, /s/, and /θ/ "th" as in *thing*. This, of course, is why those linguists who have the budget for the equipment now use computerized acoustic analysis, but this is not always available .

Even with the clearest of recordings on the best of equipment, transcription can be difficult if an investigator has to determine very fine differences in pronunciation. Since fine differences are sometimes socially significant, it is essential that transcription be accurate. There are literally hundreds of potentially important pieces of information in every interview, from fine variations in pronunciations to grammatical choices to the very organization of a narrative. All must be noted, categorized, and correlated with other factors. Giving an interview often takes hours, and it can take days to extract all of the data from each interview. Consequently, sample size must be limited.

Virtually any study of body motion, facial expression, or the like demands photographs or video recordings. Their value needs no explication.

Replicability and Variation. In order for any study to be valid, it must be **replicable**. This means that someone else can do the study exactly as the original researcher had and come up with comparable results. Years ago, there was some flurry about a book which purported to show that plants can understand language and which presented an impressive list of experiments "verifying" this proposition. The only problem was that nobody was ever able to replicate any of these experiments.

One can also do a study and change one of its **variables** and get a result accounted for by the variation. For instance, Wallace Chafe and his cohorts studied the ways people speaking different languages and coming from different cultures narrate a movie they had just seen (Chafe 1980). They all saw the same movie. The variables here were the differences in language and culture, not the movie.

I adapted this study to a population of diagnosed schizophrenics (Chaika 1990) with a matched normal population as **controls**. The variable in my study was the schizophrenia. The normals performed like other Americans in the Chafe study. Therefore, differences in features of the narrations could be related to the fact of schizophrenia.[5] McKenna and Oh (2005) recently replicated the same study with British schizophrenics, finding the same features in the schizophrenic speech that I did. A good experimental protocol can have a long life.

Interestingly, it was not that normals made no errors and schizophrenics did. Both populations had glitches in their narratives, but the schizophrenics did certain things the normals didn't. For instance, normals would break a sentence off in the middle, give a comment, and then resume, as in:

1. and then she—**her father came home from work, what-ever**—she asked her father for money.

In contrast, when the schizophrenics broke a sentence off in the middle, they never resumed it, as in:

2. he was blamed **for** and I didn't think that was fair the way they did that either.

3. and asks if she can **have** then goes to the ice-cream place . . .

Sampling. The purpose of the investigation helps determine sample size and composition. If one wishes to contrast two attitudes in a community, a much smaller sample is needed than if one wishes to delineate general social stratification. Ten to twenty speakers from each social group in the community is generally considered a sufficient number, especially if long and varied interviews are given. Fortunately, there are statistical measures that allow one to extrapolate from small samples (Woods, Fletcher, and Hughes 1986, 101–10).

Finding speakers to observe or interview is a problem in itself. Using any given source might skew the distribution of members in a sample so that it is not representative of the population at large. School enrollment lists skew toward the younger population, those with children in school as well as the pupils themselves. Voting lists do not give names of those who are unregistered, often the poorest or lower classes. Telephone books do not give names of people with unlisted numbers. If, as Anshen (1978) thinks, these are the rich, then they will be underrepresented in the sample. Nowadays, another factor is illegal immigration. With estimates as high as at least 11 million illegal immigrants, a sizable number of U.S. residents is not likely to be tapped on questions concerning health and education. Certainly, any study of how people learn a second language would do well to include this population if possible.

However one chooses from a population, one is sampling randomly within each group in the community. One can also do **quasi-random** sampling (Butler 1985, 3). This is done by selecting the first person—or unit, if people aren't the targets—randomly, and then choosing the others at equal intervals, say, every twentieth. Rarely can one study every single person within any group, unless one is studying, for example, a relatively small gang (Labov, et al. 1968). This means that within each group there is random sampling. Understanding this is important when analyzing results statistically.

In order to come to valid conclusions, there must be an adequately representative sampling of the **target population**, the population under consideration (Woods 1986, 49). For sociolinguistics, adequacy depends upon distribution as well as numbers if one is comparing or describing more than one group. Even within what one thinks is one group, say, urban blacks or women or Jews, one has to consider that there might be age and/or educational differences, or differences according to length of residency or some other factor. Therefore, rarely is it sufficient simply to have a percentage of a total population of a city or town, or even a neighborhood, unless those locales are remarkably homogeneous in the above factors.

Usually, the investigator first groups the population on such factors as age, sex, ethnic origin, race, and social class, and even gang and club membership if these seem potentially important. Investigation may show that some of the groups are not significantly different, but speakers still have to be chosen from every possible group at the outset of the sampling. Otherwise, significance or lack of it cannot be proven.

Generally speaking, the larger the sample tested, the more valid the results. However, the analysis of sociolinguistic data can be exceptionally time-consuming as one gets so many hundreds, even thousands, of potentially valuable data points from each subject. Every variation in pronunciation, grammar, word choice, voice quality, and body motion may have to be recorded and tabulated. Fortunately, powerful computer programs have made such analyses doable. Also, while one starts out thinking of every variation, as one starts tabulating, it often becomes clear that not all of them are making a difference, so one can focus just on those that do.

A good place to start is the sociology department of a nearby college or university to see if a general sociological survey of the area has been made recently. This not only points to the probable significant groupings in the community but is a source of subjects as well.

Too often, U. S. studies of standard versus nonstandard dialects and, more recently, studies of literacy versus illiteracy have really been studies of one of the regional standard American Englishes versus African American English rather than including other kinds of nonstandard speech.

Comparing standard speech of whites with African American vernacular (henceforth, AAVE) confuses issues of race and standard speech, which may be very separate factors in one's results. Since middle-class African American speech is largely ignored, readers can get the impression that African Americans are all nonstandard speakers and perhaps are also illiterates. This is certainly not true. Middle- and upper-class African

Americans usually speak the same standard speech as non-African Americans in their region do. Some are also bidialectal, mastering both AAVE and standard speech.

It is never valid in a study to ask people directly what they think of another group. Americans, by and large, will not admit that they are prejudiced, so if one wants to see if they are, one has to get at the information another way. This is usually done by matched guise testing, as described earlier.

Statistics. We also have to show that our results didn't happen by chance. For this, we have to use **statistical tests**. Some people think we can make statistics say whatever we want them to. Unfortunately for researchers, this is simply not true. Nor is it true that, as the old saw goes, "There are lies, damned lies, and statistics." It is true, however, that there are several kinds of statistical tests that can be applied, each for somewhat varying purposes. It is not unusual for a student, scholar, or researcher to be criticized because he or she didn't do a particular test, one that would give a different result. One of the reasons that scholars give papers at meetings and publish in journals is so that their analyses can be subjected to such checks. Thus, scholarship improves.

It is, of course, not possible in a text such as this to present enough material so that readers can actually learn how to apply statistical measures. It is useful, however, especially for those who have not had a course in it, to explain the purpose of statistics and, very generally, what they mean and why they must be used. That is the intent of the following discussion.

The purpose of statistical analysis in the social sciences is simple enough: to see if differences in scores, or other facts, between two or more groups occur because of the random variation that one would get in any population. If the results couldn't happen by chance, then we have a **significant difference**. This term should only be used for results that have been subjected to tests of **probability**. In order to have a significant difference, the probability of our results occurring by chance has to be less than 1 in 20, written as $p = <.05$. That is the highest our p-score can be. If $p < .01$ (1 in 100) or $p < .001$ (1 in 1,000), it is even better.

Labov did not use statistics in his dialect studies. He said that it was not necessary to use statistics when "results are repetitive" (Labov 1969). Lawrence Davis (1982) shows that this is not true. Davis analyzed Labov's results in the department store survey and found that some of the differences were not significant. For instance, he found that there was not a significant difference between employees at Macy's and Klein's when they pronounced *fourth* emphatically, but there was a significant difference in the casual pronunciation between Saks and Macy's when pronouncing *floor*. However, this is mighty slim evidence that *r*-dropping increases the lower the class, especially when we recall that Labov sampled a population, sales clerks, without knowing anything about their backgrounds. He assumed what social class people belong to on the basis of the feature he had already decided was lower class. This is a classic example of circular reasoning.

Most people are familiar with one kind of measure used in statistics: the **mean**, the technical term for *average*. By itself, however, the mean can be very misleading. For instance, Labov found that nobody pronounced certain sounds in only one way all of the time. Rather, pronunciation varied. Labov (1966) showed that people from all classes sometimes pronounced the /θ/ "th" more like *t* in words like *throw, thing,* and *death,* but that the variation correlated with feelings of identity with different social groups. Characteristically, each pronounced it in this way a different percent of the time.

Suppose I wish to replicate Labov's study. I find that two different groups, X and Y, make the *t* for /θ/ a mean of 12 times out of a possible 24. If, however, this was distributed so that X pronounced /θ/ 24 times, and Y never pronounced it at all, then these two groups are heterogeneous and probably shouldn't even be compared. In other words, they form two distinctly different groups. If, however, I find that X pronounces the /θ/ 15 times and Y does so 9 times, I still have an average of 12, but it means something quite different. The two groups are comparable, and /θ/ is a speech variable for both groups (which it isn't if one group never pronounces it and the other always does).

However, we still don't know if the difference between X and Y has occurred by chance. In order to know this, we have to see how closely the scores cluster around the mean. Thus we find the **standard deviation**.

What this tells us is:

> If the deviation from the mean is very large compared to the standard deviation, then we conclude that there is a **significant difference** between the populations. If the difference between the means is small compared to the standard deviation, then we conclude that the difference is due to chance.
>
> Where did chance come in? Recall that the members of the two groups were selected at random (by chance) as representatives of each group. When you take random samples from any group, you will observe random differences among sample means. The question is, is the difference in your study one of those random differences or is the difference greater than can be accounted for by random chance? (Richard Lambe, classroom lecture)

ETHICS

Finally, it is not ethical to make people unwitting guinea pigs. With few exceptions, if people are to take part in an experiment, no matter how innocuous, their consent must be obtained. The subjects have to be told exactly what is required of them and as much as possible about the purposes of the study without prejudicing the results. Sometimes, they can't be told the purpose of the study, but, even then, an investigator can't lie. He or she should tell subjects that reactions to a situation or a problem are being evaluated without telling them exactly what is being looked for.

Under no conditions should someone's performance be ridiculed or criticized in any way. At no time and for no reason should an investigator identify subjects or report their individual performances. If a subject tells the investigator something about his or her life or makes any comment on a topic beyond the testing situation, that information cannot be used in any way without express consent of the subject. Hidden tape recorders and bugging devices should not be used unless subjects are told about them, preferably beforehand, and even then the content of the tapes cannot be used without **informed consent**. This term means that the person taped, interviewed, or otherwise made a subject must give consent, knowing that results of his or her performance will be included in the general results of the study.

It is far better to inform subjects that they are being investigated, get their consent, and get them accustomed to the presence of a tape recorder. One has to have very strong reasons for any other procedure. If one wishes natural dialogue, one can contact a club or other groups and ask their consent to record meetings, or one can invite friends to one's home, letting them know a tape is being made and why. The tape recorder can be placed in full view, and as the interaction gets under way, people simply forget about it.

It does not take much reading in sociolinguistics to come across studies done by hidden tape recorders. This is done only in studies of anonymous people in which semantic content is not reported in print or orally, and then only if the data cannot reasonably be obtained in any other way. We will see a hidden tape recorder's being used in Chapter 10, but only in recording public interactions.

It must be emphasized that science is not an excuse for immorality. People are always entitled to privacy. Hidden recording devices are uncomfortably close to eavesdropping. Before moving in close enough to record, the investigator should make sure the conversation is not private or intimate in any way. Only public transactions qualify, such as greetings and chitchat, conversations on buses, or on benches at malls. If a conversation is loud enough for everyone around to hear easily and no attempt is being made to mask the content, it can justifiably be considered public. The same privacy limitations hold for any other method of preserving conversation, such as writing it down as one hears it. Even if one jots down only selected features of a conversation, such as the number of pauses or interruptions, there should be no eavesdropping on private interactions without prior consent.

Notes

[1] A vowel merger occurs when words that used to be pronounced with different vowels begin to be pronounced alike. As we shall see in Chapter 7, vowel mergers are going on in many dialects in North America.

[2] This is the way the British would pronounce the final sound of *teacher*.

[3] These are what most laypersons think of as "an accent," but, as we shall see, it also involves grammar and words as well.

[4] The third position is at the end of a word if the next word starts with a consonant. If the next word starts with a vowel, the /r/ will be pronounced.

[5] Actually, the Chafe movie was too long and potentially threatening to this schizophrenic population, as would be the paraphernalia of a movie. Therefore, I devised a shorter sequence on videotape, but the task itself was the same.

CHAPTER 2

Exercises

1. Suppose you wanted to discover how people ranked different accents. How would you go about setting up a study to do this? What uses might such a study have? How would you design your study so that it would work for these uses?

2. How would you go about getting a sample of subjects? From what populations would you choose your subjects? How are these populations related to the purpose of your study?

3. You want to find out whether males are more likely than females to try to solve problems than to sympathize with someone's problem, or to find out if males are more competitive in their speech than females. How would you set up a study to investigate any such topic? What pitfalls would you anticipate, and how would you try to avoid them?

4. Take a five-minute tape recording of anybody speaking. Try to transcribe it. How long does it take? Have someone else check your transcription. Do they find you have transcribed something wrong? Or differently from how they would? Were there any portions of the tape you couldn't transcribe? What does this experience tell you about dealing with large amounts of oral language in a study?

5. Make up an informed consent form that you might use in a study of your own. Also make up a questionnaire that asks for background information.

6. Suppose you were a linguist and a large corporation hired you as the director of research. What sorts of studies in language use might you devise? What kinds of language issues would you suggest to the corporation's executives as being important to the company's public relations personnel, sales, managers, and receptionists?

7. Suppose you were a linguist and a labor union hired you as director of research. What sorts of studies in language use might you devise for the union? How would you go about investigating language issues important to negotiators, speech givers, those in charge of publicity, and lobbyists?

8. Go sit on a bench in a playground for preschool-age children. How do the children get others to share or to comply with their wishes? What language skills do they evince? What kind of study might you conduct from such an observation? How would you record data? How would you organize it?

Chapter 3

Style of Speech

Speech, like dress, varies with the situation. Styles used only in certain locales and occasions are called registers. Voice quality is learned, not completely inborn. Different aspects of voice have been shown to correlate with the way one's personality is perceived. Style forms a communication system apart from linguistic messages given in words and sentences. In fact, these messages are not supposed to be conveyed by the linguistic code itself. Style controls social interaction subliminally. Messages of power and solidarity between interactants are an important function of style. Each society has its own rules of politeness. It is not certain that one society is more polite than another. What is true is that politeness may be encoded on different parts of the language.

STYLE AS COMMUNICATION

Style refers to the selection of linguistic forms to convey social or artistic effects. In recent years, the term *style* has also been used to indicate different modes of communicative strategy associated with ethnicity, a matter taken up in a later chapter. In this chapter, we consider style as alternate forms to convey mood or other social or artistic messages. In these guises, style often acts as a set of instructions. The messages it conveys are not normally conveyed in words. Indeed, the idiom "didn't get the message" refers to listeners' not picking up on style, even though they understood the actual words. Interactants mutually apply style both to guide and manipulate others. In any conversation, we often rely upon style to get others to conform to our wishes without coming right out and saying what we want. Curiously, such manipulation—or guidance, depending on how you look at it—like other backgrounded matters in social uses of language, facilitates the smooth progress of ordinary daily interaction.

Style forms a communication system in its own right, one that determines how a social interaction will proceed, or if it will proceed at all. If it is to continue, style tells how, whether formally or informally. Style may also tell listeners how to take what is being said: seriously, ironically, humorously, angrily, lovingly, or dubiously. Style is also intimately bound up with our presentation of self, the image we convey to others.

CHAPTER 3

Often when the meaning of the style of an utterance contradicts the meaning of the words and grammar used,the style is believed (Bugental, Kaswan and Love 1970; Mehrabian and Wiener 1967). Since style tells us how to interpret a message, this is not surprising. For example, if "Nice move" is said sarcastically, the style instructs 'take these words to mean the opposite of what they actually say.' Thus, "Nice move" means 'Stupid move.' Similarly, a timid "I'm not afraid" conveys 'I am afraid.' And, a cold, formal "We'll be in touch" is not going to encourage the listener to sit by the phone waiting for a call. Style forms a communication system that works along with language itself, yet is apart from it. Many stylistic messages are countered only with other stylistic messages. Style uses all the resources of language: tone of voice, different pronunciations, even the choice between synonymous words and grammar. The number of possible variations of style is far more limited, however, than the possible choices of words and their combinations in sentences.

Style overlaps with ritualistic uses of language, as in greetings and forms of address. Each language or dialect usually has several of these, each marked for a different style. Considering the function of style as the controller of the interaction, this is hardly surprising. Greetings and address start interactions. One expects heavy style-marking on them because they set the tone for what is to follow.

Registers

A style may be associated with a particular social occasion. Then it is called **register** or **functional variety** of speech. One uses one register at a funeral and another in the receiving line at a wedding. Sometimes, an occasion calls for switching into a second dialect for bidialectal speakers, or even into another language for bilingual speakers. Both dialect and language switches are associated with occasion or mood. We cannot make neat categories for style, dialect, and language. There is a continuum from style to register to dialect to language. This may disconcert readers who wish that everything can be divided into nice tidy labels and definitions. The fuzzy borders between language categories are what ultimately make language flexible. To put it another way, human beings can handle variation. The thing to remember is that the elements of speech that get varied are the same in style, dialect, and language. Styles differ from one another in the same features as dialects and languages do. Since dialect and language differences will occupy the rest of this book, only style will be discussed here.

Choosing Linguistic Alternants

John Gumperz (1971) pointed out that one's choice of linguistic alternants "reflects the positions actors [parties in an interaction] assume relative to each other." By linguistic **alternants**, he meant sets of words and/or phrases that share meaning but differ in that one or more members of the set carries a social connotation. This connotation gives information about the speaker's social status and about how he or she wishes to be treated.

In an earlier piece, Gumperz (1964) gave the example of *dine* versus *eat*. Both denote consumption of food, but *dine* connotes more formal surroundings, calling for formal manners. It also implies certain kinds of food: *coq au vin* as opposed to fried chicken. Choice of the verb *dine* also carries implications about those who are doing it. Gumperz (1964, 139) says, "Not everyone can 'dine.' Certainly not two laborers during a dinner break no matter how well prepared the food . . . and how good their table manners." How attitudes have changed! Certainly, the laborers—or professionals for that matter—don't dine during a lunch break, but laborers certainly can and do go to nice restaurants, and they certainly do dine when there. *Dine* implies a kind of environment and food, not a person of a given social class, at least in modern America.

One way to verify that words have stylistic meaning is to notice the difference in **co-occurrence restrictions**. These are restrictions on what words can go together. For instance, in English, both people and animals can be killed, but only people can be murdered or assassinated. The latter two verbs imply the victim was a human being.[1] Similar restrictions determine which style goes with certain words. Words that differ in the degree of formality do not usually **co-occur**, nor do words that give conflicting information about social status. Note, for example:

1. Let's dine on fried chicken.
2. Hey, baby, wanna dine tonight?
3. Let's go dinin' tonight.
4. Wouldja dine with me tonight?
5. Would you dine with me tonight?
6. Mrs. Whitmore wishes you to dine with her.

The first four sentences are humorous. The joke for each lies in the violation of co-occurrence restrictions. Except for *hors d'ouevres,* food eaten with the fingers is not an appropriate object of *dine.* "Hey, baby," implies that the speaker is a young male trying to put forth a macho image. Since, in our society, being macho is not associated with refinement, such speech forms clash with the formal *dine.* The pronunciation -*in* instead of -*ing* in 3 clashes with the formality of *dine,* as the variant -*in* belongs to casual speech. *Wouldja* is a more casual pronunciation than *would* you, and doesn't go with the formal *dine*. The last two sentences are not humorous because they are entirely formal, hence appropriate for *dine*, although they too could be used facetiously by, say, a person adopting a formal tone for comic effect.

Speakers give a great deal of information about themselves just by the words, grammar, and pronunciation they choose both unconsciously and consciously. This information reveals to the hearer such things as the speaker's social or educational background and regional affiliation. The style markers of a particular social group or region may be deliberately used for other purposes. For instance, the man who approaches a woman with "Hey, baby, I like yo' gear" may not be an inner-city youth. Middle- and upper-class whites and African Americans have adopted such speech. Although his own usual dialect does not normally greet with "Hey, baby . . . " nor use *gear* to mean 'clothes,' a middle- or upper-class man may choose that terminology as a way of asserting his masculinity. His "hey, baby" lets the woman know that he does not want their encounter to be formal. It is an invitation to intimacy. Of course, she may not be in accord. If she is not, she responds in a style appropriate both to her status and the degree of intimacy she prefers, as in the following:

7. I'm busy tonight, thank you.
8. Were you talking to me, sir?

She does not need to comment overtly on his style. Rather, by her responding with a formal style, she instructs him to keep his distance. Her style alone says, "Back off, Jack," although her words do not. The message also is conveyed by her intonation, inflection, and precise pronunciation. For instance, the second of the above responses uttered with a rising inflection might be interpreted as a coquettish response. It would be downright odd if she said something explicit like, "I do not want you to be so familiar to me. I do not consider myself a sexually available woman, nor do I wish to be intimate with you." Such messages are usually given by style. Actual words are used only on the rare occasions that the offending party is too obtuse to "get the message." It must be emphasized that the social message conveyed by style is not always coded directly onto actual words.

GREETINGS

Greetings are an excellent example of style as communication. Have you ever answered someone's "Hi! How are you?" with a brisk "Lousy" or its equivalent, only to get a cheerful response of "That's good" as the greeter traveled on? Conversely, have you ever answered "Fine" in a glum voice, only to have the greeter stop and ask, "Oh, what's the matter?" In both cases, clearly, the words were ignored, but the style was not (Chaika 1973).

How something is said takes precedence over what is said. Indeed, in greetings and some other social routines, it is inappropriate to state one's real feelings in words, unless the response indicates happiness and/or satisfaction and the responder genuinely has those feelings. If responders are not happy or satisfied, they still must use words that indicate good feelings. Note the implication of describing individuals as being 'the kind of people who, if you ask them how they are, tell you.' That is, they are socially inept. This sums up the social rule that Americans prefer a pretense that all is well. Hard-luck stories are not appreciated except perhaps between good friends, and then only if kept to a minimum.

Ritual greetings are supposed to convey information about someone's well-being, but not in words. Nor, today in our culture, are words usual for the messages of status and intimacy. There seem to be three reasons for this: **phatic communication** (Malinowski 1923), **control of interactions**, and **protection of the ego**, what is commonly called **face** (Goffman 1955).

The rules for greeting and other social routines are unspoken, but they are rules nevertheless. It is not surprising that in activities as complex as much conversation is, sometimes speakers unwittingly—or wittingly—break the rules. When this happens, co-conversationalists typically do not overtly comment on the infraction.[2] There are several kinds of repairs, each appropriate to particular facets of social interaction. It is revealing to examine the ways repairs are carried out as we examine the unspoken rules of conversation: the style, kinesics, and discourse routines that have to be adhered to. In each instance, the offended party attempts to right the situation without overtly commenting on the other's infractions, so that, for instance, style is repaired by one's manipulating style. We will be coming across the concept of repairing as a regulator of interactions throughout this book. Repairs differ from overt correction in that the former always gives the offender a chance to make his or her correction without losing face; that is, without being embarrassed. Looking at repairs also underscores the intricacies of interaction that we have been socialized to obey, and the regulatory functions of such behaviors.

Greetings have two functions. One is to initiate interaction; the other, which will concern us first, is what cultural anthropologist Bronislaw Malinowski (1923) called **phatic communication**, speech not to convey thoughts but to create "ties of union . . . by mere exchange of words." Phatic communication is speech for the sake of social contact, speech used much the way as we pat dogs on the head as a way of letting them know we care.

CHAPTER 3

Greeting, even if in passing, is essential to let members of society know that they count, and that "everything is all right." Most often, this is to indicate that there are no hard feelings or anger on the part of the greeter, although, in the event of a cold greeting, it may indicate that there are still hard feelings. If an acquaintance fails to say "Hi" when we know that he or she has seen us, we feel hurt. Such a trivial omission, yet we give it a name, a *snub*. We are obliged to greet even when we cannot or do not want to get into a conversation. For this reason, perhaps, the person greeted is supposed just to acknowledge the greeting phatically, not launch into a recital of "What's 'happenin'" or, yet worse, complaints about life.[3] The response "Fine" can properly end the greeting sequence. Whether or not the person is truly fine is immaterial. Phatic communication has been completed with its utterance. If the greeter wants to know more, such as why "fine" was uttered glumly, he or she can stop and ask for more information. At this juncture, it is proper to go into details. Greeting, then, fulfills two functions: first, it is a requirement of phatic communication, and second (if desired on the part of the greeter), it opens further interaction.

It is amazing how much we can be controlled by the style of a greeting, especially if it is appropriate to the person who uses it. The person with higher rank, if there is one, has the privilege of controlling interaction. This is done simply by choosing the style. Then the lower-ranking person is constrained to follow suit.

One's superior may maintain authority merely by consistently choosing formal greetings. The underling who must always respond to "How are you today, Mr./Ms. X?" with "Fine, thank you" is kept at a distance. Each time the greeting is given, the social distance is reinforced. Casual chitchat and easy confidence are almost impossible with someone who consistently greets and addresses one formally. Most important, it is difficult, even impossible, to challenge aloof, formal authority. The words metaphorically stick in one's throat. Most of us have had the experience of being at a loss to "speak up" to a teacher, employer, parent, member of the clergy, or any other dominant person. In earlier, more formal, and more authoritarian times, it was perhaps a more familiar experience than it is today in our egalitarian culture.

ADDRESS FORMS

In the United States today, the person we cannot address by a first name is not a peer. In other words, we are expected to address peers by their first names. However, this was not always so. As late as World War II, it was not uncommon even for longtime friends to address each other by titles like *Miss* or *Mr*. This is very noticeable in nineteenth- and early twentieth-century novels, as well as in plays, older movies, and newer movies seeking to recreate older times.[4]

Today in America, it is possible, but as we shall see, rare, for someone to force deference by maintaining the formality of **TLN** (Title + Last Name). Such a person can be most difficult to confront. Perhaps this is why respect always takes the form of formality. Respect implies social distance, and social distance defines formality. Being casual implies social intimacy or equality. One need not obey one's equals nor show them any particular respect beyond the bounds of normal politeness and mutual consideration.

Even if we understand how style controls us, we cannot break its barriers. For ten years, my immediate superior, a courtly gentleman who outranked me both in position and age, greeted me, "How do you do, Dr. Chaika?" Thus, he affirmed his own higher status and announced that he wished to maintain distance. Because he unfailingly greeted me that way, I, of course, was forced into a wholly uncharacteristic "How do you do, Dr. X." Even at parties, I found it impossible to say, "Hi, P. . . How's it goin'?" The round of greetings typically was, "Hey, Rich! Hi, Jane! How do you do, Dr. X?" The first time he saw me after announcing his retirement, Dr. X greeted me with, "Hello, Elaine," finally establishing us as equals.

Not all superiors wish to maintain distance, or at least not so overtly as using formal TLN. Nowadays, especially, it is not at all unusual for bosses to **FN** (first-name) their employees, and to request first names back. The late Robert DiPietro pointed out to me that such first-naming is "at least on the surface, a state which is intended to avoid confrontation." In other words, first-naming allows a pretense of equality even though one outranks the other, thus allowing the subordinate to save face. As we shall see, saving face is frequently the force behind choosing one linguistic alternant over another. This does not mean that the subordinate has no choice at all. Strangely enough, although they cannot bridge social distance by initiating first-naming, inferiors can maintain it by refusing to first-name superiors. Sometimes such refusal is virtually involuntary, as when a person simply cannot bring himself or herself to call an elder or a boss by his or her first name.

As far back as 1961, Roger Brown and Marguerite Ford said that the principal option of address in American English is either to call someone by their first name or to use their title with a surname (1961, 375). They found that mutual FN was most common, but that children called adults by TLN with adults first-naming in return. They also found that most adults, when first meeting, used TLN to each other, and that adults who were about fifteen years younger than another continued to use TLN to the older person, receiving FN in response. As adults became more intimate with

CHAPTER 3

each other, they progressed to mutual first-name. Bosses in those days were usually given TLN, with employees being addressed by FN, unless the employee was older than the boss, in which case the boss would reciprocate with TLN.

Well, things have both stayed the same and changed, largely changed. Thomas Murray, noting as perhaps most of us beyond youth have, that even older adults get first-named by younger people all the time. Upon first being introduced, adults immediately first-name each other. I've noticed that at parties, everyone from their twenties to their seventies offer new faces their first names without even bothering to append the last ones.

Murray (2002, 48–52) says that Americans mutually FN each other 75% of the time. Moreover, mutual TLN is "no longer the undisputed norm between newly-introduced adults," and for a large minority of Americans the difference between mutual FN and mutual TLN is no longer "primarily one of degree of acquaintance." Furthermore, whereas children virtually always used TLN to adults who then used FN with them, nowadays many children FN adults, often with the permission of the adults themselves. Most of my students at a conservative Catholic college say that they always TLN their parents' friends and also neighbors. When asked by adults to use FN, the students say they feel awkward and try to avoid it. In the Midwest, Murray found that FN was used by youngsters to adults 42% of the time. That figure might vary regionally.

Murray concludes that Americans today define intimacy and age-related hierarchies differently than was done forty years ago. Murray (52–53) does note that certain professions confer such status that TLN is usual, even when it is countered with FN. I have noticed, for instance, that if I give a salesclerk a credit card which has my name as *Dr. Elaine Chaika* on it, I do get addressed with TLN. In all other instances, I receive FN, even when I am clearly much older than the clerk.

Interestingly, the ubiquitous mutual FN has invaded the United Kingdom, as part of the ongoing Americanization of that island. Lynne Truss's new book on manners complains about the same thing, noting that:

> People who have spent their whole lives as "Mr Webster or Mrs Owen" do not want to find, at the end of their lives, that younger people who don't know them are calling them "Alf" and "Joyce." To them it is sheer impertinence. (Truss 2005, 155–56)

Murray himself (2002, 50–51) notes that Tony Blair, the British Prime Minister, upon taking office, vowed to stop the practice of calling his cabinet members by title.

The reason given for first-naming everyone, in government, businesses, and even in the highest echelons of corporations is that many Americans feel that is more friendly. Ostensibly, people will want to shop in a store where sales clerks are chummy enough to FN you.

As Murray also notes, Americans have changed the meaning of *social distance*, so that only very great social distance is graced by use of TLN, or, with the highest-ranked like judges, just T alone: "the semantic concepts of *distance, formality, intimacy,* and *status* . . . have indeed changed for a large portion of the American public . . ." (Murray 2002, 53). Simply put, we don't give respect except to those much more elevated than we are, and those people are mighty few.

STYLE AND INTERACTION

Style is so integral a part of social functioning that interaction cannot go ahead if one party does not speak with the right style for the occasion. Whether or not style is right depends partially on the social identity of the speaker. If a style is perceived as correct for a given speaker, then the respondent has to obey that style or, at least, normally does. Style also has to fit the social situation: a funeral does not allow for the same range of styles as a backyard barbecue.

Repairing Style

Correct use of style is a delicate matter. If the wrong style seems to have been used by one party in a dialogue, **repairs** often will be attempted by the other. These repairs take the form of the respondent's manipulating his or her own style in an effort to get the first speaker to change style. This typically happens when one person speaks too intimately to another. A response in a superformal style is a clue to the first speaker that distance is to be maintained. Style is elevated often far above what is normal in an effort to make someone switch to more formal speech. Saying, "Were you talking to me, sir?" in response to someone's overly casual style is a common example, as is a sales clerk's, "May I help you, sir?" to a too-forward customer. These illustrate both the way that style itself is the message and the way we try to control others through style.

It certainly does not seem surprising that we slap someone down for being too intimate. What is surprising is that being too polite seems just as bad socially. Politeness, as much as rudeness, calls for stylistic repairs or even anger. Garfinkel (1967) had his students act too politely at home. The results were disastrous. Mothers cried. Fathers became furious. Since politeness indicates formality, therefore social distance, the parents' reactions were perhaps to be expected. One's family interprets intimacy as a sign of affection and belonging. The converse must seem like rejection. Then, too, since the privilege of initiating a style belongs to the socially superior, and since those in authority have the right to maintain distance by maintaining formality, the students were acting wholly inappropriately to their parents; that is, the students' style usurped their parents' authority.

In a near replication of Garfinkel's work, I instructed my students to act too formally to their friends. Their results illustrate the social functioning of style even between peers. (Names changed to protect identities.)

In the dormitory:

1. *Trish*: Would it be possible for you to wait for me after class?
   Ann: Yes, of course it's possible. Why are you talking so proper?

In a car on a date:

2. *Pat*: Jacques, could you tell me how far we are from our destination?
   Jacques: [sarcastically] Yes, Patricia. We are about 50 miles from our destination. Are you satisfied?

In the cafeteria:

3. *Robert*: Hi, Dave!
   Dave: Hello, Robert. How are you?
   Robert: Not bad. You take a test or somethin'?
   Dave: Why, no. Of course not. Why do you ask?
   [Robert looks strangely[5] at Dave, and leaves without replying.]

4. *Tom*: Is this seat taken?
   Al: Why, no. Won't you join us?
   Tom: [looking puzzled] How was logic today?
   Al: Very instructive.
   Tom: Oh, was it? What did he talk about?
   Al: He talked about fallacies and associated topics.
   Tom: [laughs, looks puzzled, mimics Al, and hits him] Would you care to come over for tea?

5. *Ernie*: Hello. How are you?
   Andy: Tired.
   Ernie: And why is that?

Andy: [suspiciously] Because I haven't gotten any sleep this week.

Ernie: Oh, that is too bad. I feel sorry for you.

Andy: [antagonistically] Why are you smirking when you say that? Because you're a louse!

[The experimenter and an observer both claim that Ernie was not smirking and his tone was not sarcastic.]

In 1, Ann responded to both the linguistic and the stylistic message. She answered the question, and then attempted to find out why the style was wrong. Notice that when Ann answered the question, she matched Trish's formal style (Giles, Taylor, and Bourhis 1973). "Yes, of course it's possible" is not a usual college girl's response to her roommate. "Yeah, sure" is more likely.

We see style matching as well in 2. The respondent uses the formal variant of his girlfriend's name: Patricia. Even the "yes" is a formal answer. He continues in a superformal style, to the point of actually mimicking Pat's words. His sarcastic tone throughout indicates that this is more than mere style matching. Normally, it is very rude to mimic someone whom you perceive as not having spoken correctly. It would be unthinkable to do that to a foreigner or someone with a speech impediment, for instance. If someone uses the wrong style with you, however, apparently the social conventions can be dismissed.

We see another social convention dismissed in 3. Usually, it is the height of rudeness to leave a conversation without saying "good-bye" or one of its equivalents. It is doubly rude simply not to answer a question. Robert, like the respondents in the preceding examples, immediately perceives the inappropriate formality. His repair takes the form of asking why they are "talking so proper." His "You take a test or somethin'?" is another way of saying that.

We see a slightly different tactic in 4. Here, Tom uses humor to repair the too-formal style. He mentions "coming over for tea," which in American culture usually indicates a formal afternoon gathering, one as inappropriate for buddies as is Al's style.

Unfortunately, Andy had another typical reaction. He got angry, assuming that Ernie either was making fun of him by speaking too formally, or thought so little of him (Andy) that he was not to be given an opportunity to make amends if he had done something to offend Ernie.

Unless one considers style as a communication system in its own right, the responses in 3, 4, and 5 could seem bizarre. In 3 and 4, the responses have no relevance to anything that has been said in actual words. Clearly in 3, Robert means 'Is something wrong?' He wonders whether something unsettling happened to his friend to cause him to seem remote or cold. Tom's bogus invitation to tea in 4 is a way of saying "Come off it." Andy's anger results from his frustration because Ernie is not playing by the rules of the game: use correct style for the occasion.

Naturally, the receiver of too formal a style, especially if normally intimate (as is a buddy, family member, roommate, or lover), wants to know what is wrong. If the first speaker does not use an appropriate style in responding that nothing is wrong, then the other party, far from being reassured that the world is all right, is getting cues indicating that it is not. Properly, if someone has offended one, and that is why he or she is being too formal, then the offender has a social right to find out what is wrong and try to make amends. It shows little regard for the offender if he or she is not given this courtesy. Until and unless the hearer can localize the source of the inappropriate behavior, he or she cannot behave normally. This, in itself, bars interaction; hence the anger and the termination of conversations.

Why do people respond to style with style? Why don't they just say, "Your style is inappropriate." The most overt comments on style are of the variety "Why are you talkin' so proper? You take a test or somethin'?" These are attempts at repair, at finding out why the style is off so that the hearer can deal with the situation, but as with style, the message is often not overt.

It has already been demonstrated that style gives messages about the social status and mood of the speaker. It would be very odd to say, "I am a middle-class educated female from Rhode Island. Today I am feeling tired and irritable, and I do not wish intimate conversation with you, although I consider you my peer and acknowledge your existence." Yet, a greeting, in both the form chosen and the tone of voice of its delivery, conveys that meaning. Also, the style selected during the entire conversation either reinforces or contradicts that information. Using style carried along with a greeting and conversational message is more efficient than having to encode that information at the outset or continually during a conversation.

Having such information given via style has another advantage. It allows status and mood to be known, without ever bringing them to the fore. It saves face. The lower-status person does not have his or her social inferiority rubbed in, so to speak. Constant assaults to the ego are spared by placing messages of rank in the background, by having style carry them.[6]

Then, too, people can behave in accordance with style without any arguments about it. If stylistic messages were overtly encoded, they could as overtly be commented on. The person who said, "I am of higher status than you. Treat me with respect"— or even, "I am your equal"—would be inviting comment. Wrangling about status, intimacy, and mood is kept to a minimum if they are signaled only by style. By keeping such information backgrounded, it can be acted on virtually automatically.

Style, then, serves social interaction four ways. It saves time and egos, as well as cuts down on friction. It is also a powerful regulator of social interaction. Using the correct style is a way of "staying in line," conforming to the rules of society. Finally, if the style is perceived as wrong, as we have seen, style rather than overt comment is used to effect change. This can be viewed as an extension of using style to control social interaction.

THE ELEMENTS OF STYLE

Just as language itself can be broken down into elements that combine in various ways, so can style. There are three important differences, however. Whereas the elements of language proper can be combined and recombined into an infinite number of sentences, the system of style appears to be finite. Whereas language can be used to say anything, style is confined to messages about social status, moods, and desired degree of intimacy between speakers. Then, too, language must be broken down into elements if it is to be understood, but style is virtually **isomorphic** with the message. That is, in contrast to language itself, there is a one-to-one correspondence between the message given by style and its meaning.

Style is akin to the signal system of animals. It is not as inherently ambiguous as language itself. Every word or sound in the linguistic system proper can be used to mean many different things, and their meanings can change in new situations. Since style is processed separately from the meaning of words and grammar, it is not surprising that its messages are unambiguous. To have two sets of messages coming at once and to have both potentially ambiguous would multiply the complexity of the task of understanding. Style is an instruction to hearers superimposed upon the content of the communication. The less ambiguous the instruction, the more likely it will be understood.

The messages given by style depend heavily on features like tempo, pitch, loudness, intonation, and timbre. This last refers to voice character or quality—whether it is resonant, harsh, thin, nasal, breathy, creaky, mellow, musical, twangy, or the like (Abercrombie 1967).

Voice

The **voice quality** we use is not entirely the one we are born with. To be more accurate, each person is born with a possible range of voices, one of which we adopt as the base or normal voice. Most of us could talk either on a lower or a higher pitch than we do, and we can vary our timbre, making it more or less resonant, twangy, mellow, or harsh, for instance. Sometimes we do change our voices, making them sexier or kinder or sweeter. When we mimic others, we may change our voices so radically that we do not even sound like us anymore.

The pioneer anthropological linguist Edward Sapir (1927) noted, "On the basis of his voice, one might decide many things about a man . . . that he is sentimental . . . sympathetic . . . cruel . . . [or] kindhearted." Experimenters like Allport and Cantril (1934), Kramer (1963) and Laver (1968) have found that people judge personality and even physical appearance on the basis of voice alone. For instance, we associate a deep, loud, resonant voice with a tall, stocky man, although a slight, short man is able to have such a voice. Many radio announcers lost their jobs when television arrived because their appearance didn't match their voice. You yourself, I am sure, have formed a picture of a person you know only by their telephone or radio voices.

To some degree, the voice quality we adopt is that of our social group or dialect (Wells 1982, 91–93). The high-pitched little-girl voice of the Southern California girl, the African American man's deep resonance, and Midwesterner's twang are all examples. This does not mean that all members of a group adopt the same voice, but rather, that certain voices are associated with different groups. Individuals who fit those categories may choose not to sound that way, however. They may adopt a voice quite different from that of the group to which they belong. Alternatively, they may switch into and out of particular voices at different times.

Switching from one voice to another is part of the larger phenomenon of being bidialectal. It can also show change in topic. Blue-collar males of Italian ethnic background in southern New England may speak in a raspy, harsh, loud voice when talking about fights or other street concerns, but adopt a smooth, mellow one for recounting personal memories of a less hostile nature. Voice switching can yield voices so different that students evaluating speakers on tape consistently fail to recognize two segments as belonging to the same speaker. Furthermore, they consistently rate the supposedly different speakers in very different ways, according to the voice used.

Many people think they can identify a man as gay on the basis of his voice quality. Certainly, when talking "camp," a style adopted by gay men to self-identify usually in the company of other gay men (Harvey 1998), a particular voice quality is used. On TV and in the movies, often gay men have to talk camp so audiences will get the point. One thinks of Charlotte's gay friend Anthony, the wedding planner, on *Sex and the City*, as a prime example. Although Carrie's gay friend Sanford also self-identifies as gay, his voice is not nearly so camp.

However, gay men do not always camp it up. They do so under certain social situations as a rule, not in most daily interactions with heterosexuals. Gaudio (1994) compared the speech of men who were openly gay, that is "out," to heterosexual men. His study did not include gay men who are not out, or who never present themselves as effeminate, two omissions that weaken his findings or, rather, limit them. He found that listeners listening to recordings of the men reading both a passage on accounting and another from a play accurately picked out gay speakers from straight ones, and "their ratings of speakers on the effeminate/masculine scale corresponded to common American stereotypes of gay and straight men's speech, respectively" (48). The judgments apparently were based upon voice quality and intonation contours. **Intonation** is the rise and fall of the voice over phrases. Gay men and straight women seem to use wider intonation contours than straight men and lesbians, although there is variation in each of these populations.

My own experience has been that you can know men for many years and never know that they are gay until they tell you overtly. The opposite situation also occurs. There were three males in my high school class whose thin voices and effeminate intonations had us all convinced they were gay. Upon meeting up with them at reunions many times over the years, it became very evident that they were, in fact, heterosexual, married with children. In a city as small as ours in which so many of the professional men and politicians went to the same high school, and people remain in touch after graduation, one is likely to hear of bisexual peccadilos. Thus, their apparent heterosexuality can be inferred.

Studies of homosexuals and heterosexuals have concentrated on those who self-identify as such, thus skewing the findings. By not testing people blind as to sexual orientation, studies have not ascertained the full range of homosexual or heterosexual pitch and intonation. In other words, researchers seem to have selected straight- or gay-sounding men in order to define what straight or gay voices are. Had they instead selected speakers with a wide range pitch and intonation and then identified them as gay or straight, results might have been quite different. As emphasized in Chapter 2, field methods are all.

Most studies who mention homosexual and heterosexual differences rely on folk taxonomies of what is or isn't feminine or masculine speech. As noted, Gaudio's confines itself to openly gay men and heterosexuals who were purposely chosen because of their masculine style. In general, it is accepted that female speech style is characterized by wider intonational contours than males typically use and by raising the voice at the end of a statement as if it were a question. Male style uses a flatter intonation and a downward contour at the end of a statement. Stereotypically, lesbians adopt a more masculine style.

However, I must add to this that males in my classes, when answering a question often use an upward, questioning contour at the end of their statements. From this, I conclude that this is done when people are unsure of themselves and this is not a specifically feminine or homosexual trait. If females do it more often than males, it is because of their general social insecurity or because they think that, to be feminine, they shouldn't speak with authority. In any event, it is clear that speaking like a straight man or woman or a gay man or a lesbian is an adopted style. As such, this suggests that all gay or straight people may not adopt the style or may do so in varying degrees or in various contexts. A woman who speaks with a canonical female style is not likely to be taken as a figure of authority, nor is an effeminate gay man.

The same voice quality can give different messages to different cultural groups. What is a normally loud, friendly, and warm voice in one culture can be judged as pushy and crude in another. Similarly, what is submissive in one can indicate great inner strength in another. Each culture has its own norms for loudness, dominance and subordination, politeness and rudeness. But within those ranges, other qualities occur, such as raspiness, breathiness, resonance, or reediness, that may give clues as to personality and mood. People project images with their voices.

Just as a particular voice quality is associated with a particular style, such as being tough or formal or intimate, so may a voice quality be associated with a particular dialect or language. One may expect a more harsh voice from a construction worker than from a banker. Dialect melds into style if a given dialect is correlated with a particular voice quality.

Style is relatively minor variation in usage. Dialect indicates rather more difference, and language, the most. It is virtually impossible to pinpoint exactly when a style switch graduates into a dialect change. A working rule is that dialect signals regional variety of speech, or one associated with a social group, either social class or ethnic group, whereas style signals a change in mood or intimacy as well as gender or degree of authority.

People from the same social groups seem to assign the same meaning to intonation, tempo, and voice quality. How could it be otherwise, if such factors are to be useful in communication? However, different languages and different dialects may use the features of style somewhat differently, leading to cross-cultural misunderstanding. Also, the same elements that go into stylistic variation may be part of dialectal variation. That is, it seems as if some languages or dialects are spoken at higher or lower pitches, slower or faster rates, or with more or less of a twang.

Pitch

Like voice, **pitch**, how high or low the voice is, is also somewhat culturally bound. Although, as with voice, pitch is partially inborn and is also a physiological correlate of age, different cultures habitually keep the voice at different pitches. Moreover, as with voice, changes in pitch can be correlated with different emotions or styles. These yield different messages in different cultures. Whereas some cultures indicate threats by lowering pitch, others do so by raising it. This can cause grave cross-cultural miscommunication in public settings in which people of different cultures come in contact with each other, such as sporting events or public schools.

Many Americans feel that there are specifically black voices that have racial characteristics, but this is not so. Part of the stereotype of black males in America is that they have deep, resonant, loud voices. However, Nigerian black male Yoruba speakers of my acquaintance have high, thin voices as compared to the canonical American male voice of any race.

Labov (1964) showed that many black voices cannot be identified as such on the basis of recordings. John Baugh, an African American college professor, has conducted experiments over the years in which he answers an ad for an apartment using a "black" voice and then calling again, adopting a "white" one. He doesn't use an aggressively African American dialect in his black guise. When he first calls, in his "black" voice, he is told the apartment is rented, but when he calls back with his "white" voice, he is invited to come see it.

For many years, my only contact with Asians, specifically Chinese males, was with Cantonese-speaking immigrants who owned Chinese restaurants. Characteristically, their voices were not resonant or deep. Years ago, while visiting Los Angeles, I heard a deep male voice reporting the news on TV, and, upon turning around, was surprised to see an Asian male with a typically American male voice. For a moment, I felt a mismatch between voice and face, despite the fact that I knew that voice is a cultural matter. Since then, I have met many Chinese, Japanese, Cambodian, and Thai men who have deep voices.

One's stereotypes can even affect one's understanding. Rubin (1992) took a tape-recorded lecture made by a native speaker of English and played it to students after showing them a picture of the supposed speaker. When they showed a picture of a white woman, students had no difficulty understanding the lecture. When students were shown a picture of an Asian woman, they reported she had an accent and was difficult to understand. Furthermore, these students did worse on a comprehension test of the lecture material (quoted in Eckert and McConnell-Ginet 2003, 62).

The point is that one's voice is not a feature of one's race and certainly not of one's ethnicity, nor, perhaps, of one's gender. Think of men in drag who adopt female voices, or women with deep, raspy voices. You can change your voice quality if you want. Try saying the same short sentence in as many voices as you can muster, pretending not only to be of another race, but of another gender, region, or ethnicity.

There are definite ranges of pitch which members of a culture will consider masculine, feminine, aged, babyish, and so on. One reoccurring gimmick in television ads is to show a baby while an off-screen deep-voiced male speaks. It looks as if the baby has the deep voice. Within the accepted ranges, how deep or high the voice is gives definite personality cues. Surprisingly, Scherer (1973) found that, for American and German males, high pitch within the masculine range correlated with men's self-evaluations of their own personality as being sociable, dominant, and aggressive. Also, their peers judged them to be dominant and aggressive. Scherer (154) explains that the fact of competent and dominant speakers having higher pitch than submissive speakers does not really violate expectations because these voices don't necessarily sound high-pitched so long as they don't get into the feminine range. That is, they are high-pitched for males. Scherer explains that high pitch is evocative of "habitually elevated level of arousal" (157). Since arousal leads to muscle tension, competence and dominance may be reflected in heightened muscle tone. Depressed psychiatric patients, on the other hand, are characterized by low-pitched voices.

Many people, at least in the United States, assume that the pitch of gay men's voices is higher than that of heterosexuals. However, when Gaudio (1994) made acoustic analyses of the recordings discussed above, he found no significant correlations between listeners' judgments with measures of gross pitch range or with the median fundamental frequencies of their pitch (49). Pitch range includes the differential in the highest and lowest pitches each used. Since any pitch differences between gays and straights is accidental, at least according to this study, then the perception of gay men's voices being higher than those of straight men depends on other factors, perhaps intonation or even word choice.

Tempo

The actual tempo of speech is confounded by one's familiarity with the variety being spoken. Students learning a foreign language often find that it seems spoken too rapidly at first, but the more proficient they become at it, the slower the speech seems to occur. Within a language, typically, speakers feel as if some dialects are spoken more slowly than others. For instance, the normal tempo of some dialects of the American South seems slow to Northerners. Consequently, they may label Southerners as lazy or stupid. In turn, Southerners may find Northerners brusque and impatient.

Interestingly, people differ in their judgments of tempo. Although New Englanders may judge urban Midwestern speech as being rapid, there are Midwesterners who find New England speech fast. Many adults find that Rap songs are chanted so rapidly that they have difficulty decoding the words, but younger listeners, familiar with the idiom of Rap, report no such difficulty. The less familiar a dialect or language, the more rapid it may sound. This may be caused partially by the miscuing that results from slight differences in using allophones in different dialects, or even from differences in points of articulation for the same phonemes. As we shall see, there are also cross-cultural differences in such matters as how long a pause one requires before one can jump into a conversation. This can cause those who wait longer to feel that the other party keeps cutting them off by speaking too rapidly.

Loudness

Loudness differs according to social, ethnic, or language groups. This can lead to serious misunderstanding. The stereotype of American tourists as brash and rude may derive from such differences, as Americans may speak more loudly than those in some other cultures. Closer to home, a second-generation American who has strong ethnic ties to the Italian American community once approvingly told me about a lecturer, "I knew she was one of my kind. She talked so loud." The friendly, happy unselfconscious talk of Americans of Italian background, especially those who still identify with their ethnic group, seems to be somewhat louder than, for instance, speech of descendants of the English settlers. Jews of Eastern European origin, especially those with strong ethnic identities, are often accused of speaking loudly.

It must be emphasized, however, that many people of Italian or Jewish background do habitually speak with soft, quiet voices. Knowing many people from both ethnic groups, I can only conclude that there is great variability in loudness between individuals. What I do find is that, in those groups during a lively conversation, often one way interest is shown is by speaking more loudly than usual. Among younger and educated speakers, those now in their forties, ethnic differences in speech seem harder to find. (See Chapter 9.)

As with tempo, however, the loudness perceived by listeners of another culture may not be actual loudness at all. Many factors may lead to a judgment of loudness when, in fact, a speaker is not talking especially loudly. If the rules of conversation of one group of speakers do not usually allow one person to start talking while another is still speaking, then dialogue with a member of a group that does allow such interrupting may be uncomfortable. The member of the former group may feel that the interrupter is speaking too loudly. The same perception can occur if someone breaks into speech after a shorter pause than another person's rules for conversation allow. Speaking loudly is a way of impinging on conversational space. Therefore, if someone breaks into someone else's speech in violation of that person's conversational practices, the behavior is perceived as speaking loudly.

Whether differences in loudness are real or imagined, misunderstandings result if people feel someone speaks too loudly or too softly. People accustomed to soft voices may misinterpret louder voices as being overbearing or vulgar. However, people accustomed to louder voices often judge softer-voiced speakers as cold, distant, unfeeling, unfriendly, or mousy. Currently it seems as if adolescents adopt louder voices than their elders in public places. The elders find the youngsters rude and loud, and they in turn find their elders cold and stiff. Such judgments are easily gathered by playing tapes of people speaking with different degrees of loudness and asking subjects to rate them on a questionnaire.

MARKED AND UNMARKED VALUES IN STYLE

There does seem to be one difference between stylistic variation and that of dialect. For each feature of style such as tempo, pitch, loudness, timbre, or intonation there seems to be a base that indicates that everything is fine. The base is not a fixed point or line, but a range within which no special message seems to be given. In linguistic terms, we would say that staying within the base is an **unmarked** situation. Moving out of that range indicates that something is wrong or out of the ordinary. Hence, it is a **marked** situation.

Each dialect or language seems to be spoken at a characteristic rate. Speeding up indicates excitement. Slowing down may indicate exhaustion, boredom, or uncertainty. Raising the normal pitch may indicate a number of emotions: anger, fear, surprise, or excitement. Lowering it can be a sign of happy excitement or even rage. If loudness and slow tempo are combined, it can be a signal that the speaker's patience is wearing thin. One's normal voice can be made more honeyed when an attempt is being made to ingratiate oneself with another. That one wants unquestioning obedience may be evinced by making one's voice harsh and raspy. One's normal intonation (rise and fall of the voice) changes to show surprise, sarcasm, or exasperation. In combination, especially, these features allow the full range of human emotions to be expressed. Remember, however, that different languages may use them differently to signal somewhat different messages.

Using a Moog synthesizer, Klaus Scherer (1973) created tone sequences by varying tempo, pitch, loudness, and intonation. He found that judges could assign meanings to each sequence, such as pleasantness, activity, potency, interest, sadness, fear, happiness, disgust, anger, surprise, elation, or boredom. There was good interjudge reliability in the task. That means that a significant number of people had the same opinion about each sequence. Note that these tones were not produced by the human vocal tract—it was the actual tempo, pitch, loudness, and intonation that people responded to.

In general, Scherer found that moderate pitch variation in intonation indicates generally unpleasant emotions, such as sadness, disgust, and boredom. Extreme pitch variation produces ratings of pleasant, active, and potent emotions, such as happiness, interest, and surprise. Fast tempo is more active and potent than slow, with the former indicating interest, fear, surprise, or anger, and the latter indicating boredom, sadness, or disgust. Both fear and anger can be indicated in diametrically opposed ways, either by low, slow sounds with moderate intonation or by high, fast sounds with extreme intonation. The difference seems to be that of potency, with the lower, slower, flatter variation indicating cool anger or fear without activity. The faster, higher, more extreme tone sequences indicate hot anger and a more potent, excited fear.

Today, robotic voices on computers can be varied while showing computerized faces in order to identify the emotional bases of acoustic qualities. The expressions on the faces themselves can be varied with the tones to produce more information. It is especially fruitful to show a facial expression that is mismatched to the voice being played, as well as those that match. Much of the work of designing voices for cars and other appliances has been done by getting user's reactions to such computerized speech. When I take a wrong turn, I notice that the voice in my car's navigation device sounds agitated as it rapidly repeats "Recalculating!"

Indexical Meaning

Within a culture, people assign what Laver (1968) calls **indexical** meaning to voice quality, intonation, pitch, and other features of style. Laver means that these features serve as indexes, or markers, indicating social status, age, and personality characteristics. This is hardly surprising. It would be of little use to signal that I am angry if others in my culture do not understand my cues for anger.

Laver notes, "Listeners, if they are from the same culture, tend to reach the same indexical conclusions from the same evidence, but the conclusions themselves may on occasion bear no reliable relation to the real characteristics of the speaker." In other words, we judge voice quality according to our stereotypes of the people who, we believe, use a particular voice or style. The American stereotyping of black male voices mentioned above is a case in point. This is not as contradictory as it sounds. Members of a group do assign the same messages to certain styles, but a member may not necessarily use the stereotyped style. Similarly, one need not indicate anger or impatience if one does not desire to, even if one is angry or impatient. Hence, the absence of a style or even the presence of one, such as friendliness and warmth, may not correlate with actual feelings.

A person can adopt a particular style to project a false image. Laver mentions that a harsh voice "is correlated with more aggressive, dominant, authoritative characteristics," so it is likely to be adopted by, say, drill sergeants. Scherer (1979, 158–59) suggests that resonant, metallic voices seem to indicate emotional stability, extroversion, and dominance. He quotes Laver's doctoral research as support, saying that passive, submissive people could be assumed to have rather lax voices, but disciplined and controlled speakers would have tenser ones. A breathy voice projects an image "more self-effacing, submissive, meek." That description aptly describes the sex kitten voice, such as the late Marilyn Monroe's.

Scherer also notes that breathy voices may be indicative of introversion, neurotic tendency, and anxiety. In a study of jurors, German speakers with such voices were judged by their peers as dominant and neurotic, but not sociable. In this light, it is interesting to consider Henton and Bladon (1986). They show that breathy phonation occurs consistently in females speaking two accents of British English, despite the fact that such breathiness actually creates perceptual problems for the hearer (225). It is not a feature of male speech. Noting that breathiness is associated with "sexiness," they suggest that "if a woman can manage to sound as though she is sexually aroused, she may be regarded as more desirable" and that such a voice may be seen as "a part of courtship display ritual" (126).

In the United States, high pitch in females correlates positively with judgments of femininity and socialization, but negatively with capacity for achieving status, sociability, social presence, and self-acceptance. In other words, women who use high-pitched voices are felt to be well socialized into being women, but they are not felt to have much capacity to achieve high status, aren't self-confident, and aren't sociable. This probably says more about stereotypes of what constitutes femininity in our culture than it does about femininity. Assertive, self-confident women do not fit the cultural ideal of the passive, nonassertive woman. Women who prefer to break out of the latter mold would enhance their chances by developing low-pitched voices.

Scherer (1979) rightly deplores the copious writings purporting to designate specific voice qualities with personality types. Far too few of these have ascended above the plane of anecdote. He makes the accusation of "the happy consistency of findings and interpretations . . . which one sometimes finds in American textbooks or review chapters." These, he notes, are not due to lack of research. He himself, admirably, uses excellent field methods, including acoustic analyses, expert ratings, and systematic codings. He relates these to standardized personality measures (151). Unfortunately, space here has limited us only to his work on pitch.

Voiceprinting

In recent years, American courts have allowed identification by voiceprinting. It is popularly believed that people's voices are as individual as their fingerprints. James Milroy (1984, 52–53) criticizes such a belief. First, "voiceprints" are only printouts of spectrographic data. It has long been possible to record pronunciations to get a visual "picture," just as we can get one of brain waves or heartbeats. The problem is that these visual prints only substitute for aural ones. That is, phoneticians have to interpret what they hear or what they see, and, at the point of present knowledge, even the best phoneticians are likely to be wrong sometimes in identifying whether two voiceprints are of the same person. A second reason for approaching voiceprinting with caution is that "no one can define a finite population from which the data-sample to be analyzed is drawn; therefore, there is no way of knowing how many individuals have similar vocal characteristics" (52).

Robert Rodman (2002) tells of a heartbreaking case in which a Haitian man was convicted of drug dealing on the basis of a tape recording of a sale on the streets. The speaker on the tape was an African American dealer whose voice was very different from that of the Haitian, who happened to be a translator by profession. The prosecutor labeled the man as a "linguist." Looking that word up in a dictionary, he found that linguists studied sound changes. From this, he surmised that the defendant could change his voice and managed to convince the jury of that. The Haitian was convicted despite the fact that his voice differed greatly from that on the tape. His accent was also grossly different. The prosecutor's success rested upon the general ignorance of what linguists do, and also the perception that tape-recorded voices don't always sound like the speaker's real voice. Most people who hear themselves on tape are surprised at how they sound. The new digital voice recorders are more accurate than older tapes, but still there may be some distortion in voice quality, depending on the quality of the one used.

Testing for Cultural Differences in Style

How can we ascertain what attributes members of a society ascribe to features of style? There are two kinds of tests used extensively to measure reactions to dialects that are equally useful for testing features of style: matched guise and subjective reaction testing. The first of these entails recording the same person speaking in different styles or dialects, and then measuring reactions to each version of his or her voice. The reason that the same person is used is to ensure that reaction is to the feature tested, not to some accidental feature of voice quality between two speakers. Besides asking listeners to evaluate the matched guise voices, one can use other measures, such as giving directions over a loudspeaker and seeing how many people comply. In a subjective reaction test, people are asked to evaluate speakers using certain target features. It has been found that the features that people most disvalue in themselves, they also disvalue in others, even when they are unaware, as they usually are, of how they are really speaking. That is, people monitor themselves as speaking a certain way, usually one that they admire, but they may actually speak quite differently (see Chapter 9).

Knowing how members of social groups actually evaluate stylistic features can be very important in the training of teachers, salespeople, social workers, and even managers. These occupations demand the realization that one may unconsciously evaluate pupils and clients unfavorably just because of their pitch, loudness, tempo, timbre, and intonation. People in these fields should also be on guard because they themselves may be unconsciously off-putting. One of the complaints that people make when they have to deal with members of other cultures is, "You never know what they are thinking." Actually, one never knows what anyone is thinking, but one automatically responds to cues of style.[7] If those cues differ from the ones we have internalized, then we do not quite know how to react. Perhaps this explains the preference of some people to "be with their own kind."

However, in the United States as intermarriage between religious and ethnic groups has increased, and as people have increasingly abandoned ethnic styles, at least those whose immigrant roots are more than two generations ago, such stylistic differences seem to be leveling out. This is not so true of all working-class people or recent immigrants, however. This issue will surface again when we discuss dialects.

PHONETIC, LEXICAL, AND SYNTACTIC ALTERNANTS

The features of style so far delineated are nonlinguistic. These, along with the kinesics discussed in the next chapter, are the **paralinguistic** component of language. They do not involve the system of sounds, words, and grammar that make up language proper. Some other aspects of style do, however. These are **phonetic variants**, different ways of pronouncing the same things; **lexical variants**, different words for the same thing; and **syntactic variants**, different grammatical constructions for the same meaning. For instance, it is normal and usual in American English to convert a word final /t/ into [č] "ch" if the next word starts with a [y], as in "doncha" for *don't you*. These variants are stylistic when choice of one or the other does not change the content of the message but does signal a different social or emotional message, or belongs to a different register.

The technical term for this process is **palatalization**. That, in English, this is in the realm of style, not language proper, is shown in two ways. First, one variant is normal and usual, and a departure from it signals that the circumstances are not ordinary. Second, the words are perceived as remaining the same, whichever pronunciation is adopted. In contrast, *tin* and *chin* are perceived as being different because of the differences between /t/ and /č/. The meanings and possible contexts of usage are changed because of the presence of one or the other sound. There is no such difference between *won't you* and "woncha" despite the fact that the same sounds are alternating. We perceive the change from /t/ to /č/ as linguistic in *tin* vs. *chin*, but as stylistic in *won't you* and "wontcha." For instance, if one says to a peer or inferior "Won't you come afterwards?" with a clearly articulated /t/ and /y/, this indicates a formal party or anger or upset on the part of the speaker. In the encounters reported above with my students' speaking too formally, a prime signal of superformality was the lack of palatalization, which caused strain between speakers. If one, instead, asks "Wontcha come afterwards?" it connotes that everything is all right. Relations are normal.

Words, more technically termed **lexical items**, may also show stylistic variation. In the formal speaking exercise, we saw several lexical variants: "destination," "very instructive," "associated topics," even phrases like "would it be possible . . . ?" and "and why is that?" The choice of one word or phrase rather than another gives a stylistic message although the linguistic meaning remains the same. In all of these instances, the message given by style indicates that the speaker outranks the hearer and wishes formality, hence, distance.

Lexical variants can also give the opposite stylistic message. For example, choosing "I'm outa here" over "let's go" establishes an informal, casual mood. Referring to a man as a "dude" shows one's hipness. Saying "dichotomy" instead of "split," "division," or even "two sides to the question" shows that one is educated. The person who speaks of "shooting the breeze" instead of "chatting" is referring to a very casual conversation, and is more likely to be a male than one who "chats."

Laver and Trudgill (1979, 26) feel that lexical markers are the least interesting and the hardest and least profitable to study. They feel that linguistic analysis has little to offer in this area, and that lexical markers occur infrequently and are "liable to conscious repression." Given the strong role of lexical markers in jargons and slang, however, they are not uninteresting sociolinguistically. For instance, semantic features indicating sexuality and weakness abound in American terms for females, and these are usually used wholly unconsciously, even by women. Even after these biases have been uncovered, such gender marking in the English lexicon is alive and well. Lexical markers are very closely tied to style. There is always another word one can use to convey a message. The one that gets chosen often is the one that fits the style the speaker is adopting.

Moreover, examining how African American word coinages like *bling-bling* and *bodacious* have so rapidly been adopted by non-African Americans is very important in any analysis of American society in the 21st century. In fact, looking at how this has happened over the decades, non-African American youths' identification with African American street culture can be seen as very marked as early as the 1920's. This is hardly trivial and uninteresting. It is an important factor in understanding our society. Slang is an important feature of certain styles, and where it comes from is an important indicator of cultural influences.

Syntactic variants involve the choice of one rather than another grammatical construction for the purpose of giving a different social message. Saying "Have I not?" instead of "Haven't I?" is one example. Although the use of double negatives and *ain't* are often differences between educated and uneducated dialects, in actual fact, many educated speakers will on occasion use such forms stylistically. At casual parties, rock concerts, and sports events, educated middle-class speakers can be heard saying such things as "Ain't no way that's gonna happen," and "He never brings no beer." Use of such forms heightens camaraderie and the general informality of the occasion. Occasionally, these forms are also heard as being extra emphatic. It is interesting that the very forms which are banned in formal writing are employed for style.

Linguistic meaning can only be extracted from speech by an active decoding process. The hearer has to figure out what sounds have been used, which meanings should be extracted from the words used, and how to fit the meaning of the words into the syntax used. Additionally, the hearer has to interpret a syntactic construction if it is ambiguous. In contrast to these complex decoding strategies, to decode style the hearer must only determine which variant was used. There is little, if any, segmenting out of features and fitting them to the context. All the hearer has to do is note which variant has been used in order to get the stylistic message.

Language itself is open-ended. There is no limit on the number of different utterances a person can make. Although there are limits on the possible meanings of a given sentence or word, both can change meaning to some degree in different contexts. Style, on the other hand, is virtually a closed system. There are a limited number of pitches, tempos, timbres, and intonation contours available. There are bounds on softness and loudness. There are relatively few sounds involved in phonetic variation, and only a few syntactic constructions for stylistic manipulation, compared to the language as a whole, that is.

Perhaps the most open-ended feature of style is lexical variation as it bears the brunt of adapting rapidly to new situations. Even so, the number of lexical items available for purely stylistic choices is very limited in comparison to those in one's entire vocabulary. Furthermore, far from the changeability of meaning that characterizes language, the elements of style are quite fixed, with the element given and the message it gives being virtually one and the same. This makes it possible for style to function as it does, as a set of instructions telling the speaker how to take whatever is being said. A hearer need only note the markers of style as he or she decodes the sentence proper.

POWER AND SOLIDARITY

Brown and Gilman (1960) in a pioneering work defined social relationships in terms of **power** and **solidarity**. Both of these are matters of degree, and they work together to produce various combinations of distance and intimacy. A person in power, for instance, may elect to use some markers of solidarity with her or his employees to maintain friendly relations. Forms which indicate power establish who has authority and how much authority. Forms which indicate solidarity establish the degree of intimacy in the relationship. These concepts have been very useful in analyzing social variation in **kinesics** (uses of style and body motion). However, it should be remembered that there are many social limitations on who can signal power and who can signal solidarity, and that these often are beyond the choices of the individual speaker. Since power and solidarity are the two major variables in interactions, it is not surprising to find them well-marked in most languages, especially at the outset of interactions, such as introductions, greetings, and summonses.

Interactions typically have a formal beginning. This is an indication that the hearer is supposed to start decoding a linguistic message. At large gatherings or in public places, we hear talking all around us, but it is only a jumble of sound. Then suddenly amid the babble, a name or a key word penetrates our consciousness and we find ourselves hearing what one voice out of the many is saying. People usually tune out conversation not relevant to them, even when conditions are fine for hearing. Director Robert

CHAPTER 3

Altman's films like the original *M.A.S.H.*, *McCabe and Mrs. Miller*, and *Nashville* were very confusing to audiences at first viewing because in an attempt to stimulate actual social situations, he had several people talking at once, often carrying on several conversations. In many scenes for the first few seconds, viewers were given no clue as to which conversation to focus on. In actual social situations, we typically zero in on one and ignore the rest.

One sure way for a conversation to become relevant is for someone to give a summons or greeting. This summons grabs one's attention. It need not include names. A simple "uh" or "excuse me" can function as a summons. A summons is the verbal equivalent to catching someone's eye. No conversation is likely to proceed without one or the other.

It is not surprising that style is especially heavily marked at the outset of conversations. A summons may take many forms—*uh, excuse me, waiter, Joe, Dr. Dreidel*—and may or may not be combined with an address form. Lexical variation is prominent at the outset of conversations, although the other features of style certainly are also used. These may be modified by varying timbre, loudness, and the like, but the prime marking usually is by the form itself. This seems to be a reflection of the importance of this initial style-marking. Perhaps word variation is more perceptible, especially in the flurry of greeting, than general tone of voice.

A summons typically is followed by a conversation (or other action), whereas greetings may or may not be. Whereas the function of greeting is phatic, that of summons is not; it has a purpose. Catching someone's eye may be followed only by a greeting with no other conversation, but the fact of summoning implies more is to come. If address forms precede a greeting, they may function as a summons. A few greetings may also function as summons, notably the shorter, more informal ones, such as *hi!* or *hey!* Pitch and intonation distinguish between the summons *hi* and *hey* and the greeting version.

Address is often part of greeting. When it is, it must match the greeting in style. Together they can signal the same messages of power and solidarity. Address differs from summons and greeting in two ways. First, summons and greeting are used only at the outset of a conversation and are not repeated, whereas address may be repeated throughout the interaction. Second, we have seen that summons is used to get someone to attend to the summoner, and greeting may be used phatically. Address, however, is used almost solely for power and solidarity. Between two people, then, it remains constant throughout a relationship unless that relationship changes. An example is an older person's saying, "Oh, call me Marge" when previously she was called "Mrs. Doohickey." She is signaling that she wishes more solidarity in the relationship. My superior's eventual "Hello, Elaine" when he retired was a clear shift away from power.

If a stranger is summoned, polite forms, those that signal that social distance is to be kept, are used. An example is the common, "Excuse me, sir. Could you please tell me the time?" If a person approaches a stranger and asks, "What time is it?" without at least an "uh" or "excuse me" to act as summons, the person spoken to usually ignores the question. If the asker persists, the stranger may turn, saying, "Were you talking to me?" or its equivalent. This occurs even if the two involved are the only two present, as at a bus stop or waiting for an elevator. "Were you talking to me?" is not a request for information. It is really a repair meaning 'you are not using the correct form for this conversation.' This is generally invoked for any inappropriate approach, as when males come on too strong to females. A *sir* attached to the question has the added effect of 'keep your distance.'

The use of formal distancing style to strangers is an indication that, although a request must be made, there is no intention of intruding on the person's privacy. The request is not to be construed as a bid for friendship. If, being bored, one of the parties does wish to continue a conversation, polite forms are still used until it is evident that both wish to talk further. If the person approached does not want to converse, he or she need only answer briefly and turn away. Notice that this option is open only after the original summons and request are answered.

People feel compelled to answer a summons. If someone does not, we assume that something is wrong. Even if it is a stranger ignoring a summons, the one who gave it feels hurt and even angry, as if receiving a slight. Indeed, one has, considering the social rules that decree that people are supposed to answer appropriate summonses for appropriate purposes. In our society, queries to strangers about time or location are proper if preceded by a summons using polite forms. Their obligatory nature can be seen by the declaration "I wouldn't give her [or him] the time of day." Since we are obliged to give that to anyone who asks for it, provided that they have used the correct summons, the declaration is tantamount to saying 'she or he is beneath my notice as a human being.'

If a casual, informal style, normal between two persons who are acquainted, is used with a stranger, the recipient is under no obligation to answer. "Hi, there. Know the time?" is fresh and rude. If a male says that to a female and she answers, he may well assume that she is willing to give more than the time. If a female uses a casual, informal style to summon a male, he is more likely to assume that it is a sexual invitation. Formal interactions with strangers protect our privacy. Formality ensures that we need not spend time with a stranger. At the same time, it ensures that strangers can get necessary information such as time or directions. This is another example of how crucial style is to social interaction. It also illustrates the rigid conventions that govern even trivial interactions, as well as the social reasons for those conventions.

CHAPTER 3

Speakers of European languages, excepting of course English, have another resource of address open to them: two forms of the second-person pronoun. For instance, French has *tu* and *vous*, and German has *du* and *Sie*. This variation can be, and is, used to control social interactions by indicating the degree of power (Brown and Gilman 1960) and solidarity between the parties. As we shall see in later chapters, many other facets of communication also signal messages of power and solidarity.

On the model of French, Brown and Gilman called the singular of the second-person pronoun the *T form* and the plural the *V form*. When they speak of T forms, they include the German *du* and all singular *you*. The V form includes German *Sie* or *Ihr* as well as all *vous* and other plural *you* words. English once had this variation, the old *thou* versus *you*, but the distinction all but disappeared during Shakespeare's time, and is seen today virtually only in the *thou* of prayers.[8]

If a **dyad**, two interacting parties, exchange mutual T forms the singular, they are signaling intimacy, that is, solidarity. However, if one member of the dyad gives the singular and the other has to use the plural V form back, then power is being signalled by the one who gives T and gets V.

It is quite usual in many societies to find the same address forms being used both to keep inferiors in their place and as a sign of intimacy. Those who have studied European languages may recall that the intimate form of *you* is also the one used to inferiors. In French, for instance, one says "I love you" using the *tu* form, as in "je t'aime." The parallel use in English of using *thou/thee* for intimacy was pretty much gone by the time of Shakespeare's later plays. Then, we find the familiar *thou/thee* co-occurring with insults and a more generalized *you* in most speech. At times, in one speech, a character would alternate the pronouns to show change of mood.

Formality implies distance. Both intimacy and insulting imply little social distance. Hence, the same form can be used to insult and to show endearment. The insult occurs when the intimate form is used inappropriately to someone of higher rank who has not given permission to an underling to use it.

Because of the social upheavals of two world wars and the urbanization of society, many of the old rules for using T and V forms have changed. The French verb *tutoyer* meaning 'to use *tu*' and the German *dutzen* 'to use *du*' show the importance of employing these forms inappropriately. For instance, in World War I, officers in France used *tu* when speaking to ordinary soldiers. It also used to be correct to *tutoyer* waiters. Nowadays with less social stratification, *vous* is used in both situations. A French-speaking colleague of mine assures me that in France today, it is always correct to use *vous*. One must be careful with whom one uses *tu*. This is parallel to what happened in English in the 17th century.

Throughout Europe there has been either a steady erosion of T forms to indicate that the person addressed is inferior, as in France, or an erosion of V forms to indicate superiority, as in Germany and Italy. In either situation, however, indicating power by pronouns has been minimized.

My colleague, John Lawless, who lived in Germany for a time, tells me that his impression is that the tendency there is to get past the formality of *Sie* and the concomitant TLN with *Herr/Frau* as soon as possible, at least between near equals or in cordial relationships. My own less extensive experience with Germans at meetings and on social occasions confirms this. If I address them as *Sie,* they often request *du*. Because of class issues, Lawless says,

> waiters and shopkeepers might still be a little shocked if you began to *dutzen* them right off the bat. A certain formality always seems to exist between perfect strangers or in commercial interactions. At the same time, neighbors might keep up the *Sie* forms for years as a kind of good psychological fence. There is another wrinkle here, though. Left-leaning political persuasion and rebellious youth seem to be encouraging some to dispense with formality altogether.

He did take a few courses from younger lecturers who used *du* from the start, but he doesn't think it was because he was American and a special case since they seemed to do it with everyone except senior professors.

In Italy, among university students in the 1960's, there was an increase in the intimate form *tu* to indicate equality. Bates and Benigni (1975) investigated such changes. They administered a questionnaire orally to 117 Italian adults between the ages of fifteen and sixty-five, so that they would get both pre– and post–WWII adults. The oral format was used so that those with poor reading skills would not be at a disadvantage. The participants, who came from different social classes, were asked to imagine twenty-three different social situations, including those in which there would be conflict, such as speaking to the seven-year-old son of the president. They were allowed to tell the interviewer what forms they would use, and also were allowed to comment on their choices.

Italian not only has the T and V forms, *tu* (singular) and *voi* (plural), but also *lei*, a formal marker meaning roughly 'her ladyship,' but is used to mean 'you.' Bates and Benigni quote a university student who says that everyone uses *tu*, unless the person to whom they are speaking refuses to respond with *tu*. Then, the student said, they use *lei*.[9] He claimed that nobody uses *voi*. This last is the most respectful term. By *nobody*, the student apparently meant 'nobody among university students.'

CHAPTER 3

Working-class youth did use *voi* to older members of their family, a practice largely abandoned by the students. Workers used *lei* to shop-keepers and other such contacts. In other words, the working class was much more likely to preserve the older forms of respect than the middle and upper classes. The young of the latter groups were the most likely to use *tu* to everyone, implying a comradeship with everyone. Interestingly, on Italian television and in the comics, the working classes are portrayed as always using *tu* inappropriately, of not knowing the niceties of address,[10] when, in fact, they do. This shows the danger of assuming things in socio-linguistics.

Recently, my colleague, Giacomo Striuli, a native of Milan who visits his family there frequently, tells me that now *lei* is the form of 'you' that is preferred. The university students whom Bates and Benigni interviewed have apparently not won out. Dr. Striuli tells me that first names can be used with non-intimates, but only if accompanied by *lei. Tu* is reserved only for people with whom one is intimate, but *voi,* the most distant form, is rarely used in the north of Italy. Sales clerks never first-name customers as they do in the United States. He tells me also, "The use of titles is a good thing. Italians like it unless they invite you not to." Titles are terms analogous to our *Mr., Mrs., Dr.,* and *Professor.* They are required in Italy to a greater degree than in the United States.

Dr. Salvatore Cappelletti, another Italian colleague, tells me that *voi* is used more in the south "as a friendly but respectful form for the elderly and strangers," but is dialectal. He, who is from the south, says that his young relatives, all college graduates, address him as *voi* and if they had said *lei,* that would have been too formal in his region. This is interesting, as *lei* is less formal than *voi* in the north. Dr. Cappelletti claims that the college students interviewed by Bates and Begnini were leftists in the 1960's, and that was why they wanted to use *tu* to everyone. In contrast, in the 1930's, the Fascist dictator Mussolini banned the use of *lei*, insisting on the more formal *voi*. So, in Italy, address forms are indicative of the political situation as well as of the social one.

Historically, a similar phenomenon occurred during the French Revolution when older titles were replaced by *Citizen* and after the Russian Revolution when *Comrade* was the enforced title. Titles work with address forms like *you* in regulating interactions.

So, Italians do not use the most intimate pronoun freely, and they do use titles regularly. They also use appellatives before titles, especially in correspondence and announcements, but even in speech, as when introducing someone. *Onorevole* (Honorable) is used for government officials, so that one would say *Onerevole Presidente Bush* or *Onervola Senatrice Clinton. Egregio* (Distinguished) is used with other titles, as in *Egregio*

Avvocato (Distinguished lawyer, masculine), *Egregia Dottoressa* (Distinguished Doctor, feminine). Onorevole Dottore Cappelletti also told me that I could be called *Illustra Professora Chaika*, but if the last name is omitted, it would be even more elevated as it would imply that the person so named is the only illustrious or distinguished professor. One may also add *Signore, Signora*, as in *Egregia Signora Professora* for me. If a person has no such occupational title, he or she could still be called *Egregio Signore Smith* or, even, *Gentile Signore Smith*.

The situation in the United States is very different. Of course, except for the Quakers, *thou* was never an option, as the English who colonized North America had already lost it as a sign of intimacy or of speaking to the lower classes. However, in the 1940's, it was still usual for neighbors to refer to each other as *Mr.* or *Mrs.* + Last Name. First-naming was reserved for friends. Children, of course, never addressed adults by their first names. In older novels and movies about older times, one sees this. In fact, in movies taking place in the late 19th or early 20th centuries, often one knows that a man and woman have fallen in love when he asks her permission to use her first name. That, of course, has changed drastically since World War II. As we have already seen, mutual first-naming is now the norm in the United States and, apparently, in England. Only those in the most elevated positions receive TLN or especially respectful titles like *Your Honor* or *Your Reverence*.

There seems to be a change in progress in addressing teachers. In some U.S. schools, both high schools and colleges, it is the norm for students to FN teachers. Even in schools where it is not the norm, some teachers prefer that students FN them. During a lively discussion on this practice, I found a class of twenty-five almost evenly divided. This is not to say that all U.S. students are evenly divided. At best, it suggests the need for a formal study of this issue.

Some of the students said it feels disrespectful to do this, because they are in school to learn from a superior. Others said they have more respect for a teacher they can FN and that they still recognize the teacher's superior knowledge if they do so.

A colleague who who teaches poetry writing tells me she is always first-named in her writing classes, but insists on TLN in an ordinary classroom situation. Professors in my school's Public Service program usually receive FN. This program is very interactive. There are a great deal of internships to be supervised and visits to various locations, and often classes are divided into teams to solve problems on their own. The professor's role is to lead gently, not to teach certainties. An article some time back in *The Chronicles of Higher Education* by a professor from a Midwestern university complained that he didn't enter academia in order to be chummily first-named by students. Again, no wide-ranging study has been made about either student or teacher acceptance of FN in the classroom. Certainly, we professors are far away from the Italian practice of being termed "most honored" and "most reverenced."

The stickiest situation is that of my children's friends who call me *Mrs. Chaika*. I object to that title, as it marks me as someone's property. If and when there are titles for men which indicate if they are married or single, then, and only then, do I accept a title which categorizes my marital status. However, if I tell them not to address me as *Mrs.*, and they aren't comfortable with using FN, I'd have to insist on *Dr.* or *Professor*, which somehow sounds too snobbish. I have no resolution for this problem except to put up with the title I dislike.

Perfect strangers, even adolescents and twenty-somethings, call white-haired strangers by their first names. At the doctor's office, in banks, in stores, while getting one's tires rotated, in all situations, one is first-named. As noted previously, sales clerks also FN customers once they see their names on credit cards. One of my credit cards has my title, *Dr.*, on it. When a salesperson notices that, usually after calling me "Elaine," he or she will quickly self-correct, "Oh, I mean Dr." I have even had sales clerks ask what kind of doctor I am, checking up to see if I am a "real" doctor, an M.D., or just a Ph.D. It would be interesting to know if they would ask a man that.

If one corrects salespeople for using FN or asks them why they do that, they say that it's company policy. It's more friendly and personal. Mutual first-naming is also a sign of equality. Since a salesperson's job is to serve customers, not to be their friends, it is not clear why friendliness and equality are desirable. Being personal opens the path to intimate revelations, which is hardly the goal of selling merchandise. Of course, a salesperson should be treated with respect, but that doesn't mean he or she has to be familiar with the customer.

My powers of analysis of social uses of language fail me when it comes to explaining ubiquitous FN in sales. One wonders if the reason so many people shop from catalogues or online is that, in stores, they are not waited on. Along with being addressing customers by FN, many salespersons today don't go looking for sizes, colors or fabrics for the customer. They just passively wait until items are brought to the cash register. Perhaps salespeople would be more willing to serve customers if they use TLN rather than the equalizing FN. This is especially detrimental to the idea of shopping in higher priced department stores.

I have not been able to find any studies which test the reaction of people to being first-named in doctors' offices and other public places. I don't know if my distaste for the practice is because I'm some sort of stodgy person or if others find it equally offensive. I've done informal polls among friends and students, but that evidence can only be counted as anecdotal. It seems to me that businesses themselves would want to know how customers really feel about this practice.

Medical doctors are so honored that it is virtually impossible to FN them and they can be addressed simply as *Dr.* with no last name. There is no ambivalence about physicians in the United States. They are almost always and everywhere called *Dr.* Even if a physician is younger than the patient, *Dr.* is the usual address. Occasionally, one hears someone consistently refer to his or her physician by first name, as in "I told Mitchell just before I was put under. . . . " Since it is, indeed, a privileged patient who first-names his or her physician, one cannot help feeling in many instances that this is a way of affirming special status.

There are two reasons for this consistency in addressing medical doctors. First, their position is virtually exalted. Despite backbiting at the profession in recent years, medicine is still a highly respected endeavor. The second reason for always calling a doctor *Dr.* may be for control. Doctors have to be, or feel they have to be, obeyed.

Similarly, in the military, titles like *Colonel, Sergeant*, and *General* must always be used, and any utterance spoken to them has to be accompanied by *sir* (or *ma'am*), again because they are in a position in which they have to be obeyed. They are not there to be one's friends. Those whom we first-name are our peers. We do not usually obey them. It is difficult to argue with those who are always above us, always at a distance, by virtue of address forms. The address form governs us.

As a measure of their status, physicians can be addressed as *Dr.* without a last name, and this is still respectful. This is not so true of *Mr., Mrs.,* or *Miss.* If those titles are used without last names, they become impersonal, as in:

Hey, miss, your lights are on.
Hey, mister, you dropped your wallet.

or even rude, as in:

Where do you think you're going, mister?

But the title *Dr.* retains its respectability with or without a last name. Oddly enough, doctors who do not have M.D.'s are properly addressed only by [Dr. + last name]. The exalted *Dr.* by itself is denied them. Whenever he goes out of his office, one Ph.D. of my acquaintance tapes a sign on his door that says, "The Doctor is not in." The humor lies in the fact that *Dr.* without a last name refers to a medical doctor, not a Ph.D.

CHAPTER 3

Other titles that can or must be used without last names are *Father, Sister, Rabbi, Reverend, Your Eminence, Your Excellency,* and *Your Honor.* These denote either the religious or judges who must be listened to and whose decisions may not be disregarded. It is essential for maintaining social order to maintain the utmost respect for the courts. Even when not on the bench, a judge is always addressed by TLN, as in Judge Robertson.

The most respectful terms, like *Your Eminence* and *Your Honor,* are not paired with last names at all. It is as if their position takes precedence over their individuality. In monarchies, *Your Highness* or *Your Majesty* is used this way. In line with our own country's political base, our leader is called *Mr. President,* a title that combines the everyman's *Mr.* with the respected *President* and, like titles of the *Your Honor* or *Your Highness* category, is not used with a last name. Senators and members of Congress also retain titles, but with last names appended.

The form of address in itself is a powerful controller. Susan Ervin-Tripp (1972) recounts a sad example. Dr. Alvin Poussaint, a well-known African American psychiatrist and author, was driving in his native Mississippi in 1967. A white policeman stopped him.

What's your name, boy? [the policeman asked]
Dr. Poussaint. I'm a physician.
What's your first name, boy?
Alvin.

In a *New York Times* article, Dr. Poussaint[11] admits, "As my heart palpitated, I muttered in profound humiliation. . . . " Ervin-Tripp explains that the source of Dr. Poussaint's extreme emotion was that he was forced to insult himself publicly and that this was done through widely recognized American rules of address. We have already seen that medical doctors are accorded exceptional respect in American rules for address. The policeman's refusal to use Dr. Poussaint's correct and deserved title was tantamount to stating that no black is worthy of adult status or earned respect, even one who has a medical degree. The officer's use of address form alone conveyed that message without his having to put it in actual words.

Ordinarily in modern societies, at least, a pretense is made that all members are worthy. Those whose "face" is consistently damaged by being given overt markers of disrespect feel shamed, but also angry and resentful toward those who do this to them. Typically, they develop deep-seated prejudice against their tormenters. Because such treatment is only given to people who are totally powerless, they have no other redress. Such treatment can only occur with the consent of the government and, sometimes, of churches as well.

In Eastern Europe, for 2,000 years, Jews routinely were called *Zhid* and other derogatory terms to their faces. Worse, they were often massacred and routinely murdered. Apparently, it was not a legal offense to kill a Jew. They understandably developed deep prejudice against their tormentors. Some young American Jews are appalled by their grandparents' use of terms like *goyim*, a derogatory term for Gentiles. They can't understand it because they don't know what horrors their forebears underwent even before the Holocaust. Like blacks in America, Jews in Eastern Europe were not allowed to forget their despised status. It took a long time for many Jews to lose their distrust of Gentiles.

To show how usual such longstanding feelings are, consider the Armenians. Although they didn't have 2,000 years of such treatment, the Armenians were massacred by the Turks in 1915 during World War I. To this day, American Armenians ensure that their children keep the tradition of enmity towards the Turks. They speak of it often, and solemnly observe the date of the massacre every year. Most of them will not socialize with Turkish Americans.

African Americans in the South were in much the same position as the Jews in Eastern Europe. They were demeaned by being called *boy*, as well as *nigger*, *spade*, *coon* and other epithets. They were ordered about, barred from all but the most demeaning work, and even punished if they spoke with an educated accent. Those who disobeyed white strictures could be lynched. The sight of a black man or woman's body hanging from a tree was not uncommon as recently as the 1930's, but lynchings occurred right through the Civil Rights activities of the 1960's.

African Americans who personally have not suffered the terror of lynchings, the demeaning and humiliated treatment and subjugation of their parents and grandparents, still speak bitterly of these things. They feel justifiably embittered by what white society did to their forebears, and feel that the past injustices have not been sufficiently redressed. In time, one hopes their anger will be assuaged, but that can happen only if they are treated with respect and justice.

Address forms can have a powerful positive effect as well. My (Jewish) great-grandfather in Ukraine was the village blacksmith and a very admired man. He not only shod horses but also made farm implements and other ironware. Although he lived in a town that regularly saw massacres and random killings of Jews, townspeople addressed him as *Pan,* a title of respect virtually never given to a Jew. This was so wonderful to the family that my father and his sisters still spoke of it wonderingly sixty years after leaving the Old Country.

So address forms are powerful both in maintaining face, a positive social image, and in losing it, being given a negative social image.

CHAPTER 3

Address forms mirror a society's makeup and its attitudes. One reason for using address forms that do not humiliate or insult others is to maintain harmony within a society. That stricture can be violated when one group has no power and another dominant group has it all. In modern times, with the American ideals of equality spreading worldwide, such lopsided authority relations are being questioned. To measure how far a culture has moved toward equality, one need only study what is going on with its address forms.

Fairclough (1989, 72) claims that the reason that overt marking of power relations is soft-pedaled in Europe and America today is that "power-holders have been forced into less direct ways of exercising and reproducing their power. . . ." This is because the formerly powerless and disregarded people have protested, gone on strikes, and actively rebelled. Certainly, we have seen this with African Americans fighting for their civil rights in the 1950's.

Another kind of address is centered on nicknames. These are often used among close friends or members of teams. High school and college students often employ nicknames within their social groups as a sign of their special friendship. If the television program *Rescue Me* is an accurate portrayal, firefighters make extensive use of nicknames in each station. Nicknames foster bonding between members of a group, so one expects them in situations where a group has to rely upon each other to get the job done on a regular basis, such as winning games or putting out fires.

Nicknames are also signs of intimacy. Husbands and wives often have special names for each other and, of course, so do their children. Nicknames for bonding or signs of belonging differ from other address forms because they are idiosyncratic to a certain person in a group.

In contrast, many names have recognized nicknames that are used as a matter of course, with the given name virtually never being used. If it is, something is unusual, typically anger, exasperation, or humor. It is the rare *William* who hasn't turned into *Bill* or *Willy*. *Robert* usually becomes *Bobby*. *Charles* almost always becomes *Charlie* or *Chuck*. Of course, *James* is doomed to *Jim(my)*, and *Daniel* to *Dan(ny)*. This also occurs with female names like *Patricia* who used to be *Pat*, but, for many younger females now is *Trish*. *Katherine* by any spelling become *Kathy*, *Kate*, or, more rarely, *Kitty*. This does not seem to be a matter of solidarity, but of common usage. People with certain names are almost always called by the recognized short forms of those names. To be sure, an occasional recipient of such a name insists on the full form and, even more occasionally, manages to get it.

Some common first names are actually old nicknames. *Wendy* comes from *Gwendolyn*, *Stacy* from *Eustacia*, *Nancy* started life as *Hannah*, *Sally* as *Sarah, and Beth* or *Betty* as *Elizabeth*. Also, it is certainly not unusual for a girl to be given for her full name what is still recognizable as a nickname or even two, such as *Peggy Sue, Cathy Jo*, or *Annie May*. It seems to me that this is more prevalent in our society in names for women than for men. I have met a handful of men christened with nicknames like *Sam* or *Benny*, but, in my personal experience, it is more common for women to be given nicknames as full names than it is for men. Since the usage of nicknames implies that the one so called is to be treated as an intimate and not as one in power, it would be pertinent to investigate whether this practice is more prevalent for women than for men.

One curious disparity in American naming practices is that names for men can cross the line and become names for women, but the reverse does not happen. For instance, the names *Shirley, Joyce, Brook, Marion, Ashley, Whitney, Beverley, Casey, Kyle,* and *Dorian* were all originally names for men. Once the name becomes used for females, however, they pretty much cease being used for men. One might say that the names then become stigmatized for men. This suggests that females don't have quite the positions of males in our society, even now.

As we've seen, the function of address forms in creating solidarity has resulted in more ready first-naming than was common even fifty years ago. This probably results from the increased mobility of our population. In the old days, when people lived in the same neighborhoods for most of their lives, as did their neighbors, the progression from formal to casual, if it occurred at all, often did so slowly. After all, casual address goes with friendship. If neighbors are likely to be stuck with each other for life, they have to be careful to whom they extend the privileges of friendship. Also, when people were occupied with large families, including distant cousins, and work weeks were far longer than today's, many did not have time for a large circle of friends. In modern transient neighborhoods, however, if people waited a long time to become friendly, many would never make friends at all. With the breakdown of the extended family, that would leave lots of people mighty lonely. Easy first-naming of people at work or among neighbors seems to me to be a response to the need to replace the family with other networks of relationships. It is apparently furthered by the circumstance that the ways of youth are the reference point for much of society. Tradition, with its respect for old ways, formality, and titles, belongs to the aged, and they no longer set the pace for society.

It is well-known that the Japanese have an extensive system of **honorifics**, address forms attached as suffixes to names. For instance, in normal conversation, most adults would append *-san* to another's name (Coulmas 1992). Lee (1976, 992) says that surnames are usually used with honorifics, although married couples and relatives may use first names, again

CHAPTER 3

with honorifics.[12] -*San* is used for ordinary politeness; -*sama* is even more respectful. Ms. Mimi Morimuru, a Japanese high school teacher living in the United States, tells me that only women use -*sama*. This is not surprising, as, in general, women are more polite than men in Japan (Okamoto 1999, 53).

In speech, -*sama* is used mostly for addressing one's mother, as in *okasama*, although it may be used in writing for either gender. Similarly, the once-lofty -*dono*, originally used only to men, is now used for both men and women, but primarily in business letters. Ms. Morimuru tells me that one would use -*dono* only when joking or being insolent.

At really formal occasions like weddings and funerals, people use -*shi* to men and *hujin* for married women. For unmarried women, -*jo* is used. As in English-speaking countries, then, a distinction is made between married and unmarried women, but not between married or unmarried men. Boys either do not use honorifics with each other, or use the casual -*kun*, which can also be used for men and is roughly equivalent to English *Mr.* (Okamoto, 52). Girls, being more polite, use either the ubiquitous -*san* or -*chan*, a term of endearment often used for little children.

Married men call their wives by their first names with no honorific suffix, but they also use the term *omae* 'you,' a pronoun used for a person with lower status than the speaker, and -*kimi* 'you,' a pronoun for an intimate, an equal, or an inferior. Wives, on the other hand, address their husbands as *anata*, the form of 'you' given to a person with higher status. Men also call their wives *okaasa* 'mother,' which Ms. Morimuru says is the term she uses for her mother. Some men call their wives *okaacha*, which Ms. Morimuru tells me is an insult. It is a vulgar or 'low-class' way of referring to one's mother. Women don't use equivalent terms for their husbands.

Two terms for wives deserve mention, *tsuma* and *gusai*. When I first read about these way back in 1976, the author said that they were in the written language only and the second term was 'rather archaic.' However, Ms. Morimuru tells me that both are widely used. In fact, she teaches *tsumai* in her language classes. That word actually means 'a vegetable used as a garnish with raw fish' or 'a side plank supporting a house.' So, a wife is a garnish or a side plank? *Gusai* literally means 'stupid wife.' An older man may use it in letter writing. It is not so much that he really thinks she is stupid. Rather, "he intends to honor the person to whom the letter is addressed by lowering the status of his wife and therefore, himself." There is no equivalent term to address a husband as 'stupid husband' (Lee 1976, 995). Happily, Ms. Morimuru tells me that younger couples now often just mutually call each other by their first names.

It has long been thought that the Japanese honorifics were so codified that they were virtually a part of the grammar of the language. Apparently that has never been quite so, and, nowadays, as in Europe and America, there is much change in their usage.

Brown and Levinson (1978) posited that politeness is universal. That is, in all cultures, people employ politeness strategies in order to maintain their own public image, and to avoid threatening others with all the negative consequences that can accrue from that. Some Japanese scholars have taken strong exception to such a claim. Their argument is that, in Japan, the social situation itself elicits the politeness form, and that individualistic strategies are not important (Koyama 2004, 425). Indeed, Koyama scathingly calls arguments for universal politeness strategies myopic and egocentric. His claim is that Japanese politeness arises from individuals submerging themselves into the society, and are not used manipulatively as in Eurocentric cultures (Koyama, 416).

Oddly, he does note that honorifics are not used in rural Japan. Rather, they are part of the Tokyo dialect (Koyama, 426). If honorifics are an expression of one's identity as a member of Japanese society, and not, as in Brown and Levinson's characterization, part of our repertoire of social strategies, why aren't honorifics used throughout Japan? According to his reasoning, only Tokyo speakers submerge themselves in society, not Japanese who reside elsewhere. Koyama himself also says that honorifics mark the speaker as being urbane and knowing the proper way to speak. This is not different from Western societies, in which knowing manners, including knowing how to address another, is considered a mark of the middle and upper classes. Often, in Europe and apparently Japan, rural or small-town people are stereotyped as being "country bumpkins." We saw that such a stereotype is unfounded in Italy, where working-class speakers of regional dialects were more polite in their address forms than were college students.

Okamoto (53–55) and Pizziconi (2003, 1489–93) both show that one can't predict with certainty when Japanese speakers will use honorifics or even what honorifics they will use. Both scholars present several interactions to bolster their contentions. They show that speakers use politeness markers strategically just as Brown and Levinson predict, which contradicts Koyama's assertions.

Okamoto notes that honorifics are used to keep interpersonal distance, formal ones being used to prevent undue intimacy, just as in Europe and America. Moreover, certain situations, such as the telephone, elicit more formality than others. Women are more likely to use honorifics than men. Okamoto (56) cites a prime minister responding to hostile questions by using very polite language to younger reporters "while his facial expressions are cold as if he were glaring at them." Both authors also note that books of etiquette telling speakers when to use honorifics are very popular, showing that people don't know precisely when to and not to use them.

Using markers too formal for a situation gives negative messages. Either it shows anger or mocking or that the speaker isn't well-bred. There is disagreement among the Japanese as to the appropriateness of certain forms in certain situations. Okamoto cites a letter to the editor in which the writer complains that in some schools, teachers aren't using -*san* to students. The writer sees this as rudeness. A student wrote a response in which she said that she preferred teachers who didn't use -*san* because they were friendlier and there was more discussion in their classes.

UNIVERSAL POLITENESS

Even the most apparently polite of cultures may allow some behaviors which others find quite rude. For instance, when two Japanese exchange students in my class gave a talk on Japanese honorifics, mitigators[13] and dishonorifics,[14] the female startled the class by saying in a voice which sounded scornful to our American ears, "You Americans are so rude. You come right out and say things!" We Americans all felt immediately that she had insulted us. Afterward, I asked her if it was considered in line to say such things to people. She said, brusquely (or so it sounded to us Americans), "Yes!" I then informed her that it is very rude in America to tell someone bluntly that he or she is rude. Only during an argument would such a thing be said. Both Japanese students were shocked. It never occurred to them that there are ways in which Americans are polite and ways that the Japanese are rude according to our standards. They just presumed we have no politeness conventions because we don't use honorifics and mitigators!

The Japanese often feel that Americans are rude because we do not use **dishonorifics**, suffixes that indicate that what one has is not very good (Lakoff 1972). In English translations, these dishonorifics are usually equated with a word like *humble*, as in "Have some of my humble apple pie" or "Please enter my humble home." Such translations render the Japanese ridiculous.

Actually, what the Japanese do is put a suffix after the word. This suffix means, roughly,[15] 'Eh! It's not so hot,' backgrounding it more than the English translation of 'humble' suggests. Lakoff points out that we do have our own version of dishonorifics in English, but we don't put them on the noun. Our version of saying "my humble home" is "Please excuse the mess." Typically this is said as one enters a spotlessly neat house, and it serves the same social purpose as the Japanese suffix.

As for humble cakes, we allow our system of modal auxiliaries[16] to take on this semantic load. Thus, Lakoff says, if we are offering someone cake that we ourselves have baked, we would normally say, "You **must** have some of this cake." In other circumstances, *must* is used if we are commanding someone to do something distasteful, such as, "You **must** clean the toilet!" Therefore, by saying that someone **must** have the cake, one is pretending that a person has to be forced into eating the cake, even though we think the cake is actually delicious. The polite fiction, then, is parallel to the Japanese dishonorific. Presumably, the Japanese speaker would not think of offering someone cake which is actually 'humble.'

Notice that it would actually be somewhat rude to use *should* in this context, as it would be too close to bragging about one's baking prowess, although I can use *should* when offering cake I neither baked nor selected, as in, "You **should** have some of this cake. My mother baked it." The rudest of all to an adult is the one most accurate in terms of semantics, "You **may** have some of this cake." This is rude because it implies the speaker is socially superior to the one being offered the cake. This may be true, but our society usually adheres to the social fiction that all parties to the interaction are equal.

The Japanese may perceive that Americans "just come right out bluntly and say things" but that they, the Japanese, **mitigate** verbs by using prefixes. These, in effect, mean 'I humbly say that I heard you perhaps say that. . . .' Again, there are American analogues to such softening of assertions, as when one says such things as:

I thought you said . . .
Gee, it seemed to me, and I may be wrong, that you said . . .
Maybe I didn't hear you correctly, but I interpreted what you said
to mean . . .

English speakers also soften assertions by casting them in the future or past tenses. For instance, *will* functions as a politeness marker in:

That will be five dollars.
And this will be Mrs. Jones.

Typically, this last is said upon meeting someone one knows with a companion, and one presumes the companion is a spouse one knows of. Taking the assertion away from the present tense makes it not so direct. Compare, for instance:

And this is Mrs. Jones.

Similarly, the past tense in English is often used to indicate a situation which is imaginary:

The unicorn **was** at the pond.

or to indicate that someone is no longer alive:

My uncle **had** blue eyes.

indicates that my uncle is dead, whereas:

My uncle **has** blue eyes.

indicates that he is still alive.

Because both the future and the past indicate nonreal or nonexistent situations, they combine to produce polite forms. The auxiliary verbs used to indicated politeness typically have a sense of futurity combined with a past tense. *Would,* for instance, a combination of [*will* + past tense], gives the polite:

Would you *hold* this for me.
Would you *stand* over here, please.

Similarly, *could* (combination of *can* + past tense) and *might* (*may* + past tense):

Could you please *lend* me a hand right now?
Do you think you *might be* able to lend me five dollars?

The frequent use of questions rather than statements in politeness routines also mitigates the requests or comments. Americans don't have a specific set of formal honorifics and mitigators as Asians do, but we indicate that someone is of honored status by such verb usage. That is, by using verb tense and questions to soften statements and requests, we are, in effect, saying to the other person, "I am humbler than you. You are superior to me. I am showing deference to you." The social effect is the same as that of honorifics and mitigators: helping to avoid confrontation and saving face. The same social effects may be achieved by manipulating different language features in different languages.

Not surprisingly, some Asian speakers do not recognize the way we achieve politeness in English. They simply see the lack of overt honorifics and mitigators, not realizing that English uses syntactic means to achieve these effects. Consequently, when they request or criticize, they sound to Americans as if they are being brusque.

A previous editor of mine, David Lee, recounted two incidents involving very polite and friendly Taiwanese coworkers, people with whom he had always had very cordial relationships. Mr. Lee was taken aback by a fax from his Taiwanese colleague which stated simply, "Include market surveys in all subsequent reports, please." This was the first time such a request was asked for, but it sounded to him almost like a rebuke. As an American, he would have requested by saying something like, "I meant to tell you at our last meeting that it has been decided to include market surveys with all reports, so from now on, could you please include market surveys? Thank you." The Taiwanese colleague seemed to think that the inclusion of *please* alone was sufficiently polite even though no market surveys had been requested before. To an American, however, such a brusque, direct request can be made only if several earlier, polite requests have been tendered.

Mr. Lee had an even more unsettling correspondence from Taiwan. He had written an article about the company at the request of the Taiwan affiliate, who did reply with a simple thank you. However, the affiliate also sent Mr. Lee a note saying:

> I'm sorry can't be adopted. Please have H&H to rewrite. Please try to be interesting, knowledgeable, intelligent, and not too commercial.

Mr. Lee said that he was sure the affiliate didn't intend to give a message which conveyed that he, Mr. Lee, was stupid. I asked Mr. Lee how an American would express dissatisfaction with an article. He offered as a typical rejection: "This isn't quite what we wanted to say. How about something that talks more to the teachers?" Americans always try to give a piece of direct advice about what to do.

Also, note the indirectness of the American response, the hedging with *quite*, as if the article were almost all right, and the almost casual question "How about . . . ?" There is no actual criticism in the American response, whereas the Chinese response, saying "try to be" (a command) and then the word *intelligent*, clearly implies that the article was neither intelligent, knowledgeable, nor interesting, and, finally, it was too commercial.

Notice also that the Chinese complaint did use overt politeness markers like "I'm sorry" and "please" whereas the American one did not. The Chinese rely on overt politeness markers, but the Americans rely on mitigating through understatement and questioning.

If we are willing to look at the language system as a whole, we can often find equivalencies in politeness and face-saving rituals; that is, we must never expect the same measures of politeness to occur in the same places across languages. Still, it is difficult to say that all languages do exactly the same things in politeness (Werkhofer 1992). That is, although many languages do allow the pretense that what the giver has to offer is inferior, this is not to say that all cultures ascribe to this fiction. Certainly, all cultures do not codify a pretense that the speaker is of humbler—or equal status—than the person addressed. We have already seen some examples of cultures which did not treat all of its members with respect, respect being a pretense in social interactions that the person spoken to is of at least equal worth as the speaker. In highly stratified societies with noble ranks, often the upper classes make no attempt to save the faces of the poorer or to mitigate the lack of equality. This probably explains the viciousness of the lower classes when, historically, aristocracies were overthrown, as in the French and Russian Revolutions.

NEGATIVE AND POSITIVE FACE

Coulmas (1992) recounts the true story of a Japanese man who killed a stranger who dared to use the suffix -*kun* to him. Yet, in our culture, the equivalent of -*kun*, first-naming, is quite common among strangers. To us, the solidarity marker is a way of showing respect for someone else's worth, but to the Japanese, it is disrespectful. Apparently, this is because of different ways of maintaining face in each culture.

Wood and Kroger (1991) show that a useful concept in distinguishing between cultures is that of **positive** and **negative** face. Positive face is achieved by "positive rites of approach, exaltation, and affirmation" (146). They claim that positive face "requires the achievement of closeness and common identity (147), such as using first names or address forms like "brother" or "darling." Negative face distances, overtly shows deference, and acknowledges "the lack of common status" (146).

Earlier, Brown and Levinson (1978) had defined one's positive face wants as the desire to be seen as positive and part of the group. Negative face wants are based upon a desire not to be restricted in one's freedom of action (Harvey 1998, 302–03). This can be done by affirming one's status, one's right to be where one is and to do what one is doing.

Saying *Your Majesty*, attaching -*san,* or even just using TLN are all ways of maintaining negative face. Some societies seem to rely more on positive face rituals to protect their public image, and others rely on negative ones for the same purpose. Those societies that are abandoning negative face wants by doing away with such markers as -*san* or TLN are opting for positive face. Everybody is equal. Everybody's a pal.

Similarly, the leveling of T and V forms in Europe seem to be a move toward positive face for those who previously received *tu* and *du*. In France, however, *vous* is now the preferred address form as an expression of negative face, of maintaining one's distance. The Italian preference for titles, often embellished by words making them seem more exalted, and the general use of *lei* rather than *tu* also seems to fit Wood and Kroger's definition of negative face. I myself see it as a culture in which people are given overt respect. Those who achieve are highly esteemed.

My own take on the move to positive face rituals in impersonal social contexts, contexts in which people are interacting for a short time for a specific end, is that it shows a lack of respect for achievement and for someone who has earned higher rank. It weakens the value of friendship when everyone acts like your friend. Then, too, using FN to everyone is intrusive of individual autonomy. For an adult to be reduced to FN by everyone is to put them back into the position of being children whom everybody FN's.

Perhaps the excessive positive face rituals that have developed in countries like the United States are evidence of the rootlessness of people, of transience in relationships, and also of a lack of respect for those whose earned status used to be considered worthy of honor. There is a great deal of cynicism engendered by the media, which are driven to keep coming up with sensational stories to sell their wares. Exposés are the order of the day. Consequently, private lives of once-respected officials, including the Presidents themselves, are exposed in a way that were off-limits fifty years ago. Members of all professions are portrayed as "in it for the money," as not caring. Any error is condemned as venal, but no human in any profession can possibly never make an error. Markers of negative face, then, are lost for all but a few, like physicians or judges. Style tells us a great deal about society.

CHAPTER 3

Notes

[1] Figurative language is excepted. For instance, when organizations like Greenpeace speak of the murder of the baby seals, they do so to imply that baby seals feel the same pain as humans.

[2] Unless the rule-breaker is a child or is in a classroom situation.

[3] There are cultures which, in contrast, do expect to hear complaints, recitals of illness, and stories of hard luck.

[4] *Dreamchild*, a 1985 movie about the Alice for whom Lewis Carroll wrote *Alice in Wonderland*, depicts the brashness of American reporters who failed to use the titles an English lady expected. Much of the tension of the movie is centered on the business of address forms.

[5] The student who reported this used the term *strange*. Although he didn't elucidate, as a native-speaking American, I could picture the look and even reproduce it. This is a normal circumstance with metaphorical or idiomatic speech, as discussed in George Lakoff's (1987) *Women, Fire, and Dangerous Things*. For instance, he gives the example of how all members of our culture get same picture from "she held him at arm's length."

[6] As we shall see, however, not all members of society may be equally spared indignities to face; nor have all societies necessarily considered this a high premium.

[7] One also reacts to kinesic cues (see Chapter 4).

[8] Shakespeare and other writers of and before his time thus had a resource open to them which is denied to us. Shakespeare, for instance, played with the usage of *thou* and *you* to indicate extreme anger, humor, and sarcasm. A character, such as one of the King Henry's, would use *you* until he got angry. Then he would slip into *thou*. Often such switching is the strongest linguistic evidence of emotion.

[9] Professor Rodney Delasanta, a native speaker of a northern Italian dialect and a frequent visitor to Italy, tells me that the university students he has known while teaching in Italy always use *lei* to him. In fact, he says, *lei* is prevalent everywhere, from and to shopkeepers, within families, between friends.

[10] This is like the portrayals of the mythical American cabbies who call everyone "Mac."

[11] This is the same Dr. Alvin Poussaint who has taught at Harvard University for years and is the psychologist who advised the *Cosby Show*.

[12] She was writing in 1976, and I don't know if first names are used more today. Ms. Morimuru, my informant, didn't mention this, although she did ask me to call her "Mimi," her first name. Whether that is because

she now lives in the United States or because using first names is more common in Japan, I don't know. I would suspect that if first-naming has become more prevalent, it would be among the young.

13 These are morphemes put on verbs that make the statements less direct and forceful.

14 Expressions that indicate that one's possessions or food are not very good.

15 Robin Lakoff is not responsible for this translation. It's my own.

16 These are the verb auxiliaries: *shall, should, may, might, must, can, could, will, and would.*

CHAPTER 3

Exercises

1. How many registers do you think you usually command? Give examples of each along with a description of the circumstances that evoke each. What are the components of each register?

2. Observe the difference in address forms that you give and receive in two different social situations (work, school, home, church, party, etc.). How do English speakers compensate for the lack of honorifics or a difference between a T and V forms for *you*? Do not work from memory. From these forms, can you make any judgments about the social structure of the community you observed?

3. If you were writing an etiquette book, what rules for address forms, offering, asking, inviting, accepting, greeting, register, and style would you include for work, school, parties, sporting events, funerals, weddings, formal dances, or graduation ceremonies? Choose just one social event, and write five to ten politeness rules for it. Try to think of some rules which were not covered in this chapter, such as *please* and *thanks* or *thank you*. What honorifics, dishonorifics, and/or mitigators should be used? Explain them, pretending you are teaching a Japanese student (or one of other nationality) how to be polite in American English.

4. Make a questionnaire asking people of different ages how they feel about being first-named by store clerks, medical assistants in doctor's offices, or by other strangers.

5. Try to violate co-occurrence restrictions in greetings and address with people you know well. How do they respond? Do they attempt repairs, and, if so, how? Can you formulate any general principles of repair ?

6. Describe the voice(s) of a character or characters on a television show or commercial, and try to explain how this voice presents the person's personality. Alternatively, discuss why such a voice was adopted in this circumstance.

7. Observe the same person speaking in two very different situations, such as at a funeral and at dinner. What changes in style do you notice? Alternatively, notice whether someone's style changes as topics of conversation change. Does a person speak of a death in the

same way as a party, for instance? What are some of the signals that signal 'this is unpleasant/serious/funny, etc.

8. Note all the instances of positive and negative face rituals in contrasting interactions. For instance, what differences do you find between same-sex peers versus an older, high-status person with a younger, lower-status person (such as a professor and a student)? Do your observations substantiate the idea that Americans rely on positive face rituals? If you use interactions between people of another culture, analyze whether they use positive or negative face rituals and when.

9. If you know someone whose forebears were stigmatized, never received respect by the dominant group in their society, and were generally mistreated, ask what he or she knows about that history. How do members of the stigmatized group feel about their former oppressors today?

Chapter 4

Kinesics: The Silent Language

Kinesics is the study of body motion. Under it, we subsume all matters of interaction which are not carried out by actual words, including such matters as the amount of talking which may be done, regardless of the content of that speech. In order to equate given body motions with specific social messages, very careful studies must be made of interactions. The gestures have to be correlated with the social message given. Popular books which promulgate hidden meanings to body language are too often based upon nothing more than someone's whim, and when examined are shown to be fallacious. Although humans share a basic repertoire of kinesics (body motions, eye contact, facial expressions, gazing, postures, touching, and proxemics), each social group may have somewhat different rules for using them. There may be national, tribal, ethnic, or gender differences in all aspects of kinesics. Since these matters are important for regulating interactions, such as showing interest, politeness, submission, approval, or disapproval, people who do not share the same repertoire of kinesics may misunderstand each other. This causes cross-cultural difficulties and becomes crucial when one group of people is in a position to dominate another whose kinesics are substantially different. Special attention is paid in this chapter to valid ways of researching these behaviors.

BODY LANGUAGE

Communication is not achieved by voice alone. It is comprised of posture, gesture, facial expression, gaze, even how we space ourselves relative to others. As with the vocal cues such as pitch and timbre that give purely social and emotional information, body movement is difficult to describe and analyze because we respond to it subconsciously. In fact, it is extremely difficult to talk without using body motion and facial expression (Hall 1959; Kendon 1983). Have you ever noticed someone having a phone conversation on a landline phone, accompanying his or her speech with arm and hand gestures? You may very well find yourself doing the same thing. Apparently, gestures are an integral accompaniment to speech. (Cell phones don't allow one to swing his or her arms around while talking.)

CHAPTER 4

Body motion is such an integral part of interactions that researchers have found that people actually remember more of what is said to them when the words are accompanied by gestures, especially those that illustrate the parts of the utterances (Feyereisen 2006; Thompson, Driscoll, and Markson 1998). One of my students, Julie Hosselbarth, replicated these studies on the Providence College campus. She prepared a four-minute narrative about meeting a crazy man on her way to Dunkin' Donuts. She then identified ten words or short phrases which could be easily interpreted by using gestures. By these, she meant phrases like "slam the coffee down" and "no teeth." Then, she narrated the story to two groups of six students, one group hearing it with gestures when the ten phrases were uttered, and one who saw no gestures. After recounting the narrative, Hosselbarth asked each group to write down as much of the story as they remembered. She found that the group that heard the story with accompanying gestures recalled 28.3% more details than the group who heard it without gestures. The latter remembered only 51.7% of the sixty possible details. In contrast, the group who was told the story with gestures recalled 80% of the sixty details. Most tellingly, the group who saw no gestures never remembered a phrase better than the group who did. Hosselbarth's results were found to be statistically significant. That is, there was less than a 95% chance that the results could have been due to chance. Clearly, gestures aid recall.

If we are miscued or feel something is wrong, we frequently feel uncomfortable without quite knowing why. As with style, this can be a basis for discomfort when interacting with people from cultures different from our own. It may also cause us, in all innocence, to ascribe the wrong characteristics to those whose "silent language" differs from our own.

Kinesics is the technical term for all aspects of this silent language. Along with those elements of style that we have already discussed, it forms the **paralinguistic** system that operates along with the linguistic system proper. Together, they create the meaning of the interaction.

Like language itself, kinesics seems to be both inborn and culturally determined. There seem to be certain facial expressions, gestures, and body motions that generally mean the same things in all cultures. There are other kinesic messages that have specific meanings to particular cultures. Even if they are seen in more than one culture, it may be that they are evinced at different times in different cultures.

Charles Darwin (1965) felt that human expressive movements are the vestige of biologically useful movements that later became innately linked to emotional experience. A pushing-away movement of the hand accompanying a negative response, for example, may be viewed as the vestige of actually pushing away a danger.

Darwin and, later, ethologists like Konrad Lorenz, Jane Goodall, and Dian Fossey noted the similarities of expression between humans and other animals. One example is the brief raising of the eyebrows to indicate recognition. This has been observed in wolves and apes as well as humans. In many human cultures, this has been extended in its meaning to indicate sexual desire or invitation. Old movie buffs will recall that both male and female movie stars in the 1920's had the entire area from eyebrow to eyelid painted to emphasize looks of sexual invitation. Groucho Marx's exaggerated eyebrow lifts were a parody of this sexual message. With or without makeup, raising of the eyebrows is used for flirting in many cultures. The Polynesians carry it one step further, using an eyebrow lift alone to mean 'yes' (Eibl-Eiblesfeldt 1979, 39).

Raised eyebrows signal to another that she or he is being looked at. In our own culture, the idiom "looking at him/her/them with raised eyebrows" means that the looker disapproves of a particular behavior. *Raised eyebrows* in this instance refers to staring, as the idiom implies that the eyebrows remain lifted for more than the split second necessary to signal recognition or invitation. Like so many other idioms, this one reflects our virtually subconscious knowledge of what is going on in ordinary interactions.

Goffman (1963, 86) says that normally we give "civil inattention." We don't usually stare at strangers. He notes that one of the trials of the disabled is that people do stare at them, just as they stare at animals in the zoo. Staring may even be done to those with whom we do not speak.

Although raised eyebrows universally signal that someone is being looked at, the degree of raising, the duration of raising, and whether it is with or without eye widening may all be manipulated to give different messages within cultures and cross-culturally.

When comparing American college students to the Fore tribesmen in New Guinea who then had virtually no contacts with Westerners, Ekman and Frisen (1976) found that there is great similarity among cultures in signaling specific emotions by facial expression. Each group looked at pictures of the other group and was asked if the faces were happy, sad, disgusted, surprised, or fearful. The instructions to the Fore were couched in small narratives, like, "His or her friends have come and he or she is happy." They found that both the Fore and the Americans made similar judgments. Because people could identify emotions on the faces of people from other cultures, Ekman and Frisen concluded that specific facial expressions are associated with particular emotions for all human beings.

Eibl-Eiblesfeldt (1979, 38, 42–44) offers even more conclusive evidence for the same position. He noted that three children who were deaf and blind and had no hands still smiled, sulked, laughed, and showed surprise and anger with expressions like those of children who can see. He previously observed blind children with hands, but critics were quick to point out that such children could have learned normal facial expressions by touching faces that made different expressions.

Keating et al. (1981) specifically compared facial gestures indicating dominance cross-culturally and across species. They noted that nonhuman primates such as Old World monkeys and apes signal dominance and submission by their degree of eyebrow raising, with lowered brows indicating dominance.

When I read this study, it occurred to me that, as so often in the social and behavioral sciences, everyday idiomatic usage indicates a recognition of social cues and rules, in this instance of the lowered brow. We have words in English which refer specifically to the message of the lowered brow seen in us and the other primates: *glowering, glaring*, and *browbeaten*. Note that the first two describe the dominance expression of lowering the brows and sending the emotion of justified authoritarian anger. The third refers to a submissive person, one who is metaphorically, of course, beaten by the brows of a dominant person.

Keating et al. (1981, 615) note that all primates use such facial expressions because they signal social status and help regulate relationships by "forecasting the probable nature of impending interaction." Although humans also have language to help this along, still the facial gestures do the same work. As with features of style carried paralinguistically with speech, signaling dominance via kinesics helps avoid confrontation and battling over power. Interestingly, Keating et al. found that human facial expression of dominance is homologous with that of other primates. Before we can accept such a parallel, we have to see if all cultures signal dominance this way. If they do not, then, despite the similarities between English-speaking and nonhuman primate dominance displays, we can't say with assurance that we have a true connection.

These researchers showed pictures of smiling and nonsmiling people with or without lowered brows to a wide variety of cultural groups: Zambians, Brazilians, Kenyans, Germans, Canary Islanders, Thais, Texans, and New Yorkers. What they found was that Westerners, including Americans, did associate lowered brows as an indication of dominance, but other groups did not or did so weakly. They found "neither observers' gender nor familiarity with models' ethnic facial characteristics had any important influence on dominance attributions" (1981, 624).

Similarly, they investigated whether there was a correlation between smiling or not smiling and dominance. This seemed mostly culturally determined. Texans and Canary Islanders did not find that nonsmilers were dominant, but New Yorkers and Canary Islanders did. Why the Canary

Island students and workers have different judgments about smiling and dominance is not clear. As it happens, in many societies, different social groups may interpret the same cues differently, a phenomenon we will see in the United States in subsequent chapters. Keating et al. (624) do suggest that a dominant person can manipulate another by smiling when giving commands and that smiling can indicate social dominance. On the other hand, submissive people may also smile at those who are dominant.

In short, although some humans do signal dominance the way other primates do, human facial gestures also are culturally influenced. Apparently, the other primates' expressions can be modified by their experiences as well (625).

Smiles

Although the basic human repertoire for facial expression may be the same, there is plenty of evidence showing that each culture modifies that repertoire. Smiles provide us with a good example. All human beings smile, but there are many kinds of smiles. Each culture smiles in somewhat different ways for somewhat different purposes. Even within a culture, there are many smiles. In the United States, for instance, there are friendly smiles, placating smiles, sly smiles, skeptical smiles, derisive, threatening, and sick smiles. And there are also grins. Some cultures demand a wide smile, teeth showing, upon greeting. Others find this too forward, greeting people with close-mouthed or only narrowly open-lipped smiles. Others greet each other deadpan. Some smile when scolded or asking a favor. Others do not.

The situations that call for smiles and call for each type of smile seem to be culturally determined. In a multicultural society, this can cause misunderstanding. Persons who do not smile enough for one group are pegged as cold and unfeeling. Frequent smilers, or those whose smiles are broader than other groups, strike nonsmilers as being phony or stupid. One of the most often quoted examples of cultural misunderstanding because of differences in smiling habits is that of Japanese-American children. As a sign of respect to their elders, these children smile when they are being scolded. Their Anglo teachers construe this as rudeness. LaBarre (1947) mentions the Japanese custom of smiling even at the death of a loved one. This is not because of any hard-heartedness. Rather, the bereaved smiles so as not to inflict his or her sorrow upon others.

A particularly gruesome instance of cross-cultural misunderstanding because of smiling as a sign of respect was portrayed in the movie *Platoon*. This involved a Vietnamese peasant who was brutally beaten to death because, in his attempts to be ingratiating, he kept smiling at American soldiers, one of whom interpreted this to mean the man was laughing at them.

CHAPTER 4

Birdwhistell (1970) found that there were differences in frequency of smiling in different regions of the United States, even neighboring ones. For instance, people from Memphis and Nashville, Tennessee, smiled more than Northerners, but people in the Appalachian areas of the South smiled much less. With the migration of Northerners to the South, one wonders if this disparity still holds true. Are the Northerners smiling more when they move South, or are the Southerners smiling less, or does each group keep its smiling habits?

Keating et al. (1981, 264) said that Texans and New Yorkers should have agreed on their correlations between dominance and smiles, but they do not. When we look at data such as Birdwhistell's, however, we see that such variation in meaning should be expected, considering regional differences in frequency of smiling. It must be noted that Americans, at least, think that people who don't smile as much as they do are cold. Hence, Southerners complain that Yankees are cold. As the next section shows, such feelings don't stop at a country's borders.

Babad, Alexander, and Babad (1983) show that smiling is clearly inborn, but how much smiling someone does and the intensity with which it is done seems to be cultural. Specifically, they show that children by the age of three show clear differentiation in returning the smile of a stranger. Israeli children and adults smile far less than Americans do. It has been speculated that the Israeli children do not smile as much as American children because of the constant threat of war in Israel. However, Babad, Alexander, and Babad (1983, 91) point out that it is Israeli Jewish children who don't smile very much. Israeli Arab children smile a great deal, and they are in the same danger as the Jewish children. Moreover, American Jewish children smile at strangers a great deal, as much as any other American child in the region in which they are being raised. So the difference in this study can be seen as an artifact of culture, not religion or location.

Clearly, the correlation is between culture and smiling. What is the prime cause of such cultural differences? This, at least in such behaviors as smiling, we don't know. What we must not assume is that there are any particular moral traits possessed by those who smile a lot or smile very little. To say that Americans, for instance, are friendlier and nicer because they smile more than those from other cultures is a value judgment based on American culture and even Americans differ in smiling behaviors. All of our evaluations of behavior depend upon our own cultural standards and don't reflect universal human traits. Moreover, even if Americans rate smilers as being nicer, there is no objective evidence that they are. Someone can smile a great deal and be a selfish, uncooperative, or untrustworthy individual. Or not. Smiling alone doesn't tell the tale. What does is how members of a culture rate behaviors like smiling. The ratings don't necessarily correlate with actual conduct in other matters.

What we do know is that there is considerable misunderstanding between peoples with differences in kinesics. Americans feel that Israeli Jews are rude and hostile because they don't smile "enough," and Israeli Jews feel that Americans are insincere because they smile so much. The Israelis don't see themselves as rude and hostile, however. They see themselves as natural and sincere (Babad, Alexander, and Babad 1983, 6).

Smiling often figures into ratings of competence. Israeli Jewish elementary school teachers rated nonsmiling children as more competent socially than those who smiled a great deal. American teachers thought smilers were more socially competent, since, in America, smiling is the social norm.

In general, a cultural group which smiles less than another seems to feel that smilers are either insincere or not too bright. Although the United States is a smiling culture compared to the Jewish Israel one, even Americans downrate those who smile too much for their cultural norms. Note, for instance, the unflattering image of salespeople with superwide, toothy smiles often depicted in cartoons. When Jimmy Carter, a Southerner, was President, respectable news magazines pictured him on their covers with an exaggerated toothy smile that was distinctly unflattering.

Lying

If one wants to determine what a given body motion or facial expression means, then careful field methods must be employed. It is not sufficient to notice somebody making a motion or expression and then assume that it means a certain thing. For instance, it is useful to know if people are lying. To people in business, this may be crucial when hiring or before signing a contract. To consumers, it is crucial if one is relying on a salesperson for information. Do liars give themselves away by subtle cues? Some people believe they do. While watching the movie *School of Rock* with me, my friend suddenly exclaimed:

> "He's pulling his ear!"
> "So?" I asked.
> "Oh," she replied. "That means he's lying."
> "How do you know that?"
> "Everyone knows that," she answered.
> "When I hired sales people, I always made sure they didn't touch their ears when I asked a question. The more they touched, the bigger the whopper they were feeding me."

One has to test such a belief objectively by correlating lying and ear touching. That is, one must observe people touching their ears in a natural environment or a controlled laboratory situation. Then one has to see if the touching occurs at the point at which the person told a lie. Since a person who lies isn't likely to admit being untruthful if one asks him or her directly, if one sees this behavior outside of the laboratory, one has to research the person's background to see if a lie was told. It is not enough to do this for one or two people. One must have a wide sample of ear touchers of each gender and different cultures and regions. It seems to me that this would be a tremendously long process. What makes it more untenable is that one would have to be ready to write down the statement that accompanied the ear touching whenever one encountered it, and then have to do detective work on the person's background as pertains to the incident he or she was talking about at the time of touching. Thus, one could only verify people one knew or had data on, not on casual acquaintances or strangers.

Alternatively, one can find subjects and tell some of them to lie when they are asked something in an interview. The controls would be told to tell the truth. Then, mock interviews that could be videoed would be set up. Observers would note what movements, if any, those told to lie made when they did lie. These scenes would then have to be compared with those who told the truth for the same question.

A major problem with such a study is that, when a person is told to lie and the lie in no way brings rewards, there is no way to know if that person would behave differently when telling an actual lie for personal gain or even just for kicks. Another problem is that some non-liars might touch their ears or make other nervous gestures, and some liars may not.

As for the ear touching, one has to ask why someone would do that when lying. The whole point of lying is to seem as if the liar is telling the truth. If any one movement is correlated with lying, then liars would never be believed. Why would liars give themselves away so blatantly? It is counterintuitive that people would announce that they were lying. Searching the academic literature, I could find nothing corroborating that ear touching is a sign of lying. Indeed, the best I could find were discussions on the difficulties of determining when people are lying, mostly in critiques of lie detector tests.[1]

There are real difficulties in trying to prove that ear touching is a sign of lying. Either, like my friend, one surmises a priori that people are lying when they touch their ears, or one has to know beforehand that they are going to lie, and then observe them to see if they touch their ears at the point at which they are telling the prearranged lie. However, because the lie is prearranged, the liar may be so confident that he or she makes no visible gestures or facial expressions.

Finally, ear touching can't be inborn behavior because, in evolutionary terms, it is maladaptive. If someone needs to save his or her life by lying, then to betray the lie by a gesture could lead to death. Also, skillful lying can give the liar an advantage in many situations, but lying isn't skillful if it's obvious.

When we were discussing lying in class, one of my students, Leland Scanlon, said that he is an avid poker player. "Oh," I recalled. "Tells." A tell is an inadvertent action, gesture, or even vocalization, that indicates that someone is bluffing. A bluff in poker is, of course, a lie. It's a pretense that your hand is better than it really is, a deliberate intent to deceive.

Scanlon told me that there is a whole literature on tells, complete with pictures of what people do when they are bluffing. It occurred to me immediately that here was a way of discovering correlations between lying and visible signs accompanying it. The beauty of using poker games to study lying is that one can video the game or, acting as a nonparticipant, otherwise take notes on the players' behavior—provided that one can think of an excuse for doing so.[2] Since, at the end of a game, players show their hands, the person who is analyzing the video knows exactly who was bluffing.

Excited, I went to a website Scanlon recommended as the best: Caro's University of Poker (Caro 2006). Clearly, Mike Caro is adept in noticing signs of nervousness and hesitation, which are often, but not always, signs of bluffing. The problem with Caro's portrayals is that the videos he presents are all acted. They are not spontaneous behaviors in an actual game. Furthermore, Caro simply presents what he considers are tells, presumably from his long experience with playing. He does not verify that the gestures and expressions actually occur when someone is bluffing. He never shows that the tell correlates with a poor hand by showing the cards at the end of the game. He only gives clips of people who are supposedly using tells.

Then, too, there is always the possibility that some poker players are so adept that they have true poker faces. They don't reveal their deceptions through tells. Also, novices may just be nervous when making bets, and these signs of nervousness could be mistaken for tells. Then again, tells could be individual. The way one person behaves when bluffing may be different from the way another one does, so that one person may look at his or her hand and then at the pot hesitantly, but another may just suck harder on piece of candy. Some poker players claim that everyone has a different tell. If that's true, one can only know the tells of players one is with in many games. It also means there is no one behavior associated with tells.

One has to establish that certain gestures accompany bluffing a significant number of times, enough so that the gestures described did not happen by chance. Basically, what Caro shows is a variety of nervous behaviors that, from his experience, he claims are tells. It is important to note that his business is the selling of books and videos that purport to enlighten poker players about tells.

CHAPTER 4

However, to be valid, a study of tells should involve actual players in a real game. At the end of each hand, when the cards are shown, the researcher will have confirmation that a given tic, gesture, or expression was or was not a tell.

Scanlon tested out tells while he observed poker games. He found that such an enterprise is fraught with complexity. For instance, he found that "one of the most obvious tells is the genuine smile." He claims, "When players make a genuine smile, they have a genuine hand. A forced smile indicates a bluff." He confirmed that this is an accurate tell a majority of the time, but not all the time.

As he himself realized, he had to describe the parameters of a genuine smile as opposed to a forced one. He distinguished between the two by noting other parameters of smiling, such as whether or not only the mouth moved into a smiling curve. He found this indicated a false smile. A genuine smile, on the other hand, was characterized by concurrent facial movements like cheekbones rising and eyes becoming less wide. He surveyed the other players in the games he monitored and verified that they discriminated genuine from false smiles as he did. In other words, he got a measure of interjudge reliability, which is crucial in any study that depends upon characterizing behavior. His associates agreed that X's smile was fake, indicating a bluff, or that Y's smile was genuine, indicating he had a good hand. In other words, one can't use smiling as a criterion for lying until one first shows observable differences in smiling that people other than the researcher can verify. This Scanlon did, and smiling seems to be the only tell, although not all bluffers use it. That is, if someone gives a fake smile, he is bluffing, but if he does not smile at all, he may or may not be bluffing.

Scanlon did find some other reliable tells. One interesting one is that an anxious player, one with a weak hand, "cannot discourse in casual conversation." To establish this, he asked the player a question that required a lengthy answer. If the player had trouble focusing on what was asked or had trouble formulating the answer, then he or she was bluffing. Also, Scanlon noted that when a person bets and then shoots a quick glance at the person he bet into, it is almost always a bluff. This is especially true of inexperienced players who want to check on the other's reaction to the bluff. Experienced players eventually learn not to tell this way. Finally, Scanlon enlisted a player as a confederate in a game he was examining. The confederate was asked to "stare down" another player who made a bet. If that bettor was bluffing, he or she sat as still as possible, "like a statue." In contrast, if the bettor remained relaxed, the bet was genuine.

Scanlon found that when players had poor hands and were bluffing, they made other signs of nervousness like trembling hands, fidgeting, glancing nervously back and forth at the pot, and the like. However, he also found that when some players have good hands, they, too, exhibit such signs of nervousness, perhaps because they feel more pressured not to blow their good fortune. Scanlon cited what seems to be an adage that nervous mannerisms show both a good hand and a bad one. In other words, fidgeting per se is not a reliable clue as to the worth of a player's hand.

A further complication, as noted, is that some players never demonstrate smiling, nervousness, or other cues, regardless of their hand. They have true poker faces. In all instances, experienced players were less likely to evince nervousness or smiling. It was inexperienced ones who did. Most importantly, even when people did give evidence of unease, they didn't use any one particular tell. There was nothing that anyone did that unerringly signaled lying, except perhaps not be able to sustain a conversation. That needs replicating with more subjects. Proving the meaning of kinesic messages is a complex business.

All of this is clearly just preliminary, but then Scanlon is only an undergraduate without the funding or time to do an in-depth study. His work is worth noting, however, in that it shows us what is needed in order to uncover kinesic cues to lying. He also thought of some criteria not in Caro. Meanwhile, poker players are spending good money for books and videos that don't seem to be researched in any systematic fashion. Similarly, in the world of pop culture, we find books that aver such "truisms" as someone who stands with his arms crossing his chest is saying 'stay away,' and someone who keeps his arms wide is inviting and generous. Books saying such things sell, but the basis for such pronouncements is hardly scientific. Notice they never lay out for you carefully conducted experiments or observations proving their assertions. My point is, beware of books on kinesics that aren't based upon solid studies. They are about as reliable as the belief that tugging on one's ear indicates a lie.

Culture-Specific Gestures

Studies of kinesics and culture often confine themselves to culture-specific gestures; that is, they are concerned with the way a given message is expressed in the kinesics of a given culture. Many, if not all, human groups often express 'yes' and 'no' kinesically, although not necessarily with the nodding and head-shaking that we associate with positive and negative. Examining the signs for 'yes' and 'no' is a study in how varied kinesics can be in different cultures, even though there are some widespread similarities. The Dyaks of Borneo raise their eyebrows to mean 'yes' and contract them, thus frowning, to mean 'no.' Actually, so do Americans under certain circumstances, as when surreptitiously trying to 'throw' a message to someone. The contracting eyebrows is often accompanied by a slight shaking of the head to mean 'no.' This head shake is very common among both humans and other animals. Darwin related it to a baby's refusal to nurse when it is full. As noted above, Eibl-Eiblesfeldt (1979, 42–43) found it in children who were blind and deaf. Darwin feels it stems from the way animals and birds shake themselves to be rid of water or the like.

Still, there are many culture-specific ways to say 'no.' The Abysinnians jerk their heads to the right shoulder, in a sort of modified head shake. They indicate 'yes' by throwing the head back and raising the eyebrows. This is a neat combination of a culture-specific motion with the apparently universal eyebrow-lifting motion. Just how different cultures can be may be seen in the Maori 'yes' and the Sicilian 'no.' The two cultures use the identical motion, raising the chin while tilting the head back, but for the opposite meaning (LaBarre 1947).

Even a transparent gesture such as pointing with the finger to indicate location is not universal. The Kiowa Indians point with their lips. Sherzer (1973) found that the Cuna Indians of San Blas, Panama, use lip pointing to indicate direction, to acknowledge a joke, especially one mocking one party to the interaction, or as a greeting between people who have a joking relation. Interestingly, Americans, although pointing with fingers, not lips, can use a pointing gesture in the same ways that the Cuna do.

Efron (1972) attempted to relate differences between kinesic systems to cultural facts. He studied Jews and Italians in New York City in the 1920's at the end of the great waves of immigration. He found that Eastern European Jewish immigrants, who had been persecuted for centuries, used confined gestures with elbows close to their sides. They walked with a shuffle and stood hunched with rounded shoulders. Their entire appearance was apologetic, timid, and depressed.

In contrast, Italian immigrants moved the whole arm widely and expansively. Efron felt that the Italians' feelings of personal freedom were expressed in their arm movements, as the Jewish feelings of repression and inhibition were expressed in theirs. Because conditions were different in America, Jewish kinesics have changed. The accuracy of Efron's analysis is confirmed both by current-day Israeli and American Jews. Members of both groups maintain confident postures and gestures.

Terneus and Malone (2004) quote research showing that adolescent males and females in the United States employ very different body language signals when displaying interest in the opposite sex. Interestingly, females initiate as much as 70% of courtship interaction. They do so by flipping or tossing their hair, throwing quick glances and then averting their gaze, lowering their eyelids while tucking in their chins, licking their lips, placing a hand near their mouth while giggling, and smiling so that their teeth were exposed. Other gestures include gestures with palm up, primping, caressing their body, and even crossing and uncrossing legs.

That males recognize these as solicitation behaviors was shown by their approaching females, not on the basis of their looks, but on how frequently they indulged in such provocative movements. Of course, women also engage in refusal behaviors like looking away, yawning, frowning, and avoiding eye contact for more than ten seconds while the male is speaking. Males gaze longer at females they are interested in and, given the right cues, will walk over to them to initiate social interaction.

Terneus and Malone assert that adolescent females really control adolescent males in courtship behaviors. Given that our culture expects males to make the first overt moves, this is not surprising. If a male is to walk over to a female to ask her to dance or to go out with him, he wants an indication first that the girl will assent. That is, if males show an interest and it's not returned, they feel a blow to their egos, a loss of face. This would explain why they are more attracted to females who engage in solicitation behaviors. Like females, however, if the male isn't interested, he will avoid eye contact and otherwise ignore the soliciting female.

PROXEMICS

In order to carry on an ordinary conversation, people have to learn the correct patterns for their society. This includes learning how near or far to stand from those with whom they are conversing. It has been long noted that normal distance between speakers varies from culture to culture and between subcultures of the same society, although, as is shown below, proving this is not easy. There are many variables to consider when talking about personal space.

Many have noted that Americans stand with more distance between them when they are speaking than do Latin Americans and Middle Easterners. Scheflen and Ashcraft, quoted in Milroy (1980, 90–92), claim that Cuban men stand only 18 inches apart when talking in quiet and uncrowded places, but African Americans (by which I suppose they mean males) stand more than 36 inches apart even in fairly intimate conversations.

Early observers of proxemics like Edward Hall (1959) often relied upon impressions of how far people positioned themselves, without carefully measuring those distances. Hall, for instance, claimed that people from "warm" cultures like the Mediterranean ones stood closer together and touched each other more than people from "cold" cultures, such as northern Europeans. Remland, Jones, and Brinkman (1995, 292–94) videotaped naturally occurring interactions in several countries. Their measurements showed that Irish and Scottish pairs actually stood closer to each other than did Greek and Italian pairs. However, Greeks and Italians touched each other more than did the English, French, and Dutch, which Hall did predict.

CHAPTER 4

Remland, Jones, and Brinkman (282) observe that some of the research on proxemics is anecdotal, inconclusive, and even nonsupportive of the idea of strict cultural proxemic behavior. However, they also cite studies that have shown cultural influences on proxemics. It seems to me to be more accurate to say that studying proxemics isn't a simple task. Many variables are involved, such as age, degree of intimacy, power, and the place and purpose of the interaction being observed. Even measuring distances isn't simple. One can't just gauge the distance from toe to toe. Jones and Aiello (1973) found that one must measure the distance between interactors' heads and torsos, as well as adjust for height differences in figuring out interpersonal distance, as people lean into each other—or lean backward—to adjust distance.

One of my students found very systematic behavior in some aspects of personal space. Paul Goebelbacker decided to investigate how consistently students at Providence College maintained distance while standing in line. He chose this situation because lines formed daily in the cafeteria and at an ATM machine in the student center. Therefore, he could easily observe lines on successive days and even photograph them. At the ATM machine, 30-centimeter tiles covered the floor,[3] so he could measure the distance that students maintained by examining the photos. What he found was that students spontaneously, but consistently, placed themselves at a distance of 45 centimeters from each other. The lines were very orderly, even in this casual setting, and the equality of space between members was very striking. One would almost think the students measured. Goebelbacker concluded that a line is a social structure and people unconsciously follow the rules for its formation as part of their socialization. His argument is bolstered by the fact that frequently one person would come up to another in line to talk to her or him, but the newcomer never got in between that person and the next one in line. Rather, he or she stood just outside the line, positioned at right angles to the one being talked to, so that the 45-centimeter distance was maintained between those waiting and the line was not disrupted, but the conversation could still go on.

This lining up seems to be a self-regulatory behavior, and one which helps maintain an orderly society. These students stayed far enough from each other so that their bodies did not touch at all. This is not at all surprising among middle- and upper-middle-class students from the Northeast United States. This region is apparently not a "touchy-feely" one and, even when engaging in casual conversation on campus, one notes equal distances being maintained among speakers. However, intimacy can affect these distances, a fact also noted by Remland, Jones, and Brinkman.

This self-regulatory behavior is not necessarily universal in all cultures. One of my students, Kaitlin Callahan, went to a wedding in Ireland of an Irish-American bride to an Irish groom. Callahan's family, although Boston born and bred, has maintained close relations with their Irish relatives, and her own sister had gotten married to an Irish-American in November 2005, a few months before the April wedding in Ireland. Ms. Callahan thought it would be interesting to look at pictures taken at both weddings to see if the Irish-Americans showed different proxemics from their Irish-born relatives. The snapshots were very revealing. The Irish varied in the distance they maintained from each other as they interacted, but the Americans, even at the Irish wedding, did not. That is, Americans self-regulated the space around them, but the Irish didn't. Sometimes they stood further away from each other than Americans did, but at other times, they stood markedly closer together. In circles, for instance, the Irish usually formed much tighter groups than Americans did. However, what really set their behavior apart is that the Americans kept set distances from each other, but the Irish did not.

In American society, among others, if someone stands too far away in an interaction, it is virtually impossible to continue a conversation. Because of this, one way to signal the end of a conversation is to walk backward slowly[4] while maintaining eye contact. As one crosses an invisible line, the boundary of interactional distance, the speaker will suddenly stop even in midsentence, saying the equivalent of, "Oh—see ya!"

It would be interesting to see if the distance changes in other regions or among different social groups. To test this out, one would need an accomplice to videotape interactions in which one party deliberately starts walking backwards while maintaining eye contact. If one tapes in a place which provides easily marked physical features, one can go back and measure while looking at the video. This would result in discovering accurate interactional distances for different cultures and regions. Such information would be very useful for business people, lawyers, physicians, educators, and others who have to interact with a variety of people.

Terneus and Malone (2004), quoting Edward Hall, say that there are four interpersonal distances in the United States: intimate (0–1.5 ft.), personal (1.5–4 ft.), social (4–12 ft.), and public (12–25 ft.).

If one habitually stands too closely to those who are used to more personal space, one makes them feel crowded, even threatened. Conversely, if one stands too far away, one gives off inadvertent messages of dominance or coldness. Cross-culturally, since the distance for ordinary, non-intimate interaction varies, those who are used to less distance will keep moving closer if they are conversing with someone used to a greater gap. The latter will keep stepping backwards, and so it goes. Once, entangled in just such an uncomfortable conversation with a male student whose ethnic conventions were different from mine, I realized that I was dancing around my office with my co-conversationalist in hot pursuit. At one point, I found myself in the hall outside my office! What made it even more uncomfortable was that I am less than five feet tall and he is over six feet. To minimize the distance between us, as he was explaining his problem, he also kept leaning towards me, craning his head downwards. So, there ensued a dance around my office and out to the corridor and back. My feelings of being crowded were palpable, almost suffocating. Finally, I had to put my hand out, palm up, and say, "Stop! Please sit on that chair." He couldn't talk over my normal distance, and there was no way I could listen if he tried to lessen that distance.

The extreme discomfort caused by someone's moving in too close was well illustrated when one of my students did so experimentally. She placed her tray adjacent to that of a casual acquaintance in the cafeteria. Returning from getting some drinks, she found her tray had been pushed across the table. She pushed it back and sat next to the hapless acquaintance. The victim sat fiddling with her napkin, not contributing much to the conversation. When the experimenter moved even closer, the subject moved away, and finally asked, "What's your problem?"

Repeating this procedure in a student lounge, the experimenter kept moving in too close to a boy eating a grinder.[5] He abruptly picked himself up, leaving about three-fourths of it. Before his hasty departure, he signaled discomfort by looking tense, speaking abnormally little, and nervously jabbing at the ice in his glass. A third subject, approached while sitting in a library carrel, finally laid her head down and said, "I really can't help you anymore. I'm so tired from studying." Perhaps the most original repair tactic was displayed by a girl chewing bubblegum. When the experimenter started walking out of class far too closely by her side, the gum chewer proceeded to blow a huge bubble. This forced the experimenter to move aside before the bubble burst in her face. As with style, it is rare for violations of proximity to be commented on overtly. Rather, people try other adjustments to force a proper distance to be maintained.

An interesting gender disparity in repairing behaviors occurred when Terneus and Malone (2004) asked adolescent mixed-gender groups to position themselves in a circle while standing. Terneus and Malone found that when asked to form a circle, males adopt the "buffalo" stance: legs straight but not close together, arms crossed over the chest or hanging by their sides with muscles flexed. In contrast, females adopted a "model's pose," pivoting hip, bending the knee and pulling the foot inward, while standing with body weight on the other leg. The female pose lessens the space occupied, as the legs are closer together.

When females wanted to talk to males, they turned their torso at the waist, but males, when talking to females, turned their head almost 90 degrees. Within each group, the teenagers maintained intimate distance for about ten minutes. In each of the groups, a female's behavior caused males to leave, apparently without first trying to repair the situation. This occurred when females talked to each other, excluding males, or when one squeezed herself in between two males. These illustrated the two apparent reasons for males leaving the group. The first, females talking to other females, implied a rejection of the males, causing them to leave. The second, violations of personal space by a female, also resulted in a male's leaving. Violations occurred, for instance, when a female brushed against two males as she positioned herself between them after the circle was formed, and when another female flipped her hair to each side apparently into the males' territory.

Such behaviors resulted in the males' leaving the group, often stepping back and making eye contact, then leaving together. Terneus and Malone posit that this shows that females control male behaviors, at least in adolescence, but there is another explanation. If females do not please males because they seem to be excluding them or if they appear to be invading the males' space, then the males simply leave and do their own thing. Invading someone's territory implies disrespect for a person, something that males apparently do not tolerate well.

The amount of space one takes up also gives clear messages about dominance. It is well known that dominant mammals take up more space than those who are nondominant; that is, the dominant ones demand that more space be left around them than for inferiors. Thus we have the image of inferiors huddling together with a space between them and their leader. Examining the behaviors of American males and females gives us some disquieting confirmation of this.

American males tend to fill up the spaces around them. They stand with their legs wider apart than females do. Shannon Case, a student in my 2006 sociolinguistics class, observed male-female proxemics in casual interactions in the dorms at Providence College. She found that women, whether men were present or not, took up less space than men do, and men, whether or not females were present, maintained more space.

Most telling is what happened if a male came into a room of females. When this happened, the females lessened their personal space. For instance, they drew their legs even closer to their chests as they sat hunched over, their arms wrapped around their knees. In contrast, when females walked into a male's room, the males adjusted to get more space than before. For instance, before the female entered, one male was leaning on a bunk bed closest to the door, leaning on one arm, with the other across his stomach, and both of his legs spread over the edge of the bed. A second male was sitting in a chair before a TV, legs spread out in front of the chair. When a female entered, the male on the bed spread out across the entire bed. His legs were on one bed, with one leg nearly against the wall and the other slightly over the side of the bed, so that he was sprawled with his legs as far apart as possible, thus maximizing the amount of space he was taking. Additionally, one arm was placed on his stomach, but the other was spread out behind him as far as it could go, resting on the metal bar of the bed. The male watching TV draped one arm over the back of the chair and placed one leg on the chair next to him. His other leg was spread in the opposite direction so that effectively he was taking up three spaces in front of the TV!

The female who caused this shift in male space-taking sat down on the lower bunk of the empty bed across the room, opposite to the bed occupied by the first male. She sat with her legs pressed together and her arms close to her side, hands in lap. Case noted that the dominance of males is shown by their adjusting their already greater personal space so as to take up even more when females enter a room, whereas females, who already were taking less space, shrunk themselves even more when males walk into a room.

Over the years, my students have reported—and I have observed—that men spread their arms out over backs of chairs and assume asymmetric leg positions with one leg up on a chair and the other on the floor or another chair or stool, legs as far apart as the human body allows. Men lean their torsos way back while their legs are stretched forward. It often seems that the males at a social gathering expand in every possible direction.

Women, in contrast, sit with their knees together or legs crossed tightly, arms close to their sides, or hugging their knees close to their chests. My student Elizabeth Brown, who did a term paper on elevator behavior, carefully noted the different behaviors of men and women. As expected, women took up less space than men, crossing their arms and even legs, often also keeping their heads down, another way to minimize space. If they carried a briefcase or bag, they held it close to their legs or chest, thereby setting up a physical barrier between themselves and others. Men were more likely to spread their legs apart, keeping their arms at their sides. Some put their hands in their pockets with their elbows out to the sides, another way of maximizing their space. Whereas women could best be described as being huddled, men leaned against the walls with legs stretched forward.

Considering that men are used to claiming a wide space around them as a mark of their dominance, Terneus and Malone's finding that adolescent males leave when their space is invaded by females is an unsurprising result.

Men walk with a wide-legged stance, a ten to fifteen degree angle, but many women walk not only with legs close together but actually crossing one leg in front of the other. This results in exaggerated hip motions which are sexually provocative. Fashion models walking down a runway are prime example of such a walk taken to its physiological limits.

Men often appear far more relaxed both when standing and sitting than women do. Only when women become old are they likely to sit with legs wide apart. In old age, many gender markings in body language become less overt (Remland, Jones, and Brinkman 1995, 283).

Other studies have shown that behaviors evinced toward inferiors are regularly evinced toward women but not men. For instance, both men and women stand closer to women than to men (282). Invading another's space is permissible for the dominant party, so this is a sign of nondominance in women. Both men and women touch women more in conversation than they touch men, another sign of feminine lack of dominance, even in these enlightened times.

EYE CONTACT

Very rarely can interaction begin until eye contact is made in our culture. When a person is summoned by another, it is not sufficient to answer verbally. One must turn his or her head toward the summoner. Then the interaction can begin. In many, but not all situations, once eye contact is made one is compelled to respond. This is why waitresses as they rush about will not look at patrons. By looking away, they are not compelled to take any more orders. Once they allow eye contact, they might feel that they have to stop and listen, even at another waitress's table.

So strong a cue for interaction is eye contact that anger is frequently signaled by refusal to make eye contact. Such refusal means 'no' to social interaction.

Sometimes technology creates social dilemmas. We have all known the discomfort of waiting for elevators with strangers. Where to put one's eyes? If we inadvertently make eye contact with strangers, either we look away quickly, embarrassed, or we are compelled to engage in chitchat. In general, Americans, at least, prefer to avoid conversations in elevators. Interestingly, a friend of mine who lives in Orlando, Florida told me that elevator conversations are usual there.

Whether her observation results from the fact that she is exceptionally likely to talk to strangers or it is a regional difference, I don't know, but I do know that, over the years, my students who have researched elevator behaviors have all confirmed that people practice what Goffman (1963) called "civil inattention" in elevators. This includes a 2006 project by Jennifer Barnaby. She cites a six-year German study by Stefan Hirschauer that corroborated the evidence from New England. Barnaby noted not only how many instances of eye contact she observed over a ninety-minute period riding elevators in the Westfield Shopping Town Mall in Trumbull, Connecticut, but also how people placed themselves and maintained personal space. She found that nobody maintained eye contact. Out of fifty people, thirty-nine made no eye contact at all. Of the eleven who did, four gave brief glances, lasting on average, one second. Another three looked at her or another passenger for an average of 2.5 seconds, and the remaining four made eye contact for three seconds, and these were the only riders who spoke to any of the passengers. The utterances consisted of a joke, comment, or request for help.

Where people directed their gaze was interesting. Thirty-three stared at the floor indicator for the entire ride. Nine gazed at the elevator door. Four stared at their watches, three stared at the floor, and one at the ceiling. Ms. Barnaby explained that looking at the floor indicator is a good way of avoiding eye contact and is visible from every part of the space. Also, staring at it gives the impression that one is in a hurry and has somewhere specific to go. Staring at one's watch serves the same purpose. Being in a hurry conveys the idea that you are important to someone. It also serves the purpose of civil inattention. If you're in a hurry, you have no time for chit-chat. What I find interesting is that even in such an impersonal and commonplace setting, people are concerned with their self-image, their face! Even in such a insignificant anonymous circumstance, face needs are important and govern seemingly trivial behaviors.

What was also interesting is where people positioned themselves when they got into the elevator. It is obvious that this was determined largely by the requirements for not making eye contact. Out of the fifty riders, twenty went immediately to the right side wall. Fifteen others walked straight to the left wall, and twelve chose the back wall. Only three, 6%, chose to stand in the middle. Positioning oneself at the sides or the back minimizes eye contact, whereas standing in the middle means that you look at everyone who comes in. You're also in the way of people leaving the elevator. In fact, people usually stood in the middle only when the the other locations were taken.

During a conversation, eye contact is never steady. Steady gaze is staring. In most if not all cultures, staring is impolite. Perhaps this is because, even in creatures as lowly as chickens and turkeys (Sommer 1965), staring is both threatening and cowing. If dominant birds, for instance, stare at lower-ranking ones, the latter look away submissively. Staring in human beings can also be a sign of dominance and may be taken to mean haughtiness. Only a dominant person can "stare another down."

Many a teacher knows how often a class can be quelled simply by staring. And many a mother controls her children in public just by staring at them across a room. Staring also implies that the one stared at is outside the pale of society. One deserves staring if one's behavior is out of normal bounds or if one is some sort of freak to society. That is another reason that staring is rude. It implies that the one stared at deserves it, and only outcasts are believed to deserve it.

During conversation, regular fluctuations of eye contact are followed by looking away. The length of time eye contact is held and the number of times it is made during a conversation depends partly on the topic of conversation. Within cultures, there may be differences in eye gaze between the sexes, different age groups, and those whose status differs on other parameters.

Culture determines both the frequency and length of eye contact. This can cause severe cross-cultural discomfort. Those who are used to little eye contact feel that those who habitually engage in more are staring. This is a common complaint about Anglos by members of some tribes of Native Americans. Conversely those who are used to more eye contact, the Anglos, feel that those who give less, the Native Americans, are not paying attention, are passive, or are sneaky.

As with features of style, deviation from the conversational norm connotes a special message. For example, in American culture, sexual attraction is signaled by two people looking into each other's eyes. Thus, flirting can be initiated by prolonging eye contact.

Women look at one another more while they are speaking, while they are being spoken to, and while they exchange simultaneous glances. Whatever the sex of the other partner in the dyad, women look at the other more than men do. There are two possible reasons for this. One is that women are more willing to establish and maintain eye contact because they are more inclined toward social relations (Grumet 1983, 117). Another is that women are more sensitive to visual cues (Eakins and Eakins 1978, 50).

However, another explanation is more likely. It seems that, frequently, the subordinate person in an interaction looks at the superior more than the superior looks at the subordinate. Looking to the superior is a way of getting approval, of gauging the effect the subordinate is having on the one whom he or she wishes to please. In conversations, listeners look more at speakers than speakers look at listeners. One is reminded of the stereotypical blushing bride who keeps looking adoringly at her husband to see his reactions to her words.

This is not to say that gazing is always an indication of inferiority or of willingness to have social interaction (Kleinke 1986, 80). Kleinke shows that "gaze influences evaluations of liking and attraction, attentiveness, competence, social skills and mental health, credibility, and dominance."

Interestingly, he found that studies have shown that Americans say that people like each other if they gaze into each other's eyes. Direct eye contact increases credibility, and a person with a relaxed facial expression is seen as more powerful except when someone is attempting to coerce another (Agunis and Henle 2001, 539).

One disquieting discovery was that people gaze more at interviewers when they are intentionally giving false information (Kleinke 1986, 82). Yet, Americans rate people as being truthful if they look directly at someone. The shy person who can't bring herself or himself to look into another's eyes, or one whose culture forbids such gazing, is likely to be rated as being shifty and dishonest by Americans.

Having people rate participants in movies of job interviews indicates that the interviewee who gazed at the interviewer 80% of the time was rated more favorably, but more tense, than those who gazed less (Kleinke 1986, 80). Gaze seems to indicate intensity of feelings, but the feelings can be either good or bad (Kleinke 1986, 81). As we have seen, prolonged gazing, which is considered staring, can be threatening or an indication of dominance, as well as an indication of interest and liking. Within a culture, the particular meaning given to the gaze depends on mutual social rankings, situation, posture, facial expression, voice quality, and, of course, what is being discussed.

There is a body of research which says that people are likely to increase their gaze when they are trying to be persuasive (Kleinke 1986, 82), as well as when they want to be friends. In fact, gazing seems to be the thing to do to get others to comply with one's requests, at least in the United States. People have been shown to be more willing to accept leaflets, to donate money to charity, and to change money for experimenters who gazed at them. Similarly, drivers were more likely to pick up hitchhikers who gazed at them. People were more likely to pick up coins or leaflets that were dropped by someone who gazed at them (Kleinke 1986, 83). Professors who make a good deal of eye contact with students not only get rated highly, but their students perform better than those under the tutelage of professors who gaze less (Kleinke 1986, 84). We must remember, however, that the amount of gazing and what it means varies from culture to culture. Those students who come from cultures in which direct gazing is avoided might feel threatened by teachers who gaze at them. In turn, the teachers might construe the student who refuses to gaze back as being uninterested, bored, or sneaky. It is imperative that teachers and others who deal with the public understand the differences in kinesics.

Gaze also helps regulate social interaction. Typically, in many but not all American social groups, listeners look more at speakers than vice versa (Bavelas, Coates, and Johnson 2002, 571). When the speaker does look at the listener, it can be a cue that the speaker is willing to give up the floor.

Bavelas, Coates, and Johnson (2002, 576–78) showed that listeners and speakers coordinate their gaze behaviors not only to regulate who will speak next but also to seek and provide listener feedback, to see how their remarks are being taken. The listener's gaze behaviors encourages the speaker to continue, so that the interaction is a collaborative process. They found that gaze was fully integrated with words and other visible acts such as facial displays, head movement, and pauses. From this, they conclude that meaning in conversation cannot be separated into audible and visual components, but must be considered as a whole, as a reciprocal and collaborative endeavor.

Gaze can mean many things, such as disapproval, approval, anger, or flirting. Other factors, including the appearance of the gazer, will also influence the message of the eyes. It has been shown, for instance, that an unkempt person staring at pedestrians at a stoplight will make them hurry across the street.

Like style, eye gaze and head position must be correct for interaction to continue smoothly. We are all familiar with the discomfort caused by the person who persists in looking down or away as we attempt to talk with her or him. As parents know, young children have to be taught to look at someone who is talking to them or to whom they are talking. Two-year-olds for instance, often look down at their toys while talking to parents or when they are spoken to.

In an Anglo group in the United States, those addressed behave differently from others in the group (Philips 1976). This does not seem to be so among the Warm Springs Native Americans. Speakers there do not align their bodies toward anyone in particular. Non-Native American observers often get the feeling that Native American speakers are talking in general to the entire group because no one in particular aligns herself or himself with the speaker. In the interactions between other Americans, aligning motions are prime determinants in who will take the next turn. In classrooms, for instance, often the student who aligns her or his body motions to the teacher is the one who gets called on. Such alignment is taken as a sign of interest. One can see where Anglo teachers might misinterpret Native American or other children whose kinesics do not align themselves to show their interest. This doesn't mean that they don't have other subtle ways of indicating interest. It is just that the teacher may not recognize another culture's way of doing so.

TOUCHING

Cultures also vary in the degree of touching that they do during normal social interaction. When we think of touching, frequently we think of sexual advances, such as pinching bottoms or making "a pass." This does not mean that we don't ever touch or are never touched nonsexually. We greet each other with a handshake. Heslin and Alper (1983, 51) say that the handshake "neutralizes status." Handshaking "is used to signal that the persons involved are starting off on status levels that manifest each other's personhood." So long as it can't be construed as a sexual advance or sign of superiority, touching can be bonding.

Although little has been written about it, touching in the course of professional activity is allowed and even sought out by the middle-class. Many people are routinely touched by hairdressers, manicurists, massage therapists, estheticians,[6] tailors, and of course, doctors and nurses. As part of their training, health professionals have to learn when to touch and under what conditions to do so. Their touch may be comforting or procedural, the latter being an integral part of the patient's treatment. Estabrook and Morse (1992, 453–54) are concerned with the dearth of research into how nurses learn to touch. They show that touching is intertwined with kinesics and talk. The nurse has to gain permission to enter the patient's personal space or "bubble," a vital step toward connecting with the patient and helping in the healing process.

Typically, we barely notice certain kinds of touching: the unintentional and unavoidable, as when one is jammed together in a full bus or standing in a long line to get tickets for a rock concert. Bumping, momentary contact, is also often permissible, as when trying to navigate an airplane aisle while carrying a suitcase. The sting of such touching is lessened by the one bumping repeating, "Excuse me, Excuse me" while making her or his way. Other kinds of touching can set off an argument. If one male pokes the other on the shoulder as they argue, that can be construed as inciting blows. In contrast, a light touch on the shoulder or just below it as one male says something friendly to another may be construed as a sign of bonding.

Very little research has been done on these impersonal or threatening kinds of touching, but there is evidence, even for middle-class Americans, that some touching by strangers and acquaintances can have a positive effect. For instance, people have been shown to comply with requests more frequently, perform favors more readily, be more likely to sign a petition, fill out a questionnaire, and even return money found in a phone booth when they are touched lightly (Heslin and Alper 1983, 68). However, Remland and Jones (2001, 94–96) found that when students were asked both to touch strangers in an airport and to speak with different intensities, touch was not a factor in getting people to mail a postcard. Rather, speaking in a medium-loud voice was the major determinant in gaining compliance. Speaking in a soft voice was apparently too weak, and a loud one too strong, perhaps threatening.

Some ethnic groups touch more than others. Brady and Eckhardt (1975) studied African American girls in the schoolyard in the South. They found that for these girls, the welfare of the group is more important than individual success. Everything is done in terms of the group, both to get its support and to give it. Although there is competition, it always involves the group. It is not for personal gain. Understandably, then, a major component of play is hand-clapping. The girls clap in time together, sing the same ritualized tunes in unison, and form circles when playing, thus invoking strong affirmations of friendship.

All of these behaviors indicate strong bonding and solidarity. Clapping, of course, is touching, and touching can be bonding. Singing together is also bonding, which is why in many countries there are national anthems which citizens sing together, and, of course, why hymns and responses are sung by the congregations in churches and synagogues. The circle itself is universally a symbol of solidarity. Hence, campfires, pow-wows, square dancing (which is actually circular), and folk dancing take place in circles.

So important is the concept of the circle to these girls that even when they are sitting around just talking, they form a rough circle. At the same time, they touch each other, even if it is a foot stuck out to touch someone else's foot. In most of the circle games, they hold each other's hands, a further display of solidarity.[7]

Brady and Eckhardt show that these girls don't lose all individuality. One at a time, they go to the center of the circle and there they can dance and sing as they wish. As Brady puts it, "Surrounded by the support of her friends, which is echoed in every clapped beat, [she] is free to act out whatever she wishes." Moreover, the others will imitate what the girl does in the center, showing that they accept her both as a performer and as a member of the group.[8]

One striking thing is the degree to which these girls look out for each other. They constantly literally look at each other, reinforcing solidarity with eye contact, teaching each other, and making sure none of them is in trouble. They have very few of the competitive games that girls (white and African American) indulge in, games in which one person emerges as the winner. One of my students, Kate D'Addabo, volunteering in a charter school for girls in Providence in 2006, with a predominantly non-middle-class African American enrollment, has confirmed this cooperative behavior among the girls, showing that, when they are working on projects in groups, they spontaneously form circles and help each other out. Then, when they have to report on what they've done, they go back to their seats as in a traditional classroom. However, being allowed to cooperate enhances both their liking for school and their performances.

CHAPTER 4

Although middle-class British and Irish, like many Americans, do little touching, the working class in Belfast differ (Milroy 1980, 91). Milroy describes a common occurrence especially among women there. Women who are not especially intimate sit "squeezed" together with arms linked. As she was visiting them, she found that sometimes a hand was placed on her arm or around her shoulder. As the women conversed, they slapped, squeezed, and nudged to reinforce what they were saying.

Men, too, evinced both closer proximity and touching in daily interacting. One speaker placed a hand on a listener's shoulder, standing within a foot of each other, at right angles, with his mouth only inches from the listener's ear, avoiding eye contact. Milroy observed these two men, who had never met previously, adopt this pose for over an hour in a crowded dance hall. The speaker was talking about the fact that he was illiterate, a fact which he wished to keep secret.

Milroy says, and I agree, that in Belfast such proximity and touching is not intimate, but it is done to achieve solidarity. The male-to-male conversational stance noted above also signalled that the conversation was private and shouldn't be interrupted. Also note that neither the female nor male stances fostered eye contact, although there was touching.

Eye contact frequently interacts with touch. Both give strong messages about intimacy, solidarity, and power. For instance, it has been long known that couples who make a great deal of eye contact are perceived as liking each other more than couples who make less eye contact (Abbey and Melby 1986, 285). Abbey and Melby also found that both genders perceived females, but not males, in terms of their sexuality when photographs of males and females were viewed in different poses involving touch, gaze, and proximity. The woman who touches a man and/or gazes into his eyes is very likely to be interpreted as having sexual interests (Abbey and Melby 1986, 284, 296). When we discuss gender, we will see that this is part and parcel of a larger tendency to define women in terms of their sexuality.

In many cultures, if not all, touching between adults can indicate sexuality; however, the conditions under which it does varies greatly. For instance, in the United States, men do not walk around holding each other's hands, unless one is blind or otherwise infirm and the other appears to be helping him get around. Between able-bodied males of similar age, this is seen as a strong indication of homosexuality. This is true of female pairs as well. Yet, in some countries, such as Egypt or some of Latin America, same-sex handholding or arms around the waist or shoulder indicates solidarity. In those cultures, typically, a man wouldn't touch a decent woman in public, although in the United States, hand-holding across sexes is considered harmless enough.[9] Similarly, the American locker room habit of one man playfully slapping another on his behind is misconstrued by those of other cultures as being homosexual, although, in the United States, this only indicates camaraderie.

Recall that, in Belfast, neither males nor females make eye contact, although they certainly make physical contact. Perhaps having both kinds of contact at the same time is simply too powerful and indicates too much solidarity, sexuality, or both. Eye contact, so long as it isn't construed as staring, indicates willingness to interact. When combined with touching, it can be a potent force. Jennifer Barnaby's study of elevator behavior discussed earlier similarly showed that, although people have to stand very close together in elevators, they minimize the impact by avoiding eye contact.

The combination of having to be close together and of making eye contact can be threatening especially between strangers. For instance, Goldman and Fordyce (1983) had a confederate approach a passerby and ask people to participate in a survey. Just before the last question was to be asked, the confederate touched some of the passersby softly on the shoulder. Others weren't touched. The touching was combined with eye contact for some, but not others, and some eye contact was made without any touching. Variation in voice was also combined with the touching and eye contact, so that some heard a "warm and expressive" voice, and others a flat, monotonous one. After the last question was asked, the confederate "accidentally" dropped the sheaf of questionnaires. The dependent variable was whether or not the passerby helped to pick them up.

Every possible combination of touch, eye contact, and voice was used. The most help was obtained if the confederate did one or the other, but not both. That is, the confederate made no eye contact but did touch, or made frequent eye contact but didn't touch. Making both eye contact and touch, or no eye contact and no touching got the confederate less help.

One of my students, Susan Pinkerman, replicated this study. She confirmed the results, except that she found a gender difference: males helped females far more than the reverse under all combinations of touch and gaze. Overall, less help was offered with the combined approach. Apparently, both together are perceived as an invasion or even a threat of undesired intimacy. Pinkerman saw this nonhelping behavior as an attempt at repairing the situation, a way of keeping the experimenter at bay. A little friendliness goes a long way.

I suspect that using two such signs of intimacy to strangers is very threatening; however, using one or the other makes the encounter just personal enough so that the respondent feels cooperative.[10] If the person asking another to respond neither touches nor gazes, the respondent gets no bonding whatsoever, no feeling except that of being a cipher. Ciphers don't fill out forms or do favors. Also, Fordyce and Goldman found that significantly more help was forthcoming when requests were made in a warm, expressive tone rather than in a flat one.[11] Again, the feeling that someone cares is conveyed by expressive tones, whereas flatness conveys a lack of interest .

The degrees of solidarity that we see in both the African American Southern girls and the Belfast working class are, as noted, not usual in more competitive groups in Western cultures, especially among the upwardly mobile middle and upper middle class. In fact, one requirement for such upward mobility is the willingness to become more competitive and to lessen behaviors intended primarily to achieve solidarity. Milroy cites the cases of bright working-class children in Belfast who reject scholarships because they do not want to have to leave their neighborhoods. It seems to me that the major reason for this is that people raised in neighborhoods in which solidarity is constantly affirmed find middle-class culture frightening with its apparent coldness. Moreover, those who are used to having the support of the group in their endeavors find it difficult to stand alone, so to speak, and constantly to have to compete against others. Mere money and elevated social position aren't always enough reward to those used to being part of a close and caring group that reinforces its strength by constant touching, looking, talking, visiting, and general caring.

Actually, there seems little reason beyond custom for the "every person for himself or herself" ethic in business or the professions. Rather than requiring those who are raised with solidarity to learn the ways of power, perhaps those who are raised with power should learn how to achieve solidarity in education and industry. That is, instead of blithely assuming that, in order to get ahead, one must learn competitiveness, perhaps the upper middle class in Europe and America can learn achievement through solidarity. Typically, the assumption is that those who wish to raise their socioeconomic status must become like those who have higher status, but it is just as reasonable to change work and educational practices so that cooperative and caring group behaviors lead to higher socioeconomic goals.

AMOUNT OF TALKING

People often seem to judge each other on the basis of social behavior rather than on acuity. It is not always what people say that causes others to evaluate them in a certain way, but how they say it, and even how much they say. Bales (1955) found that people in small group interactions who speak more than average and give more than the average rate of suggestions and opinions will be judged as "having the best ideas." This is true regardless of the worth of the ideas expressed. In getting others to think that one is bright, one's ideas themselves are not as important as their frequency. Furthermore, the member ranked the highest by a group addresses considerably more remarks to the group as a whole than to individuals. Lower-ranking members address individuals more than the group.

Riecken (1958) went one step further than Bales. Riecken provided both high-ranking and low-ranking members of groups with a solution to a human relations problem that the groups were considering. Using 32 four-man groups, he verified Bales' finding that those who talk the most are ranked the highest. He also found that those who are ranked highest by the group got their ideas accepted. Lower-ranking members who advanced the same ideas did not get them adopted. Moreover, Riecken found that the high-ranking members influenced others because of their ability to win support by talking the right way and using the right techniques of kinesics and eye contact.

My student Casey Frosch (Spring 2006) doubted that the amount of talking someone does is the determinant of whose ideas get accepted. For her paper, she wrote scripts for three speakers who were asked if they would help raise money for a certain cause. She manipulated the scripts so that speaker A, who had the longest discourse, presented the worst idea on how to raise the money. Speaker C, who spoke the least, had the best idea, and B was midway between the other two both in length of utterance and worth of solution. Frosch recorded each speaker and then had fifty students respond to each by filling out a questionnaire which had both pertinent and nonpertinent questions on it. She found that 84% of those surveyed ranked C as having the best idea and also as being the brightest; 64% rated A as having the worst idea; and 62% found A the least bright. Contrary to expectations, then, the person who spoke the least (14 seconds) was considered the brightest with the best idea, and the one who spoke the most (52 seconds) was deemed the least intelligent with the worst idea. There is actually a dearth of research on this topic, but these findings should tempt some graduate student looking for a good dissertation topic. Certainly, the world of sales would be most interested in the results.

BODY MOTION IN CONCERT

It can be seen that even the simplest of conversations requires a good deal of learned behavior, all fine-tuned. Whether one may speak at all depends on the situation and whether one's culture allows speech in it. Not only does the content of the message have to be appropriate for the context, but the speaker has to encode her or his meaning with words and grammar that hearers can understand. Even that is not enough. The style used must be appropriate for the occasion. Then, too, the speaker must stand just the right distance away, making the right amount of eye contact, holding it just the right length of time, remaining tuned to the requirements of turn-taking as well as topic of conversation. Heads must move to signal points as well as to signal turn-taking. Gestures must correlate with meaning and, again, with turn-taking.

This is part of a larger phenomenon of the way interactants organize their postures, patterns of looking, proxemic configuration, nods, and gestures in "cooperative, reciprocal, rhythmically coordinated ways" (Chick 1990, 227; Pelose 1987). In a successful interaction between members of the same culture, conversational behavior is synchronized "like ballroom dancing partners of long standing . . . moving in smooth harmony," whereas interactions between persons from different cultures may be "marked by a series of uncomfortable, asynchronous movements" as Erickson, quoted by Chick, says. As we shall see, maintaining synchrony is part of doing a conversation successfully, including giving appropriate turn-taking cues (Pelose 1987, 186–204). Typically, we are so unaware of these behaviors that when we can't get in synch with another, we find the interaction stressful, thinking that person is uncooperative, aggressive, or otherwise difficult. Different cultures maintain different rhythms in their conversations, use more or less subtle body motions, and so on, making intercultural interaction difficult, and leading to negative cultural stereotypes (Chick 1990, 228).

Even though participants in an interaction are generally unaware of the fine adjustments they are making while talking, these have to be made accurately. As Harumi Befu (1978) has shown, this holds true even when participants cannot see each other, as in Japanese bowing. Both the depth and the timing of each bow vary with the status and degree of intimacy of participants. Furthermore, the bows have to be synchronized with the other party's. Once a bow has begun, however, one cannot see the other. "Bowing occurs in a flash of a second, before you have time to think. And both parties must know precisely when to start bowing, how deep, how long to stay in a bowed position, and when to bring their heads back up" (Goody 1978). With the changes in Japanese society in the past decades, bowing behaviors seem to have been modified greatly, so that as one Japanese friend told me, her mother complains that her brother never bows anymore. That will mean a loss of this kinesic skill.

American cultures do not include such bowing, and in fact, during and after World War II, Japanese bowing was frequently ridiculed or held up as an example of Japanese slyness and deception. Of course, the Japanese evaluated the American failure to bow very negatively, thinking that Americans were rude, proud, and aggressive. During World War II, American and British POWs were often treated very harshly because they refused to bow to their Japanese captors. Neither side understood the social messages bowing gave to the other. If the incidence of bowing is diminishing in Japan today, when once it was so important, it is a powerful testimony to the Americanization of that country.

Violations of Expectations

It has generally been assumed that all facets of gaze, kinesics, and proxemics must be exact for interactions to take place successfully. If someone violates expectancies, it prompts changes in others' behavior and evaluations. For instance, as seen above with proxemics, the offended person tries to repair the situation by putting up barriers or walking backward. However, Burgoon (1983, 77) claims that there are situations in which it is beneficial to violate **expectancies**, her term for 'expectations.' In studies of small group interaction, it has been found that high-status members get better evaluations by not following the group's consensus when given a task demanding creativity. However, low-status people who conform to group norms are more attractive to others. That is, it's okay to be different if one is highly ranked, but not if one isn't.

Burgoon found that one important variable in how people are rated is how physically attractive[12] they are. For instance, attractive people are more likely to be rated as sociable, composed, and extroverted. When distance norms are violated by someone coming in too closely, the attractive people are rated as sociable. Furthermore, attractive people may stand farther away than our social norms dictate, but they can get away with it. They seem to communicate an unspoken message of high status.

Burgoon also finds that if someone speaks unexpectedly temperately in an intense situation, he or she will be judged more favorably and will foster greater changes in attitude. It seems to me that this is not really acting against social expectancies. It is to be expected that the one who keeps coolest shall prevail, since we associate overt anger and emotional stress with unclear thinking. The assumption is that hotheads are incapable of thinking straight or planning wisely.

Moreover, it must be stressed that the violations of expectations that Burgoon cites are quite different from what has been shown in previous sections. She does not show, for instance, that Northern Irish working-class women can interact successfully by being competitive. Nor does she show that an American woman—or man—can interact successfully by hiding her—or his—mouth behind a hand while he or she is trying to talk. In fact, her violations do not seem to be violations at all. They are variations in gaze and proxemics, variations which convey definite messages of authority when done by those who are perceived as having the right to do them. I would even quarrel with her lumping together creativity and unexpected response. She does this by giving as an instance of unexpected response the creativity of a high-ranking member in a small group. Presumably, if a group is getting together to solve a problem, it is hoped that at least one person will have some new and unusual ideas. The true violation of expectation in such a situation would be for no original ideas to come forth, or for one member suddenly to haul out a whip and start beating others into submission, or for one to suddenly pelt the others with rotten eggs.

Regulating Conversation through Kinesics

Like gaze, body motion is implicated in regulating conversations. Again, like style, this backgrounds messages of control, submission, and cooperation. Since conversations are regulated differently from culture to culture, often outsiders do not catch the cues. Members of the Warm Springs tribe in Oregon, for example, use much less body motion, shifting of body and moving of head, than most other Americans to indicate the course of an utterance (Philips 1976). Instead, these Native Americans rely on movement of the eyes and eyebrows: widening, lifting, and narrowing. They themselves refer to the eyes most when describing emotions. For instance, "they were snapping eyes" means 'they were very angry.' Lips are not moved much in this culture. Arm and hand movements are more confined than for most Anglo groups. They make much less eye contact and complain that Anglos stare too much, even when Anglo observers verify that they were just glancing. One person's glance is another's stare.

For most other American groups, however, kinesics plays a large part in controlling turns. There are speaker-distinctive movements such as head bobbing in rhythm with speech and gesturing to punctuate speech. By stopping such movements, a person signals that she or he is giving up the floor. In general, as noted above, in our culture listeners look at speakers more than speakers look at listeners. When a speaker gets ready to let another take over, she or he will look at that person. Before long utterances, speakers look away until nearing the end. Looking away prevents the listener from breaking in (Clarke and Argyle 1982). Looking at the other person invites that person to speak. If someone actually stops talking in most Anglo groups, someone else rushes in to fill the silence.

Susan Philips, who sat in on meetings at the Warm Springs reservation, says that Warm Springs interactions seem vague and unstructured to outsiders, so much so that outsiders get the feeling that nothing is being responded to at all. At the reservation, if an issue is raised or an accusation made, the next speakers do not necessarily even mention it. If someone does bother to comment, she or he may do so almost as an afterthought.

Philips gives the example of a woman who complained, "[a tribal member] goes to Washington too often." After eight others spoke, the apparent accused got up, read a fifteen-minute report, then entered into a discussion of the report. During this discussion, the accused said, "I can account for all of my trips to Washington." During the entire meeting, Philips notes, no one spoke directly to anyone, and no one ever asked for any response to the statement. Nobody interrupted, and there were no visible kinesic clues that someone was no longer listening or wanted to talk as there are in Anglo conversations. Philips feels that the Native Americans control when they speak. They are not "forced" into it as Anglos are by having to respond to another's statement. Also, since nobody interrupts, they control the length of their own turns.

Actually, Anglos also exercise control over when they speak and for how long. They just do it differently. The Native Americans' control over their turns is not necessarily greater than that of other Americans. If someone is not free to interrupt or to give kinesic signals that he or she wishes to speak then that, in itself, is a very great restriction. One is not controlling when and for how long one may speak if one has no way to make the other person give up the floor.

It must be stressed that none of these social behaviors is a matter of one culture's being superior to another, but of understanding how each culture regulates social interactions. There are many ways of doing conversation, and each culture has its own. They all can and do work to create orderly social interactions, and none is superior or inferior to another. It's all a matter of what one is used to. Anglos might misinterpret tribal members as being unresponsive and vague, but, in turn, tribal members might misinterpret Anglos as being too intense and impatient, just because of differences in eye contact and kinesics in conversational turn-taking.

PROBLEMS IN RESEARCH IN PARALINGUISTICS

We can close this chapter with some observations by Knapp (1983) on some problems in all aspects of studying kinesics, gaze, and proxemics. He points out that many studies of paralinguistic communication are based upon studies of people who are not intimate and haven't had a relationship with each other. Furthermore, he shows, we judge the same actions very differently when done by those we are intimate with as opposed to those with whom we are not. For instance, in a video, if we see an interviewer sit erect with eyes on a sheet on paper, we would judge that professionalism is being evidenced, but that doesn't mean that we'd rate our spouse or sibling the same way if he or she read while talking to us. Furthermore, Knapp points out that researchers are concerned with visible behavior, but in ongoing relationships it's often the nonvisible behaviors which are important. The timing and location of behaviors is often the most important. He gives the example of someone holding out a hand to someone with whom one has just had a vicious fight. This is more important and has a greater meaning than the number of times the same pair has been observed holding hands previously (Knapp 1983, 184). He claims that most of our knowledge of paralinguistics has been gleaned from nonintimate encounters, and this makes it all woefully incomplete. I would counter such an assertion by noting how many studies quoted in this chapter are of people who interact with each other on a regular, even daily, basis.

Knapp (1983, 188) also points out that nonverbal behaviors often mean more than one thing. For instance, silence can be used both for intimacy and remoteness. Squeezing a child's shoulder can mean 'pay attention,' 'do what you were told,' and/or 'I am capable of really hurting you.' He has also found that one must consider interaction of behaviors. For instance, although it has long been accepted that invasion of someone's space leads to that person's stepping back, Knapp (1983, 189) has found that, in an argument, the person who "has made a strong stand" is not vulnerable to those who invade space. Again, we see a common idiom accurately encoding what is going on socially.

Finally, Knapp (1983, 190) sees as another serious problem in paralinguistic research the problem of training a confederate to behave in a neutral or even deviant manner, as in participant observations. He points out that the very quality of neutrality actually may give a message of lack of interest. Similarly, if one is instructed to gaze 100% of the time in an experimental situation or to gaze 50%, these gazing behaviors are so abnormal that it simply isn't safe to generalize to the population at large .

We must recall that Knapp is concerned with the paralinguistics of ongoing relations, what happens when relationships become more or less intimate. This doesn't invalidate research with those who have transient or distant relations. Papers like Knapp's are invaluable in their ability to prod us, to ask questions we haven't thought of asking, and to make us look carefully and with clear eyes at the research we read about.

Notes

[1]   Note that these difficulties are also inherent in lie-detector tests. It is assumed that people will show changes in physiological reactions like blood pressure and rate of heartbeat when they are lying, but there is no evidence that this is indeed true. That is, studies have not been done in which a person is known to be lying and who is having his or her blood pressure and heartbeat measured as he or she is lying. Even if such a study were done, the very fact that the liar knew he or she was being measured might allow him or her to control spikes in physiological reactions.

[2]   Scholarly ethics prevent one from using hidden recording devices, so participants have to know they are being recorded, but not necessarily why. It would negate the purpose if they were told the experimenter was looking for symbols of lying, so one has to come up with a viable excuse, such as, perhaps, finding out what kinds of jokes people told while playing or what topics of conversation were acceptable.

[3]   This space was recently renovated, so the telltale tiles no longer exist.

[4]   This is done, in my experience, when one announces that he or she has to go and the other party continues to talk. Looking at one's wristwatch, another cue that one wishes to end the interaction, may not help. Finally, one starts to move away.

[5]   Known in various places in the United States as a *hero, hoagie, submarine, poor boy, wedgie,* or *torpedo.*

[6]   These give facials and apply cosmetic makeup.

[7]   An even more solid display of solidarity in play is seen in scenes of apparently usual play among children of the Bushmen in the Kalahari Desert in the movie *The Gods Must be Crazy.* Here children are shown dancing in a circle, each on one leg, and the other leg lifted and entwined in the leg of the child behind him or her. The entire group hops around thus intertwined as if it is one being.

[8]   Again, this is generally human behavior. A close parallel occurs in Ukrainian folk dancing, in which women dance in a circle and men go into the center to show off their acrobatic ability. Women are cooperative and men competitive.

[9]   Except among Orthodox Jews who refrain from handholding or touching a member of the opposite sex except for their spouse, and then only in private.

[10]   Goldman and Fordyce made no such interpretation and aren't responsible for this one.

[11]   Pinkerman did not attempt voice quality as a variable.

CHAPTER 4

[12] Many studies of nonverbal behavior use as one variable the dimension of physical attraction. Interestingly, however, this is never really defined. One assumes that the researchers assume that certain metrics of attractiveness are uniform within a society, an assumption which I suspect should be investigated.

Exercises

1. Watch a video of at least one blind entertainer (or observe a blind person of your acquaintance). Describe his or her facial expressions, gaze, head movements, and hand movements. To what degree do these seem to differ from those of seeing persons? To what degree are they the same? From this, what conclusions do you draw about the relation of nature and nurture in kinesics?

2. Observe people interacting in public places, such as the library or cafeteria. Compare a dyad or a group that seems to be very much involved with each other as opposed to one in which the members are not. What behaviors distinguish between the two groups? How accurate is the idiom "in synch with" in describing the involved versus the uninvolved groups? Alternatively, you may analyze a television commercial or other video.

3. Observe a group at a party or other gathering. Is there a difference in the amount of space around different members? That is, do some members take up more space than others? If so, what is the gender, social class, and/or ethnicity of those who do? What conclusions can you draw about power and/or solidarity from these observations?

4. Observe eye contact in your home or social group. What seems to be the "normal" amount of eye contact in an interaction? What topics or situations seem to call for longer eye contact? Alternatively, try to compare the eye contact behavior of two different groups (ethnic, gender, social class) and determine what differences there are, if any, between them.

5. Keep a log of all the touching you do and all those who touch you at school, work, or home for part of a day. How much touching actually goes on, under what conditions, and for what reasons? What kinds of touching evoke excuses, and what seems to be unnoticed? Exclude sexual touching from your observations.

6. Watch a group of children at play. In what way(s) do they signal solidarity and/or competitiveness? Alternatively, watch a team sport on television and describe the kinesics of members of the team to each other as opposed to nonmembers.

7. Try to analyze a few minutes of a movie or other video source, correlating facial expressions and kinesics to the verbal message. How much of the message is being given in words alone? How much in kinesics alone? How much by interaction of both? Alternatively, observe people interacting, and estimate how much of their messages are being overtly stated and how much is given in kinesics.

Chapter 5

Pragmatics and Conversation

Much speech is a way of effecting actions, a way of doing things with words. Cultures have different rules for when people can speak and when they must be silent, including rules for interrupting. We must use shared discourse routines for much interaction. We are not free to say anything we want or even to say it in the way we want as we converse. Utterance pairs must be responded to in certain ways and, if they are not, repairs are attempted. Simply knowing the language is not sufficient because true meaning often lies not in the actual words uttered but in a complex of social knowledge.

DOING THINGS WITH WORDS

People usually think of speech as a way of stating propositions and conveying information, and they think that this is done by selecting the exact words and grammar that add up to what they are trying to convey. So persistent is this "commonsensical" idea that for generations, linguists were primarily concerned with trying to elucidate the rules of grammar and the meanings of words in order to explain language.

It remained for philosophers to point out the obvious. Much of what we say means things quite different from the words and grammar used. Furthermore, much of what we say is not concerned with conveying ideas, even those utterances which are not part of phatic communication. Austin (1975) stressed the functions of speech as a way of "doing things with words." For instance, one may use the same proposition to do quite different things. Searle (1969, 23) says one may use it "to 'describe,' 'assert,' 'warn,' 'remark,' 'comment,' 'command,' 'order,' 'request,' 'criticize,' 'apologize,' 'censure,' 'approve,' 'welcome,' 'promise,' 'object,' 'demand,' and 'argue.'" These are all examples of **illocutionary** force. The illocutionary force, expressed implicitly or explicitly, tells how the proposition is to be taken. For instance, if I say, "I'm eating with Berthold tonight," I might mean this as a warning to Berthold's girlfriend that I intend to steal him from her. Alternatively, I could mean it as a description of my current social life. I could phrase it as, "May I eat with Berthold tonight?" if Berthold is a student who needs permission to go out. Or, I could mean it as an apology to someone who has asked me to dinner.

CHAPTER 5

Sometimes it is clear from the context what the illocutionary force is. For instance, one could say, "I'll clean up that mess before you come back." This is clearly a promise even without prefacing it with, "I promise . . ." Often, a promise is effected just by using the modal auxiliary *will* or its contraction, *'ll*. Interestingly, the stronger *must* doesn't indicate a promise. "I must clean up that mess before you come back" doesn't promise the other person. Similarly, "I should clean up that mess . . ." acknowledges that one is responsible for cleaning it up, but doesn't promise that one will.

Verbs like *bet, promise, guarantee, order,* and *request* are known as **performatives**, and these explicitly state the illocutionary force of one's utterance. Frequently, one can determine that a verb is performative by putting *hereby* before it, as in "I hereby request that you leave this property." In contrast, note the absurdity of "I hereby detest chocolate soda." That is because one's detestation of chocolate soda conveys information and does not do something with words like *betting, promising, guaranteeing,* and the like.[1] If one's utterance actually makes another person do something such as carry out a command, take defensive action, or even to change someone's mind as when one persuades, then the speech is a **perlocutionary act**.

Speech Acts and the Law

The reality of speech acts has long been recognized in law. The Bill of Rights protects freedom of speech so long as the speech is about personal opinion or statement of fact, but it does not protect all speech acts. That is why crying, "Fire!" in a crowded building is a crime. Despite the fact that it is clearly speech, it is also primarily an act, as it is intended to make people flee the building. It is not someone's opinion, or shouldn't be since it has the perlocutionary effect of panicking people, potentially causing a great deal of harm. The fact of crying out "Fire!" is tantamount to commanding everybody to get out as fast as possible.

Similarly, conspiring to bribe a jury or to commit another crime is illegal even though both are done in speech, because they have the effect of inducing illegal actions. Other crimes which are essentially speech acts are perjury, libel, and slander. Wills, contracts, and appointment of an agent on one's behalf are also speech acts. Wills give something to someone. Contracts are reciprocal acts of offering and accepting (Tiersma 1993, 133). Appointment of an agent permits that person to buy or sell for you, to act, in other words.

PRAGMATICS AND CONVERSATION

Speech Acts and Social Interactions

Speech act theory has prompted sociologists, anthropologists, and educators to investigate the ways people use language to manage social interactions. It has prompted linguists to consider how meaning is achieved regardless of what words are actually used (Chaika 1981, 1990). As we shall see, this has impacted on the study of literature, legal documents, psychotherapy, and a myriad of other human activities. Threatening, complimenting, commanding, even questioning can all be manipulative, as we shall see. Another person's behavior may be affected quite differently from what one might expect from the actual words used. "See the belt?" may be sufficient to restrain a child from wrongdoing if he or she has reason to fear spanking.

SPEECH ACTS AND DISCOURSE ROUTINES

Because speech acts operate by what amounts to pragmatic principles, the study of speech acts in daily interaction is called **pragmatics** to distinguish it, for instance, from rules of syntax and lexical choice, such as the rule for making a passive sentence or using a word denoting time with the verb *lapsed*. Speech acts carry heavy social implications. The responses to them are typically conventional, so that we speak of **discourse routines**, such as questions and answers.

Much of our everyday talk consists of discourse routines, and cultures vary considerably in the modes of routines they prefer. The degree to which one requests or orders directly, the occasions on which one compliments and one's response, how one invites others to do something, all of these are done by socially recognized discourse routines, which are speech acts. Asking questions causes others to answer; therefore, questions are speech acts. So are apologies and excuses. All of these are embedded in our daily conversation.

Since cultures vary in how they carry out discourse routines, learning them is an important task if one is to become socialized to a given culture. Unfortunately, foreign language classes often focus on correct grammar and vocabulary building. They teach us how to speak directly, how to say what we mean. However, much interaction has to be effected by not speaking directly, by not saying what one means. One also has to learn to make the proper responses in one's culture in discourse routines. This can cause cross-cultural difficulties. The social facts of responsibility and saving face determine how discourse will be routinized in a culture. That is, whether or not one can issue a command to another is determined according to whether one has the obligation or the right to do so. How one phrases a request or a criticism may be determined by the desire not to insult another or to make them lose face.

FRAMES

Many scholars have shown that the way we make sense of the myriad impressions that assail us daily is to use **frames**, also known as **scripts**, **schemata**, and **structures of expectation** (Gumperz 1982a, 21–22). We use these to decide what is important, what inferences we can and should be getting from an interaction, why someone is speaking the way he or she is, and what our reaction should be. If we did not use such interpretive frames, we would have to treat every conversation separately, examining it word by word. This would hinder communication drastically. Nothing would ever get done. We would never be able to make sense of things.

Goffman (1974) speaks of frames somewhat differently, as self-presentation. Generally, Goffman portrays people as giving performances as they go about their daily business. Corsaro (1985, 178) complains, "Goffman makes major assumptions about what people do in discourse without ever studying discourse," a practice also criticized by Stubbs (1983, 91). Their criticisms don't take into account qualitative analyses (Johnstone 2000). These are acceptable in sociolinguistics. That is, studies to which statistical analyses of the data cannot be applied, such as studies of responses in conversations or analyses of narratives, can be very accurate. One must set up good field methods and ask the right questions to get scientifically acceptable results in such studies, but that is true even of quantitative analyses.

Many issues in conversational analysis and pragmatics admit only of qualitative, not quantitative, analyses. The kinds of observation employed by Goffman are valid in qualitative analyses with due regard for the dangers of random observation. Although some of Goffman's studies do seem to be based upon random observations, such as his mentioning the behavior of people he saw on a bus, much is derived from more principled investigation. You shouldn't ignore Goffman. His works still apply today. His writings are seminal and should—and do—inspire valuable research.

Since subsequent chapters will show how people use language to project an identity, in this one we will consider only frames as expectations. Ironically, one obstacle in using frames to interpret is that they are based upon an individual's personal experiences. Another is that cultures differ in their frames. Tannen (1979a) illustrates how we can figure out such differences by analyzing what people say. She specifically analyzes how Greek and American women narrate what they have just seen in a short film and how their frames can be deduced from what they say. The film showed a pear picker in a tree, who had left his fruit in a basket under the tree. A boy came along and stole the pears. Then he fell from his bike and dropped the pears. Other children riding by helped him pick up the pears, so he gave each one some fruit. When the picker came down from the tree, he discovered his empty basket. Then he saw the children eating the pears (Chafe 1980).

Americans revealed more expectations about what a film should be than Greeks did. For instance, several commented that the film had no dialogue, showing that they expected it (Tannen 1980, 151). Tannen explains that negative statements are the most frequently used clear indications that an expectation is not being met (148). Americans also thought that the task was a test of memory. This was revealed in comments like "How picky do you want?," "That's all I remember," and "You should have caught me . . . ten minutes ago when I remembered. . . ." Greeks, on the other hand, expected the film to have a message (155, 160) which they revealed by their judgmental comments. For instance, one woman commented on the pear picker, "He lived that which he did, he liked it." Of the children she said, "this was something that showed how children love each other" (156).

Other kinds of expectations are similarly revealed. Both Greeks and Americans commented on the fact that the picker didn't see the boy. Clearly, they expected that the worker should have seen the boy. This is very evident in "But he's [the boy] very brazen. I mean . . . they're only three feet apart." Tannen points out that the words *brazen* and *only* both show that the speaker would normally expect to see the boy (161).

SPEECH EVENTS AND GENRES

A **speech event** is a situation calling forth particular ways of speaking (Gordon and Lakoff 1975). **Genre** refers to the form of speaking. Usually, it has a label, such as *joke, narrative, promise, riddle, prayer,* even *greeting* or *farewell.*

Members of a speech community recognize genres as having beginnings, middles, and ends; they also recognize them as being patterned. For instance, "Did you hear the one about . . . " is a recognized opener for the genre *joke* in our society. "Once upon a time . . . " is a recognized opener for the genre *child's story*, and "They lived happily ever after" is the *stock ending*. The end of a *joke* is a *punch line*, often a pun, an unusual or unexpected response to a situation or utterance, or a stupid response by one of the characters in the joke. Frequently, the stupid response to a situation is one that reveals that the character is lacking in some basic social knowledge. For instance, an old Beetle Bailey cartoon shows Sarge saying to

CHAPTER 5

Zero, "The wastebasket is full." Zero responds, "Even I can see that." The joke lies in the fact that Zero took Sarge's words literally rather than interpreting them as a command, which was their actual social force.

Sometimes, but not always, the genre is the entire speech event. Church services are speech events, for instance. Sermons are a genre belonging to church, but sermons do not cover the entire speech event. Prayers, responsive readings, hymn singing, and announcements also constitute the speech events of church services.

The way that participants carry out the demands of a genre is their **performance**. In some communities this is more important than others. Also, performance is more important in some speech events than others. A professor's performance is usually far more important than that of students in her or his classroom.[2] Perhaps *important* is not quite the right word. It might be more accurate to say that the professor's importance will be judged more overtly than a student's and will be judged according to different criteria. These are the criteria judged in public performance, such as clarity of diction, voice quality, logic of lecture, and coherence. Correct performance in less formal speech events is just as important, but judgments may be limited to how appropriate the speech was to the situation. Everyday discourse routines are as much performances as are preaching, joke telling, and lecturing.

INTENTION

In all interaction the parties assume that each person is speaking with a purpose. Hearers get meaning partially by what they think the speaker's purpose is. Esther Goody (1978) says that people impute intentions to others' words. In fact, she notes, they "positively seek out intentions in what others say and do." A person's assumption of what another's intention is colors the meaning he or she gets from messages. How often has someone suspiciously said to a perfectly innocent comment of yours, "Now what did you mean by that?" The question is not asking for literal meaning but for your intention in saying what you did.

One important determinant for interpretation of intention is the **presequence**. Presequences are recognized opening sentences which signal that a particular kind of speech act will follow, such as commands, demands, or threats. For example, the child who hears an adult's, "Who spilled this milk?" may rightly perceive the question as the precursor to a command, "Wipe it up!" So important is intention to verbal interaction that deBeaugrande and Dressler (1981, 112) say that the only way utterances can be used to communicate is if the speaker intends them to be communicated, and the hearer accepts them as intended.

Often intentions are not perceived correctly, causing misunderstandings as harmless as hearing an honest question as a command or as serious as hearing an innocent comment as an insult.[3] To illustrate, consider a man who, in front of his slightly plump wife, looks at a model and says, "Boy, is she skinny!" The wife immediately bridles or dissolves in tears, depending on her personal style. She assumes that his comment is a way of complaining about her fat. However, he might be commenting that the model is too thin to be attractive and that he prefers curvier women.

If a speaker gives false information, then his or her intent will largely determine whether or not it is a lie, an error, or a fantasy. If the speaker gives false information but believes that it is true and is intending to inform, then he or she is simply mistaken. If the speaker gives false information but knows that it is false and is intending to make the hearer believe it is true, then he or she is lying. If he or she gives false information and knows it and is representing it as not true, then he or she is creating a fantasy. The difference between an error, a lie, and a fantasy, then, is not only a matter of actual truth but also of the speaker's belief and intent.

CONVERSATION

We are not mere creatures of conditioning when it comes to language. Noam Chomsky's most potent insight, perhaps, was that we can say things we have never heard before as well as understand what we have not previously heard. Language makes us free as individuals but chains us socially. We are not free to say what we really want to in many social situations. We are limited by what has just been said or by the social situation itself. Fairclough (1989, 84) points out that **discourse**, any connected body of speech or writing, such as conversation, is, in itself, social interaction. He claims that "people internalize what is socially produced and made available to them" and that what they internalize gives "the forces which shape societies a vitally important foothold in the individual psyche, though . . . the effectiveness of this foothold depends on it being . . . below the level of consciousness." Discourse, then, involves social conditions, thus helping maintain the social order (25). In other words, our unconscious compliance with social rules of discourse helps keep us and others in their place.

In contrast to Chomsky's dictum, when we consider discourse rules we find that the social rules of language often force us to respond in certain ways. Frequently, we are at least constrained, if not forced, to limit sentences to conform to a topic previously introduced by another (Duranti and Ochs 1979). However, each new utterance may open up new possible topics.

There are socially acceptable ways to change topics. If one does this, as we shall see, the topic change in itself may have a meaning. For instance, someone may make a negative remark about somebody and you respond by, "Did you get to the Nordstrom's sale?" The fact of the topic change itself indicates that you didn't like the remark and are refusing to talk further about it. If the topic change can't be construed so that the hearer can figure out why it was abruptly changed, the speaker may be accused of being uncooperative. When I first began examining schizophrenic speech, I found that some psychiatrists blamed patients this way because of their chaotic topic switching.

The topic need not be overtly stated, and seldom is. Also, there are times when we must respond whether we want to or not or respond in very limited ways when we would prefer to say more (Sacks 1964–1972, 1970; Schenkein 1978).

Grice (1975, 45–47) claimed that there are certain maxims which guide conversation. He calls these the **maxims** of **quantity**, **quality**, **relation**, and **manner**.[4] **By** *quantity*, he means that one should say no more nor no less than is required for current purposes. By *quality*, he means one should say only what one has evidence for and what one believes is true. By *relation*, he means that everything one says should be relevant to the interaction. By *manner*, he means that one should try not to be obscure or ambiguous, or say anything more than necessary, and that one should be orderly. These maxims can be **flouted**, that is, not obeyed. When they are, they typically entail or imply another meaning. Thus meaning is effected both by adherence to the maxims and by flouting them.

For instance, Grice says that the person who is over-informative may mislead hearers into thinking that there is a reason for the excess of information. One possible reason that something is mentioned when it could be presumed to be known is to put someone down, to say in effect, the speaker thinks you're so stupid that he or she has to tell you the obvious. In 1978, when I brought my computer in for repair, the technician, a male, patronizingly said, "You know you have to put in a diskette." (This was before hard drives and before women were considered as computer users.) Since this was so basic to operating a computer, it was as if the technician assumed that I didn't know how to operate my own computer. I naturally took this as an insult.

Gordon and Lakoff (1975, 92) give a wonderful example of the violation of quantity. If you were to go up to a married friend and say, "Your wife [or husband] is faithful," the friend would probably do a double-take and even get angry. The friend would figure that you were casting doubt on the spouse's fidelity. Otherwise, why say it at all? Spouses usually assume their partners are faithful unless the marriage is bad. Telling them that the partner is faithful, then, indicates there was some doubt about the matter. Part of the reason that it means this is that there is a violation of the maxim of relation. Why would you say such a thing? What relation does it have to the interaction?

Of course, if there had been an earlier interaction in which the spouse's fidelity had been an issue, the married friend would be glad to hear the news. The maxim of relation would not have been violated, as the utterance would be related to the prior one. Nor would the maxim of quantity have been violated. Notice that there is a meaning **entailed** by "Your wife is faithful," a meaning not directly attributable to the actual words used. In a very real sense, words in an interaction usually mean a great deal more than they say. We "get at" that surplus of meaning by our assumptions.

Intentionally or not, people frequently violate the maxim of quality. That is, they misinform unintentionally or misinform intentionally (that is, lie) or both. The lie consists as much in the hearer's assumption that the speaker is telling the truth as it does in the actual words of the speaker. Similarly, the unintentional misinformation is effected because of the hearer's assumption that the speaker knows what he or she is talking about.

All people at some time are obscure when they are trying to explain or recount something, thus violating the maxims of relation and manner. Fortunately, the hearer can initiate repairs so the speaker can sharpen his or her manner. People who wander off the topic or who say things with no apparent relation to the context can also be asked for repairs, unless, of course, they are insane or under the influence of drugs or alcohol. Indeed, one of the criteria for insanity is that the speaker not only violates the maxim of relation, but also cannot repair what was said. For instance, one schizophrenic in an interview said:

> I have distemper just like cats do, 'cause that's what we all are, felines. Siamese cat balls. They stand out. I had a cat, a manx still around somewhere. You'll know him when you see him. His name is GI Joe. He's black and white. I had a little goldfish, too, like a clown. Happy Hallowe'en down.

In my experience, patients who say things like this cannot answer questions about it. Nor can they repeat what they just said. If you were to ask where GI Joe is now, for instance, and the patient responded at all, it would not be to tell you about the cat or anything else in the discourse.

Mentioning too much, even if it is related to the topic and can be construed as being new information to the hearer, can be as distracting as actual departures from the topic itself. People assume that anything known to all parties in a given conversation will not be overtly stated unless there is some special reason for so doing. Searle (1975) says that mentioning extraneous matters leads listeners down false trails as they try to figure out how those matters fit the topic at hand. It seems to me that this is why our courts of law have such strong rules against introducing irrelevant matters. To do so clouds the issues for the judge and jury.

Applying these maxims, which are actually presuppositions about discourse, is one factor in our being able to make sentences cohere so that they are perceived as being a discourse. Since the term *maxims* has long been in use in discourse analysis, I use it here, but, actually, they are **strategies** based upon presuppositions about conversations and text which we use to interpret.

Although Grice is not wrong, more detailed analyses of conversation by linguists have shown that adherence to the maxims is not quite so cut and dried. Indeed, in order to do conversation skillfully, sometimes more needs to be said than is strictly necessary for conveying information. This, as we shall see, however, does not take the form of over-informing in a business encounter, such as dealing with repair technicians. Moreover, the entire concept of a topic around which all statements revolve belongs more to writing than to speech.

It has become increasingly clear that people do a conversation together as a social action. Both hearers and speakers are involved, and their roles rotate in the course of a conversation. If one person speaks and the others just listen, then one is hearing a lecture or a sermon, either of which primarily inform. In contrast, while conversation may inform, it just as importantly serves as a bonding activity, a way of maintaining social relations with others. Examining some actual conversations, one sees that the maxims are often not so much flouted as that they are irrelevant, and that society cannot be understood without understanding conversations, just as a sentence cannot be understood without considering the entire discourse in which it is embedded. Linguists, therefore, have become very interested in **discourse analysis**, both written and spoken.

Strictly speaking, the term *discourse* refers to any stretch of language above the level of the sentence which, in some sense, coheres as a unit. The term *text* usually refers to written language rather than spoken, although some use the term *discourse* for writing as well.[5] People who come from cultures which have writing systems typically think of language as being what is on the written page and are frequently amazed to discover that ordinary speech is as important an object of study as texts are. Indeed, it can be argued that analyzing ordinary speech is more important for understanding a society than analyzing texts is. As Stubbs (1983) says,

Conversation is basic: the commonest use of language, a pervasive phenomenon of everyday life that deserves systematic study . . . If only because of its massive occurrence, spontaneous unrehearsed conversation must provide some kind of baseline or norm for the description of language in general. (10)

PRAGMATICS AND CONVERSATION

Clearly, there is no way of understanding any society unless one understands its conversation. There are cultures which have no writing, but none which have no conversation. Besides conversation, there are more formal uses of spoken language, such as lectures and eulogies, which are quite different in form and purpose from conversation.

Topic

Although spoken sentences are not like written ones, they still are usually governed by a topic (VanDijk 1977). Once a topic is introduced, it must be adhered to unless some formal indication of change is being made. Paradoxically, in American English, this often is, "Not to change the subject, but . . .," which always changes the subject. "By the way . . ." also indicates that the topic is about to be changed to something which has been mentioned before. Among the other changes of topic signals are, "Ooooh, I meant to tell you" or "That reminds me . . ." or "Speaking of Harry. . . ." It is also possible for a speaker to announce a topic, as when one prefaces a remark with phrases like, "About last night . . ." and "You'll never believe this one. . . ."

These are valid ways of changing a topic. The very fact that we have so many devices to do this indicates the importance of keeping to a topic or at least ensuring that one's contribution is understood in light of the topic currently on the floor. In any conversation, one's response or utterance must relate in some way to what has already been said, or is about to be, but frequently one can't show that the utterance adheres to an overriding topic that governs the entire conversation. In an ordinary conversation, topics change as the interaction progresses. In interactions for a selected purpose, such as a meeting at work, topic is severely constrained, and each utterance must be able to be seen as relevant to the purpose of the meeting.

In a casual conversation, the interactors are typically limited only by the speakers' ingenuity in presenting statements so that hearers can deduce the "point." Erickson (1984, 126) speaks of **topic associating** in a conversation. As people talk, giving anecdotes, listeners use a strategy of figuring out what the semantic connections between the anecdotes are. It is the listeners as much as the speakers who create the topic. Erickson also speaks of **rhapsody**, a stitching together of a conversation (97) between speaker and hearer. Thus, often a friendly conversation starts out on one subject and ends on quite another without anybody overtly announcing change of topic. Still, it will be a coherent, sensible conversation because the adjacent parts of it go together in a relevant way.

When conversation is going well, when the speakers are all "in synch" with each other, it can be set to a metronome (Erickson and Shultz 1982).

CHAPTER 5

Movements, whether micro movements like head nodding, or larger ones like leg crossing, are synchronized with utterances. Tannen (1989, 18) likens joining a conversation to joining a line of dancers. One must first be able to share its rhythm. Erickson and Shultz found that people being counseled were able to derive more usable information from interviews when they and counselors were able to establish such a rhythm.

Maxims of Quantity and Manner

The maxim of quantity is constantly being violated in conversation. For one thing, repetition which does not further a storyline or add new information is, nevertheless, a very important part of successful conversation. Tannen (1989) shows that repetition serves many conversational purposes. It is a way of showing that one is still participating even if he or she has nothing new to add. It also shows support for the views of a co-conversationalist, or agreement. Repeating the end of someone's sentence can be a way of showing that one understands what the other is saying. Repeating also shows appreciation of what the other has said. Then, too, it emphasizes a point, and a way of establishing a rhythm. I've had students collect instances of repeating of the "I can't believe . . ." variety. They have found this common, especially for emphasizing how much somebody ate or drank. It works by punctuating a conversation about parties. For instance, "You drank the whole pitcher of beer" with an upward rise in intonation may be repeated several times.

Other examples of repeating are:

In telling about a fight:

1. And I says to him, you're bleeding, you're bleeding. Jack, you're bleeding.

At the dinner table:

2. *Bobby*: I've stopped drinking.
   Susanne: He's stopped drinking.

3. *Mother*: Use your napkin, Johnny.
   Father: Use your napkin, Johnny.

Or, upon leave-taking:

4. *Mother*: You'd better button up. It's cold out.
   Aunt: Yes, it's very cold out.

Similarly, when one repeats the punchline of a joke while laughing, one is letting the joke-teller know that one thinks he or she is very funny. Orators like Dr. Martin Luther King, Jr. made great use of repetition to keep his speeches memorable and rhythmic. Think of his famous "I have a dream" speech.

Another way in which the maxim of quantity is violated, and has to be violated, is that in conversation, a good speaker will pepper his or her talk with details not strictly necessary to convey the information or will supply anecdotes by way of illustration. Parables, in which the stories illustrate one main idea, are an extreme example of the latter. Tannen shows that use of details and anecdotes is a way of involving others in the conversation. They help the other(s) to visualize events being spoken of, so that they feel as if they have actually participated. For example, in telling a friend how my husband always buys more than he is supposed to, I recounted a time when I asked him to bring me home some candy:

5. Well, he stuck his hand in his pocket and out came jujubes and fruit drops. Then he went to another pocket and produced crunch bars and chocolate covered cherries, light and dark. He handed me a bag too. I opened it. Baby Ruths and sour balls, caramels. So I screamed, "Why did you get so much?" He answered, "I wasn't sure what you were in the mood for.

Interestingly, the friend then repeated, laughing, "He didn't know what you were in the mood for," showing that she appreciated the story. The reporting of actual dialogue, even though it is not strictly necessary for the message, adds to the immediacy of the scene; hence, adds to the hearer's involvement. It helped that I can imitate my husband's facial expressions, shoulder shrugging, and intonation when repeating his words. Had I merely said, "He brought me too much," the friend couldn't have visualized the scene, wouldn't have seen the latent humor in the situation. It occurs to me that by recounting this story in such detail, I conveyed to the friend a great deal about my husband's character and behavior, which wouldn't have been conveyed had I strictly adhered to the maxim of quantity. Had I just said that he always buys too much, it would have sounded like a complaint, not an affectionate portrait of him.

Paul Drew (2003) studied the amount of precision with which people describe events, and what happens when they exaggerate. Both situations are, of course, related to quantity: How much should you say? How much is too much, and how much is too little? He points out (919–20) that in the courts, one must supply much more detail and be much more precise than in other conversations. For instance, a defendant (D) accused of speeding told the prosecutor he was going fifty-five as he approached a sign giving the speed limit. The prosecutor (P) persisted:

6. *P*: Exactly fifty-five?
    D: Somewhere in that vicinity.
    P: Well, did you look at your speedometer?
    D: Yes, I know I was under fifty-five.
    P: Well, do you remember what you were going?
    D: No, I don't.

In an ordinary conversation, not only would nobody keep asking for verification, but if D had said something like:

7. I was going around fifty-five n' I know that because I looked at my speedometer just before I saw the traffic sign although I have to admit I don't know precisely how much I was going, a little more or a little less . . .

a co-converationalist would consider him or her to be a windbag, a bore. Who goes on and on about the precise number of miles per hour like this?

Similarly, in ordinary conversation, when asked how long one waited for the door to open after she knocked, someone might answer, "It seemed like three days." This exaggeration is perfectly all right, but in a courtroom when a defendant answered this way, the judge refused to respond and the defense attorney persisted, elongating words and using long pauses between phrases:

8. An:d [clears throat] (2.1) asi:de for the moment (0.3) of how long it see::med to you (1.5) because of your then state of mind d'you have any: (0.3) are you able to: (0.3) come to any (.) estimate (.) now with respect to real ti:me. (0.3) Was it er: minute was it a minute an' a ha:lf? Or (.) can you give us your best judgment. (0.8) Not how long it see:med to you (0.5) to have th' ( ) door opened but how long it was. (0.7) J'st your best estimate. (918)

The number of words used for this request, combined with the portentous manner of it, is appropriate for a courtroom but not other situations. Far too much was said to ask so little. Basically, all that was needed was, "Yeah, but how long did it really take?"

Drew shows that how much one says depends upon the particular context in which one is speaking. In casual speech, we use hyperbole all the time without being questioned. For instance, people commonly say things like, "I have absolutely no money," or "There's no food to eat in this house" (932–937). They do not elucidate about how much money they really have or what food is actually in the house, but that's okay in casual speech. Of course, there may be people with absolutely no money and with a totally bare larder, but these conditions don't have to be true for someone to make such claims. In a courtroom or to one's social worker, on the other hand, they would have to be true, and the speaker would have to justify the claims.

If a co-conversationalist has some reason to doubt one's veracity, or doesn't want to take the claim with a grain of salt, he or she can respond by saying "You haven't?" or "Really?" This allows the first speaker to modify his or her claim by weakening it somewhat, like "Well, I have five bucks . . ." or "Only some stale bread. . . ." Interestingly, speakers usually don't retract their original exaggeration; they just modify it downwards. Drew (937) says that, in conversation, hearers may repair an exaggeration, but they don't do the kind of cross-examining done in court.

Whether or not a speaker has made an exaggerated claim in ordinary conversation, it would be inappropriate to ask such questions as "Do you mean you don't have a penny in your possession?" or "How long has it been since you put a morsel of food in your mouth?" "Are the cupboards completely bare? Isn't there a box of crackers? How about flour and baking soda?" It is a real violation of quantity to ask too much about the veracity of another's statement. Adhering to the maxim of quantity, then, is a delicate business. It is context-bound behavior, and it must take into account picturesque language which may employ repetition, anecdotes, and exaggerations.

It seems to me that in everyday conversation, it is all right, even good, to exaggerate occasionally to make one's speech more vivid. Hearers expect this and, for the most part, don't question it, understanding that what was said was hyperbole. Speakers have to know with whom and under what circumstances it is all right not be precise.

It is not that the maxims don't guide much of our speech and writing, but that they don't explain a good deal of our ordinary conversation. What is needed, perhaps, is a strict taxonomy of when the maxims apply and when and how they should be ignored.

THE ETHNOGRAPHY OF COMMUNICATION

Studying the dynamics of communication within or between social groups is the **ethnography of communication**. The ways that one studies and records such fluid phenomena as ordinary speaking is ethnomethodology. Garfinkel (1967; 1972, 309) says he uses that term to refer to "various policies, methods, results, risks, and lunacies" to localize what parts of behaviors are important to study as well as to investigate the reasons for the "organized artful practices of everyday life." The work of the ethnographers has shown us that the seemingly random behavior of ordinary daily activity is actually highly structured, often as much so as texts are. It has also been discovered that the rules for carrying out conversation and other speaking activities vary not only from country to country, but both regionally and ethnically within a country.

In order for social interaction to proceed smoothly, all societies employ some kind of speech exchange system. Some cultures allow the person speaking to continue until he or she wishes to give it up. Others regulate turn-taking more overtly. The early research on turn-taking gave us a picture of a smooth transition between conversationalists with little or no interruption of the speaker. At some point in the speaker's turn, he or she signaled by a downward intonation curve that it was the other person's turn. If one participant overlapped his or her words with the speaker's, it was considered an interruption. After a suitable pause to ensure that the speaker really was giving up the floor, the other person would speak. This is a highly idealized picture of much ordinary conversation.

Analyzing Conversation

Conversational analysis (CA) treats talk and social interaction as an object of social scientific study. It emphasizes the role of social interaction as an autonomous reality in its own right rather than as a window into other social processes (Arminen 1999). What is different about conversational analysis is that each utterance has to be considered in relation to the preceding ones and also to those that follow. Each turn in a conversation is both a reaction to the context of a prior one and itself establishes a context for what comes next. The *next turn proof* is used for making sense of a prior turn (252). That is, if you think an utterance means a certain thing, to prove it, you consider how the person who spoke next responded. The analysis one makes in CA is not theoretical. It is measured against what actually transpired.

Arminen (252) admits we can't make infallible predictions of what will come next, nor is there necessarily only one response that could be made to any utterance. Someone may take a remark quite differently from what the speaker intended, but the way that remark was taken will provide the context for the response to it. She stresses that "a property of talk that looks innocent and insignificant may be relevant" (253) when looked at from another angle. She insists that one should try to find *order at all points* (italics hers), and shows that CA makes the research process a never-ending quest. It seems to me that its value lies in the fact that one doesn't jump to conclusions or rely on everyday assumptions in analyzing a conversation.

This doesn't mean you won't find regularities in the ways that people of different cultures respond; that is, regularities in the way speaking turns achieve certain intentions. However, you can never be sure that the turn will yield what the speaker wanted, except in the more routinized parts of interactions like greetings and questions, which demand certain responses. Also, certain formal institutional speech exchanges are rigidly constrained so that speakers must respond in certain ways and with certain information. Of course, these aren't conversations, which are more open-ended. Still, conversations can be analyzed.

In CA, one analyzes the way talk in interaction performs social actions within the context, considering how context is constantly being built up within the conversation. The applications of CA in such spheres as psychotherapy are obvious, but it is good for sensitizing people to others' motives in what they say, and also to highlight the various motives which can be construed from quite simple observations. CA also sheds light on interactions like survey interviews, human–computer interactions, business meetings, effective sales techniques, and communication problems of deficient speakers like aphasics and the mentally ill.

A simple instance of CA is seen in

E: That Pat, isn't she a doll?
M: Yes, isn't she pretty?
(Arminen, 254)

E's question invites M to assess Pat. On the surface, it is a simple question answerable by *yes* or *no*, but M doesn't treat it that way. Instead, M gives a downgraded opinion of Pat, also phrased as a question. If Pat is merely pretty, she's not a doll, which encompasses the idea of prettiness and also of being an easygoing person. By responding with a question, M hasn't cut off further discussion, but she has also indirectly let E know that she (M) doesn't agree with the first assessment. Also, M has provided an opening for discussing why Pat is not a doll. However, if E doesn't want to hear it, she is at liberty to change the subject at this point. If M had given a true question, E would be obliged to answer it, but, since her question can be seen only as an indirect way of correcting E's statement, then it need not be answered. It's always a ticklish business to contradict someone else's evaluation of another person. It can lead to hard feelings. Here, M has phrased her negative evaluation in such a way that this is not so likely to happen. Moreover, she has left the way open for E to explain why she thinks Pat is a doll.

CHAPTER 5

Harvey Sacks, some of whose work is discussed below, was a major instigator of CA. Working at a suicide prevention hotline, he wondered if conversations were just strings of propositions or, in contrast, methodological ways of doing things. For instance, he considered such problems as how to get someone's name without asking for it. This was important at the hotline. Another problem was how to avoid giving help without refusing to give it. His answer to this was to treat the circumstance as a joke. He paved the way for considering how turn-taking in ordinary conversations contributes to the organization of an activity, as well as for showing the work that a simple phrase can do interactionally. We will see this below when we discuss such things as "What is that, chocolate?" Unfortunately, Sacks was killed in an auto accident in 1975, but his work has been continued by many scholars.

High and Low Involvement Behaviors. As it happens, length of pause between turns in a conversation varies cross-culturally, causing problems. For instance, Southern friends and colleagues have complained about how difficult it is to interject their words in conversations with Northerners (like me), because just as the pause is long enough for them to take the floor, the Northerner figures that the other doesn't want to say anything and takes the floor back. Thereupon, the Southerner feels as if the co-conversationalist is not giving him or her a chance to speak, and is being very rude. Even within a region this can happen with people from different ethnic groups.

The person who interrupts another's turn is felt to be invading the space of the other. In fact, Tannen (1984, 78) cites an article about a psychologist who considers "fast talkers" and those who don't allow a pause between turns to be "conversational menaces" who "crowd" others, thereby leading to lack of communication.

But what of the invaders? Do they perceive themselves to be rude? Are they being rude? Tannen (83–87), in her study of spontaneous conversation between friends at a Thanksgiving dinner, shows that, to the contrary, for members of certain cultures, overlapping is a sign of bonding of showing rapport (56), even of helping the other speaker (118–119). Tannen says that overlappers are members of **High Involvement** (HI) cultures, as opposed to those who don't overlap, who are members of **Low Involvement** (LI) cultures.

Rapport and bonding for HI speakers are shown by clearly extraneous questions and comments as the other talks. Tannen gives as an example **cooperative prompting** (118), in which a listener keeps asking things like "What'd she say?" "Did it really?" "What did you say?" This is done although it is very clear that the speaker is going to tell all with or without prompts. The prompting is a way of showing enthusiasm, interest, and encouragement for the other's narrative. Obviously, when someone says, "Did it really?" for instance, she is not maligning the speaker's veracity. There is variation in how this is done in different HI cultures, as when ethnic blacks murmur, "Tha's right," "Talk dat talk," "Right on brother," and other such encouragements. This is done in church in response to a preacher's words, at banquets when a formal speech is given, as well as to each other in intimate conversations. These responses are frequently accompanied by overt head nodding. To those used to such encouragement when speaking, it is extremely unnerving to face people who remain silent when another is speaking.

Perhaps the most important thing to remember in dealing with those from other cultures is the list of common misperceptions that HI and LI members of society have of each other. We have already seen that LI conversationalists may consider HI ones to be rude and pushy. In turn, the HI speakers may feel that the LI ones are cold and wishy-washy. The Scollons (1981, 36) present lists of misunderstandings between Athabaskans, who are LI, and non-Native Americans, who are not. The latter group are "confused" (their term) because the Athabaskans don't speak, keep silent, never say anything about themselves, talk in a flat tone of voice, are slow to take a turn in talking, talk only to close acquaintances, and avoid direct questions, among other LI traits. The Athabaskans, in their turn are confused by English speakers who talk too much, always talk first, talk to strangers, brag about themselves, always interrupt, don't give others a chance to talk, always get excited when they talk, only talk about what they are interested in, and so on. These are virtually classic LI versus HI conflicts arising from the differences in speaking styles.

Bonding through the act of conversing seems to be widespread if not universal, especially if the parties are able to agree. Adrienne Lehrer (1983) reported that her subjects in a wine tasting experiment expressed good feelings when they were able to negotiate an agreement about what words to describe wine they had just tasted. Many of the words subjects used, like *oaky*, were not usual words for beverages, so subjects had to define meanings. Good conversations and discussions that lead to agreement or at least compromise are bonding behaviors. Such good feelings can also occur if participants agree to disagree, just so long as no anger is aroused. It's the good conversation that promotes satisfaction in a social encounter.

In the thick of talking, speakers often can't think of an event or a place, or the right word or wording. They make slips of the tongue and false starts. In some HI cultures, co-conversationalists feel free to break in on the speaker and help him or her by supplying the right word or fact. Tannen points out that not only is this expected, it is virtually required. Such overlapping gives a message of, "I understand you so well that I know what you are going to say."

In HI cultures "overlap not only does not impede but in fact enhances communication" (Tannen 1984, 79). Overlapping is a sign of interest, enthusiasm, and encouragement. Tannen sums it up, saying that in such cultures

> it is not the business of listeners to make sure that others have "room" to talk. It is their business to show interest and enthusiasm. Finding room to talk is up to speakers. Indeed, it is incumbent upon speakers, if they are observing this system, to find things to say and places to say them. A person who gives up after a single try is perceived by overlap-favoring speakers as being uncooperative, withholding, even sulking. (Tannen 1979b)

Tannen's observations were specifically on Jews from New York City of Eastern European background and may not be true of Jews from other backgrounds or locations. Also, it may be that Eastern Europeans in general or New Yorkers in general would fit Tannen's description of members of HI cultures. She did not explore these possibilities. Certainly Jewish New Yorkers are not the only people who overlap other's words in conversations. Several of my students have attempted to replicate Tannen's investigation at family dinners. So far, it appears from these studies that people who identify ethnically with being Italian, African American, or Irish seem, generally, to be HI.

However, many of my students over the years have distinguished between HI cultures and HI situations. That is, they find that, within their respective cultures, some situations, like family dinners, are characterized by HI behaviors, but others, like funerals, talking with relative strangers, job interviews, and visiting in hospitals evince characteristically LI practices. This certainly would be true of Tannen's HI speakers. She was investigating only behavior at a Thanksgiving dinner.

In any event, it is not the case that all members of any group are equally talkative or verbally aggressive or equally quiet and passive. There are always variations in individual personalities, but those from a HI culture, for instance, are not likely to be offended by someone's butting in as much as an LI person is, provided the situation is right for such behavior.

Another thing that must be borne in mind is that there is probably no sharp dividing line between HI and LI cultures. For instance, Native Americans in the West are clearly LI. But virtually all other groups in America, including LI groups like descendants of French Canadians in New England

and the original English settlers, would probably be more HI than Native Americans but still far less HI than Russians. It is doubtful, however, that the bundles of behavior patterns that have been labeled HI and LI will be shown to be all or nothing. We should think, instead, of a cline, with a gradient of HI to LI characteristics, and different cultures lying higher or lower on the gradient.

Those who come from LI cultures were probably shuddering as they read about those who interrupt, overlap, and leave no pauses. The normal conversational behaviors of High Involvement cultures are exceedingly rude in the eyes of others. An anecdote illustrates: My friend B from the very background Tannen identified as very HI, married a man from a very LI one. When B's mother-in-law regaled her with the doings of illustrious ancestors, B would, of course, constantly ask little questions and make little remarks, whereupon her mother-in-law would stop and glare at her for her rudeness. As it happens, B is an exceptionally quiet, polite, and soft-spoken person. The impression she gave of rudeness rested solely on the fact that her way of being polite did not jibe with that of her husband's family.

Note that someone who is considered *pushy* metaphorically crowds others. The feeling that certain ethnic groups are pushy seems related to their normal practices of overlapping and interrupting. Social scientists again and again have shown that often the way we perceive people is not always the way they actually have behaved. For instance, the common belief that women talk more than men has been disproved. Men talk more than women, and even interrupt women more than women interrupt men (see Chapter 10).

Tannen (1984, 132) counted the amount of time and the number of turns taken by each of the guests at the Thanksgiving dinner. Afterwards when she interviewed the participants in the Thanksgiving dinner, everyone was surprised that David (HI) had actually spoken less frequently than had Chad (LI). Everyone had come away with the impression that Chad had talked very little. One thing that caused this misperception seemed to be that David made a far greater percentage of ironical or humorous remarks than Chad, who made virtually none. In fact, the three HI speakers in the group were most likely to indulge in humor, which seems to be part of their normal style, especially irony and self-mocking, such as exaggerating their own ethnic speech styles (131–36). This implies that the "use of humor makes one's presence felt" (132).

Tannen (54–58) shows also that HI conversationalists talk about themselves a great deal and do this as an invitation for the other to do the same. LI speakers often view this with distaste. Not only are they unlikely to reciprocate with tidbits of their own lives, but one has to drag things out of them by questioning. In turn, HI speakers may find LI ones secretive and cold.

Finally, the persistence of HI speakers (87–94) bears mentioning. Not only do they overlap when they wish a change of topic or a chance to question or comment, they persist in talking while others are. They do this until they get the floor.

Direct and Indirect Statement. We all are willing to say some things directly, and others we have to indicate indirectly. Still, as perhaps might be expected, it seems that HI speakers frequently prefer more bald on-record statements. By this, I mean bald statements, statements that are on the record, as opposed to off- the-record implications. LI speakers may prefer subtlety, whereas HI speakers prefer to "lay it on the line." Again, it is Tannen (1981, 1984) who provides succinct examples:

1. *Wife*:   John's having a party. Wanna go?
   Husband: OK.
   Wife: [later] Are you sure you want to go?
   Husband: OK, let's not go. I'm tired anyway.

2. *Husband*:   Let's go visit my boss tonight.
   Wife: Why?
   Husband: All right. We don't have to go.

Tannen asked both Greek and American informants to interpret 1. More Greeks than Americans felt that the husband's "OK" meant that he really didn't want to go, but he thought she wanted to go, so he would go along with it. They thought this because of the brevity of his first response. In contrast, the Americans thought that the very brevity of "OK" is what showed he really did want to go. The Greeks wanted a greater display of enthusiasm to indicate genuine willingness, and the Americans felt that intimates say what they really mean. Moreover, the husband, when later asked to comment, said that since she mentioned the party in the first place, to him that meant she wanted to go, but by asking the second time, it meant she had changed her mind. He was trying to be solicitous and caring, so he made up an excuse for not going. The real problem is that the wife expected to give and understand outright statements, not subtle cues, but the husband was responding, he thought, to subtle cues.

In 2, the husband reported that when she countered with "Why?" he assumed she didn't want to go and this was her way of saying so. On her part, the "Why?" was a genuine request for information. The wife felt that her husband was very erratic because he was "always changing his mind."

Both thought the other mercurial. The husband in both sequences was Greek, and the wife was Deborah Tannen herself, an American of HI culture. Miscommunication resulted from the use of directly opposing strategies. Such are the shoals of communicating in a marriage between people of such different communication styles.

Speech Occasions

The occasion itself is crucial in determining who will speak and even if anyone will. There are times when it is all right to speak and times when it is not. These are frequently bound with place. For instance, in a Northern European or American middle-class neighborhood, if a group of adults congregate in the streets, everyone would assume that something bad has happened, such as someone's house catching fire. In other neighborhoods, however, it is usual to see groups talking and laughing on the street. In some cultures, it would be fitting only for men to do this; in others, both men and women would. In African American neighborhoods of some Northern cities, men congregate on the street corners or in front of a business establishment. Women sit on front porches or "stoops" of residences.

What middle-class people in the United States do once they cross the thresholds of their home, other groups will do in public. Milroy says that working-class men in Belfast congregate in the streets to talk and they will have very personal discussions in quite public places. This is succinctly called **threshold behaviors.** One of the things that young children have to learn is what is permissible beyond the threshold of their homes. Such things as shouting or crying loudly are not allowable behaviors in the United States. Parents become very embarrassed and unnerved when their toddlers throw a tantrum in public. It seems to me that this is because one is not supposed to stand out of the crowd in public places. Conversations, even disagreements, must be spoken in a low enough voice so that others can't hear them, and attention is not to be drawn specifically to oneself.

There is, as one would imagine, considerable cross-cultural variation. In my local pharmacy, for instance, I have heard Arabs speaking to each other loudly enough for people who are at the opposite end of the store to hear their entire conversation clearly. Since they are speaking Arabic, I can't understand them, but it doesn't sound like angry speech. When one looks at the speakers, they seem to be merely engaged in friendly talk, comparing items and the like. Other patrons express disapproval and even anger at what they see as a violation of space. What Americans hear as rudeness seems to be normal, friendly conversation between these speakers.

CHAPTER 5

SILENCE

In order to carry on a successful interaction, one must know the rules of silence, as well as the ones for speech. Silence can say as much as speech. Accompanied by the correct kinesics and among those of the same culture, it says, "We're friends," "I'm hostile to you," "This is a reverent occasion," "I disagree with you," or, even, "Shut up!"

Jaworski (1993) shows that silence itself may be defined in different ways. It may mean either 'the absence of sound' or 'the absence of speech.' It may even mean 'failure to speak about something,' when someone has actually spoken. In fact, in Polish, there are separate words for silence meaning 'no speaking,' and silence meaning 'not speaking about something one was expected to mention.'

Jaworski (43) stresses that silence has different functions and qualities. Silence is not *just silence*. It may come from an inner state or be imposed by others. There is anticipatory silence, the silence of reflection, or even, although Jaworski doesn't mention it, the silence of boredom or of opposition. That is, one may remain silent when speech is seen as complying with whatever one disagrees with. Silence in itself, then, may be a contradiction or disapproval of what was said.

Cross-Cultural Disjunction in Silence

In American English, I have noticed that silence may entail making some noises, like "mmm" or "uh huh." In other cultures, making such noises wouldn't be silence. We take it for granted that upon meeting someone, we must speak in order to be friendly and social. In some cultures, silence is employed when first meeting someone. The classic example is Basso's (1989) discussion of Apaches, who do not speak until they feel they know somebody well enough. That is, situations that call for phatic communication, small talk, in Anglo culture call for silence for the Apaches.

In the United States, we speak of dinner table conversation and how it is carried out, but in Finland, they do not consider it necessary to speak while eating (Jaworski 1993, 54). In the United States, a person who can converse easily with strangers and others is someone to be admired, a socially savvy individual. In Japanese, in contrast, a reticent person is trusted as honest, sincere, and straightforward (67). In that culture, silence is an active state, but speech can be construed as delaying activity. Worse yet, speaking a lot is associated with falsity, disguise, and deception. As we shall see, even so common a thing as religious feelings, connecting to a higher power, falls on a spectrum of complete silence to overt noisiness, with each group claiming spirituality by their silence or talk, which here includes chanting, singing, and shouting out.

It would be hard to find any communicative behavior that causes more intergroup misinterpretation than the rules of silence. For many Americans and Europeans, silence when with another indicates hostility or social malpractice. In the United States the ideal is to fill silences up, but there is variability in silence practices. Milroy (1980, 80–89) tells of a Danish couple who were so exhausted and angered by an American guest's constant chatter that they had to retreat to the privacy of their room. Of course, the American was just trying to be polite.

Milroy herself suffered from a disjunction between her rules of having to fill up the silences and those of the working-class Catholic Irish she was investigating in Belfast. As you may recall, Irish female guests would sit with their elbows entwined and bodies otherwise touching, and when they did talk, they gave little slaps and pokes to each other. Often, they didn't speak at all. They sat close together, arms entwined, and silent. Guests frequently entered the home and sat down, sometimes for hours, not saying anything. In contrast to most American and Northern European groups, stepping over someone else's threshold clearly was not a signal for chit-chat.

Milroy (89) suggests that this is similar to what has been reported of the Eskimos, who would visit a researcher every day for an hour to make sure he was all right, but said nothing. The visitor just sat down quietly and apparently observed. It has occurred to me that one reason that such rules of silence are prevalent in working-class Belfast and the Eskimos is that these groups are closely knit, with everyone pretty much knowing each other. Friends and neighbors do not expect invitations of any kind. They just visit frequently, and, of course, homes are always open to visitors. Frequent visiting in itself is an important mark of solidarity. Talking is both superfluous and beside the point. It would be too exhausting otherwise in such a culture. Requiring talk as a show of solidarity seems more necessary in a society in which people visit far less and, typically, only by invitation.

Milroy (89) says that "[a] fairly familiar (but not necessarily intimate) visitor . . . in Belfast may sit in total silence without the host feeling the slightest obligation to say anything at all." In such a culture, people in the family usually go on with their business, even when visitors drop in. This makes perfectly good sense. If people stop by frequently, how would anyone get their work done if a host had to be one in the American middle-class sense? Whereas in Belfast, such uninvited, frequent visiting is a show of solidarity, of belonging, for most Americans, it would be considered very rude and a severe violation of privacy.

CHAPTER 5

Religion and Silence

The rules for silence vary greatly among religions. There is a cline from complete silence to constant noise, often, but not always hushed. Interestingly, the noisiest services I've ever attended, Orthodox Jewish ones, don't have the loudest calling out. By *noisiest*, I mean amount of noise, not volume. The loudest I've heard is at Protestant Evangelical services. English has no word to differentiate the two meanings of *noise*.

In some religions, prayers at services are said in unison under the direction of a leader (minister, priest, imam, or rabbi). At others, they are said at each person's individual pace. Still others have variations between these extremes. Muslims, for instance, stay in synch with the Imam if they attend communal prayer as a congregation, but if they say their prescribed prayers after the communal prayer is over, they go at their individual pace even if others are praying with them in the mosque. So long as they've correctly said all the prayers prescribed for that time of day, they are considered as being as spiritually connected whether they prayed alone or with the Imam. Catholics at Mass pray only as the liturgy directs, under the leadership of the priest. Most Protestants also pray when told by the minister, as do Reform Jews. Orthodox and Conservative Jews may sometimes pray at their own pace during a service, stopping their private prayer to join in communally at certain junctures. Yet, all of these differences in prayer are intended to enhance the individual's spirituality and communion with God.

In a great cathedral, if a worshiper disagrees—or even agrees—with the homily, she or he does not stand up to encourage the preacher by shouting out, "Ain't it so, brother" or "Hallelujah!" In contrast, in an English chapel or an American Pentecostal church service, parishioners do call out affirmations, but they would never criticize. Their calling out is considered evidence of strong religious feeling, of really feeling the spirit, just as silence is evidence of deep religious feeling in masses at cathedrals. Those who practice silence typically feel it indicates respect. Yet, the Pentecostal is not being disrespectful by calling out. To the contrary, he or she is showing great reverence for God by praising Him aloud so others can hear.

In mainstream Catholic and Protestant services, parishioners are silent except when praying and singing in accordance with the requirements of the ritual as carried out by the priest or minister leading the service. The only other noise comes from the choir and organist or other musician(s). Typically, while people are seated waiting for mass to begin, at the Catholic churches I've attended, they don't speak. Of course, as they exit the church, friendly conversation resumes. At some Protestant services, I've heard quiet talk before the service officially begins, but not at others.

Maltz (1985) explains that, among Pentecostals, speaking out in church is both a way of showing their commitment and of demonstrating their joy. He says, "The expression of joy is not merely permitted, but openly encouraged" (126), especially since Pentecostals believe that calling out "Amen," "Hallelujah," and other expressions of support show that one has received the Holy Spirit. "Speaking in tongues," that is, producing streams of sounds not identifiable as a language, is another such expression also associated with the Pentecostals. Although Americans often identify such a display as being a feature of certain American Protestant churches, this is known in Scotland and England as well. It has to do with Pentecostalism, not ethnicity.

To show how variable practices for the same ends can be, the Quakers, in order to let the Light of Christ enter into them, are silent at worship, with individuals speaking out only when they are sure that they have received a message from the Light (Maltz, 123). Jaworski (1993, 38–40) notes that their silence is "functionally equivalent" to the exuberant noise of Pentecostals. He also says that the amount of silence at a Quaker meeting varies. At times, there is no talk. At others, two or three hours may pass before someone talks, and at still others, many may talk. The Quakers' silence is to them a desirable state for communal worship, and when one speaks, it is not to invite other speech. Rather, it enhances the silence that is already occurring (41).

Muslims are enjoined to pray five times a day. Each one knows all the prescribed prayers for each time, and the order in which they must be said. He or she prepares for prayer by ablution, carefully cleansing the body five times a day. Then, the person goes to a mosque and says the prayers in synchrony with the Imam leading the session. Prayers are said aloud, but not necessarily loudly. As the Imam prays, he stands, bows, kneels, sits, puts his head down, and so forth, at appropriate times in the prayer, and the congregation follows suit. When the prayers are over, someone might greet another or, upon seeing a stranger, invite him to dinner, but there is no conversation during the reciting of prayers. If someone misses the particular prayer service, he may come to the mosque later, although not so late that the prescribed time for the prayer has passed. My informant, Cemal Ekin, a Turkish Muslim, gives as an example someone coming in just after the noon prayer has finished. In the absence of the Imam, he says the prayers at his own pace. If a person can't make it to a mosque at all, then he or she puts down the prayer rug, faces towards Mecca, and says the prayers. Since each Muslim knows the prescribed prayers for each time of day, and knows the order they are said in, prayers can be said anywhere. Both in Egypt and Israel, I regularly saw people walking, carrying their prayer rugs,[6] so they would be ready to pray wherever they were, at a mosque or not.

CHAPTER 5

In an Orthodox Jewish congregation, each individual is also free to chant the prayers at his or her own speed regardless of where the rabbi and cantor are. Some men drape their prayer shawls over their heads to isolate themselves during intense prayer. This is a reflection of the fact that, in Judaism, the rabbi has no special powers and members of the congregation can and do participate in every aspect of the service. The name *rabbi* means 'teacher,' and a cantor is a singer who has had special musical training. The congregation is not in a subservient position, and each member is presumed to have a thorough enough religious background, including knowledge of Biblical Hebrew, to officiate at services. In fact, a thirteen-year old's Bar or Bat Mitzvah, which you may have heard of, celebrates the first time a young person stands before the congregation and reads in Hebrew from the Torah,[7] also giving his or her interpretation of the passage. Sometimes he or she actually conducts the entire service.

For Orthodox and Conservative Jews, noise other than that from the pulpit is fine, as it indicates that congregants are praying the entire service, often by chanting, in a one-on-one communication with God. A cantor, choir, lay leader and/or rabbi will also be praying, speaking, or singing from the pulpit. They are singing or saying prayers for the congregation as a whole. Even if the members of the congregation just say "Amen" it is considered that they have each sung the prayer themselves, so that both individual and group prayer can go on at the same time. Similarly, sporadically through a service, one will hear a voice singing a short refrain, or joining in on the last few words being sung by the cantor or choir. Heath (1983, 209) chronicles the same kind of "support" in an African American church when a layperson is praying: "On one occasion . . . a member of the congregation broke in with a supporting bar of melody."

If each person is capable of chanting the entire service and is free to move along at his or her own pace, then noise other than that from the pulpit is all right, providing of course that the noise is associated with praying. Reform Jews, who aren't as well-versed in Hebrew prayers, are more likely just to follow in the prayer book and, like non-Pentecostal Christians, to do responsive readings and sing hymns together as directed by the pulpit.

Although little of the praying noises of Orthodox services survives amongst the less traditional Jews, one thing does: when they are sitting and waiting for a service to begin, Jews are likely to be chatting with their friends and families. When they are invited to Catholic or mainstream Protestant weddings or other church services, the Jews may upset the Christians because they sit and talk, not knowing that this is not done in churches.

The thing to remember, however, is that these highly diverse and conflicting practices are all intended to enhance communication with God, and those who practice them feel that they are evincing true piety. There are many ways to do this.

RITUAL NATURE OF CONVERSATION

The ritual nature of conversation as well as the role of social convention in determining meaning is easily seen in rules for the telephone (Schegloff 1968). Considering telephone routines also illustrates how new situations, in this situation, technology, creates new ways of interacting. Although phones were invented at the end of the 19th century, not all families had them until after World War II. Still, the rules for their use were well established by then. Exactly how such rules arise and become widespread through society is not precisely known; they just do. When a social need arises, language forms evolve to meet the need.

The first rule of telephone conversation in the United States is that the answerer speaks first. It does not have to be so. The rule could as easily be that the caller speaks first. That makes perfectly good sense, as it means that the one who calls is identified at once.[8] Of course the American way makes equally good sense, as it ensures that the receiver is at someone's ear before the caller starts to speak. There are often several equally logical possibilities in conversation rituals, but any one group will adopt just one of the possible alternatives. All that seems necessary is that members of a culture agree on the form of the ritual. This allows people to know what to expect and how to respond.

In any event, in the United States the convention is that the answerer speaks first. If the call could conceivably be for the answerer because she or he is answering the phone at her or his home, the usual first utterance used to be "Hello," and, for most situations, this may still be true. In places of business or in a doctor's or lawyer's office, wherever secretaries or operators answer the phone, "Hello" is not proper. Rather, the name of the business or office is given, as in "E.B. Marshall Co." or "Dr. Sloan's office," or "George J. West Junior High." Giving the name in itself means, 'this is a business, institution, or professional's office.'

Godard (1977) recounts the confusion on both her part and on the part of American callers because her native French routine requires that callers verify that the number called is the one reached. Violation of discourse routines, like violations of style, hinders social interaction at least a little, even when the violations otherwise fit the situation.

As simple as the telephone rules seem to be, and they surely constitute one of the simpler social routines, there are still many other rules to follow for a good result. After the answerer says "Hello" (or its variants), the caller asks "Is X there?" unless the caller recognizes the answerer's voice. In that instance, the caller must greet the answerer before asking for the party she or he wishes to speak with. Some do not bother to do this. Whether hurt feelings result seems to depend on the length of acquaintanceship and degree of intimacy. Students in my class report that their parents feel snubbed if a frequent caller does not say the equivalent of "Hi, Mrs. Jones. Is Darryl there?" Sometimes callers wish to acknowledge the existence of the answerer (phatic communication) but do not wish to be involved in a lengthy conversation, so they say, "Hi, Mrs. Jones. It's Mary. I'm sorry, but I'm in a hurry. Is Darryl there?"

On the surface, "I'm sorry, but I'm in a hurry" seems to have no relevance to phone greetings. It makes perfect sense, however, if one takes phatic communication into account, as well as telephone routines. The apology acknowledges that the caller recognizes acquaintance with the answerer and, therefore, the social appropriateness of conversing with her or him.

In terms of social rules, perhaps what is most interesting is that the person who answers the phone feels compelled to go get the one the caller wants. This compulsion may be so great that answerers find themselves running all over the house, shouting out the window if necessary to get the one called.

A student of mine, John Reilly, reported an amusing anecdote illustrating the strength of this obligation. He called a friend to go bowling, and the friend's sister answered the phone. She informed John that her brother was cutting logs but that she would go fetch him. John, knowing that the woodpile was 100 yards away, assured her it was not necessary. All she had to do was to relay the message. Three times she insisted on going. Three times John told her not to. Finally, she said, confusedly, "Don't you want to talk to him?" John repeated that she could extend his invitation without calling the friend to the phone. Suddenly, she just left the phone without responding to John's last remarks and fetched her brother.

As extreme as this may sound, it is actually no more so than the response of a person in the tub when the phone rings. She or he leaps out of the tub to answer it[9] and, still dripping wet with only a towel for protection, proceeds to run to another part of the house to summon the person for whom the caller asked. It is the rare person who can say, "Yes, X is here, but I don't see him. Call back later." Indeed, there are those who would consider such a response quite rude. It is as if the person who answers has tacitly consented to go get whoever is called, regardless of inconvenience, unless the called one is not at home. The sense of obligation, of having to respond in a certain way, is at the core of all verbal social routines.

Because of the ubiquity of cell phones, I have suggested to a few classes that perhaps this compulsion to get someone may not occur so much today. I know I have said to someone, "Call him on his cell," if my husband is outside or in the cellar and I am busy. However, my students insisted that they do run outside or to another part of the house to get the person who was called. They suggest the cell phone only if they know that the person has left the premises.

Caller ID has also caused some changes in telephone routines. First, and most obviously, one may decide not to pick up the phone if a certain caller is displayed. This is common with telemarketing. Another change is that people don't necessarily answer with *hello*. They often, instead, say [*hi* + first name]. I overheard a man answer his cell phone (which also had caller ID) with "What do you want now?" Other phrases indicating a continuation of a preceding conversation can be used, such as, "As I was saying . . . " or "Okay, I spoke to Ken and. . . . " I've even heard in lieu of a greeting, "How did you get this number?" Of course, calls to cell phones are almost always intended for whoever picks it up, ostensibly its owner, so there are no protocols for getting another person.

On a landline phone, if the one called is not at home or does not live there anymore, or never lived there at all, the semantically appropriate response to "Is X there?" should be "No." In fact, however, "No" is appropriate only if X does live there, but is not now at home. For example, if X once lived there, but does not now, an appropriate answer is:

1. X doesn't live here any more.
2. X has moved.
3. X lives at ___ now.

Although a plain *no* carries the correct meaning, it cannot be used if X no longer lives there, but once did. If X has never lived there, one may answer:

4. There is no X here.
5. What number are you calling?
6. You must have the wrong number.

Again, *no* would seem to be a fitting response, but it cannot be used with "Is X there?" Notice that 4 semantically fits a meaning of 'X no longer lives here' but it not likely to be used for that meaning by someone socialized into American society.

In discourse routines, frequently an apparently suitable response cannot be used in certain social situations or the response will have a greater or different meaning than the words used. For instance, one apparently proper response to:

7. Where are the tomatoes? [in a store]

is:

    8. I don't know.

Most people would find such an honest answer rude, even odd. More likely is:

    9. I'm sorry, but I don't work here.
    10. I'm sorry, I'll ask the manager.
    11. I don't work here, but the tomatoes are in the next aisle.

If one is not an employee, then she or he explains as in 9 why no answer is forthcoming. If the one asked is an employee, then 10 is appropriate. As with the telephone, the answerer feels obligated, as evinced by prefacing each remark with "I'm sorry." This apology makes no sense if we consider the question alone. It makes perfectly good sense, however, when we realize that the response is to the **precondition** that there is an assumption that an employee knows where items are. Notice that there is no reason at all to say "I don't work here" in 11, except that the respondent is correcting the asker's assumption that she or he works there. That is, again, the response is understandable only if we realize that people respond to the social assumptions behind questions and other remarks as well as to the actual words given.

Preconditions for asking questions in our society are:

- The questioner has the right or duty to ask the question.
- The one asked has the responsibility or obligation to know the answer. (Labov and Fanshel 1977)

Preconditions for speech acts are as much a part of their meaning as actual words are. The giveaway in 11 is the *but*. It makes no sense at all unless it is seen as a response to the second precondition. When *but* joins two sentences it often means 'although,' so that 11 means 'although I don't work here, I happen to know that the tomatoes are in the next aisle.' That is, 'although I am not responsible for knowing since I don't work here, I will tell you anyhow.'

The phenomenon of responsibility as in telephone routines and answering questions is part of a larger responsibility that adheres to the discourse routines that Harvey Sacks called **utterance pairs**.[10] These are conversational sequences in which one utterance elicits another of a specific kind. For instance:

- greeting–greeting
- question–answer

- complaint–excuse, apology, or denial
- request/command–acceptance or rejection
- compliment–acknowledgment
- farewell–farewell

Whoever is given the first part of an utterance pair is responsible for giving the second half. The opener of such a sequence, in our society, commands the person addressed to give one of the socially appropriate responses. As with the telephone, these responses often have a meaning different from, less than, or greater than the sum of the words used. The only time that we are freed from the obligation to carry out the socially prescribed roles in conversation is when the other party is incapable of acting with a purpose, as when drunk, stoned, or insane (Frake 1964). Perhaps one of the reasons that we get so angry when someone does not act or speak appropriately for the situation is that we cannot figure out his or her intentions. Without knowing those, we do not know how to act ourselves when dealing with the person.

Interestingly, the first half of the pair does not necessarily have to sound like what it really is. That is, a question does not have to be in question form nor a command in a command form. All that is necessary for a statement to be construed as a question or command is for the social situation to be right for questioning or commanding. The very fact that a speech event is appropriate for a question or a command may cause an utterance to be perceived as such even if it is not in question or command form. As with proper style, the situation includes roles and relative status of participants in a conversation. Situation, roles, and social status are an inextricable part of meaning, often as much as, if not more than, the actual form the utterance takes in terms of words used and sentence construction.

Utterance pairs are not necessarily universal, at least not in demanding a rapid response. For instance, for mainstream American society, if a question is asked, it must receive an answer even if that answer is "I don't know." The Warm Springs Indian does not have to answer right away. One may be asked a question but may not give the answer for hours or even days. Similarly, in much American culture, if one receives an oral invitation, one must give some sort of answer right away. If a Warm Springs Indian gets one, she or he need not respond at all (Philips 1976).

Goody (1978) points out that questions, being incomplete, are powerful in forcing responses in our culture. We have already seen that certain preconditions exist for questioning and that an answer may be to a precondition rather than to the question itself. In the following discussion, it is always assumed that the preconditions for questioning are fulfilled. We will then be able to gain some insights into how people understand and even manipulate others on the basis of social rules.

CHAPTER 5

There are two kinds of overt questions, *yes-no* questions and *wh-* ones. The first, as the name implies, requires an answer of *yes* or *no*. In essence, if the *yes-no* question forms are used, one is forced to answer "yes," "no," or "I don't know." There is no way not to answer except to pretend not to hear. If that occurs, the asker usually repeats the question, perhaps more loudly, or even precedes the repetition with a tap on the would-be answerer's shoulder or the verbal equivalent. In the past few years, saying "hello-o" with upward intonation has been used for this purpose. This sounds especially insistent, and, to me, borders on the rude. Alternatively, the asker could precede the repeated question with a summons like, "Hey Bill, I asked. . . ." It is because members of our society all recognize that they must answer a question and they must respond "yes" or "no" to a *yes-no* question that the following question is a recognized joke:

Have you stopped beating your wife/husband?

Since you must know what you do to your spouse, "I don't know" is not an answer. Only a "yes" or "no" will do. Either answer condemns. Either way, you admit to spouse beating.

Yes-no questions can also be asked by ending a statement with a **tag**:

You're going, *aren't you*?
It's five dollars, *right*?

If the preconditions for questioning are present, as Labov and Fanshel (1977) point out, a plain declarative statement can be construed as a *yes-no* question, as in:

Q: You live on 114th Street.
A: No, I live on 115th.

The *wh-* questions demand an answer that substitutes for the question word. An "I don't know" can also be given. The *wh-* words are *what, when, why, who, where,* and *how* appearing at the start of a question. These words are, in essence, blanks to be filled in. *What* has to be answered with the name of a thing or event; *when* with a time; *why*, a reason; *who*, a person; and *how*, a manner or way something was done.

There is actually yet another *wh-* question, "Huh?," which asks 'Would you repeat the entire sentence you just said?' That is, the "huh" asks that a whole utterance be filled in, not just a word or phrase. It also may be voiced to indicate disbelief after a statement. The "huh" means something like, 'Did I hear you correctly?' or 'Are you kidding?'

The answer to any question can be deferred by asking another, which creates **insertion sequences** (Schegloff 1968), as in:

A: Wanna come to a party?
B: Can I bring a friend?
A: Male or female?
B: Female.
A: Sure.
B: O.K.

Note that these questions are answered in reverse order, but all are answered. Occasionally insertion sequences can lead conversationalists "off the track." When this happens, participants may feel a compulsion to get a question answered even if the topic has changed; hence, comments like, "Oh, as I was saying. . . ."

Note that *oh* serves as an indicator that the speaker is not responding to the last statement but to a prior one. Seemingly innocuous words like *oh, well,* and *by the way* frequently serve as important markers in conversation. The importance of *oh* as an aid to comprehension was shown by Fox, Tree and Schrock (1999), who played tapes consisting of students telling stories to each other face to face. Subjects heard either the taped version with an original *oh* in it, or a version in which the *oh* was excised from the tape, replacing it with a pause. Subjects had to detect a word in the stream of speech. Those who heard the tapes with *oh* were faster at detecting the word than those who heard the tapes either with the *oh* replaced by a pause or excised with no pause.

Similarly, in a test in which people had to respond to a word that had occurred earlier in a discourse, they responded more rapidly if they heard a tape with *oh*'s intact than if it was excised, with or without a pause. *Oh*, in all these discourses, were repair items. That is, they referred back to something that was said, and were followed by a correction of some sort.

The experimenters explain that the information after the *oh* always refers back to something that was said before, so that listeners are warned to prepare for a change in information (291). Upon hearing *oh*, listeners know they have to focus on what's coming because there is going to be a change from what was said before. They conclude that "[hearing *oh*] . . . helps avoid the confusion that would arise had the speaker merely stopped one train of thought and begun another without a marker" (293). I suspect other oral discourse markers like *well* or *so anyways* also have important functions in helping listeners keep track of what speakers are saying.

The actual meaning of any utterance depends partially on the social context in which it occurs (Brown and Yule 1983, 27–58). Rommetveit

(1971) gives a classic example of this. He tells a story about a man running for political office who is scheduled to give a talk in a school auditorium. When he arrives, he sees that there are not enough chairs. He calls his wife at home. Then he goes to see the janitor. To each, the candidate says, "There aren't enough chairs." To his wife this means 'Wow! Am I popular!' To the janitor it means 'Go get some more chairs.' The full meaning evoked by the statement "There aren't enough chairs" is largely a product of the context in which it is said, including the relative social statuses, privileges, and duties of the speaker and hearer. Society places obligations upon us in discourse, and the real meaning of an utterance cannot be derived independently from social context.

Manipulating by the Rules

It is easy to manipulate people subtly by plugging them into the presuppositions and preconditions behind statements (Elgin 1980; Labov and Fanshel 1977). Putting *even* before someone's name can be a powerful manipulation, as in "Even Oscar is going." The assumptions are that Oscar doesn't usually go, so that if he is, then everyone is going except the person being addressed. There is a further unspoken proposition that if everyone else is doing something, then so should the addressee. Readers may recognize in this rather common ploy the childish, "Everyone else has one" or "Everyone else goes to sleep at ten. "

Elgin (1980) also discusses the manipulations of the "if you really love me" variety. These are actually subtle accusations. What they mean is 'you should love me but you don't. The guilt you feel for not loving me can be easily erased, though, by doing whatever I want.'

Another manipulation is the "even *you* should be able to do that" type. Here we have *even* again, the word that tells someone that he or she is alone in whatever failing is being mentioned. Its use with *should* is especially clever because it implies that the hearer is stupid or some sort of gross misfit, but it backgrounds that message so that it is not likely to be discussed. Rather, the hearer is made to feel stupid and wrong, so that he or she will be likely to capitulate to the speaker's demands in an effort to prove that if all others can do it, so can the hearer.

A variant to this is "even a child/baby/idiot/moron/etc. can do it." This is a gross insult, as it says that those with little intelligence can do it, so if one can't one is are truly unintelligent. Using *even* in this way may uncover social attitudes, for the person(s) who are the butt, so to speak, of the *even* are inferior. For instance, it is possible to find contexts for "Even a woman can do it," as in "Even a woman can pump gas." This implies that women usually cannot pump gas, which, after all, takes little skill.

The contrasting phrase, "Even a man can do it," seems harder to find a context for. Men are not presupposed to be inept or stupid. However, "even a woman" implies that women are so ditzy that if they can do something, anyone can.

One can achieve manipulation and insult by preceding a comment with "Don't tell me you're going to . . . " or "Don't tell me that you believe. . . ." Notice that these are questions in the form of a command. They are actually a way of asking:

Are you really going to ___?
Do you really believe___?

Both of these also mean 'Your action or belief is stupid.' The *really* indicates disbelief that anybody could do or believe such a thing. A likely response to either of these is:

Well, I thought I would, but now I'm not so sure.

But responses like:

Of course I am. Aren't you?
Of course I do. Don't you?

while rarer, could be humorous simply because they violate the presuppositions behind the *don't tell me*'s. In any event, such rejoinders certainly would deflate the manipulator and make her or him seem to be the stupid one. Moreover, they are a way of informing the *Don't tell me* speaker that you are not going to be manipulated.

The really clever ploy of the "Don't tell me . . ." variety is that the hearer, H, is instantly made to feel foolish because of the presuppositions. However, since the speaker, S, has not overtly accused the hearer of stupidity, argument is difficult. H is not even allowed the luxury of anger at the insult because it has not been overtly stated. It is contained only in the presupposition or the word *really*. H might become immediately defensive but still feel quite stupid because of the implied insult. Not only does S usually get H to capitulate, but S also establishes that H is the stupider of the two. As a manipulatory device, this is a "double whammy" unless, of course, H stands her or his ground and delivers the unusual retort.

Labov and Fanshel (1977) show that some people manipulate in even more subtle ways by utilizing common understanding of social and discourse rules. Using patient–therapist sessions, which they received permission to tape, Labov and Fanshel describe the struggle of a woman named

CHAPTER 5

Rhoda for independence from a domineering mother. The mother finally leaves Rhoda at home and goes to visit Rhoda's sister Phyllis. Rhoda cannot cope, but neither can she ask her mother to come home, because that would be an admission that the mother is right in not giving Rhoda more freedom. Labov and Fanshel say that Rhoda employs an indirect request both to mitigate her asking her mother for help and to disguise her challenge to the power relationship between them. Rhoda calls her mother on the phone and asks:

1. When do you plan to come home?

Since this is not a direct request for help, Rhoda's mother forces an admission by not answering Rhoda's question. Instead she creates an insertion sequence:

2. Oh, why?

This means 'Why are you asking me when I plan to come home?' In order to answer, Rhoda must admit that she cannot be independent, that the mother has been right all along. Her mother has the right to question by virtue of her status and Rhoda has the duty to answer for the same reason. So Rhoda responds:

3. Things are getting just a little too much . . . it's getting too hard.

To which the mother replies:

4. Why don't you ask Phyllis [when I'll be home]?

Since it is really up to the mother when she will come home, and also, since she has a prior obligation to her own household, Labov and Fanshel say that it is clear that Rhoda has been outmaneuvered. The mother has forced Rhoda into admitting that she is not capable and she has, in effect, also refused Rhoda's request for help.

It seems to me that this mother has also conveyed very cleverly to Rhoda that Phyllis is the preferred daughter and has said it so covertly that the topic can't be openly discussed. Clearly it is the mother's right and duty to come home as she wishes. By palming that decision off on Phyllis, she is actually saying to Rhoda, "No matter what your claim on me is, Phyllis comes first." That is, for Phyllis's sake, she will suppress her rights as a mother and allow Phyllis to make the decision. Notice that all of this works only because at some level both Rhoda and her mother know the rights and obligations of questioners and answerers.

All indirect requests do not arise from hostile situations, although most are used when individual desires conflict with other social rules or values. Classic examples, spoken with an expectant lift to the voice, are:

Oh, chocolates
What are those, cigars? (Sacks 1964–1972)

Assuming that the above are spoken by adults who have long known what *chocolate* and *cigar* denote, these observations are perceived as requests. This is shown by the usual responses to either:

Would you like one?
I'm sorry, but they aren't mine.

or

I have to save them for X.

Toddlers just learning to speak do practice by going about pointing at objects and naming them. Once that stage is past, people do not name items in the immediate environment unless there is an intent, a reason for singling out the item. All properly socialized Americans know that one should never directly ask for food in another's household or for any possibly expensive goods like cigars. That would be begging. Therefore, one names the items in another's home or hands so that the naming is construed as an indirect request. There is rarely another reason for an adult to name a common object or food out of the blue in the absence of a previous question or utterance which could elicit the name of the object. The responses to "Oh, chocolates" and "What are those, cigars?" make sense only if the hearer construes those as really meaning 'I want you to offer me some of those chocolates/cigars.'

Commands and Questions

Requests for food are not the only discourse routines arising from conflicts between general social rules and the will of the individual. Commands share virtually the same preconditions as questions:

- The speaker who commands has the right and/or duty to command.
- The recipient of the command has the responsibility and/or obligation to carry out the command.

The problem is that, even more than with questioning, the one who has the right to command is usually clearly of higher status than the one who must obey. The United States supposedly is an egalitarian society, but having the right or duty to command implies that some are superior to others. This runs counter to our stated ideals. Therefore, in most actual situations in American speech, commands are disguised as questions. The substitution of forms is possible because both speech acts share the same preconditions. Moreover, phrasing commands as questions maintains the fiction that the one commanded has the right to refuse, even when he or she does not. Consider:

Would you mind closing the door?

Even though this is uttered as a *yes-no* question, merely to answer "No" without the accompanying action or "Yes" without an accompanying excuse would either be bizarre or a joke. In the movie *The Return of the Pink Panther,* the late Peter Sellers asks a passerby if he knows where the Palace Hotel is. The passerby responds, "Yes," but keeps on going. The joke is that "Do you know where X is?" is not really a *yes-no* question, but a polite command meaning 'tell me where X is.'

Direct commanding is allowed and usual in certain circumstances. For instance, parents normally command young children directly, as in:

Pick those toys up right away.

Intimates such as spouses or roommates often casually command each other about trivial matters such as:

Pick some bread up on the way home.

Often these are softened by *please, will ya, honey,* or the like.

Direct commanding in command form occurs in the military from those of superior rank to those of inferior. During actual battle it is necessary for combatants to obey their officers without question, unthinkingly and unhesitatingly. Direct commands yield this kind of obedience so long as those commanded recognize the social rightness of the command or the need. It is no surprise that direct commands are regularly heard in emergency situations, as during fire fighting or surgery:

Get the hose! Put up the ladders.
Get me some bandages! Suture that wound!

In situations that allow direct commands, the full command form need not always be invoked. Just enough has to be said so that the underling knows what to do, as in:

Time for lunch! [meaning 'come in for lunch']
Scalpel! Sutures! Dressings!

Note that such commands are contextually bound. They are interpretable as commands only if the participants are actually in a commanding situation. Similarly, Susan Ervin-Tripp (1972) comments that:

It's cold in here.

can be interpreted as a command only in a specific commanding context. The speaker must somehow have the right to ask another to close a window if that is the cause of the cold, or to ask another to lend his or her coat. In this situation, the fact that one person is closer to an open window may be sufficient reason for him or her to be responsible for closing it.

The duty or obligation to carry out a command need not proceed only from status, but may proceed from the physical circumstances in which the command has been uttered. That is why in the right circumstances, ordinary statements or questions may be construed as commands, as in:

Tom: Any more coffee?
Ann: I'll make some right away.
Tom: No, I wanted to know if I had to buy some.

If it is possible to do something about whatever is mentioned, an utterance may be construed as a command. It was possible for Ann to make some more coffee, and she must have been responsible for making it at least part of the time. Hence, Tom's question was misinterpreted as a command to make some. The same possibility of misinterpretation can occur in questions like:

Can you swim?

Said by a poolside, it may be interpreted as a command, "Jump in!" but away from a body of water, it will be heard merely as a request for information.

Although questions are often used as polite substitutes for commands, the question-command can sometimes be especially imperious:

Would you mind being quiet?

Similarly, an *if* clause by itself yields an especially haughty command:

If you would wait, please . . .

CHAPTER 5

I suspect that both of these carry special force because the high formality signaled by *would you mind* and *if you would please* contrast so sharply with the banality of keeping quiet and waiting that the effect of sarcasm is achieved.

Compliments

Compliments are another utterance pair type that can create conflict. There is a great deal of cross-cultural variation in the amount of complimenting that is done, on what one may be complimented, and if complimenting should be done at all. Basso (1989) shows how the Apaches ridicule the amount of complimenting by "the whiteman." The overabundance of complimenting is actually embarrassing to them.

Sometimes, even in the Anglo culture, people feel that a compliment is an implied judgment that the complimenter had no business to make. For instance, I heard a supervisor of student teachers complain in high dudgeon, "What a colossal nerve!" because one of the students had dared to judge the supervisor's class by saying, "That was wonderful!" The supervisor felt that, of course, she was wonderful. What else would the student expect?

Knapp, Hopper, and Bell (1984, 13) report that two-thirds of 245 people who were observed while being complimented reported later that they felt "uncomfortable, defensive, or cynical" about the praise and, to me most telling, have problems responding appropriately. I strongly suspect that this is because of general social convention and the rule that the first part of an utterance pair must evoke a response. Compliments call for an acknowledgment. The acknowledgment can properly be acceptance of the compliment, as by saying, "Thank you." The problem is that to accept the compliment is very close to bragging, and bragging is frowned upon in middle-class America. Hence, typical responses to a compliment are disclaimers like:

1. This old rag?
2. I got it on sale.
3. It was a Christmas present.

An exception is special occasions when compliments are expected, as when everyone is decked out to go to a prom or a wedding. Then, not only are compliments easily received with "Thank you," but not to compliment can cause offense or disappointment. One of the little sadnesses of old age was brought home to me when my then eighty-five-year-old mother sadly commented to me after a family wedding, "Nobody said anything about my clothes all weekend, and I bought them especially. People don't notice how I look anymore." It is as if, being old, one's appearance doesn't count. This reflects the American attitude towards being elderly. Only youth looks good.

Persistent complimenting can lead to social embarrassment. If one gives compliment after compliment, the recipient feels uneasy. "Oh, I love your hair. And what a nice dress. You're so thin! You look good in everything. And the shoes? They match your bag perfectly!" Such an effusion is off-putting. The object of the compliments feels uneasy, even suspicious and angry. She may try to avoid the person who heaps such fulsome praise. The suspicion is either that the complimenter is being patronizing, or is trying to "butter her up." There may also be a feeling that the complimenter is implying that the recipient usually doesn't look or dress very well. Otherwise why go on and on about every facet of her appearance? Or, she may suspect that the complimenter is jealous of her. If the compliment is about behavior, overdoing may lead to a suspicion that the recipient isn't expected to behave so well, which is an insult. This doesn't mean that one shouldn't compliment at all. Knapp et al. (27) claim that most people who give compliments and who receive them say that the compliments are deserved. A compliment can make another person feel good. It's nice to be admired. Overdoing them, however, gives off undesirable messages, achieving the opposite result of a sincere compliment.

Requesting and Apologizing

The speech acts of requesting and apologizing vary greatly across cultures, both in what must be apologized for, what may be requested, and how either is to be carried out.

Requesting varies according to whether or not the speaker chooses a more or less direct request in a given situation, such as requesting a ride from someone (House 1989, 111). Some apologize first, explain why they need the ride, and then make a request, as in:

1. Excuse me, I'm Bob Miller. I live on the same street you do. I wanted to ask you if you may possibly take me along in your car because I missed my bus and the next bus goes in one hour.

This was elicited from an American. Note the degree of apology and indirectness: *Excuse me, I wanted to ask you if you may possibly* . . . followed by the request for a ride. In contrast, a British speaker simply said:

2. Look, if you are going my way, could you possibly give me a lift? I've missed the bus and there isn't another for an hour.

CHAPTER 5

The British man also uses politeness markers like *could you possibly*, but doesn't embed it in a string of *if you may possibly*. Note that the British request starts with a simple and direct, "Look, if you are going my way . . ." whereas the American both excuses himself, gives his name, explains his relationship, and then says, "I wanted to ask you. . . ."

House (107) establishes that such differences depend on the degree to which the requester has a right to ask, whether the hearer has a social obligation to comply, and if the request is associated with social or communicative difficulty. For instance, if the person asked would lose face by complying or it would violate the hearer's privacy, then the requester would have to hedge the request in increasingly more convoluted politeness phrases. Apparently, the American feels that asking for a ride is more of an imposition than the British person does. If the same request were made to a spouse, the American might simply say "Hey, I need a ride. I missed the bus." One must be less direct with strangers, as they don't have the same obligations to do one's bidding.

Blum-Kulka and House (1989) show that, in many instances, the tendency toward a particular speech act pattern may be similar, although there are always differences. Whereas we might suspect that one culture is more polite than another, it is equally true that cultural attitudes and facts are important determinants in how a request or apology will be conveyed. For instance, Israeli Hebrew speakers and Germans show close agreement on avoiding overt apology words like "I am so sorry" for insulting a worker, but they vary in apology strategies in other instances. In general, however, it was found that there weren't significant differences in the kinds of strategies used in different situations eliciting apologies. This may be because the four groups studied, Israelis, Germans, Australian English, and Canadian French, are all basically Eurocentered Western industrialized cultures who share similar values.

Presequences

An interesting class of discourse rules is what Harvey Sacks (1964–1972, November 1967) called **presequences**, particularly **preinvitations**. Typically, someone wishing to issue an oral invitation first asks something like:

1. What are you doing Saturday night?

If the response includes words like *only* or *just* as in:

2. I'm just washing my hair.

or:

    3. I'm only studying.

the inviter can then issue an invitation for Saturday night. If, however, the response is:

    4. I'm washing my hair.

or:

    5. I'm studying.

the potential inviter knows not to issue the invitation. Following such responses, the inviter typically signals a change in conversation by saying, "Uh . . ." and then speaks of something other than Saturday night. Issuing of preinvitations is an ego-saver like the use of style to signal social class. Having been spared overt refusal, the inviter is able to save face. Additionally, Blum-Kulka and House (1989, 130) suggest that prerequests check the feasibility of compliance, thereby overcoming grounds for refusal.

Collapsing Sequences

Sometimes utterance pairs are collapsed (Sacks, November 2, 1967), as in the following exchange at an ice-cream counter.

    1. *A*: What's chocolate filbert?
        B: We don't have any.

B's response is to what B knows is likely to come next. If B had explained what chocolate filbert is, then A very likely would have asked for some. By explaining what it is, B would be tacitly saying that she or he had some to sell. In a selling situation in our society, explaining what goods or foods are is always an admission that they are available. Imagine your reaction, for instance, if you asked a waitperson what some food was like and she or he went into detail telling you about it. Then, if you said, "Sounds good. I'll have that," and the response was, "We don't have any" you would think you were being made a fool of.

Another common collapsing sequence is typified by the exchange:

    2. *Q*: Do you smoke?
        A. I left them in my other jacket.

CHAPTER 5

Such collapsing sequences speed up social interaction by forestalling necessary explanations. They are used for other purposes as well, as when a newcomer joins a discussion in progress:

3. Hi, John. We were just talking about nursery schools.

This either warns John not to join the group or, if he is interested in nursery schools, gives him orientation so that he can understand what is going on.

In utterance pairs, the first half strongly controls what is coming next. The larger conversation beyond these is not so strongly constrained as to form. The syntax of the language can be drawn upon to encode new ideas, not just the syntax of greetings or questions. In questions, for instance, the first sentence or so is predetermined by the question just asked, but the speaker becomes even freer as soon as an answer is given that fills in the *wh-* word or supplies the *yes, no,* or *I don't know.* The constraints upon topic, however, remain very strong.

Repairs Revisited

As we have already seen, if a person uses the wrong style for an occasion, the other party to the interaction tries to repair the error. Schegloff, Jefferson, and Sacks (1977) collected interesting samples of self-correction in discourse: people repairing their own errors. Sometimes this takes the form of obvious correction to a slip of the tongue, as in:

1. What're you so *ha* -er- unhappy about?

Sometimes speakers make a repair when they have made no overt error, as in:

2. Sure enough ten minutes later the bell r—the doorbell rang.

Because such repairs do not show a one-to-one correspondence with actual spoken errors, Schegloff et al. preferred the term *repair* over *correction.* In both of the following, for instance, neither repair is preceded by an error that actually occurred in speech.

Schegloff et al. found an orderly pattern in speech repairs. They did not occur just anywhere in an utterance. They occur immediately after the error as in the previous two, or at the end of the sentence where another person would normally take the floor, as in the following:

3. . . . all of the doors'n things were taped up—I mean y'know they put up y'know that kinda paper stuff, the brown paper.

or right after the other person speaks:

4. *Hannah*:   And she's going to make his own paintings.
    Bea: Mm hm.
    Hannah: And—or I mean his own frames.

If the speaker does not repair an obvious error, the hearer will. Usually this is done by asking a question that will lead the speaker to repair his or her own error. Some examples:

5. *A*: It wasn't snowing all day.
    B: It wasn't?
    A. Oh, I mean it was.

6. *A*: Yeah, he's got a lot of smarts.
    B: Huh?
    A: He hasn't got a lot of smarts.

7. *A*: Hey, the first time they stopped me from selling cigarettes was this morning.
    B: From selling cigarettes?
    A: From buying cigarettes.

Often the hearer will say, "you mean . . ." as in:

8. *A*: We went Saturday afternoon.
    B: You mean Sunday.
    A: yeah, uhnn we saw Max . . .

In most of the repairs by hearers, it seems that the hearer knows all along what the intended word was. Still, it is rare, although not impossible, for the hearer only to supply the word without at least putting it in a question. It seems to me that this is a face-saver for the person who made the error. The hearer often offers the correction or the question leading to correction tentatively, as if she or he is not sure. That way, the speaker is not humiliated as she or he might be if the hearer in positive tones asserted that an error was made. I also suspect that another reason that hearers offer corrections tentatively may be that in doing so, the hearer is in the position of telling someone else what must be going on in her or his mind, a right we accord only to psychiatrists.

Schegloff et al. (38) state that "the organization of repair is the self-righting mechanisms for the organization of language use in social interaction." In other words, it maintains normal social interaction. We have already seen this in attempted repair of inappropriate style. Fairclough (1989) suggests that this is also a way of maintaining the status quo in society.

The importance of the self-righting mechanism is shown in the following almost bizarre interactions. These involve repairs in greetings and farewells collected as part of a participant observation by a student, Sheila Kennedy. While on guard duty at the door of her dormitory, she deliberately confounded greetings and farewells, with fascinating results.

> 9. *Sheila*:   Hi. [pause] Good night.
>   *Stranger*: Hello. [pause] Take it easy.

Note that the stranger also gave both a greeting and a farewell, even matching the pause that Sheila used between them. This is highly reminiscent of the exchanges in which subjects matched the experimenter's style even when they questioned it or objected to it. Another exchange was:

> 10. *Friend*:   Bye, Sheila.
>   *Sheila*:   Hello.
>   *Friend*:   Why did you say "hello"? I said "goodbye."
>   [pause] Hi.

Even though the friend questioned the inappropriateness of Sheila's response, she still felt constrained to answer the greeting with a greeting.

> 11. *Friend*:   Hi!
>   *Sheila*:   So long.
>   [both speak at same time, so Sheila starts again]
>   *Sheila*:   Hi!
>   *Friend*:   Bye. [laughs] Wait a minute. Let's try that again. Hi!
>   *Sheila*:   Hello.
>   *Friend*:   Bye.
>   *Sheila*:   So long.
>   *Friend*:   That's better.

What is interesting here is the lengths the subjects went to in order that the appropriate pairs were given. Note that the friend had to get both greeting and farewell matched up before she would leave.

The degree to which we are bound by the social rules of discourse is well-illustrated by the phenomenon of repair. The very fact that people go through so much trouble to repair others' responses seems to me to be highly significant. It shows the importance of discourse routines to social interaction and that one cannot be divorced from the other. Even when people know what the other must mean, they want the discourse righted. Even when it makes no difference in a fleeting social contact, interactors demand that the right forms be chosen. This establishes the importance of maintaining social routines in the overall maintenance of social order, and that such maintenance is not merely a matter of overt laws and policing, but of our internalized assent to modes of conversation. This is another example of Fairclough's (1989) thesis that ordinary speech activities have as part of their purpose the maintaining of the status quo in society.

JARGONS

The sensitivity with which language mirrors society is highlighted in jargons. **Jargons** are varieties of language created for specific functions by the people who engage in them regularly. They are like minidialects, but used only for the activity for which they were created. Jargons are not only sensitive to the requirements of the activity but also to the personal and social needs of the speakers. Jargons arise so rapidly and are so fitted to specific events that they give us insights into both the mechanisms and causes of language change by ordinary conversational practices.

A student of mine, Timothy Rembijas, an experienced league bowler, took down a conversation between a nonbowler, F, and another member of the league, S, during a match. S used jargon words like *cranking, turkey, bellying, gyro*, as well as common words used with special meaning, such as *buried, inside, outside*, and *carry*. In this lingo, *cranking* means 'throwing ball with much velocity and curve'; *turkey* means 'three strikes in a row;' *bellying* is 'too much curve'; *gyro* is a kind of bowling ball; *buried* is a way of saying 'perfect'; *inside*, 'left side of approach;' *outside* 'right side of approach;' and *carry* is 'get strikes or knock down pins consistently.' F pretended that he understood S by comments like "Yeah, I thought so too," but his kinesics told a different story. He was clearly uncomfortable and bewildered.

Dell Hymes (1974) mentions two ways in which speech function can be mismatched to the participants in the speech event:

- The intent is understood, but not the actual words.
- The words are understood, but not the intent.

The one-sided commentary just quoted is a beautiful instance of the first. Given the nature of jargons, the situation is not unusual. One function of jargons is to exclude lay persons or novices, those who do not belong. It is well-known that usually speakers adjust to listeners' needs (Giles, Taylor, and Bourhis 1973), defining words when they notice confusion, slowing down speech to foreigners or speaking more loudly. Despite F's overt kinesic signaling that he was bewildered, S barreled on, piling jargon word on jargon word.

S behaves like those who display their brilliance by spouting jargon, cowing lesser beings who do not know it. Doctors and lawyers are often accused of such behavior, but the practice is not confined to them. Displays like S's underscore that those who do not understand are outsiders. In other words, jargons are one way to play one-upmanship. Rembijas explains that in order to be regarded as an expert bowler, one must not only bowl well but also be able to use the language. The bowler who cannot, even if he or she gets high scores, will be regarded by bowling peers as being simply lucky. Jargon is a clear case of language being used for social identification.

Jargon also serves the purpose of bonding. Whenever people use special words to let others know that they share interests or background, this bonding is achieved. Claiming something in common, especially language use, is a request for at least some degree of intimacy: "We are friends and others aren't invited to share our special bond." We have seen that style may be used the same way. In both jargon and style, the choice of word itself, not its actual meaning, gives the social message. If jargon is used for bonding, it is a request for less social distance between parties. Also, as in style selection, using features that heighten differences between speakers is a way of forcing distance. Thus, the jargon word lessens distance between those who know it and heightens difference between the person uttering it and those who do not know it.

Sometimes close friends will create their own jargon. Bridget Hurley and Maureen Sullivan, my students, made me promise that I wouldn't use theirs until they graduated because they didn't want friends not in their immediate circle to understand it. They devised this to comment on male-female relationships in close contact. Their jargon centered on words for kissing. They give as a typical conversation:

1. [topic is previous night's dating]
   M: What time did you get in this morning?
   S: Early enough to reap the crops.
   R: How was the harvest?
   S: Better than last season's crops, but not as good as consistent corn that other people get.
   [group laughter]

What this meant was that S found her date's kissing to be better than the last boy she kissed, but not as good as one would expect from a steady relationship with real involvement between a couple. In this jargon, *corn* means 'kiss'; *reaped the crop* means 'a casual date'; *last season's crop* is 'male previously kissed'; and *consistent corn* is 'involvement in a relationship.' There are other words in this jargon, all related to corn, such as *kernel's worth of corn* 'a kiss on the cheek,' *imported corn* 'males visiting females,' *potential corn* 'looking towards the prospect for involvement,' and *bad crop*, 'male expecting too much.'

Only words associated with the activity eliciting the jargon are used for excluding and identifying those who belong. All of the jargon words for bowling describe different aspects of the game. If the markers for a jargon center on the activity that calls for it, they will normally appear early on in an encounter. Thus, they are effective as signals for identification.

Another motivation of word creation in jargons is communicative efficiency. If something has to be mentioned often, it is more economical to have a single word to refer to it than a lengthy phrase. It is more efficient to say "carry" than "get strikes or knock down pins consistently," especially in the heat of a bowling contest, when rapid encoding of the events is important.

CB radio jargon was developed for quite different reasons: to prevent boredom and to keep drivers informed of the presence of highway patrols monitoring speed. Because of the noisy road conditions under which it operated, CB has actually developed new syntactic forms so that its messages can be more readily interpreted. This gives us insight into how grammars of a language can change, and how rapidly if need be (Chaika 1980).

There was (and is) a great deal of noise on CB channels, both static and road noise. Since it was necessary to locate where the police were, new markings developed on expressions showing location. In mainstream English, most locative phrases do not take demonstratives and articles, such as *the*, *this*, or *that*, but in CB talk these developed:

2. *CB English*   *Mainstream English*
    this 95   95
    that exit 23   exit 23
    that Maine town   Maine

Similarly, names for people also took on demonstratives, as in the *handles* (on-air names for people):

3. The One Outlaw   Outlaw
    The Jungle Jim   Jungle Jim

CHAPTER 5

By violating the usual grammar rules of English and putting *the, this*, and *that* where they do not usually appear, two things were achieved. The ones who really belong use the new grammar rule, thus being identified as real CB-ers. Also, the innovative use of demonstratives warns listeners to be alert, that a location is about to be named. This helps counteract the noisy conditions of the road. The reasons for the same kind of marking on names are that it is difficult to know to whom one is speaking as, typically, several conversations are going on at once, making a generally noisy environment even more confusing.

CB-ers never use their own names. Instead, they give themselves **handles**. Why, then, do they want to mark these names? After all, one would assume, they want to keep their identities secret. DiPietro (1977) remarked that these are handles that only open outward, and that they are "devoid of any allusion to [the CB-er's] own social status." As an instance, he comments that Henry Ford II preferred his handle to be "Beer Belly" rather than "Hank the Deuce" or "Chairman." Therein, I believe, lies the answer. The kinds of handles CB-ers choose indicate that they wish to project an image. They prefer pseudonyms like "Outlaw," "Rocky Raccoon," and "Jungle Jim." Typically, handles seem to refer to stereotypical lower-class images, fighting prowess ("Rocky") and animal imagery. We see these last two combined in "Rocky Raccoon." Raccoons are animals noted for their thievery. The animal imagery also conjures up back-to-nature images with its overtones of sexuality and toughness unrestrained by civilization. "Jungle Jim" was a seminary student and is now a priest. "Outlaw" was a happily married college graduate. Thus, through their handles, CB-ers can hide their true identity and vent their most taboo fantasies. But what fun would it be if nobody knew whose voice and handle it was? Even in fantasy, people usually want to be somehow identifiable.

Jargons, like conversations, and discourse routines in general, are not random. They serve communicative purposes, regulate social interaction, and allow people to feel as if they belong in society. They demand that interactors follow rules so that what they say can more easily be interpreted. All interpretation depends upon the social situation and also on what the speaker's intent seems to be.

Notes

1   However, one could say "I detest chocolate soda" in response to someone's offer of one, so that the person will not actually place a chocolate
soda in front of you. Notice, however, that saying this does not prevent someone from trying to force the soda on you anyway. Conveying one's dislikes does not necessarily do or prevent anything, whereas
a bet or a promise is doing something even if it is ignored. That is, the
bet has still been made, as has the promise.

2   The exception would be those classes in which students have been
assigned special speaking tasks, such as oral reports.

3   The adjective *innocent* refers to the fact that we so associate intention
with speech that we must distinguish between comments meant with
the intent to insult and those that have no such intent. When such
matters get encoded as part of the speech activity, we know how in-
grained it is in our everyday use of language.

4   Gordon and Lakoff's term *conversational postulates* refers to essentially the same phenomena, although their term does convey the idea
that we are operating on these assumptions.

5   See Stubbs 1983, pp. 9–11, for a full discussion of the different implications of using these terms.

6   These may not be used to walk on. They are clean and represent a pure
place upon which the praying is to be done. Nothing impure is allowed
to impinge upon a Muslim's prayer.

7   The Old Testament written by a scribe in Hebrew on a parchment
scroll.

8   Now, with the ready availability of caller ID, this is no longer necessary. Often one knows who it is before one picks up the phone.

9   Not to answer at all is very difficult. The ring itself is akin to a summons that cannot easily be ignored, if at all.

10   These are also called **adjacency pairs**. Some authors use the terms
interchangeably. Because it is possible to have utterance pairs without
their being adjacent, this text uses the former term.

CHAPTER 5

Exercises

1. Record a short, but not intimate, conversation in a setting of your choice and count all of the repetitions in it. Did they enhance the conversation or make it boring? What seemed to be the purpose of the repetitions? Warn the speakers that their words are being recorded.

2. Poll friends of different religions about when it is all right to talk in church and when it is not and under what conditions one calls out responses. How much variability do you find? Try to explain the varying practices in accordance with religious beliefs.

3. Observe two or more people in conversation. What evidence do you see for synchrony between them?

4. Using evidence from dinner-table conversation, explain whether your family belongs to a High or Low Involvement culture. Alternatively, determine the kinds of culture friends are by observing their behavior during a meal or a visit. Another approach is to determine which situations call for High or Low Involvement behavior. Do you think this is a matter of culture or of situation, or something of both? Defend your answer by giving actual examples.

5. Give the first part of utterance pairs to friends or family and record the responses. Do your results conform to those presented in this chapter? Can you find a type of pair not mentioned here?

6. Collect several instances of repair and explain how they work. Do these verify the regulatory nature of repair and/or the ways that repair helps maintain the status quo? Can you find examples of a speaker error that nobody repairs? If so, what is the situation that allows an error not to be repaired?

7. Try to tell the same story in two different frames. What is the effect of the frame on how the story is perceived? Alternatively, collect an example of misinterpretation because the hearer misperceived the speaker's intent.

8. Collect examples of speech acts as opposed to communicative speech among your friends or family. How can you distinguish between the two?

9. Do you participate in a jargon? If so, describe it and show how it fulfills its purpose. What difference is there between a jargon and slang? Do they overlap? Defend your answer.

Chapter 6

Orality and Literacy

All societies grade members on verbal skills, either oral or written. Literate societies prefer displays of book learning, although there is a continuum from oral to literate activities even in literate societies. That is, some written activities, like instant messages and chat rooms, are closer to oral productions, and some oral activities, like eulogies, are closer to literate ones. It has been difficult to prove that being literate creates new mental skills, although oral cultures seem to stress thematic thinking more than literate. Uneducated people may display very sharp logic and often show greater knowledge of vocabulary and history than the educated would assume they have. People use verbal displays as a way to boost their egos and to relieve tensions safely in a community. The topics of verbal displays reveal social attitudes and underscore social conditions under which participants live.

VERBAL SKILL

Almost every social group grants high status to members with good verbal skills, but different social groups value different skills. In middle-class American culture, the skills most respected are those associated with formal schooling: reading books designated as texts and reproducing part or all of their contents on paper. This is known as "passing tests." A good deal of adult rank depends upon the skill with which this was done in childhood and how long into adulthood test-passing was carried on. Cultures that value this are **literate**. But there are more kinds of verbal activity than book learning. So much do we forget this fact that when we come into contact with people to whom book learning is not important, we assume that they are nonverbal. They, too, have their tests, but these are spoken. Such cultures are considered to be **oral**.

Nonliterates and those to whom written skill is not important engage in oral dueling of all sorts. Ong (1982, 43–44) takes this to mean that oral cultures are **agonistic**, that is, that much of their speech is combative and strains for effect. He feels this is an inevitable characteristic of oral societies, and he certainly implies that this is a limitation.

Here, I will develop the thesis that people lacking formal education and formal high status use such oral displays as a way of gaining status. Wit,

CHAPTER 6

repartee, and drollness are all admired by the formally educated, but for them, a person's ultimate status is not determined by oral performance but by bookish or business skills, both of which demand their own kind of competitiveness, and both of which are relatively recent arenas.

LITERACY

For most of human existence, language and the knowledge based upon it resided only in the human brain. Writing systems, even primitive ones, have been in existence for only about 5,000 years.[1] Those of us raised in a largely literate world assume that writing is language. Indeed, it is difficult for us to think of language as being anything but what is written. For instance, most of us think of ourselves as pronouncing letters, not sounds.

We even justify our pronunciation on the basis of letters in the spelled version of a word. Midwesterners visiting Eastern New England complain that the natives don't pronounce /r/'s where they should and do pronounce them where they shouldn't. This complaint is made because they hear *heart* and *hot* pronounced alike and *saw it* is pronounced as "saw-r-it." They base this judgment on the standard spelling. What is interesting to me is that they use modals like *should* that imply moral obligation to express their judgments. In other words, it is morally wrong not to pronounce /r/'s where they are written in standard spelling. Of course, the Midwesterners don't realize that they may not distinguish between certain "letters" themselves, as when they make homonyms of *hairy* and *Harry* (which the r-droppers would never do). Similarly, just as Eastern New Englanders may put in a "letter" where it doesn't "belong" so do Midwesterners and Northwesterners, who pronounce *wash* like "warsh." Nobody pronounces English as it is spelled. Nor, given the inconsistencies in English orthography, could anybody do that. How does one distinguish between the pronunciation of *red* and *read* (past tense)? Who pronounces the <ea> in *dead, beat, great,* and *heart* alike? Still, literate people presume their true language is the written one. For those with no writing systems, and that includes most of the human beings who ever lived, and most of the time that *homo sapiens* has lived, language is what is in the mind.

In the modern world, a world in which increasingly everyone must be able to handle reading and writing, literacy has become not only an educational concern but a political one as well. Those who are illiterate are severely handicapped. If these illiterates disproportionately belong to certain ethnic and racial groups, many suspect deliberate neglect of those groups. Since we can certainly find that those are the people who have historically been shortchanged by those in power, it is easy to blame their lack of success on the government and schools. In all fairness to politicians and teachers, however, we should remember that literacy is not inborn in humans the way spoken language is. Children don't have to be taught to speak, but they do have to be taught to read and write. Although children denied language through normal channels will create a language on their own, they will not create an **orthography**, writing system, in the absence of written input. Children learn reading by being raised with books before they get to school.

Indeed, we could make quite a case for saying literacy is unnatural, an accident of human history. There are intelligent people from literate cultures who have dyslexia, causing them difficulty in learning to read. Thus, it is not only the economically disadvantaged who have such problems, although the burden may be heavier on them than on dyslexics from other groups.[2] It has only been comparatively recently that we have begun to learn the dynamics of culture on successful literacy.

ORAL AND LITERATE CULTURES

In the 1960's it was assumed that all we had to do to create a literate society was read to little kids, have books lying around the house, and have adults be seen reading. For those children who didn't come from such homes, we assumed that Head Start programs and the like would be adequate substitutes, as would remedial reading classes. In those halcyon days, we thought money spent on "programs" was the answer.

Then came the first disquieting observation: there are literate and oral cultures, and, some think, these produce children with different kinds of minds, different ways of interacting with the world. This is not to say that those from oral cultures are stupid or deficient in any way. In fact, the entire *oeuvre* of scholars like Labov and Abrahams showed that those from oral cultures are as intelligent and logical as those from literate ones. What is different is what they are intelligent about.

Ong (1982, 44–45) thinks that oral cultures foster "a celebration of physical behavior" and that they are far more violent than literate cultures, an arguable premise at best. American culture hardly confirms this, and, as we shall see, nonliterates are not necessarily violent. Indeed, many of their typically oral activities are designed to minimize confrontation and violence.

In general, Ong's explanations of the differences between oral and literate cultures depend on post hoc analyses, not from a consideration of the functions of oral language in nonliterate cultures. For instance, he says that the reason for oral descriptions of violence is that gore is "less revulsive" when spoken than when read. Actually, gore might well be more revulsive when described orally, complete with intonation and verbal sound effects. The printed word is not so immediately graphic. Whenever we try to construe the meaning of any social act, we must first consider its function in society, and then see how it fits its purpose.

Scholars have long known that nonliterates are often capable of prodigious feats of memory, feats we literates are frequently incapable of. Poetry seems to have as its origin the need for remembering in the absence of writing. If one encodes thoughts in rhyming words, so long as one retrieves one member of the pair, the other is likely to come to mind. If one encodes using a strong repeated beat and/or latches the words to a tune or chant, then one need only recall the beat or the tune to start remembering. If one encodes thoughts in highly unusual language, metaphor, simile, and metonymy, one is more likely to recall the image.

Keyser (1976) observed that most poems say quite ordinary things, but do so in extraordinary language. Poetry once served the function of record-keeping: genealogies to inspire great deeds, information on weaponry, food finding and/or growing, and even records of attacks and defeats so that warriors could be whipped into enough frenzy to fight victoriously. This is the stuff of the *Iliad, Beowulf,* and even parts of the Bible.[3] Ong (1982, 38–39) sees the necessity for such devices as leading to redundancy in thought. In contrast, he finds literate thinking sparse and analytic because one need not fill up one's mind with what can be looked up in a book. Members of oral cultures could argue that books have wreaked havoc on memory skills. Some scholars—and nonscholars—take pride in being able to memorize large passages of literary works and to give performances of them. It is essential for scholars to be able to recall what they've read in order to use it in their arguments. Before you can look something up in a book, you have to be able to recall that relevant arguments have been made on a certain subject in that book. In writing a book such as this, which depends upon a vast array of writings on diverse subjects, one relies on one's memory of what one has read. How else could it be done? Yes, then, one can go to the particular piece of writing to get exact wording or statistics or whatever, but remembering comes first.

The Oral and the Literate Mind

Because they perceive regular differences between oral and literate cultures, some scholars theorize that there are differences between oral and literate minds. With much justice, Ong (78–108), for instance, declares that literacy restructures consciousness. Because writing transfers speech to the visual plane, Ong maintains that the literate are capable of more abstraction and distancing. Thinking becomes less bound to a specific or personal context. He points out that the Sumerians developed a code of law almost as soon as they developed writing, a feat not feasible in the absence of writing. Even our concept of time, our habit of dating from specific years, is a matter of literacy. Our seeing history as the accumulation of points in time is a literate habit. I am certain that so are the kinds of categorizing which are dependent on outlining, diagramming, and other visual displays of language. One would expect that the kinds of accumulated fact learning typified in game shows like *Jeopardy* and *Scrabble*—or in "objective" tests—are not found in oral cultures. Bits of information not related to themes are not a concern of such cultures.

Ron and Suzanne Scollon (1981) maintain that oral cultures rely on thematic abstraction both for memory and for making sense out of the world. They show that the Athabaskans abstract themes from what they observe and hear (159–62). Knowledge is organized around central themes. Consequently, narratives are important in socializing children. The Scollons claim that in this culture, "Human variability is organized around typifications and the typifications further are taken as norms for behavior" (159).

Those from literate societies have to be taught to abstract themes from what they read. They have to learn such abstraction in formal lessons in school, but those from oral ones learn to do this on their own as a vital part of their socialization.

Scribner and Cole (1981) investigated literacy among the Vai in West Africa. The Vai are exposed not to one but to three kinds of literacy: English, via formal schooling; Arabic, taught by the local Imam who teaches children to chant the Qur'an each morning at daybreak (30); and Vai script, which was developed by the Vai themselves in the nineteenth century. Scribner and Cole tested both literate and nonliterate Vai with a battery of tests designed specifically to see if literacy does have an effect on the mind. They came up negative on almost all counts:

> On no task—logic, abstraction, memory, communication—did we find all nonliterates performing at lower levels than all literates . . . We can and do claim that literacy promotes skills . . . but we cannot and do not claim that literacy is a necessary and sufficient condition for any skills we assessed. (251)

Any advantage literacy conferred was highly specific, being related to given tasks associated with that script. Literacy didn't even make individuals more objective about parsing sentences grammatically (157). Nor did literacy lead to superior communication skills (212). Each kind of literacy was virtually exclusive of the others (107). This last suggests to me that there is no generalized literacy effect. Being literate in Vai script confers no educational or vocational advantage in that culture. Nor does it "open doors to vicarious experience, new bodies of knowledge, or thinking about major life problems" (238). Of this conclusion, I would have to ask what kinds of texts are available to the Vai. Certainly, one great advantage of literacy is that one can learn a great deal not attainable by one's immediate physical and cultural environment. For this benefit, however, a large number and variety of texts must be available. Scribner and Cole do not say that the Vai have access to libraries. If they do not, then, of course, literacy will not open doors to vicarious experience.

Scribner and Cole's conclusions directly contradict those of Ong and the Scollons, who assume that literacy restructures the mind. Scinto (1986) has objected to their conclusions on two grounds. First, Scribner and Cole based their conclusions on a separation of literacy and schooling practices themselves. Scinto (94) points out that the use of a written language norm and the process of schooling are interfunctional. One is learned in the context of the other, and both together determine how literacy will be used. Scinto (96) also points out that literacy is marked by **decontextualization**. That is, one learns to handle language apart from the physical context one finds oneself in. This is a sharp difference from most oral communication, which depends on the social and physical context of utterance for its meaning and force. This decontextualization involves learning different means of expression from those used in oral production, and this learning is affected by school and by literacy together. Scinto (96) avers:

> Schooled discourse values knowledge insofar as it is objective and depersonalized, that is, knowledge or rules of inquiry into things which are divorced from immediate perceptual experience . . . Schooling as an institution honors rational and logical knowledge that in its most extreme form is what we have come to call science.

This does not mean that nonliterates are not as capable of thought or reasoning as literates. Indeed, we shall present much evidence that it is entirely possible to be logical in an oral culture.

Still, why Scribner and Cole found no difference between literate and nonliterate Vai has to be explained. If they are correct that literacy makes no difference, then Ong, the Scollons, Scinto, and I are wrong. Moreover, their study was careful. What they didn't take into consideration is the continuum of oral and literate activities. I strongly suspect that Vai literacy was associated with more oral endeavors, such as learning prayers and relevant passages of the Qur'an. Even though they learned to read and write English, it seems likely, as I noted above, that they didn't have available large numbers of books, nor do Scribner and Cole show that literacy was taught in conjunction with science. Merely learning how to handle a kind of script without corollary readings is not enough to produce a literate mind.

The Oral/Literacy Continuum

Moreover, there is no sharp break between oral and literate language. Rather, there is a continuum. There are oral productions that are very "literary" in character. These range from papers given at scholarly meetings, to sermons, to political speeches, to inaugurals, eulogies, and valedictorian speeches. These are more literary than oral because they use the grammatical devices of writing: a great many subordinate clauses, long sentences, words usually only seen in print, and a tightly organized structure, complete with topic sentences and formal summations. Then, too, there is writing that is oral in structure: humorous pieces, novels like *Catcher in the Rye* and *Finnegan's Wake,* informal notes or lists, chatty letters, and electronic communication like e-mail. Tannen (1981) shows that telling someone to "get to the point" is an extension of requirements of writing (3). It also seems that much of what has been deemed oral vs. literate may really be a matter of focus (Scollon and Scollon 1984). If the focus is on the social interaction itself, oral strategies are more likely. If it is on content, then literate ones are.

Moreover, all oral cultures are not alike, nor are all literate ones. Tannen demonstrates this in her comparisons of Greek and American narratives. The Greeks, who are certainly literate, use what Ong and others have regarded as "oral" strategies, such as insisting on a moral in a movie (Tannen 1980). On the other hand, as we see in the studies of African American street gangs, logical reasoning is used in oral argumentation (Labov 1972a).

It may be, however, that those from cultures that focus on social interaction rather than depersonalized knowledge have difficulty making a transition to what schools teach. Gumperz, Kaltman, and O'Connor (1984) show that an ethnic black college student transferred his oral narratives to his written themes with little use of literary techniques. Similarly, in the same volume, Michaels and Collins (1984, 224) show that the African American children they studied used an **associating** style in Show and Tell rather than a **topic-centered** one as did the white children in the class. Apparently, the African American children they studied were not from middle-class homes. It is unfortunate that these authors—and so many others—use African American non-middle-class children and adults for their examples as they then confound issues of race, ethnicity, and social class. Middle-class African American children from literate homes behave like white children from the same kinds of homes.

The associating style of these African American children is characterized by their using seemingly unrelated anecdotes to tell their story, using prosody instead of actual words to show connections (234). Of course, prosody is denied to writers, but it is normal in speech. One thing a literate person has to do is to learn to use actual words and grammatical forms to do what one does with voice in speech.

At first blush, it appeared that these children were flitting from topic to topic (224), but careful analysis showed that there was an implicit theme of the story, which one had to deduce, as one would expect from those raised in an oral culture (Scollon and Scollon 1981). Middle-class children in the class subordinated all of their sentences to an overtly announced topic and used actual words as connectors (Michaels and Collins 1984, 236–38).

Shirley Brice Heath (1983), in a monumental study of African American and white rural families in the Piedmont of the Carolinas, investigated the ways that children learned how to use language in their social group and how they used literacy. Like Scribner and Cole, she found no sharp division between oral and literate traditions. The two function together as "part of the total pattern of communication . . . For both groups, as for the Vai, the residents turn from spoken to written uses of language . . . as the occasion demands . . ." (230).

One surprise in this study is that African American children actually begin to read before entering school (192–94). Despite this, they do poorly once in school. The reason they fail is that their socialization with regard to language use differs so drastically from what schools require. At home, they are allowed to break into adult conversations (167); they are not socialized to answer factual questions directly, nor to be still when others are talking. Also, they don't come from a culture in which activities occur at a special time or place. Even their church services are open-ended, ending when they end, so to speak. Further, in their communities, reading is done aloud as a performance, not silently. Even so in school, the African American children seek out books, reading them through again and again (295).

White rural children are socialized to answer factual questions and to be silent until called upon. Although they do well at the outset, they, too, fail as time goes on. It is their socialization as well that causes this. At home, great store is set on their learning facts and accepting what they are told. Life is explained in proverbs and other pat sayings. Creativity is often considered lying. In their narrative performances, these children show no evaluation of what they have related, no indication of emotional involvement, and no causal links between events (304). Although they seem to start out more in tune with the schools, they fall behind once creativity and problem solving become more highly valued by teachers.

Logical Argumentation in an Oral Culture

Labov, Cohen, Robins, and Lewis (1968) give a very good example of logical argumentation in a speaker of a nonstandard dialect, one from a clearly oral culture. At the time of their investigation, the Harlem street gangs were heavily involved in the Muslim religion. The same boys who were virtually illiterate in regular schools were studying history, science, and reading in the Muslim schools. They often took oral tests, which was called "being put on the square" or displaying "heavy knowledge," although that terminology may not have been used in other black communities. The ability to win arguments by quickness, facts, and logic was at a premium.

Labov et al. often took gang members on trips. Since one tenet of the black Muslim religion is vegetarianism, this posed a problem in providing lunches. Once, unthinkingly, Labov and his team prepared tomato sandwiches with mayonnaise. Since mayonnaise has eggs in it, several boys objected, saying, in effect, eggs are from chickens, chickens are meat, so eggs are meat. To this, one boy, Quahab, responded, using the dramatic intonation of black preaching style. This includes chanting as well as an elongating of the final word of a sentence, often the one crucial to the argument. The hairsplitting arguments are worthy of theologians, even those who write their thoughts for others to read:

1. No, bro', we din't eat no meat. You might as well say we drunk it because it was in a liquid fo-orm.

In other words, the injunction is against eating meat, not drinking it. Eggs are liquid. One drinks liquid, so it's all right to consume eggs. To hammer home his point, Quahab continued:

2. Dig it, it ain't even in existence yet, dig that. It ain't even in existence yet. It didn't come to be a chicken yet. You can detect it with a physical eye, you can detect that.

THE USES OF SPELLING

We've already seen that literate people equate the rightness and wrongness of some pronunciations on the basis of spelling. In reality, standard spelling in English is so chaotic that nobody can pronounce words the way they are spelled. The same letters stand for different sounds; different letters stand for the same sounds; some letters are not pronounced; other sounds are not represented by letters. For instance, consider the different pronunciations of <ough> as in *through, cough, though,* and *rough,* or the <o> in *not, so,* and *son,* or the <ea> in *head, meat, heart, ear, heard,* and *great.* In words like *use* and *music* the /y/ before the <u> is not spelled.

Some letters like <c> and <x> stand for sounds spelled by other letters. A <c> before an <i> or <e> is pronounced like /s/, and before an <a>, <o>, or <u> is /k/, as in *city* and *come.* The <x> stands for either /ks/ as in *ox* or /gz/ as in *anxiety.* As we shall see, because of these overlaps, the letter <c> especially has become a vehicle for creativity and rebellion. Most commonly, where one would expect a <c> for <k>, the <k> is used, although in standard spelling, that appears only before <i> and <e>, as in *kite* and *keep.*

In any event, for most purposes, such as school, formal letters, tests, publications, and the like, it is expected that writers use standard spelling. Not only is this enforced by editors and teachers but also by employers. No matter how brilliant and capable one is, if one sends a letter of application for a job with misspellings, one is not likely to get that job, or even an interview. Some publications may allow some nonstandard spellings to indicate spoken nonstandard speech, but the bulk of a text must conform to accepted orthographic practice. Therefore, an important part of establishing that one is literate is to use standard spellings.

Because English orthography has such a misfit between letters and the sounds they represent, a space is created that can be exploited for creative spellings, spellings that defy the standard orthography but indicate the same pronunciations as the standard does.

For purposes of publication in newspapers and magazines, exceptions to the standard are allowed in advertising in creation of names for products, like *Lite, Rite, Nite, Kool,* or *Q-buddy* for a pool cue cover. Typically, however, the text of the ad is in standard orthography.

The spelling of personal names is less regulated than other spheres of spelling. Nonstandard spellings are regularly employed here, so Kristofer or Kristoffer instead of older Christopher is seen, although even in the 18th century, its nickname Kit was seen. Similarly, Christine is now sometimes Kristine or even Kristeen. I know a Carol, Carole, Caryl, and Karryl, and, I'm sure somewhere there is a Karrill, Karrille, Karyl, Karrylle, Carrill, Carryl, or Carryle. Each spelling is pronounced identically. Doubled consonants are pronounced like single ones in modern English, and both <i> and <y> can be pronounced alike in certain contexts. Thus, we have Meryl, Merril, and Merrille, Cheryl, Sherril, Sherrille, and Sheryl or Sherryl. We associate such deviant spellings with modern practices, but at least one similar one has been in effect for centuries. The name Katherine and its short form Kate both violate the rule that /k/ is spelled <c> before an <a>, but even Shakespeare used the <k>. In standard spelling these should be

Catherine and Cate. I have only recently seen this "correct" spelling of the short form. Now I'm seeing older Caitlin, spelled Catelyn, Katelin, and Kaitlyn.

None of these variant spellings violate the rules of possible correspondence between English letters and sounds. English orthography somewhere allows each letter to have the sound intended. Also, double consonants, like <rr> are pronounced exactly like single ones, <r>. Interestingly, one rarely if ever sees variant spellings allowing doubled vowels like <aa> or <ii>.[4] When vowels are doubled, they seem to be in accordance with accepted digraphs like <ou>, <oi>, <oo>, and <oa>. A digraph is composed of two letters that indicate one sound, as in *join, soon,* and *road.*

Spelling as Rebellion

Not surprisingly, those out of the mainstream, especially adolescents, defy the conventions by exploiting the irregular correspondences between letters and sounds in standard orthography. African American rappers and filmmakers have been using a <z> where standard spelling demands an <s>, as in the movie title *Boyz in the Hood.* Similarly, they defy the standard in other instances such as where an <s> stands for a /z/ sound as in <waz> for *was.* They spell *the* as <da> and *gangster* as <gangsta>, mirroring African American Vernacular English (AAVE) pronunciation. This seems to be simultaneously an act of creativity, a way of indicating rebellion against the middle-class power structure, a way of commenting on the vagaries of the spelling system that is such a bar to accepted school performances, and, ultimately, the silliness of conventional spelling standards.[5]

Mark Sebba (2003) shows that deviations from the standard orthography are a means of rebellion. He cites examples from graffiti, and other writings in British Creole. Graffiti itself is a rebellion (158–61) because it involves writing on surfaces not intended and even outlawed for writing upon. He also looks at the writings of other nonstandard speakers in England. He notes that most writing is regulated, so that only those texts that are marginal, such as deliberately oppositional ones or those considered trivial, escape regulation.

In Spain, for instance, standard orthography uses <c> or <qu> for the sound /k/. However, because of borrowed words, the Spanish are familiar with the letter <k>, so, in graffiti and in anarchist publications, the <k> is used rather than the standard letters. The very word *ákratis* (meaning anarchists, anti-establishment teenagers, university students, and gays) uses such an "unauthorized" <k> as a sign of deliberate opposition.

CHAPTER 6

Graffiti in England shows similar unconventional spellings. Sebba (163) offers:

K.O ov B/w
woz ere
livin' ina
dredd time
runnin' tings

He says that using <woz ere> for *was here* is actually a conventionalized nonstandard spelling. The lack of <h> on *here* reflects British nonstandard /h/-dropping and <woz> is just a variant spelling of *was*. The <v> for *of* reflects its actual pronunciation for virtually all English speakers, as does <dredd> for *dread*.

Sebba notes similar creative spellings in poetry and fiction, especially that intended to capture nonstandard speech, both when the pronunciation would be nonstandard ("ting" for *thing*) and when it is not (<kommit> for *commit*).

In many representations of dialogue in America as well as Britain, we see such spellings, <bizness> for *business*, <sez> for *says*. Explaining their prevalence in British Creole writings, Sebba (165) says that the writers claim they spell this way in order to represent the sounds of Creole more accurately. However, given the plethora of misspellings that represent pronunciations used in the standard, it is clear that these writers are emphasizing their otherness. A sample of misspellings that do not indicate a nonstandard pronunciation in poems is seen mixed in with standard forms:

We wi mite haffe kommit
Some dreadful krime

He also cites spellings like:

waan 'want' (?)
Jamaka 'Jamaica'
kum 'come'
funki 'funky'
ah 'of'
de 'the'
kean 'can't'

COMMUNICATING BY COMPUTER

Nowhere is the intersection between orality and literacy seen as vividly as in electronic discourse: e-mail, chat rooms, instant messaging, and mobile text messaging. Here we see writing used for the kinds of social interaction formerly believed to be served only by oral communication. I would note that before the advent of e-discourse, in novels and in personal letters, there had already been a movement to use conventions of orality, such as sentence fragments, discourse markers like *well, gee,* and *oh* preceding sentences.

In novels, so far as I know, this started with stream-of-consciousness novels like *Ulysses* and *You Can't Go Home Again* from the 1920's on and was reinforced by the wholly "oral" 1950's *Catcher in the Rye.* By the 1950's, that was the style being used in personal letters, at least by my friends and me, although I doubt that we were the only ones or the instigators. Actually, although writers on literacy rarely seem to mention them, starting in the 1930's, the comic books used oral styles in their text and nonstandard spellings to give an aura of speech. Of course, the only texts they used were put into balloons emanating from characters' mouths, a device honed by political cartoonists in the previous century. Comic books also made use of printed sound effects like *Bam!!*

Scholars and nonscholars alike often look at e-discourse[6] and its nonstandard forms as if they were new and had no precedence. Indeed, many express fear that computerese will be the death of literacy. I would argue that, not only are there precursors to e-language, but it is simply one more item in the repertoire of the literate. Even more so, I think it opens literate practices up to people who never willingly took pen to hand, but will go on a chat room or do instant messaging or text messaging on a cell phone.

Sebba (167) examines a website for a British comic, Ali G, who affects nonstandard speech forms, both British Creole and other dialects. Not surprisingly, he found that the contributors created a pseudo-Patwa (patois) like that of Ali G when they visited his website. It may or not be the case that contributors were themselves speakers of nonstandard dialects, but that is how they present themselves on the computer:

1.   Just 'coz you went 2 jail 4 dealin'
2.   dave u rude gal if u is finkin dat ali g is an eejat . . .
3.   Wot I is sayin is dat instead of sittin on ur batty

What is interesting is that, in the United States, adolescents using chat rooms, instant messaging, text messaging, and e-mail, henceforth all called e-discourse, also present themselves as nonstandard speakers, especially copying AAVE pronunciations, although in many instances, they would never use these themselves, as in:

playa   'player'
da   'the
ting   'thing'

CHAPTER 6

As Sebba (160) noted in British graffiti, in American e-discourse, one finds numbers and individual letters used for words, as in *4 eva, 4giv, 4c, b4, 2 b, 2 c.* In America, acronyms also abound in e-discourse: *cwot* (complete waste of time), *lol* (laugh out loud), *brb* (be right back), *imho* (in my humble opinion), and the like. Sergestad (2002) mentions "unconventional and not yet established abbreviations" in Swedish e-discourse. However, Sebba doesn't mention these in England, nor does Dürscheid (2000) note them in German chat rooms, although both do show other parallels with American practices.

Nonstandard spellings, including simplifications, are common in e-discourse, including many of those we saw in Sebba's data, such as *u* for *you, uz* for *use, ur* for *your. Pleez* for *please*, and more common simplifications like *rite, tho, thru,* and the like are usual. These approximate spoken language, often using only as many letters as there are sounds in the words. These are also mentioned by Dürscheid in German and Sergestad (2002) in Swedish.

Computer discourse also simplifies the mechanics of writing. It is not at all unusual to find a whole message with no capitals, even from another scholar. Such niceties as colons and semicolons may be missing, as well as quotation marks or italicized titles. Capitals are often used to indicate shouting or emphasis, rather than for opening a sentence or glorifying a proper name.

E-discourse tries to approximate kinesics and facial expressions by the use of emoticons, like :) to indicate a smile. These have also been reported in the European texts. Another way of approximating oral communication is the use of *hi* as the greeting. Again, even scholars open e-mails with *hi Elaine.* Christa Dürscheid gives several examples of the American *hi* in German[7] e-discourse. Tanskanen (1998, 150–52) also notes the practice of inserting one's comments into those of an e-mail one is replying to. This can be done, of course, by copying their comments and then inserting one's own after them. More commonly, at least in my experience, is that one just hits the reply button and then goes to each comment one wishes to respond to. Either way, the result is an e-discourse that looks more like conversation between two people. To sum up, e-mails and related texts aim for an informal, friendly tone as close to face-to-face communication as one can get in writing. Interestingly, I have found this true even in e-mail correspondence dealing with essentially business matters, so that all of the transactions between my editor and me on this text have been in the form of informal e-mails (with chapters attached separately). It is almost unheard of to get an e-mail that uses Title+Last Name. Scholars I've never met, not to mention other people who e-mail me, always greet me with my first name. Even my students address me as plain *hi* or even *hi doctor*. The latter seems to come from freshmen.

Many noting such misspellings and mispunctuations voice angst for the future of literacy. Sergerstad (2002) argues that e-discourses are merely variants or repertoires, such as we saw with registers and styles. Her claim is that e-language is a creative adaptation to the computer. She says that the syntactic and lexical reductions in computerized communication are a way of reducing time, effort, and space. They also act as a way of increasing interpersonal intimacy. She concludes that the written language has been enhanced to suit the conditions of computer talk.

As a professor, I do have to say that even in formal papers in the past five or so years, I have noted a great, even an escalating, increase in spelling errors, especially involving homonyms, so that students tell me they are going to "sight" an author, or that something is "plane," that they liked a "seen," or that someone is "meated" out punishment. Of course, little words like *too, two, to* are constantly confused, as are *see* and *sea*. One explanation for this is that spell checkers don't pick such errors up, but we've had spell checkers for twenty years, and two decades ago, even one decade ago, I rarely saw such errors. I also am finding errors like "cidy" for *city* and "beaudy" for *beauty*. This occurs because, in American English, a /t/ or a /d/ in between a vowel is pronounced as a *d*-like sound, so that *wedding* and *wetting* are pronounced alike. However, when students were more literate than they apparently are now, they did know the conventional spellings of words with the collapsed distinction between /t/ and /d/. That is, they knew the spellings <city> and <beauty> from their readings.

Perhaps I should have said, "When students were more literate in the way I was taught." What I think is happening is not that people are becoming illiterate. Far from it. Electronic discourse is an extension of literacy. However, literacy as we conceive of it today, or as older people do, is changing. English is long overdue for spelling reform. Perhaps e-discourse will be the vehicle that finally brings it about. As for the oral character of e-mail, that doesn't preclude more literature-bound productions in other media. Scholarly writing will remain formal and not oral, as will legal, theological, and medical treatises. Competence in e-discourse will just be added to a person's competence in communication and interaction.

VERBAL PLAY

Many researchers into African American speech, including Labov, have made a very strong case for the verbal agility of its speakers. Very little research has been done on such skills among whites, and the little that has been done (Schatzman and Strauss 1972; Bernstein 1971; Bereiter and Engelmann 1966) has compared lower- and working-class whites with the middle class. Since such studies use the middle class as their norms, naturally the lower-class whites have come out badly. In contrast, African American oral activities have been studied for their own sake, without measuring them against the yardstick of middle-class skills. The thrust of the literature, therefore, has clearly been that African Americans are superior to comparable whites in oral ability, and, because there is so little research into non-African American speech activities, of necessity this text will seem to be perpetrating the same misconception. People of all ethnic groups with little formal education argue about weighty matters like politics, religion, and life in general as well as engage in verbal play. If I do not here give examples of Hispanics, Arabs, French-Canadians, Chinese, Japanese, or any other group, it is not because their speech practices are uninteresting. It only reflects a lapse in research.

Different ethnic groups may engage in different kinds of verbal performance, but skillful verbal jousting exists for them in one form or another. Verbal play may consist of any or all of the following:

- Being quick on the uptake.
- Verbal thrusting such as joking insults.
- Making a joke out of something another has just said.
- Conning others by telling outrageous lies with a straight face.
- Dueling verbally in boasting contests, riddles.

(Dundes, Leach, and Ozkok 1972)

We can also include joke telling, song writing, storytelling, and making up rhymes of various kinds. Certainly, the educated do the same things, but such activities among them appear to be more a matter of individual taste than of social obligation.

Punning as Play

The following dialogues show a punning game very prevalent among working-class white males in Rhode Island. A student of mine, Jean Shields, collected the examples in 1 below from Len, an unskilled kitchen worker in a cafeteria. I collected the samples in 2 from three white males with education ranging from eighth grade to high school. Their occupations were carpenter, carpenter's assistant, and delivery truck driver. Len, an urban dweller, is ethnically Irish, and those in 2, from rural New England villages, were all descendants of the original English settlers. For both groups, the oral sparring is typical unplanned speech behavior.

1. *Jean*:   I have a date tonight.
   Len: Last night I had a date with a fig.

   [a day later]
   Jean: I used your line about a date with a fig on my linguistics test.
   Len: Oh, lines. I've got a lot of 'em. [points to his face]

   [during inconsequential chatting about Len's family]
   Jean: What's the difference between your coat and his?
   Len: Oh, well, the blue jacket means he has big hours and the tan ones mean we got little hours.
   Jean: What are little and big hours?
   Len: Little hours are four hours a day, and bigger ones are eight hours.
   Jean: I gotta go—you're a peach.
   Len: I may be a peach on the outside, but I'm a nut on the inside.

2. *Pete*:   [to me] You still studying schizophrenia?
   Charley: Schizophrenia? That's in the genes, isn't it?
   Ed: I got something in my jeans once.
   Pete: Pig ripped my jeans last night.
   Dave: The pig in the field or the pig you was out with last night.
   [continues for two hours nonstop]

Len is so intent on making his every utterance colorful that he uses *big* and *little* to describe the number of hours men work rather than *more* and *less*. This works because in some contexts *big* and *little* mean *more* and *less*, as in "give me more cake" when it means 'give me a bigger piece of cake.' Such unusual usages, so long as they fit the topic at hand, are the heart of creative language use.

The game in 1 and 2 consists of making a pun out of another person's statement. For the New Englanders, if one can also include an insult to the conversationalist whose words are being punned, that is even better. The resulting conversation is reminiscent of the repartée common in older sitcoms like *Friends* and *Seinfeld*. The difference is that these speakers do not have anyone writing their material. The speakers in 2 are old friends who hunt, snowmobile, and play pool together regularly. During their weekly pool games, the bantering never ceases, and no one is immune. There is never apology or hurt feelings. The activity is understood for the game it is.

Unlike the verbal sparring of African Americans described in the next section, there is never overt judgment on any statement beyond general laughter, although some members of the groups are acknowledged to be more skillful talkers than others. It is interesting to note that on shows featuring African Americans like *In Living Color* when someone made a telling pun or other remark, the audience gave a "Whoo-ooo" that acts as an evaluation such as, "He zinged you" whereas in other sitcoms, canned laughter is the usual response. This parallels the responses given to such activities in different cultures.

In the Appalachian mountains there is a tradition of song making among descendants of the original Scots-Irish and English settlers. Any devotee of American folk music is familiar with one version of this song making, the talking blues. The talking blues are spoken, but with a strong rhythm, usually accompanied by a guitar or banjo. The Appalachians write songs about many topics: love, death, hard times. If asked about an event such as a mining disaster, an Appalachian might answer, "I've written a song about that," and proceed to sing it. One can see such a sequence in the documentary *Harlan County, U.S.A.* Those not into that kind of music often find it tuneless at first, more of a chant than a song. Occasionally, country and western singers will lapse into a segment of talking blues in their songs. Both the Appalachian song making and talking blues have always reminded me of the epic poetry chanted by the minstrels of early Europe. Often accompanied by a stringed instrument, this poetry told of the history of the people, its hard times and good times.

In different parts of the country and in different ethnic groups, undoubtedly many other kinds of verbal activities can be found. The situations that call them forth, however, may differ from group to group.

The Original Rap

Although it has largely been ignored in whites, the gaming aspect of speech and the concern with rhetoric has been well studied in African American culture. Claudia Mitchell-Kernan (1972) gives an example of a young man **rapping** to her. Note that this original usage of the term *rapping* differs considerably from that activity today. Sitting on a park bench, she was approached by three young men, one of whom started a conversation:

1. *M*:   Mama you sho is fine.
   M-K: That ain' no way to talk to your mother.

The conversation continued. Mitchell-Kernan told the man what she was doing. He immediately adjusted his rap:

2. *M:*   Baby, you a real scholar. I can tell you want to learn. Now if you'll just cooperate a li'l bit, I'll show you what a good teacher I am. But first, we got to get into my area of expertise.

M-K: I may be wrong, but seems to me we already in your area of expertise.
[general laughter]

M: You ain' so bad yourself, girl. I ain't heard you stutter yet. You a li'l fixated on your subject though. I want to help a sweet thang like you all I can. I figure all that book learnin' you got must mean you been neglecting other areas of your education.

2nd Man: Talk dat talk [meaning: olé]

M-K: Why don't you let me point out where I can best use your help.

M: Are you sure you in the best position to know?
[laughter]
I'ma leave you alone, girl. Ask me what you want to know. Tempus fugit, baby.
[more laughter]
(170–71)

This man used the grammar and words of what is often termed AAVE. Both Mitchell-Kernan, a respected scholar, and the man in the park, apparently uneducated, use recognizable features of AAVE.[8] I must stress that many African Americans command standard speech of their region but also can switch into AAVE when appropriate. Also, not all people of color speak AAVE. Many, such as Haitians, Caribbeans, and Cape Verdeans, have a cultural and linguistic history quite different from African Americans descended from slaves.

The young man's rap to Mitchell-Kernan is a typical ethnic black activity between men and women. Even though he probably has not received much formal education, he uses the jargon of scholarship: *expertise, fixated,* and the Latin *tempus fugit.* Mitchell-Kernan herself did not present M's credentials. However, having been raised in a mixed African American and white lower- and working-class neighborhood, and having taught such students both in public school and an Upward Bound program, I can vouch that even virtual illiterates often have amazingly erudite vocabularies, as well as a facility with words that puts many a scholar to shame. Typically, those in the lower-classes are more familiar with upper-class speech than the upper-classes are with the lower. Actually, it makes very little difference whether M is educated. Mitchell-Kernan's aim was to show the characteristic black ethnic skill with language. It is not likely that M realized that he was going to meet a female scholar while strolling through the park that day. His innuendos based upon scholarly speech had to be made up on the spot. Mitchell-Kernan comments:

> By his code selection . . . the speaker indicates that he is parodying a tête a tête and not attempting to engage the speaker in anything other than conversation.

She means that despite the sexual double meanings, M's display is actually a verbal one and is not necessarily intended as a real invitation. Notice that once the young man has demonstrated his virtuosity, it is he who ends it.

In the encounter just presented, once the young man finds out that Mitchell-Kernan is a scholar, he adjusts his rap toward scholarly language. The adjustment is significant. For successful rapping, it is not enough merely to make innuendos; they must be made in language appropriate to the person being spoken to. Like the dialogues in 1 and 2 above, the rapper takes what the other conversationalist says and builds on it.

M does this, for instance, by offering to be Mitchell-Kernan's teacher. The "other areas of your education" imply sexual ones, especially since she is a "sweet thang." When the man says, "I ain't heard you stutter yet," he is complimenting Mitchell-Kernan's quick comebacks. The "talk dat talk" from M's friend is an African American congratulatory comment when a speaker uses language both colorful and appropriate to the social context. That the juxtaposition of scholarly and street language is deliberate and intended for humor is shown by both that comment and the laughter at "Tempus fugit, baby."

The term *rapping* originally indicated such displays of verbal skill, often but not always entailing the use of ordinary language in such a way that it took on a sexual double meaning, a use we also saw above with white rural males. In the 1960's, it also began to be used to describe a conversation in which political and social issues were being discussed. Although the term *rap* originally was used for spoken displays and discussions, today it is most associated with rap songs, which are also displays of verbal skill, but of a different kind.

Rappers Today

The rapping that Mitchell-Kernan describes seems to have little in common with the raging testosterone driven lyrics about ho's, bling-bling, fast cars, and guns spoken against the loud pulsating beats that characterize rap and hip-hop of today. Certainly, the rappers today, with their mega-bucks and megapossessions, have little in common with M in the park. The two usages of the term *rap* should not be conflated. Rap songs did develop out of older African American speech activities and music, but not the older practices of rapping.

Some rapping today seems to be little more than bragging about sexual prowess or the ability and willingness to commit violence. However, many rappers speak out against social and racial injustices. Rap has been going on for so long and there are so many rappers that many topics make their way into the genre. The ones that don't are expressions of romantic love, the beauties of nature, expressions of ideals, or anything that smacks of a fairy tale. These are not songs of moon in June, tender breezes caressing trees.

The emphasis in rap is of being real. Realness means looking at the world in all its awfulness. Sudden death for young men, poverty, cruelty, fighting your way through life, these are real. The rewards are always monetary. Jewelry, cars, fancy houses, these are real.

Even if you don't like rap and rappers, you cannot discount them. They are not only popular among African Americans, but to a great cross-section of American youth. My own very white upper-middle-class male students engage in free-style rapping in imitation of African Americans. These boys don't know from social injustice, or from want, or from life in a public project. It seems that the messages of sexual prowess, male strength, and potency are what is attractive to them. They tell me that they know they can't compete with African American rappers, but still they rap as often as they can. They also adopt African American clothing styles, slang, pronunciations, body motions, and even activities like bragging about their sexuality, ability to fight, and consuming large quantities of alcohol and drugs. Rap music has a profound effect on these boys. Unfortunately, the messages of rap about poverty and injustices to African Americans are not what these boys focus on. Unlike my schoolmates in the 1960's, rap hasn't made them social activists.

Rap has affected young people all over the world. For instance, on television news one night, I heard Japanese rappers. Memorably, Arab rappers in the Middle East were presented singing of their situation with great emotion, using the exact beats and kinds of tunes and instruments that African American rappers do. It was uncanny. One can't ignore a genre that speaks to so many so deeply. One also cannot ignore such large numbers of youth, female as well as male, who can believe only in what is real, when real does not include the softer, more loving aspects of life. This is certainly a comment on our society.

CHAPTER 6

SPEECH ACTIVITIES AND SOCIAL PRESSURES

Rap songs are, of course, the most prominent African American verbal activity today. However, they derive from a long tradition in the African American community, one well worth examining. Indeed, one cannot truly understand rap without understanding where it comes from and what social conditions produced its forebears and now rap itself.

M's quick allusions to sex, above, are seen in other ghetto speech activities as well. Polite fictions about sex are stripped away again and again in black oral performances. The pinnacle of these performances occurred in **toasts,**[9] although they are rarely if ever recited today. These were poems recited on street corners and in bars. The name *toast* in and of itself is a parody of the polite and laudatory practice of toasting at weddings, testimonials, and the like.

The toasts were actually epic poems. Admittedly, most people would not think of epic poetry when they first hear black toasts. The ubiquitous profanity and taboo subjects so shock middle-class listeners that most cannot appreciate the skill it takes to compose them. Although they now belong to the realm of esoterica, examining toasts is a valuable lesson in the ways language activities mirror social realities and fulfill the need for ego satisfaction. As we shall see, the themes of the toasts are still present in current rap songs.

The toasts—and other oral displays—are not braked by any coyness in language or topic. In fact, one suspects that taboos are deliberately woven throughout. Although they offend sensibilities, profanity and taboo subjects are an integral part of any sociology of language, as they reflect social conditions and attitudes. This is true for all people, not just African Americans. We are using that group for our examples because their productions have been well collected, African Americans have raised speech performances to a high art, and, for the young, their speech and music have become the ones to copy today. Because the message of the songs is as important as the form of the music itself, its influence on all of American society is considerable.

The original toasts are actually oral epics like the *Iliad* or *Beowulf:* long poems, originally meant to be spoken, that recount magnificent deeds of a hero. The hero is a model epitomizing the way men are supposed to be. The epic not only entertains and thrills but also teaches. Examining epic poems, then, reveals cultural attitudes.

The hero of the toasts is often a pimp or lawbreaker. He is just about always a misogynist. Even if he is not, he is overtly antisentimental and tough. Gambling, drinking, procuring, prostitution, and the treachery of women are common themes. These were the facts of life to the anonymous composers of *The Fall, The Signifying Monkey, The Sinking of the Titanic,* and other tales of the black folk heroes Shine and Stackolee. The attitudes found in the toasts presented below have not changed very much, as an examination of the lyrics of current rap songs show. The major difference, so far as I can see, is that, whereas toasts had the attitude of "that's the way it is and you might as well be resigned to it," the raps have an attitude of "it's bad and must be changed."

Epic poetry sets its scenes in war. There heroes can exhibit the traits that society expects of its men. The battlegrounds of the black epics are the slums of the large cities, as in these opening lines from one version of *The Fall:*

1. It was Saturday night, the jungle was bright
    As the game stalked their prey;
    And the cold was crime on the neon line
    Where crime begun, where daughter fought son
    And your mom lied awoke, with her heart almost broke
    As they loaded that train to hell
    Where blood was shed for the sake of some bread
    And winos were rolled for their port.

    Where the addicts prowl, where the tiger growl
    And search for their lethal blow,
    Where the winos crump for that can heat[10] rump
    You'll find their graves in the snow;
    Where girls of vice sell love for a price
    And even the law's corrup'
    But keep on tryin' as you go down cryin'
    Say man it's a bitters cup
    $\qquad$ (Labov, et al. 1968, 56)

This stark and graphic opener leads into a tale of a pimp who exploited a whore shamelessly, ending with his arrest:

2. Now as I sit in my 6 by 6 cell in the county jail
    Watchin' the sun rise in the east
    The morning chills give slumber to the slumbering beast

    Farewell to the nights, and the neon lights,
    Farewell to one and all
    Farewell to the game, may it still be the same
    When I finish doing this fall. (58)

CHAPTER 6

In *Honky Tonk Bud*, the hero is convicted of a narcotics charge. Before sentence is passed, he tells the judge:

> 3. He said, "I'm not cryin' 'cause the agen' was lyin'
> And lef' you all with a notion
> That I was a big deal in the narcotics fiel'
> I hope the fag cops a promotion.
> It's all the same; it's all in the game.
> I dug when I sat down to play.
> That you take all odds, deal all low cards.
> It's the dues the dope fiend must pay." (58)

"The game" is the way things are. Labov et al. point out that the toasts do not claim that the game pays off in any way. The satisfaction comes from playing with dignity and according to the rules. The rules dictate that one never complains about what happens. Justice is not expected, nor is injustice bemoaned. Heroism consists of great courage as it does in the middle-class world, but, in the toasts, the courage consists partly of being willing to face the penalties of crime.

Certainly, these are poems of despair. Achilles had a battlefield with potential honor. Beowulf could become a bonafide hero by killing Grendel. These were heroes to their entire people. African Americans in the slums often saw no way to become the kinds of heroes general American society set up,[11] at least not before the 1960's and the first glimmerings of the civil rights movement. This does not mean all black males sought their honor in playing the game of drugs and pimps. Most blacks did not and do not. But the message was the same to all: "You keep on tryin' as you go down cryin,' You take all odds" and you don't complain.

The toasts taught other lessons as well. Clearly, throughout, no sympathy is to be shown, no self-pity, no pity for others. This is well-illustrated in *The Sinking of the Titanic* when Shine, the hero, starts swimming across the Atlantic away from the disaster. He encounters several doomed passengers who plead with him to save them. Despite the rewards they promise, he rebuffs them all harshly and coldly. Finally, he meets a crying baby:

> 4. Shine said, "Baby, baby, please don't cry.
> All little motherfuckers got a time to die.
> You got eight little fingers and two little thumbs
> And your black ass goes when the wagon comes."

Labov et al. (1968, 60) compare this to Achilles' speech in the *Iliad*:

5. Ay friend thou too must die: why lamentest thou?
   Petroklos too is dead, who was better far than thou.
   See thou not also what manner of man am I might and good-
   liness?
   Yet over me too hang death and forceful fate.

However, Achilles says this to another adult, not a helpless baby. What can this mean, and why is it in the toast? Certainly, blacks love their babies. Shine shows some feeling for the baby, "Please don't cry." In fact, the baby is the only one of the doomed to whom Shine uses politeness markers. To the others he is brutal. We have ample evidence from this toast and from others, such as *The Fall,* that pity for others is to be squelched at all costs. Many verses in *The Fall* are devoted to first establishing that the prostitute served her man fantastically well. When she becomes ill, however, he throws her out and several verses recount the particular heartlessness with which he does so, such as:

6. You had your run. Now you done.
   I can't make no swag off some swayback nag
   Whose thoroughbred days are past.
   Why I'd look damn silly puttin' a cripple filly
   On a track that's way too fast. (57)

My interpretation of such passages is that they are intended to underscore an important message to the urban slum dweller. It is not good in that life to have too much pity for others. In a world as harsh as that pictured in these toasts, the only way to survive is to cut off compassion. The passage from the *Iliad* had the same message for the ancient Greek youths: in war, one must not be compassionate. In essence, the world of toasts is a world always at war. Just as Shine's swimming the ocean to safety is a tremendous exaggeration, so is his encounter with the baby. It is the message "be dispassionate" carried to the point of hyperbole.

African American storytelling is suffused with tales that teach people not to trust, not to pity. This theme has even been grafted onto stories originally from Africa, such as the talking animal genre like the "Bre'r Rabbit" stories. The difference is that in Africa, these stories were used to teach children to beware of antisocial creatures who disrupted friendship. In America, these were changed so that they taught instead that everyone must look out for him- or herself. Thus are the realities of society mirrored in speech activities.

The attitude toward women in the toasts goes beyond mere lack of pity. It is actively hostile. In one toast, Stagolee casually shoots women at the slightest provocation. In another, Shine makes the cruelest fun of the romantic notions of two young girls, telling them in the bluntest of terms that the sexual act itself, not love or romance, is all there is to relations between men and women.

In *The Fall,* the whore is called a "sex machine" and in an extended metaphor is likened to a racehorse. A general bitter vindictiveness characterizes all dealings of men with women in the toasts, a vindictiveness matched by the cruel insults hurled at women in verbal games like ranking (see below) long played by black male adolescents (and now by whites as well). In movies like *The Boyz in the Hood*, black adolescents typically address girls as *ho, hooch,* and *bitch*, as they do in the raps today. When one girl protests being called a ho, Doughboy sarcastically answers, "Sorry, bitch." Perusing the lyrics to rap songs confirms this misogynistic attitude. Labov et al. (62) points out that the hostility revealed in all such verbal activity makes it especially difficult for female teachers to deal with male members of this culture.

The pimp as hero in the toasts and on the streets is another expression of this hostility. Again, the reason is perhaps to be found in social values and conditions. African American culture is, after all, American. In our society, as indeed in most, men are traditionally supposed to dominate women. Until recently this has meant that men should make more money than their wives and even control any earnings their wives brought in. This is no longer true, but even on a "progressive" recent TV series, *Sex and the City*, there was a set of shows about Carrie's being dumped by a man who couldn't deal with her making more money than he. So such attitudes aren't completely dead.

During the years when the toasts were being composed, the ideal was that a man should be able to earn enough so that his wife didn't have to work. That was a particular point of pride during my growing-up years. It must be emphasized that most African Americans have been raised in families with wage-earning fathers. In fact, when I was growing up, the only stay-at-home mother on our street was our African American friends', and their father was the sole breadwinner.

Still, for many years, a much higher percentage of African Americans than other ethnic groups have came from families in which males were not the principal wage earners. There were few jobs for men of color, and those that were available were usually at the lowest end of the economic scale and, worse, not steady. It was easier for women to get jobs. If nothing else, they could be domestics, although some more prestigious jobs like nursing were open to them.

It must be emphasized that having an education or specialized training did not often improve the lot of African Americans until long after the civil rights movement of the 1960's. One of the African American men in our neighborhood was a college graduate, but the only job he could get, pre-1960's, was as an elevator operator. The only other thing open to him was to be a stevedore or to do other heavy labor.

For some men, then, the way to dominate women as well as to make a great deal of money was to pimp. Pimping is the rawest exploitation of women as sex objects, of women being subservient to men. Pimping is a way, a very depraved way to be sure, of achieving the American ideals of making money and dominating women.

Spike Lee in his book *By Any Means Necessary* angrily speaks of 1970's blaxploitation movies like *Superfly*, charging that the unflattering portrait of a drug-dealing, drug-using misogynist "hero" was a pandering to white tastes. Actually, these movies come straight out of the tradition begun by the toasts. These were among the first movies written and directed by blacks. Like the toasts and other ghetto speech activities, they had a real "in your face" attitude toward whites. For the first time, blacks could publicly express the disdain they had for white society, and the anger they felt toward that society. They also charged that white dealers targeted African American neighborhoods, and that law enforcers did not overly concern themselves with drugs until white suburban youths began to take them. The directors of these films, like Melvin van Peebles and Gordon Parks, Jr., stressed that there were few legal options for the intelligent person of color in the United States.

They also portrayed white society and government as hopelessly corrupt and hypocritical, and attacked every middle-class value. For instance, in *Superfly*, the "hero" is named "Priest" and he regularly is shown snorting cocaine from a cross he wears around his neck. Given the traditional intense commitment to religion by African Americans, this is hardly a just portrait, but justice wasn't the point. Letting "Whitey" know how blacks felt was.

Some decades later, black directors like Spike Lee and John Singleton, while still blaming white society, offer very different messages. These directors are anti-drug, anti-crime, anti-pimp, and pro-education. While some characters in their movies, like Doughboy, may be misogynistic, some women are portrayed very positively in movies like *Jungle Fever* and *Boyz in the Hood*. The leading women in these movies are intelligent, articulate, beautiful, honorable, and capable. However, American society has changed in many ways since the 1970's, both in attitudes toward women and toward people of color, and this change is evidenced in movies. Unfortunately, too many lyrics of rap songs, which are closer to the art of the ghetto culture, still advocate a violent lifestyle which deprecates women.

CHAPTER 6

Street Poetry as Art

Perhaps a defense is in order of the proposition that the toasts parallel the great epics of the past. It is very easy to look at the topics of the toasts —the profanity, the lawbreaking, the nonstandard speech forms—and dismiss them as being unworthy of scholarly attention. However, examining such productions tell us a good deal about the lives of the people who composed and recited them. It tells us how they saw the world they lived in and why they held certain attitudes. Granting all that, still, why call the toasts poetry? Yes, they had heroes of a sort. They told their listeners how life should be lived: stoically, unromantically, unpityingly. This makes them epics, but does it make them poetry?

Without any philosophical haggling about Art and what it is, we can see that the toasts made use of all the devices of poetry and did so skillfully. Poetry manipulates language while expressing even ordinary meanings (Keyser 1976). Often this manipulation makes us see old things in new ways.

Rhyme is a frequent, but not a necessary, feature of poetry. If it is used, in order to detect rhymes, poetry must be read in the dialect in which it was composed. For instance, in order to appreciate the skillful rhyming in the toasts, the reader must realize that the following sets of words rhyme in AAVE:[12] *odds, cards; cell, jail; deal, field (fiel')*. It is not easy in any dialect to find rhyming words that can fit in the rhythm of a poem as well as give the poet's desired meaning. Still hundreds of lines of toasts and other African American oral activities manage perfect rhyme, many highly clever and unusual. This feat is all the more impressive when we consider the intricate rhyming scheme of the toasts. The basic scheme of many toasts consists of a long line divided in two, with internal rhyme, as in:

7a. She tricked with the **Greeks**, the Arabs and **freaks**
. . .
She tricked with the **Jews**, Apaches, and **Sioux**
    (*The Fall*)

8a. He said, "I'm not **cryin'** 'cause the agent was **lyin'**
. . .
That I was a big **wheel** in the narcotics **fiel'**
    (*Honky Tonk Bud*)

These long lines form sequences with short lines that rhyme with each other, as in:

7b. . . . To her they were all the **same**
She tricked with the Greeks, Arabs, and freaks

> And breeds I cannot **name**
> She tricked with the Jews, Apaches, and Sioux
> (*The Fall*)

And:

> 8b. He said, "I'm not cryin' 'cause the agent was lyin'
> And left you all with a **notion**
> That I was a big wheel in the narcotics fiel'
> I hope the fag cops a **promotion**"
> (*Honky Tonk Bud*)

Another very important feature of poetry is figurative language such as metaphor. The image of addicts as vicious felines is reinforced by the metaphor of people as jungle animals ("as the game stalked their prey . . .," "Where the addicts prowl . . .") and is tied together by the rhyme of *prowl* and *growl*. The metaphor of the city streets as a jungle in which game stalks prey sets the moral tone as well as the physical aura of *The Fall.* "And the cold was crime on the neon line" emphasizes the misery and ugliness of the streets. Jungles can be warm and beautiful as well as vicious and unlawful, but these lines make it clear that only the latter meanings are to be taken. Images of heat are followed by images of cold throughout *The Fall.* The winos have canned heat such as sterno, but still die in the snow. Even at the end the sun rises, but it is the morning chills that put the slumbering beast to rest. The word *slumbering* itself is literary, even poetic. This is another instance of the supposedly unlettered being familiar with the language of books. Throughout, this toast shows skillful use of language, all bringing to us vividly, as only poetry can do, the terror and the feel of the city jungle, the contemptuous feeling for women, the bravery and resignation of the heroes.

The Blues

Erickson (1984) shows that conversations are characterized by a **rhapsody** that "stitches" utterances to each other. This is achieved partially by shared knowledge both about the world and about the rules for discourse in a given culture. Disjointed sentences are transformed into a coherent conversation by such shared knowledge. This applies as well to art forms, including popular songs.

Jarrett (1984) describes the blues and demonstrates that they make sense only to an audience that knows the rules for the genre. The same audience would know if a verse could even belong to that genre. What strikes an outsider as incoherent and meaningless may be perfectly coherent to members of the culture itself. If we analyze what the audience knows and expects, we see that is what makes for coherence. Jarrett suggests that the **genre** by itself is a pragmatic device "which constitutes a kind of signal with which to orient an addressee" (160). The blues are songs of complaint, but not just any old complaint. Both in the verse structure and in permissible topics, there are powerful constraints on the bluesman in the guise of a narrator, who is presented by the singer-composer of the song.

This narrator sings only of what one person can subjectively know (167) so that the singer is, in effect, commenting on life. It is for this reason, I think, that the ordering of the blues is not temporal. That is, there is no "first this happened, then that" (163).[13] The bluesman is not interested in nature; therefore, a song that sang of someone's going out to look at the moon would not be acceptable to the blues audience (161). The bluesman, however, is knowledgeable about women, booze, and preachers. The form that these comments are encased in is a stanza with the first two lines repeated and the third one as a comment that rhymes with the other two, as in:

1. Baby you so beautiful, you know you're gonna die someday
    Honey, you know you beautiful, you gonna die someday
    All I want's a little loving, before you pass away. (160)

This is highly reminiscent of the humorous wordplay of sexual invitation that we saw with Claudia Mitchell-Kernan. Notice the wheedling logic, the implication of 'c'mon baby, what's a little sex among friends?' (my interpretation, not Jarrett's).

Jarrett shows what an audience has to know to interpret the blues correctly. He claims that Hispanic and white listeners experience such lyrics as incoherent, but African Americans, understanding their conventions, have no difficulty with them:

2. Oh, I wish I had me a heaven of my own Great God Amighty
    Yeah, a heaven of my own
    Well, I'd give all my women a long, long happy home
    Oh, I have religion on this very day
    Oh, I have religion on this very day.
    But the womens and the whiskey they would not let me pray
    (162)[14]

Jarrett explains that in order to understand such lyrics, one has to be aware that there is a long tradition of teasing preachers for being hypocrites. He points out the satire in many blues lyrics, including this one, in that they incorporate regular calls heard in very serious church services, such as "Great God amighty," "Lord have mercy," and "amen" (165). We see virtual parody of church in:

3. Oh, I'm gonna preach these blues and choose my seat and set down
   Oh, I'm gonna preach these blues now and choose my seat and set down
   When the spirit comes sisters, I want you to jump straight up and down.

As with M's rap to Mitchell-Kernan, skillful *double entendres* abound.

The currently popular rap songs are very much in the tradition of toasting and the blues. In them, too, one might find references to preachers, as in *Yvette* in which L.L. Cool Jay raps, "The preacher says that you are God." This was said to the promiscuous girl of the title. Rap songs also owe a great deal to the dozens and to sounding (see beow). Noticing the continuity of themes, rhyme, and beat, one of my students, Crystal Jones, examined the tradition that has produced rap songs. She calls the raps "toasts set to music," noting that they "insult all women, talk a lot about sex and drugs." More than a decade has passed since her analysis, so one can find counterexamples today, but her observations are still valid for many raps. Like toasts, rap songs make extensive use of internal clever and even improbable rhyme.

There appears to be no change in the kinds of insults thrown at women in rap. Often, they graphically delineate the depths of what we could term *sluthood*.[15] Jones, quoting from Jackson (1974, 4) notes that "sexual relations in the toasts were invariably affectionless" with the female existing "as a device for exercise and articulation of female options."

Interestingly, one ghetto speech activity has for decades centered specifically on insulting women. This was and is such an important activity that it has had many names over the years. *Sounding, chopping, ragging, ranking, cutting, woofing, giving shit, joning, giving S,* and *giving J* are some of the local or older terms for the same activity: competitive insulting between African American males (Abrahams 1972), an activity now engaged in by white males as well. One of my colleagues says it was called *crowing* in her Kansas neighborhood. Two more recent terms, but perhaps not current as you read this, are *dissin'*[16] *and illin'*, although these last two can refer to any kind of negative commenting about a person. In this text, the term *ranking* will be used.

CHAPTER 6

Ranking arose from an earlier competition called "playing the dozens," rhymed couplets with four strong beats per long line. In the following, the boldfaced words have the strong beat. In my childhood neighborhood, one heard young men being "put in the dozens" by:

4. I **don't** play the **dozens**, I **don't** play the **game**
   But the **way** I had your **mother** is a **god** damn **shame.**

This started a round of such couplets, all insulting an opponent's mother, implying that she was promiscuous. By the early 1960's, perhaps because both the structure and topic of the dozens proved too limiting, they had given way to ranking, such as:

5. Your mother's like a doorknob, a turn for everyone.
6. Your mother is like McDonald's, fun for all ages.

The opener "your mother" is so prevalent in these, that a boy could insult another by simply saying, "your mother!" When employed as a verbal dueling, however, ranking always involved unrhymed one-line similes followed by a "kicker." This, like the structure of toasts, blues, and rap songs, was an almost invariant structure that had to be conformed to. Early rap songs, those of the mid-1980's, such as *Yvette* by L.L. Cool Jay, showed a similar structure with a strict rhyme scheme and the addition of a chorus (Chaika 1981, 161–62).

This has been largely abandoned, and although rhyme is still utilized, it doesn't have to occur at set intervals as before and there is no necessary length of lines. Rather, current rap utilizes series of phrases, some of which rhyme, all chanted to the strong rap beat. Instead of regular choruses, some of them repeat phrases internally two or three times, but there seems to be no rule for this. There are few overt linguistic transitions between the phrases. It is up to the hearer to make the connections. Although, on the surface, the lyrics seem to ramble, on closer inspection it can be seen that they are subordinated to a topic or theme. These have also changed. Instead of female relatives, we now find topics like anger at the police, exhortations to make something of one's life, lectures against eating swine, admonitions about AIDS, and advice about how to deal with faithless partners.

Even ranking did not confine itself to mothers and sisters. Although they were prime targets, two other general themes could be ranked on: poverty and physical attributes of the opponent and his family. Again, these don't seem prevalent in current rap music. Ranking often took the form of a verbal duel between two boys. Onlookers overtly commented on the quality of each sound, much as onlookers to the early dialogic rapping between a man and a woman commented "talk dat talk" or "rap city baby." The more original the ranking, the higher it was graded. As with the white repartee mentioned earlier, ranking that elaborates on an opponent's previous statement was considered better than an unrelated one. For street kids, ranking and other verbal displays were—and are—often major determinants of social status.

Although far more data have been gathered on non-middle-class blacks' speech, what little has been gathered suggests that similar attitudes toward middle-class values may occur among working-class whites. There is verbal dueling, for instance, which deals wholly with taboo topics, including those rarely if ever heard from blacks. As with black ritual insulting, what is said in the dueling is not necessarily true. Rather, each person tries to build upon a previous remark either by introducing a taboo subject or by insulting another person, preferably with his or her own words. Puns are not necessarily a feature of such exchanges. The repartee can be between men and women, and the entire subject matter of the discourse can deal with subjects that are especially taboo in middle-class speech. Although the topics are taboo, taboo words are not necessarily used.

A sample of such dialogue, gathered by a student, Cynthia Marousis, in an urban coffee shop after midnight, started with a male customer's asking a waitress if she was married. When she responded, "Yeah," he asked, "How's your lover?" The assumption, pretended as much as real, that she was immoral enough to have a lover started an entire sequence of exchanges about menstruation, incontinence, oral sex, and homosexuality. The waitress commented, "My husband's good, but my lover's not doing good. He's got the rag on." This comment about her lover shows that the object is to raise a taboo subject somehow. It makes no difference how absurd, impossible, or bizarre the rejoinder is, just so long as the taboo subject is raised. Such exchanges are displays of verbal skill, especially one-upmanship. The topics chosen indicate hostility toward middle-class mores about what can be talked about.

EGO-BOOSTING IN SPEECH ACTIVITIES

The men who created toasts could gain ego satisfaction from both their creation and their performance. As we have seen, African Americans overtly praise and encourage someone who is giving a good display of speech. With the toasts, men could fantasize as they boasted about the great exploits of their heroes. Similarly, African American men have long exchanged boasts about their prowess in fighting and other street activities, just as rappers still do today.

CHAPTER 6

In a study of white barflies, a student of mine, Robert Walling, found patterns of conversation also designed, in his words, to "reinforce and stabilize egos." Their pattern was simple. The conversation started with criticism of current government, society, or sports figures. This, apparently, served as a way of establishing the man's superiority over those in power. An unfavorable comparison of the present to the past was then made. This is not surprising, since they always claimed that their glories were in the past. Finally, the barfly gave a sketch of his past life and, if he was a father, his children's fate. These sketches proved to be untrue, though not wholly so. There was always some germ of truth in these tales. Unlike African American street youths, these older white men do not claim fantastic exploits. They only upgrade the past a few notches. The bars they frequent are in stable neighborhoods. Most of the men are lifelong residents, and the bartenders and other patrons could all verify the truth of each tale. Walling found no difficulty in getting the men to talk. Indeed, as soon as they saw a new face, they accosted him and insisted on telling him their tales.

One man who many years ago had driven a city bus for ten months until he was fired for drunkenness claimed:

1. I was a bus driver and a damn good one too. My wife used to work at the Outlet [a local department store] and now my two boys drive truck for them.

The bartender confirmed that his boys were doing no such thing, nor as their father also claimed, was it likely that they could have gone to college.

Another oldster who had been a janitor at an elegant hotel claimed:

2. I worked at the Biltmore. You name it and I did it. There wasn't much in that place that I couldn't do. That used to be the best hotel in southern New England. All the big shots who came to Providence stayed at the Biltmore [shows autographs from Jack Benny and Jack Dempsey].[17] Pretty impressive, huh? I talked to those two for about an hour apiece. Ya, they were great guys. I still remember what Demps told me, "You got to fight to win in this world." I'll never forget those words and that was almost forty years ago . . . When I had my big job with the Biltmore I never complained once.

Note the use of a pseudo-nickname, Demps, to indicate familiarity or intimacy with the great fighter. For these men, part of the reason for going to bars seems to be to have a chance to tell their stories, to present themselves as worthwhile people.

234

Most people apparently use language somehow to boost their own sense of worth, to gain status and maintain their egos. Erickson (1984, 145) confirms this. He dissects an ordinary conversation, showing that an African American speaker and his audience "were doing" the conversation together. The speaker was able to display his skill and to persuade the others, but the conversation, which Erickson aptly described as "call and response," allowed a strong manifestation of solidarity between the interactors. Although the principal speaker was able to establish how good a talker he was, this wasn't done at the expense of anyone present. His superiority was achieved "by collaboration with, rather than at the expense of less . . . creative and assertive members of the audience." Thus, says Erickson, "soul" is achieved. Notice that the boasting of the barflies reported on by Walling are not done at anybody else's expense either.

Ritual Insulting

Casual, rough talk can be very revealing of social attitudes and conditions. Labov (1972c) has termed activities like ranking "ritual insults." Unlike true insults, ritual insults do not evoke anger or denial. Instead they evoke other insults, laughter, or, occasionally, a change of subject. Although probably all human societies have ritual insulting activities, some seem to indulge only sporadically. Others, such as American urban black youth, have codified the activity. It is virtually an everyday business, and one important in determining social rank.

The frequency of ritual insulting changes throughout one's lifetime. There are times and situations when one is very likely to indulge in ritual insulting. Adolescence seems to call forth a good deal of play insulting. Examples are easily gathered from athletic teams, cafeterias, and school-yards in the United States as well as in other countries (e.g., Dundes, Leach, and Ozkok 1972). Brothers and sisters often tease each other playfully but with a barb. College students tell me that insulting often reaches a peak in the dorms during exams. Some husbands and wives playfully insult each other. More rarely, and only in some really relaxed family situations, do children "bust up" their parents. In earlier times, when children had to be far more formal with their parents than today, playful insulting was unthinkable. Ritual insulting seems most acceptable when the participants are of equal or near social status, and it occurs most frequently at times of stress, such as adolescence in general and exams in particular. The business of living together as a family can create small tensions. Thus siblings, college roommates, or spouses insult each other jokingly, whereas casual acquaintances are not as likely to. When we see an entire cultural group regularly engaging in ritual insulting, we have good reason to suspect that they are under special strain.

CHAPTER 6

The topics of all ritual insults, including ranking, seem to be constrained. To overstep the bounds leads into genuine insulting. The limits shield participants from inadvertent hurt. However insulting ranking may be, for instance, calculated not to bruise egos. To the contrary, the activity of ritual insulting provides ego-boosting for boys to whom the ordinary ego satisfactions are denied. The street kid who may never make it into college or a prestigious job, who cannot participate in the American dream of upward mobility, can get daily proof of his intelligence and wit by these verbal duels. Abrahams (1972) says that verbal jousts are a safe arena in which to seek success and to exercise aggressiveness.

Labov et al. (1968, 101–02) convincingly demonstrate that mention of a true incident is not taken as part of the game; it is not heard as ritual insulting. Rather, it brings forth angry denials. For instance, although poverty itself may be sounded on, to mention something showing someone's actual poverty is taken as a grave insult. It is all right to say that the cockroaches in Junior's house are so bold they pull a gun on you, but it is not all right to tell about the chair that broke when you sat on it. Labov et al. reported that when one boy mentioned that, the other hotly responded, "You's a damned liar, 'n you was eatin' in my house, right?" In that community, remarking that someone ate at someone's house implies hunger, a real need for food. Thus it is a true insult.

The reader may recall that asking for food is difficult for Americans in general. With all the profanity and vulgar images that the boys proved capable of in the Harlem study, one of the worst insults that Labov et al. collected was "Yeah, but you sure be eatin'." It proved easy to determine true from ritual insults. The true ones were not only highly plausible events, but the boy sounded on angrily justified what was said. Telling the truth about one boy's father, that he stuttered and had gray hair, evoked heated denials, even tears.

Nonetheless, a germ of truth exists in ritual insulting. Poverty is ranked on; so are physical attributes like fatness or black African facial features. Although they have some foundation in fact, the sounds are saved from truth by being so fantastic that they could not possibly be true. Perhaps for this reason, bizarre and absurd imagery abounds in sounding. For example, the following was collected from two college students by another student, David Aldrich. It is an excellent example of earthy, even raw language that in reality serves both social and psychological purposes for the speakers. As casual as it is, it follows the rules of the game:

1. *Craig*: Man, if I was a chick, I wouldn't kiss you with my dog's lips.
   Greg: With the size of your lips, you'd drown her for sure.

Craig: I may not be the best kisser, but man, I'm hung like a
baseball bat and swing it like Willie Mays.
Greg: Well, you got your chance tonight. Baby, I got my
goggles on and I'm ready to do some heavy divin'.
Craig: Just call me Jacques Cousteau

The germ of truth here is that Craig's lips are characteristic of black Africans. So are Greg's. However, the very absurdity of the image allows it to remain in the realm of joking. Notice how deftly Craig turns Greg's ritual insult into a boast about his other physical attributes. In verbal dueling and one-upmanship, one can best one's opponent by taking another's insult and using it to lead into a self-glorification. Greg then shows his own skill by turning the sexual reference into a metaphor for deep-sea diving. Craig's "Call me Jacques Cousteau" is a way of saying that he is the best deep-sea diver of them all.

Comparing oneself to a famous historical figure or a modern celebrity is quite usual as a way of boasting in the African American community. Although this exchange is undeniably vulgar, as are many insulting rounds, it still is the subtle comment that wins the game. The entire discourse takes a good deal of wit and skill.

Labov found a good deal of ranking on shared physical characteristics of African Americans. This does not necessarily indicate self-hatred, as some suppose. I think, rather, that there is a larger principle of social behavior. It seems to me that things which are involuntary, short of deformity, can often be joked about. This seems to be true in many different cultures, although which topics are to be excluded are specific to each culture. Among most Americans, teasing about freckles, red hair, and short stature is permissible, so that a short red-headed boy of my acquaintance was nicknamed "Strawberry Shortcake." If he were a genuine midget, his height couldn't be mentioned. Similarly, if a normal person trips, someone might joke, "Whatsa matter, forget your crutches?" But the same statement to a paraplegic would be outrageous.

Labov et al.'s (1968) samples of sounding do include those about poverty, but they were all impossible exaggerations. They were collected on the streets of Harlem from boys who were really poor. Note the difference in sounding on poverty initiated by Craig, an African American college student, and Bill, his white roommate, as they were playing cards:

2. *Craig*: Hey, man, you got another trump card just as sure as a
bear shits in the woods.
   Bill: I sure as hell don't got no trump card, just as sure as
your mother shits on the floor.

CHAPTER 6

> *Craig*: Well, Mr. Cool, at least we got a floor to shit on. They don't let you shit on the welfare office floor.
>
> *Bill*: You're pretty bad with the mouth. How about the cards?

It is all right for Craig to tease Bill by implying that his family is on welfare because it is neither true nor likely. To a genuinely poor person in an inner city neighborhood, this would be a true insult. A variant of the "your mother" insult was collected in the same dorm between white students:

> 3. *Al*: I can read 350 words a minute.
>
> *Bob*: Shit you can't even turn the pages that fast.
>
> *Al*: I turned your mother that fast.

In 1973 in my first sociolinguistic classes, white males unanimously agreed with great vehemence that any slur on their mothers' or sisters' characters would be a grave insult. The question is why did African Americans develop such a game, and why, later, did whites start to imitate it? Some have posited that the dozens were devised as a way of turning aggressions inward. They see such gaming as a result of oppression by whites. Those with a Freudian bent explained it as the need for African American youth in female-dominated homes to cut the Oedipal bond. As with glorification of pimping, put-downs for women give black males the opportunity to assert their virility. This does not explain why middle-class suburban white elementary schoolboys glory in "your mother" jokes, however; nor do these explanations elucidate why middle-class blacks from intact homes also do. Then, too, why did whites borrow ranking when they did, rather than, for instance, in 1941?

It would be comforting to mothers to be able to say that such joking is innocent enough, just a way for adolescent boys to get things off their chests, but then it would have to be explained why it isn't fathers who get ranked on, or other male relatives or friends, or any of the host of possible topics that could serve as ritual insults. In Turkey, for instance, adolescent males often insult each other ritually by creating riddles that imply that the other is homosexual. It is hard to escape the conclusion that the devaluing of mothers is part and parcel of a more general devaluing of women in our entire society.

We have already seen that ritual insulting provides two benefits to a social group: lessening of tensions and ego-boosting by besting others in competition, or at least by getting a good line or two in. It can also be used as a regulatory mechanism in conjunction with another activity. Examining such an occurrence is in itself a study in the sensitivity of language use to social needs.

ORALITY AND LITERACY

The Verbal Game and the Real One

In African American neighborhoods, games of pickup basketball are prevalent. They constitute a very important activity for the youths of the community. Since there is no referee at such games, the players have to keep score and generally regulate the game by themselves. Such a situation is potentially explosive: unsupervised boys playing a competitive game with no one to judge what is foul or out of bounds and scores kept only in the heads of individual players. Allan Baker, himself at the time a member of the basketball team, shows how the activity of sounding and general verbal gaming is used to regulate the score. The exchange below occurred during a dispute about a score in a game played in a college gym between black male college students from several Northern cities. Baker was watching, taking down the exchange under the guise of doing his homework. A dispute was started when B called a foul on A. Because pickup games are rough, fouls are not usually called. Baker says that the person who does call one can expect to be sounded on. Therefore, A says that B plays like a girl:[18]

1. *A*: Look man, you play like my sister at your best.
   B: Shit. Your sister is better than me. She can dunk on Wilt! [Chamberlain]

B's response is typical, and, for the moment, gives him the advantage, since he turns A's words back into an insult about A's sister. This exchange allows both players to shed their irritation with each other—B because he has a foul committed on him and A because the foul is, in his eyes, unjustly called. Dissipating anger by verbal exchange works because both boys understand the ritual nature of the insults. Then came the following sequence:

2. *A*: Look man, you cheatin'
   B: Your ass, I don't have to cheat-ya to beat-ya.
   A: I know we got more points than that.
   B: This ain't the welfare building, we don't give shit away here, sucker.
   A: You ain't givin' us nothin', we takin' it sucker.
   B: You ain't no damn gorilla cool.
   A: Look man, we got ten baskets.
   C: Now I know you jumped out of your tree, fool! You can't count to no fuckin' ten!
   D: Look, man, give them ten and let's get it on. Shit, we been arguin' all night. Other people wanna play.

> *B*: I ain't givin' them no ten, no way.
> *D*: OK, man! Let's start back at eight, tie score, all right?
> *A*: Hell, yea. I just ain't gonna get beat out no points.
> *B*: Man, ain't nobody tryin' to beatcha. You always cryin'.
> You got over this time, but I'm going to bust your ass.
> *A*: Sure, man, you jus' keep talkin' that Jeff Davis shit.

During a pickup game, each team keeps its own score. Although a running patter accompanies the game, whenever one team falls behind, one of its members starts insulting the opposition. The point is to con the other team into thinking the losers have more points than they do. Allan Baker comments, "This is not to say that blacks thrive on cheating, but rather that if the opportunity presents itself and debate occurs, the advantage goes to the most verbal." The technique that A uses is typical. He lures the other side into debate, thereby stalling the game. Baker points out that A sets the other side up by naming a ridiculous number of points, here ten baskets. In order to get the game going again, the opponents have to give A's team some points. Baker, sitting on the sidelines, had been keeping score. In actuality, A's had only five baskets, and B's had ten. A's ploy resulted not only in his team's getting more points but in B's giving some up! In 1992, the movie *White Men Can't Jump* opened with an analogous dispute that was resolved in the same way by the same kind of ritual insulting.

The reason that such ploys are so successful is the shared cultural behavior of the participants. They know and understand that if an insult has been given, it must be answered and that this will go on until one side can claim victory. The only way to stop the round before then is to at least partly accede to the opponent's demands. Even the team that is actually ahead knows that they will have to give a little as well. In this particular round, some of the insults are quite blunt. "You cheatin'" is a bald accusation. Baker emphasizes that because the participants are all friends, they do not become angry at such insults. Within the context of the athletic contest, the insults are taken as ritual ones. The verbal requirements of the insulting contest take precedence over the game for these players. The entire sequence can be taken as a subcategory of ranking, one used to gain an advantage in a usually nonverbal activity. Baker comments that although none of these boys were professional players, they were all what he calls "professional talkers." Also, he notes that the verbal game is as important as the basketball game in pickup games.

Because ritual insulting can go on concurrently with the game, it has a strong regulatory function. It allows disputes over scoring to be settled on another plane by utilizing the well-known rules for ritual insulting. Here we see a beautiful example of what is probably a universal phenomenon, ritual insulting, as it is adapted to a specific social situation. Verbal sparring takes the place of a referee and scorekeeper.

The apparently mundane matter of how people insult each other in a community is a highly complicated set of interrelated behaviors. They reflect general social conditions as well as the requirements of particular social situations.

CHAPTER 6

Notes

[1] See Gelb (1963) for the chronology of writing.

[2] This is clearly an arguable question, as those from educated homes may carry an especially severe load of shame because of their poor reading skills. Financially, they may not be so badly off, but finances are not the only yardstick by which to measure a disability.

[3] It has also occurred to me that the big truths of epic poetry had to be said again and again lest people forget. If they were in ordinary, straightforward language, people would soon get tired of hearing them. By putting these truths in figurative and unusual language, people are more likely to listen. Also, people are forced to interpret figurative language. This, too, aids recall. Then, too, having the enjoyment of music and chanting as part of the human baggage makes it more likely that people will want to sing, and when they do, they are reiterating the messages of songs and poetry on their own. Notice that in the toasts, the message of bravely accepting what comes one's way is reiterated, as is the message of untrustworthy officials, but they are saved from being boring by the many different ways they are encoded.

[4] In standard spelling, one does get *aardvark* and *skiing*. *Aardvark* is one of only three words spelled that way: *aardwolf* and *Aaron*. *Skiing* is a result of the fact that *ski* ends with the vowel, and the suffix *-ing* begins with it. Also, the double <ii> indicates that the vowel is pronounced twice.

[5] One of my own children, at the age of 7, asked me one day if all languages spelled the way English does. I finally figured out he was trying to find out if spelling is as universally irregular as it is in English. At the end of the discussion, he announced, "It's silly. I'm not going to learn spelling any more." This was long before the African American rebellion against conventional orthography.

[6] The *e-* prefix is here used to mean 'electronic.'

[7] This isn't so surprising, considering that Germans have borrowed American *okay* as well.

[8] Although some people rank AAVE as being nonstandard, it actually is simply an ethnic variety of speech which may be spoken by those descended from Africans who were brought to the United States as slaves. Its origins and history are quite different from those of other dialects.

[9] Younger African Americans and even somewhat older middle-class ones are largely unaware of these toasts, or, at best, recall a snatch or two from *The Signifying Monkey,* or vaguely recall Shine, the hero. In

the movie *House Party*, however, the protagonist's father plays a recording by Domitian of *The Signifying Monkey*. Fortunately, folklorists have preserved many of these toasts before they were forgotten.

10   This refers to Sterno, which is a fuel that comes in a small can. One lights it like a candle and it burns slowly. It is often seen in buffets keeping the food trays warm. It was used in the streets to warm hands and feet in cold weather.

11   Even in World War II, most blacks were relegated to janitorial and other personal service capacities. The Army camps were segregated, and blacks were given little battlefield operation. This in a war which stressed human rights as its motivation.

12   Other dialects rhyme some or all of these pairs. For instance, in my dialect, *odds* and *cards* rhyme, but not all of the other pairs here.

13   This effectively rules out "Frankie and Johnny" as being a genuine blues song, since it is temporal, recounting what seems to be an actual event.

14   "Preachin' the Blues." Recorded on *The Legendary Son House: Father of Folk Blues*. Columbia CS 9217.

15   I am very aware of the sexist meaning of *slut*. This is my coining, but a coining made while being most aware that female sexual habits are judged quite differently from male's. Jones is not responsible for this term nor for my comparison with dozens and ranking, although, as indicated, she noted the parallels with toasts.

16   This word has become part of standard English both in the United States and the United Kingdom.

17   Jack Benny was a well-known comedian and Jack Dempsey, a well-known prizefighter.

18   Note the inherent sexism in using the word *girl* for an insult. This is not confined to the African American culture.

CHAPTER 6

Exercises

1. In light of what you have learned about literate and oral cultures, evaluate such programs as President Bush's "No Child Left Behind." A Lexis-Nexis search on this topic should give you the particulars of this act. Alternatively, if your state has a unified exam for high school graduation that all students must pass, try to find how much of it depends on good literacy skills. How fair or even useful is such testing for all students? To what degree does it presuppose that a high school education should be only a preparation for college? Should all American students have college as the goal of their education? Defend your answer.

2. Examine the lyrics of a rap song of your choice. What topics and attitudes are like the verses of the toasts? What has changed?

3. Examine the structure of a selection of rap songs. Do they show evidence of strict form? In what ways are they structured like toasts, blues, or ritual insults? In what ways are they different?

4. Jarrett says that one recognizes immediately that a song does not belong to the genre of the blues if it contains references to nature. Analyze the lyrics of your favorite kind of music, and note what topics are never mentioned and/or what ones are. What are the usual topics of these songs? You may instead want to compare two groups. Country and western has a great many adherents. You could compare its forms and lyrics with rap or with another genre of music that you like.

5. Collect some ritual insults among your friends. What topics are permissible? What topics are not? That is, what insults are taken as true insults? What reactions do you find when someone gives a ritual insult to someone else? How do these differ from reactions to true insults? Some of my students say they can insult anybody on any topic and still have it seen as a ritual insult. Does this square with your experience?

6. Listen to some comic monologue on TV, audio recordings, or at a live performance and count the derogatory jokes about females. How many of these concern a female's sexual activities? What other characteristics of females are joked about? Are there similarly derogatory jokes about any other segment of society, such as all males, the Chinese, Native Americans, or fathers?

7. What kinds of boasting activities can you collect from your peers? What is permissible to boast about? Do you find any ego-boosting or tale-telling (such as the stories of the barflies discussed in this chapter), or are the boasts fantastic (like those of Craig in this chapter)? Who seems to boast? Who doesn't? How is this boasting evaluated by others in your group? What isn't it permissible to boast about? To what degree does the locale or social situation determine the degree to which boasting is positively valued?

Chapter 7

Everybody Speaks a Dialect

Every variety of a language is a dialect, even the standard. There is no sharp dividing line between dialects and languages, although considering a speech variety a separate language rather than a dialect can have important political and social consequences. The identity one projects is bound up with one's speech; hence people are concerned with using language properly. Unfortunately, too often those who set themselves up as experts rely on their own personal prejudices more than on scientific studies of how people actually react to various speech forms. Consequently, there is variation in agreement among the experts. The original dialect studies were focused on creating linguistic geographies, finding out how people of each region spoke. Americans increasingly want to sound as if they don't have a regional accent, but there is no General American. There is a great variety in regional and ethnic accents. People use ethnic accents to reaffirm their identity. Dialects differ in their lexicon, syntax, and pronunciation, but all are equally rule-governed. People often misinterpret what speakers of other dialects actually mean. Despite the onslaught of the media, regional, social, and ethnic dialect differences remain strong in America, although educated speakers are sounding more and more alike, at least when they are speaking carefully. In order to render the actual pronunciations used in speech, it is necessary to use the symbols of the International Phonetic Alphabet (**IPA**). This is because, in ordinary spelling, the same letter can stand for more than one sound and two letters may stand for the same sound. Therefore, it is necessary as you read this to refer to the Appendix, which lays out the requisite symbols and the sounds they represent.

LANGUAGE VERSUS DIALECT

Dialect is the technical term for what Americans usually think of as an accent. Strictly speaking, *accent* refers only to differences in pronunciation between one variety of a language and another. *Dialect* refers to all the differences between varieties of a language, those in pronunciation, word usage, and syntax. Often, as indicated in Chapters 3 and 4, there are paralinguistic differences between dialects: timbre, tempo, and the like, as well as kinesic differences. These are usually ignored in traditional dialect studies, but that does not mean they are unimportant. To the contrary, they are often vital in rendering a dialect and in perceiving it. However, only the linguistic differences—the phonology, lexicon, and syntax—will be considered in this chapter. In themselves, they are complex, and analyzing them serves to illustrate the important points about dialects and how and why they are used in social groups.

No sharp demarcation exists between language and dialect. As a rule of thumb, if two varieties of speech are mutually intelligible, they are considered dialects. If they are not, they are considered separate languages. In actual practice, the situation is far more complicated. There are dialects of one language which are not mutually comprehensible and separate languages that are. The fact that we can't establish an airtight difference between dialect and language might seem a bit of the usual academic nitpicking about definitions, but anything dealing with language has consequences for speakers.

For instance, Geneva Smitherman (1984, 2000) as an expert witness in a class action suit against the city of Ann Arbor, Michigan, argued that African American Vernacular English (**AAVE**) is a separate language, not merely a dialect of English, and that schools must take this into account in educating African American students. The Equal Educational Opportunity Act decrees that states must not "fail to overcome language barriers that impede equal participation by its students in its instructional programs." The judge ruled that AAVE, being a dialect, did not count as a language barrier, so that children who speak it are not being denied educational opportunity by a system which doesn't recognize it. Smitherman contends that AAVE should be considered a separate language on the grounds of structural and sociolinguistic differences between it and other varieties of English. She argues that the schools should have to adjust their methods to AAVE speakers as they supposedly do for speakers of other languages like Spanish or Portuguese.

Smitherman (1984, 103), claims that, often, when people think they understand another's dialect, they are misunderstanding it. For instance, non-African Americans misunderstood Muhammad Ali's assertion:

> There are two bad white men in the world. The Russian white man and the American white man. They are the two baddest men in the history of the world.

Smitherman points out that *bad* in the Websterian tradition means 'evil, wicked' but in AAVE it means 'powerful, omnipotent, spiritually or physically tough, outstanding, wonderful, and with emphasis, very good.'

The problem with her contention that AAVE should be considered a separate language is that all dialects have structural differences from each other, even standard ones. Yet, we wouldn't consider Los Angeles English a different language from Boston English because of their differences. A teacher from Los Angeles wouldn't dream of teaching Bostonian fifth graders as if they spoke another language. Part of belonging to a language group is adapting to the vagaries of the different accents that it is composed of. Yes, teachers should be aware of AAVE and how it's structured, but AAVE speakers also have to handle what's said in another American dialect. There is no solid evidence that I've been able to find that AAVE speakers can't do that. They may not choose to speak a standard variety (hereafter SE), but they do understand it. I believe it is wrong to label AAVE as a nonstandard dialect because it is primarily an ethnic one used for social bonding. It is important to realize that AAVE is a full-fledged language with its own rules of grammar, as are all dialects. Dialects are not deficient, nor do they represent a falling away from the standard.

Comprehension Difficulties across Dialects

Consider the following utterances from the American Midland, a collection of dialects which extend from parts of Pennsylvania westward through portions of other states, culminating in a wedge in South Dakota on its northern boundary, and through Oklahoma to upper Texas on the southern one (Ash 2006, 35):

1. I need to talk to John or Malcolm one.
            (Montgomery 2006, 152).
2. That's all the fast it can fly.
3. That's all the faster he can run.
4. That's all the farther I've read.
5. That's all the coat he has.
6. The baby likes cuddled.
7. We always use coupons anymore when we shop.
8. What all were you expecting to see today?
9. Whenever I first heard the news, I about fell over.
10. You'ns are welcome.
            (Murray and Simon 2006b, 15–16)

If you don't come from the parts of the states that comprise this dialect, or even if you do, you may not quite understand all of these sentences, or you may think you understand them but are getting the wrong nuances.

It is important to realize that these sentences are not mistakes. They are not a random collection of funny sentences or grammatical errors. In the dialects in which they are spoken, they follow specific grammatical rules and are used only in the circumstances that allow such sentences to be formed. They fit in their dialects. As we shall see, different dialects have different grammars, and what we think of as "proper" grammar belongs to one kind of speech, that which is taught in schools as being "correct." However, all dialects, like all languages, have their own rules, and these rules are systematic, not random. Some of the sentences in 1–10 are spoken by educated standard speakers, and others are spoken by working-class or uneducated ones, but all are evidence of different grammar rules.

Although such sentences taken together are indicative of the Midland dialect area, not all of the cities and towns there share all of them. That is, 1, for instance, might not occur in Pittsburgh, but might be understood in southern Illinois.[1] St. Louis, which is geographically right in the Midland area, has only three features of that general dialect, although other cities and towns have more. Some Midland features are found elsewhere. Using *one* as in 1 above also occurs in parts of the South. Someone from the Smoky Mountains would understand it with no problem.

If you come from New England, North Dakota, Oregon, California, or many other states, even though you're a native speaker of American English, at least some of 1–10 might not only sound weird to you, it may not be comprehensible. However, there may well be constructions you use unthinkingly that other Americans would have similar problems with. Of course, if you come from a Midland city that uses any or all of the above grammatical forms, you're wondering what I find so different.

When I first read sentence 1, I had no idea what *one* could possibly mean in that context, "John or Malcolm one." Montgomery not only explains it, he shows the probable historical development of the construction. When he did so, it made perfectly good sense. After all, I do say, "I need to talk to John and Malcolm both." That's similar to using *one* after the nouns to indicate 'either.'

I had more problems with 2–6, as they translate very differently in my dialect. 2 seems to mean 'as fast as it can fly,' and 5 probably means 'the only coat he has.' Neither would have an *all* in such sentences in my speech. 3 and 4 pose the biggest problem for me. I don't have a handy equivalent at all for those comparatives. Does 3 mean 'he can run no faster' and 4 'I've read no farther'? In my dialect, neither sentence can start with "That's all the. . . ."

The point is that dialects can vary widely in the syntactic rules they have and, sometimes, even in these days of mass communication, speakers of a language may have problems with some parts of a dialect they're not familiar with. However, that doesn't mean we speak different languages. We just have to tweak our own dialects a bit. Midland speakers don't have to be taught as if they speak another language, nor do speakers from other dialect areas.

In the main, we understand each other, and when we don't, we can always negotiate the meanings. There are sentences in virtually every dialect that speakers of other dialects might not understand. I've selected the Midland ones because I've just been reading a wonderful book about that cluster of dialects: Thomas Murray and Beth Lee Simon's *Language Variation and Change in the American Midland.* There are hundreds of dialects of American English, more than we can even begin to discuss here, and many which have been only barely studied.

Language versus Dialect

There is no dividing line between language and dialect. The rule of thumb is that if two varieties of a language can be mutually understood by their speakers, they are dialects. If they cannot be understood, then they are two languages. However, as so often in language, there are fuzzy boundaries between these categories.

In Barbados, as elsewhere in the Caribbean, one dialect of English spoken primarily by blacks is called "talking bad" or "speaking broken" (Abrahams 1972; Chaika 1982b, 93–94). American and British visitors usually can't understand it at all, although they have no problem with standard Barbados English. However, natives to whom I have spoken, black and white, say that "bad talk" just sounds like another kind of English to them.

It is not only English that has such instances. In Italy, for instance, bordering dialects are mutually comprehensible, but those farther apart become increasingly less comprehensible, so speakers of rural dialects from the south of Italy often couldn't be understood by those from the north. Rodney Delasanta, a native speaker of a northern dialect of Italian, says he could not understand bus drivers in Naples, even though he only asked for directions. His parents, one from the eastern border of Italy and the other from the western, could not understand each other's native dialect.

Political boundaries, in themselves, often determine whether two speech varieties will be considered different languages. For instance, some varieties of Swedish, Norwegian, and Danish are mutually comprehensible, but they are considered different languages because they are separated by national borders. To show just how similar these are, Yvonne Sandstroem, a native speaker of Swedish, remarked to me that Scandinavian Airlines hires stewards and stewardesses from all three countries. They all make announcements in their own native tongue and do not have to translate for the other Scandinavians on board.

Conversely, the so-called dialects of Chinese are as different as French from Italian, but because of national and ethnic feelings, they are not considered separate languages. Sometimes ethnic and social factors determine whether two varieties of speech are considered separate languages. A Norwegian scholar once complained to me that when Norwegian speakers appear on Swedish television, subtitles are used, but in Norway they are not used when Swedes are on Norwegian television. To say the least, the Swedes annoyed him. It's like saying that Norwegian isn't "good enough" to be considered mutually comprehensible with Swedish, although, in fact, it is.

A similar situation can occur across generations. The Yiddish[2] dialects that were spoken by Jews of Eastern Europe are mutually comprehensible with many varieties of modern German. Both Germans and Jews regard Yiddish and German as separate languages, however. This is a direct reflection of the separate religious and cultural affinities of Yiddish and German speakers. Older Germans of my acquaintance, those who lived through World War II, tell me that when they hear Yiddish spoken, they can't understand it at all. However, younger ones, those born after the war, whom I met at a summer German program, told me that, when they heard it spoken on Miami Beach, they understood it just as if it were German or English. In other words, whether a variety of a language is understood can be a result of attitude as much as similarity of language.

In Africa, the Kalabari are a powerful and important people, but the Nembe who speak a closely related language are not. There seems to be no linguistic reason for the two speech varieties not to be mutually comprehensible. Yet the Kalabari claim that they do not understand the Nembe, and all communication between the two must be in Kalabari or Pidgin English.

A similar situation with dialects occurs in the United States. In public schools, standard-speaking teachers confronted with nonstandard-speaking youngsters often claim difficulty in understanding them. The teachers complain that the students' speech is deficient or broken. However, it has been shown time and again that dialects perceived as nonstandard are as systematically rule-governed as standard ones. Standard speakers don't perceive this because of their attitudes toward those who speak the nonstandard.

Another example of the fuzzy border between language and dialect is given by Trudgill (1983a, 57–58). Although we consider a change in pronunciation to be confined to a language, spreading from one dialect to others, Trudgill shows how a dialect feature, the uvular /r/,[3] has spread across national boundaries since its origin, supposedly in Paris in the seventeenth century. It hit Copenhagen by 1780, and has spread to Germany and even northwest Italy (56). What one would normally think of as spreading of a dialect feature has spread from one language to another.

The Development of Standard Dialects

Many languages today have one dialect spoken throughout their countries. Although these dialects may have arisen as regional ones, they transcend region by now. One reason for the emergence of such dialects is the need for a speech variety that all people ruled by one national government can understand. As this need has grown in modern technological societies, the development of national standards has become widespread. Fairclough (1989) claims that a standard dialect is also a means of a certain class, those who have mastered it, to maintain power as well as to be gatekeepers, declining to admit nonstandard speakers to those positions that lead to power.

As we shall see, however, this is not necessarily true today, at least in some countries. That is, nonstandard dialects may have a covert prestige and be better for use in some circumstances and for some purposes than the standard is. We will consider this later.

The standard dialect can be understood by just about everyone in a modern nation. Because it is based upon the speech of the educated, which in most countries concurs most closely with the written language (or perhaps most accurately, the written system is made to coincide with the standard), people often assume that the standard is the "true" language, not realizing that it, too, is a dialect. Many people think that dialects refer to substandard, even defective, speech. The French dismiss such dialects as *patois*, implying that these are not real languages, but they are.

British Caribbeans who speak Creole refer to their speech as "patwa." Creoles, which have their origin in the mixture of two languages, are often considered some sort of bastard concoction, but they are full languages. Some major modern languages derived from Creoles. There is evidence, for instance, that Proto-Germanic, the language that gave rise to modern German, English, Dutch, and the Scandinavian languages, was a Creole formed from a native language and an early Indo-European[4] one.

Any variety of a language is technically a dialect, even the educated standard. Everyone speaks a dialect. Everyone has an accent, except perhaps in those languages with so few speakers that there are no varieties at all. The dialect that becomes standard is an accident of history. It has nothing to do with intrinsic worth of the standard. All dialects are inherently equal, just as all languages are, although they aren't socially equal. Some dialects command more respect and power in some situations than others do.

CHAPTER 7

A British scholar might deliver a scientific paper in British received pronunciation, spoken by the educated, but not in Cockney, although that might be better in a brawl. A Brooklyn accent does not seem appropriate for lecturing college classes, but it could be very convincing if one were running for political office in a working-class neighborhood. Television commercials often gear the speech variety to the product being sold: Shake and Bake and a Southern accent; Poland Springs water and a Maine accent; barbecue sauce and a Texas accent. The accent suitable for a given purpose is related to the generally held image of people who speak that way. Typically, at least in modern America and Europe, nonstandard dialects are perceived as tougher and more masculine than upper-class ones. Often dialects are as stereotyped as the people themselves.

Frequently, because we associate certain kinds of speech with activities, a dialect will take on a vocabulary especially efficient for those activities. Hence, educated dialects have developed a tremendous number of scientific and other learned words. These differ from jargon only in that they are used by more diverse groups in broader social situations. Other dialects could as easily include the same words, but they do not because they are not used for the purposes that demand the particular expression.

Nonstandard speech is as intelligent and complete as standard. Effective education and politics depend upon such understanding. This does not mean that I or linguists in general think that in speech anything and everything is all right. Even if one recognizes that all dialects are equally complete for their users' purposes, one can still recognize that educated dialects are necessary for many kinds of social functioning. James Sledd once forcefully condemned attempts to teach standard varieties of American English in school as "the linguistics of White supremacy." In my opinion, such a view ignores the functions of dialect and the realities of social interaction.

It is necessary for students to be able to command educated varieties of speech if they wish to be able to hold certain kinds of jobs, but not others. A car mechanic, a house painter, a plasterer, or an electrician don't need or perhaps don't want to speak a standard. Any attempt to teach a standard dialect to a nonstandard speaker must take into account why people speak as they do. It must also take into account why there are different dialects of a language in the first place and what conditions favor dialect learning.

Proper Speech. A good measure of the importance of speech variety is the anxiety it evokes. In the United States, because there is no one acknowledged standard as there is in countries like England, Italy, and France, the anxiety at times almost borders on hysteria. Proper speech is pursued with what can only be called religious fervor. Witness this advertisement for

Fowler's *Modern English Usage*: "The most practiced writer will only too often find himself convicted of sin when he dips into Fowler." Clifton Fadiman, a respected scholar, author, and editor, wrote of Fowler that "it is the final arbiter of our language" and "it shows me how bad a writer I am, and encourages me to do better." The equation of grammar choice with sin, with being bad, makes it appear that *Modern English Usage* is on a par with the Old Testament. New Testament status has to be reserved for Nicholson's *American English Usage*, which is based upon Fowler's.

For most Americans, however, the dictionary is the final arbiter of correctness. Fowler and Nicholson are reserved for the select few whose sins are too subtle for *Webster's*. In 1961, *Webster's Third* unabridged edition innovated. Rather than acting as prescriber of "correct" usage and condemning "substandard" usage, it just listed how words are actually pronounced and used in American English. It lacked convenient labels like "vulgar," "preferred," and "slang." Dr. Max Rafferty, then superintendent of schools for the State of California, said:

> If a dictionary doesn't exist to set standards and maintain them,
> what possible use can it have? . . . when I go to a dictionary I want
> to know what's right. I already know what folks are saying. What
> I want to know is what they *should be saying* [emphasis mine].
> (Pyles 1972, 167)

The intensity of concern about proper language forms is startling. One would think that any form short of profanity is proper so long as it's comprehensible. Why can an advertisement promising to convict writers of sin sell a book? The ad for Fowler's reads like a call to that old-time religion, not a reference book. Why should an exceptionally literate writer feel that Fowler had the right and competence to show him that he is bad? That word *bad* in itself in the context that Fadiman uses it has a strangely moralistic ring. Dr. Rafferty, an outspoken man, was certainly not one to be swayed by mere public opinion. Why, then, was he willing to take the decision about his use of words from a dictionary? The answers to these questions are found when we consider the role of dialects in social functioning.

Over the years, many have warned, wailed, and predicted direly that the language is decaying. No matter that people are understanding each other with perfect ease, and no matter that there is no evidence at any time in history that a language can decay so that speakers no longer can understand each other. John Simons and Edwin Newman, neither of whom are scholars, have had great success castigating the educated for their writing. The fans of their books, *Paradigms Lost* and *Strictly Speaking*, respectively, object, "But they're trying to save the language from decay."

CHAPTER 7

In fact, John Simons claimed on the 2005 PBS program, *Do You Speak American?*, that the language has become so debased that he fears it can never be fixed. On the same PBS broadcast, he called linguists (like me) "a curse upon the race." Apparently, he feels this way because linguists explain language change, and don't condemn it. Therefore, linguists, in his view, are causing the decay of English.

Even if linguists did condemn certain usages, what effect could they conceivably have on others? By what authority could they stop language change? Generations of teachers have tried to rid students' usage of "seen" for *saw*, and "ain't got no" instead of *haven't got any*, with no luck. And they have the power to grade. What power could linguists exert? Make nonstandard usages a felony? Call in the police when they hear someone say "I wish I coulda saw dat."

Often such self-appointed arbiters of language have very little understanding of how English or any other language really works. For instance, one can find commentators railing that English is in a state of decay because it "confuses" nouns and verbs. That is, nouns are being used as verbs and vice versa. Jean Safford, a Pulitzer Prize winner, excoriated a writer for "Her hair *haloed* her head."

The problem with her reasoning is that English has always done this. Surely even the most careful writers use words like *love, group, kill, hunt*, even *man* or *police* both as nouns and verbs, and for that matter, as adjectives. The practice is not confined to English. Most and probably all languages allow words to cross part-of-speech boundaries in some way. If a language did not allow slipping across boundaries, many of the meanings one wished to convey would need at least two distinct roots: one for a noun, another for a verb. It is much more economical to use the same root as a noun, a verb, and an adjective simply by changing the grammatical signal slightly. This may be done by changing suffixes, prefixes, or other syntax markers such as sentence position or putting *the* before a noun. To give an English example, there is no confusion in interpretation of *love* or *group* in any of the following:

> The *love* I had for him is gone. (noun)
> I *love* candy. (verb)
> That was quite a *love* tap. (adjective)
> That's a good *group*. (noun)
> Let's *group* them this way. (verb)
> It's a *group* project. (adjective)

Great poets often demonstrate their artistry by using old words in new ways, helping us to make new connections by just such violations of part-of-speech boundaries. Think of Shakespeare's "But me no buts" or Dylan Thomas's "the cargoed apples" or "the sweethearting cribs."

It does make sense to suppose that changes in the language could lead to its decay, except that all language is always in a state of change. That is what makes it such a delicate social instrument. In the past 1,000 years, English has changed so that its earliest writings have to be studied as if they were written in a foreign language. At no one time in these thousand years has such natural change led to a breakdown in communicability, at least among those living in the same regions. Someone who does not understand a new coinage can always ask the speaker who uttered it to paraphrase it. It takes centuries of change before incomprehensibility sets in.

Many historians of the language have taken special delight in poking fun at the preachers of the doctrine of correctness and their followers. This is easy to do, especially since many of the supposed sins of language are among the oldest forms in English and have been found in the best of English writers: Chaucer, Milton, Shakespeare. Worse, there is no justification in the history of the language for many of the rules prescribed by those who would save our speech. They were made up out of whole cloth by self-styled educators like Bishop Robert Lowth in the eighteenth century or self-appointed experts who have never examined language objectively. Such criticism of the purists misses the mark, though, for historical justification has nothing to do with what should or should not be considered correct. Sometimes a new usage comes into play to mark out those in the know or those of elevated status.

Neither, apparently, does it make much difference who is telling us what is or is not all right. Who was Fowler that he could condemn speakers of verbal "sin"? Who are writers of dictionaries? Why are they privy to divine revelation denied the rest of us? Scholars like Thomas Pyles, W. Nelson Francis, and Elizabeth Traugott, who are authorities on the history of English, are far less likely to be heeded than prophets like Fowler, Nicholson, Safford, or Newman. Who ever asks the qualifications of an arbiter of language?

What is perhaps most puzzling of all is that people who unquestioningly accept the authority of such arbiters are often precisely those who have been the best trained in questioning what they read, examining all arguments for flaws, or accepting nothing without empirical proof. All this training flees when they hear a lecturer or a writer criticize middle-class usage, prophesying doom and decay. Even the best-educated leap into the lap of the saviors of language. It is they who equate language with sin, who want to be told how to talk, who seek some authority to tell them what is correct, and, even better, what is incorrect. Others may not notice if you use phrases correctly, but they will notice if you do not. For an educated person publicly to commit a grammar error is profoundly humiliating, like being caught slobbering over food.

Since those who delve into dictionaries, flock to Fowler, and kneel to Newman are clearly among the best and brightest, they cannot be dismissed as unintelligent. For that matter, both Newman and Safford, like most who plead for correct speech, are highly intelligent, perceptive, and literate. Newman is correct, I think, in his judgments about the clumsiness of academic and government writers, but this is not necessarily indicative of mind mold. Language is patently an emotional issue, not wholly an intellectual one. As we shall see, the concern with keeping language pristine, if in fact it ever was pristine, stems from social and psychological needs. More is at stake in the forms of the language one uses than communicating per se.

Standard vs. Nonstandard Speech. Dialect studies show that how one speaks is inextricably bound up with one's identity. Who one is, how one may be treated, and how one may treat others are all proclaimed in one's speech. In earlier times, in stable societies, people in a community knew one another and knew where everyone belonged on the social scale. Where there is little social mobility all one needs to know to assess another's social rank is what family the person belongs to. In many cultures, there are other indicators as well: clothing, hairstyles, jewelry, dwelling place, and the make of one's automobile. Today in the United States, none of these is exclusive to any one social class. The son of a janitor might be a college president. A high school dropout may drive a Mercedes and be loaded with bling-bling. A wealthy contractor with little formal education may own a home next door to a high-ranking business executive with two master's degrees. Even occupation fails as a guide. Your local woodcarver might hold a Ph.D., and the driver of your cab might be an expert on Jane Austen. Nowadays, rich or poor, lawyer, doctor, plumber, or ditch digger all wear the same sorts of clothes, style their hair the same ways, and even wear the same expensive watches. The differences between individuals have less to do with money than with other attitudes, such as identifying with punks, gangstas, or preppies. Because of the homogeneity of other aspects of culture, speech is likely to be the most reliable determiner of social class or ethnic group.

This is a matter of great concern to the educated middle class, which above all wishes to be identified as educated. The recognition of its members as those to be listened to hinges strongly on language. When people say they want to know the right way to speak, they do not mean the right way to communicate their ideas but, rather, the right way to announce that those ideas are to be respected. To some degree, perhaps, people who fear innovation and change in language may really fear that they will no longer know the rules. That is not as petty as it may sound. Not to know social rules is a serious business to eminently social creatures such as human beings.

When we speak of talking "properly," we are not talking about some objective standard that can be shown to be superior to any other. Rather, what is considered proper is quite arbitrary and depends on who is speaking, the history of a region, and many other accidental and historical facts. Still, unlike many linguists, I do not put *properly* in between quotations, because in terms of social class, speaking properly is exceedingly important for certain people. Certainly, I wouldn't be credible if I didn't speak properly.

The rebels among us might ask, isn't it irrational to dread not speaking right or being caught in a solecism? Using incorrect—that is, nonstandard —forms can have consequences that strike right at the heart of middle-class privilege. One field method used to test this out has been the matched guise technique, in which a speaker who commands both the standard and a nonstandard dialect equally well records the same speech in each of his or her guises. For instance, in Great Britain, Bourhis (cited in Giles and Powesland 1975, 104) had an announcement made over a loud-speaker in a theater asking patrons to fill out a survey questionnaire. On successive nights, the announcement alternated between a nonstandard dialect and **received pronunciation** (RP), the upper-class educated dialect of British English. On the nights that RP was used, more people filled out the forms, and they wrote longer answers. It had already been established that people will write at greater length at the request of someone whose accent they admire (Giles, Baker, and Fielding 1975). By having the same speaker in both instances, the investigators were assured that it was dialect that people were responding to, not voice quality.

Crowl and MacGinitie (mentioned in Giles et al. 1975, 91) had six white and six black[5] speakers read identical answers to two questions. The blacks spoke in AAVE. The whites spoke one of the educated standard American dialects, SE.[6] Although exactly the same answers were read, the judges consistently rated the SE answers as better. In this study, judgments were on race, not just social class.

It is not what is said but how it is said that counts. Intuitively you probably knew that. Imagine a philosophy professor lecturing, "To tell you da trut' da problem of good 'n evil ain't gone away" as opposed to, "A consideration of the problem of good and evil entails a realization that definitive answers may well be impossible." Although both statements mean the same thing, the second one sounds more authoritative, even more intelligent. Notice that the nonstandard utterance is just as intelligent as the standard one, but listeners are more likely to rate the second as sounding more intelligent than the first. One can be brilliant and say brilliant things in nonstandard dialects, but whether or not people will take one seriously in intellectual matters is another matter.

Speech variety may also influence how willing people are to help. Gaertner and Bickman (1971) had both African American and white callers telephone 540 African American and white subjects, pretending to get the wrong number. Callers told each subject that they were stranded and had used their last dime. Then they requested that the subject call another number to send help. At this number there was a confederate of the caller who recorded which subjects had responded to the caller's request for aid. African American subjects helped African American and white callers equally. Whites helped blacks less frequently than they helped whites. This, of course, might also be explained on the basis of racial prejudice; however, it does show that the dialect used does in and of itself affect how others treat you.

Giles, Baker, and Fielding (1975) developed an experiment to test the effect of nonstandard English that did not entail racial differences. Theirs was based upon SE in its British RP form and the nonstandard dialect of Birmingham, England. They used a matched guise technique, so that a male speaker who was equally proficient in both dialects addressed two groups of high school students. The students had to write letters of recommendation stating their opinion of this speaker as a suitable candidate to lecture high school students about the nature of university studies. The students also had to evaluate him on traditional rating scales. Giles et al. based this experiment on earlier findings that subjects write longer letters about someone they like than about someone they don't like. Also, it had previously been demonstrated that subjects speak more when they are conversing with someone they like.

Giles et al. figured that if more students wrote letters for the fake candidate and wrote longer opinions when he was speaking in one guise than in the other, that would constitute proof that the dialect alone caused him to be rated differently. What happened was that the high school students to whom the speaker had used SE wrote a whopping 82% more about him than those who heard him speak nonstandarly. Finally, 13 out of 18 found him "well-spoken" when he spoke as a standard speaker, but only 2 out of 28 who heard him speak nonstandardly described him that way.

It must be emphasized that the task in the experiment by Giles et al. is one in which standard speech is considered suitable. One expects educated speech from a man lecturing students about preparation for the university. Nonstandard speakers are typically judged higher than SE speakers on some traits, such as being humorous, hard working, sincere, and more trustworthy in a fight (Lambert, Giles, and Picard, 1975).

Dialect and Identity

Bernstein (1971) points out that the selection of an nonstandard dialect is a way of indicating bonding, but SE exhibits status. Subsequent research has proven him correct. There is strong evidence that the "in" group of African American urban youth prefer those who speak AAVE. Those who don't used to be called "lames," and were treated like outsiders (Labov 1972a). Whether or not the label *lame* is still prevalent, it is still true that African Americans have to command AAVE if they want to be regarded as a homie or a dawg, a true member of the African American community.

However, this speech variety is no longer limited to African Americans. It is used by Chicano youth in Los Angeles and white youth all over the United States. What is most interesting is its adoption by upper-class white youth. My own students, who are attending an almost all-white school, claim that they speak AAVE all the time when they are out of the classroom. In fact, one of my classes criticized me for labeling that variety of speech on the grounds that there isn't a distinctive AAVE because "everybody" speaks that way at times. When I showed them certain features of AAVE that they didn't know to use, such as its verb system (as shown below), they were chagrined. And here they thought they could speak just like African Americans because they had learned a few expressions!

In Britain, Hewitt (cited in Cutler 1999, 429) showed that some white teens pass through a phase of allying themselves culturally with blacks. Cutler (1999) gives a case history of Mike, an upper-class white teen who attended exclusive private schools in New York City. At around age thirteen, he started to identify strongly with hip-hop culture, wearing baggy pants, a reverse baseball cap, and designer sneakers, as well as listening to rap music. He also joined a street gang, a white one, and engaged in street fighting and creating graffiti. He was not unique. Cutler says he belonged to a group of white, well-to-do teenagers called "prep school gangsters." He also changed the way he spoke. For instance, he repaired his pronunciation of *ask* when speaking to a friend, saying:

I gotta ask, I mean **aks** my mom

This pronunciation is identified with AAVE (although it does occur in some white dialects, such as some Appalachian ones). He also prefaced statements with "yo" and liberally spiked his speech with AAVE forms like *phat*.

CHAPTER 7

Like my students, Mike's adoption of AAVE is largely phonological with a sprinkling of AAVE lexical items. Cutler (431) cites research which shows that people can imitate these features of other dialects, but do not, as a rule, pick up on the grammatical differences between them. For instance, he didn't omit a form of *be* where AAVE does (shown below).

Although *r*-dropping has been a nonprestige feature in New York City speech since at least the 1950's, and Mike grew up pronouncing that sound wherever it is spelled, as did his parents, he frequently did drop the /r/ at the end of a word. What is interesting about this is that white /r/-droppers do pronounce that /r/ as in *four o'clock.* So, Mike's *r*-dropping aligned his speech with AAVE, not nonstandard white speech. Other nonstandard pronunciations adopted by Mike were "duh" for *the* and "wit" for *with.* Substituting /t/ and /d/ for the two <th> sounds occurs in all varieties of nonstandard English and AAVE. Mike also left out some vowels and lengthened others in line with AAVE prosody, so that *suppose* was said as "spo:z" with the vowel held longer than in SE.

It must be emphasized that many white youth who adopt hip-hop styles and AAVE have very little direct contact with African Americans. They pick it up from movies, TV, the Internet, and rap music, of course:

> Rap music videos have animated hip-hop cultural style . . . cross neighborhood [and] cross-country . . . Rap fans can consult lyric sheets in CD cases allowing them to learn the latest expressions coming out of New York City and Los Angeles . . . the words and expressions from these have become incorporated in the speech of teenagers across the entire country. (434)

There are also several websites which have dictionaries of hip-hop and sites which provide rap lyrics. Actually, my experience is that hip-hop lingo remains a part of the male verbal repertoire throughout college, at least, although African American styles in dress and headgear may be abandoned or used only on certain occasions. At what point hip-hop speech is dropped, or if it is dropped completely, we don't know yet. Certainly, some terms have passed into SE. Everybody *disses*, loves (or hates) *bling-bling*, thinks something is *mad cool*, and admires something as *phat*, not to mention apologizing with *my bad* or describing a girl as a *bomb bitch.* I've even heard British RP speakers use the verb *dis* and the noun *bling.* It seems to me that the reason some AAVE terms have been mainstreamed is that they are associated with youth, and even middle-aged speakers want to be identified as being young in mind, not stuffy oldsters. An analogous situation is manifested with surfer talk in Los Angeles, so that businessmen still use surfer terms they learned as teens. Now in America, it seems as if AAVE is a major force in language change, but, as we shall see, it's not the only one.

With hip-hop, however, AAVE speakers actually resent what they see as privileged whites as co-opting their culture without having the history of slavery and poverty that it evolved from. Cutler remarks that Mike and his friends "demand the erasure of differences in race and class history and position" (436). She quotes a conversation in which he and his friends expressed anger at African Americans who keep themselves completely separate from whites and who emphasize their African American identity as much as possible. Mike cited *Def Comedy Jam*'s cracking on whites. Cutler (435) points out that whites "feel they have the right to appropriate the hip-hop look and language, and that black adolescents who oppose them are racists." To be sure, these "wiggas" or "white niggas," as Smitherman (1994, 168) calls them, see that their coming from an affluent stratum of society invalidates their claim to be part of hip-hop. Consequently, they lie about the schools they go to, use addresses of friends or relatives who don't live in an obvious upper-class neighborhood, and otherwise pretend to a poverty they've never had.

Why do members of hip-hop culture resent whites' copying them? African Americans feel separate from whites. Their history and culture is unshared by even poor whites. Whites can't possibly know what it feels like to be black, to be visibly "the other" as soon as people see them. That is, whatever whites are or whatever their history, it doesn't mark them out visibly. Swapping tales of oppression with an African American one day, I was told, "Look, if your ancestors didn't want to be persecuted, all they had to do was to become baptized. And if you didn't want people to know you're Jewish, all you had to do is pretend you're not, but me, I can't deny being black. I can't do anything to stop being black." African Americans are not necessarily being racist when they resent white co-optioning of their culture. They are just asserting their difference as a group, a group which has been demeaned, used, and abused. Whites enjoyed being entertained by them, but historically stole their music from them. For years, white artists playing for white audiences simply took the songs of African American singers and writers without paying them any royalties. Also, white historians and other scholars have seldom given African Americans credit for their accomplishments. In other words, whites have always been willing to co-opt African American culture without compensation for it.

AAVE and hip-hop are ways of African Americans bonding with each other, as well as of showing identity with their forebears who suffered so much. Rap is also used to voice African American complaints against white society. The "wiggas" aren't offering to ameliorate the plight of African Americans. They're not donating time or money to African American concerns like terrible housing or lack of money to go to the kinds of schools that Mike and his friends go to. All they've done is co-opt the exterior: the dress, the lingo. So, as fast as white youth pick up on the latest hip-hop, rappers make up new terms to remain different.

Why do privileged youth want to be part of a culture which has historically suffered greatly? Well, AAVE is associated with being tough and being survivors. Also, as an examination of rap lyrics show, hip-hop is very masculine-oriented. It puts down women, calling them bitches and ho's. It glorifies pimping, an exploitation of women. It also is associated with great sexuality. Teenage boys are often very insecure with girls, and very unsure of their own sexuality. Therefore, they copy a group which seems to be very sure of its sexuality, as well as its masculinity.

AAVE can be considered an ethnic dialect, as it marks its speakers as belonging to a specific cultural group with a specific history in the American experience. However, regional nonstandard dialects also have survived the massive onslaught of the media and the general mobility of people from one region to another in the United States, although they have changed in some respects, not necessarily towards SE, however. It is clear, then, that nonstandard dialects have a value for their speakers. Furthermore, the very fact that SE speakers adopt nonstandard forms from time to time suggests that even they value them positively for some purposes.

TRADITIONAL REGIONAL DIALECT STUDIES

So far, we have seen that the way one speaks affects how one is treated and is also tied up with the image one seeks to project. In Chapter 9, "Speech Communities," we will show how finely grained dialect studies of a locale reveal social divisions more accurately than any other single sociological study. However, dialects are not wholly social. They are regional as well. In fact, the oldest dialect studies were linguistic atlases. That is, field workers elicited pronunciations and words for certain things from informants within communities. The workers then mapped where certain pronunciations and words were used, drawing lines known as **isoglosses**[7] between areas where an item changed. There is almost always room for disagreement about the exact location of each isogloss, but these are usually not large. What is perhaps more disputable is deciding which items should be counted as indicating a different dialect region, as we shall see below. The first published atlas study in the United States was *The Linguistic Atlas of New England*, known as *LANE*. The plan was to extend this eventually to the rest of the country. Hans Kurath and Brown University began their first atlas investigations in the early 1930's, but the complete atlas mapping of North America was not published until 2006. Then it was done by different scholars under different auspices.

Since every pronunciation and every dialectal word did not coincide within one boundary, the maps produced for atlas studies had bundles of isoglosses. That is, each word and each pronunciation had its own isogloss. Within a dialect area, the isoglosses were close, but still had different boundaries. A group of these isoglosses was called a bundle. At the outermost limits of these bundles, a major dialect area was drawn.

As examples of how isoglosses differ in a dialect area, we can consider two pronunciations. In New England, west of the Connecticut River, /r/'s were (and are) pronounced wherever they are spelled, but east of it, /r/'s were dropped before consonants. Consequently, the isogloss for *r*-dropping includes Rhode Island, eastern Massachusetts, and points northward up to Maine. As of now, this is a recessive feature in all of these areas. That is, more and more people are becoming *r*-full there, but in Kurath's study, it mirrored a real distinction in New England dialects. On the basis of this feature, Kurath divided New England into two dialect areas, Eastern New England (ENE) and Western New England (WNE).

However, from Boston to the north, the words *cot* and *caught* are pronounced alike, but in both Rhode Island, which is solidly ENE, and in WNE, they are pronounced differently, so that /ɑ/ "ah" is used in *cot* and an /ɔ/ "aw" is heard in *caught* (Boberg 2001, 15). Therefore, the isogloss for this distinction in pronunciation occurs in ENE south of Boston and includes much of WNE. In other words, the isogloss for *r*-dropping in New England differs[8] from the one for pronouncing different vowels in *cot* and *caught*.

During my many visits to western Massachusetts, I have noted the term *grinder* for a large sandwich on a torpedo roll and *jimmies* for chocolate bits on ice cream. Boston and points north in New England call the sandwich a *sub* but Rhode Island and neighboring cities call it a *grinder*. The chocolate bits are also *jimmies*. WNE, then, patterns with the southern part of ENE in pronunciation of certain vowels and in the usage of certain words, but historically differs from all of ENE in being *r*-full. This means that *r*'s are pronounced wherever they are spelled. The complexity of determining dialect areas by looking at isoglosses is apparent by this example.

Part of the decision in declaring two locales as belonging to one dialect or another is partially dependent upon what features the researchers decide are going to be the defining ones. For instance, on the basis of vowel pronunciation and lexicon, one might group Rhode Island with WNE, but on the basis of *r*-dropping, it has historically been grouped with ENE, which includes Boston. Yet, Rhode Island and Boston vowels differ considerably. Dialectologists have considered *r*-pronouncing more important than other features in grouping the New England dialects.

CHAPTER 7

The original Atlas studies did not investigate ethnic or racial dialects. What they looked for was the speech of those descended from the original settlers of the region, usually defined as white Anglo-Saxon Protestant or at least Northern European. Those Atlas studies were interested in the linguistic history of the white population of each area, how they spoke during colonial times, and how the original dialects spread from focal points to other areas. For instance, Boston was a focal point northward up the East Coast.

Trudgill (1983b, 33), a British linguist, complains that no attempt was made in *LANE* to correlate the New England data with the regions of Britain with which it shares certain features, such as the so-called intrusive *r* in phrases like "saw-r-it" for *saw it*, and "Martha-r-is" for *Martha is*. Given the excellent dialect geographies done in England, this is a bit surprising, but since *LANE* is readily accessible, this could be done even now. In fact, the Atlas studies should prove excellent for such purposes as locating where settlers, especially on the eastern seaboard, came from. Moreover, as shown in Chapter 9, dialectologists can delve into the colonial records still available and, by examining spelling errors, ascertain some features of the original colonists' speech.

An example will suffice to show the limitations and yet the need for speech geographies. Linguistic geography shows that the working class in ENE and New York City share the same rules for dropping /r/'s as speakers of southern British dialects. That tells us a great deal about the history of the dialects and their range, but it does not tell us anything about the social worth of the *r*-rules in the different countries and the social purposes for which they are used. I often hear Americans say that British *r*-dropping accents sound intelligent and urbane to Americans. Still, American *r*-droppers today are stigmatized. Interestingly, the *r*-dropping rules are the same in England as in New York City, ENE, and the coastal South, but they are perceived and evaluated differently when heard as part of different accents. It is no surprise that all the formerly *r*-dropping U.S. locales are increasingly becoming *r*-full. Given the British admiration of all things American, it will be interesting to see if, in the future, they start pronouncing all their /r/'s too.

The Atlas originators did interview both educated and uneducated speakers, which gave some information about social class differences in dialects. City dwellers were underrepresented overall, despite the fact that language change historically moves from the cities to the outlying areas. Because rural speech was considered more conservative than urban dwellers, Kurath and his associates gave undue attention to rural speakers. Labov, Ash, and Boberg (2006, 7) blame this on the fact that the sampling grids were based upon geography and not density of population. This is true, but it is also true that the linguists who designed the Atlas were using European models which valued rural speech because it was supposedly more like the original speech of an area, which they termed the **basilect**.

In any event, the original word geography of the eastern states (Kurath [1949] 1966) is replete with quaint old terms like *cade* and *orts*. These mean, respectively, an orphaned lamb and the leftovers one gives to pigs. Needless to say, such words were unknown to city speakers who comprised most of the region in which these words were collected. Yet, to this day, I hear these words cited as indicative of New England speech (especially by people who have gotten ahold of *LANE*). Carver (1987, 25) claimed that in the 1960's, *orts* was known only by two informants, one in Maine and one in Massachusetts. Actually, when I was doing some dialect work in rural western Rhode Island in the 1980's, I found several informants familiar with that term and with *cade*, although they said they never used either themselves. They belonged to their grandparents' generation.

Kurath and his associates were not interested in changes in progress in a region. Since these typically occur in younger urban dwellers and Kurath's studies concentrated on the educated older speakers in cities, he couldn't have picked up on ongoing changes anyway. These sampling errors have been corrected in newer studies.

Although Hans Kurath (1939) started what he hoped would be a complete atlas of American speech, after years of painstaking work, he had completed only the East Coast and the Southern and Middle Atlantic states. The work was started in the early 1931, but only *LANE* was published by 1941.[9] The field work for the Atlas eventually took 52 years, ending in 1983. By that time, the eastern dialects, indeed, dialects throughout the country, had changed or were in flux so that the original Atlas work became in many respects outdated.

Even so, it is useful as a base for later studies (Labov et al. 2006, 7). They note that the original Atlas was actually the most accurate kind of investigation, but if it were applied to the whole country, the time required to complete it would take so long that when it was done, you could no longer compare the speech of speakers from one area with those of another, as the language would have changed in the interim.

Before Labov, Ash, and Boberg's new *Atlas of North American English* (*ANAE*), the only atlas other than *LANE* to be published in book form was Harold Allen's *Linguistic Atlas of the Upper Midwest* (cited in Carver 1987, 3). However, Frederic G. Cassidy's (1985) *Dictionary of American Regional English* (*DARE*) covers just about the entire country. This was possible because it included only words, not the painstaking phonetic transcriptions of the Atlases. From 1965–70, 82 field workers "netted some two-and-a-half million individual responses" (Carver, 5).

CHAPTER 7

Where *DARE* went over the original Atlas regions, it was able to show the changes during the dynamic years since Kurath first started his work.

Carver himself took the *DARE* data and, with the help of computers, created dialect maps of the United States from them. His maps concentrate on the migration and spread of words, not the words themselves. Together, they give us a comprehensive overview of this country. Timothy Frazer (personal communication) says that comparison of maps based on the original Atlas studies and the *DARE* field records show a remarkable consistency in the distribution of words and phrases.

The New Studies

Starting with Labov's famous studies of Martha's Vineyard and New York City in the 1960's, dialect studies have concentrated on the social variation within a speech community (Chapter 9). These actually enhanced Atlas studies by giving us a great deal of information about how to elicit natural speech, as well as new insights into what dialect variation means socially. There are now excellent studies of different regions in America and the country as a whole (e.g., Frazer 1993; Murray and Simon 2006a; Labov et al. 2006).

What has changed is the way studies are carried out, both in technology and in elicitation techniques. The early Atlas investigations were conducted before there were even tape recorders, much less lightweight portables with good acoustic representation. Now, not only are there high-quality recording devices, there are sophisticated spectrographic computer programs which visually show the actual phonetic output of informants, accurately portraying the actual vowel sounds they were making. This is important because American dialects differ mainly in their vowel sounds. *ANAE* (Labov et al. 2006, 9) was produced in a relatively short time because acoustic analyses could be performed on between 300 and 500 vowel tokens of a speaker in one day. Earlier, it took a week to produce only 120 tokens. Of course, there were no acoustic analyses for the earliest studies.

ANAE resulted from an innovation in interviewing. Researchers conducted telephone surveys (which they label Telsur) both across the United States and in Canada. The telephone had been used earlier in much smaller studies, showing that it provided good information. Had they not done the Telsur study, *ANAE* would have taken much longer than the decade it did, as field workers would have had to be sent all over the continent.

The Telsur interviews were recorded and then subjected to acoustic analysis. This was important for two reasons. The telephone does not give the full acoustic spectrum, so fine points in pronunciation may be masked to the human ear. Also, even when a trained linguist transcribes someone's speech in person using IPA, he or she must make decisions about how high or low the tongue is and how far front or back it is for a given vowel to be pronounced as it was. Often what we hear as a different accent depends on very fine gradations of the tongue's position, but to transcribe these so that others can know precisely what sound was made is exceedingly difficult. Often, two linguists hearing the same recording will not agree with the other's choice of symbols. The acoustic analyses do away with such disagreement by showing the exact formants (sound waves) produced by the speaker (9). Since all speakers vary their vowel sounds slightly as they talk, the acoustic analysis can give an accurate picture of the range of sounds that will be heard as one phoneme by speakers in a given dialect area.

The sampling problems of the traditional atlas studies were solved by limiting the Telsur interviews to people in urban areas of 50,000 or more. This is precisely the population which was underrepresented earlier, and also the population in which most change is going on (8). Since Telsur was specifically set up to examine language change in progress, the obsolescence problem was solved. That is, the pronunciations for each region will be valid long after the 2006 publication. The older atlases which dwelled upon older, conservative speakers were often obsolete by the time their investigations were complete. That is, the children of the first set of informants who were recorded had already changed their accents. In *ANAE* the maps show clearly that even where certain distinctions noted in the earlier atlases have almost disappeared, the areas where they are still used form distinct geographic patterns today (49–57).

Perhaps the biggest problem with the *ANAE* data is that it was collected from only 439 speakers over the entire United States and Canada. That doesn't invalidate it, however. Each interview yielded hundreds of pieces of data. Having such a small base, however, means that only large dialect areas can be discerned. The variation that occurs within a large area cannot be. Labov et al. (3) specifically say that *ANAE* is not "a study of social variation within cities." Rather, "[t]he Atlas traces the geographic distribution of dynamic patterns that determine the direction of change. . . ." In other words, it shows how American accents are changing within broad regions. Although American dialects have been changing rapidly over the past few decades, and are still in the process of change, there are still separate geographical dialect patterns. We all don't speak alike, although most of us probably don't speak like our grandparents.

The vast Western expanse is treated as one region in *ANAE* (148). The boundaries for the West include all or part of New Mexico, Arizona, California, Oregon, Washington, Montana, Idaho, Wyoming, Nevada, Utah,

Colorado, and small parts of Nebraska, Kansas, and Texas. There is a good deal of variation within this region, however. For instance, one of my students who grew up in Oregon mentioned that she pronounces *bag* as [beyg], so that *bag* and *vague* rhyme. She claims that this is how *bag* is pronounced in her home town. Labov et al. (2006, 181) cite this pronunciation as being found in Wisconsin and Minnesota, but not in Milwaukee. However, when the Oregon speaker mentioned the way she said *bag*, a Milwaukee native in the class told us that she pronounces it the same way. Minnesota and Wisconsin are not part of the West according to *ANAE*, but Oregon certainly is. Labov et al. don't mention this pronunciation as occurring in the West at all. This is most likely an artifact of his sampling size.

Speakers from Washington state say they come from "Warshington," and things are "innerestin" (*interesting)* but my California cousins don't use those pronunciations at all, nor do they pronounce *bag* as [beyg].

Because of the variability within the West, the dialect map of the United States presented here is based upon, but is not identical to, map 11.16 in *ANAE*. That map shows Labov et al.'s map 11.15 (148), with the boundaries by Carver (1987, Map 8.1) superimposed on their Telsur results. Since the previous edition of this book also used a Carver map (Chaika 1994, 281), I have reused Carver's boundaries subdividing the West into the Southwest, Southern and Northern California, the Northwest and Central West, including them within *ANAE*'s boundaries for the West.

Since Carver did not agree with designating the Midland as a dialect area, Chaika (1994) did not do so, either. Since then, the work by Frazer (1993) and excellent in-depth studies of the Midland (Murray et al. 2006a) have convinced me that the Midland is one dialect region and not, as Carver had it, two: the Upper South and Lower North. Therefore, the map presented here agrees with all of the other dialect boundaries presented in *ANAE*'s Map 11.15.

As valuable as it is, *The North American Atlas* is just a beginning. For instance, Map 8.4 (Labov et al., 56) shows whether speakers pronounce *Mary, merry,* and *marry* alike or, as I do, with three separate vowels. However, it includes no speakers from Washington state, Oregon, Idaho, Montana, Wyoming, Utah, Arizona, North Dakota, or Kansas, and only one speaker from California and one from Colorado. Labov et al. say that, nevertheless, they have collected enough data to show that the West is a coherent dialect area. It would, in fact, be almost impossible to show all the variations possible within one dialect area. That is, not all speakers in any one region speak the same way. Speakers from Alabama do not speak exactly the same way as those from Mississippi, but they are still recognizable as Southern.

Dialect investigation sheds important light on the social stratification of an area, social and political trends, and how urban or rural the populace feels, changing social conditions, and migratory patterns. What we find in dialect study often cannot be derived from any other kind of sociological or political survey, as the information people give is truthful. They can't lie, as it's based on how they talk. Even if they try to talk more upper- or lower-class than they actually do, that alone gives information about who they admire, and what kind of persona they wish to project. Dialect studies are an important entré into understanding human behavior.

THE MYTH OF GENERAL AMERICAN

A particularly persistent myth is that there is a dialect which is General American or there is a way of speaking which is accent free. This is not, however, true, nor apparently, has it ever been. Van Riper (1986) demonstrates that the term "General American" changed drastically with each new dialect study. That is, originally it was assumed to be a variety of English that was neither Southern nor New England, but as other areas were investigated, its domain has been variously considered to be:

> . . . westward to the Rocky Mountains or the Pacific Coast from the Connecticut River, from the Hudson River, from New England, from parts of New York City, from New Jersey, or from Ohio. It has even been given territory as far northeast as Maine (123).

Most of these domains were a result of happy ignorance on the part of researchers. They had not bothered with gathering comprehensive data (131). Kurath as early as 1949 created a dialect boundary separating the Northern and Midland areas in the Great Lakes and Ohio Valley regions, an area formerly thought to be General American. Timothy Frazer (personal communication) has told me that one cannot go twenty miles in any direction in Illinois without encountering dialect differences.

The Midlands include states that are considered "Midwest" by some people, such as good chunks of Indiana and Illinois. Yet to Eastern ears, the Midland area in parts of Indiana sound like the South, although Southerners don't necessarily hear it that way. My grandson, who went to University of Iowa, was surprised by the "Southern" accents of some native Iowans.

As close as Milwaukee and Chicago are in distance, their dialects are as different as Boston's is from Providence's, and these two cities are even closer together. People visiting New England may not distinguish between Boston and Providence at first, but anyone who has lived in the region for any length of time hears the differences very clearly. The same is true of visitors to what they think of as the Midwest. They are not likely to hear the real variation between, for instance, Columbus, Cleveland, and Cincinnati in Ohio, although Ohioans surely do. Midwestern speech can actually be divided into the Midland, the North, North Central, and the Inland North, as shown on the map on the next page.

Van Riper concludes that so-called General American is actually a professional dialect taught in schools that train announcers, although one can hear differences in pronunciation between different TV and radio announcers. Usually these center on pronunciation of a particular word or a difference in the way a vowel sounds.

One thing is certain and that is that pronouncing /r/ wherever it occurs in spelling is now associated with General American speech, but vowel sounds differ considerably from dialect to dialect. Certainly, the common pronunciation of [iə] "eeya" in words like *happy* and *bad* in the Great Lakes cities is not perceived as accent-free by many Americans. Avis (1986) claims that Canadian English has a more uniform standard than American English does. The *ANAE* map does show one Canadian boundary from the Pacific Ocean to the Atlantic Provinces (Labov et al., 148).

I am often asked, "What is the right way to speak?" or "Which region has the best speech?" In England, one knows that RP is the right speech. This is a social-class dialect, not a regional one. In that country, most educated speakers, regardless of regional origin, speak RP at least some of the time, and the regional dialects are all considered nonstandard to some degree.

The United States, being a considerably larger and more culturally diverse country and one without the traditional sharp class divisions of England, has always had several regional standards in speech. One could always sound educated in any of the regional standards, especially if the hearer was familiar with the regional dialects. When I was a newly minted linguist at a scholarly meeting in 1972, I met an elderly gentleman who spoke with a very pronounced old Southern accent, one no longer heard, I must add. Not being that familiar with speech of the Old South, I actually had difficulty understanding him. When he heard who my dissertation adviser was,[10] this fellow scholar said, "As you can tell, I come from an old family in Columbia, South Carolina" (which he pronounced as "Cayuhlina"). To my Yankee ears, it just sounded Southern. Undoubtedly, my speech just sounded Northern to him.

What has been happening, as we shall see, is that some of the older regional standards are changing so that educated speakers from all parts of the United States sound somewhat more alike than they did, for instance, fifty years ago. Even so, regional differences are remaining. Many people in the regions which have historically *r*-dropping accents think that if they

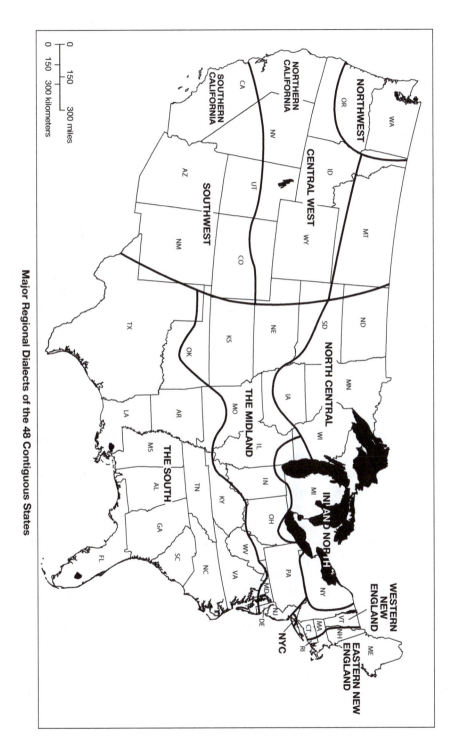

EVERYBODY SPEAKS A DIALECT

Major Regional Dialects of the 48 Contiguous States

pronounce their /r/'s wherever they appear in spelling, then they don't have an accent. However, a Californian can still tell that an *r*-full Boston speaker comes from "back East." One's vowels give one away.

The Myth of Regional Dialects

Not only is there no one General American dialect, but there is really no one Southern, New England, California, or other statewide or region-wide dialect. Although people think of a Midwestern accent, there isn't any dialect which can be considered Midwestern. As noted above, where one would expect a Midwestern boundary, instead there are Midland, North, and other dialects. Each region is characterized by several inter-related dialects. It is not the case that each dialect is sharply split off from all the others. Rather, dialects are alike in some features and different in others. Dialect boundaries can be very broad, based upon a few features, or very small, discriminating between more features. For instance, with justification, we speak of British English as opposed to American English. The latter is one dialect when opposed to Britain. However, within American English, there are dialectal differences within cities, within states, or across several states. It depends upon how one is cutting the pie, and for what purposes.

The Dialect Areas of American English

Although there is not complete agreement on how to cut up the American pie, the following areas would be considered as valid dialect areas by most scholars. The major point of disagreement, as noted above, is whether or not to consider the West as one region. Today, the major dialects in the United States are Eastern and Western New England, which include the different parts of the New England states of Maine, New Hampshire, Vermont, Massachusetts, and Connecticut, with Rhode Island considered entirely ENE, as it isn't west of the Connecticut River. The North includes New York outside of the New York City focal point, Michigan, northern Indiana and Ohio, most of Wisconsin, Minnesota, northern Iowa, most of South Dakota, North Dakota, a small piece of Nebraska, and northern Illinois including Chicago (Labov et al. 2006, 134 Map 11.8). The Midland starts in Pennsylvania and includes Delaware and northern Maryland, most of Ohio, Indiana, Illinois, southern Iowa, Missouri, Kansas, Nebraska, northern Oklahoma, and even a piece of Kentucky and West Virginia. The South includes much of West Virginia, Virginia, North Carolina, South Carolina, Kentucky, Tennessee, Georgia, Alabama, Louisiana, Arkansas, southern Oklahoma and Missouri, and Texas. The Southwest includes a small part of Texas, Arizona, New Mexico, part of Nevada, and

Southern California. The West is northern California, Colorado, Utah, Nevada, Wyoming, much of Idaho, and western Montana. The Northwest is Washington, Oregon and part of Idaho.

Notice that dialect boundaries rarely stop at state lines. In fact, many states have more than one dialect boundary within them. In contrast, a dialect area may include parts of several states. Notably, the Great Lakes cities[11] form a definable dialect area although they spread from New York to Illinois. Labov et al. refer to these as the cities of the Inland North. There is no one South Dakota or California or Iowa accent. Outside of the West and deep South, few states are wholly within one dialect area according to the Labov et al. maps. This doesn't mean there are no differences between the states designated as the South and the West. It is just that they did not investigate all of the features which would differentiate between them. For instance, it is improbable, in fact, that North Carolina, Texas, and Mississippi natives all speak alike. However, they do share general features which characterize the entire South, so they can be justifiably said to share a Southern variety of speech. And, some of these features spill over into the contiguous Midland states.

The Midland: A Case in Point. Dialects differ in phonology (accent), lexicon (word stock), and grammar. In order to define dialects, we have to consider all three. A good illustration of how dialects differ yet group together is the Midland, or as Timothy Frazer (2006) calls the region, the Midlands, because it can be subdivided into North, South, and West areas. Murray and Simon (2006b, 12) point out that the term *Midland* is a scholarly one. Most people think of the "Heartland" as the Midwest, although the actual Midland region doesn't cover the entire part of the country known as the Midwest. In fact, there is no single Midwestern dialect. The latest dialect investigations reveal no region in the country that can be labeled "Midwest" for purposes of dialect labeling.

I've already noted that highly respected and respectable scholars have disagreed upon the issue of there being a Midland region at all. Murray and Simon (15) offer seventeen[12] grammatical constructions that define the Midlands, some of which are:

1. That's **all the fast** it can fly.
2. That's **all the faster** he can run.
3. That's **all the** coat he has.
4. We always use coupons **anymore**. (positive *anymore*)
5. The baby **likes cuddled**.
6. The car **needs washed**.
7. The cat **wants fed.**
8. **What all** were you expecting?

9. **Whenever** I first heard the news, I **about** fell over.
10. **You'ns** to mean 'two or more of you.

The positive *anymore* in 4 means 'nowadays,' although people who aren't familiar with it are likely to interpret it as 'still.' *Whenever* in 9 means 'at the particular time that something happened,' but to people who don't have this in their dialects, it almost makes no sense because *whenever* means 'at any time.' That is, the word has diametrically opposed meanings in different American dialects.

Montgomery (2006, 152–54) discusses one usage that is in the South, the South Midland, eastern Tennessee, the Smoky Mountains, central Georgia, no farther north than southern Ohio, Indiana, and Illinois. It is often not understood by Americans from other regions, a common situation in dialect differences:

11. . . . you can put [your paper] in my mailbox or my door **one** by the end of the week.
12. I'll go down there and get him dead or alive, **one**.

When Montgomery gave a class directions by saying 11 above, one student "found himself befuddled and asked, 'Where is your door one?'" He says that he has tried out this usage of *one* on his students over the years. The Southerners understand it, but the Northerners draw a blank. What it means is 'one or the other.'

Some of the features mentioned as Midland (Murray et al. 2006b) occur elsewhere, such as:

13. The dog **wants out**. I **want off** at the next stop.

Using *want* with a preposition as in 13 is certainly common in Rhode Island, which, so far as I know has little connection with the Midland. I strongly suspect it is usual elsewhere in the country. For instance, I regularly hear "Do you want in?" on television, as when someone is asked to join a betting pool.

What is interesting to me is that many of these Midland features are virtually incomprehensible to people outside of the region. Yet, as noted above, the Midland dialects cover a large chunk of the United States.

Geographic Influences on Dialect

It has been long known that geographical features like mountain ranges and rivers create dialect differences, as did trade routes. These were formed in places which could be easily traversed, so geography has also influenced them. Major migratory routes also influence dialect formation, often persisting as dialect boundaries for two hundred years or more. Geographically, in the United States, the Appalachians created dialect boundaries between the coastal South and the mountain areas, and the Connecticut River is a major line between ENE and WNE, as are the Green Mountains in central Vermont. In each instance, the physical barriers of a wide river or of a mountain range prevented dialect features from melding together.

The Midland is an excellent example of the influence of topography and roads on dialect formation. Sharon Ash (2006, 53–54) shows that the degree of Midlandness, so to speak, is explicable by the location of the cities. That is, the number of features of the Midland dialects that are exhibited in any one city is related to its geographical situation. Ash (54) says that Columbus, Ohio is the "quintessential Midland city," exhibiting ten of the features she considers markers of the area.[13] It is as far away as possible from both the South and the Inland North.

Philadelphia exhibits only three Midland features, positive *anymore*, pronouncing *on* so it rhymes with *dawn* rather than *John*, and the expression *come with*. Although it is believed that Philadelphia is the origin of the Midland dialects, it is isolated by the Appalachians from other cities in the region. It is also on the Atlantic, so that it can more easily look to the north, south, and east than to the west.

Pittsburgh, also in Pennsylvania, stands as a gateway to the heart of the Midland and uses seven features of the region, including *you'ns* for plural *you*. Cincinnati also exhibits seven Midland features, but its location on the Ohio River just across from Kentucky influences its dialect. A transplanted Cincinnati native recently told me that much of her speech is like Kentucky's.

Indianapolis uses even more Midland expressions as it is in the middle of the Midlands, so it is not so in touch with other dialects. Ash explains that the small cities of central Illinois, Kansas City, and Omaha all exhibit nine of the ten features she considered as Midland markers.

The most interesting case is St. Louis. Speakers there used only three Midland features although, geographically, they are within the Midland borders. They use the positive *anymore* to mean 'nowadays,' as in "Meat prices are high anymore," and they rhyme *on* with *dawn*, using the /ɔ/ "aw" vowel, but they present scant evidence of the typically Midlands *needs swept* construction. In fact, this city has features of both the North and the South. Ash (55) explains that this is because St. Louis sits at the confluence of the Mississippi and Missouri rivers, which provide important links upstream to the North and West, as well as downstream to the South. By car, it is a straight 250 miles to Chicago with no major urban centers in between. It is also equidistant between Kansas City in the Midlands and Louisville in the South. Consequently, its dialect is influenced by these other regions. Interestingly, the one native St. Louis speaker I know claims that she has a Midwest dialect. She does not admit of any Southernisms at all.

Not all dialect differences within a region can be explained by location. For instance, Boston and Providence are less than an hour apart, and have had good routes between them both by water and by land since colonial times. However, the vowel distinctions in Providence are very similar to those in New York City, not Boston. In both Providence and New York, *cot* and *caught* are pronounced with two different vowels, whereas in Boston, they are pronounced the same. Furthermore, the Boston vowel in those words isn't used at all in Providence. Instead, Providence pronounces *cot* and *caught* the same ways New York does. Providence and New York City also pronounce the first vowel in *orange* and *Florida* alike, as /ah/. In general, all of the Boston vowels have slightly different pronunciations than the Providence ones, again with Providence sounding more like New York City. I have never found a satisfactory reason for this situation. Both Providence and Boston share a similar settlement history, except that Providence was founded because Roger Williams got kicked out of Massachusetts Bay Colony. Also, both have the same ethnic mix and the same historical immigration patterns in the late 19th and early 20th centuries.

Where Do the Features of a Dialect Come From?. An obvious influence on dialect formation is where early settlers came from and the routes they took. These are evident in some dialect boundaries today, some as long as 200 years after pioneers made their way inland. The first colonists in the coastal South and Eastern New England came from the London area. These colonists brought *r*-dropping with them to those areas, which, with the exception of New York City, are the only American ones that have ever had that feature. There is no way that *r*-dropping could have been uniform up the Atlantic Coast, excepting Pennsylvania, in the interior farmlands, and on the mountains in Eastern New England, unless the original settlers were *r*-less.

Labov says that people in this region and the coastal South copied the British in the 19th century, but as he himself proved (see Chapter 9), people don't copy the accents of those they don't identify with, and few New Englanders identified with the British. As for the South copying the British, again, one would have to ask why sharecroppers, artisans, and ordinary people with no contact with the British would be copying aristocratic British. Furthermore, the rules for *r*-dropping are so complex, they can't be copied casually in imitation of British speakers that Americans had no steady contact with. Indeed, most of the Americans had no contact with the British at all.

It is true that Martha's Vineyard, off Cape Cod, has always been *r*-full, but it wasn't settled by the Puritans. It was settled later, and, being an island, was largely unaffected by mainland speech until the twentieth century, so it didn't become *r*-less like the descendants of the original settlers. Elsewhere, when *r*-full speakers settled in the already established ENE region, their children became *r*-less, as did the Irish in 19th-century Boston and Providence. The Atlas linguists considered Martha's Vineyard a relic area. That is, they presumed it had the original accent, and the rest of ENE changed. Well, if Martha's Vineyard was a relic area, why didn't field-workers find other such *r*-full relic areas in remote villages in Maine, for instance? In other words, other places in ENE were very remote, their residents rarely or never interacted with people in cities, never traveled more than a few miles from their homesteads. Yet, none of them were *r*-less when the first Atlas study was done.[14] The entire Atlantic Coast except for Philadelphia was *r*-dropping. ENE and New York City also had an intrusive *r*, as described below.

Philadelphia was founded in 1681, later than either the South or ENE. It was settled by people from the north of Britain who were *r*-full. In the 18th century, large numbers of Scotch-Irish came to Philadelphia, then spread west across Pennsylvania to farmlands across the Shenandoah, across the Blue Ridge Mountains to the Piedmont of the Carolinas (Ash 2006, 36). They were *r*-full and, unless they migrated to *r*-less communities, they remained so. Where they became original settlers themselves, they established *r*-full speaking areas.

The reason that WNE is *r*-full is that, it too was settled by "a considerable admixture of Scotch-Irish in the half-century preceding the Revolution . . ." (Boberg 2001, 9). Many of the descendants of these settlers moved westward toward the better farmlands in Illinois and Wisconsin. WNE settlement was also prevalent in upstate New York, Cleveland (which Connecticut claimed as its Western Reserve), northern Ohio, Indiana, Illinois, southern Michigan, and Wisconsin. The latter were the future sites of the major northern cities, Detroit, Chicago, and Milwaukee. So, WNE migrants to the west helped establish *r*-full speech in the United States away from the Atlantic Coast. The *r*-full speakers from the Appalachians and Pennsylvania also reinforced this as the most typically American pronunciation as they, too, moved westward. Early on in the history of American settlement, the *r*-less speakers were outnumbered by the *r*-full ones.

Ash (2006, 37), says "There is a remarkable coincidence of the path of migration of Northeasterners to the Upper Midwest and isoglosses between The Midland and Inland North cities, as if the route established the boundary." Frazer (2006, 201) notes that a dialect boundary between the North and the Midlands follows both Interstate 80 and the old Illinois-Michigan

Canal, the east-west flow of the Illinois River, and an even earlier Native American route to the west.

Other clues as to paths of settlement are words clearly from an earlier settled region appearing in a cluster far away from it. Frazer speaks of a "Pennsylvania wedge" in Ohio, stopping at the Indiana line. Several Pennsylvania words also turn up occasionally in northwestern Illinois, such as *spouts* (for *gutters*), *firebug, clingstone peach,* and *clook.*[15] This is in a part of Illinois settled heavily by Pennsylvanian Mennonites. German immigration, starting in the 1830's, had an influence on Pennsylvania and the westward settlements of what is now the Midland and the Northern Cities region. For instance, *come with* is not only very widespread in the Midland, but is a feature of Chicago speech.

Callary (2006) shows how one can ascertain who the settlers of an area were by examining the names of geographic features like brooks (also known as creeks) or place names. He investigated areas outside of the original colonial settlements. Using The National Geographic Names Database (http://geonames.usgs.gov), he looked for southern terms in Illinois, such as *branch* for the name of a stream. He didn't ask people what they called a stream. He (Callary, 96) only noted its name, pointing out that a field worker might get a response like, "Oh, that creek over there? That's called Turkey Branch." In other words, the Southern word is used as the name, but the speaker in that region calls it a *creek.* He points out that many immigrants to Illinois came directly from Kentucky and Tennessee from the Revolutionary era to about 1830. Their settlement patterns can be deduced by the toponym *branch.* Further, by noting the percentage of times this toponym is used in different counties, he followed the path of settlement from a region, in this instance, the South. He found that the Southern influence was rather uniform in the southern one-third to one-half of the state. Then it moved west following the Mississippi River Valley, losing strength as it moved north. However, northern Illinois was settled later, supposedly by New Englanders. Their term for a stream is *brook*, but Callary didn't find this word as a toponym. The only linguistic evidence New Englanders left was the name of a few towns, like *Cambridge, Barrington*, and *Andover* from Massachusetts. He also found *Aurora, Batavia,* and *Geneva* from New York. Why Northerners transplanted their town names but not their toponyms is not explained. I wonder if it is because, when they settled Illinois, it was already settled by others who had appropriated the toponyms. That is just a guess.

He gives a more fascinating example of the words *fork* and *prong* to indicate a bifurcation in a stream. These originated in different parts of the south, as in Crooked Fork, Tennessee and Coopers Prong, Georgia. The distribution of *fork* in Illinois mirrors that of *branch* (101). The hearth area for *fork* is West Virginia and eastern Kentucky, whence it apparently moved on to Tennessee (103). What is most remarkable however is that, when plotting this toponym onto a U.S. map, Callary (104) found a second hearth area in the Salt Lake City Valley of Utah. From there it has spread northward and westward. Callary says that this is a mystery. Was it taken to Utah by Mormons from the South or by Mormons from Illinois? There's a topic for a master's thesis!

DIALECT DIFFERENCES

You already know that people have different accents, ways of pronouncing the same sounds, but accents are only part of the story. Dialects differ, as we have seen in the words they use for the same things, and also in the grammatical constructions they allow. What is interesting is that these differences coincide. That is, where we find certain accents, we also find certain words and grammatical constructions in roughly the same area, although, as noted above, the isoglosses for each will differ somewhat.

As noted, the original settlers brought their pronunciations with them, setting the base dialect at least for the Northeast and South. Then, with westward expansion, settlers from the earlier regions established their dialects in new settlements. Over the years, the speech changed, both in the original colonies and the newer inland ones, but it changed in different ways. Even so, we can still tell who settled certain regions in the Midwest by the way certain sounds are pronounced. For instance, Erik Thomas (2006) demonstrates that the particular ways that the phoneme /æ/ is pronounced in Ohio shows where heavy concentrations of speakers from New York and New England settled, as well as the areas where Pennsylvanians and Southerners did. Each of those areas pronounces /æ/ differently. In some cases, the original sound changed in the new place, but the way it changed gives us a clue as to who settled there. For instance, as Boberg shows, the raised sound for <a> in *cat* is a result of the pronunciation originally brought there by WNE settlers. WNE does not pronounce that sound the way current Buffalo speakers do, but the Buffalo pronunciation is an outcome of the WNE one.

Also, individual words get carried along with settlers as they migrate. We saw this with Callary's investigation of Southernisms in toponyms in Illinois. To some degree, grammatical forms may be carried to new areas, such as Southern *might could* (for *might be able*) appearing in the Midland. Another Southernism that has spread to the Midland is the use of *one* to mean 'either,' as discussed above.

Let us now look at what you may expect in accent, word choice, and syntax as you travel across country. The following discussion is not complete, nor could it be in a book devoted to so many topics pertinent to sociolinguistics. Here, only broad dialectal differences will be considered. For very finely grained analyses of vowel differences across the United States, see Labov, Ash, and Boberg (2006).

Phonological Variations

One of the most diagnostic differences in sounds across dialects is how the *a* in words like *bad, gas, happy,* and *last* is pronounced. It ranges from a low monophthong[16] [æ] sound to a vowel made with the tongue as high as it can go. Listen to the way national newscasters pronounce *bad* to hear the sound represented by [æ], or, if you pronounce the vowel very differently in *bad* and *ban*, you probably have the [æ] in *bad*, and a higher variant [ɨ] before nasals (*n*, *m*, and *ng*). Virtually no Americans have the low [æ] before nasals. If you have the low /æ/ sound as in *bad*, then you will notice your tongue lies flat as you say it in a word. Also you will notice that when you make the *a* in *ban* as /ɨ/, your tongue is raised. Just say the two sounds together to feel the difference. If you come from New England, all but a few areas in the West, and most of the Midland, you probably have the low vowel /æ/, raising it to [ɨ] before a nasal. Timothy Frazer (personal communication) tells me that much of the lower Midwest, including downstate Illinois, and the Plains states also have this alternation in pronouncing short <a>.

In Chicago and other Great Lakes cities like Gary, Buffalo, Milwaukee, Albany, Rochester, Detroit, and Cleveland, the short <a> in words like *bad* is pronounced as [ɛə] or even [iə][17] "eeya." The sound in these cities is similar to the one of speakers who pronounce the short <a> as [æ] before a nasal as in *ban* except they add a little glide to it. Labov et al. chart the [iə] in Omaha, Nebraska and Aberdeen, South Dakota, as well as in Los Angeles, Tucson, Boise, Eugene, and Portland, Oregon and Spokane, Washington. The boundaries of this raised <a> are roughly those of the Inland North leaking into North Central on your map, and even going into the Midland city of St. Louis (Labov, Ash, and Boberg, 179, Map 13.4) and then leapfrogging into a few cities of the West.

What is interesting about these western cities is that they are surrounded by large regions which apparently don't use the [iə]. Either that, or Labov et al.'s sampling didn't get speakers in between the North and the West who did. To sum up, in the Inland North and a few other points, the original /æ/ has been raised, (the tongue moves upward) and also turned into a diphthong, not a monophthong, a process called **breaking**. Labov et al.'s acoustic analyses revealed that both the degree of raising in these areas and the tongue movement varies slightly from place to place. But most people wouldn't hear the differences. What they do distinguish is the low /æ/ as opposed to the raised /iə/.

The South also has breaking of the <a> in *bad*. This is heard as the Southern drawl. The vowel is a very long /æ/. While making it, the speaker glides the tongue into a *y* and finishes with an [ə]. The result is an [æyə] as in [bæyəd] (Labov et al. 178). The Southern pronunciation of "cayunt" for *can't* is another example of this breaking. Not all Southern speakers drawl, but speakers who did were found in North Carolina, South Carolina, Tennessee, Alabama, Mississippi, Arkansas, and Texas. In Georgia, it was found well south of Atlanta, and in Virginia, only in Roanoke.

The Northern Cities Shift and Mergers. In the Great Lakes cities and areas around them which have the very high, tense /iə/ for short <a>, other vowels have been affected because of changing the original low /æ/. When one vowel changes, it leaves a space in the mouth where no vowel is pronounced for a while. For reasons we don't understand, whenever this occurs, it causes another vowel to shift to take the place of the original one.[18] Especially for those in the Inland North but also the North Central region, seven vowels have shifted (Labov et al., 187–90). Space does not permit a full elicitation of this shift, but two examples show it. The "ah" sound in *not* and *John* has moved forward and is now pronounced [æ], so they say "nat" where most other Americans would say "naht." You can hear this in the speech of the actors Dennis Franz and James Belushi. Also, the original [ʌ] "uh" in *bus* has now become [ɔ] "aw," the sound many Americans have in *boss*.[19] This shifting is most pronounced in the Inland North, which seems to be its hearth site.

Interestingly, this is the region that broadcast English adopted in the mid-twentieth century, replacing educated ENE. On national news, however, today it is not used. As Labov et al. note, "the sharp split between the vowel systems of the Inland North and other areas makes this dialect an unlikely candidate for 'general' or unmarked form of American English." It must be emphasized that educated speakers have these vowels as well as uneducated ones. It is not lower-class speech, by any means. I do get a number of students from the Chicago area who don't evince this vowel system, although they can imitate it. Most of them are from the suburbs and not the city itself.

Throughout North America including Canada (Labov et al., 19), several mergers are occurring. Vowels which once distinguished words are now becoming the same, producing **homonyms**, words spelled differently which sound alike. There are so many of these mergers either completed or going on that here I will discuss only the ones which characterize large regions or are currently in progress.

In the South and parts of the Midland, as well as in much of AAVE, [ɛ] and [I] are collapsed before nasals, so that *penny* is pronounced /pIni/

'pinny' and *meant* and *mint* are pronounced alike, as are *many* and *Minny*. Many speakers of this region who have lost all other regional vowel differences still retain this pronunciation. This doesn't mean that these speakers are more careless than anyone else. The rule is that every dialect has its own homonyms. That is, every dialect pronounces certain sets of words alike, but distinguishes between others.

Another longstanding merger in the South and South Midland and AAVE is [aɪ] (long *i*) with [ɑ] "aah" (Bernstein 2006). In these dialects, *Tom* and *time* are often alike, and *fire* and *tired* sound like *far* and *tarred*. This is an example of a diphthong becoming a monophthong. There is variation within the region in exactly what kinds of consonants the vowel precedes for a merger to take place. In other words, a speaker may not merge *tight* and *tot*, but will merge before other consonants. Vowels in English are affected by the kind of consonants which follow them.[20]

What is most important, however, is how Southerners feel about this merger. Some see it as a symbol of the South and even equate it with old money. It used to be a feature of all classes of Southerners. Others, like those Bernstein interviewed in Alabama, now see it as country or even being a hick. This contrasts with Texas, where Bernstein found it not only widespread, but spoken by upper-class, educated speakers. Interestingly, Mexican-American Texans do not have the merger. Bernstein (221) says this is not because of a Spanish influence.

A widespread merger, still ongoing in many regions, involves the vowels in *cot* and *caught*, *wok* and *walk*. These pairs are pronounced differently for some speakers and the same for others. Rhode Island, New York City, WNE, the Inland North, and the South pronounce in the words in each pair differently, but in Boston northwards in ENE and the West, the words in each pair are pronounced the same. So saying, this doesn't mean there is uniformity across regions which have merged or which have not. The Providence, New York City, and WNE vowels are [ɑ] "aah" in many words spelled with <o> and [ɔ] "aw" in words spelled with <al>, <aw>, <aught> as well as those spelled <of> (*soft*) and <os> (*loss, lost*). Although the vowels are distinct in other regions, the members of each pair may not be pronounced with the same vowels in each one. Certainly, the Inland North, while distinguishing *cot* and *caught*, does so differently from New York City and so does the South.

Similarly, those places that have merged use a different vowel. The Boston focal area, for instance, has had this merger for a very long time. They use a vowel not heard in the rest of the United States, so far as I can determine, an /ɒ/ which can be approximated by saying "ah" as far back in your throat as you can, and then slightly rounding your lips. In Los Angeles, which has merged these vowels, they are both distinct /a/ "ah."

However, in all of these places, the pairs *talk, tock* and *walk, wok* are pronounced alike. Similarly, the vowel used in those words appears in *soft, saw, boss, taught, daughter,* and myriad other words which have an /ɔ/ "aw" in other dialects.

An example of miscommunication with the merger occurred when my granddaughter called me from school, very upset because, she told me, she had *locked* her cell phone. I was very confused until it hit me that she had *lost*[21] her phone. She lived in Los Angeles until she was nine, and when she is upset, often reverts to that accent. I have an [ɔ] "aw" in *lost* and an /a/ "ah" in *locked*, but she has /a/ in both words.

Matthew Gordon (2006, 58) says that this merger is well-known as a feature of western Pennsylvania and is well established across Canada. In the West "it appears to be a relatively new development." In fact, Labov et al.'s map of the West showing the merger (61, Map 9.2) shows that cities as far apart as Seattle and Bismarck, Santa Fe and Duluth are in transition, so that some people have the merger and others do not. Los Angeles natives in 1953, interviewed for the *Linguistic Atlas of the Pacific Coast,* did not have the merger, but twenty years later there was a steady increase in the merger across the generations.

This squares with my own observation of my Los Angeles cousins in the 1970's. By then, they had absolutely no distinction between [a] and [ɔ] except when an <o> in spelling occurred before an [r] as in *orange, horrible,* and *corridor.*

Gordon (2006, 58–68) says that the merger is a relatively recent arrival in his native eastern Nebraska. In Kansas City, Missouri, it was found that 80% of speakers over sixty maintained separate pronunciations in pairs like *Don* and *dawn, odd* and *awed,* and *cot* and *caught.* In contrast, only 12% under twenty maintained the distinction. Different parts of Missouri had different ratios of speakers who have merged these vowels. In fact, some have merged them in some word pairs, but not others. This merger is not a big factor yet in Rhode Island and New York City, but Philadelphia has some people in transition. The first glimmerings that the merger will come to Rhode Island is seen in upper-class high school girls, especially those in private schools. I hear them pronouncing *walk* like *wok.* Interestingly, where they are beginning to merge those vowels, they are not adopting the well-established Boston merged vowel. Rather, they are adopting the Los Angeles pronunciation.

Although some linguists often pooh-pooh the effect of the media on regionalisms, I think that, today, young California-speaking actresses who are very much in the media and followed by young females are influencing regions far away from southern Cal. The long-noted upward contour of a sentence so that a statement sounds like a question, and now the low back vowel merger both seem borrowed from that region. It's always dangerous making a prediction about speech change in the future, but I do think that within a generation or two, the *cot–caught* distinction in American speech will have disappeared. And the vowel used will, in the main, be the Los Angeles one.

The last merger is a general one of most vowels before an /r/ between vowels. Many North Americans pronounce *Mary, merry, marry* the same. Some pronounce them all alike. Others pronounce *Mary* and *merry* alike, but *marry* differently, and others, *merry* and *marry* alike, but *Mary* differently. Still others, use three distinct vowels in all three words. *ANAE*'s map 8.4 shows only a small cluster of speakers pronouncing them all differently, concentrated in the Northeast: Rhode Island, New York, Philadelphia, Wilmington, Delaware, and scattered speakers in Roanoke, Virginia, Greenville and Columbia, South Carolina, New Orleans, and Miami. Most of the rest of the country pronounces them alike, with a few who pronounce two alike and one different. There is no particular pattern, except that the map shows eight speakers in the West who pronounce them the same, and none who distinguish between them, but this is a mighty small sample of a very large expanse.

Similarly, for much of the country, *Barry* and *beery* are pronounced alike, as are *Harry* and *hairy*. Labov et al. (57) show a merger for young people in Philadelphia for *spirit* and *spear it, nearer* and *mirror*. I suspect this is far more widespread, but they didn't happen to elicit these terms in the rest of the country. I have also noticed, even in newscasters, a general merger in other vowels before /r/'s so that the first vowels in words like *current, thorough*, and *tournament* are pronounced like the vowel in *her*. The same speakers also pronounce words like *for, sure,* and *fur* alike. Other speakers maintain clear vowel differences in these words.

These mergers seem to be relatively recent as defined in dialect studies. That is, in listening carefully to old movies, those from the 1930's to the 1950's, one doesn't hear these mergers before /r/. In my admittedly older, conservative dialect, *current* has a distinct /ʌ/ "uh" and *tournament*'s first vowel is /ɔ/ "aw." Similarly, *for, sure,* and *fur* are all different. My students from the northern part of WNE, upstate New York, the Midwest, and West have mergers in these sets. So far in Rhode Island, vowels are kept very distinct, but I would not be surprised if the pressure from the rest of the country leads to more mergers. It is likely that other regions also have not merged all these vowel distinctions. New York City hasn't, nor has Boston, but none of the dialect studies I could find mention words like these specifically.

Another merger not mentioned in the dialect studies, and, again, one that seems relatively recent, is that of the first vowel in *Florida, orange, corridor, forest,* and *horrible* as opposed to *story, more, bore,* and *shore.* In much older Eastern speech, the <o> vowel in the first four is pronounced as /ɑ/ "aah," and the vowel in the second set is /ɔ/ "aw." In most of North America, these two vowels have merged, so that any words spelled with <o> before an /r/ is /ɔ/ "aw." My Midwestern friends, now in their sixties, tell me they grew up with the merger. However, a local DJ, who doesn't come from ENE or New York City, told me that as late as the 1970's in broadcast school, he was taught the correct form was to say "ahringe" for *orange.* I doubt that anyone would be given that advice today.

Investigating old movies, again, I have found that the distinction between /ɑ/ "ah" in *Florida* vs. /ɔ/ "aw" in *story* is regularly made. Doris Day, in the 1950's, pronounced her name "Dahris" not "Dawris." The first entertainer I heard use the /ɔ/ was John Denver when he sang "like a light in the forest" and didn't pronounce it "fahrist." So far, even young speakers in Rhode Island and most of my students from the New York City focal area maintain the old distinction. But, again, upper-class private school students are beginning to merge the two. One of my grandsons, who went to Berkeley, told me that was one of the first changes he made in his speech because of the ribbing he got. The other, who is at a university in Houston, says he is also called on that pronunciation but hasn't yet changed it.

Vowel mergers are a natural sound change. English has more vowels than most languages, more vowels than I've had space to discuss here. For example, in a conservative enclave like Rhode Island, most speakers make seventeen different vowel distinctions. Compare that to five in Spanish. When a system becomes out of balance phonetically, by some process we do not fully understand, speakers simplify it.[22] In linguistic terms, English has a **marked** vowel system. Mergers cause a simpler phonetic system by doing away with some of the vowel distinctions. It seems as if most of the mergers have progressed from west to east. This mirrors the cultural influence of the West.

It is not surprising that the region which still makes the most vowel distinctions is historically *r*-less. Labov et al. (57) make this connection explicitly, saying one would not find *r*-full speakers who make many distinctions before an /r/, explaining this is a result of how /r/ is pronounced. There is another explanation as well. The English /r/ is a marked consonant, found in few languages. Dialects which drop it before consonants maintain more vowel distinctions, but those who pronounce it favor vowel mergers. In other words, each dialect gets rid of one marked phenomenon in the language, either /r/ or too many vowels.

CHAPTER 7

Consonant Differences in Dialects. Consonants, which seem more crucial to identifying spoken words, show fewer dialectal differences than vowels do. There are only two major difference in consonants between most British and American dialects: merging /d/ and /t/ in between vowels and r-dropping.

Both American and British English aspirate the /t/ at the start of words like *toy*. Put your finger to your lips as you pronounce *toy* and you will feel the puff of air, which is called aspiration. The /d/ does not get aspirated, ever. In fact, perceptually, the major way English speakers distinguish between words like *to* and *do* is the aspiration. In between vowels, as in words like *kitty* and *kiddy,* the British make a clear /t/ or /d/. For them, *kitty* and *kiddy* are pronounced differently. But Americans pronounce both words the same. In American dialects, /t/ and /d/ in between vowels are the same sound, a light flap of the tongue, sort of a /d/ and sort of a /t/, but not quite either.[23] The British hold the /t/ and /d/ as they enunciate, but Americans just flick their tongue tip to the ridge behind the front teeth. You can easily hear this by saying the following pairs rapidly, as in conversation: *latter–ladder, betting–bedding, wedding–wetting.*

The pun in the name for a store that sells water beds, "Off Track Bedding," would not work in England as it does in the United States. Puns are tied to the accent they are said in and in British English, those words aren't homonyms. Also, spelling errors reflect pronunciations. In student papers, I have seen words like *city* spelled as <cidy> and *beauty* as <beaudy>.

If a scholar wanted to find out when Americans started pronouncing /t/ and /d/ alike between vowels, he or she would look in old diaries, ship logs, handwritten wills, old letters, and the like to find such misspellings. I recall an elderly linguistics professor, William Twaddell, telling me that this fluke of pronunciation started in the Midwest in the 19th century and made its way eastward year by year. How accurate this is, I don't know.

When I lived in rural Maine in the 1950's, there were people who still pronounced the /t/ as a full stop, as in "That'll be ninety cents, please." The /t/ in *ninety* was as crisp as the /t/ in *toy*. In clips of old newsreels, you can hear President Franklin Delano Roosevelt during World War II also enunciating his /t/'s and /d/'s between vowels. They were distinct, not merged. Some think this is because he was imitating the British, but it is more likely that, since he was born in the East in the 19th century, he learned to speak before the pronunciation of these two sounds merged there. If he were just imitating, he wouldn't have been able to pronounce them consistently as two separate sounds. Also, I can still hear in my mind the voices of elderly neighbors from my childhood clearly lingering on /t/'s that I knew I never said. The Maine speakers who did this reminded me of the old-fashioned speech of my childhood. Interestingly, older Providence

African American speakers were very likely to use this pronunciation. As one genteel elderly woman told me, "We talk like the old English."

The other consonantal difference in dialects is, of course, *r*-pronouncing. Speakers of the *r*-full dialects often accuse those of the misnamed *r*-less dialects of putting /r/'s where they don't belong as well as leaving them out where they do. The term *r*-less dialects is actually a misnomer because all English speakers, British, American, and Australian, do have /r/ at the start of a word, as in *ran*, and, for most such dialects, between vowels, as in *marry*.

The American South is rapidly becoming *r*-full (Labov et al., 47–48). The rapidity of this change is seen in the statistics. Each older generation is about 14% lower in *r*-pronouncing than the generation just after it. Younger white speakers are consistently *r*-full. Labov et al. say that this is because of the influence of Appalachian speech, which has always been *r*-full. It seems to me, also, that the tremendous influx of Northerners into the coastal South must have influenced this change.

Americans criticize *r*-dropping, considering it an error, often associating it with lower-class speech. Since educated, upper-class, even aristocratic British, Australian, South African, and older upper-class East Coast American speakers drop /r/'s, then neither carelessness nor ignorance can account for it. In fact, when one examines actual speech of *r*-droppers, one finds very definite rules for when and when not to pronounce that sound. If the /r/ occurs before a consonant, it is not pronounced, so that *heart* and *hot* are homonyms. Also, if a word-final /r/ occurs at the end of a sentence or in a word uttered alone, it is not pronounced, as in:

How are you getting theya [there]?
By cah [car].

These dropping rules are actually similar to the elision rules in French in which final consonants of words are dropped when said in isolation.

ENE and New York City speakers also put an *r* in "where it doesn't belong," as in expressions like "saw-r-it" (saw it) and "sofa-r-is" (sofa is). This so-called intrusive *r* occurs only when the speaker is going from a mid-back or central vowel to a front one. That is, it occurs when one word ends in an /ɔ/ "aw" (*saw*) or an /ə/ "uh" (*sofa*) and a following word starts with /I/ "short i" as in *it* or an /æ/ "short a" as in *at* or *and*. As the speaker goes from one of these vowels to the other, his or her tongue glides into the position of an /r/. Thus, the so-called intrusive *r* is actually a glide caused as the tongue is moving from the back to the front of the mouth. This causes pronunciations like "thaw-r-it out" or "my sofa-r-and chair."

Virtually all Americans have an analogous glide when they go from an /u/ "ooh" to another vowel, as in "who-w-is" or from an /i/ "ee" to another vowel as in "see-y-it." The ENE speaker simply has another glide so that whenever he or she has two vowels together, it is broken up by either an /r/, /w/, or /y/. Those who don't have the *r*-glide often get rid of the second vowel by omitting it, saying "sawt" for *saw it* in rapid speech. Socially, that is acceptable and using the glide is not, but these are social judgments and do not reflect any inherent qualities in pronunciation. A very small minority of Americans are now consistent *r*-droppers, and the regions they come from are not dominant in any way. Therefore, their speech is dis-valued. In earlier times, as a crash course in old movies reveals, this was not always true. In British, South African, and Australian speech, *r*-drop-ping is still the norm, with some dialects having the intrusive *r* and others not. In the United States, again being aware of the danger of predicting, I foresee all the *r*-less speakers, except perhaps AAVE ones, becoming *r*-full.

Word Differences

There are small differences in lexicon from dialect to dialect. These are not **slang**. Slang consists of words used for a relatively brief time in informal situations. It is often associated with adolescents. If a slang term persists for several years, it becomes part of the vocabulary, and is no longer slang.

The lexical differences in different regions or in certain ethnic dialects involve the names of commonly used items. For this reason, misunder-standings can and do occur, even in this land of television and national advertising. In a Rhode Island supermarket, a male customer just ahead of me in the checkout line asked the boy packing groceries to place a large bag of dog food in a "sack." The boy looked puzzled, then said dubiously, "I'll have to ask the manager." The customer reddened angrily. I inter-vened, hastily explaining that, as in many other regions, groceries are placed in *bags*. *Sacks* are made of cloth. The customer, from Oregon, said, "I never heard of such a thing," and the boy had never heard of *sack* for *bag*. Usage of these words varies considerably all over the country. Some regions reverse the usage just mentioned, so that *bag* means 'a cloth container,' as in *burlap bag*, but *sack* is made of paper. Tuscaloosa County uses the two words interchangeably. For the item made from burlap, Alaska uses *gunnysack*, and Honolulu, Hawaii has one group which calls it a "gunnysack," but another which calls it "burlap bag." There are, or at least used to be, Southern areas in which the word *poke* was used for a bag. Hence, the expression "to buy a pig in a poke."

The upset over the use of *sack* for *bag*, discussed above, is not as unusual as one might think. At O'Hare Airport in Chicago, a thirsty woman with a strong Boston accent asked an attendant where the bubbler was. The attendant kept saying, "What?" to which the traveler, raising her voice, kept answering "The bubbler!" Given the proximity of Chicago to Milwaukee, one would have thought that the attendant would be familiar with *bubbler* for a public drinking facility. That term is also used in Wisconsin. And, given the fact that only parts of Boston use the term *bubbler*, one would have thought that the traveler would have dredged up *fountain* in her moment of need.

Even so, the traveler seemed unaware that most of the country calls it a "fountain," "drinking fountain," or "water fountain." To those who call it a *bubbler*, fountains are the big, gushing water decorations in parks or in front of buildings. *Water fountain* seems redundant, at least nowadays, but at one time there were soda fountains in drugstores where Coke and ice cream sodas were dispensed.

Mike Kenny, a writer for the *Boston Globe*, expressed surprise to me that an ex-governor of Massachusetts, Michael Dukakis, on the campaign trail for a presidential nomination somewhere in the West, remarked, "They don't know what a frappe is." Kenny was surprised because, in this day and age, one would expect everyone to know that the "general American" term is *milkshake*. I countered with an even more narrow provincialism. As I disembarked a plane from Los Angeles to Rhode Island, I noticed a very excited young man joining three male friends who had come to pick him up. As I was passing by, I heard him saying in a high, buoyant voice, "C'n you believe it! They don't know what a cabinet is, and they never heard of coffee milk!" (A *cabinet* is a *milkshake*, and *coffee milk* is lowfat milk with coffee syrup in it, a drink not known outside of Rhode Island.)

I was married to my New York–bred husband for twenty-five years before I discovered that he said "rubber band" for what I term *elastic* and what Pittsburgh speakers call *gum band*.

As an ENEer, I go *down cellar* and *downcity* rather than *down the cellar* and *downtown*, and wash up with a *facecloth* rather than a *washcloth*. The venerable L.L. Bean Catalog advertises facecloths instead of washcloths. Often, advertisements gave away the dialect of their writers by their word choices. Midwestern companies like Bird's Eye frozen foods had *green beans* on their labels instead of *string beans* or *snap beans*. Now *green beans* are found in regions which formerly used the other terms. Similarly, Midwest *swimsuit* has replaced *bathing suit* in ads, so that term has become widespread.

In ENE, one *graduates high school* or *graduates Columbia* with no *from* before the school name. This usage may be more widespread, however, as I have heard a few TV announcers use this construction. As a child, I separated *swill* from *rubbish*, although nowadays it is all *garbage*.

CHAPTER 7

Swill survives only in the sense of "swill it down," an uncouth pouring of drink down one's throat, and *rubbish* has been replaced by *trash*.

I always was fascinated with *fireflies*, but visitors from the South insisted they were *lightnin' bugs* and Midland speakers know them as *firebugs*. Similarly, my husband's *dragonflies* were my *darning needles*, and a Midland speaker's *snakefeeders*.

I carry a *pocketbook*, which my husband insists is a *purse* and which people from other regions call a *handbag* or just a *bag*. I have tried to explain to my husband that a purse is a small item in which one puts coins, but the pocketbook is what you put the purse in.

In the East, one orders *soda,* which, in the Midwest and the West is likely to get you an ice cream soda (if you get anything at all). Sharon Ash (2006, 44) says that *soda* is universal in Philadelphia, but that from Pittsburgh throughout much of the Midland, *pop* is the term. When she grew up in Chicago, she says that *soda* was completely unknown, but *soda pop* could be used. St. Louis differs from the rest of the Midland by using *soda*, but that term is beginning to encroach on Chicago and Detroit. The South calls carbonated beverages *coke*, as does Indianapolis in the Midland. I presume that if you want orange soda, you would ask for orange coke. What happens if you want cherry soda? Cherry coke is a particular kind of kind of cola drink, different from regular cherry soda. Massachusetts and points north had the most unusual term of all, *tonic*, but younger speakers seem to use *soda* nowadays. Of course, one way to get what you want anywhere would be to ask for a *soft drink*, but that also could net you lemonade or juice, at least in the East. In New York City and environs, the bottled stuff is *soda*, but a drink made at a soda fountain with chocolate syrup, milk, and plain soda water is an *egg cream,* which has neither egg nor cream in it. Unflavored carbonated water used to be called *seltzer* in ENE and New York City, but *club soda* from brands bottled elsewhere invaded the region. Now, with the advent of fancy carbonated bottled waters, it's either *bottled water, sparkling water,* or *mineral water,* all at a heftier price than seltzer or club soda.

There are also regional differences in the name of the drink made from ice cream, syrup, and milk beaten together. Most of the country calls this a *milkshake* or *shake*. Other terms are *frappe, velvet,*[24] and *cabinet* in Massachusetts, Maine, and Rhode Island respectively. Because of national fast-food chains, *shake* or *milkshake* has moved into those areas as well. Often, Rhode Island customers order cabinets[25] at the *creamery* (ice cream parlor[26]), but a *shake* at a fast-food place. Since the fast-food shakes typically contain gelatinous thickeners, whereas cabinets are only milk, syrup, and ice cream, the two drinks are not alike. Traditionally, *milkshake* in Rhode Island and parts of Massachusetts has referred to milk and syrup beaten together with no ice cream at all.

With the advent of Massachusetts chains into Rhode Island, *frappe* has crossed the border. Some ice cream parlors list *cabinets*, *frappes*, and *milkshakes*. The difference is usually that the cabinet has the most ice cream, the frappe somewhat less, and the milkshake either none or very little. Other stores, may differentiate the three differently. To my amusement, I saw a sign advertising "Cabinets (frappes)" in Bristol, Rhode Island, a historic town frequented by tourists from all over America. The owners seem blissfully unaware that most Americans would have no idea what either one was, although, clearly, the word *frappe* was intended to define *cabinet*. What is surprising is that very insular terms like *cabinet* and *frappe* are surviving despite pressure by national chains. This seems to be a result of their being deployed as different kinds of milkshakes.

Chocolate bits on ice cream are *sprinkles* in New York, but *jimmies* in parts of New England, *ants* in others, and *shots* elsewhere. A *roll* is a small round crusty kind of bread in the East. Other regions call that a *bun*, but buns, to me, aren't crusty, as in hamburger or hot dog buns. Otherwise, they are sweet, often with *frosting* on them. Or is that *icing*?

Students in my linguistics class in Spring 2006 showed a good deal of diversity with usage of *frosting* or *icing*. Some use one or the other exclusively. Others use one for the top of a cake and the other for in-between the layers. Others consider *icing* thinner and smoother than *frosting*, but not so thin as *glazing*. As a verb, some *ice* the cake and others *frost* it. Some, like me, have *frosting* on both the top and between the layers, but they *ice* the cake with the frosting. I use *frost* and *frosting* in all situations. Notice that all these terms carry connotations of coldness. Roads get *glazed* with *ice* when it's *frosty* out.

Other dialectal variations similarly use different words for the same thing, but the words are semantically similar. For instance, the British have a *bonnet* on their cars, but Americans have a *hood*, both being a form of headdress on people. However, our *trunk* is their *boot*. These words are not semantically similar at all. The Brits take a *lift* while we take an *elevator*. Both words do refer to the same thing, but the British term is less erudite. The American term *eraser* has as its British counterpart *rubber*. To erase something and to rub it are semantic counterparts, but, unfortunately, in America, the latter term is the name for a *condom*. This has caused both confusion and embarrassment on both sides of the Atlantic.

What do you put in the turkey? *Stuffing* or *dressing*? The latter, to me, is only what you put on salad. Southerners eat their turkey with *fixins*, a term which is occasionally seen on a menu even in Rhode Island to indicate traditional side dishes, including the stuffing.

Rhode Island, parts of Connecticut, and western Massachusetts eat *grinders*, a very large cylindrically shaped sandwich on a roll. Nearby Boston and vicinity order *subs*. New Yorkers refer to them as *heroes*, and

CHAPTER 7

one sees in the New York City *Yellow Pages* advertisements for "Hot heroes to go." Whether the image that conjures up is deliberate or just a lapse, I don't know. Other terms for these sandwiches are *hoagie, torpedo (sandwiches),* an *Italian sandwich,* or *poor boy*, depending on where you eat them. It is not unusual to hear a Rhode Islander order a *grinder* in a Boston-based chain that advertises *subs*. Some Rhode Islanders have replaced native *grinder* with Boston *sub*, one of the amazingly few adoptions from eastern Massachusetts dialect.

It is surprising that local terms are retained even in regions close to each other both geographically and culturally. The persistent differences in regionalisms between Rhode Island and eastern Massachusetts are of note not only because the states are adjacent to each other, but many people commute to work on both sides of the border. Still, the Rhode Island dialect is largely untouched by Massachusetts features. Such a situation is not unique in the United States as we saw with a Midland city like St. Louis, which doesn't use Midland terms although it's surrounded by them.

Ethnic terms for food are clustered in the regions where a given group has settled, so in the Midland, you can get *smearcase*, a spreadable cheese, and in New York City, with its large Eastern European Jewish population, you can find *knishes, blintzes,* and *flanken*, or have a bagel with a *shmear*, cream cheese. A knish is like an English pasty, a baked crust with a tasty filling of potato, meat, or buckwheat. Blintzes are a kind of crepe stuffed with cream cheese or blueberries, and flanken is pot roast. Italian and Mexican food have become so much a part of the American diet that terms for them are widespread throughout the country. Who doesn't know what a pizza is, or a tamale?

Much of the East Coast put their *stockings* on, but the Midwest put on their *hose*. The latter is often not comprehended in the East, where *hose* refers only to the long snaky thing used to water a garden. The newer *pantyhose* is used alongside *stockings* for many East Coast women. They put on their stockings, even when their stockings are pantyhose. Younger speakers just use the term *nylons*.

When I was growing up, we put on our *stockings* every day, referring to what today are called *socks*. In recent dialect investigation, I have found that *stockings* for *socks* survives primarily in educated African American native Rhode Island males of my age or older. Other than that, it seems that only Santa gets stockings.

In building, Northwesterners put *shakes* on the side of homes, but Northeasterners put on *shingles*, referring to the same item: wood squares, usually made of cedar. There are variations on this theme all over the country, with some also putting shakes on their roofs, whether or not they are wood, and others putting shingles on if they are not wood. Yet others use shingles for both siding and roofs, wood or not. Others put shakes on the side, and shingles on the roof. As with *bag* versus *sack*, the material used may affect the word, so that cedar shakes can be used for either roofs or sides, but asphalt ones will be shingles. With the advent of national housing supply stores, the Northwestern term *shake* has moved to New England, but it is reserved for siding. The roof is still shingled.

In mobile societies, words from one dialect may conflict with words from others. That is, some regions have had an influx of newcomers, each bringing his or her own regionalisms. When conflict occurs, two things can happen. Either one term drops out, or each word starts to refer to slightly different aspects of the thing originally designated. English *shirt* and *skirt* are old examples of this, originally having been British dialect variants for the same article of clothing.

In the United States, the hardware on a sink from which one gets water is called a *faucet, tap*, or *spigot* (or *spicket*). In areas where two or three of the terms compete, people will assign a slightly different meaning to each, so that *faucet* may become what's in the bathroom or laundry, *tap* is in the kitchen, and *spigot* is on the outside. Others may assign the meanings differently, so that, although *tap* is still where one gets drinking water, *faucets* may be both inside and out, and the *spigot* is what's on a beer keg or on the heating oil tank. Until about twenty years ago, the term *tap* in Rhode Island referred only to an upscale bar. There were painted, often gilded, signs on windows like "Billy's Tap." Also, bars advertised "*beer on tap*," otherwise known as *draft beer*. Both of these usages survive in Providence. Other than that, a *faucet* was both in the kitchen and the bathroom or anywhere else in the house, and a *spigot*, if used at all, was the outside faucet. *Tap* was not used for a kitchen faucet as it is in other parts of the country. I was familiar with the term *tap* for the water faucet only from dialect studies.

With the advent of bottled waters, restaurants began asking customers if they wanted *tap water* or *bottled*. That introduced *tap* as the term for faucet in the kitchen sink. Younger speakers began to say, "Get me some water from the tap." People also use *faucet* this way. Some of my students report that they just say, "Get me some water from the sink." Many of them, mostly from the East, but not Rhode Island, didn't know the term *spigot* at all. It seems that those who refer to faucets both inside and outside don't have *spigot* at all. Several students told me that they even refer to the knob and spout on a keg of beer as the *faucet*. Others who use *faucet* both inside and outside the house reserve *spigot* for liquids other than water. Some communities have yet to settle on which word refers to what, so that different residents use the terms differently.

A number of vocabulary differences distinguish American and British English. Besides those noted above, the British have *hire, lorry*, and *ladder* (in a stocking) while Americans say *rent, truck*, and *run*, respectively.

CHAPTER 7

Americans buy on *installment plans*, but British do the same thing with *hire purchases*. The British love *chips*, which Americans call *fries*, and they eat *crisps*, American *potato chips*. On my last trip to England, in many pubs I was offered potato chips instead of crisps. Considering how the British have co-opted American culture, this shouldn't be too surprising. They have Pizza Hut, KFC, and McDonald's, so why wouldn't they use the other words associated with American food? They have also borrowed American idioms like *sell someone down the river*. What is odd about that is that the idiom refers to selling slaves on the Mississippi, which certainly never applied to England. As noted above, they have also adopted AAVE words.

One British term, *bunk* meaning 'escape' or 'leave someplace without telling others,' used to occur in southern New England in the meaning of 'stay out of school with no excuse,' although younger speakers increasingly don't use it except in the expression "National Bunk Day" (when, putatively, everyone bunks school). In Philadelphia, that would be to *bag* school, and in other places it would be *play hooky* or simply to *cut* school.

English is too widely spoken a language, and there are far too many dialect differences in word choice for anything approximating a comprehensive discussion here. As you read this, you probably thought of many local terms that you know other places don't use.

Syntactic Variation

Dialects differ in syntax as well as phonology and lexicon. Americans are generally familiar with the well-known signposts of uneducated dialects such as double negatives and lack of agreement in number of subject and verb. The dialect markers that signal social class distinctions often occur in common constructions of the type that crop up frequently in conversation. The markers must appear early on in an interaction, or else they would not be reliable as cues to identity.

Syntactic markers center on marginal constructions, grammar rules that are relics of bygone days. Consider the major differences between educated and uneducated American dialects. The educated ones use the forms of *be* (*am, is, are, was*, and *were*) that agree with the subject of the sentence in which they appear. These different forms for one verb are a relic of the **inflections** used long ago when verbs agreed in person and number in the present tense and in number in the past tense. Besides the inflected *be*, the only other survival of that system is the -*s* that marks the present tense third person singular, as in the singular *he goes* as opposed to the plural *they go*.

Be usage is a particularly effective marker of social class in both American and British English because it is hard to talk for very long without one of its forms cropping up. It is quickly evident whether a speaker uses the correct form of *be*; hence, whether the speaker is middle-class is quickly established. This is because almost none of the nonstandard varieties of English uses the inflected forms of *be* in the standard way. Some speakers say, "I is"; others say, "I be," "You is," "You was," or "You be." Some do not say *be* at all, as in "He good." These are differences in *be* usage from one nonstandard dialect to another, but all seem to differ from the standard varieties of English, whether British or American. In this respect, the standard educated varieties of English are alike.

Similarly, although all educated dialects still use the -*s* number agreement marker in the present singular, nonstandard speakers often omit it there, saying, "He go," "He don't." Some varieties of English use the -*s* agreement marker, but not necessarily on the third person singular. Rather, they say, "We sits, "You sits," and /or "They sits," but "He sit." Many speakers, educated and not, use what I call a "narrative -*s*" in the singular, as in "Then I sits myself down and. . . ."

Verb inflections work beautifully as signals because they stand out in the stream of speech in English, which has long since shed the large system of inflection and agreement its words once had to use. The very fact that the *be* forms, relics of the old system of inflections, no longer fit the general grammar of English means that people will notice how they are used in speech. That these relics remain suggests to me, at least, that they may have survived because they are so useful as social class markers.

Another social class marker that is a relic of an earlier stage of the language is the retention of now irregularly formed past tenses of certain verbs. Here sometimes the older form is now nonstandard, while the newer regularized one is standard. Appalachian *holp* was the original past tense of *help*. In fact, *helped* originally must have been the kind of kiddie error we saw in Chapter 1, like *sitted* for *sat*.

Have went, which is today nonstandard, reflects the original past participle of *went* as in "She wends her way." *Wend* used to have the past tense *went*, thus "She went her way," and the past participle *went* as well, just as today we have *spend, spent, (have) spent*. For some reason the present tense of *wend* was replaced by *go*, and the old participle of *go, gone*, was retained, resulting in the **paradigm** (set of forms) *go, went, gone*. When the paradigms of two words are collapsed (coalesce) this way, the process is called **suppletion**. This process typically affects common words in the language. We see another example in the paradigm *good, better, best*. The *good* clearly comes from an originally different set than *better* and *best*. The speaker who says "have went" is just using the old participle form of *wend*.

In general, all over the United States, the past participles (the form used with the auxiliary *have*) of irregular verbs are being replaced by the simple past, so that one hears, "I have spoke . . . ," "He's wrote . . . ," and "You should've saw. . . ." One freezing day in winter, as I was pumping gas, a man came by and offered to do it for me so I could sit in the warm car. When I thanked him, he wistfully replied, "I wish I coulda did it for my mudda."

Actually, this is not new. Examples can be found as early as 1565 (Bloomer 1998), "Such things as I *have wrote* of the most holy father." From 1865, "We *woulda took* the bottle, but it *was broke.*" Abraham Lincoln, in an 1863 letter, wrote *had strove* for *had striven.* Bloomer notes that most instances of using the wrong past participles involve a modal auxiliary (*may, might, can, could, will, would, must*) followed by *have* or its contracted forms, *-ve* or *-a*. He argues that one doesn't find *That has been knew for a long time* or *a knew entity.* It is true that *a knew entity* for *a known entity* doesn't seem to occur, but that phrase belongs to formal speech, and *That has been known for a long time* is a set phrase. That is, it is a sentence one hears with some frequency.

Like Bloomer, I have found most of the erroneous verb forms in phrases with a modal auxiliary, but not all. There are a fair number which occur after the full form of *have* or after a clearly articulated *'ve.* I have been collecting phrases like *has gave,* and *have ran.*[27] A reverse situation is one in which the past participle is used as the simple past, as in *I seen it.*

It seems to me that we are seeing a change in progress in the verb system in which the simple past like *broke* is being used as a past participle. Except for a relative handful of irregular verbs, this is already the case with English verbs, so that we have *he played* and *he has played.* Even some of the irregular verbs have identical simple pasts and past participles, like *she brought* and *she has brought.* What's happening, then, is that the grammar is being regularized so that all verbs use the same simple past and past participle. Those worried about language decay because of these mistakes can rest easy. All that's going to happen is that a more uniform verb system will be created.

Negatives also have to be used frequently in conversation. They are, by their nature, not part of large sets so that they, too, stand out in the stream of speech. Negation in English has become a social marker and, by extension, a stylistic one as well. Double negation as in "I didn't do nothing" signals the working and lower classes, but "I didn't do anything" signals the educated middle class. Double negation sometimes is affected by educated speakers as a marker of casual, informal style. They attempt to emulate the naturalness and informality which they presume to be characteristic of formally less-educated classes. Therefore, speech forms readily identifiable as belonging to their speech, especially double negatives, have become stylistic as well as grammatical. As it happens, the lower-class practice is the older one in English, and the educated *anything* is the newer.

Some regional grammatical differences are unrelated to social class. These are more subtle, not necessarily concentrated in constructions that have to be used a great deal. People are often unaware that these differences exist, just as they are often unaware of lexical differences. These regionalisms involve variation in prepositions, positive *anymore* mentioned above, and double modals.

Prepositions. Prepositional differences offer a good example. Prepositions have a habit of slipping and sliding around over the years. Often prepositions in themselves have little meaning, and the selection of one over the other has little consequence for meaning. Old English prayed to God "on heaven" rather than "in heaven." Today, *in* and *on* vary regionally. New York City and environs wait *on line* to buy tickets instead of the more common *in line*. Of course, with the advent of the Internet, everyone now is on line, but not in the New York sense. In the South and the Midland *wait on* means what Northerners do by *wait for*, although sometimes I hear Northern lovers of jazz and blues say "wait on" for *wait for*. In the North, *wait on* refers to serving another person. In Pennsylvania and parts of the South and Midland, one might hear *sick on his stomach*, *sick at his stomach*, or *sick in his stomach*. The usual Northern phrase is *sick to his stomach*. Appalachians speak of *at the wintertime*, rather than *in*. Rural Downeast Maine says *to home* for *at home*. The Midlands tell time with *quarter till* instead of *quarter to* or *quarter of*. Some speakers in New York City, parts of Wisconsin, and Pennsylvania *stay by* a relative's house when they visit rather than *stay with*, perhaps because of the influence of Yiddish and German in those areas.

Because choice of preposition is determined by arbitrary grammar rules rather than by selection on the basis of meaning alone, much preposition use is considered syntactic. Prepositions in many European languages have replaced old endings on nouns that tell how the noun is being used in a given sentence. For instance, in English, the surviving inflectional suffix on nouns, the possessive *'s*, is also paraphrasable by using the preposition *of*.

***Anymore* Revisited.** We have already seen that *anymore* used without a preceding negative term is characteristic of the Midland dialects. Parker (1985) notes that in some parts of West Virginia, Pennsylvania, Delaware, upstate New York, Ohio, Kentucky, Indiana, and South Carolina one hears:

Things are getting busier for me **anymore.**
That's what plane travel is **anymore.**
You really talk a lot **anymore**.

CHAPTER 7

As prevalent as this is, and as widespread, my students who don't come from these areas misunderstand that it means 'nowadays,' and not 'still.' For their part, the ones who do use positive *anymore* are surprised to discover that it is a dialectal variation.

Even more subtle syntactic differences occur across America. An educated Detroit speaker told me "that squirrel *is keeping on getting into* my bird feeder." Polling students and friends, I find most would say "that squirrel *keeps on getting into* my bird feeder." British RP speakers regularly say "I *am wanting to know the answer.*" Most Americans I've polled confine themselves to *want to know.* Possibly because of the influence of Italian, Yiddish, and other European languages, one hears from New York City and Los Angeles speakers, "We *are married for* forty years." In some other areas, it is, "We *have been married for* forty years."

Might, Could, **and** *Fixin' To.* In all varieties of English we can use a **modal auxiliary** followed by the base form of a verb for a variety of meanings:

I *can do* that.
He *may do* that.
I *will see* to it.
Marissa *could study* harder.
Max *might go.*

However, most English speakers wouldn't say:

I *can might do* that.
Jane *may should go.*
You *might could see* him.

That is, most dialects do not allow two modal auxiliaries to be used in the same phrase. Still, there are large numbers of speakers in the South and South Midland who regularly use double modals like those above. DiPaolo (1989) has collected a plethora of such usages in East and West Texas. She shows that such usages are not random. The two modals cannot occur in just any order. For instance, she found that *may can* is used, but *can may* is not (198). Di Paolo suggests that these are frequently used as hedging so as to sound tentative; hence, pragmatically, they can occur as politeness forms. For instance, a sales clerk in a fabric store suggested to a customer who wanted to redesign a shirt:

1. You *might* still *could* keep the cuff the way it is.

followed by:

2. You *might could* keep the cuffs . . .

We have already seen (Chapter 3) that all varieties of English make verbs more polite by use of modals rather than, as the Japanese do, using a set of honorific endings on the verb. Therefore, it is not surprising to see those dialects which use double modals do so also as politeness markers or ways of making statements seem more tentative.

Another Southernism is the use of *fixin' to* as an auxiliary verb. This is quite different from the use of *fix* as a main verb, as in:

3. I'm going to *fix* dinner.
    I have to *fix the car.*

in which *fix* means 'make' and 'repair,' respectively. All Americans would fix a car, and most would fix a meal, but they wouldn't be *fixin' to do* something.

Ching (1987, 338) reports that in those dialects that do, there are a variety of meanings for the auxiliary use of *fixin' to*, although all include the meanings of 'immediacy, priority, definiteness, certainty, and preparatory activity.' Additionally, there seems to be a meaning of 'short delay' in all the usages he reports. He gives as examples of proper usage of this auxiliary:

4. I'm *fixin' to* take care of it [cleaning up a spill].
    I'm *fixin' to* get to work [on homework].
    I'm *fixin' to* wash the dishes.

But, he discovered most respondents to a survey said they could not use this form in sentences like:

5. *I'm *fixin' to* leave in the next five years.
    *I'm *fixin' to* lose weight one of these days.

Perhaps Ching's most interesting finding is that people assigned different meanings to *fixin' to* depending upon the situation in which it was said and the relative social status of the speakers. For instance, when a maid said to a faculty member, "I'm fixin to take care of it," it was interpreted as her finishing her task at hand, and then immediately going to clean up the spill. A faculty member has the social right, in that situation, to ask a maid to clean up, and she has the social duty to do so as soon as possible, whereas a student's telling her adviser, "I'm *fixin' to* get to work" doesn't necessarily carry the meaning of finishing another activity and immediately doing the homework.

He also found, by asking people to choose meanings of several statements, that Southerners disagreed on many of the usages. For instances, 67 said one can't say, "I'm fixin' to lose weight one of these days" but 37 said one can. Similarly, 57 respondents said that they would say, "I'm fixin' to have a baby" upon discovering she is pregnant but 46 said they wouldn't expect to phrase it that way.

Troike (1989) noted that there is an added meaning to *fixin' to*. It signals that the speaker is already aware of the situation, so the maid who said, "I'm fixin' to take care of it" is also indicating that she is aware that the job needs doing. Ching verified this among his students, who told him that the only way one can use *fixin' to* in the first person without prior awareness is in a joke, but in the third person it can be used without a notion of prior awareness, as in:

6. It's **fixin' to rain** [speaker looks out of window].
7. He's **fixin' to get hit** [when speaker sees car out of control and ready to collide with another].

The intricacies of the meaning of syntactic forms and the difficulties of nonnative speakers in using them accurately are well illustrated by this example.

The *fixin' to* usage developed in the South. It has no counterparts in British, Irish, or Scots dialects. It is strongly associated with the South. Some Southern speakers stigmatize it as being country, associating it with being a hick. Northerners who have moved to the South stigmatize it as well. One friend of mine so derides it, that he criticizes me for saying, "I'll fix dinner." This, despite my explaining to him that *fixing dinner* is not the same thing as *fixing to fix dinner*.

As this section has shown, however, stigmatized or not, there are definite rules as to when one may or may not say, "I'm fixin' to do something." It is not a mistake. It is a bona fide syntactic construction in its dialect area.

With the continued migration of Northerners to the South, it may well be that the auxiliary use of *fixin' to* will either disappear or only be used in uneducated speech. When outsiders move into a region, they often ridicule local speech. If large numbers are moving in, as has happened in the South, the attitudes of the newcomers could affect the native speakers' dialects. As an example, Hazen (2006) believes that Appalachian dialect in West Virginia is a dying one. However, he concludes, that this area will still show regional variation, specifically retaining the South Midland mountain dialect.

BLACK ETHNIC SPEECH

Despite American folk beliefs, there is no one Black English. All African Americans do not speak the same way. Not all Americans who consider themselves black are African American. There are Haitians, Cape Verdeans, and African Africans whose histories and cultures differ, as does their speech. For this reason, the term AAVE refers specifically to African American speech. Among African Americans there is variety. Many speak the regional standard, and their speech is indistinguishable from whites among whom they reside. Others command two dialects, one the white regional and one of the varieties of AAVE. Despite the many differences in these dialects, some features are acknowledged to be markers of AAVE; that is, they occur widely or universally in those dialects.

Although AAVE is usually characterized as sounding Southern, it does differ from white Southern dialects. However, it is obviously more like those dialects than Northern ones. In pronunciation, historically, AAVE has clearly been influenced by white Southern coastal *r*-less dialects (Mufwene and Gilman 1987). Exceptions to this occurred in at least one African American population in the North, the Olney Street neighborhood of Providence, which was settled by freed or runaway slaves during the Colonial and Federal periods. Many of their ancestors were among the slaves brought to New England who never did get to the South, or who escaped when slavery was abolished early on in the Northeast. My dialect investigations into older members of this community showed no Southernisms. As I mentioned above, one of my informants proudly told me that they spoke like the old English. Certainly, their speech is a clear variant of Rhode Island English. Most of my students who have heard tapes of these speakers do not identify them as African American.

In the 1950's and 1960's, however, the migration from the South and the identification of southern-based AAVE with black ethnicity brought more traditional AAVE speech to this area. However, many of the descendants of the older population of Rhode Island African Americans still do not use such speech or do so rarely.

What we might call canonical AAVE, what most people are referring to when they speak of the AAVE vernacular, is quite traditionally Southern in pronunciation. *Time* is pronounced "Tom," *hard* is "hahd," *aunt* is "ahnt," not "ant," and /ɛ/ and /I/ are merged before nasals even in northern cities like Chicago, so that *pin* and *pen* are both pronounced like *pin*. As with other *r*-less speakers, younger African Americans are beginning to pronounce the pre-consonantal /r/ at least some of the time (Myhill 1988), although a quick course in rap music shows these dialects are still essentially *r*-less.

Another feature of AAVE is the dropping of final consonants, so that *field* rhymes with *wheel*, and *whore* has become *ho*. We saw this in Chapter 6 as a significant source of rhyming in AAVE speech.

All varieties of American English simplify final consonant clusters. All Americans usually say, "roas' beef" for instance, dropping the final consonant when the next word begins with a consonant, but retaining the /t/ on *roast* in "roast in the oven" where the next word begins with a vowel. Many AAVE speakers are likely to drop this final /t/ as well, saying "roas' in the oven." We don't notice that we simplify the consonant cluster in "roas' beef." But we do notice when a consonant is dropped that we wouldn't drop. Therefore, non-AAVE speakers think that AAVE speakers drop sounds willy-nilly. One result of this general final consonant dropping in AAVE is that the plural of words like *desk* and *test* becomes "desses" and "tesses." This is because when the final consonant is omitted, the word then ends in -*s*: "des" and "tes." Words that end in -*s* form a plural by adding -*es*.

The syntax of AAVE verbs has long been acknowledged to differ from most white varieties of American English. A major difference is the existence in AAVE of a **durative** versus a **nondurative** aspect in the verb system. This is the contrast of "He **be** bad" with "He bad." The first means 'he is always bad' (durative), whereas the second means 'he is being bad right now.' Richardson (1991) comments that:

Them boys **be beating** up girls

has no ready counterpart in what she calls SAE (standard American English), noting that the use of the invariant *be* here means both 'habitual' and frequent behavior. Her study of African American and white teenagers in East Palo Alto showed that AAVE speakers use the *be* to express habitual behavior, using fewer adverbials than whites. White speakers "mark habituality semantically" (301) by using adverbs like *always*. Since white speakers do not have a durative form, not surprisingly, they do not contrast it by leaving out the **copula** (a form of *be*) as do AAVE speakers when expressing a nondurative or nonhabitual circumstance as in "He all right." Besides the durative *be*, AAVE uses *steady* to indicate a habitual action. Edwards and Ash (2004, 171) quote Tupac Shakur's "Smokin' blunt after blunt and *steady drinkin'*."

This difference in dialects carries over to questions as well. In AAVE, a question like "*Do* babes *be* willin'?" means "Are babes always willing?" The lack of an -*s* agreement marker on *do* is another feature of AAVE. However, Bernstein (1988) found that Southern blacks then over the age of forty-nine use an inflected form of the durative copula *bees* that does not seem to occur in other dialects. She found no instance of this in white speech.

AAVE also uses *ain't* as an auxiliary in the sense of *didn't*, as in "I *ain't do* nothin'." They also use it, like white nonstandard speech, in the sense of *isn't*. Edwards and Ash (2004, 169) give the example, "It **ain't** easy tryin' to raise a man."

An especially interesting use of *be* as an auxiliary verb occurs in emphatic expressions like "You *be sat* there" meaning 'you'll remain sitting there.'

Two other auxiliaries used in AAVE are *done* meaning 'action completed in past' and *been*, 'action completed in the further past.' As the examples below show, both can be used to indicate that what happened in the past is still relevant, although they can also mean 'It's done and over.' Wolfram and Fasold (1974, 152) claimed that these were disappearing, especially in northern cities. In 2006 they seem to be alive and well. Not only have I had a young woman tell me, "Girl, I *been had* those shoes," but Edwards and Ash (2004, 171) report "Cuz we *been beat* those [people]" from an interview with Tupac Shakur. An African American friend, now forty years old, once told me she didn't use *done* as an auxiliary, and a few minutes later said, "I *done told* her not to do that." She laughed immediately. In fact, she uses it frequently. Another example I've found from younger speakers is "I *been* settled the score," meaning, 'I have already settled the score once and for all.' An African American neighbor of mine told me, "We *been had* those dogs since they were puppies." Apparently, the reports of the demise of the AAVE *done* and *been* auxiliaries have been premature.

One future marker in AAVE is *I'ma*. This can combine with the durative, as in "I'*ma be* workin' in a office" meaning 'I'll be working steadily doing office work.' Another example, is "I'*ma be* somebody. . . ." The *be* is the durative mentioned above. This seems to add a feature of determination to the future. It is very emphatic, "I WILL BE someone."

Spears (1987, 51) notes two other grammatical features of AAVE. One is what he terms the "semi-auxiliary *come*" used in a negative sense, as in "She *come callin'* me, *come yellin'* in my phone." He glosses this as 'She had the nerve to call me and to yell in my phone.'

He also notes that, although AAVE often doesn't use the third person singular agreement marker *-s* (*she come* for *she comes*), it does use an *-s* to indicate that a narrative is being related which took place in the past, as in "Jackie *comes* out of the hospital," meaning that she came out of the hospital. Actually, this usage occurs in other dialects as well under the same circumstances when someone is relating a string of events, as in "First, Jackie comes out of the hospital, then she gets into her car, turns on the motor, and crashes the car into the gate." This is all to be taken as past action. Only if such forms are used by an announcer doing an on-the-spot will this present tense be interpreted as a contemporaneous event.

Another feature of AAVE is the lack of a possessive marker, as in "That *Tyrone car.*" The plural *s* is also frequently omitted in AAVE, resulting in phrases like "two *boy.*" However, if the plural is irregular, it is used, as in "two men." Similarly, the past tense in *-ed* is often not pronounced, leading to sentences like "We play yesterday." Again, if the verb is irregular and doesn't have the *-ed* ending, it will be used in the past as in standard English, "The car broke down yesterday." Another feature of AAVE is not using the auxiliary *do* in a question, like "*why* they *take* another soldier?" and "Ah, Suge, *what* I *tell* you . . .?" (Edwards and Ash 2004, 171)

Some scholars have claimed that there is no difference between AAVE and other Southern dialects matched for socioeconomic status, e.g., McDavid and Davis (1972), yet others insist that it is a separate language (Dillard 1973; Smitherman 1984, 2000). Still others claim that African American speech affected white Southern speech. For generations, both before and after slavery, African American women were charged with the care of white children. The slave term *mammy* is but a variant of *mama.* Perhaps this influenced the speech of Southern white children. The problem with this line of reasoning is that all the evidence shows that children learn to speak like their peers, not their parents or other caregivers.

It has also been suggested that Southern *r*-dropping was caused by slaves who couldn't pronounce the /r/, but, again, historically, people don't imitate their slaves or employees. African Americans weren't a dominant class in the South. Today, young people imitate AAVE, but that is because African American entertainers and sports figures are admired. They are influential. This wasn't true during the days of formation of Southern speech. Also, since *r*-dropping was a feature of British speech, that is its likely source.

Fasold (1986) investigated the matter of black and white speech similarities in the South and found eight features exclusive to AAVE. One difference is that in single syllable words or on stressed syllables, AAVE speakers often pronounce a word-final /d/ as a glottal stop followed by a [t], so that *bed* is pronounced [bɛʔt] (Fasold 1986, 453). A second is the omission of the *-s* agreement marker in phrases like *he walks* and *he kisses.* One study in Mississippi found that AAVE speakers omitted this 87% of the time, while whites did so only 15% of the time (454). Parallel omissions of plural and possessive markers are also prominent features of AAVE (457) and not of white southern speech .

Some scholars explain the durative *be* and the auxiliaries *done* and *been* as deriving from verb systems in African languages. This may well be the origin of these forms. As anybody does when learning a new language, the African speaking slaves would have used the syntax they were familiar with and just substituted English words for them. However, the remote aspect *been*, as in "You won't get your dues that you *been paid*," has been found in Newfoundland speech. Here it means that the dues have long since been paid. That indicates some dialects of English had that form, as Newfoundland speakers had no contact with Africans. The overseers on the plantations were often Irish, and Gaelic has a durative. Other dialects spoken in the 17th century might have had the remote aspect as well. This doesn't negate the influence of African languages on AAVE, however. If the slaves heard forms similar to those they were used to, they would have easily incorporated them in their English. In the United States, these features belong only to AAVE and not other varieties of English. Other speakers seem never to use them. It seems very reasonable to me that AAVE shows influence from Wolof and other African languages, as well as influence from the white Southern speech the slaves heard around them. The ubiquitous *okay* derives from the Wolof word meaning 'all right.' In New England, where a population of African Americans lived who never suffered through slavery in the South, their speech, while identifiable as AAVE, showed none of the Southernisms. Moreover, it didn't have a durative *be*, nor did it have the omission of the copula as in "He tired" to indicate a temporary state. Their speech understandably was strongly influenced by the Providence accent.

DEVELOPMENT OF AN AMERICAN STANDARD

Since World War II, migration from birthplace has become so common that regional loyalties have been weakened. Concomitantly, social networks have also been weakened. This seems especially true for people most likely to move: the educated middle class who go where their jobs take them. More and more, at least on the East Coast, educated speech is losing some of its historical regional qualities. Many middle-class speakers seem almost aggressively pleased if they can claim, "No one can tell where I come from." Although this is truer of speakers about fifty and younger, occasionally informants as old as seventy make this boast. When East Coast middle-class speakers are asked to participate in a dialect study, they frequently respond, "Yes, but I don't have a [name of locale] accent."

On the other hand, people from other regions presume they don't speak with an accent at all. Once, on the phone to place a catalogue order, I asked the operator if she was from Washington state. There was a dead

CHAPTER 7

pause for a second, and then she asked, "Can you hear that I have an accent the way I can hear that you have one?" When I said that I could, she responded, "That's funny. I never thought we had an accent here." I've had similar experiences with speakers from Los Angeles, Minneapolis, Philadelphia, Connecticut, Kansas City, and many other points across the country. My Connecticut students are quite aggressive about claiming they have no accent. They are also the most likely to say that their speech is the American standard. Strangely, the Midwestern students, those from Chicago and Milwaukee, whom most New Englanders assume are accent-free, are quick to say they have an accent.

On the American Dialect Society's tape *American Tongues*, there is an interview with a man from Columbus who says that their speech is bland, neutral, without an accent, middle America, middle everything. You may recall that Columbus is at the heart of Midland speech, using expressions like "The house needs painted." When I was a child, my family moved briefly to Los Angeles. I recall how the kids made fun of my accent. I was shocked on two grounds. One, at that time ENE speech was still considered prestigious and most of the movie stars were trained to speak that way. Two, it was very evident to me that the LA kids had an accent. After all, they pronounced *your* as "yerr" (rhyming it with *her*), whereas I pronounced it as it "should" be, [yɔr] "yawr." A man once remarked to me "An accent is something you get when you leave home." That is no longer precisely true, especially for those who come from regions whose speech has been stigmatized, such as New York City, ENE, and the coastal South, the historically *r*-dropping areas.

Many Northeast and Southeast educated speakers by the 1950's became convinced that whatever they learned in childhood is not "General American." Therefore, throughout the formerly *r*-less dialect areas of the East Coast, both North and South, the /r/ is increasingly pronounced in words like *park* and *car*, especially amongst younger and educated speakers. *ANAE* (Labov et al. 2006, 47–48) reports that in the South "younger white speakers are consistently *r*-full." In contrast, African American speakers in the South are still largely *r*-dropping.

Labov et al. report that in New York City and ENE there is increased *r*-pronouncing among educated and younger speakers. However, it is not as consistent as in the South, occurring mostly in formal speech. Their interviews show the level of *r*-dropping in ENE as 75% (226–27). They said that New Hampshire is the only ENE state in which people rarely drop their *r*'s, although other features of their speech put them squarely in ENE. The *ANAE* Map 16.1 shows six Telsur interviews in Rhode Island, all of them evincing almost complete *r*-dropping.

However, I am a native of this region and have long-standing ties with other native Rhode Islanders. At my high school reunions, it has been notable for years that everyone is *r*-full. I rarely hear educated speakers under the age of fifty or so who aren't *r*-full. Dropping *r*'s is diagnostic of ethnic and uneducated speech.

The student body at the college that I teach in has a majority of students from ENE, New York City and environs. They, too, are uniformly *r*-pronouncing. Even my manicurist who never went to college and identifies strongly with her Italian ethnicity is *r*-full. When I lived in rural Foster, Rhode Island from 1970–1995, high school students who were planning to leave the region, even if they weren't college-bound, didn't drop *r*'s, but those who intended to stay did.

There are two possibilities for the Telsur results. One is, simply, six people taken at random aren't sufficient to find the actual situation in a population of just over a million. The second is that the pronunciation of /r/ in ENE is not as strongly constricted as it is in other parts of the country. This consonant is produced by tensing the tongue tip and there is variation in the degree of tension used in different dialects. The telephone acoustics may not have registered a lightly tensed /r/.

Labov et al. (4) note that the telephone interview doesn't give reliable information on the vocalization of /l/. Well, /r/ and /l/ are acoustically similar, and I suspect a lightly constricted /r/ may not have been noted, especially since the investigators didn't expect to find one at all.

In ENE, like New York City, *r*-dropping is a matter of age, gender, and social class. Younger people do it less than older ones. Women do it less than men. Educated people do it less than uneducated. Still, I have observed speakers in ENE who are over seventy but don't *r*-drop as a rule.

One can contrast Ted Kennedy's increased /r/-pronouncing in many words with the complete lack of /r/ before consonants in the speeches of his brother John F. Kennedy.[28] Their children, the Kennedy cousins, seem all to be consistently *r*-full, even those like Patrick who was raised in Massachusetts and is now a Rhode Island Congressman.

The many differences in vowel usages that mark out dialect regions do not seem to carry the same status-marking messages as /r/ pronouncing has. Why has /r/ become such a distinct social marker in America? As a Civil War buff, I came across a diary once in which a New England woman said of a Southern gentleman, "His speech was so fine you could hardly hear an *r*." As part of the myth that there is a General American dialect out there somewhere in the great Midwest, people associate *r*-full speech with being American. So do British linguists, even those who are specialists in dialects like James Milroy (1984, 54) and J. C. Wells (1982, 473), although one would expect them to know differently.

CHAPTER 7

After World War II, the United States rose as a world power and Great Britain declined. In national terms, so did ENE. Southern dialects, the other *r*-less ones, had largely lost their prestige in the aftermath of the Civil War. No longer was *r*-lessness associated with power in America. With the phenomenal growth of the great midwestern and western universities, the Eastern bastions were no longer considered the repository of learning and culture. And, large cities changed their sociological mix, requiring new pronunciation variables to distinguish people of different social groups (Chapter 9).

The *r*-full pronunciation prevalent in most areas of the United States and Canada already was a natural candidate for new prestige marking in formerly *r*-less areas. Thus, the encroachment of a new /r/-pronouncing standard is evident up and down the eastern seaboard. It is easier to pronounce /r/'s wherever they are spelled than it is, for instance, to try to adopt the vowels of the Great Lakes cities. So, it appears that *r*-dropping will remain in American English mostly in AAVE, blue-collar, and uneducated speech.

Notes

1   This is strictly a "for instance" on my part. Montgomery says that Southerners understand this construction, but Northerners are confused by it. Exactly how he delimits Southerners from Northerners is not clear. Timothy Frazer (personal communication) has told me that many central Illinois speakers sound Southern to East Coast speakers.

2   Yiddish is the term for the many dialects of German spoken exclusively by the Jews of Eastern Europe as a result both of their enforced isolation from Christians and of their being persecuted for centuries. Because of these factors, they developed into an ethnic group with its own language. As these factors have disappeared, American and Israeli Jews no longer speak it, and it is largely dying out. It survives almost entirely amongst the very old. Do not confuse Yiddish with Hebrew. The latter is the language of Jewish prayer and the Bible. A modern version of Hebrew is spoken in Israel.

3   This is the [r] associated with German and French, as opposed to the American retroflex or Italian trill.

4   The Indo-European languages are those spoken from modern-day India, Pakistan, and Bangladesh to the Slavic and Germanic languages to the Romance languages and Iranian, Greek, and Armenian. There was once one language, known as Proto-Indo-European, which broke up into dialects and separate languages as its speakers spread from Asia east to west, reaching India to Europe.

5   In reporting on these studies, I am using the terms for race and ethnicity that the original researchers did. Usually, as is the practice in this book, I prefer the term *African American* to refer to American blacks.

6   This is not to say that all blacks speak nonstandard English or that only whites speak Standard English. Apparently these researchers preferred for their example of nonstandard speech to record blacks speaking that way. By no means can one always tell if someone is black by hearing a tape recording of their speech. Many blacks speak indistinguishably from whites, and many blacks command both Standard English and ethnic black dialects, switching between them as they wish.

7   I am using *isoglosses* here to indicate a boundary between two pronunciations and a boundary between two different words for the same thing. Strictly speaking, *isophone* is the term for the boundary between two pronunciations, but, especially since isophones and isoglosses occur close to each other and often delimit the same dialect areas, many linguists simply use the term *isoglosses* to refer to both kinds of boundaries.

CHAPTER 7

8   Boberg claims that all of eastern New England pronounces *cot* and *caught* alike. However, this is not true. All of Rhode Island and neighboring Massachusetts cities like Seekonk, Fall River, and parts of Attleboro pronounce them differently, as does western New England.

9   For a more complete discussion of the older atlas studies, see Chaika (1994, 273–81).

10   W. Nelson Francis, who had done dialect investigations in England.

11   I refer to them as the Great Lakes cities both because I have met residents of those cities who refer to them that way, and because, to me, it's easier to visualize them as being on the shores of the Great Lakes. The part of Indiana included in this dialect area is the part closest to the Great Lakes. Of course, the dialect features of these cities go somewhat beyond the borders of the cities themselves.

12   They say that there are a total of 629 language items that have been identified as belonging to the Midland.

13   Different authors claim different numbers of Midland features. Ash lists 10, but Murray and Simon list 17, and mention that there is a total of over 600. What is interesting, however, is the widespread agreement on the differences cited in 1–12.

14   When I lived in the mountain areas of Aroostook County and the Moosehead Lake regions of Maine in the 1950s, I met many people who lived in isolated outposts, making their way by small farming, lumbering, and hunting. Such people lived in the mountains of New Hampshire and in isolated villages in western Rhode Island and contiguous areas of Connecticut. All were *r*-less despite their lack of contact with city folk. It is inconceivable that their ancestors could have been influenced by British speech. In fact, many of those I talked with were proud of how their ancestors fought the British.

15   I have no idea what this word means, as I can't find it in any dictionary and Frazer doesn't supply the meaning.

16   A monophthong is a vowel made while the tongue stays in one position. It contrasts with a diphthong like the *i* in *time* in which the tongue moves from one position to another as you make the vowel sound, which is actually /ai/. That is, you start saying "ah," and move your tongue upwards to "ee." However, the two vowels are said and intended as one. If one comes from the South, the diphthong *i* may be pronounced as a monophthong /ah/, but diphthongs will be pronounced in other vowels.

17   There are many ways of representing this particular sound. Labov himself has employed different notations for it over the years, from calling it æ-1, æ-2, æ-3, etc., to raised /æh/. Others have designated it

as [ɛə], and I myself have used the IPA symbol [ɨ], which comes from the original IPA. In light of the "breaking" which Labov et al. found in acoustic analyses, that is, that the sound is actually produced as a diphthong, with the tongue moving either from [i], [I], or [ɛ] to an [ə], I have also adopted these symbols as the cover symbol for the raised variants of short <a> in *bad*, *happy*, and related words. However, the transcriptions /iə/, etc. only refer to speakers from the Great Lakes cities. Other American speakers do not necessarily make a glide on that sound, so their pronunciation is /ɨ/. When you make the vowel sound in *ham*, notice your tongue is both high and in the front of the mouth.

[18] Historically, this happened in the late 15th century when the vowel in *time*, which was originally pronounced like "teem," shifted to the modern *i* sound. Then because the position for the original vowel was vacant, the vowel in *knee*, first pronounced "nay," got its modern pronunciation of "ee." Then that vowel space became vacant, so the vowel in *name*, which was originally pronounced "nahm," got its modern form "ay," and so on. Because of The Great English Vowel Shift, to this day, English pronunciations of long vowels represented as *a*, *e*, *i*, *o*, *u* do not jibe with the pronunciations of those vowels in other European languages.

[19] Los Angeles speakers pronounce *boss* as "bahs."

[20] Consonants differ in whether they are voiceless, like /p/, /f/, /t/, /θ/, /s/, /ʃ/, /k/, and /h/ or voiced, which includes all others. Other groupings of consonants, like fricatives (/s/, /f/, /θ/, /z/, etc.) and stops (/p/, /t/, /k/, /b/, /d/, /g/) also affect preceding vowels. The vowel is held longer before /d/ than /t/. You can hear this by saying *bat* and *bad*.

[21] *Locked* ends in the sounds /kt/, and *lost* ends in /st/, which are phonetically similar.

[22] A prime example of this occurred in Indo-European, the parent language of most of the languages spoken in Europe today, and many of those spoken in India, as well as Farsi, spoken in Iran. Indo-European had only one consonant that was a fricative. This was an /s/. It had twelve stops, however, sounds like /p/, /b/, /t/, /d/, /k/, /g/, with each of these having a counterpart produced by puffing air, as still seen in Hindi spellings and pronunciations like *dhal*. When the first Germanic speakers adopted Indo-European, they changed three of the stops to the fricatives /f/, /θ/, and /h/. This made the consonant system more balanced, with four fricatives and six stops. Nobody decided to do this. Indeed, those primitive tribesmen certainly didn't consciously know

about stops and fricatives, but they still righted the system. In most of the Indo-European daughter languages, some of the stops became fricatives.

23 Strictly speaking, Americans make a flapped *r* for both /t/ and /d/ in between vowels, as in the British *very,* spelled <veddy> when authors want to approximate a British accent. The phonetic symbol for this sound is [ɾ].

24 I do not know if this is still used in Maine, as I never drink these concoctions and keep forgetting to look on menus when I go to Maine. So far as I know, this is not a term that has been elicited by field-workers. At least I can't find mention of it in the literature on dialects. I just know it from my residency in that state.

25 I am often asked where Rhode Island got this unusual (when referring to a drink) word. It's actually an example of *metonymy.* The early blenders were housed in small wooden cabinets, so people referred to the cabinet for the thing it made. This is like saying, "The baby wants his bottle" when it's not the bottle the baby wants but what's in it. Rhode Islanders are very aware that others find the word strange, and middle-class blacks and whites and Rhode Islanders who have lived elsewhere will sometimes deny knowing the term or will use the generic *shake* when asked in a dialect interview for the term for a mixture of milk, ice cream, and syrup. At the end of an interview, if I casually say, "Have you ever heard of someone drinking a cabinet?" this always elicits a "Oh, yes" sort of answer followed by an apology like "I haven't had one in years . . . I forgot." Interestingly, my younger (now in late teens or twenties) informants are not so self-conscious about this term, and freely use it, although they are aware that it is called *milkshake* elsewhere.

26 I don't know if *ice cream parlor* is a New England regionalism, as I've never seen it elicited in a dialect study. I suspect that there is much more regional diversity in words than we know of, simply because field-workers have not attempted to find out what certain things are called.

27 I have heard such constructions from Ph.D.s.

28 Clips of JFK speaking are played regularly on programs about his assassination or about the sixties in general. I presume most readers have heard these.

Exercises

1. Listen to a song or view a movie or television sequence in which a dialect of English different from yours is spoken. What seem to be the differences between this dialect and your own?

2. Make up a list of words which you think have dialectal variants. Make up a definition for each word. Then poll your friends to see what they call them. For instance, "What do you call the square of toweling that you wash yourself with?" Alternatively, ask people if they know what a *facecloth* or *hoagie* (or any other dialectal variant) refers to. Do they know or use expressions like "The car needs washed"?

3. Ask several people what kind of "accent" they have. How many say something like "General American" or "Vanilla English"? Ask them where they were raised. Can you detect differences in their speech from yours or others you know? Who is likely to say that they have an accent? Where were they raised?

4. Ask a dozen people, preferably from different regions, how they would pronounce the following pairs:

talk	tock
orange	coffee
cot	caught
since	cents
tournament	urn
hurry	her
right	ride

(Add any items you think will be pronounced differently by your participants.) Do all of them pronounce these the same way?

5. Look in three or four college writing handbooks (Harcourt-Brace, Prentice-Hall, etc.), books on advice to writers, or books commenting about how to use English (like Fowler, Newman, John Simons) for advice on using the phrase *in regard to*. Alternatively, take another "don't" such as using *whether or not*. Do all of your sources agree? Take any of the alternatives any of them suggest (e.g., *as regards, with regards to, regarding*, and look those up. Do the sources agree? What can you conclude about the validity of such pronouncements? If you wished to express the thought encoded in any of these, how would you do so, based upon your research?

6. Watch television commercials that feature speakers using regional or ethnic dialects. Recently, many commercials have been featuring British male speakers, some of whom do not speak upper-class British. That is, they do not speak like the actors Jeremy Irons or Hugh Grant. Why do you think these Brits are chosen for these commercials? What are they advertising? What features of the dialect do they seem to be using so that you will identify it as such? If you are familiar with the dialect in question in any of the commercials, how accurate is the actor's representation of it?

Chapter 8

Bilingualism: Individual and Social

Many people speak more than one language. They may have different levels of proficiency in each of their languages, and use them for very different social purposes and in different social situations. Both the errors a bilingual is likely to make in learning the new language, and the cultural attitudes bilinguals have toward each of the languages have been well studied. In educational and legal settings, it is important to know how a bilingual's native language may affect his or her functioning in other languages. It is also important to find out how to teach people foreign languages efficiently. This entails knowing how people go about learning other languages in adulthood. In countries forged from speakers of many languages, it is important to plan which language or languages are going to be used officially in education, the legislatures, and the courts, as those whose languages are not used may be at a serious social and political disadvantage. Under the pressure of modernization, languages not widely spoken in urban areas are becoming extinct, so that we may never be able to know what the human mind is capable of in creating languages.

MONOLINGUALISM AND BILINGUALISM

In the United States, many assume that every person usually speaks one language, the language of his or her country. However, in much of the world, it is usual for people in the same country to speak two or more languages. Many countries simply do not have just one language. Different ethnic groups or tribes retain their native languages as well as speak others common to their country. That is, most of the countries in the world are bilingual or multilingual. In contrast, the United States is virtually a monolingual nation, or so many think.

Bilingualism is both a societal and an individual concern. In terms of society, we consider what languages are spoken in a country, by whom, and for what purposes. Also, scholars should study what effect bilingualism has on the economic and social lives of ethnic groups. Additionally, when considering the individual bilingual speaker, scholars have to investigate how best to teach languages, what difference the age of a learner makes, and what kinds of interference a first language can have on learning a second.

CHAPTER 8

Bilingualism in the United States

Although the United States is usually considered a monolingual nation, it actually never has been. This supposedly monolingual monolith plays—and has played—host to Spanish, Italian, German, French, Polish, Yiddish, Swedish, Norwegian, Danish, Russian, Ukrainian, Greek, Chinese, Armenian, Finnish, Hungarian, Czechoslovakian, Portuguese, Japanese, Korean, Cambodian, Thai, Laotian, Hmong, Mien, Vietnamese, Cambodian, Arabic, and Hebrew, as well as various languages from India and Africa, several Filipino languages, and many other languages not native to these shores. Of course, there is also a variety of Native American tongues, such as Navajo and Cherokee, remnants of the incredible variety spoken before European colonization.

Not only are these languages different from each other, but so are the cultures of the people who speak them. Because their cultures are so different from that of mainstream urban United States, Southeast Asian refugee youth must contend with significant cultural differences and long-term adjustment problems in school (Ascher 1990). Hmong and Mien speakers have the added problem that they do not have a long tradition of writing their languages, so they are from basically oral cultures. As we shall see, people who do not come from literate traditions may have greater difficulty in schools than those who do. As a result of the great cultural differences, Southeast Asians often have not assimilated as well as other non-English speaking groups, including Hispanics (Wong-Rieger and Quintana 1987). However, Vuthy So, a student of mine in 2006, tells me that Cambodian teenagers of his acquaintance haven't learned their parents' or grandparents' language. This has been historically the first step in assimilating to American culture.

The 2003 census showed that there are at least thirty-four home languages spoken in the States: Spanish or Spanish Creole, French, French Creole, Italian, Portuguese or Portuguese Creole, German, Yiddish, Scandinavian languages, Greek, Russian, Polish, Serbo-Croatian, Armenian, Persian, Gujurathi, Hindi, Urdu, Chinese, Japanese, Korean, Mong-Khmer, Cambodian, Miaio, Hmong, Thai, Laotian, Tagalog, Navajo, Hungarian, Arabic, and Hebrew (U.S. Census Bureau 2006, 47). Of these, Spanish speakers comprise the largest minority by far, with 29,698,000 who report speaking Spanish at home, compared to 214,809,000 who speak only English.

Besides the individually listed languages, the census lumps together an unknown number of others into multilanguage categories starting with "other." These languages are labeled: West Germanic, Slavic, Indic, Indo-European, Asian, Pacific Island, and Native North American. Then, there is a catchall category of "other and unspecified languages." *Scandinavian* is a cover term for three languages: Norwegian, Swedish, and Danish.

Diversity is even greater than the above listings indicate. What are termed *Chinese dialects* are actually as different from each other as French is from English, so we really should consider them different languages such as Cantonese, Mandarin (Beijing speech), and the Miao-Yao languages spoken by recent immigrants from southern China. *German* includes both the Pennsylvania Dutch of the Amish and the more "mainstream" German found in groups more assimilated into the general culture. *Italian* refers to both northern and southern dialects, which differ considerably. *Portuguese* encompasses both Brazilian and mainland Portuguese, as well as Cape Verdean and Azorean. Similarly, *French* includes Canadian and Louisiana dialects as well as Haitian, and, of course, Continental French.

There have been so many different languages brought to the United States, that it has been a practical necessity for newcomers to learn English. Obviously, a unified country stretching over 3,000 miles could not be run in fifty or more different languages.

The Impact of Bilingualism. What is the impact of our society on the speakers of these languages and on the languages themselves? How many will survive alongside English? What kinds of problems might they pose for our educational system? During the great waves of immigration, foreign-speaking children were simply left to their own devices, being expected to learn English on their own. Those who could manage the feat were able eventually to use the schools as a springboard to a better life. Those who could not learn English were happily absorbed by the great wave of industrialism, the steel mills and factories. Those who didn't learn English on their own were not necessarily stupid or backward. Often, they didn't have the leisure. They had to work, to bring money into the house to help support their families. Fortunately for those in the cities, night schools were available for those who worked days, and many were able to get a high school education there after they learned some English on their own. In any event, their children were usually English-speaking, many on their way to assimilating into American culture.

Nowadays, we have bilingual education for children who are immigrants, but this is primarily a stopgap until they learn English well enough to be mainstreamed into English-speaking classes. The number of schoolchildren receiving English language learning (ELL) services in the United States according to the National Center for Education Statistics, is 4,029,340 (Hoffman et al. 2005, 7).

Language retention is not an insignificant issue. When people lose the language of their culture, their family ties can be weakened, and with them often their religious ties as well, and their sense of ethnic identity and community. A shared language strengthens social and familial bonds. Only the bilingual speaker knows the rush of warmth of suddenly hearing his or her mother tongue in a land where few speak it.

When Languages Meet. When two languages come into contact, they inevitably affect each other. In the most extreme cases, languages known as Creoles are formed from the languages in contact, resulting in a new language which is actually a combination or blending of two or more parent languages. Although most people think of Creole French in Louisiana when they hear of Creoles, actually any two languages can result in a Creole. As will be demonstrated later, many scholars believe that the varieties of black speech in the United States and the Caribbean emerged from a marriage between various African languages and English, Spanish, or French.

On the individual level, if adult speakers have to learn another language, they usually try to learn it in its entirety. Typically, this results in a foreign accent and errors in discourse, syntax, and vocabulary (Odlin 1989). These are usually not shared by the speaker's native-speaking offspring. There is no clear evidence that such foreign accents have left permanent marks in American English pronunciation, although words from many immigrant groups have been adopted.

Commonly a second language learned in adulthood is acquired as if through a filter, the filter being the first language. Some speakers retain strong accents, making grammar errors based on their first language and misusing words in accordance with their first language even if they have spoken the second for more years than they were monolingual. Moreover, they retain the accents even if they have spoken the second language more frequently than the first during those years. Immigrants who came to America in their twenties may still speak with an extremely thick accent when they are in their seventies. Others will learn the second language with no trace of an accent. The amount of formal education the speaker has received does not seem to be a determining factor in whether an accent is retained, although the amount of formal instruction specifically in the new language may be, apparently because adults need somewhat simplified input to help them acquire the second language (Krashen 1983). This is not surprising if one considers the amount of time that a child can devote to extracting vocabulary and grammar rules from the language he or she has to learn. The adult not only has the interference from a native language, but his or her time to learn is limited. Some immigrants never learn the language of their new country at all. Others learn just enough to get by at work. Social and economic factors, such as a desire to integrate into the new society or to achieve success in business or the professions, probably influence the degree of language learning and the ultimate freedom from a foreign accent.

The movie *Stranger Than Paradise* (1984) depicts the Americanization of Hungarian youths who have recently emigrated from Hungary. The tone is set as the movie opens with the male lead, visibly annoyed by a phone call from his aunt, interjecting "Speak English" to whatever she is excitedly telling him, although he himself certainly can speak and understand Hungarian. When people lose the language of their traditions, they may also start to disvalue the traditions themselves. When that happens, the old who are seen as the guardians of tradition become disvalued as well. What happens to immigrant languages is a vital question for any society, even our own. Can we achieve a melting pot without stirring out all the lumps of different cultures and languages? What do we have to know about language learning and language use to make our decisions wisely?

The Critical Age Controversy

Many linguists believe that sometime after the onset of puberty, a person's ability to discriminate new sounds becomes impaired. *New* here is used in the sense 'different from those in any language(s) already learned by the speaker.' Whether this is purely developmental or whether it is at least partially social is not certain. Folk wisdom claims that adults lose their ability to learn new languages without an accent. It may be, however, that adults do not have the same motivation as children do to learn a new language rapidly without an accent (Lambert 1969; Lambert and Gardner 1972). In light of what we know about the reasons why people retain certain accents, it is not unreasonable to assume that adults retain foreign accents as a way of signaling that they still identify with their homeland.

There is considerable variation in the degree to which second languages are acquired. One famous and important statesman in the 1970's, Henry Kissinger, could not manage accent-free English although he came to the United States at age 15,[1] but many other immigrants who arrived here in their teens speak English with no foreign accent at all. This alone shows that age per se is probably not the sole factor in learning to sound like a native in a second language.

Second languages do not appear to be learned by mimicking any more than first languages are. People who have learned two languages in their childhood seem to learn third or even fourth languages more easily than a monolingual adult can learn a second. Even so, most such bilinguals, but not all, have an accent in the language learned as an adult. Krashen (1983, 30) claims that it is important in language learning to be presented with data just a bit more complex than what is already known. In first language learning, this is typically provided by caregivers' expansions of a toddler's utterances. Few adult language learners get this kind of correction. Therefore, he suggests that one of the most important functions of formal instruction for adults is providing just such input. Many adult second language learners never get formal instruction, however, but they become competent in the new language anyway.

Foreign accents are caused by actual misperception of sounds (Odlin 1989, 113–19). Speakers seem to hear the sounds in a new language through a filter of their own language, converting new sounds to one already in their linguistic repertoire that shares some phonetic features. Some inroads into misperception can be made by good teaching, by focusing the learners' attention on certain sounds and how they should be made.

The attitude of the learner may play a role as well. For instance, German speakers seem to hear the English /Θ/ "th" as in *thing*, and /ð/ "th" as in *the*, as [s] and [z], respectively. Many Germans who resettled in America during the 1930's and 1940's still say "zis sing" for *this thing*. However, younger Germans born since the end of World War II, who live and have always lived in Germany, often pronounce those sounds as native-born English speakers do. One supposes that at least some teachers of English in Germany concentrate on those sounds. Then, too, these speakers have usually started to learn English before adulthood. As surprising as it is to Americans, in many European countries, children start learning new languages in elementary school. Many younger Germans are extremely proud of their accent-free English. For young people virtually the world over, English is a prestige language. Such a desire to be proficient in a second language may make the difference in breaking through perceptual barriers.

Grammatical interference may also arise from misperception, or perhaps, failure to perceive at all. The kinds of grammatical errors that bilingual speakers make usually can be traced to the grammar of their native language (Weinreich 1968; DiPietro 1971; Burt and Kiparsky 1972; Odlin 1989). Uriel Weinreich pointed this out in his landmark study *Languages in Contact*. For instance, my grandmother always spoke of "washing her hairs," she always put her hand "in the pocket," not "my pocket," and she often complained "I am waiting since four hours." All of these were transfers from her native languages.

Are Second Languages Learned or Acquired? Krashen (27), quoting Newmark, attributes such grammar errors to ignorance of the rules in the new language, not to interference. Yet people speaking a second language often make systematic errors in grammar, errors based upon their native language, even after being taught the correct rules in school. One example that comes to mind is the failure of Russians to use the noun determiners *the* and *a* correctly in ordinary conversation. For instance, Mikhail Baryshnikov, on a TV salute to Broadway, told Liza Minelli that they could "go through mirror" (to Wonderland), and on *Sex in the City*, he asked Carrie, "Are you comic?" meaning 'a comic.' A Russian-born friend told me about the results of an interview, "I will get letter." A former colleague of mine, a Ukrainian-born anthropological linguist, virtually never used these determiners when speaking.[2] However, in her scholarly writing she always used them correctly. Knowing the rules helped her writing, but not her speaking. Similarly, Germans whose English is otherwise impeccable may still say things like, "I always to the beach go." Adverb placement differs greatly in English and German, so that German speakers simply transfer their own rules to English. American speakers frequently fail to use the correct subjunctive forms when speaking French, Spanish, or the other European languages[3] despite the fact that they are drilled over and over on them.

It may be true that people make such errors because they are not wholly sure how and under what conditions all of the grammar rules apply. Alternatively, even if they do know, in the heat of encoding ideas in the new language, they fall back on the grammar they have most thoroughly internalized. Probably both factors are at work in grammatical error, or, for that matter, in any kind of bilingual interference.

Krashen (1983, 83–87) has long claimed that there is a difference between acquiring a language, as a baby does naturally, and learning it by being taught. In his view, *acquisition* refers to the process of learning a language without consciously dissecting or otherwise examining its rules. He claims that acquisition is what is responsible for our being able to speak our native language. What he terms *language learning*, on the other hand, is what is formally taught and it may not lead to acquisition. That is, one may learn a language without internalizing it. For instance, as noted above, although English speakers can give the rule for using subjunctives in European languages, in actual unplanned conversation, many still cannot use them correctly.

Krashen's distinction is both precious and doubtful to many scholars. Surely, many people who speak English with foreign accents and who regularly make syntactic errors in it are not stopping to dissect rules or thinking of what rules to apply. If they have not acquired and internalized the language, how can they speak it at all? Moreover, a major problem for foreign speakers is that they often don't even hear the errors they are making. They misperceive the sounds coming from their mouths as being identical to the ones native speakers make. That is, the French speaker who says "zat is ze troos" for "that is the truth" literally doesn't hear the difference between /z/ or /s/ and the two "th" sounds. The same, of course, holds true for English speakers who learn a second language. This is the adult parallel to the child's inability to learn by imitating that we saw in Chapter 1.

We have little understanding of how children actually figure out the rules of their native tongues. It is very difficult, if not impossible, for adults to explain the rules they use in creating sentences of any kind. Try to explain to someone, for instance, exactly why you would ask a question by saying, "Do you know the answer?" Why do you start the question with *do*? You don't start all questions with *do*. Clearly, there is a rule you must follow that tells you when to use that word and when to use others, like "Have you been studying?"

In any event, one need not be a perfect speaker to be understood and to function well both socially and professionally. One need not be able to rattle off rules. In teaching second languages, the focus should be on teaching people to speak well enough for their purposes, not to be impeccable in every utterance. It has long seemed to me that one reason Americans so rarely learn to speak a foreign language that they've studied in school is that American teachers often correct each mistake that the student makes, no matter how minor, giving them little chance for actual give and take in a conversation. In real conversations, we must expect that a language learner—or even one who speaks the language as a second one—will make mistakes. So long as he or she can be understood and speaks fluently, that poses no real problem for interactions.

To me, the interference of rules across languages is reminiscent of the baby who persists in saying "goed" or "'nother one spoon." The rules the child has figured out for himself or herself seem to act as interference, much as the rules of an older speaker's first language interfere with learning a second.

Yet another factor may also come into play in such interference. Unless there is some strong reason for so doing, speakers usually do not remember the exact words and phrases used in a conversation. They remember semantic content or actual lexical choices, not syntactic form. The parallel to this phenomenon is that people do not always notice the syntax that another speaker is using to encode an idea. Much of the so-called bilingual interference perhaps proceeds from the same cause. That is, the speaker simply does not always notice the exact form of the syntax used by native speakers, much less all the particulars of where it differs from his or her own first language. This explains why people can live in a country, not their native one, for most of their lives and never get the grammar rules of the newer language down pat. They can get their ideas across well enough without knowing all the fine points, so they don't necessarily notice them.

Furthermore, it is an economy not to get hung up on all the details. Some grammatical errors are acceptable when uttered by persons who are patently not native speakers. If speakers were not willing, or not able, to communicate in a new language without native-speaker competence, it would hinder them greatly in social interaction. Imagine if one had to stop and analyze every single grammatical form one wanted to use, making sure one wasn't using one from Language A in Language B! Perhaps bilingual interference may result as much from the need to hurry up and speak the new language as from any loss of ability to learn new grammars after a certain age, just as baby errors may arise from the need to communicate before all the rules can be learned.

Tran (1990) investigated problems in learning English among 327 Vietnamese refugees over forty. In general, older speakers had more problems becoming acculturated than did younger, and women had more problems than men, but these factors seemed to be related to cultural attitudes. Historically, in immigrant groups, women, who were more likely to remain in the home and to be the guardians of traditions, did not learn English as rapidly as men.

Even men sometimes failed to learn English if they didn't have to interact with English speakers. This was the situation with Portuguese speakers in some of the mills in southeastern New England. Typically, the mills hired foremen who spoke Portuguese to communicate with the workers and tell them what the owners wanted of them.[4] The Portuguese also lived in ethnic neighborhoods in which most people spoke Portuguese, including store owners. Therefore, they had little need to learn English, and didn't. Their children did, however.

Vocabulary Borrowings. What people do seem to pick up in the new language, however, are American words for things. In fact, immigrant languages have historically become riddled with Anglicisms in America.[5] There are far more words in any language than there are sounds or grammar rules. Learning new words continues throughout a person's lifetime, especially in societies where there are always new objects being invented, new ideas requiring new labels, even new words for old things. For instance, who today speaks of a *piazza* rather than a *porch* or *deck*? If you do, you would be marked as an out-of-date person. Your grandparents probably did not speak of *parenting* a child. They *raised* their children, but younger, educated speakers may prefer the word *parenting*, which makes the process seem more scientific, especially if they feel that they have *parenting skills*.

Even if two languages both have a word for the same thing, other meanings of that word will not necessarily be the same. In no language does a word have just one meaning. That would be most uneconomical, requiring that speakers have separate words for each and every concept. Also, it would prevent language from being flexible. Only if a word can mean many things is flexibility ensured, so that old words can be used in new ways. Each word has attached to it a constellation of meanings. During a former U.S. President's[6] visit to Poland, a United States government translator embarrassed the United States by mistranslating the verb *desire*, accidentally choosing a completely inappropriate word translatable by one meaning of English *desire*. Unfortunately for the dignity of the United States, the word chosen by the translator was the Polish word for 'sexual desire, lust.' The Polish have a completely separate word for English *desire* in the sense of 'would like to,' as in "We desire (would like) to be friends." English happens to attach both a sexual and a neutral meaning to that one word, but Polish does not. Another example is the English word *light*, which refers both to visual sensation and weight. This dual meaning may not be—indeed, probably is not—mirrored in another language, so someone learning English not only has to learn what *light* means, but that it means what two separate words do in his or her native language.

Similarly, Americans are unfamiliar with the older Germanic meaning of *corn*, meaning 'grain.' They think that the Bette Davis movie *The Corn is Green* refers to American ears of corn, missing the metaphor of the title completely, since corn on the cob when ripe is green on the outside. *Corn* in this title refers to unripe wheat in the fields. Wheat becomes tan when it is ripe. When I was growing up, there were Jewish bakeries that sold "corn bread." Americans, even those who were Jewish,[7] often thought that such bread was made entirely of corn meal, such as that used in such American dishes as grits or cakelike corn bread, but it was not. It is made from rye, one of the grains called *korn* in Yiddish. In older English, *corn* also meant 'rye' as well as other grains.

Often general words, words without very specific semantic features, are transferred from one language to another. For instance, the Pennsylvania Dutch say, "It gives rain" under the influence of *es gebt rejje*. Yiddish speakers (or nowadays, their descendants) might say, "Give a look" on the model of "gib a kik."

If a bilingual's original language has a word that sounds like one in their second language but has a different meaning, frequently that word will change to the meaning of the new language. This has been the fate of the Italian *fattoria*, which in America means 'factory' but in Italy meant 'farm.' Greek *karro*, now 'car' originally meant 'wagon.' American Portuguese *pinchar* now means 'pinch' as well as its original 'jump' (Weinreich 1968).

Transferring words alone from one language to another is not hard. For this reason, English words have crept into virtually all of the immigrant languages. One of my colleagues, a bilingual Italian American, told me that when he first visited his family in Italy, they laughed when he said "raincoat" as if it were an Italian word, but now, they regularly use English words in their Italian. Listening to a Portuguese-language television show recently, a student of mine, Manuel Vasconcelos, heard the newscaster announce "hamburgers" and "steak" being served at the "Boy's Club" in "Fall River."[8] These English words popped out of the stream of Portuguese sentences. When he played a tape of this newscast, students who had never heard a word of Portuguese in their lives recognized the English words immediately. In Beijing in 1991, I saw a restaurant sign proclaiming "California Barbecue." While watching a Japanese movie a while back, I was surprised to hear words like "fish" and "soup" interspersed with the Japanese. Part of the fun for me in watching Japanese films is counting the prevalence of English words in the script. One needn't go so far afield to hear this. The recent French movie *Love Me If You Dare* is suffused with English words, especially American taboo terms.

Earlier on, Florida Spanish developed *pelota de fly* for 'fly ball' (Sawyer 1964). American German has *fleysch pie* for 'meat pie.' Italian restaurants now offer *zuppa di clam* rather than *zuppa di vongole,* a delicious dish of clams in tomato sauce. Mexican-American boys can be very *tufo* (tough) as they race cars with tires that are *eslica* 'slick.' A car has a *breca* 'brake,' *bomper* 'bumper,' and *guipa* 'wiper.' To be out of control is *esta de control* (Ayer 1969). A great number of such examples could be supplied from every language spoken in the United States and Canada. Even where immigrant languages have survived, often they have become Americanized in vocabulary.

This doesn't happen only with English. A French-speaking Belgian friend told me that, while visiting relatives overseas, she wanted to make linguine with clam sauce for them. She went to several stores, asking for clams, using the French word for them. French is the language of this part of Belgium and the storeowners all spoke it. Baffled because she couldn't find clams, she went home and reported this oddity to her relatives. They looked at her surprised, telling her that she should have asked for *vongole*, the Italian word for clams. Apparently, that has supplanted the original French word. Immigrant workers in European countries have adopted German or French words into their native languages. This is just something that happens when languages come into contact.

CHAPTER 8

Communicative Competence

One usually assumes that if one is fluent in a language, then one can speak it. Yet, one may be very proficient in a language and still not be competent in using it socially. For instance, one may not know rules of politeness or shades of meaning not listed in vocabulary lists. Such rules are not usually taught in foreign language classes, which concentrate on the rules of grammar appropriate for formal writing styles. Moreover, most such classes typically concern themselves with the grammar of the written sentence. However, the requirements of spoken discourse ultimately determine the actual forms sentences take in actual oral communication.

Because of the attention linguists and sociologists have been paying to the analysis of discourse in the past decade, a whole new set of problems have been uncovered, especially those caused by the unwitting connotation foreign speakers give by transferring the discourse rules from their native language to a new one. An excellent example is Gumperz's (1982b) study of courtroom testimony. He analyzed the errors made by Filipino defendants on trial in American courtrooms. These defendants were bilinguals with a very good command of English.

One, a doctor, was put on trial for perjury in a child abuse case, one in which the child died of burns. The charge was that he lied to the FBI when he said he did not realize that she had been abused.[9] The FBI claimed that he knew that the girl had been deliberately burned by fuel oil and was not just suffering from a severe sunburn as he had told the authorities. They reasoned that he did not want to get involved in a child abuse case, so he let her go with her parents.

Gumperz shows in detail how the doctor's native language caused him to use English verb forms and pronouns incorrectly, leading the FBI to think he was lying. For instance, the doctor said he noticed the child's "sunken eyes" (179). This made the FBI suspect perjury because he had previously said that he had seen no serious symptoms. In English, the participle *sunken* indicates a preexisting condition, whereas the nearest equivalents in the Filipino languages, Tagalog and Aklan, do not. At another time, the doctor used the present tense rather than the past, again making it appear as if he had lied. This problem, again, derives from a natural bilingual error because his native languages don't have tense forms on the verbs. Finally, those languages do not have gender in pronouns. The same pronoun stands for males, females, and neuters. Consequently, he mixed up the English *he* and *she*, which further gave the impression that he was lying.

Gumperz shows that in another case Filipina nurses were charged with murder because they made errors in their English. The insidious thing about such cases is that the speakers are clearly fluent and may not have too much of an accent. Therefore, English speakers don't suspect the subtle miscuing that is occurring because of first language interference. In instances like this, not to understand how greatly languages differ and what kinds of interference can occur leads to gross injustice, as well as apathy, suspicion, and downright distrust. Conventional translation is not enough. It's the small differences that hurt, those wrought by unintentional and subtle cues of presupposing and implying, of little-expected errors that, in a native speaker, would indicate he or she was lying. Notice that none of this means that either English or Filipino languages are incapable of saying or implying the same things. It is only that one needs somewhat different grammatical or lexical choices in each for the same implications. That is, it is not a question of one language not being able to communicate what the other does. It is a question of knowing precisely how to do it in each language.

Then, too, there are rules in every culture of when it is permissible to speak, when one must speak, and what style of speech is expected. These differ across cultures and are also important considerations in understanding nonnative speakers of a language.

DIFFERENT LANGUAGE, DIFFERENT MIND?

Does bilingualism change the workings of the mind? Does it make one more intelligent? Able to think better in any way? Claims and counterclaims have abounded about each of these issues. In the nineteenth and early twentieth centuries, during the great waves of immigration to the United States, it seemed very obvious to earlier comers that foreign speakers were at best stupid. In fact, psychologists "proved" it. Early IQ tests, such as the Binet,[10] were administered to new arrivals on Ellis Island. One director of a school for the feeble-minded greeted thirty Jews just off the boat by having them take this test. Since twenty-five of them flunked, it reinforced the tester's convictions that Europe was dumping its undesirables on American shores.[11] The fact that the immigrants were in no shape to take such a test seemed not to have occurred to the tester. It is even unlikely that they spoke English! Such misconceived testing was also used to prove that other groups like Italians were unfit to enter the country.

Even when the test and the conditions under which it was administered were refined, the less English someone spoke, the worse he or she did on it. It seemed not to have occurred to anyone then that the tests depended on one's command of English and/or American cultural conventions. Rather, it was thought that bilingualism was a mental handicap (Hakuta 1986, 21). What is especially ironic about such conclusions is that, in those days, foreign language learning was a large part of both a high school and a college education. The ability of researchers to ignore the obvious in their quest for "scientific" proof can be a never-ending source of amazement.

More recently, studies of bilinguals have sought to prove the opposite, that knowing two languages results in cognitive flexibility. The claim that knowing two languages allows one to think in two separate systems is another statement of what is known as the Whorfian hypothesis. This is a belief that one's language influences the kinds of thinking one can do.

There are recent studies indicating that there are benefits of bilingualism. Before summing these up, it is important to understand that there are many different degrees of bilingualism. Perhaps only a few bilinguals are equally proficient in both or all of their languages. As is demonstrated later, even if bilinguals are equally proficient, they may speak each of their languages only in different social situations.

Other bilinguals, and perhaps this is most common, know one of their languages far better than the other. That is, one language is **dominant**. Some may sound very fluent, but when excited or trying to talk of difficult matters, their second language falls apart and they have to fall back on the dominant one. Also, as when comparing monolinguals, one must take care not to compare bilinguals from one social class with monolinguals from another. If one does, then the variable is not necessarily bilingualism vs. monolingualism, but social class.

In order to decide if bilingualism confers mental flexibility or any other benefit, one has to test speakers who are equally good in both languages and who are of the same social class and age group. A pioneer in devising studies which take such care is Wallace Lambert, along with his associates and his followers. Starting in the early 1960's, Lambert has devoted his academic career to showing the benefits, both social and psychological, of bilingualism. Lambert (1977, 24) claims that, through the years, it has been demonstrated that bilingual students in Canada are "more likely than monolinguals to be advanced in their schooling in French schools, to develop a diversified and flexible intelligence. . . . " Lest one think that it is only the French who fare better when they are taught English, Lambert says that English-Canadian children also do better when their elementary school classes are conducted in French.

Ben-Zeev (1977) confirms Lambert's position by her studies with English-Spanish bilinguals of low socioeconomic class and English-Hebrew bilinguals of the professional class (32). She devised a series of tests requiring analysis and categorizing. The bilingual children did "significantly better" (34) than the monolinguals. Williams (1984, 195) says that one factor in retaining Welsh as the medium of instruction in many schools in Wales is "the very high academic attainment records of the initial bilingual students. . . ." These results agree with the folk wisdom guiding traditional education. It used to be assumed that studying Latin and Greek as well as modern languages was a necessary component to learning analytical skills. Even today, social groups who insist that their children be bilingual, such as Ukrainians now living in New England, credit their children's success in school to their bilingualism. However, there are bilinguals who don't do well in school because their cultures do not value book learning. If a bilingual comes from a home which is education oriented, he or she does have an advantage in school, but there is no proof that the advantage accrues to those who see no need for schooling. Those immigrant groups who felt that getting a job in a mill was sufficient attainment didn't usually produce scholars.

Kenji Hakuta (1986, 36–41) considers that studies like Lambert's or Williams' are flawed because the investigators did not utilize random sampling. The very fact that Lambert and his cohorts selected bilinguals equally proficient in both languages (**balanced bilinguals**) may have prejudiced their results. Hakuta asks if those children were balanced bilinguals because they were more intelligent at the outset. Considering societies in which everybody has to speak more than one language, such as the Phillipines, or Africans who must master both Swahili and English along with their tribal language, this objection seems ill-founded. In societies in which multiple languages are required to get along, all members speak them, not just the more "intelligent" ones, however Hakuta wishes to define that term.

A Critical Period?

There is no doubt that children can learn any and all languages that surround them if they perceive a need to do so. In many parts of the world, as just noted, even uneducated people speak three or four languages as a matter of course. My grandmother, who had no formal schooling at all, spoke three languages fluently. The corollary to this, which American and Canadian linguistic history can attest to, is that children will not learn any languages that they see no need for. Before examining this claim, let us consider the question of age itself as a factor in second or third or more languages. Again, folk wisdom has it that children find it much easier than adults to learn new language, a position for which there is more than ample evidence, both historically and now.

Although few would doubt that children learn new languages more easily than adults, there is still a question of the degree to which this is a result of changes in the brain as opposed to changes in motivation. One position is that children's brains have a special elasticity, so to speak, and this is what enables them to learn many languages, and that in puberty, this elasticity disappears.

CHAPTER 8

This position seemed to be bolstered by the case of Genie, a girl found after puberty who had been confined to a dim bedroom virtually since infancy. No one in the family was allowed to speak to her, and she had been obviously punished for making noise, so she had never learned to control her voice. Despite her willingness and enthusiasm for learning, there were limits to the amount of language she could master. Specifically, her grammatical ability quickly topped out. Her syntax remained that of a toddler, although she would string more words together at a time than a toddler at the same stage would. The reason for this was uncovered when they found that the left side of her brain, the one responsible for syntax, seemed to have atrophied (Curtiss 1977). This was seen as evidence that the language center of the brain loses its plasticity after puberty, making it more difficult to learn new languages. Thus, Curtiss and her cohorts, including Krashen mentioned above, concluded there is a **critical period** in language learning.

While the Genie tragedy is suggestive, it is not adequate proof for this position. One case doth not a generalization make. Although the researchers claim that she was normal until she was isolated, we don't know for sure that she was. Apparently, one reason that her father confined her was because he thought she was retarded and he was protecting her. Since we cannot repeat the Genie "experiment" to see if the results can be replicated, we cannot prove Curtiss's theory.

Hakuta (1986,146) offers some different and more compelling evidence from adult language learners themselves. He cites studies showing that the older adults are when they have to learn a language, the more quickly they hit a plateau. For instance, the level of Hebrew achieved by adult males who emigrated to Israel was directly related to their age. Those in their twenties learned more and better than those in their thirties and forties. Hakuta points out that this doesn't argue so much for a critical period as for a gradual decline with increasing age.

He cites two studies of Spanish-English bilinguals in the United States, both of which confirmed that age is important in foreign language learning (147). One of these actually divided children into two age groups, six to ten and eleven to fifteen. A sixteen to twenty-five year-old group was studied as well. The results showed that the younger the group, the better the English. Another study measured how accurately native Spanish speakers could distinguish between certain sounds as native English speakers pronounced them. Again, the younger people were when they came to the United States, the more accurately they identified the sounds (147–148). However, it has also been shown that individual adults may learn a second language as perfectly as a child does (153). It has even been shown that in at least one instance, twelve- to fifteen-year-olds were more accurate in their ability to use and understand a second language, Dutch, than younger ones were. It is difficult to reconcile the critical age theory with such a result. As Hakuta demonstrates, however, it is very difficult, but not impossible, to come up with accurate testing that truly taps the skills learned, and many results are based upon the opinions of raters, not on any objective measures. With the advent of such sophisticated devices as spectrographs and speech synthesizers, Hakuta (149–53) notes that it has become more possible to devise objective measures.

Scovel (1988, 183–86) disagrees, concluding that speech, by which he means phonological output of language, is subject to a critical period. That is, if a language is not heard or spoken before puberty, he claims, the speaker will not achieve perfect pronunciation (122). However, "other aspects of language—vocabulary and syntax, for example—are free from any ultimate learning period." Still, Scovel concludes:

> Indeed, from the experimental studies . . . we see that regardless of how quickly or slowly you acquire a second language, if you pick it up after the age of 10 to 12,[12] you end up easily identified as a nonnative speaker of that language. (Scovel 1988, 123)

Another factor that one would expect to be important in second language learning is that of length of residence. One might suppose that the longer a person lived in a country or spoke a given language, the fewer errors he or she would make. This apparently is not necessarily true. Krashen took as proof of his critical age theory the demonstrable fact that length of residence alone cannot explain the degree of proficiency in the new language. What he found was that after a few years, adult learners simply stopped improving. He claims that this has been confirmed in other studies. Somewhere between three and a half and five years of exposure to the new language, improvement stops (146–149). After that, apparently, only formal instruction can make a difference. However, it may be that after this time, the person speaks well enough for his or her purposes, so that others can understand. Therefore, he or she doesn't concentrate on language per se so much.

As mentioned previously, it is erroneous to claim that children who are balanced bilinguals simply are "highly gifted and [have] . . . a flair for language learning" (Macnamara quoted in Hakuta 1986, 39). There are simply too many societies ranging from what we consider the most primitive to the most advanced in which everyone speaks more than one language. There are countries that are officially multilingual like Switzerland and Israel. An American visitor to Israel cannot help but be impressed by the high levels of proficiency in English that one hears from everyone, Israeli Jews and Arabs alike, of all social classes, from chambermaids to peddlers to physicians and professors. Indeed, one reason Americans give for not bothering to learn other languages is that wherever in the world they go, people speak English. It can't be that all those people are especially gifted in languages. Language learning is a human ability and doesn't depend upon special gifts.

Grosjean (1982, 176–77) reports that Yaqui Indian children acquire their second and third languages at about ages five or six. Yaqui, of course, is their first language. Spanish learned from Mexican Indian children is learned next, and English is the medium of instruction in school. Tanzanians all speak at least three languages: their tribal tongue, Swahili, and English, again, as the medium of instruction in school. Similarly, in the Phillipines, everyone is at least trilingual, speaking a home language like Pangasinense or Aklan, then Tagalog as the official "trans-Phillipine language" and English as the language of instruction in school.[13] Looking at humankind, not just Western technologically advanced nations, we see that people are naturally as bilingual or multilingual as their societies and their geographies require them to be.

Again and again scholars have pointed out that it is monolingualism that is unusual, not bilingualism. Americans say they have no aptitude for languages and do poorly in language studies at school, despite the fact that they may be descended from people who spoke two or more languages. Language learning does not seem to be a matter of individual heredity as much as it is of cultural attitudes and social necessity.

Certainly, knowing more than one language is a great resource both in social interactions and in intellectual activities. There is no substitution for bilingualism when it comes to reading or hearing works of art such as novels, poetry, and plays or intellectual works like philosophical and psychological treatises. To have to rely on others' translations for artistic work is to miss the fusion of form and meaning of the original. To have to rely on others for the intellectual content is to take the chance of getting the message garbled to some degree or other.

In business nowadays, being monolingual is a great disadvantage. When one commands the most widely spoken language in the world, one will find someone who speaks it just about everywhere. In business dealings, however, much can be hidden or unspecified because American businesspeople don't speak the language of those they are negotiating with.

Moreover, it is arrogant to expect that of the 5,000 or so languages on earth, everyone should speak to us in our own and no other. At a German-owned chemical company in Rhode Island a few years ago, a delegation of Germans came to inspect operations. When they sat down and realized that all the carefully prepared materials for them to study were written only in English, they were so insulted that they left the meeting, even though they knew how to speak English.

BILINGUALISM: INDIVIDUAL AND SOCIAL

The fact that we can make everyone speak to us in English shouldn't blind us to the fact that monolingualism is not particularly natural, nor is it economically or politically beneficial. In both trade and diplomacy, Americans too often rely on the ability of foreigners to speak English, not on American ability to speak "their" language. Thus, Americans are at the mercy of translators. Also, they can't understand any byplay going on between delegates. By not speaking the language of those one wishes to do business with, one is very much in their power, knowing only what they want one to know. The same is true of government dealings with other countries.

LANGUAGE AND THOUGHT

The degree to which our languages control our thoughts has been an important philosophical issue for centuries. Wilhelm Von Humboldt in the nineteenth century and, later, Edward Sapir argued that people who speak different languages perceive the world differently. That is, people are prisoners of their language. All that we have seen about the flexibility and creativity of language use seems to deny such a proposition. Yet such notions, especially as promulgated by his protege Benjamin Lee Whorf, persist.

Whorf famously used the example of a man who tossed a cigarette butt into a gas drum marked *empty*. Whorf claimed that English forces the use of the word *empty* even though fumes are still in the drum. He argued that the use of the word *empty* allowed the careless smoker to think of the drum as having nothing in it, thereby disregarding the vapors and behaving as if they were not there. One flaw in such reasoning is that Whorf did not show that the careless cigarette smoker knew that an empty drum could still have dangerous vapors in it. Assuredly, not everyone does. I do only because I have long known about Whorf's examples. In other words, the mistake could have been caused by sheer ignorance, not the English language. English certainly allows one to label an empty gas drum, "Danger! Flammable vapors."

Similarly, Edward Stewart (1979) claimed that the atomic bomb was dropped on Japan because the Japanese had marked the Japanese equivalent of *ignore* on the United States communique informing them of what was going to happen if they did not surrender. Stewart argues that the Japanese, in line with their culture, needed time to deliberate and that is what they meant by their *ignore*. Our culture, supposedly being more hasty, puts another meaning on *ignore*. So we dropped the bomb. To me, this is an example of poor translation. Hasty and fast-acting culture or not, English is perfectly capable of expressing the idea of holding off on a decision. *Delay decision* would have been an appropriate translation. Surely Japanese has some way of saying that. *Ignore* means 'do not pay attention.' Whoever chose that word for the concept "delay decision" was not a proficient translator. Americans who read the Japanese response *ignore* could not have known that the Japanese wanted time to think it over.

Too often those who claim that we are prisoners of our language base their claims on insufficient knowledge of both languages. Whorf (1956), for instance, made much of the fact that the Hopi did not conceive of time linearly, as a row of days following each other. He said that they conceive time only as a cycle. They didn't say things like "10 days." Instead, they conceived of "day" as being when daytime is happening, not as a sequence of separate days. The word for *day* in Hopi is supposedly an adverb, not a noun. Therefore, it can't be conceived of as a thing which can be placed in a row.

However, Shaul and Furbee (1998, 48–50) show that the Hopi certainly do conceive of time linearly. Later anthropologists, who learned the language apparently more thoroughly than Whorf did, discovered that Hopi say things like "the beans will come up in 10 days." Whorf said they couldn't say that. Moreover, the Hopis use the word *qeni* to mean 'place/ position' and 'time.' They see time as both cyclic and as a series of events, just as English does. Just as English uses the same word to indicate time and place, as in *over time* and *over the door* or *behind time* and *behind the sofa*, so does Hopi with the word *qeni*.

Similarly, Shaul and Furbee (1998, 47) cite a scholar who claimed that Chinese doesn't use counterfactuals, expressions like *if . . . then,* followed by *would have*. If true, this would mean that the Chinese couldn't express a notion like, "**If** you **had** read the paper, you **would have** seen the report." The English-speaking researcher who made this claim didn't recognize the fact that the Chinese word *yaoshi* expresses counterfactual propositions. True, Chinese doesn't mark it by paired subordinators or verbs with auxiliaries as English does, but it expresses the same idea by using one word which applies to a statement. As we have also seen with politeness, two languages may do the same thing, but mark it on different words and grammatical constructions. In politeness forms, you may recall, what the Japanese do by adding an ending on a word, English does by using phrases.

Again and again, when Whorfians or others insist that something cannot be said in one language, it turns out to be just such a case of translation difficulty. Having been raised in a multilingual environment, I am familiar with people saying, "You can't say X in English" (or some other language), and then proceeding by circumlocution to tell the hearer exactly what they have just claimed you can't say in that language!

To be sure, there may be no one word in English to correspond to the one word in the other language or vice versa. What makes translation so difficult is that no two languages cut up the semantic universe in the same way. Meanings and connotations get attached to words differently. English, for instance, uses *eat* for what both people and other animals do. German has a separate word for human eating and eating by other animals. For humans, one uses *ess(en)* and for other animals *fress(en)*. It is not that English speakers do not perceive a difference between animal and human eating. They do, as witnessed in the simile *eat like a pig*. English[14] just does not happen to codify that difference as German does, although it makes other distinctions that German does not make. For example, English distinguishes between *tall* and *long*, whereas German uses the same word for both.

Polish has two words for that English translates as *silence* or *to be silent*: *cisza* 'absence of sound' and *milczenie* 'absence of speech.' The former means one doesn't talk at all, and the latter, one doesn't talk about an expected topic (Jaworski 1993, 71–78). One may use either noun to refer to a person, but *cisza* not only means the person didn't speak at all but also that he or she wasn't expected to. *Milczenie* may refer to someone's not talking at all, but with the connotation that talk was expected. What is interesting is that this can mean the person did talk about other things, so one of the Polish words for *silence* can indicate speech, whereas, in English, it can only refer to lack of speech. Of course we can say *silence about* or *silence on the topic of* to indicate speech, but not on the expected topic. The point here is that to translate English *silence* into Polish, you have to choose which noun to use, whereas in English, you have to choose whether to use the noun alone or the noun followed by a prepositional phrase. Languages are suffused with these little differences, some involving different lexical items, some involving different grammatical structures. Therefore, accurate translation demands a thorough, even intimate, knowledge of both languages as well as vigilance against passing over a difference in connotation of a word. Jaworski didn't mention it, but it seems to me that the English *quiet* can be used in the sense of *milczeni*. If you say someone was quiet at a social gathering, it doesn't mean he or she said nothing. However, in contrast to the Polish word, it doesn't imply expectation of speaking on a particular issue, although it does imply that one would have expected more speech from that person. Again, there is no easy matchup of words to meaning across languages.

Another problem with translation is that words with the same gloss may have very different sociolinguistic connotations. Eugene Nida, a linguist to whom the science of translation owes a considerable debt (Nida 1975; Nida and Reyburn 1981) gives the example from the New Testament

CHAPTER 8

Gospels of Jesus calling Mary by the Greek word which means 'woman.' In English, this is intensely rude, but researching other Greek writing of the day, Nida discovered that "woman" was a common, highly respectful address form for 'mother.'

Sometimes these differences do reflect cultural attitudes, as we shall see in our discussion of gender. If so, whole sets of words will be implicated. Sometimes these differences are accidental. No language can have a separate word for each and every concept a speaker might wish to convey. If it did, vocabularies would be horrendously large. Also, language would be static with a one-to-one correspondence between word and meaning. Metaphors and other types of figurative language could not exist, as these are the product of the fact that in all natural languages any given word can mean many different things.

Because languages are constructed so as to have a great deal of polysemy (multiple meanings on a word), related words often take on different meanings in different languages or even different dialects. As an example, in the United Kingdom the notion of a hike in pay is attached to *rise*, but in the United States to *raise*. The time between acts of a play is called an *interval* in the United Kingdom but *intermission* in the United States. Both dialects are perfectly logical. It seems to be quite accidental which one became usual in each dialect, just as it is accidental that one language uses the word *casa* and another *house* to refer to a domicile. One is no better or worse than the other. The same is true of such things as grammar rules across languages.

Despite the flaws in the writings of Whorf and his followers, the idea that our language influences our thoughts and perceptions is still engaging researchers. Lera Boroditsky (Cook 2002), a professor at MIT, has been experimenting with the time it takes speakers of different languages to respond in certain tasks. She is also investigating what kinds of words they use to describe different things. For instance, in Mandarin Chinese, people say that time moves down, in contrast to English, which has time rushing forward. Boroditsky found that Mandarin speakers who viewed time sequences moving vertically on a video screen answered time questions faster than English speakers do when viewing the same video. English speakers do better than Chinese ones when the time sequences are played horizontally. This implies that Mandarin speakers' brains process time differently from English speakers.

Since many European languages classify nouns according to gender, which English no longer does, Boroditsky studied whether gender assignment affected how an object was thought of. For instance, the word for *key* is masculine in German and feminine in Spanish. She found that German speakers used masculine terms to describe a key, like *hard, jagged, heavy,* while Spanish speakers favored more feminine descriptions like *golden, intricate, lovely*. One problem I have with this research is that German uses a different gender for the words for *fork, knife*, and *spoon*. Do they think of one of these utensils as more masculine, another as more feminine, and the third as neuter, whatever that would entail in adjectival selection? Similarly, different languages use different gender markings on words for *door* or *bridge*. Does a speaker of one that treats *door* as feminine think of it as being weaker than someone whose language expresses it as masculine? If a language marks a bridge as feminine, does a speaker think of it as fragile? If so, who would want to go on it? In any event, Boroditsky's work, so far as it goes, is suggestive.

Boroditsky claims that because Americans are monolingual, they do not have access to the alternate realities present in other languages. Steven Haskos, one of my students, who is a Greek-English bilingual, commented upon hearing this, "One world, one set of perceptions, even if you know two languages." However, he learned both languages as a baby. Therefore, he has long since made the connections between the two and wouldn't be conscious of learning a new way of looking at something in one of the languages. One of my friends, a native speaker of French, tells me she doesn't even know what language she thinks things in. She is more conscious of the situations which call forth each language, so that speaking to her children has always been a French situation.

Bilinguals do admit that they typically choose the language to use in any given circumstance according to the topic. Haskos, for instance, reports that, in his family, people automatically switch into Greek when they are talking about traditional foods, like the Easter lamb, or soccer. Jan Svartvik, a Swedish linguist, once told me that it seemed unnatural to speak English to his children. Spanish speakers have been found to use Spanish when talking about family and social matters, but English when talking about business, often switching from one language to the other in the same discourse.

The question still remains of how one's perceptions may be changed according to one's language. That is, if one's language doesn't have a word for a concept, does that mean one doesn't perceive the world the way someone does whose language does have such a word?

The earliest work on this situation that I know of was Paul Kay's studies of how rapidly people named colors. It seems that no two languages cut up the color spectrum in the same way. Some languages, for instance, use one word for what English designates as two colors, and vice versa.

Kay and Kempton (1984) investigated the difference between English speakers and the Tarahumara in Mexico in their perception of blue and green. The Tarahumara use one word for the two words English uses for blue and green. That is, English distinguishes blue and green as two colors, and the Tarahumara do not. Using eight chips of varying shades of blue and green, Kay and Kempton posited that because English has separate primary terms for those colors, they would perceptually "push" apart the colors of two blue-green chips, which were very close in actual hue, but the Tarahumarans would not, perceiving those chips to be more alike. Indeed, this is what happened when they were asked which of the three was most different from the other two. English speakers said the closely matched green-blue and blue-green chips were farther apart in color than did the Tarahumarans. This showed the influence of having separate categories of blue and green.

But in a second procedure, one in which subjects could not use naming strategies because all three chips were not in view at the same time, the difference between groups of speakers disappeared. Kay and Kempton concluded that one's language does affect certain perceptions if one is in a situation that allows reference to the language system (e.g., "hmm, this is green and this is blue"), but this is not a perceptual prison and can be overcome.

Most of us have had the analogous experience of buying a shirt or tie to go with a piece of clothing at home. When you visualized the non-present article, let's say, as red, you selected what seemed to be a perfect match, but when you got the purchase home, it didn't match at all. Often, your mental image of red was primary red, and the clothing turned out to be a different hue.

A more interesting problem occurs with the Pirahã tribe in Brazil. According to one account, they have no words for numbers at all (Douglas 2006, 45–46). Consequently it seems that they can't be taught to count. Nor could anthropologists teach them to do sums or anything else that involves quantification, such as telling time. Moreover, the tribespeople have proven to be very resistant to learning Western ideas and skills. They see no value in learning to read, for instance. They can make a straight line in the earth with a stick to represent one of their spirits, but they can't learn to make the number 1.

Naturally, the anthropologists conclude that the Pirahã's language prevents them from having number concepts. If this were indeed true, then if a mother had three children and one disappeared, would she not know she had lost one? If a child had two pieces of food in front of him or her and someone took one away, would the child not notice?

Is the answer to the Pirahãs inability to learn simple arithmetic simply that they see no need for it in their society? It's boring, and one can't even say to them that they must learn it to get a better job. They don't need jobs. They live off the land.

The article itself admits that, when an attempt to teach them to read was made, they succeeded in reading the word *bigi* 'sky.' However, they then laughed. When asked why, their response was that it was their word for sky. When told that was correct, the Pirahã rejected all further efforts to teach them reading on the grounds that they don't write their language. Clearly, they could see no need to do so. Couldn't that be the answer to their supposed innate lack of number perception? Perhaps they perceive the numbers of things, but see no reason to codify it, to write numbers down or manipulate them.

Indeed, an earlier article on the same tribe in *New Scientist* online (Biever 2004) claimed that Pirahã is a "one, two, many" language. That is, they have words for *one* and *two* and a word for *many* and that's all. That reseacher, Peter Gordon, who tested them says, "There are not really occasions in their daily lives where [they] have to count." He found that if he laid out a random number of familiar objects, the Pirahã could match them from their own piles of the same objects, but only up to the number three. Similarly, they also failed to remember whether a box they had been shown seconds ago had four or five objects on the top. When the researchers "tapped on the floor three times, the Pirahã imitated correctly, but failed to mimic strings of four to five taps."

Did their language cause the Pirahã to fail, or did they fail because they saw no reason for concentrating on longer tasks? If they did see a reason for quantifying larger numbers, then, it seems to me, they would develop words for them. All languages can make up new words. Every language has an unused stock of possible sound combinations with which they create new words. Think about the words we have today that didn't exist 200 years ago, like *google, netpal, website, internet, dvd, voicerecorder*. Such things didn't exist, so there was no word for them, but that didn't stop people from developing them and then giving them verbal labels.

`As for the Pirahã having no concept of number because they have no words for numbers, I would have to wonder about their basic mammalian intelligence. Sheepdogs who herd regularly notice if one of the flock is missing and, after herding the rest, immediately run back to the fields and look for the missing one. My dog, a Maltese, bred for nothing but being a human companion, thinks it is his duty to greet every person who comes into our house. Recently, I had thirteen students over, already seated before the dog came in from a walk. He immediately surveyed the group sitting in a semi-circle, then, starting from the rightmost seat, went to each person in turn, doing his greeting routine. When he got to the leftmost end of the semi-circle, after greeting the student who was at the end of the line, he suddenly sat down. Remaining motionless for less than a minute, he looked upwards towards the ceiling with a "whom did I forget" look.[15]

Then he suddenly shot to one person sitting six seats from the end, where the semi-circle curved. He greeted her as enthusiastically as he had the others. When I asked her if he had missed her the first time around, she said "yes." The others verified that he had greeted each of them. Apparently, he had some image or perception of how many students there were and, when he came to the end, realized he had missed one. Certainly, he has no word for thirteen, but he is able to quantify in some way. To him, greeting everyone is important, just as the lost sheep is to the sheepdog. Somehow, the dogs quantify without words. I strongly suspect that to the Pirahã, tasks given by psychologists and anthropologists are clearly not important, so they don't bother to expend the effort to do them. Surely, if dogs can count, so can they.

One problem in measuring differences in cognition is the difficulty of finding appropriate tests to measure the skills we want to know about. Some groups, such as the Kpelle in Liberia, have been found to flunk a supposed test of cognitive abilities, but when observed in daily activities, they were seen to be using those abilities (Scribner 1977; Scribner and Cole 1981). No one knows how to test unerringly for cognitive abilities. Therefore, we cannot claim that people do or do not have abilities on the basis of what we think we know about their language.

One provocative collection of essays (Cooper and Spolsky 1991) suggests that a weak form of the Whorf hypothesis is highly tenable. They show that the way people categorize is influenced by their languages and that the differing semantic loads of words in different languages can affect cognition. The argument is that speakers of one language are more likely to think in certain terms, or more likely not to challenge certain assumptions. Therefore, they claim, if one learns another language, one is introduced to new ways of thinking. Perhaps this explains the finding that bilinguals seem to become more cognitively flexible.

It seems to me that the evidence from English and Portuguese sexist vocabulary presented in Chapter 10 supports such a view. In sum, if your language is loaded with derogatory words for females indicating that they are sexually immoral and stupid, you will tend to think of them that way. However, as well-oiled as some of our thinking is because of our language, it can always be changed. When I first started reading about sexism in language, I was amazed that I had never noticed, but once I did notice, the effect on my thinking was galvanized. It is possible to change language and it is possible to change one's thinking.

BILINGUALISM ACROSS GENERATIONS

During the great waves of immigration to the United States in the nineteenth and early twentieth centuries, most who came learned English.

Their children learned it, often with no trace of accent of the native language. Usually immigrants' children born in this country learned their parents' language at home, although sometimes not very well. Often older children knew the language better than the younger, some of whom never learned it at all. The grandchildren usually did not learn it at all, except for a few words here and there. Some groups, worried about deculturation, instituted after-school instruction or parochial schools in which at least half-days were done in a foreign language. Greeks, Armenians, French, Chinese, Poles, Germans, Ukrainians, Italians, and Jews are among those who have tried, or are trying, such schooling.

This is quite different from public bilingual schooling for children who come to school already speaking a foreign language which might or might not be their only language. The special after-school or weekend schools usually are a salvaging attempt. Most have been for children who do not know their grandparents' language or do not know much of it. If that language is not used regularly in the home, these schools are not likely to be successful.

There used to be foreign language church-run schools such as French-Catholic parochial and German Lutheran schools. Many of these now teach in English, but one can still find French, German, Italian, Spanish, or other schools that don't run classes in English. Most of these are in cities and are private, so that only parents who can afford the tuition can send their children there. Even so, many of these schools are very successful and offer a way for American parents to ensure that their children are bilingual.

Both after-school instruction and day schools run by Jews illustrate especially well the general factors in keeping second languages alive. Rarely was it the goal of Jewish schools to keep Yiddish alive. Their mission was Hebrew, the language of Jewish prayer, of the Bible, and of much Jewish exegesis of the Bible. Yiddish is actually a form of German and is as different from Hebrew as English is. It was spoken only by the Jews of Eastern Europe, not those from the Mediterranean or Arab countries.[16]

Most of the Jews in America today are of Eastern European origin. Their ancestors brought Eastern European pronunciations of Hebrew to their praying and Bible reading. Many American Hebrew schools ignored these traditions, teaching instead the pronunciation of Hebrew used in modern Israel. This is based upon the traditions of Jews in the Arab nations. American Jews largely rejected their Eastern European origins, a fact reflected in the dramatic loss of Yiddish within one or two generations, as well as the change in Hebrew pronunciation. Over 1,000 years of degrading and humiliating persecution is associated with both Yiddish and Eastern European pronunciation of Hebrew. The Israeli Hebrew is associated with bravery, independence, and victory. Hence, that is the language taught.

A similar tale can be told of Canadian-French as spoken in southern New England.[17] The language spoken there was not considered proper. The ideal was the French spoken by the educated French on the Continent, not that spoken by the workers in the shoe and textile factories and the lumber mills. There were French churches, with masses in Canadian-French and the parochial schools run by French-speaking nuns. Classes in religion were taught in French, and there was formal study in Continental French, albeit taught by Canadian-French speakers. Because Canadian-French stood in relation to Continental French the way Yiddish did to High German, those of Canadian French background who wanted to be French scholars went to great lengths to get rid of their native pronunciations. Over the years, as barriers to higher education and jobs were hurdled, fewer and fewer children from Canadian-French homes learned the language at all, and in time, the French parochial schools, although retaining French names like Mount St. Charles, became like any parochial school with their student bodies drawn from many different ethnic groups.[18]

To some degree, then, one reason for loss of many languages of different groups is that the variety they spoke was associated with poverty, persecution, and even ignorance. So long as the members of such groups could not get ahead, the principle of solidarity reigned, but as soon as opportunity presented itself, some opted for power (Chapter 3). That is, so long as members of a group feel they cannot get ahead, they retain a native language for intimacy, but they may abandon it when they get an opportunity to rise socially and materially.

When the language was taught in schools, it was the standard dialect, or as standard as the teachers could themselves use, not necessarily the dialects the immigrants themselves brought with them. Inadvertently, this, too, led to loss of the immigrant language, as the schools taught the dialect of power, stigmatizing the dialect of solidarity. Ultimately, however, the *coup de grace* for the immigrant languages was the opening of doors for their members.

Not all immigrants are poor people wanting to elevate themselves to the middle-class. Some, like two Chinese families I know, were professionals when they came to the United States, and spoke a valued dialect of their native language. It is instructive to note the outcome of becoming bilingual by comparing these families. In both, the fathers were professors of physics at the same Ivy League school. In one family, no English was allowed to be spoken in the house ever. Crossing the threshold meant speaking in Mandarin, the prestige dialect in China. In the other, who lived two houses away, the children were allowed to speak English. If the parents spoke to them in Mandarin, the children answered in English. These children never did learn Chinese, but the ones who weren't allowed to speak English grew up completely bilingual. Modern language professors of my acquaintance, whether they teach Italian, Spanish, French, Russian, Portuguese, or any other language, have the same experience. Those who allow English in the house and who respond when their children speak English usually don't have bilingual children. Those who insist on speaking the other language in the home have bilingual children. Also, those who take their children to the country where the language is spoken have bilingual children.[19]

Does becoming proficient in another language harm the child's English? Not one bit. Children start learning English as soon as they start playing with American children. The children I've mentioned above whose parents made them learn another language are all high-achieving, many of them scholars in their own right.

Even if parents don't speak another language, they can help their children to become bilingual, especially if they live in a good-sized city and can afford a private school tuition. German-speaking schools operate in areas as diverse as New York City, South Carolina, and Oregon, as well as points in between. French-speaking schools are also fairly widespread. Even in a small city like Providence, there is a good French school. The students who go to it are not necessarily from French homes, but their parents want them to become bilingual. Searching the Web, I found forty French-language immersion public schools in the United States!

There may well be all-day schools which educate students in other languages, like Greek, Armenian, Turkish, Japanese, Polish, Italian, Chinese, Russian, or Arabic, but googling the Web yielded only notices for private lessons, after-school programs, college programs, or study-abroad opportunities. I was especially surprised that I could find no mention of all-day schools teaching in Arabic at the elementary and high school levels. This doesn't mean they don't exist. In Rhode Island, the *Providence Journal* newspaper has reported the opening of a Muslim day school in response to the increased Arabic population, a development one would expect in other areas as well. However, there does seem to be a dearth of programs to teach children Mandarin as part of a regular school day. As that language is increasingly important both politically and economically, such schools might be instituted. As of now, Chinese schools exist primarily as after-school add-ons, much like Hebrew, Greek, and Armenian schools.

I would have to conclude that, although the United States aren't quite a desert when it comes to becoming proficient in a second language, they still don't offer widespread opportunities for young children, the ones who can learn languages the best, to become bilingual.

Maintaining Bilingualism

The larger the community of speakers of a given language, the longer the language is likely to be retained. In earlier decades, in regions with large populations of non-English speakers, business, social, and church matters were often not conducted in English. Foreign-language newspapers, societies, and radio shows flourished for speakers of Polish, German, Portuguese, Italian, Swedish, Norwegian, French, Chinese, Hungarian, Serbian, Japanese, Greek, Ukrainian, Yiddish, and assorted other languages. Over time, there has been a steady erosion of many of these non-English languages in the United States (Fishman 1966). However, new ones have been added to the mix, such as Southeast Asian languages like Cambodian and, of course, Arabic. Actually, some Arabic languages, like Lebanese, have been spoken in the United States for decades. However, in recent years, there has been an increase in others.

Nowadays, there are non-English television programs. Not only are there several cable networks in Spanish, but many movies and popular TV shows in English have Spanish subtitles. In southeastern New England, there is a Portuguese language network as well, and at least one satellite service advertises that it provides programming from many Southeast Asian channels. Cable has made it much easier to program non-English shows, thus enhancing second language retention. The languages offered may depend upon the immigrant mix in different parts of the country, although Spanish is offered even in New England, which doesn't house as large a percentage of a Hispanic population as the Southwest.

It has already been noted that foreign languages survive best where there are large enough populations so that daily social activities can be carried on in that language. The corollary to that is that languages survive where their speakers live together in the same neighborhoods or communities. A further corollary is that the languages survive where people are somewhat isolated physically or psychologically from the mainstream.

As each originally foreign group has produced college graduates and other upwardly mobile young, their old neighborhoods dispersed. The younger members of each group moved into the suburbs along with other middle-class Americans. The population of the German neighborhoods of Chicago, for instance, decreased from 161,567 to 99,413 in the ten years from 1960 to 1970. Despite the existence of German shops, churches, radio programs, children's singing groups, soccer teams, choruses, clubs, and Saturday schools to teach German, the language is less and less spoken

(Taylor 1976). Many of those who spoke German joined the rest of the middle class out of the ethnic neighborhoods. With this often comes weakening of ethnicity and second-language speaking.

This occurs even in tightly knit groups determined not to lose their identity. For example, many Ukrainians sought refuge from Communism in America after World War II. Hoping to return to their homeland, they made very sure that their children learned to speak Ukrainian with native speaker competency, to cook Ukrainian foods, to dance all the traditional dances, and to do all the traditional crafts, including the intricate art of dying Easter eggs in exquisite patterns. Above all, they tried to instill in their children a love for their ancestral homeland. To Americans, these Ukrainians seem to have done a marvelous job of keeping their language and traditions alive. However, Olenka Hanushevsky, an American-born Ukrainian, informed me that the older generation exclaims, "How American the young are becoming!" Similarly, Hungarian refugees from the Russian invasion in the 1950's who did not become acclimated to the United States have children who are proficient in English and are becoming increasingly American (Janda 1975). The only Jews in America who have been able to maintain Yiddish are the minority of ultra-Orthodox and Hasidim who live in largely segregated communities. Virtually all other Eastern European Jews have lost Yiddish as a part of their complete assimilation to American culture.[20]

Since Israel eschewed Yiddish as one of its official languages, except for the Orthodox speakers, Yiddish will certainly continue to dwindle. American Jews who are familar with Yiddish are often disappointed to find nobody who speaks it when they visit Israel. The only other sources of Yiddish speakers, Romania, Poland, Russia and Ukraine, lost the language with the advent of the Holocaust and Communism.

Still, for many other speakers, one other factor bodes well for continued bilingualism in the United States. Now, when immigrants come, modern communication and transportation make it possible to maintain close ties with families and friends in their countries of origin. When my grandmother and her children escaped from Ukraine in 1919, they knew they'd never hear their family's voices again, much less see them. Nowadays, immigrants from Russia, Greece, Poland, Hungary, the Middle East, or virtually anyplace can fly back as well as keep in regular contact by phone. Earlier languages were retained as long as there was immigration from the old country, but immigration from much of Europe was cut off by 1924 and by the time easy access by phone and plane came, their languages were no longer being spoken by descendants of the original immigrants.

CHAPTER 8

To a large degree, this movement toward monolingual English may be viewed as natural. The young want to be like their peers, and, after all, this is their country. It can be and has been argued that abandoning ethnic languages has been a necessary factor in forging a national American identity. However, the experiences of bilingual countries like Canada and multilingual countries like the Phillipines attest to the fact that a country can be open to multilingualism and still share an identity through one or more official languages.

Besides the general intolerance of foreign languages in the United States, youngsters may see little need to learn other languages because, worldwide, English is the language to know. The young elsewhere identify with American youth, liking their music, their clothes, and, ultimately, their lingo. Foreign scholars and other professionals often feel that some proficiency in English is necessary, especially since so many textbooks are published only in English. I was astonished at a scholarly meeting several years ago when a German scholar proudly told me he had hosted a meeting in Germany at which every speaker and every moderator spoke English. All the papers were subsequently published in English. There was no German used at all, despite the fact that the participants were all born in Germany and lived there.

Still, German is in no danger of disappearing. Unfortunately, this is not true of the indigenous languages of other places. In general, worldwide, non-European languages have been disappearing at a rapid rate whenever they come into contact with European ones. Trying to salvage at least descriptions of dying or moribund languages has become a grave concern of linguists. Whether it is the languages of Amazon tribes, Native Americans, or those of the smaller tribes of Africa, many languages are disappearing. The reason is not that English and other European languages are in any way inherently superior to the ones disappearing. It is just that the conquerors of those lands spoke English, Spanish, French, Portuguese, or German, and these are the languages used in textbooks, by the governments, on television shows, and certainly are the languages needed for working in the current social and political scenes. Moreover, typically when the Europeans came into contact with those who spoke other languages, they disparaged those people, so that speaking the European language became the prestigious thing to do. Many New World Spanish speakers are descended from people who spoke now defunct Amerindian languages.

Spanish and French in the United States. Spanish was spoken in the Southwest when the Anglos conquered it. Since, for years, many Mexican Americans were barred from all but the most menial jobs, both factors for retaining their ethnic language were present: lack of a chance to get ahead and fear of the loss of solidarity if they gave up Spanish. These are the factors that lead to retention of nonstandard dialects as well. Still, the reasons for retaining Spanish were not all negative. Continued contact with families in Mexico, continued migration to the Southwest, the historical precedence of Spanish rather than English, all these contributed to its retention.

Donald Lance (1972) offers a neat example of generational differences in speaking Spanish, an example verified by Garcia (1981). The grandmother did not speak English at all, although she appeared to understand it. She was only receptively bilingual. The grandfather, a gardener, spoke English only if the hearer did not know Spanish. The daughter and her husband seemed equally proficient in both Spanish and English, although when speaking Spanish, they would throw in a few English words. When speaking English, they did not seem to interject Spanish words. In the presence of an Anglo, they relied on English. Their children were also bilingual but were inhibited about using Spanish in the presence of Anglos. They found it impossible to speak it to non-Hispanics. This indicated that they had been socialized to speak Spanish only with Spanish speakers and to do so with others would be as impossible as arguing with a priest's homily during a mass at church. The words just would not come out! One is reminded of schoolchildren who do poorly in testing situations that do not conform to the conditions for verbal performance for their culture.

Janet Sawyer (1964) found that, even that long ago, Southwest Spanish speakers avoided using Spanish terms whenever they could, even terms that Anglos typically use like *corral, lariat, frijoles,* and *chaps*. If they had to utter a Spanish word, even their own name, they would anglicize it.

Such behavior is typical of other originally foreign-speaking groups as well. Yiddish speakers anglicized the names of their foods, so in New York City, *kishke*, a kind of sausage, became *stuffed derma*.[21] *Kneydlach*, literally 'little dumplings' became *matzoh balls*. People with Yiddish names Americanized them so that *Bayla* became *Bella* and *Yakov* became *Jack*.

Like the Spanish, the Italians have anglicized Italian words borrowed into English. The pronunciation of *spaghetti* and *linguine* are wholly American. Italian *Roberto, Vincenzo,*[22] and *Allessandro* became *Robert, Vincent,* and *Alex*. In Italy, a g before a consonant is pronounced like a *y,* so that a last name like *Scagnelli*, should be the liquid "ScaNYELLi" with the stress on the "nyell" and the double *ll* held for two beats. This has been Americanized into "SCAGnelli" with the stress on "scag," a hard g, no *y,* and the *l* just glossed over. Such anglicizing, to the point of losing the beauty of the original, has generally characterized those who eventually gave up the languages of their ancestors. Yet, despite the similarities in language behavior, what happened to speakers of other languages won't necessarily happen to Spanish speakers.

Until recently, Spanish has been retained for two reasons: the real alienation of a large proportion of Hispanics by their inability to enter the mainstream, and the solidarity provided by maintenance of social networks. The former situation is slowly changing so more Spanish speakers are achieving upward mobility. Still, there are positive reasons for Spanish to be retained where other languages weren't.

First, the very numbers of Spanish speakers in the United States are a big factor in that language's not dying out. Not only are there the Southwest Spanish speakers in Arizona, Texas, and California, and the Puerto Ricans and Cubans in the East, but there are Spanish speakers from South America, such as those from Colombia, and others from Central America. Those who move upward still have plenty of relatives and friends who speak Spanish.

The need for Spanish bilingual professionals is very great: Spanish-speaking physicians, nurses, lawyers, teachers, and social workers. In these days of international business, both business and financial institutions also need Spanish-English bilinguals. Moreover, Spanish is the second most widely spoken language in the world, with English being the first. None of the earlier immigrant languages were needed for middle- and upper-middle-class jobs and professions as Spanish is, nor was any other immigrant language spoken by such numbers of people spread all over the country and all over the world. Except for Native American languages, no other language had as much legitimacy as Spanish has in the Southwest, a legitimacy conferred because the Spanish speakers were there before the English ones. In many states, Spanish is not truly an immigrant language for all its speakers. It was the native tongue until Americans took over.

The Spanish colonized Central and South America before the English colonized North America. Some Hispanics in the Southwest are actually descended from the original Spanish-speaking population and some even feel that Spanish should be the official language in their locales. More recent Mexican immigrants feel this as well.

Indeed, many Mexican immigrants feel that they have a historical right to residency in this region, and disclaim the term *illegal immigrants.* President Vicente Fox of Mexico has actually said that illegal immigrants who come and reinforce Spanish speaking in the United States are doing Mexico a favor. He sees the influx of these immigrants as leading to a reconquest of the United States. This attitude seems to be confined to Mexican activists in the Southwest and not to other Hispanics like Puerto Ricans or Colombians.

The point, to me, is that Mexican-Americans do have a historical justification for retaining Spanish that only one other non-English-speaking group has had, the Native Americans, whose claim to legitimacy precedes even the Hispanics. The town of El Cinzo, Texas actually tried to pass an ordinance that Spanish should be the official language there. It failed. It also brought about a great deal of hostility among English speakers.

The continued illegal immigration of Mexicans into the Southwest has increased Spanish speaking more than the official government census has shown. As of this writing, there are an estimated 11,000,000 such immigrants already here, with large numbers crossing the border every day. The widespread use of Spanish in the Southwest and parts of Florida has caused some Anglos to push for an amendment to the Constitution to make English the official language of the United States. However, given the primacy of English in education and the law, and its necessity for upward mobility, it doesn't seem that English is in any danger. Rather, what does seem likely is that Spanish-English bilingualism will thrive.

A different story for the loss of Canadian French occurred in Maine. As late as the 1950's and 1960's, Canadian-French-speaking children who also spoke English were fined or otherwise punished for speaking French in the schoolyard. Teachers even rewarded Anglophone students for ratting out the use of French by classmates ("French in Maine," 2006). This was largely the result of prejudice and discrimination on the part of the descendants of the original non-French citizens in that state. As it happens, I lived in Maine in the late 1950's and can attest to the low esteem accorded to the French-Canadians. They were considered at best as amusing objects of fun and were largely relegated to low-paying jobs, unless they were careful to get rid of the French lilt in their English, anglicize the pronunciation of their names, and never, ever speak French so a Yankee could hear it.

Maine didn't elect its first openly French congressman until 2002. The State Legislature has recently declared a Franco-American Day, the Pledge of Allegiance is now recited in both French and English, and the national anthem is sung in both languages. Now French speaking is making a comeback, with "reacquisition classes" springing up all over the state. About 5.3% of Maine's population speaks French at home, the largest percentage of any state. Given the stigma associated with speaking it in the past, it is miraculous that so many do speak it now.

Still, the children of those who were fined and ridiculed for speaking it were often not taught it, and it is not clear that they or their children are now willing to try to learn it. Howard Paradis, a public school teacher who was once forced to fine his students for speaking French, "made the painful decision not to teach French to his own children" and is quoted as saying,

CHAPTER 8

"I wasn't going to put my kids through that" ("French in Maine," 2006, A13).

It is not certain that French bilingualism will take root among the young. It is noteworthy that the classes for its maintenance are reacquisition ones for older speakers who learned it as children. There is no mention of classes for children now to learn it, nor could I find any evidence that Canadian French is taught in the schools, despite the extensive literature in that dialect and the prestige that it holds in Canada.

The problem is, as I see it, that at least a generation hasn't learned the language as a home one. Therefore, preserving it is a matter of resuscitation. Children already acculturated to non-French friends have to be convinced to start being more French. Also, over the years, many of the Franco-Americans have intermarried into other ethnic groups. In other words, whether Canadian French is preserved in Maine or not depends on the degree to which its potential speakers have retained their ethnic loyalties.

Besides the northern Canadian French, there is Creole in Louisiana. This is yet another variety of American French. There seems to have been a falling-off of younger bilingual speakers of that dialect. I was disheartened when speaking to young New Orleans guides who told me that although their parents still speak it, all they know are a few words of it and that this is true of many of their friends as well. The very term *Creole* suggests that its speakers don't regard it as true French, but a mixture. As younger people become upwardly mobile, this might inhibit their use of it.

Canadian French speakers in Canada believe that their French is as legitimate and standard as American English is. That is, despite the existence of Continental French and British English, the North American varieties of those languages are not inferior in any way, nor are the literatures written in them. Whether Creole speakers feel the same way about Louisiana French, I don't know.

Historically, the trend has usually been that the language of those in power becomes dominant one, even the prestigious one. However, the nondominant language does leave its traces in names for food, geographical features, and other common words. Native American place names survive in abundance: Pawtucket, Nipmuc, Niantic, Narragansett, Tuscaloosa, Shenandoah, Mississippi, Alabama, Missouri, Dakota—the list goes on of all the places taken over and of the tribes which were destroyed. Many Spanish words have entered American English, like *mesa, canyon, tostida, frijoles, nada, dinero, amigo,* even *mi casa su casa,* not to mention the terms associated with ranching, including the word *ranch* itself.

Native American Languages. Ironically, the original inhabitants of America, the Native Americans (**NA**s), commonly and erroneously called

Indians, were never able to claim their languages as American after the Europeans colonized. Many people naively think of NAs as being a monolithic group. Actually, different tribes with very different cultures and languages extended from Maine to Florida, Alaska to California, and all points in between. It is estimated that there were between 500 to 1,000 separate languages spoken in America north of Mexico. Arlotto (1972, 57–61) shows twelve large and extensive Indian language families. Each family has or had several separate languages and dialects. A language family is a group of languages that can be shown to have sprung from one common language. For instance, the Algonquin family included several languages spoken throughout central Canada, the Great Lakes, parts of the Southwest, and the eastern seaboard, with two distant relatives in California. Some examples of these were Narragansett, Cree, Cheyenne, Delaware, and, of course, Algonquin itself (59–60).[23]

The true extent of this diversity can perhaps best be seen by comparison with one language family. Most of the languages of Europe and some of India descended from one now dead language called Proto-Indo European. English, Russian, German, French, Italian, Spanish, Swedish, Hindi, and Rumanian are all members of this family, for example. Imagine twelve language families among the American Indians! The languages within each could be as different as Sicilian is from Prussian, and the language families themselves could be as different as Gaelic is from Chinese.

Perhaps one factor contributing to the demise of NA languages was the very fact that there were so many different ones, most spoken by a relatively small number of speakers (Leap 1993). Because there were so many different NA languages involved, the problem of maintaining any one of them was magnified as each language was spoken by so few individuals. None of them could be used as a general language for all Native Americans. They also were so different from each other that learning one wasn't necessarily a help in learning another.

There was no one widespread Indian language that could have been used to unite the NAs. This, of course, was a reflection of the fact that the social organization of the NAs was tribal, with no larger governmental authority to unite them. Therefore, they were virtually sitting ducks for the technologically superior European colonists who came armed as well with the concept of governmental authority that made it possible for them to mobilize more efficiently than the NAs.

The other factor in the loss of NA languages, and the major one, is the "time-honored" circumstance that the vanquished lose their language. The original language of England was a Celtic one. It disappeared when Germanic tribesmen overstayed their welcome and took over England. Originally, in what is now Italy, there were four Italic languages: Oscan,

Umbrian, Faliscan, and Latin. But when the Latin-speaking Romans took over the rest of the peninsula, the language of Rome overcame the others. Then, as the Romans fanned out over Europe, their spoken language[24] fanned out with them, leading eventually to the Romance languages. *Romance* here does not mean a love story. It simply means 'a language of Roman origin.'

Needless to say, when Europeans came, saw, and conquered the New World, they were not terribly interested in the NA languages. As conquerors, they wouldn't be expected to care a fig about the language of the conquered. Besides in this instance, the conquered were far more "primitive" both in social organization and technology (but not in culture) than were the conquerors. Consequently, many NA languages disappeared with their tribes.[25]

Grosjean (1982, 82–84) reports that according to the 1970 census, there were an estimated 764,000 NAs in the United States, belonging to about 150 distinct cultures. The 2003 census (U.S. Census Bureau 2006) reports 302,000 NAs speaking an NA language at home. They do not report how many NAs there are who speak only English at home. Most of those that Grosjean reported on were English-speaking, as only 34% reported an NA or Eskimo language as their first language. About 25,000 reported Spanish and 8,000 French as a home language. Grosjean claimed that there were about 300 NA languages still in use, mostly by older speakers, but Leap (1993) estimates that there are only about 206, including dialects. The number may well be less than that, as the 2003 survey reports that 136,000 claim to speak Navajo at home and 133,000 speak other NA languages. That is, there are fewer speakers of all the other languages combined than there are of Navajo. By 1993, Leap (207) reported that a 1962 survey showed that forty-nine of these languages had fewer than ten speakers, all over fifty years of age. It would be safe to assume that these languages are moribund if not dead. Six other languages in 1962 could report more than 10,000 speakers "within all generational groupings in each community," and fluency in the remaining 151 "can fall at any point between those extremes." Similarly, levels of English fluency vary widely, especially among the older generations (Leap 208). Not surprisingly, younger speakers may be more fluent in English than the oldest members of their tribes. This situation is enhanced by the fact that more than 70% of NA children are enrolled in public schools rather than in the older, segregated Bureau of Indian Affairs schools.

Of course, television has had its impact as well. What do NA children see on TV? There aren't enough speakers left of virtually any tribe except the Navajo to warrant cable channels conducted in their ancestral languages, and what opportunities are there for NA-speaking people? English is what they need. When I was in Alaska in 1998, I was surprised to hear members of the Tlingit tribe who said they were now trying to learn the language pronounce their tribal name and language as "Klingit." Such an error is to be expected of monolingual English speakers with no familiarity with the language. English does allow /k/ and /l/ to be pronounced together, as in *clean* or *close*, but it doesn't have words which begin with /t/ and /l/, so, upon hearing the name Tlingit, English colonizers simply substituted /k/ for /t/, a common foreign-speaker error. These younger Tlingit had clearly not heard the language very much. People exposed to other languages a great deal in childhood may not speak the language, but they can pronounce the sounds of the language correctly. The fact that these young people could not even pronounce the name of their own people correctly means they virtually never heard the language.

As we've discussed, when people hear unfamiliar sounds in a new language, they substitute ones in their native language that are close. My grandmother always "vanted" something. There is no /w/ in her native languages, so she substituted /v/ for all English /w/'s, like "vindow," "vill," "ven" and "vy" (window, will, when, why). The same things happen when a language doesn't allow a certain combination of sounds. For instance, on the 1989 tape *American Tongues*, a Southern man was asked if he knew the word *shlep* (Yiddish for *drag, carry something heavy*). Since English allows *sl* together, as in *sleep, slurp, slim,* and *slice,* but never has *shl* together, the man pronounced *shlep* as "slep," even though the announcer had just said it to him correctly.

The Tlingit youth I spoke to earnestly told me that, although some words were spelled *tl*, they were pronounced "kl," and, they also assured me, Tlingit was the hardest language in the world to learn, that being their excuse for not knowing it. Interestingly, most foreigners claim that English is a very hard language to learn. The Tlingit think their abandoned language is harder only because they grew up speaking English and Tlingit is a very different language. In any event, when a people can no longer even pronounce a language's name correctly, it bodes ill for their ever learning it.

At least part of the reason for the rapid disappearance of NA languages can be attributed to early government policy. Compulsory schooling run by the Bureau of Indian Affairs made children board at school, did not allow them to speak their NA tongues, and discouraged their parents from visiting them. Grosjean (1982, 84) says that "All ties with the nation or tribe were broken. . . ."

Since 1979, however, the government has funded bilingual education for 14,000 NAs in fourteen states. Some of these have even attempted to revive dead languages like Seminole, teaching them as second languages. As with African American parents who complain if AAVE is encouraged in the classroom, some NA parents want their children schooled in English so that they will not continue to be second-class citizens.

We have already seen that the particular language that a speaker already knows when learning another will influence the second language. This was true of NAs as well, so that Leap (209) reports that NA English varied according to the languages of each tribe, pointing out that "[t]ribally distinct English codes emerged—each formed off the grammar of the particular Indian language" (209). To some degree, these differences have remained, with consequent results for education and for the students' eventual success in Anglo society. For instance, NA students may "interpret material on the printed page in terms quite different from those intended by the writer . . ." (210). This occurs even when the NA speaker no longer speaks the original tribal language. Studies with speakers of other dialects have shown that such problems in dialect differences contribute to failure in Anglo education, thus resulting in lower socioeconomic status for the speakers.

The kinds of salvage work on fast-disappearing languages[26] that we have seen for other groups is being attempted for some endangered NA languages, but the fate of Gaelic (next section) suggests that governments would do well to assess the attitudes of the speakers before setting up programs.

The Fate of Gaelic. On another continent with a situation parallel to the stigmatized groups in the United States, the Irish, despite centuries of brutal treatment by the British, largely abandoned Gaelic as their first language. By 1850, only about 5% of the Irish were monolingual Gaelic speakers. Macnamara (1971) claims this is because English is the language one must know in order to get and hold a job. Of course, this doesn't explain why Irish Gaelic has all but died out even in the Irish Republic, which has been independent of British rule for decades now.

Furthermore, Irish has steadily declined even though the Irish government has made a strong effort to save it. When the Irish government took over in 1922, most of its speakers were in the poorest, rural parts of Ireland. To save the language, then, the government poured money into those regions, elevating them considerably. They made Irish the national language, gave subsidies to families whose children spoke it, as well as other perks such as house-building grants and scholarships. Teachers were specially trained to teach all subjects in Gaelic (Fennell 1981). The result? Irish has been steadily eroding.

Still, students of mine who come from Ireland insist it is still being learned by young people. One has a mother who teaches it and claims that most secondary school graduates are fluent in it, but I have not seen any statistical verification of these claims. Perhaps more importantly, I have seen no studies showing under what conditions Gaelic is used socially, and this is the true test of whether a language is living and well. A proficiency test administered before graduating high school is no proof that students really speak the language in social interactions. Nor is it proof that high school graduates will even remember the language in ten years' time.

Fennell blames what he sees as its erosion on the Irish government because all of these programs were administered in Dublin. However, many things are beyond a government's ability to control, and making people speak a particular language is one of them. Ultimately, however, Fennell correctly attributes the failure to the fact that the Irish simply had no will to save their language (39), something that he believes requires a "prophetic individual" to inspire the people (39). I disagree. If people have no social or economic reason to speak a language, they won't, no matter how charismatic a leader they have. At least I know of no instance in which populations abandoned one language for another because of a leader. Indeed, to influence the people, such a leader has to speak the language they already speak.

Alternatively, it may be that the Irish perceived Gaelic as the language of the oppressed and so preferred not to speak it. This certainly is one reason for the near-demise of Yiddish among descendants of Eastern European Jews,[27] and shows how important it is to discover the attitudes of speakers toward a given language if one desires to teach it.

There are fears of a similar fate befalling Welsh Gaelic (Jones 1981; Ambrose and Williams 1981), which, in many respects, has been and still is more robust than Irish despite 800 years of anglicization. One factor that saved it from the Irish fate was that evangelical Methodists in the eighteenth century adopted it as their church language, thus tying the national tongue to religion.

Still, perhaps as one would expect, it is declining even in areas with many bilinguals, despite the fact that there is Welsh-language television and books in Welsh were still being published in 1980 (48). The number still being published, I don't know. In some respects, Welsh has actually extended in use in that it is now used for public administration and is utilized more in education, including government schools.

Still, Jones says that Welsh-speaking people say they see no need for it. Because of the widening of social networks and the general utility of English, Jones fears the same homogenizing of language use that has occurred in the United States. Ambrose and Williams paint a less bleak picture, however. They have not only mapped the geographical extent of Welsh speakers, but they have also mapped areas according to the social situations in which Welsh is still spoken. As they say, the fact that Welsh is now a minority language is no cause for alarm. Languages have died out even when their speakers were a majority, and many minority languages have survived.

The key is whether the language is used for many social purposes. My guess, from a trip through Wales in 1996, is that the language is declining. I met young parents who spoke no Welsh at all, but whose children are studying it in school. When I looked through a Welsh primer, however, I realized how unlikely it was that the children who studied it would ever become Welsh speakers. The entire book was about children playing cowboy—American cowboys complete with holsters and chaps. This, of course, is an artifact of American culture, not even British![28]

If Welsh can't be linked to things Welsh, if there is nothing in Welsh culture per se that children want to emulate and if, besides that, their own parents don't speak it, why will they? Wherever we went in Wales, we saw signs urging people to speak it, signs saying, "Use it or lose it." That is the problem. If there is little social reason for using it, they will lose it. I did hear older people speaking Welsh, but not younger ones. Perhaps I'm being pessimistic, but history shows what happens when speakers no longer see an advantage to speaking a language.

The original language of Scotland, Scots Gaelic, a relative of Irish Gaelic, has been all but dead for centuries, except among isolated populations, such as rural fisherfolk in East Sutherland (Dorian 1982, 25). The British actually banned its use after they conquered Scotland. The Scots, however, developed their own brand of English. The issue in Scotland now is not to resuscitate the Gaelic but to keep Scots English alive as a separate dialect of English. Educated Scottish speakers are more and more learning British English. Aitken (1981) feels that without their own dialect of English, the Scot will completely lose their identity.

There is concern in Europe today that minority languages like Romansch, Basque,[29] Walloon, and Flemish will die out in the general crush toward speaking the major European languages. Therefore, the European community funds committees whose business it is to foster the speaking of minority languages, such as the Bureau for Lesser Used Languages, which is situated in Dublin, and the International Association for the Defense of Menaced Languages in Liege, Belgium.

OFFICIAL LANGUAGES

Despite the extensive bilingualism in the United States, for official purposes, so to speak, it is essentially a monolingual country. Therefore, it is hard to realize how important the issue of language choice is in much of the world. The issues have always been clear for our own foreign speakers.

English is the official language of the land for all purposes and if one wishes to enter into mainstream society, one must learn it. This is not entirely a bad thing.

A unified country requires that one language be understood and be used by virtually everyone. Additionally, our entire body of legal precedents, our constitution, and our laws are all written in English. So are many of the textbooks of higher education and this is true throughout the world. In many disciplines, it is essential that scholars master English. But none of this is an excuse for people speaking only one language.

We have already seen that a common language forges social bonds. The corollary is that different languages reinforce separation, even hostility. For example, utility bills are now printed in English and Spanish throughout most of the country. In southern New England, they are in Portuguese as well. As harmless as this may seem, it has excited resentment and hostility. My cousin, who lives in the Bay area of California, angrily told me that in restaurants, people speak Spanish and they don't care who hears them. He clearly feels that speaking Spanish is a bad and even rude thing to do! Such attitudes toward speaking another language are incomprehensible to me, but, apparently, in the United States it is seen as non-American or just plain wrong to speak anything but English. Such provinciality in a country founded on diversity can only be explained by an overweening chauvinism.

All modern nations require official languages in fact if not in law. Even though a country like the United States has no law proclaiming that English must be its official language, in fact, English operates as one. Laws are written in English. The courts are conducted in English. Classrooms are conducted in English unless they are specifically set up as part of a bilingual program—and even then the goal is to have the students learn English as rapidly as possible. Except in higher education in foreign language classes, no other language is used in instruction.

Countries that have recognized the legitimacy of more than one language have actually set up official languages by law. Often this is done in multilingual nations and more than one language is designated as official. In Israel, for instance, Hebrew, Arabic, and English are the official languages. In Canada, both French and English are. Given the political underpinnings of the United States, its educational system, bureaucracy, and laws, there seems to be little reason to designate English as official since it is so *de facto*.

In Canada, the French Canadians have an equivalent, actually a prior, claim to official status for their language. They bitterly resented the concept of English as the official status for everything, wanting French to have equal status in education and law. Accordingly, for some years now, laws have instituted bilingual education so that younger speakers of different ethnicities can converse with each other and even read the same books. Classes are taught in both languages.

Teaching in French legitimizes that language. Children taught French as a medium of education are more likely to feel that it is as good as English than they do if French remains only the language of the home and the streets. It must be emphasized that in Canada, bilingualism extends through the university levels. French is equal to English at all ranks of education. Laws are written in both languages, as are contracts. Advertisements appear in both, as do signs, road markings, and the like.

Various ethnic groups in the United States want similar bilingual education. When the United States government funds bilingual programs, typically they cover the elementary grades, and most have the aim of turning foreigners into English speakers. Teaching English proficiency is not necessarily a bad thing in and of itself. As I mentioned earlier, academic conferences, including those in non-English-speaking countries, are often held in English.

As students go further up the educational ladder, English becomes more and more important, especially since so many textbooks are written in English. Some aren't, though. As a scholar, I sometimes have to read a journal article or book in another language. Besides, not all bilinguals want to go to college. Those who do can benefit from knowing more than one language. There are the famous junior year abroad, college classes in French novels or Italian films that aren't conducted in English, not to mention courses in Chinese or Russian or even Swahili.

In terms of the job market, English proficiency can be very important. But, as noted above, it is equally important for businesses to have members of their staff who know how to speak other languages. Government, of course, needs speakers of myriad languages. Bilingual education for those who wish to retain their native language would be a boon for the United States. So would foreign language instruction designed to teach monolinguals to speak other languages fluently. The United States is one of the very few places in the world in which this is not done as a regular part of the curriculum starting in the early grades. A Swedish friend told me that she had to be fluent in German in elementary school. Then, she had to demonstrate fluency in French by the equivalent of high school, and then she had to be conversant in English by graduation. That is standard in Sweden.

There is some question about teaching basic skills in one language when the higher studies based on those skills have to be done in another language. This is a consideration, especially in mathematics. It is not known to what degree, if any, learning basic mathematics in one language can hamper a student in complex mathematical formulations in advanced studies.

Paradoxically, it would be advantageous to teach reading to future English users in languages like Italian and Spanish rather than English. Once someone learns to read in one alphabetic system, it is not difficult to transfer those skills to another, especially to one that uses pretty much the same letters. Since both Italian and Spanish spelling have a good fit with the actual pronunciation of both languages, it is relatively easy for their speakers to learn to read in them.

English spelling shows a very poor fit to even the standard forms of the language. Furthermore, it is chaotic: /š/ can be spelled <sh> as in *shoot*, <ch> as in *machine*, <shi> as in *fashion*, <ssi> as in *mission*, <su> as in *sure*, <ti> as in *nation*, <ci> as in *crucial*. Besides the superfluity of having one sound represented by so many spellings, the same spellings can indicate different sounds, as <ch> in *child*, and *machine*, <su> in *Susan* (where one <s> is /s/ and the other is /z/), and <ti> as in *till* and *nation*.

It is far more difficult to learn to read English than it is to read Spanish and Italian. Because of this, the children who learn to read in those languages learn more quickly and are thus able to get a jump start on subject matter. It has been found that if Spanish-speaking children are taught to read first in that language, they accelerate more rapidly than when they have to learn to read in English. Once children have cracked the code, so to speak, it is easier for them to transfer their reading skills to English.

Translating

Americans assume that bilinguals are able to translate from one of their languages into the other. Given the traditional American-style language teaching, this is not an unlikely assumption. Typically, we assume that what one does in a foreign language classroom, translating English into the target language, and the foreign language back into English, is what bilinguals do. More usually, it seems that the bilingual keeps his or her languages separate, drawing on one or the other as the occasion demands. They may be able to switch very rapidly from one to the other, but it seems as if they draw upon each as a separate system rather than trying to find the equivalents from one to the other.

Actually, bilinguals may find it very difficult to translate from one language to another. Neither words nor grammars of languages show a one-to-one correspondence with each other. One has to use a phrase in one language to translate a word in another and vice versa. Even when one can translate by substituting one word for another, the rest of the grammar of the sentence may have to be very different. Then there is always the problem of connotations that occur in one language, but not the other. Grosjean

CHAPTER 8

(256) mentions the case of a French-English bilingual who wrote his dissertation in English but then couldn't translate it into French. His wife had to do it for him.

Many foreign language teachers are themselves not native English speakers and regularly make all sorts of errors in English, which nobody ever seems to remark on. It's all right to make errors. Too fine an attention on every single point defeats the purpose of trying to learn another language. All it does is inhibit the would-be speakers, confirming them in their belief that they can't learn another language. Nowadays, readily available interactive computer programs can be used for correcting both phonological and grammatical errors, leaving more class time for encouraging actual conversation. There are even such programs for your Ipod! The virtue of the computer programs is that the learner is never embarrassed by making mistakes. It's between the computer and the learner. Also, the learner can practice as much as necessary, going over the same material until it's learned. These programs also give instantaneous feedback all the time. In a class, a student may sit for an hour and be lucky to be called on even once, only to be embarrassed by saying something wrong that the whole class can hear.

Language Planning

Many modern nations have been forged from disparate groups or tribes, all speaking radically different languages, all having a stronger commitment to those languages than to their governments or other peoples in the new nation. Yet official languages are needed both for government and education.

In most instances, a colonial power bequeathed its language: French, Dutch, Spanish, Portuguese, or English. By itself or with other languages, the colonial language is retained for government and higher education. The colonial languages might seem to be good choices as national languages for the new countries that inherited them. The only reason this might not work is that language is a very personal, very emotional issue. Former colonies often hated their European rulers. European languages, therefore, are anathema to many in the Third World. Even those who see the need for European languages deplore them for primary-school children or even for local government. They do not want four-year-olds to have to learn any of them as the sole language of school. Nor do they want business conducted in the colonial language, or broadcasting in it on radio or TV shows. In regions where as many as ten or even twenty languages are spoken, this is no trifling matter.

The problem is compounded by the lack of writing systems for many native languages. Phonetic transcriptions can be devised by linguists, but even if they are, what will become the official orthography of the country? What script will newspapers use? What will be chosen for business communication? All of these problems are further complicated by the intense emotional commitment of people to their own language. After generations of terrible oppression, blacks in South Africa finally rioted over the issue of what language would be used in the schools of Soweto. Language riots have occurred in other countries, as in India after the British withdrew.

Because of the problems caused by multilingualism in new nations, some linguists and sociolinguists have become involved in language planning. Before a language is made official, a careful study is needed to determine the attitudes toward it. Planners must decide what language(s) will be employed in elementary schools. It must be one that will not repulse natives, one that they feel comfortable speaking in social situations, including school and business.

Planners must acknowledge that such decisions have far-reaching social and political effects. If a given language is not used for schooling, business, or government, it is likely to lose prestige socially. Judging by the experiences of the United States, if enough speakers get an opportunity to learn an official language, their children will make less and less of an effort to learn their family's original language(s). This can lead to weakening of both family and social bonds. The old grandmother or grandfather who cannot speak the new language cannot converse readily with the younger generation, thereby losing prestige, not to mention love.

Worse, perhaps, grandparental authority is weakened. If the language becomes outdated, then the traditional wisdom of the old is also considered outmoded. Many an immigrant mother has found herself in such a position. And, many an immigrant grandmother in twentieth-century America found herself denied traditional grandparenting because her children's children literally could not speak her language. If she could speak theirs, it was with an accent, perhaps one lampooned in jokes or in the movies.

Choosing official languages must take such potential problems into account. What is the role of the elderly in a culture, and what language(s) are these roles encoded onto? How can these language(s) be preserved as worthy means of communication even if another must be made official for other reasons? Such questions and their solutions must be a part of any language planning.

When an official language (or languages) are chosen, those to whom it is not native can be encouraged to speak it, but not give up their home language. For, ultimately, that does have repercussions both on the extended family and the feelings of self-worth on the individual. One way that schools can help is to set up mock situations in which the different languages would be switched into and out of according to the drama being enacted. Studies like history, sociology, and psychology lend themselves to such role-playing techniques. Such activities can also be used to spur discussion. In other words, bilingual schools could teach and encourage code-switching as part of their regular curriculum.

Language planners, in their selection of one language over the other, must also be very aware of political consequences. Natives who already speak the language selected have an advantage over those who do not. In terms of carving out sinecures and of getting advantageous connections, this edge can last for generations. The fact that one language is chosen also makes its speakers seem more important than those of languages not chosen. If Western experience is any guide, usually the language not chosen is doomed unless its speakers are isolated. The reverse may also become true, as those who do not speak the official languages are likely to become isolated. Remedies for these eventualities must be part of the original planning. When we think of Hispanics and NAs in the United States itself, we must remember that this country still needs language planning.

There is no way to consider language use without considering its impact on the very fabric of society and government. There is no way to consider any human group without considering how it uses language.

Esperanto

One way to overcome these problems would be to use a language which has no political or social connotations. Devotees of Esperanto think that is the answer (Quick 1989; Carvalho 1990; Fettes 1991; Welger 1992). Esperanto is an artificial language created in 1887 by L. L. Zamenhof. Noting that natural languages were all capable of ambiguity and variable interpretations, he decided to develop a completely neutral, unambiguous language in which a word or sentence would always mean just one thing. The advantage to Esperanto, besides its precision, would be that ostensibly it would offend nobody's nationalistic feelings. Unlike English or French or any other candidate for an international language, Esperanto would not be associated with any one political or cultural group.

However, Zamenhof was writing during the heyday of colonialism and formed his language out of European, specifically Latinate, features. Thus, it is hardly neutral in terms of the mass of Chinese, Thai, Japanese, Native American, Austronesian, and other non-European languages, which, it must be noted, comprise most of the languages of the world. Esperanto is as Eurocentric as English or French.

Moreover, any language in use, if it is a full, flexible language, allows speakers to use old words and constructions in new ways. Ambiguity is a byproduct of flexibility. Communication would be severely hindered if people had to think up a brand-new word each time they wanted to convey a new shade of an idea, then had to explain what the word was and what its meaning was for all time. Rather, language is structured so that one can use an old word in a new way in such a fashion that another speaker can instantly fathom the new intended meaning. Nobody has ever found any way to stop living languages from changing, so how would we stop Esperanto from gaining new meanings? And why would we want to? If we did, it would then be isomorphic, with a one-to-one correspondence between message and meaning. This would mean that it would be difficult to express new thoughts in the language, or to name new items or situations. Lack of isomorphism, of course, is the defining characteristic of nonhuman communication systems vis-à-vis human language.

Moreover, people learn the languages they want, and one thing that makes them want to learn certain languages is that they admire the culture of those who speak it. We know of no way to force people to speak a language not identified with a culture. Certainly, if Esperanto were adopted as an international language, then the spread of English as the international language would be checked. However, English is already spoken all over the world, more widely than any other language has ever been. People have already learned it. They have shown that they want to learn it. What are we to do? Tell Africans and Japanese and Chinese and the French and Spanish and Germans and Dutch and Russians and Yugoslavians and Aleuts to forget English and try to learn a new, made-up Eurocentric language just because it is not identified with any one culture? One could say that English is no longer identified with any one country because it is so widespread. It is difficult to see another way for an international language to take hold.

CHAPTER 8

Notes

[1] My father and his sisters came to the United States when they were twelve, fourteen, and fifteen, respectively, and all three gained complete native speaker competency in English with no accent or evidence of interference from their original languages. My grandmother was thirty-five, and, although she spoke English fluently, did have an accent.

[2] Speakers of declined languages like Russian are accustomed to endings on words that show what part of speech they are and how they are being used in a sentence. In languages like English, both word order and noun determiners like possessives, articles, and auxiliaries give the same information. Typically, then, declined languages do not use articles before nouns and may rely more on verb endings than auxiliaries with verbs. As a language changes from declined to nondeclined, determiners develop. One can often tell if a speaker's native language is declined because, if it is, he or she will make many errors in using determiners.

[3] Americans are typically told that English no longer has subjunctives other than the "If I were . . ." variety used to indicate an impossible situation, as in "If I were 6 feet tall, I'd become a Rockette." However, there is another subjunctive used daily, but largely unnoticed in English grammar books, to wit:

1. I prefer that you **be** here.
2. I insist that he **come** immediately.
3. He suggested that she **leave** by the first boat.
4. They preferred that Patriarca **flunk** the lie detector test.

The use of *be* with no auxiliary is subjunctive, as is the lack of agreement on third person singular verbs. As in other European languages, the subjunctive occurs following a verb of indirect speech or when stating a proposition that is not necessarily going to happen.

[4] From the point of view of employers, this was an ideal situation. The Portuguese workers were immune to unions that might want to organize them. They also had little idea of demanding more in wages or asking for benefits. Such practices by companies employing people who don't speak English must still exist. One student of mine who majored in Spanish was hired by a national firm in Texas so that she could be a liaison with the Mexican-speaking employees.

[5] This is now happening all over the world because of the influence of American popular culture.

[6] President Jimmy Carter.

7   They were monolingual speakers of English.

8   Vasconcelos taped the show and played it for the class. The English words popped out of the stream of speech very clearly and with no hesitation before or after them. They were an integral part of the Portuguese sentence.

9   Sunburns and other burns may not appear fully until hours after exposure, and severe sunburn can look like any other severe burn.

10 This was originally created in French and was translated into English in 1910. Later, it was improved, becoming the Stanford-Binet, long used to assess the IQs of American schoolchildren.

11 What is especially ironic about this is the fact that disproportionately more Jews are research scientists, mathematicians, physicians, surgeons, concert musicians, and scholars than people of any other group. Their forebears, however, were usually the kind of desperately poor immigrants who came out of steerage and were subjected to this test.

12 This is belied by my own family's experience. As noted, my father and his older sisters were beyond this age period when they came to the United States, but all spoke English with absolutely no trace of an accent. Perhaps the one advantage they had, besides their determination to be American, was that they were already bilingual when they came to this country.

13 Ayessa DeLeon, a native Filipina who speaks Panasinense, Tagalog, English, and Spanish, tells me that there is no concept in the Philippines of having a special flair for languages. Everybody just expects to learn more than one. She was very proud of the fact that now even kindergarten is conducted in English. Also, children regularly hear English and Tagalog along with their native language. This is not a matter of social class. This applies to all classes of people.

14 Old English did make this distinction, however. Yiddish, like German, has both *essen* for people and *fressen* for animals, but, I think more than German, *fressen* is used of people who eat a great deal or eat a lot at a specific time. *Er fresst* 'he eats' indicates he has a large appetite, and *er ist a Fresser* 'he is a big eater' (like a horse) although these are usually said in fun, not as insults. In contrast, English *he eats like a pig* is an insult.

15 I am aware that this is an anthropomorphic description, but he looked towards the ceiling for a moment while sitting completely still. He didn't focus on anything on the ceiling, nor did he sniff, look around, or make any kind of noise. It looked to the students and to me that he was somehow calculating how many people he had greeted. His subsequent behavior suggests the veracity of this judgment.

CHAPTER 8

16   Spanish and Portuguese Jews spoke Ladino, based upon an early form of these Romance languages. As with Yiddish, this was a language born of isolation and persecution. This is another reflection of what we saw in dialects: people who are not allowed to assimilate develop or retain their own forms of speech.

17   It may well be true of the French throughout New England. My direct experience, however, has been with the southern New England populations.

18   This is decidedly not true of Canada. There, educated varieties of Canadian French are considered as proper as educated varieties of American and Canadian English.

19   My French-speaking friend had an unusual experience with one of her four children. She, of course, spoke only French to him, but he always answered only in English. Then she took him to France for an extended visit. Once there, he immediately began speaking French.

20   I myself have never met one below the age of sixty-five who knows more than a smattering of Yiddish words and phrases.

21   *Derma* is not a Yiddish word at all. It comes from the same Latin root as *dermatologist*, and means 'skin.' So, a kind of sausage became literally 'stuffed skin.' Despite that yucky name, it is delicious. The very fact that immigrants preferred to take a Latin root to name their ethnic food shows how determined they were just to become American and how willing they were to abandon their cultural roots.

22   In Italian, this is "VinCHENzo." A *c* before an *i* or *e* in that language is pronounced as a *ch*. Also, the stress in a three-syllable word is on the second syllable and lilts upward, with the vowel held for a longer time than in English.

23   The distribution of these languages shows the migrations of the earliest speakers of Algonquian. As separate groups settled elsewhere, their language changed over time, eventually splitting off from the parent group. This is how all the languages belonging to a parent language are formed. We can learn a good deal about the prehistory of a language by determining which languages are related. This was one of the earliest tasks of linguistics.

24   This was not, as popularly believed, Latin, but a later spoken version of the Roman language. One proof we have that this was different from Latin is that certain words for common things occur in all of the Romance languages, but not in Latin. For instance, in Latin the word for *mouth* had a root form *or-*, but in all of the Romance languages, the word *mouth* derives from *bucca*, which originally meant 'cheek.' What had to have happened is that the Romans transferred the meaning

of *bucca* from 'cheek' to 'mouth.' Then, over time, as Roman started to break up into separate languages, the word for mouth was derived from *bucca*, such as French *bouche*.

25 Sometimes an interested European wrote down lists of words with or without grammatical descriptions, and missionaries and anthropologists did get some languages well described in the 20th century and the latter part of the 19th.

26 They are disappearing in the United States, that is, when we are considering Europeans and Asians. Their languages are alive and well in their countries of origin.

27 Of course, the loss of Yiddish in Eastern Europe initially began because of the pogroms (massacres) starting in the late 19th century and then the Holocaust.

28 The only place I have seen children recently playing cowboy, dressed with appropriate Western hats and wearing holsters with toy guns as well as chaps and boots, is in the United Kingdom, and I mean the one overseas, not Disney World.

29 Basque is now being taught in the United States to children of American Basques. Their parents take them to visit in Spain so that they will not only get to speak it, but also to see its relevance to their lives.

CHAPTER 8

Exercises

1. If you come from a bilingual or multilingual home, try to observe code-switching in your family or among your friends. Chart the topics of conversation which seem to cause the code-switching. What emotional message, if any, does each language seem to signal? Do more formal situations elicit one form of language rather than another?

2. Do a computer search, such as a Dialog search, or look in published abstracts, such as *Language and Linguistics Abstracts* or those for sociology and anthropology. Create a bibliography of recent works on retention or loss of Native American languages. Check the same sources for studies of Southeast Asian languages—or any other languages—in the United States and create a parallel bibliography. Do the research efforts in each area seem equivalent? (This exercise is probably best undertaken by two or three students working together. Perhaps a jointly authored term paper could result. This exercise could also form the basis of a paper on the likely survival of Native American languages, or a report on the extent of loss of those languages.)

3. Check a historical dictionary such as the *Oxford English Dictionary* or *Random House* as to the origin of words used in science, religion, music, native American animals (such as the raccoon, possum, and squirrel) or any other sphere of interest you wish. Does the set of words you chose show heavy borrowing from another language or languages? By checking an encyclopedia or other source, try to formulate a hypothesis to explain the borrowings from the language. Remember that no language ever has to borrow a word from another language. There is always some way to create a new word in one's own language. In your response, consider the reasons that people are likely to borrow rather than create a new word in their own language.

4. Poll your English-speaking peers as to their attitudes toward foreign languages. How many languages does each speak? What languages would he or she be willing to learn? Why would they or would they not want to learn any other language? How do they feel about the foreign language classes they have already taken? Alternatively, poll immigrants or other bilingual peers, creating a questionnaire which would uncover their attitudes to English and their other language(s).

5. Look up five words in a bilingual dictionary (such as Spanish/English or German/English). Note what English words are used to translate the non-English word. Then look up each of those English words in an English dictionary. How different is the translation of the English word from its non-English equivalent? Does the English word contain more meanings or different meanings than its equivalent in the other language? Alternatively, look up the English word in a thesaurus and see how different its equivalents are to the foreign word.

6. Look up newspaper and magazine articles written in the past two or three years about resistance to bilingualism in the United States. This has taken the form of organizations—or individuals—devoted to making English the official language of the United States or of severely limiting such conveniences as bilingual signs in public places or bilingual notices on telephone bills. What are the arguments given for "English only" sentiments? In light of what you have learned in this chapter about bilingualism, prepare a short report on the wisdom of such attitudes toward bilingualism.

7. Pretend that a position becomes available to head up a new bilingual program for speakers of a language or group of languages of your choice. Apply for the position, explaining why a study of sociolinguistics and bilingualism is vital to setting up an effective program. Consider especially issues in individual bilingualism, such as problems of languages in contact, attitudes toward native and target languages, and the social situations in which bilinguals are likely to use each language.

8. Watch a foreign language movie with subtitles. As you listen, match up any words in the subtitles that the character is saying as an English word while speaking the foreign language. The characters will, of course, pronounce the English word with an accent, but if it is recognizable as an English borrowing, count it as one. For instance, the character may say "soupu" for *soup* or "les drugs" for *drugs*. How many such borrowings can you find? Listen especially for expressions like *okay* and *right*. If possible, a few classmates should each watch one movie so that the number of borrowings in different languages can be compared. What kinds of words seem to be borrowed from English?

Chapter 9

Speech Communities

Studies of speech communities reveal the social stratification, social networks, and relevant social groupings within them. Careful field methods for eliciting speech in a variety of conditions are essential for such research. People within one community do not necessarily speak the same way. Moreover, people may belong to several speech communities simultaneously, with consequences for changing their speech behaviors. Sociolinguistic studies reveal that each community has different values and these are reflected in different social markers in speech. There is no universal marker that one can expect to find in all communities. Bilinguals may switch their languages according to the social situation, just as monolinguals switch their styles. Attitudes toward different groups are readily discovered by examining whose dialects they copy as well as by asking people to evaluate their own and others' speech. Even such matters as the singing of songs and telling of jokes reveal social attitudes. The deaf show the same kinds of variability in their manual languages as the hearing do in oral ones. Dialects have many origins, which affects their present form. Some dialects are a result of creolizing of African and European languages. The course of decreolization is affected by social factors.

WHAT CONSTITUTES A SPEECH COMMUNITY

Unavoidably, our discussion of dialects implied that some are more valued than others for different purposes. There is no universally correct dialect for all segments of society or for all situations. Moreover, what one community values, another might deplore. There are no speech forms which will be admired or disliked by all communities of speakers. The operative word here is *community*. Each community has its own standards. Saying this, one might think that it is easy to define what a **speech community** is. One definition is that a speech community is a group of speakers who share a set of norms about the use of a language or languages. Romaine (1982) notes that:

in different speech communities, social and linguistic factors are linked not only in different ways but to different degrees so that the imbrication of social and linguistic structure in a given speech community is a matter for investigation and cannot be taken as fact. (13)

More recently, this has been narrowed down to **communities of practice**, which are composed of people who:

develop activities and ways of engaging in those activities, they develop common knowledge and beliefs, ways of relating to each other, ways of talking—in short, practices. (Eckert and McConnell-Ginet 2003, 57)

The community of practice is smaller than the larger speech community in which it is embedded, and people may belong to several communities of practice. Unless one moves to a different city or state, however, one's speech community is usually more permanent than one's communities of practice. Also, one usually belongs to one speech community, but may belong to several communities of practice, especially throughout one's lifetime.

In contrast, if one changes jobs and starts to use quirks of speech like one's coworkers, then one's community of practice changes. Similarly, if one joins a certain organization or team, one might adopt still other speech forms which are used with other members of those groups. One's overall speech is like that of the speech community, but the variations within it are those of the communities of practice one belongs to. One may speak with a Boise middle-class educated accent. This may differ from working-class Boise speech, but both will be recognized by people within the speech community formed by Boise residents. However, one may also engage in a community of practice at work in which still other aspects of speech are varied.

Nowadays, it is common for people to move to different speech communities for work or for retirement. This situation may lead us to change our concept of a speech community. When one moves, does one keep the standards of one's original speech community, or does one adopt new ones? The age at which one leaves one's original speech community may well affect the degree to which one alters one's loyalty to a speech community. Much work remains to be done on this issue, but, still, it is clear that there are community standards and also variation within a community which allows its members to identify other members' social position.

Labov's early work uncovered a very straightforward variation in speech behaviors allied to social stratification within a community. However, Leslie Milroy, in a very different setting, found that her data didn't admit of such a clearly stratified community. Rather, she found that:

sociolinguistic structure is woven in a complex way throughout the community with different phonological elements being associated with various social groups. (Quoted by Romaine, 14)

Romaine argues that speech communities can be quite messy. All of its members may not use the rules of language the same way. Actually, this is precisely what Labov showed. Romaine argues that the varieties of a dialect cannot be considered simply a falling away from the rules of the standard, a position many linguists concur with. This contradicts Labov, who compared all speech variations to the educated standard of the community. Romaine also noted that people belong to several speech communities at the same time: occupational, regional, social, ethnic, foreign language(s), age, race, gender, education, common disabilities or illnesses, and perhaps even others; and these interact in highly variable ways for each speaker. These are what were later named *communities of practice.*

The biggest counterexample to the idea of a speech community is that any individual in a community for whatever reason may have his or her own set of rules. This is true, but not usual. As part of our socialization process within peer groups, we adopt certain ways of speaking. The individual or individuals who speak differently from their peers are sometimes social isolates, at least in their native speech community, or they are signaling that they intend to leave it. As we shall see, members of a speech community categorize others by their recognition of certain features of speech.

As we have seen, we each learn our language(s) by ourselves, so individual variation is inevitable. Additionally, different members of a speech community may have had very different experiences. Some may have gone into the military where they met people of many different dialects. Consequently, they may have modified their own speech. Others may have gone to schools in different regions, and that has affected their speech. Others adopt speaking practices to present a particular persona. It has also been shown that the more people interact with each other, the more alike they sound. In turn, this may be affected by community standards.

For instance, a female speaker from New Haven, Connecticut sixty years ago might have tried to emulate the admired actress Katherine Hepburn. However, sixty years ago, *r*-dropping speech was considered correct in many parts of the United States. British upper-class speech was considered very fine. Today, *r*-less speech in America is generally frowned upon, and Katherine Hepburn's accent seems affected, so a female who wished to sound like an admired actress would have to pick someone like Meryl Streep or Reese Witherspoon to emulate. The trend towards young upper-class girls in Eastern New England picking up on Los Angeles "girlie" talk is such a phenomenon, but it isn't individual. It's occurring within the communities of practice of private schools and colleges.

Clearly, both factors operate in the details of how one speaks: individual motivation and community standards, be they nationwide, region-wide, statewide, citywide, or even village-wide (Dorian 1982). For individual variation to have its desired effect, however, the individual must consider the community standards. It does no good to talk like a "good ol' boy" if one doesn't know what speech features are associated with good ol' boys. Moreover, it is hard to account for language change unless we consider both individual variation and social standards. Labov's work, presented below, is undoubtedly a simplification of the true complexity of the communities he studied. However, it seems to me that he does show some methodologies for getting at general community standards. In contrast, Milroy's study of Belfast, also presented below, shows the greater complexity caused by individual circumstances and concerns.

DIFFERENT DIALECTS, SAME REGION

Whereas older dialect studies concentrated on relatively large areas, trying to find uniformity in speech, recent studies by sociolinguists have concentrated on smaller areas, and within those areas have interviewed more informants from more social groups than the older ones did. William Labov pioneered far more in-depth investigation. His inspiration, in part, appears to have been a small study by John Fischer (1958), who investigated schoolchildren's alternating the suffixes -in' and -ing as in runnin' or running. Each child was found to use both pronunciations, but the percentage of times each was employed varied according to how genteel or rough the child was or wanted to appear to be. In particular, boys used the informal variant far more than girls.

In the early 1960's, Labov (1963) noticed that young people on the island of Martha's Vineyard spoke differently. Specifically, those who intended to stay on the island after graduation spoke with a pronounced Vineyard accent, but those who were planning to leave the island spoke like people from Boston. He also found that those social groups that felt the island belonged to them, the descendants of the original English settlers, spoke with a more pronounced Vineyard accent than those who were newer comers, like the Portuguese fishermen and their families. Labov gave people both an attitudinal survey and a linguistic one, having them read passages loaded with the three sounds that varied among the groups, terming these **linguistic variables**, thus confirming his hypotheses.

The Variability of Variables

In his later New York City study, Labov (1966) proved even more conclusively that examination of phonological variables is a remarkably exact way of analyzing a community's social organization. Furthermore, it reveals attitudes unerringly, attitudes that people often would never admit to having. New York City, being sociologically more complex than Martha's Vineyard, has more phonological variables. Labov investigated the following:

- Whether or not /r/ was pronounced before a consonant.
- Whether the /θ/ "th" in words like *thing* was pronounced as [t] or [θ].
- Whether the /ð/ "th" in words like *the* was pronounced as [d] or [ð].
- How high the front of the tongue is when pronouncing the [æ] in words like *bad* or *dance*.[1]
- How high the back of the tongue is when pronouncing the /ɔ/ "aw" in *more* and *coffee.*

Just because a feature is sociologically significant in one region, it does not follow that it will be in another. The pronunciation of [æ] as [ɨ], disvalued in New York City, is quite normal for the Inland North and even much of Canada, as we saw in Chapter 7. Educated speakers in the Great Lakes cities like Chicago, Buffalo, Cleveland, and Detroit may show far more raising than any New Yorker. However, in those cities, that sound does not mark social class. In the Midwest, the person who pronounces *bad* as [bɨd] or even [biəd] is showing a regional, not a social pronunciation.

Similarly, using an [ɔ] "aw" for the first vowel in *more* and *coffee* may not denote lower-class speech outside of New York City. It appears in the speech of those with impeccable ancestry and schooling, even one Harvard Ph.D. of my acquaintance who was raised in Philadelphia.

Substituting [t] or [f] for [θ], and [d] or [v] for [ð] marks social class throughout the English-speaking world. For centuries saying [də] for *the* and [tro] for *throw* has marked an adult speaker of English as uneducated, as has pronouncing *mouth* as "mouf" and *mother* as "muvuh." This does not mean that there is anything intrinsically wrong with [t], [d], [f], or [v]. They are all just fine in other words, those in which standard speakers feel they belong, as in *time, dime, fine* and *vine.*

Swedish, which like English once had [θ] and [ð], has long since converted, so that the Swedish counterpart to *that there* is "dat dere" for all speakers, and it sounds right to even the most educated Swede. Those sounds are not social class markers in Swedish as they are in English. The two sounds spelled <th> in English fit all the requirements for social class markers. They are **marked** sounds, appearing in few of the world's languages. When they do appear, as in Swedish, they have a tendency later to disappear.

In English, these sounds have disappeared in most dialects. Although they appear in only a few words even in the dialects that have retained them, those few words must be used frequently. One can barely complete one sentence in English without having to use *the*. The sounds are rare enough to stand out and cannot be avoided even in casual conversation.

Like agreement markers in grammar, they may have survived mainly because of their utility in social class marking. This does not mean that all marked sounds that survive do so only because they are social markers. The reverse may well be true, that the marked sounds which survive become social markers. However, it is remarkable how frequently social class markers are either marked sounds or irregular relic forms in English (Chaika 1973). If the same is found to be true in a wide variety of languages, then we can claim that markedness is a major factor in social marking.

Eliciting Styles

In his New York City study, Labov elicited speech in all styles, from formal to casual. The pronunciation that people use in formal styles indicates what they think is correct in formal situations. If the same pronunciation is typical of a particular group or social class, we know that the group is admired, the **point of reference** for the society being investigated. Copying the speech of another group for other purposes, as when being supercasual or recounting a fight (Labov 1964), reveals points of reference for those situations as well. Everyday, casual speech reveals an individual's true feelings of social identity. Labov (1966) proved this by correlating pronunciations that occurred only in casual speech with a person's membership in ethnic and social classes.

Labov elicited the most careful, formal style by asking people to read lists of words that contain the variables suspected of being important in a community. He found it especially fruitful to include **minimal pairs**, pairs of words that differ by just one sound, especially a socially significant one. For his New York study, Labov included pairs like *guard* and *god* because he felt that the /r/ was socially significant, as many New York City speakers did not pronounce it in casual speech, although they did pronounce it in the reading task. Labov regarded this as proof that the /r/ before consonants has become the prestige pronunciation in New York City. Whether or not someone attempted to pronounce it in the reading task depended strongly on the person's social class. This in itself is significant.

It is not to be supposed, however, that one can uncover prestige pronunciations this way in all societies. Milroy (1980, 100–1) found that her subjects in Belfast did not try to use prestige pronunciations in reading tests. Every community is likely to have its own standards for styles, just as it has its own socially significant variables.

Labov used another reading task as well, one that yielded a slightly less careful style. As in Martha's Vineyard, he asked subjects to read passages loaded with **variables**, sounds that are articulated in more than one way by different groups in the community. The passages formed a story, with each paragraph concentrating on one phonological variable. For instance, one was about chocolate milk and coffee cake around four o'clock. This tested for [ɔ] "aw" as the first vowel in *chocolate, coffee,* and *four.* For *r*-lessness, he used a passage with words like *over, far,* and *corner.* The passage testing for [æ] was awash with terms like *past* and *can't.* Another passage tested for [θ] and [ð] with shibboleths like *thing* and *this.*

One warning to the reader who wishes to use such reading passages. Many subjects get tipped off to what you are after very soon, and either become so tongue-tied that they stumble over every key word or they turn it into a joke. I find it best not to load the same sound throughout one sentence, but, rather, to strew them throughout several sentences.

Besides the reading task, Labov also noticed responses to questions in an interview. The pronunciations in the responses were usually careful, but not as careful as those elicited in reading. He found that it is possible to elicit informal and casual speech in an interview, however, by asking informants to describe games that they played when they were children and to recall childhood rhymes. The rhymes often work only in casual style with nonprestigious pronunciations. Both the rhythms and pronunciations of prestigious pronunciations ruin, for instance, the jump rope rhyme:

1. Cinderella dressed in yellow
   Went downtown to get some mustard
   On the way her girdle busted.
   How many people got disgusted.
   1, 2, 3, . . .

The only way this works is if the /r/ in *mustard* is left out so that it rhymes with *busted* and *disgusted.*

Labov also found that even when the disvalued pronunciations were not important to the rhyme scheme, subjects still resorted to them. For instance, in:

2. I won't go to Macy's any more, more, more.
   There's a big fat policeman at the door, door, door.
   He takes you by the collar.
   And makes you pay a dollar.
   I won't go to Macy's any more, more, more.

Labov found that informants pronounced *more* and *door* with a vowel close to /u/"oo" as in [muwə] "moowa" even though /ɔ/"aw" would have fit as well. They also didn't pronounce the final /r/ in *collar* and *dollar*, although again the rhyme is preserved if it is pronounced.

Sometimes certain pronunciations are no longer in use by adults, but are retained in children's games. The pronunciation "podada" for *potato* was already gone when I was growing up, but in a working-class neighborhood in Providence, my peers and I pronounced the counting out rhyme as "one podada, two podada, three podada, maw (*more*)." Apparently pronunciation in childhood rhymes can preserve relic pronunciations.

Sometimes other questions, such as those dealing with sports or hobbies, will yield unself-conscious speech in an interview. Labov asked about TV shows, fights, and personal aspirations. He even asked questions about others in the same social group, such as, "Is there one guy everyone listens to? How come?" In order to get casual, unself-conscious speech samples, interviewers must induce consultants to lose themselves in a topic.

To achieve this end, Labov relied most heavily on a "danger-of-death" episode. Informants were asked to relate a personal experience in which they had felt themselves to be in danger of death. While recounting the episode, people became progressively less formal, lapsing into their normal, everyday speech. In my own dialect collecting, I have found that many informants are daunted by being asked to share their danger-of-death experiences. Many simply say they have never had one. Consequently, I ask them for any unusual or funny anecdote: a time that they were surprised, frightened, or excited, or the like.

Shuy, Wolfram, and Riley (1967), in their Detroit investigation, relied on a variety of questions, being careful to pick cues up from their informants about what they were interested in. I have also discovered that terms like *story* or *anecdote* make the informant insecure. They seem to think that they will be judged on their ability to recount a tale. Instead, then, I ask them to tell me about an experience they've had. There is no instantly magical way of doing a dialect or sociolinguistic study. The community's value systems and social structure finally determine what methodology will yield the information an investigator is looking for.

Speech Studies and Other Sociological Measures

Since he had at his disposal the results of a previous sociological study, Labov was able to correlate his findings with information about social class, occupation, education, income, and personal aspirations. If a pre-existing study is not available, however, a researcher determines the social status of consultants by using the *Index of Status Characteristics* (ISC), a common sociological measure that divides populations according to occupation, education, income, and residence. These criteria have repeatedly been found to be important in uncovering the division of communities into social groups. Since language is social behavior, the ISC is useful in deciding which groups to study to uncover dialect differences within a community or society.

Labov found in his New York City study that use of variables within a community not only reveals its social stratification but also reveals changing patterns of stratification. Each social division that he found was characterized by distinctive pronunciation of at least one phonological variable. Although each group varied in the utilization of variables according to formality or lack of it, Labov found no overlap between groups in their total behavior.

He found that older speakers used pronunciations associated with belonging to different ethnic groups. Jews could be identified by the pronunciation of [ɔ] "aw" as [u] "oo' in words like *coffee* and *more*. Italians signaled their ethnicity by the height of their tongues as they pronounced the vowel [æ] in words like *gas* and *dance*.

Significantly, younger speakers, those aged twenty to thirty-nine at the time of the study, did not show differences according to ethnic identification. This finding mirrored the changing social stratification of New York City. By the time of Labov's study, the older loyalties to ethnic groups like being Jewish, Italian, and Irish were giving way. The new divisions were rich or poor, white or black or Puerto Rican, educated or uneducated. The key sounds had shifted to /ð/ and /θ/ as in *this* and *thing*, and enunciating the /r/ wherever it was spelled.

This finding in New York City is pertinent to East Coast cities like Providence and Boston. When I was growing up, it was easy to tell that someone was Jewish, Italian, Cape Verdean, Portuguese, African American,[2] or Irish with seconds of their opening their mouths. By the '60's, these ethnic variables were disappearing, and now remain mostly among non- middle-class African Americans and working-class Italian speakers, especially males.

The oldest informants in New York City made no attempt to pronounce preconsonantal /r/, even in the reading lists.[3] Labov surmised that they did not consider it necessarily correct or upper class. Younger edu-

381

cated speakers clearly did. They made a maximum effort to articulate all /r/'s on the word list and reading passage tasks, but pronounced it less often in casual speech. The percentage of times /r/ was pronounced in all contexts varied according to social class, but the higher the social class, the more /r/'s in every context.

The lower class produced no preconsonantal /r/'s in casual speech, or almost none. Although they did produce more in formal tasks than in the casual, they still pronounced it the least number of times overall. One interesting exception to this rigid social class differentiation in the use of /r/ was the lower middle class. They actually out-/r/-ed the upper middle class in the most formal styles. The lower middle class **hypercorrected**. This has been historically typical of lower-middle-class behavior. That class is often extra careful to be correct. They do not have the assurance of the middle and upper classes, who feel they are the ones to set the standards. Unlike the poorest classes, however, members of the lower middle class believe that it is possible for them or their children to move upward. The lower classes do not attempt to pronounce the variables that signal middle-classhood, as it is not likely that they will have a chance to become middle class.

Since the oldest speakers did not try to pronounce /r/ wherever it occurs in spelling, even in the most formal task, Labov concluded that variable was a relatively new one in New York City. Articulation of /r/ as a prestige factor apparently emerged shortly after World War II. At that time, the social stratification of New York City began to show changes as the flight to the suburbs began. A good number of children and grandchildren of immigrants began to "make it" during those years. Labov noted that being *r*-full correlated with earned status more than any other feature.

Timothy Frazer (1983) investigated a similar phenomenon, but in a rural area in Illinois. As has happened virtually worldwide, the poorer farmers with small holdings have abandoned the land, selling it or leaving it to those who can afford both larger holdings and the expensive machinery that goes with modern agribusiness. Because of this, a rural, nonprestigious pronunciation has become more frequent and invaded nonrural settings as well. This is noteworthy because, historically, pronunciations have gone in the opposite direction, from the town to the farm.

The sound he investigated is the way the diphthong in words like *cow* and *town* are pronounced. The elocution scene in the musical *Singin' in the Rain* shows the teacher drilling actors by having them say, "How now brown cow" with the prestige /au/ "ah+oo." This is done by starting to say "ah" and then moving the tongue up to an "ooh." This was the prestige pronunciation. Formerly, in nonrural Illinois, the prestige form was common, but now is changing to /æu/ "a+oo." Here, speakers start with the vowel in *cat* and then move it up to an "ooh." The latter pronunciation is common in many areas of the United States, including Pennsylvania, New York, New Jersey, California, and the Great Lakes cities. It is like the Australian /æ:u/ "æ:+oo" except that Americans don't hold the /æ/ quite as long as the Aussies do.

Frazer's findings contradicts Labov's because Labov claimed that change was in the direction of prestige pronunciations and, in Illinois, it is in the direction of a formerly nonprestige pronunciation. The whole Northern Cities' vowel shift shows the same movement away from prestige norms, or what were prestige norms, which Labov et al. (2006) especially note.

Women as Innovators

This new pronunciation in Illinois apparently started with women, but took a generation for men to adopt. Labov has well documented the phenomenon that sound change in the United States often starts with women, and women of all classes are more likely than men to try to use prestige forms, those associated with the standard. This is not so in all countries, however, and why it is in the United States admits of different explanations.

One explanation is that women are more socially sensitive than men, but this doesn't explain why their sensitivity would lead them to use more prestige language. It seems to me, rather, that women would be more likely to match their speech to that of those they converse with. In interview situations, that may well lead to a woman's using more prestige forms, but women's prestige usage has been documented in ordinary conversations with friends, children, and strangers. This doesn't mean that all women speak SE. They don't. They just seem more likely to try to.

Another possibility is that lower-middle-class women are more likely to hold jobs in which they hear SE and may feel that they must speak it. For instance, women may be hairdressers and manicurists, hostesses in restaurants, waitresses, school aides, and nurse's aides, whereas their husbands work with other men doing construction, road building, pipe laying, and the like, where they neither regularly hear SE nor have occasions to use it regularly. Deborah James (1996, 100) calls this the "market forces hypothesis."

A related factor in adopting prestige speech may, for some women, be to make themselves more attractive to upper-class males so they can marry them. I do not mean to imply that this is necessarily a plotted course. It just occurs. For instance, one career open to working-class girls in the days before a bachelor's degree was required was nursing. Nurses regularly worked closely with physicians. In those days women were rarely physicians. This often meant that the nurses were the females that young doctors saw the most. Naturally, then, it was not uncommon for physicians to marry nurses. The possibility of marriage, then, was an incentive for the females to use SE. I do not mean to imply that their adoption of SE was solely for the purpose of marriage, or that it was even conscious. Being in close proximity with SE-speaking males and having to impress them as being competent nurses, it was natural for these women to use SE. Another situation in which marriage could result was with working-class women who became secretaries. Again, the phenomenon of marrying the boss was certainly not unheard of. As James reports:

> A classic piece of evidence that such economic factors are important is provided by Nichols (1983) who showed that different patterns of sex-related usage . . . in two small South Carolina communities could be explained in terms of differences in the economic options open to women and men. . . . (James, 100)

In some cultures, women's speech is as nonstandard as men's, or even more so than men's. In Belfast, Irish Catholic women had very strong social ties in their neighborhoods, did not work in jobs requiring or encouraging prestigious speech, and had a strong sense of solidarity with their neighbors (Milroy 1980). These women talked like each other as an indication of their solidarity. Similarly, working-class men who frequently work in jobs characterized by group cooperation, such as construction or firefighting, or work in the presence of other men holding equal status, such as mechanics in a garage, also show solidarity by using nonstandard forms. Such men have little reason to use SE.

Another factor in the above scenario is that nonstandard speech is associated with masculinity, with being tough, rough, and breaking the rules (James, 113). This has been established in many countries including Holland, Ireland, Australia, England, and even China. The Australian study showed that girls speaking with a standard-speaking interviewer had more standard features in their speech, but boys did not. Also, the boys' most common themes during the interviews were conflicts with the police, teachers, and parents (James 1996).

We see a similar phenomenon today with upper-middle-class American boys adopting features from AAVE, especially from gangsta rappers. In a very disturbing video presented by Sut Jhally of the University of Massachusetts, I saw clean-cut looking young American boys boasting of how much pain they could inflict on girls during sex, using terms like *banging, ramming,* and *smashing* coupled with adverbs denoting ferocity, intense force, and destructiveness. The point is not the boys' social class, it is that masculinity is seen as a willingness by males to be violent. If standard speech is equated with politeness, respect, and decency toward others, and nonstandard is not, then our conception of gender roles explains the difference between prestige forms in male and female speech.

Another reason that has been put forward to explain women's propensity for prestige forms is that women are more polite because they are less powerful than men. The reasoning is that, by using prestige forms, the women present themselves as deserving of respect but also as not threatening the face of interlocutors. As we have seen, nonstandard speech is associated with aggression. Some think that the corollary of this is that standard speech isn't aggressive. I find this very unconvincing. First of all, it is entirely possible to be ruthless using prestige forms. Second, it doesn't explain those instances in which women, like the Belfast ones, use as many or more nonstandard forms than men. Third, it doesn't explain the finding that women's speech may use more prestige features than men's even in everyday talk with family and friends (James, 111).

I will present one more possibility. At least in the United States, there is what I call the "Mae West factor."[4] That is, a woman who speaks like a man may be seen as sexually forward because she sounds tough. Certainly, part of my socialization into my gender role was to speak and act quietly and with propriety, because to act otherwise would lead to a man's thinking I was not a lady.

In a culture in which males are the ones who use the polite speech and females do not, then such a factor would not apply. Such cultures do exist. In rural Madagascar, it is considered that men are the experts in polite communication and that women lack the skill to master it. Therefore, the women are the blunt, tough speakers, and the men are not.

To sum up, although there is evidence that in some societies women use more prestige speech forms than men of their own class, still there are other societies in which this is not true. There is nothing inherently female in using prestigious speech. If this is gendered behavior, it is because of the social system the woman is in, and also because of the economic realities of that system.

Why Social Markers are Variables

People categorize each other according to the phonological variables they use. If they did not, there would be no reason for the systematic way that variants of sounds are pronounced in a community and their tight correlation with social facts. Labov's New York City study, even more than his Martha's Vineyard one, showed that it is the percentage of times that someone uses a variable in each context that reflects social class. It is not a case of uttering a particular sound as opposed to not uttering it at all. Virtually all speakers occasionally used disvalued pronunciations, and all occasionally used valued ones.

Why are social differences so often indicated by frequency of usage rather than by absolutely different pronunciations between groups? Why is the middle class in New York City, for instance, marked out from the upper middle by using a smaller percentage of /r/'s? If the upper middle class is delimited by /r/, why isn't the middle class designated by another sound, say /l/, and the lower middle by yet another, say /m/?

Any answer is partly speculative, but it seems to me that this phenomenon is related to what we saw in development of jargons. Old material in the language is frequently made to do new duty. Human beings are already geared to handle flexibility, matching what they hear to the social context and deriving meaning accordingly. Variables in pronunciation fit into regular decoding strategies, demanding no new techniques.

Marking social groups by percentage of times that a feature is used may well be more efficient than having separate markers for each group. In a complex speech community, there would have to be a great many markers floating around, one for each group. Instead of having to listen for five or six markers, noting frequency of usage in order to categorize people correctly, residents would have to listen for as many separate markers as there are separate groups. Add to this the burden of recognition of regional markers, attitude markers, and purely stylistic markers, and the whole becomes so complex that efficiency in social functioning could well be impaired. In order for social interaction to proceed smoothly, categorization of all sorts has to be swift. Perhaps this is why dialect markers themselves are sometimes used stylistically, as when middle-class youths lapse into AAVE on appropriate social occasions.

Obviously people do not attend conventions to decide how to use speech socially or what markers to adopt. In fact, pronouncements by experts who have tried to legislate speech have rarely, if ever, been successful. Any teacher who has struggled valiantly with trying to get youngsters to speak "correctly" knows how little such efforts help. Yet, patently, people do change their speech patterns. What does make them do so?

Rarely are people wholly conscious of all that they are actually doing with speech, much less why. All of these signaling behaviors seem to be inborn in humankind, as is speech itself.

Social markers on language are not products of formal instruction. We may speculate about the origins of such behavior, but the results are clear. In Martha's Vineyard, when a need to signal allegiance to the island became important, sounds already in the dialect began to function as markers of that attitude. In New York City, when it became important to signal social class, becoming *r*-full developed for that purpose.[5] Stewart (1972) says that in Appalachia, where age is especially important to social groupings, children signal that they are not yet adult by using infantile pronunciations long after children in less age-graded societies. The research of the past two decades has confirmed that as societies change, speech behavior becomes modified to reflect the new situations. If age-grading is no longer important in Appalachia, then children will no longer use infantile pronunciations.

NETWORK THEORY

Milroy (1980) found that Labov-like studies, which neatly correlate social stratification with pronunciation, did not work in her study of the Belfast working class. She cites the case of two middle-aged women, neither of whom went to school beyond the legal leaving age, both unskilled workers married to unskilled workers, and both satisfied with "the warmth and friendliness" of their neighborhood. Yet, the speech of one consistently evinces more vernacular pronunciations than the other does. Milroy says, "Any attempt to explain the consistency of the difference . . . in terms of some kind of social status index would, therefore, be inappropriate" (132). In other words, Labovian studies do not necessarily account for individual variation. Considering that Labov's aim was to find what was common to members of each group, not to account for idiolects, he really can't be faulted. He did an admirable job in what he set out to do, and, in the process, changed linguistics, dialectology, and sociology forever. Of course, even finer-grained analyses remained.

John Gumperz (1982c) claims that "ethnic identity does not show a one to one relationship to language" (39). Even members of one family may differ in their speech because of differences in their social networks. These show the relationship between members of a community, who they converse with, and for what purposes. Milroy's studies differ from Gumperz's in that she utilizes sophisticated statistical analysis to bolster her claims. Milroy (1980, 174) claims that the concept of social network as contributing to both language change and language maintenance can be applied everywhere, and is less ethnocentric than are studies of caste or class. More recently, Salami (1991) has found that social networks, area of residence, education, gender, and ethnic background all contribute to pronunciation differences among Yoruba speakers in Ile-Ife, Nigeria. Studies in Wales, Newfoundland, and England have also shown that the density and nature of social networks explains speech patterns. Interestingly, all of these showed that women spoke with more nonstandard features than did men, the reverse of the American situation.

Basically, what one does in such a study is plot the network structure of individuals in a group, here, members of the working class in Belfast. By *network structure* I mean who visits or otherwise talks with whom and how often every day or week. Milroy made friends with the people she was investigating, visiting their homes regularly, virtually becoming part of their neighborhood, indeed, part of their network in the status of "friend of friend." Thus, she was a participant observer. This was how she was able to plot the social networks of the people.

The concept of networks actually comes from anthropological investigations. This concept works well in working-class neighborhoods, because these foster social relations much like that of people in close-knit villages in, to us, culturally and physically remote places. That is, the neighborhood itself is like a village. In a country like the United States, this may not be so true, as many people do not stay in one neighborhood for all or even most of their lives. Certainly, upper- and middle-class people don't, and, historically, lower- and working-class people have migrated to cities with more job offerings. Also, it has been common for lower- and working-class people to move into the middle class in United States, with a concomitant move to the suburbs. This doesn't mean that one can't find stable U.S. neighborhoods that foster village-type relations. One can, but my sense is that they are less numerous than in many other countries. African Americans who still live in the "'hood" often have dense networks, for instance, although many of them also are upwardly mobile.

However, in Belfast and other regions, the working class maintains a **dense** network of **multiplex** relations within a territory. *Density* here refers to the frequency with which the same people talk to each other and socialize. Working-class neighborhoods typically foster dense networks in which people live, work, marry, and converse with each other. Moreover, network relationships of such people are **multiplex**. That is, people are bound to each other in more than one capacity, as neighbors, relatives, and coworkers (Milroy, 21, 135, 140). In contrast, the middle class typically has **uniplex** networks which are not dense. Whether dealing with shopkeepers, coworkers, or going out for an evening with friends, middle-class relationships are more compartmentalized. Relationships are more likely to revolve around particular functions.

What Gumperz, Milroy, and others have found is that dense, multiplex relations foster the retention of vernacular, nonstandard pronunciations. Such relations are based more on solidarity than on power. Differences within the group can be explained by individual differences in the network. In other words, people talk like those with whom they communicate. In far less rigorous terms, this actually is what early dialectologists and linguists thought. Leonard Bloomfield (1933) in his monumental work *Language*, a work long considered hopelessly out of date, gave as the explanation for dialect change "density of communication and relative prestige of social groups" (345).

The work on social networks does not necessarily invalidate Labov. Dense, multiplex communities are characterized by a lack of change. There is little social mobility. However, the middle class, which has networks that are both less dense and uniplex, signal their social class in their speech. Perhaps it is for this reason that in modern nations the educated professionals and executives talk more like each other than like others from their region. Standard dialects are one result of social mobility and weaker, less permanent social networks.

Communities of Practice

Middle class speakers typically speak like those in their community of practice. Such a framework considers language as one of many social practices an individual engages in. That language varies according to a particular social practice is well-known. The acknowledgment of registers is an example, but the community of practice concept covers a wider range of activities, activities that are not as prescribed as proper register is.

A person who is part of a dense social network interacts primarily within that network. However, someone who is not may have instead several communities of practice. It is also possible to be part of a dense network and still be part of a community of practice. An African American choir director is part of the community of practice in his or her church and also may be in another community of practice at work, and each site yields some differences in speech. At the same time, he or she may be part of a dense neighborhood-based social network which determines his or her basal dialect, which changes somewhat in each of the other communities of practice.

In contrast, an individual may not be part of a dense social network, but is a participant in one or more communities of practice. My husband, for instance, participates in at least three communities of practice: that of trial lawyers, league pool players, and avid sports fans. His vocabulary and even grammar changes in each setting. His basal dialect is the New York City one he grew up with, somewhat modified by his years in New England, not that of the neighborhood. It's not exactly like mine or any of our friends, all of whom speak with somewhat different regional dialects. Typically, one is in a community of practice at work, characterized by specific word usages, oblique references that only one's coworkers understand, intonation contours, and general stylistic features specific to that setting.

The community of practice may be organized around any social or linguistic practice, no matter how marginal from the perspective of the Labovian concept of the speech community. Therefore, it "brings marginal members to the forefront of analysis" (Bucholtz 1999, 210). Linguists have long spoken of **idiolects**, individual variations in speech behaviors, but virtually all speech is social, and the concept of communities of practice allow us to account for individual speech practices within a larger social organization without dismissing them as merely singular. In other words, many instances of what have been called idiolects can be seen to be part of a social group.

For instance, Bucholtz (211) cites Eckert's investigation of Jocks and Burnouts in a suburban U.S. high school. The Jocks are overachieving students with middle-class values, and the Burnouts are underachievers who expected to go to work after graduation, not college. Both groups were concerned with being cool, but each defined coolness differently. Yet, they both belonged to the same social organization of the high school. A third group, the Nerds, defines itself by not being cool at all. Studies of Nerds typically treat them as failed Burnouts or inadequate Jocks, kids with deficient or invalid identities. Bucholtz argues against such a characterization of Nerds, one that equates nerdiness with social death.

She claims that Nerds choose to be Nerds, and that is their identity. They proclaim this identity through their language practices. They specifically reject the idea of being cool. Rather, they differentiate themselves from mainstream students by speaking very formally. They deliberately make intellectual displays, using knowledge as symbolic capital. In general, the Nerds use standard speech to stress their identity, not resorting to slang or nonstandard speech forms adopted by Jocks, for instance, who wish to be seen as being macho. The Nerds are not social misfits.

Bucholtz (211) stresses that Nerds are "competent members of a distinctive and oppositionally defined community of practice. Nerdiness is an especially valuable resource for girls . . . in US high school[s]." They reject the Jocks, the Prom Queens, the Burnouts, and the other groups in their school. She (212) found that the Nerds used super careful pronunciations, super correct grammar, and formal word choices such as saying, "Is anyone here knowledgeable about . . . " (215) rather than, "Who knows about . . ." and "I have to incorporate these words into a poem" (217) rather than "use these words." They also engaged in a great deal of word play, like rhyming and alliterating and parodying of others (213).

Bucholtz introduces the idea of positive and negative identity practices. Negative ones, like eschewing slang or particular pronunciations, distance the speaker from a rejected identity. Positive ones, like displays of intellectuality and individuality, are employed to actively construct a chosen identity (212–13). Nerds, unlike Burnouts or Jocks, do not have to toe the line in dress or other activities. For instance, Burnout girls have to speak in a nonstandard tough way as a symbolic way of displaying aggression. Nerds attain empowerment by the high value they place on intellectuality and cleverness in speech. Whereas Jock or Burnout girls are constrained in the kinds of clothes they may wear, Nerds are not, except that they consciously refrain from dressing like either of the other groups.

Bucholtz (221) lauds the concept of community of practice, as it allows researchers to view language within the context of social practice. More importantly, it also allows them to describe and explain complexity within larger social groupings, including local identities and the linguistic means of displaying them. To me, Bucholtz's major achievement is to show that a group that others might consider misfits are far from being misfits, but are as positively definable just as more conforming individuals are. Perhaps that's because my friends and I were nerds. In fact, I find it odd that scholars would consider nerds as being socially dysfunctional, because most of the scholars I've ever met were nerds in high school, not prom queens.

Changing Variables

The same ways that sociolinguists use to ascertain how people evaluate voice quality can be used to discover how they evaluate various pronunciations. Labov (1966) created a tape from the recorded interviews, one which included all of the variables. Then he asked the participants in the study to listen to the tape, pretending that they were personnel managers interviewing job candidates for a large corporation. They were given a rating form on which to indicate which job would be suitable for each speaker on the tape. The jobs listed ranged from TV personality to factory worker.

The results matched those of the original interviews; hence, they confirmed those results: the variables rated as appropriate for the highest-ranking jobs were exactly the ones people tended toward in the formal reading tasks. Significantly, no matter how they themselves regularly talked, everyone rated speakers on the tapes the same way. Just because someone habitually says "dese" for *these* does not mean that he or she has values in speech much different from those who use the standard pronunciation. Labov found that, even more than others, speakers who used a stigmatized pronunciation the most were most likely to downgrade speakers on the tape who used the same pronunciation.

CHAPTER 9

At least, this was true in the United States at the time of his New York study. Nowadays, with the phenomenon of the prestige of AAVE, the more nonstandard the better, different results might accrue. It might be that saying "dese" wouldn't cause someone not to be considered as an executive for a record company or even a radio announcer. Certainly a college coach could be acceptable using such speech, and, for all I know, maybe it would be considered all right for a school teacher or even a college professor. A poor Ph.D. whom Labov cited as not being able to be hired in the 1960's might fare better today. It seems to me that the time has come for a reevaluation of how people evaluate speech. As society has changed, has our evaluation of standard and nonstandard changed with it?

Labov also found that people don't always talk the way they think they do. In fact, one sure way to get people angry is to tell them they are using a particular pronunciation that they criticize in others. This, I can attest, is still true. When people make fun of how the locals speak and I point out their own pecadillos, they do get angry. Labov played a tape with different pronunciations of seven key words: *card, chocolate, pass, thing, then, her,* and *hurt.* Each word was pronounced four different ways and subjects were asked to circle the number that correlated with their own pronunciation. In most instances, people reported themselves as using prestigious pronunciations even if they really used them no more than 30% of the time.

I would like to see this study replicated, including AAVE pronunciations in which, for instance, /r/'s are dropped, so that *card* is pronounced like *cod* and the final syllable of *player* or *other* would be pronounced as "uh" with no final /r/. In Labov's study, such pronunciations were stigmatized and people claimed they didn't say them. However, I suspect that young males, those who try to speak AAVE, might claim to be *r*-droppers even if they are not.

Labov's New Yorkers monitored their own speech according to the community's standards of higher-class features. However, the way they actually talked correlated with their social class or ethnic group. In other words, people talk according to their feelings of identity without realizing it.

This has not proven to be a universal finding, however. Trudgill (1972) found that in Norwich, England, people claimed they used fewer prestige pronunciations than they did. This must be because the working- class pronunciation has its own prestige. We have to disabuse ourselves of the notion that elevated social class is what constitutes prestige for everyone.

Rebels in a Speech Community

Nobody is immune to the community's values. Even tough street kids who rebel against established institutions in every way can show a surprising concern with correct speech. In the Harlem study mentioned earlier, Labov et al. (1968) got some unexpected results from a subjective reaction test. Because African American youths respond best in competitive situations, the test was given to the whole gang at once in the form of a **vernacular correction test**. An African American field worker read sentences to the group, having asked them to correct the sentences to make them conform to the boys' usual way of saying them. If the sentences were correct according to the AAVE dialect they spoke, the boys were to make no correction. When reading the following examples, remember that the entire exchange was performed out loud so that all could hear and verify the truth of the responses. One sentence read to the boys was:

1. That's Nick boy.

One feature of AAVE, you may recall, is that it does not ordinarily use the possessive *'s* ending. Even so, Boot, one of the toughest, roughest members of the group, one who spoke virtually pure AAVE, shouted out three forms using this possessive marker:

2. That's Mr. Nick**'s** son. That's Nick**'s** son right there. Do you know that's Nick's son?

Later, the field worker gave:

3. She a real stab bitch.

Again, Boot was on his toes with a response:

4. She a real [laughs]—she **is** a real stab bitch.

That *is* was important. Boot started to affirm the AAVE version, then caught himself and inserted standard *is*. Although, as we have already seen, AAVE doesn't use it in such a sentence, Boot again reported himself as using the standard form. Then the worker asked, "What does *stab* mean?" Boot answered, "She bad." He left out the *is* when caught off guard. Boot talked AAVE but reported himself as using the "correct" form. That he knew the community's standards is shown by his response to the field worker's sentence. The worker also gave the AAVE form of a question:

5. *Interviewer*: Why he do that?
   Boot: Why did he do that, man?
   Interviewer: Don't people say "Why he do that?"

> *Boot*: Some people that don't speak correc' English do. *Calvin little brother do.*

The italicized phrase shows that he failed to use the very possessive marker that he reported himself as using in the second exchange. Note, too, that in each instance, he zeros in on the very constructions that SE considers correct. He knows just where AAVE differs and what forms have to be supplied.

With the increased prestige of AAVE among all groups of youth today, it would be interesting to administer tests asking which forms are being used. I suspect that even middle-class males would report themselves as using AAVE forms. As we've seen, some upper-class males in New York City do make a strong attempt to speak that way. I wouldn't be surprised if AAVE speakers themselves made less of an effort to claim that they use SE forms. Since such studies haven't been done recently, I can't predict the outcome with any certainty, however.

Attitudes in Dialect Copying

With the advent of the 1960's and the accompanying questioning of middle-class values and new admiration of naturalness, nonstandard dialects took on new value for American youth. This was reflected in the increased use of AAVE and other nonstandard dialects in popular songs, even those sung by SE speakers. Today even middle-class SE speakers sing with overtones of AAVE and Appalachian dialects, or British working class accents. This contrasts with crooners like Frank Sinatra, who was one of the most popular teen idols ever at the start of his career in the early forties and who always rendered song lyrics in SE with an occasional "ain't" for liveliness. Whites have been borrowing from African American music at least since the 1920's, but, until the past decade or so, usually by converting the style to make it more palatable to a general audience.

The converse of today's singing dialects was found in the forties and fifties with many African American singers such as Lena Horne, Nat King Cole, and Johnny Mathis singing in SE. This was essential if their music was to be accepted by mainstream white America.[6] Some, like Sam Cooke, switched from AAVE to SE in different songs. Harry Bellafonte sweetened up black Caribbean songs, which appealed greatly to mainstream America. Charley Pride, an African American singer who prefers country and western to traditional black music, sings in a dialect completely indistinguishable from other Nashville performers. One has to see him to realize that he is a person of color. One cannot hear it. Today, of course, we see the opposite phenomenon in singers like Eminem, a white rapper. AAVE is an asset in appealing to all audiences now, the more urban and the more African American, the better.

Peter Trudgill (1983a) examined the pronunciations of British rock singers from the late fifties, Cliff Richards through the Beatles, to 1978 and 1979 albums from rockers like Dire Straits (*Dire Straits*) and Supertramp (*Breakfast in America*). It's very evident that when you hear British rock stars interviewed, they sound much more British than when they sing. Why? Obviously because they want to. Americans have been exporting pop music for years, but this escalated with fifties rock 'n roll. Americans were the rock scene and British singers wanted to sound like them.

Just as Americans have stereotypes of British speech, stereotypes that don't take into account dialectal differences in the United Kingdom, so do the British have stereotypes of American pronunciation. They characterized all American speech as:

- Pronouncing /r/ in words like *car, girl, bachelor*, and *park*.
- Pronouncing words like *can't, aunt*, and *dance* with [æ] rather than the British [a:].
- Converting both the /d/ and /t/ in between vowels to [ɾ] so that *bedding* and *betting* are homonyms.
- Pronouncing the vowel in words like *life* and *my* like [a:] as in American southern and AAVE dialects.
- Pronouncing the vowel in *love* and *done* with the American [ə] rather than British [ʊ].
- Pronouncing the vowel in *body* and *top* as [a] rather than [o].

In addition, they used Americanisms like *guy* instead of *chap* or *bloke* and *call* for *phone* or *ring*. Obviously, they did this because "it is appropriate to sound like an American when performing what is predominantly an American activity" (144). The African American origin of rock led the British to try to imitate AAVE, just as white Americans have done. This is shown by the borrowing of specifically AAVE features like dropping *is*, as in "He livin' there still" (Beatles *White Album*) and "My woman she gone" (Dire Straits *Dire Straits*), dropping the -*s* on verbs, as in "She make me cry" (Stranglers *Rattus Norvegicus*) and "Here come old flat top" (Beatles *Abbey Road*), and using *ain't* as *there isn't*, as in "Ain't nothin' new in my life today" (Supertramp *Breakfast in America*). Despite this general dialect copying, the British singers did have *r*-less rhymes, as in the Beatles' rhyme of *Rita* and *metre* in *Sergeant Pepper*.

As in any dialect copying, the rock singers hypercorrected. This happens because the copiers don't really know the details of the dialect they are trying to imitate. For instance, they know that Americans put /r/'s in where the British don't,[7] so sometimes the Brits pronounce /r/'s where they never occur and never have, as in Cliff Richards repeatedly singing [ər] for the article *a* ([ə])in "you'll be **uhr** bachelor boy," the Kinks singing "Mar and **Par**" for *Ma and Pa* in *Sunny Afternoon*, and Paul McCartney in *Till There was You* warbling "I never **sawr** them at all." Because these errors are repeated, Trudgill feels that they arise from ignorance, not from slips of the tongue in the heat of encoding (153). Of course, Americans would make equivalent mistakes if the tables were turned.

Trudgill also shows that as British groups made their mark and began writing more and more of their own music, there was a decline in the total number of their Americanisms. Of the myth that the Beatles, for instance, began to sound more Liverpudlian, Trudgill says that their early records used both more American and more Liverpool features than in their later ones. Punk rockers singing on British themes use fewer Americanisms and more British "low-prestige south of England" pronunciations. Trudgill feels that this is because of their conflicting identities. It seems to me that this could be because this set of dialect features is associated with denial of middle-class standards, freedom (from middle-class mores), and natural-ness (by their definition, not possible with middle-class mores).[8]

Negative Attitudes in Dialect Copying

Not all copying is so benign. Negative attitudes can also be revealed by dialect copying. Labov (1964, 492) cites the example of an African American, Mr. McSorley, who spoke SE in a "quiet, pleasant, and culti-vated manner." There were no traces of AAVE in his normal speech, and on tape nobody could identify him as being black. However, in the danger-of-death story, Mr. McSorley recounted a frightening experience he had as a guard at a YMCA when he had to investigate a man who was threatening others with a gun. In imitating this gunman, Mr. McSorley used AAVE. When asked what the man's background was, Mr. McSorley answered, "I don't know. Some kind of Hungarian I think." Labov explains, "In this incident, we see a process of unconscious substitution taking place in accordance with the value system of the speaker." For this speaker, rough, uncultured speech was associated with AAVE.

A similar kind of dialect copying is often heard in ethnic jokes. If these are about Jews, joke tellers frequently lapse into a pseudo-Yiddish accent. If they are about Italians, a supposed Mafia accent ensues, com-plete with rough voice and "dese, dems," and "doses." Although the tell-ing of the joke itself is sufficient for showing the jokester's prejudices, the dialect copying underscores the teller's feelings that Jews and Italians are foreign, not like "real Americans," and that the Italians are not only rough and coarse but uneducated. Ethnic jokes typically feed off of stereotypes, such as that African Americans are oversexed, Polish people are stupid, or Jews are miserly. Needless to say none of these has any basis in fact. There are African American men who need Viagra, Polish Ph.D.s, and Jews statistically have been shown to give a higher percentage of their incomes to charity than any other group. Ethnic jokes are major vehicles for spreading ugly stereotypes and reinforcing them.

THE VALUE OF A SOCIOLINGUISTIC SURVEY

Sociolinguistic surveys are especially valuable for determining social stratification of a community for three reasons. First, a tremendous amount of pertinent information is obtained in every interview, as much as 400–500 pieces. Therefore, only ten to twenty representatives of a given group need be interviewed to obtain reliable data. Second, subjects do not usually know what is being specifically looked for if it is looked for skillfully, even if they are told that it is a language survey.

Labov found that subjects' unconscious use of phonological variables was more consistent with their social and ethnic group than were their answers to any single question on the original sociological survey that he used for selecting subjects. People asked directly what their attitudes or feelings are often give the answer they think is correct or say what they think the investigator wants to hear. Of course, they do the same in language surveys as well, but the very lie contains valuable information about social attitudes. It reveals what is considered the prestige speech or the points of reference in the community. Frequently, for example, lower-class white boys live in open hostility with African American youths, engaging in urban guerrilla warfare with them. The whites express open disdain and even hatred for the African Americans. Yet when discussing fights, the same white youths frequently lapse unconsciously into AAVE (Labov 1964, 493). In their fieldwork my own students have frequently gathered samples of white youth lapsing unconsciously into AAVE when discussing sports, especially basketball and football. When discussing nonclassical music—jazz, blues, bluegrass—SE speakers often replace SE with AAVE expressions. Much American slang, dead and alive, like "real cool, man," "groovy," or "jammin'" seems to have entered SE by such borrowing.

Hidden Attitudes in Dialect Evaluation

Although few northern college students would seriously venture to claim that southerners are stupid, lazy, and intolerant, when asked to evaluate a tape recording of a woman speaker with a strong Alabama accent, they consistently peg her as having those traits. The woman in question is in fact a practicing medical doctor, comes from a definitely upper-middle class family, and is most tolerant.

Feminism has made enough strides so that college students would not claim that women are more emotional and less intellectual than men. Yet their true feelings surface when they are asked to evaluate a man and a woman with the same regional accents, reading from the same speech. In such a test, the two read different paragraphs, but the paragraphs were matched for various speech features. The woman was consistently rated by listeners as less intelligent, more emotional, and less logical than the man.

If subjects are asked to check off the character traits of speakers they hear on tape, clear pictures of stereotypes often emerge. We discover what speech and what groups are associated with intelligence or toughness, with sincerity, honesty, humor, diligence, or laziness and even general attractiveness. Lambert, Giles, and Picard (1975) studied attitudes toward French Canadians, both in Canada and in Maine. They found that in the St. John's Valley in Maine, both those who were not ethnically French Canadian and those who were evaluated French speakers favorably; in contrast, Quebec French Canadians were inclined toward self-deprecation, mirroring the prejudice of those who are not French. The authors explain that the explanation for the difference in self-evaluation between the two Franco-American populations is explicable by the attitudes of those in power. In Canada, there used to be considerable demeaning of the French.[9] The authors claim that there was less prejudice in Maine, but, having lived there in the 1950's, I can attest that there was. As we have seen, French speaking was even banned in the public schools.

Carranza and Ryan (1975) found that in Chicago, Mexican-American adolescents assigned Spanish speakers the same social rank as non-Hispanics did. Both groups evaluated the Spanish speakers lower in status than English speakers. Whether or not they are conscious of it, people do take society's evaluation of their own group.

Hypercorrection

It is easy to make fun of people who make mistakes because they are trying too hard to be correct. For example, one hears schoolteachers ridiculing parents who say things like:

1. We wants the best for our children. They tries hard, but that Mr. S. he give them bad grades.

2. He don't belongs with them.
   (Labov et al. 1968)

In both of these, the speakers seemed to have formulated their own rule. Knowing that -*s* marks the plural on nouns, they assumed that it also marks the plural verb rather than the singular. This is certainly a logical assumption, even if it is not correct from the viewpoint of standard speakers.

Some speakers are not sure which person gets the agreement marker, so they put it the wrong ones, as in the paradigm:

I trusts my friend.
You trusts my friend.
He trust my friend.
We trusts my friend.
They trusts my friend.

The important thing to remember is that the very fact that a speaker is hypercorrecting means that he or she does perceive social norms. Moreover, it means that he or she wishes to be well thought of by educated speakers.

An odd circumstance is that my students, who certainly do use the singular agreement marker correctly, as in *he goes, she sees*, and the like, will tell me in my grammar course that the -*s* is a plural agreement marker. Yes, -*s* is a plural on nouns, but why they think it indicates the plural on a verb when they never use it on a verb except for the singular is something I can't understand. If SE speakers make such an error in analysis, is it any wonder that speakers of a dialect which doesn't regularly use verb agreement markers make errors when they do try to use them?

We have already seen that AAVE drops final consonants where other varieties do not. Such dropping may result in conflict. In reading classes, for instance, if a child pronounces *cold* as "col," the teacher might say that the word was not read correctly, thus baffling the child who has indeed read it correctly for his or her dialect. Worse yet, because AAVE speakers frequently do not pronounce the final consonant that indicates past tense, saying "kick" for *kicked* or "love" for *loved*, other speakers have assumed that AAVE is lacking in verb tense. This became a political issue when researchers like Bereiter and Engelmann and Deutsch concluded that AAVE speakers are therefore verbally deprived and that their speech is too defective for its speakers to learn to do well in school, a claim hotly disputed by linguists. Many languages, such as the varieties of Chinese, do quite well intellectually without a past tense in their grammar. However, AAVE speakers do use a past tense, especially in the irregular verbs so that one hears:

I lef' it.
We play yesterday.

CHAPTER 9

With irregular verbs like *leave–left*, the past tense is preserved even though the /t/ is dropped, but with *play*, it is not. AAVE speakers often seem to be aware that such consonant (or "past tense") dropping is stigmatized by middle-class speakers. Therefore, in careful speech, they may hypercorrect by adding an extra past tense ending as in:

> I loveded it.
> But it did tasted like chicken.

Lest we chuckle, we should be reminded that standard English also bears traces of the same kind of hypercorrection. The modern-day plural *children* actually has two plural endings on it. At one time in English, there were several ways to form a plural. Originally, the plural of *child* was *childer*. Other nouns had other endings, such as *-en*. Still others changed their vowels internally, as they still do, such as *foot–feet*. And others used *-s*. Gradually, more and more nouns switched to using the *-s* ending until the only survival of *-er* as a plural was on *childer*. Since *-en* was already an unusual plural by that time, surviving only in *oxen, brethren*, and *kine*,[10] speakers endeavoring to be correct put both plurals, the *-er* and the other irregular plural ending, *-en*, on *child*. The hypercorrect double ending on *children* remains to this day.

There is another hypercorrection rampant in educated varieties of English today:

> Between you and I . . .
> He gave it to Jake and I.
> He saw Mary and I . . .

In all of these, *I* should be *me*. The system of signaling subject versus object pronouns has been dying out for centuries in English. The old *ye/you* distinction was moribund for Shakespeare. The original object of *it* was *him*, but this died out shortly after *ye*. Nonstandard English speakers often got rid of the rest of the alternations, uttering sentences like "Him and me went." Actually, left to itself, this probably would have become the norm in English. In French, one says "Jeanne et moi sommes allés," literally translating to 'John and me went.' French also says "C'est moi," literally, 'It's me.' Both of these usages are decried in English, but are standard in French. Those who find them ugly in English do so because of social norms, not because there is anything inherently wrong with them.

Despite the purists, most educated speakers follow a general rule of using the object form after intransitive verbs, as in "It's me." This is not new. In *The Two Gentlemen of Verona*, Act II, scene iii, Shakespeare wrote "Oh, the dogge is **me**. . . ." He used the object after *as*, too, another usage purists abhor, as in "Is he as tall as **me**?" (Antony and Cleopatra, Act III, scene iii). The opposite occurrence, that of using the subject form where an object is clearly indicated, is seen in *Othello*, Act IV, scene ii, "Yes, you have seene Cassio and **she** together." Of course, *her*, the object form, should come after *have seen*. It's not "have seen she." I have heard analogs to this from television newscasters, as in "saw Mr. Jones and **he**" and even, "told **he** and the police." These should be "saw Mr. Jones and **him**," and "told **him** and the police."

Selecting the subject pronouns *I, he, she,* or *they* instead of the object forms *me, him, her,* or *them* is rampant after prepositions, as in "between you and I," and "to Sigrid and I." In these, the use of the subject pronoun is wrong.

Strictly speaking, the object pronoun follows a preposition, as in "between you and **me**," "to Sigrid and **me**." I hear analogs to erroneous subject pronouns after prepositions from college professors, newscasters, editors, and many educated speakers, including those who poke fun at people who say "between you and I." Also, these pronoun errors appear in print in all kinds of publications, including scholarly ones. It seems likely to me that within a generation, such usage will be standard. In the thirty-five years since I have been teaching a course in modern English grammar, I have seen more and more students who are completely unfamiliar with phrasing like "for Max and me," and "after him and Tony." They even tell me that "between you and I" sounds more elegant than the supposedly correct form.

This situation has been blamed first of all on Bishop Lowth, who wrote the prescriptive *A Short Introduction to the English Tongue* in 1762, a book which bluntly told people what and what not to say. Some of his strictures were based upon Latin, some on mathematics, and some, apparently, on personal preference. Most commentators blame the generations of schoolteachers who, following Bishop Lowth's strictures, taught grammar as it should be, not as it actually was. They drilled students in the correct forms, "He and I went," and "It's I."

Since the old subject/object alternation in forms has not really been a part of the language since the late 15th century, students didn't understand why they were supposed to use *I* and *he* instead of *me* and *him*. What happened was that Old English had different endings on nouns as well as different forms for pronouns when they were objects or subjects. In fact, Old English used certain endings on a noun after a preposition and a different one when a noun was the object of a verb. That way, the word order of a sentence wasn't so important because one could tell if a noun was a subject or an object just by the ending on it. These endings were so important that often a preposition came after the noun, the equivalent of *John to* for *to John*. For a variety of reasons, including social ones, these endings eroded, and, instead, word order became the prime cue to how a noun was being used. Thus, if it came before the verb, it was a subject and, if it came after the verb, it was an object. That is, in *Beowulf slew Grendel*, one knew that Beowulf did the action and Grendel was its recipient because of the word order. In older English, one could say *Grendel Beowulf slew* or *Slew Grendel Beowulf* but there were endings on Grendel and Beowulf that told one who did the slaying and who got slain.

Once those endings eroded, word order was prime. Hence, "It's me" seemed natural because the object form came after the verb, not because it was a true object. Why speakers of both French and English also used the object form of pronouns after *and*, I don't know, but they did. If this had not become the object of intense correction, perhaps English would have become like French and used the subject pronoun only when it was the only subject. In any event, because children were told that *I* was correct and *me* was not, they hypercorrected and substituted the subject pronoun even when the object one was correct.

One of my colleagues once gave a lecture in which he claimed that because we confuse subjects and objects, we are losing our ability to analyze. Obviously, if this has been going on since Shakespeare and before, this is not so. The language is not decaying because subject and object pronouns are interchanged.

It can easily be seen that the fate of a hypercorrection depends upon who is doing it. *Children* became the correct plural of *child*, and it looks as if *between you and I* is going to become the correct form, unless we professors can make such an impression that it becomes a strong social marker to say *between you and me*. It has nothing to do with grammar, and nothing to do with logic. What becomes standard is what the people who make the standard say. If speech forms that mark the standard no longer are seen as necessary or desirable, then nonstandard forms will replace them. Language itself will lose nothing in terms of expressibility or creativity. Older speakers may find it less elegant, but language changes as society does.

Variables as a Sign of Group Membership

The way people speak tells us where they come from and who they are. It also tells us who they are not. There used to be a term in AAVE for a person who doesn't belong, a *lame*. Although it is not so current now, the original metaphor is still apt. The person who doesn't use the membership markers of the community operates somewhat on the outside, like a lame person. The term did not denote a true outsider, but a person who should belong but did not.

A lame might be an African American youth who rejected the street life and attempted to be middle class. Females could be lames as well, as seen in one line of *The Fall*, "Girl you ain't no lame, you know the game." Labov (1972a) claims that lames in Harlem literally did not sound like gang members. Both by the percentage of times certain pronunciations were used and also by using other pronunciations entirely, lames were differentiated from gang members. For instance, lames, but not gang members, occasionally pronounced the ending -*ing* as "-ing" not "-in." Lames also used the verb *be* (*am, is, are*) more than twice as frequently as gang members in sentences of the "he (is) good" variety. These findings accord with social network theory as well. Gang members talk more with each other than with the lames. Wolfram (1969) found a high correlation between the isolation of African Americans and their retention of an AAVE dialect in Detroit.

Edwards and Ash (2004) found that the slain rapper Tupac Shakur chose more SE forms in his lyrical poems than in his six solo rap albums. Although his published poems were praised both by his fans and critics, they have met with only moderate success. In contrast, his rap albums, which are filled with AAVE speech features, have been phenomenally successful. Edwards and Ash (166) say that "keeping it real" or "realness" is a mantra in the African American working-class community. People who keep it real eschew deception, fakery, and mind games. They tell it like it is. For these people, realness means struggle for jobs, with the police, and the general difficulties of life in the 'hood. AAVE is associated with realness.

Shakur's rap songs contain all the features of AAVE listed in Chapter 7 in lines like:

1. A nigga tired of feelin' sad
2. This is how we gonna do this
3. It ain't easy tryin' to raise a man
4. Girlies was laughin'
5. Damn homies is dissin' you
6. Tears in everybody eyes

In the poems, in contrast, there were no examples of omitting *is*[11] or other forms of *be,* no double negatives, and no unmarked possessives. *Is* with a plural subject occurred only 3% out of a possible 107 occurrences, and there were no uses of *ain't.*

In contrast, in his rap songs, he omitted *is* 31% of the time, used *ain't* 80%, double negatives 30%, *is* with a plural subject 45% of the time, and so forth. What is interesting is that when he spoke in interviews, his use of AAVE features was midway between the raps and the poems. For instance, he omitted *is* only 16% of the time and used *ain't* only 30% of the time.

Edwards and Ash (173) posit that in his poems, Tupac was consciously aware of "the different sociolinguistic arenas in which he dealt." In his poetry, he was "accessing the world of the conventional bard." The poems were not as real as the raps, nor were they intended to be. In them, for instance, Tupac voiced idealism and looked toward a promising future. They conclude that his poems "fit well into the traditions of reflective and romantic poetry . . . [in which] the protagonist works toward a noble resolution of the psychic or emotional conflict." Also, whereas, as we have seen, rap songs glorify sex without love, Tupac's poems celebrate romance with phrases like "Nothing can come between us," "My dear one," and "Things that make hearts break." The speech community that revels in rap does not take to such sentiments. They are not real in their world.

DIGLOSSIA

Some countries normally have what Ferguson (1959) termed **diglossia.** This refers to "two or more languages (or varieties of a language) in a speech community [that] are allocated to different social functions" (Saville-Troike 1982, 56). Ferguson, discussing Arabic, originally conceived of diglossia as a switching from a vernacular to a higher form of the same language associated with a "glorious tradition" such as religion and art.

However, it soon became clear that diglossic situations can involve different languages. Before the demise of the Latin mass in Roman Catholicism, for instance, Latin was in a diglossic relationship with other European, Asian, and even African languages. Prerevolutionary Russians of noble birth spoke French to their peers in Russia, especially on social occasions, but spoke Russian to their servants or in everyday activity. The term *lingua franca* itself refers to a general European diglossia in which the upper classes could command French on formal occasions, including political activities like treaty making. In Paraguay, the Indians speak Guarani for intimacy and other matters relating to solidarity, but Spanish for education, religion, government, and high culture (Rubin 1985). Spanish for them is clearly the "high language."

Reserving one language—or one form of a language—for purposes such as religion, law, and education makes those activities special. Typically, in such instances, the language used for higher functions has a long tradition associated with erudition and sanctity. Religions commonly depend upon dead languages and archaic dialects, a form of speech no longer used for daily business, for their scriptures and prayers. Sanskrit, Hebrew, and Latin are examples of dead languages so used. The dead language separates religion from mundane activity and, since it is ancient, it has an aura of purity about it that spoken languages ordinarily lack. Religions that do not have dead languages often use archaic forms for the same purposes, such as English *thou art* and *he leadeth.*

There are other factors in choosing one language over another. Deborah James (1996, 102–05) cites studies that show that the choice of language for women is bound up with their choices in favorable marriages or retaining respect. For instance, in Austria, in one community, both Hungarian and German are spoken. The latter is the prestige language. Although men and women have similar social networks in this community, the women preferred German. Hungarian-speaking males were poor peasant farmers, but could feel independent in that role. Being the wife of such a farmer conferred no independence but did confer very hard work and subservience to the husband's authority. By speaking German, the women could hope to marry into the German-speaking urban middle class (103).

In contrast, in South Africa, among the Thonga people, women are respected and have more power than in the dominant Zulu culture. Men, however, can improve their status by speaking Zulu, so they do. The women stick to the stigmatized Thonga language as a "form of resistance to the loss of power and respect" (104) which adopting Zulu would bring them.

An interesting example of diglossia occurs in the American deaf community. Manual languages of the deaf show the same kinds of divisions into dialects and languages that oral languages do. Moreover, there are different styles in each deaf language. Many of the deaf are, in essence, bilingual or even multilingual, with one of their languages being oral English. Although some deaf people are virtually balanced bilinguals in spoken and manual language, others show varying degrees of competence in spoken language. In other words, just like bilinguals of two or more spoken languages, degrees of competency vary in each language. A person deaf from infancy or early childhood may be a native speaker of American Sign Language (ASL), as may a hearing person whose parents are deaf and regular users of ASL. Lucas and Valli (1989, 11) explain:

ASL is the visual-gestural language used by members of the deaf community in the United States. It is a natural language with an autonomous grammar that is quite distinct from the grammar of

English. **It is also quite distinct from artificially developed systems that attempt to encode English and can include the use of speech, ASL signs and invented signs used to represent English morphemes**. (emphasis mine)

Besides true ASL and signed English, there is *contact signing* (15), "an interface between deaf signers and hearing speakers" labeled Pidgin Sign English. There is also finger-spelling of English words, so that the deaf resources for communication range from ASL on one extreme and a continuum to English on the other, with signed English, contact signing, and finger spelling in between. Researchers consider this a diglossia situation with the high language (superposed or high variety) being English.

Lucas and Valli studied the varieties of sign that ASL speakers chose in interacting with both a deaf and a hearing interviewer. They were testing out the twin assumptions that native ASL speakers would always use ASL with other deaf people, but use contact signing or Signed English with hearing people. Deaf people can detect an "accent" in sign, just as hearing speakers can detect one in oral language. That is, one who has not learned ASL in childhood will, like any other bilingual speaker, have different degrees of competency in it, but will usually be distinguishable from a native speaker.

Contrary to expectation, Lucas and Valli found that the deaf subjects didn't always use ASL with deaf interviewers, although most used either signed English or contact signing with hearing ones. Three of the informants did use ASL with the hearing interviewers, contrary to the widely held belief that deaf native signers automatically switch away from ASL with the hearing. Another surprising finding was that although the deaf interviewer consistently used ASL, some actually used contact signing or Signed English with the deaf interviewer, despite the fact that they knew ASL natively.

The decision to use contact signing or Signed English with another deaf person appears to have been motivated by the formality of the interview situation, including the presence of a video cameras. In other words, some deaf subjects chose the higher (English) part of the continuum in the presence of cameras in a formal interview, despite mutual knowledge of ASL. This argues for a diglossic situation. However, two deaf persons used ASL throughout, even with the hearing interviewer and despite the taping. Apparently, for them, the desire to establish their identity as a "bona fide member of the deaf community" superseded considerations of formality (24). The researchers conclude that "[d]ifferent sociolinguistic factors motivate the language choices of different individuals."

Because the deaf subjects did not always choose the higher varieties in all formal situations, this indicates that there isn't a classic diglossic situation in this community. However, this finding may be mitigated by recalling that, currently, the issue of the validity of being deaf, of belonging to the deaf culture, is a big one. Like other minorities, deaf people are insisting on their right to be themselves, to their own culture.

Many resist the new cochlear implants which aid hearing because they fear the implants will make them outsiders to the deaf community without allowing them to be full participants among the hearing. It must be stressed that the implants do not give deaf people the same sound signal as hearing people get. What they get is highly distorted, so they still don't hear speech as it is perceived by the hearing.

Also, nobody is born able to distinguish all the sounds of their language. The kinds of errors babies make when learning to talk shows that it takes three to five years to distinguish between sounds as adults do, years of intensive listening and practicing. Adult deaf speakers with implants have to learn to differentiate between closely related sounds, and to do so with the handicap of acoustically distorted devices in their ears.

A desire to remain within the deaf community may be the reason some deaf persons do not bother with the high language, which is associated with the hearing culture, even in formal situations. That is, this would show an awareness of the diglossic situation, but a conscious refusal to conform to it.

LANGUAGE CHOICE AND SOCIAL BONDING

We have seen that one reason for maintaining a language is the need for solidarity. Shifting between two languages is a way to show camaraderie. Fishman (1970) presents a long dialogue between a Hispanic employer and secretary. He shows that the man used English to dictate a business letter and the woman responded in English. As soon as the dictation was done, however, conversation moved to the topic of a coming Puerto Rican parade. Concurrent with the topic shift came a shift in language. The switch into a second, shared language symbolizes the values associated with a cultural activity such as the Puerto Rican parade, itself an affirmation of group loyalty.

This is an excellent example of what Gumperz (1964, 55–99) terms **code-switching**. He defines this as

the juxtaposition within the same speech exchange of passages of speech belonging to two different grammatical systems or subsystems.

CHAPTER 9

This definition includes changing languages according to topic of conversation within the same social situation. This can occur with dialects as well.

Gumperz and Hernando-Chavez (1972) show code-switching between Mexican Americans:

> *Woman*: Well, I'm glad that I met you, okay?
>
> *Man*: Andale, pues, and do come again, mmm? . . . Con ellos dos. With each other. La senora trabaja en la caneria orita, you know? She was . . . con Francine jugaba . . . with my little girl.

Gumperz and Hernando-Chavez point out that this kind of switching is not necessarily related to differences or setting, factors that often determine style shifting within a language. Rather, lapsing into Spanish signifies more warmth. It is akin to using a more casual, intimate style within a language.

Sometimes a language switch is used for emphasis, as in, "I say Lupe, no hombre, don't believe that." The change from one language to another, in itself, has meaning. No matter what else such a switch means, it reinforces bonds between speakers. It may be done in the presence of those who don't know the language as a way of excluding them, a phenomenon that we have seen in the use of specialized jargons. Such language switching emphasizes that the participants belong to the same speech community or the same network in a larger community.

Sometimes a foreign language phrase will be thrown out to see if a stranger really belongs or is "one of us." Italians, for instance, often interject a "Capiche?" meaning 'understand?' Or Jews ask "Fershteyst?" African American "dig" for 'understand' has been traced to West African *dega*, which apparently was once used the same way. Throwing out a word like this can be done by people who have no real knowledge of their ancestral tongue, commanding only a few words or phrases. Paradoxically it can also be used by those of other backgrounds as a way of saying, 'Even though I am not of your group, I still feel warmth for it' or even 'Just because I am not one of you, don't think you can put one on over me.' All of these messages can be made across dialects as well by someone deliberately throwing out a word or pronunciation in another's dialect. It is also heard stylistically, as when someone raises or lowers style either to achieve more intimacy or to sound tougher or more in the know.

Switching to a second language when talking about cultural or home affairs is also a way of reinforcing that the cultural heritage belongs to the country that speaks that language. Susan Ervin-Tripp (1967) found that Japanese-born wives of Americans often slipped into Japanese when talking about domestic concerns. It may also be that the person is used to discussing certain matters in one language rather than another, and the grammar and vocabulary in the more familiar language are therefore more accessible than in the second language. Then, too, use of the first language may be associated with warmth and love. For this reason, in many families the ethnic language may be all but forgotten except for words and phrases spoken to babies, usually in games or just terms of endearment.

THE ORIGINS OF AMERICAN DIALECTS

Our knowledge of speech communities helps cast light on the origin of American dialects. Some linguists have claimed that the first settlers were *r*-pronouncing but that in the nineteenth century East Coast speakers began dropping the /r/ out of admiration for the British upper classes whose dialects had dropped it. Surprisingly, Wells (1982, 470) affirms just such a scenario. Supposedly, the Easterners became *r*-droppers because they had more contact with the British than those who lived further inland. He offers no explanation of the fact that Philadelphians, also on the eastern seaboard, is and was *r*-full. As it happens, there is evidence that the original settlers brought the *r*-dropping with them. Even if there was no actual evidence, however, our knowledge of sociolinguistics tells us that this must be the case, for there is no other way that so much of the East Coast would have adopted *r*-dropping rules after independence from Great Britain.

What is really surprising to me is that in the 2005 PBS broadcast of *Do You Speak American?*, William Labov, who so brilliantly proved that people talk like those they identify with, repeated this frankly absurd account of Eastern New England, New York City, and Coastal Southern *r*-less speech. Until recently, there was a chain of *r*-less dialects from the coastal South to New York City to all of New England east of the Connecticut River, all the way up to the Canadian border with Maine. It was broken only by Pennsylvania.

How could isolated rural farmers in Foster, Rhode Island, Maine guides in Aroostook County, and fishermen on Block Island all have suddenly decided to adopt upper-class British speech? Where would they even have heard it? Before modern transportation and mass media, these people rarely spoke to anyone outside of their communities. Also, they rebelled against the British not only in 1776, but in the War of 1812. Why would they copy their speech?

Another factor to take in account is the twin assertion of scholars like Wells and Labov that British *r*-dropping dates only from the late 19th century. As one who has studied and taught the history of the English language, I can affirm that one finds evidence of *r*-dropping in manuscripts dating from very early Modern English, as discussed below. Wells and Labov apparently have not read these texts and letters.

Study after study has confirmed that people speak like those with whom they wish to be identified and those with whom they interact. There is no reason to suppose that early Americans, striving for their own nationality, were likely to adopt innovations in British speech. Even if a few wealthy families did remain in contact with Britain, this wouldn't have affected the speech of the large working-class, artisan, and farming populations. Similarly, it is not likely that the upper and middle classes copied the *r*-lessness of Cockney sailors visiting coastal towns, as some have posited. For one thing, the *r*-dropping rules are too complex to have been borrowed from casual contact with a few people. The prevalence of *r*-less speech up and down the East Coast by speakers of all classes also argues strongly that the original settlers were already *r*-less, except for the settlers of Pennsylvania. After the local dialects had been established, later immigrants conformed to what was already there. The reason that the speech of other areas such as Pennsylvania, the Appalachian Mountain regions, and WNE are *r*-full is that the settlers there were British *r*-full speakers. For instance, the Quakers who settled Philadelphia came from northern England, which was strongly *r*-full (Williams 1975).

Although our knowledge of how people speak and why tells us that the above scenario is correct, it still is nice to have some concrete proof that there were British *r*-droppers before and during the initial colonization of these shores. There is such evidence, much of it derived from examining rhymes, puns, or spelling errors. Schlauch (1959) points out that the Pastons, a married couple who kindly left us some of their fifteenth century correspondence, made spelling errors that showed that the /r/ was already being dropped. For example, they spelled *answer* as <arnswer>. We know from older manuscripts dating from the 10th century that the word never had an <r> after the <a>. It originally was *andswer*, with the *and* from the same Indo-European root as in Latin *anti-* 'against,' and *swer*, the ancestor of *'swear.'* Originally *andswer* meant 'to swear against, to rebut a legal argument.' Why, then, would a writer suddenly insert an <r> where it never existed before, and where it still is not pronounced? That would happen if the /r/ after an /a/, as in *park*, was no longer being pronounced, so that the spelling <ar> indicated the pronunciation of "ah," as it still does for *r*-less speakers today. The /a/ in *answer* originally was pronounced as "ah" as it still is in much British speech today. The misspelling <arnswer> was a logical way to indicate [ansər] "ahnser" to people who had already lost the preconsonantal /r/. Children today who are *r*-less misspell words like *socks* as <sarks> because the <ar> indicates [a].[12]

Recently, while teaching the Paston letters, I found many more misspellings that indicated *r*-dropping, like <mo> for *more* and <dor> for *do*.

The latter spelling indicated that an <or> was being pronounced as "aw." That is, that the writer dropped a word-final /r/ in speech, so that the spelling <or> just indicated a vowel sound. The experts on the phonology of early Modern English claim that the <o> in words like *do* was pronounced similarly to "aw." The Pastons were writing well before colonization of the New World by the British.

Kökeritz (1953) pointed out that Shakespeare rhymed *John* with *forsworn*, *death* with *earth*, and *dyrst degree* with *high'st degree*. He also made a pun of *food* with *ford*. Such rhyming and punning show that Shakespeare, and by implication, his audience, was familiar with *r*-less pronunciation, although he himself was probably *r*-full. Shakespeare was writing just before and at the time of original colonization of America.

On the other side of the Atlantic, colonists were keeping records. Often they spelled the way they pronounced words, as people still do today. These spellings provide us with definite clues as to articulation, as do sporadic misspellings today. For instance, in contemporary America one occasionally sees a misspelling <ornge> or *orange*. This only occurs from strong *r*- pronouncers who leave out the vowel after the /r/ in *orange*, just as the <sarks> misspelling comes from *r*-less speakers.

Celia Millward (1975) delved into Colonial records and found convincing evidence that the Eastern New England /r/-dropping rules were in Colonial times the same as they are today. She investigated spelling errors as evidence of pronunciation and found:

1. | Misspelling | Word Intended |
    |-------------|---------------|
    | brothe | brother |
    | therefo | therefore |
    | administe | administer |
    | furthe | further |

The above show that the writers did not pronounce the /r/ at the end of a word.

2. | Mach | March |
    |---------|---------|
    | Osbon | Osborne |
    | orchad | orchard |
    | Sanphod | Sanford |

These show that the writers dropped /r/ before consonants.

3. | piller | pillow |
    |----------|--------|
    | Marthere | Martha |

These show the *r*-glide on words ending in /ə/ "uh."

CHAPTER 9

The reader may have noticed that some <r>'s that would not be pronounced by *r*-less speakers today do occur in the spellings. Does this mean that the /r/-dropping was more sporadic than it would be today? Probably not, for there is no reason to suppose that the Colonial record keepers always spelled everything phonetically. Although spelling was not as standardized as it is today, there were spelling conventions. Literate people were familiar with spellings of words that represented pronunciations different from their own. Therefore, the misspellings were not wholly consistent.

Furthermore, as we have just seen, spellings represent different pronunciations to speakers of different dialects. Just as <ar> represents /a/ "ah" and <or> represents /ɔ/ "aw" to *r*-less speakers today, to a consistent *r*-dropper, the <ar> in *Marthere* and the <or> in *orchard* did not necessarily represent an actual /r/. For them, the letter *r* was silent after a vowel, indicating how the vowel should be enunciated.

To give a modern example: for *r*-less speakers the donkey's name in *Winnie-the-Pooh* is Eeyore, that is 'ee-aw' (for *heehaw*). He is a Cockney donkey, one who drops /h/'s as well as /r/'s. Most Americans miss the point entirely because they do not realize that in Milne's British English, <ore> represents /ɔ/ "aw." Neither puns nor rhymes work well in dialects other than the one which the writer speaks. So strong is the connection between the <ore> for /ɔ/ "aw" that many *r*-less speakers think they are hearing an /r/ when they hear that vowel. For instance, a South African *r*-less speaker complained to me that in London, he was disgusted by the way people put /r/'s in where they don't belong. Thinking he meant the *r*-glide, which he certainly used, I asked him for examples. He said, "Why the /r/ they put in *off*!" Bewildered, I asked, "What /r/ in *off*?" He proceeded to use a strong [ɔ] "aw"[13] for the vowel in *off* with nary a trace of an /r/.

The Virginia Tidewater and Eastern New England were settled by colonists from the East Midlands and southeast of England. These settlers were already using *r*-less pronunciation. They also pronounced the so-called broad a [a] "ah" in words like *half, calf, ask, aunt,* and *can't*. The Middle Atlantic states were settled by Quakers from the north of England who used /r/-full. Western New England and the Great Lakes regions were also settled by northern British.

A second source of dialect features in this country is migration from East to West. One can still trace old migration routes on a map that shows dialect features. Marietta, Ohio, for instance, was colonized by New Englanders and until recently speech there contained vocabulary features of the New England dialects, such as *pail* rather than *bucket*. Los Angeles speech shows some features of Oklahoma dialect because of the great

412

migration from that state during the Depression. The strong Los Angeles /a/ "ah" in words like *talk* and *law* has been traced to that source. Because of the influence that Los Angeles now has on fashion, entertainment, and trend setting, that pronunciation is also being imported into locations which used to pronounce it [tɔk] "tawk."

Conversely, words which used to have an [a], as in *Florida* and *orange* (pronounced "Flahrida" and "ahringe") are now being pronounced as /ɔr/ ("Flawrida," "awringe.") In other words, /a/'s and /ɔ/'s have flip-flopped, each occurring precisely where it didn't used to. These changes, like the *r*-pronouncing changes, show a distinct pattern of West to East influence. Like the changes in Illinois that Frazer documents, these are pronunciations moving into a region even though they are not prestigious for older speakers.

Pidgins and Creoles

A third source of dialect differentiation is creolization. The term *Creole* in linguistics does not refer to French nor to cooking. Rather, it is the technical term for the process of a new language being formed when two—or more—languages mix together to form a new one. The first stage of this process is the formation of a Pidgin, a limited speech code typically used for business dealings between people who don't know each others' language and don't want to. Pidgins also arose out of the slavery and near-slavery of plantation workers in places as far-flung as Hawaii, Mississippi, and the Caribbean (Bickerton 1981). There, the owners and their overseers weren't about to learn the West African, Polynesian, or Asian tongues of their workers. Indeed, even if they wished to, it would have been impossible to learn them all, for even on the plantations serviced by African slaves, many different tongues were spoken, so slaves had the double handicap of not knowing the masters' language and not necessarily sharing their native one with others. In Hawaii, workers spoke Japanese, one or the other Chinese dialects, or a Polynesian tongue, so again the workers didn't necessarily share a language with their cohorts.

Consider the plight of children born on these plantations. There is no native language for them to learn. There is the Pidgin based upon a European language, European only because it was they who owned the plantations and businesses. The Europeans were a distinct minority, and their language was not really available for the workers or their children to learn. So, by a mysterious process, the children created a full-blown language out of the Pidgin. Consequently, there are French, Spanish, Portuguese, and English-based Creoles. Bickerton (1981) says that all of these Creoles are more like each other in their grammars than they are to the European languages which provided much of their basic vocabulary, despite the fact that the speakers of one Creole had no contact with those of others. We know that deaf children denied oral language or a preexisting sign will make up their own. This is a similar situation. The process is, to me, both wonderful, in the original sense of that word, and mysterious. The details of the characteristics of Creole languages are beyond the scope of this book, but Bickerton claims that examining the grammars of Creoles provides insights into what the original human language must have been like, hence the title of his book, *The Roots of Language*.[14]

The issue of possible Creole origins of AAVE has become a political one, and one which has excited bitter scholarly debate. Some scholars claim that AAVE is not a nonstandard variety of American English but an African English Creole. Because of this, some have argued that it has its own validity and even that schools should not try to modify AAVE speech. Certainly, AAVE is as complete, flexible, and intelligent as any other variety of English; however, there still may be good reason for schools to teach what are considered standard forms, such as not using double negatives.

Fairclough (1989) demonstrates that the imposition of a standard dialect is one way to maintain power by those who already have it. Those who can learn the standard will have an edge over those who do not. The corollary to this is that the standard should be at least available to all speakers if there is to be equality of opportunity. Not to attempt to teach it at all does speakers a disservice. Whether or not they choose to employ it at least some of the time is ultimately their decision.

Many scholars feel that the substantive difference between AAVE and other forms of English must be recognized in classrooms, as the differences are a result of various West African tongues mixed with English (Turner 1971; Stewart 1968; Dalby 1971; Smitherman 1984). Certainly, there are similarities in words. To *badmouth* is a direct translation of a Vai expression meaning 'to curse.' AAVE *dig* 'to understand' seems to be derived from *dega* 'understand.' Words like *goobers, jazz, banjo, jumbo, voodoo*, and *okra* are clearly derived from African languages. So is the ubiquitous *okay*, from Wolof *wahkay*.

Gullah, spoken on the Sea Islands of Georgia and South Carolina, is a distinct Creole, although it is dying out today. And, if we can believe the literary representations of African American speech in the 18th and 19th centuries, it was far more different from white varieties than it is today. Geneva Smitherman (1984) points out when African Americans were first emancipated, they erroneously thought they would assimilate into white society. This, of course, would lead to their speaking a less creolized English. With the continued alienation of many urban African Americans, their speech has been developing more ethnic markers, although these are not necessarily Africanisms. In many ways, AAVE is becoming less like SE than it has been for a long while. As we have seen, part of the impetus for this change is that whites are imitating African American speech. Therefore, AAVE speakers keep changing their speech to keep it distinct from white speech.

The notion of speech community as being composed of speakers from all parts of the country, some 3,000 miles away from others, has not been considered in the scholarship. However, it is clear that AAVE speakers form a community which stretches from coast to coast, and that they consider their speech representative of that community's. I think we have to expand our idea of speech community beyond the borders of a city or even a state to include a population of speakers who define their speech as belonging to a population even if it is dispersed, as AAVE speakers are.

Some black scholars, like Geneva Smitherman (2000) and Tamura (2002), have gone so far as to claim that AAVE is a separate language and, in 1996, tried to have the city of Oakland, California recognize it as such so that African American students could receive bilingual education. Their argument was that AAVE, which they term Ebonics, because of its African and Creole origins, is a different language from SE.

As we've seen, there is no hard and fast line between a language and a dialect. Whether we call two varieties separate languages depends on political and social factors as much as linguistic ones. Certainly, nobody has shown that African Americans don't understand SE, nor have they shown that SE speakers don't understand AAVE. Admittedly, I don't always understand the lyrics in current rap songs, but I recognize the grammar and sound system as being English. I just don't recognize the lexicon, but then I don't understand all the words used by an English-speaking nuclear physicist discussing his or her subject. That doesn't mean we speak different languages.

I don't doubt that AAVE had its origins in a creolization of African languages and English. How else could it have been? The earliest slaves didn't attend English classes. Of course, they learned what English they could through the filter of their native tongues. One example of this is that West African languages don't have a /v/ sound, so slaves are reported in the literature as saying "riber" for *river* and "debil" for *devil*. This is a typical foreign language error.

However, these origins were over 300 years ago. Since then AAVE has increasingly become Anglicized. Wolfram, Thomas, and Green (2000), having carefully studied the speech of whites and blacks in a remote rural area in North Carolina, concluded that the African Americans there spoke much like the whites. Historical written records confirm this. Now, however, younger African Americans there are using more AAVE features in their speech. It may be that since the area studied was sparsely populated, African Americans and whites historically had more interaction with each other than in other areas. Certainly, slaves who lived on large plantations had little contact with white speakers except for overseers and owners, and they certainly didn't engage in conversation with them.

The other thing is that some features that have been advanced as evidence for a Creole origin for African American speech can also be traced to some British or Irish dialects. Even if the feature did not appear in slave owners' dialects, slaves could have picked them up from overseers, many of whom were Irish.

Two good examples are the AAVE verb forms of durative *be*, meaning 'all the time,' as in "He be good" and the *been*, indicating completed action in the distant past. Much of the claim that African origins of AAVE cause its difference from other varieties rests upon these two forms. The *be* is supposed to be a translation from West African durative *blan*. Such carryovers are quite usual in bilinguals.

One objection to this interpretation is that there was a durative *be* in Old English as well as in Irish, and it has been found in Newfoundland white speech. Joseph Williams (1975) believes that it must have submerged into a lower- or lower-middle-class social dialect in England, so it did not appear in writing for many centuries. Then it was brought to this continent by settlers, where it surfaced again. He argues, and I believe correctly, that the whites in Newfoundland were not likely to have learned this form from African Americans. His arguments appear to be bolstered by the fact that *been* meaning 'completed past' has also been found in Newfoundland. Perhaps the slaves learned English from those who spoke the same dialect as that from which Newfoundland English is derived. The fact that they were already used to a durative in their own languages would have made it natural for them to adopt even a vestigial one still existing in an English or Irish dialect.

Another objection to saying the durative *be* shows that AAVE is a Creole is that in the recordings made of ex-slaves in the 1930's, this *be* doesn't occur, and there is little evidence of creolisms in their speech (Bailey, Maynor, and Cukor-Avila 1991). Sutcliffe (1999) shows that this is partially an artifact of how the ex-slaves' speech was transcribed. Bailey, Maynor, and Cukor-Avila aimed for a noncontroversial transcript, and any disagreement was purposely resolved in favor of standard speech. As you can imagine, the quality of the recordings was quite primitive in 1930, involving large pieces of equipment that created discs, not tapes, all done well before anyone had ever even heard of "high-fidelity sound." Sutcliffe did find some evidence of Creole in the use of pronouns, a past tense marker *-uh*, and the use of *duh* as a marker before a verb to indicate continuing activity, as in "whuh I *duh work* at" (where I was working). So far as I know, this feature does not appear in modern AAVE. What seems surprising is the lack of the durative *be* that has been made so much of as proof of Creole origins.

It's not so surprising, however, if you consider how these recordings were elicited. White men carrying heavy, imposing machinery came into this sparsely settled rural community and asked people to talk. We know from Labov's studies that this is likely to elicit someone's most careful speech. These ex-slaves might be as aware as the gang member Boot was that whites didn't use certain forms in their speech, such as *be*. Therefore, they may simply have avoided them. The other explanation is that slaves were spread over a very wide area of the South. It is very probable that their speech developed differently in different places, but, in the 20th century, when descendants migrated to large Northern cities, their speech melded into what we know today as AAVE.

The issue of the development of AAVE speech is clearly a complex one, complicated by the conditions of the original slavery and the years of social and psychological isolation of African Americans themselves, an isolation attested to by the fact that a distinct AAVE group of dialects still exists all over the United States (Smitherman 2000). The isolation is probably what is important, not the specific origin of verb forms.

The idea that Ebonics (AAVE) is a separate language is not dead as of this writing. It seems to me that we should make a distinction between the undoubted Creole origins of AAVE and its present status. The very existence of Creoles of African and European languages, including English, all over the Caribbean and on the Sea Islands off Georgia where Gullah persisted into this century, argues for such an origin for AAVE. But this doesn't mean that AAVE is still a Creole. Geneva Smitherman believes that on historical and sociolinguistic grounds, AAVE should be considered a separate language even though, she admits, it is very much like white varieties of English.

One of the proofs that creolists invoke in favor of their claim is that AAVE is systematically different from other varieties of English. However, all dialects are systematic, hence systematically different from each other. In my opinion, no matter what its origins, AAVE is now far more like other varieties of English than it is like African languages. It certainly should be recognized as an ethnic dialect, not a nonstandard one, and teachers should learn the sociolinguistic rules of the ethnic groups their students belong to and adjust their classrooms accordingly. It is not unusual for African Americans or anyone else to command more than one dialect or language: one used for status situations, and another for social bonding. Perhaps part of the schools' task is to teach students appropriate times to talk in each of their varieties. We cannot redress 300 years of slavery and persecution by not making an effort to allow students to add SE to their linguistic repertoires to use or not as they want in adulthood. This should also be an aim of teaching whites who speak with a non-standard dialect.

Notes

1   Labov found that there were five ways of pronouncing this <a>, ranging from the tongue being held low enough to produce a very low [æ] to a high [ɨ]. (See "Appendix of Phonetic Symbols" for the values of these symbols.)

2   It must be emphasized that Providence African-American speech was not at all Southern in its pronunciation. It was recognizably Providence, but with a few vowel differences from their white neighbors, such as saying "leyg" for *leg*. They also said *aks* for *ask*. They did drop their [r]'s, but all Rhode Islanders did that until the 1960s. It was in the 1960s that black males began to copy AAVE, much to the distress of some of their mothers. Friends of mine cried to me, "He's sounding so Southern."

3   These speakers are almost all dead by now. It is safe to assume that all New Yorkers now would try to pronounce the /r/ at least in careful speech.

4   Mae West was a vaudeville entertainer who also wrote and starred in her own movies in the 1930s. She always acted like a tough-speaking, forward, sexually active woman. She was the actress who immortalized the line, "Why don't you come up and see me some time?" and who singlehandedly brought censorship to Hollywood by saying to a man, "Is that a gun in your pocket or are you just happy to see me?" This was in the days before movies were rated, and it was assumed that children could see any movie shown.

5   Obviously, speakers in the community don't get together and decide such matters consciously. Still, it is amazing that social markers in speech uniformly get adopted within a speech community. Literally millions of speakers are affected by the norms that develop, either because they adopt them or resist them. Either way, their speech is consistent in using or not using a given variable.

6   However, blues and jazz singers did not modify their BE dialects.

7   The British are often not aware that there are /r/-dropping accents in the United States, and, since British dialects are /r/-dropping, in order to sound American, the singers try to pronounce /r/'s everywhere.

8   Of course, middle-class mores have undergone a tremendous shifting since the '50's, a shift towards the values espoused in rock 'n roll.

9   Things may have changed considerably since this study was done, especially since Canada has become officially bilingual and the French Canadians have reasserted pride in their ethnicity. However, the principles uncovered in this study are still valid. If a group is stigmatized

by society, it will not value its own variety of speech, even as it clings to it as a sign of solidarity.

10 This is an old plural of *cow*.

11 For the sake of simplicity, I use *is* to stand for any form of the verb *be* here. With plural subjects, *is* is used here to indicate any singular verb form.

12 The Berlitz guide to Italian for English speakers uses British and American *r*-less speech as its basis for rendering pronunciation. Consequently, it indicates the [a] "ah" pronunciation by using the spelling <ar>. This can cause trouble for *r*-full Americans. For instance, the real pronunciation of Italian *mange* is is rendered as "marnge." One wonders what happens to *r*-full Americans in Italy. They must have [r]'s all over the place where Italian doesn't.

13 Think of the TV sitcom *The Nanny*'s strong "aw" in *talk*. That is a typical British sound also heard in *off*.

14 This is not to say that all scholars agree with him, scholars being the feisty lot they are, but he makes a good case for his general thesis, I think.

Exercises

1. What speech community do you think you belong to? What communities of practice? Do you or people you know have a social network that influences your speech? If so, how is it different from a community of practice?

2. What variable(s) seem to operate in your speech community? How do these seem to relate to national, regional, or ethnic variables? Do you use different ones in your communities of practice? For instance, your home dialect may make use of different variables from those you use with your roommates and friends.

3. Make up a brief speech evaluation survey and poll your friends to see their attitudes toward some variable pronunciation in use in your community. Alternatively, play rap music to your friends and have them evaluate the speech on traits like pleasantness, toughness, sociability, or whatever other traits you deem important. Alternatively, ask subjects if they use a pronunciation or speech form. What does each friend report him- or herself as using?

4. If you are bilingual or know someone who is, investigate the conditions under which code-switching occurs.

5. If you have access to the papers of an elementary school student, examine these for misspellings caused by dialect. Alternatively, examine the class notes of friends from different regions. Explain how the misspellings relate to the dialect in question.

6. Can you find evidence of features of creole in the AAVE of a rap song, or the dialogue of a movie like *Barbershop*?

Chapter 10

Vocabulary and Gender

A society's attitudes are revealed in its vocabulary and speaking practices. Examination of euphemisms show what members of a society are uncomfortable with. Words for females in English typically take on meanings of sexual availability and desirability. Once equivalent, words for males and females diverge in meaning over time so that the feminine counterpart takes on a trivial meaning. Moreover, words which indicate strength in women take on negative connotations. These combined with an examination of male-female practices in speech show gender differences in our society.

VOCABULARY AS A MIRROR OF SOCIAL REALITIES

So far as linguists know, all languages are mutually translatable. What can be said in one language can be said in any other—somehow. To put it another way, if a speaker of any language wants to express something, he or she can make up new words or make up new sentences in their languages which will express that new thought. All languages are so constructed that new thoughts can be expressed in them. To be sure, it is easier to express some ideas in one language rather than another. This is because the vocabulary of each language develops partly according to the priorities of its culture. The objects, relationships, activities, and ideas important to the culture get coded onto single words, which are often highly specialized to express subtle nuances.

Everyone's favorite example is the Eskimos, to whom snow is a central feature of life. For this reason, it has been claimed, they have anywhere from eight to hundreds of distinct words for it. Unfortunately, this is a major myth. Eskimos have four words for snow, *aput, qana, piasirpaq,* and *qimuqsuq,* meaning, respectively 'snow on the ground,' 'falling snow,' 'drifting snow,' and 'a snow drift' (Shaul and Furbee 1998, 29). Eskimos do have grammatical modifications to their basic vocabulary to express such thing as different duration or conditions of snow. African languages, spoken where there is no snow, do not have a word for it. Still, they could describe it, as, for example, white, cold flowers from the sky that turns to water when they are touched.

CHAPTER 10

Friendship is more important in Russian culture than it is in American, as witnessed by the fact that we have but one word *friend*, which can be modified by words like *best* (Weirzbicka 1997, 55–84). In contrast, Russian has six separate words, each denoting very different friendly relationships with a person: *drug, podruga, tovarišč, prijatel,* and *znakomyj.* These words are not at all interchangeable. One is either a *drug* or is not. One is a *prijatel* or is not. This is in sharp contrast to American English in which people can have ten best friends, one from college, one from their old neighborhood, and so on. Also, in America a friend can be someone you just met at a party or someone whom you have known for forty years. *Friends* in America is a very loose term.

In Russian, on the other hand, a person's *druz'ja* "form this person's life support" (59). A *drug* is a person you can rely upon for help and support. Seeing one's *druz'ja*, talking with them, confiding to them, and spending time with them is an important part of a Russian's life, but this is not true of the other categories. *Tovarišč,* for instance, refers just to someone one has gone through an experience with. *Podruga* can be a temporary relationship. *Prijatel* refers to someone who is friendly but not intimate. It's not that we can't express such differences in English, but our language doesn't easily codify them. Russians have to categorize these distinctions in relationships every time they go to mention another person with whom they have a relationship. There is no cover term like English *friend* in Russian. In the United States we make friends, find them, and lose them. They are not permanent fixtures in our lives, but in Russia they are of vital importance, they are durable and consistent, and this is reflected in the careful terminology for friends in that language.

As we shall see, oddly, things which are taboo in a culture are also often marked by having many words refer to them, frequently, none of them directly naming the taboo action or item.

People make their language say what they want it to, as we saw with jargons. They make it easy to reference the things important to them—or disgusting to them—by having many vocabulary items referring to different aspects of a concept, or to allow speaking of taboo things by never directly naming them.

If it were possible to say certain things in one language but not another, then we would have the problem that people who speak one language could know things that those in another could not. Bilinguals might have the problem of being able to know something in one language but not another. In fact, although it may be more difficult to express a given idea in one language rather than another, there has never been any proof that it is impossible.

This, however, does not mean that there is a one-to-one correspondence between languages. If there were, it would be possible to translate any language into any other by machine. However, this has proven to be a very knotty problem. Computer translations are still limited after three decades or more of intensive research. They founder on the fact that any word in any language potentially has many meanings, and that the same idea can be expressed by grammatically different sentences. Computers can't match what is said to the cultural context or even to the context of utterance the way any human can do.

The major problem is that, although all languages can potentially say the same things, the way they say them is considerably different. Each language carves up the semantic universe (the universe of all things which can possibly be said) differently. Even when two words mean the same thing in two different languages, the entire semantic load of those words differs. For instance, in English *climb* can be used in:

Maxine climbed the tree.
Maxine climbed out on a limb.
Maxine climbed out of bed.
The airplane climbed 20,000 feet.
Maxine climbed the to the top of her company.
What a social climber Maxine is!

There is no reason to suppose that in any other language on earth all of these meanings of *climb* would be combined in one word. In other languages, there might be separate words, each with its own semantic load (the entire complex of meanings of a word).

Prototype theory and modern theories of metaphor (Lakoff and Johnson 1980; MacLaury 1989) have shown that cultural models underlie the variable meanings of words such as English *climb*. For instance, in English, the prototype of *climb*[1] consists of:

- vertical movement
- use of hands in grasping position
- use of legs, bent at knee, in sequence[2]
- purposeful activity

It is not necessary that all of these features be present in all usages of *climb*, but all use some combination of them. For instance, "climbing up in a tree" uses all of these features. "Climbing out on a limb" refers to the prototypical hand and leg movements, but to horizontal motion, rather than vertical. Climbing out of bed uses vertical movement and perhaps leg movement, but not the grasping hands. The airplane's climb is vertical motion without hands or feet. The metaphor for climbing up the corporate ladder depends on the entire picture of climbing, including the prototypical motion of the hands. This last adds a picture of grasping, of ruthlessness, so that the metaphor "climbing to the top of a corporation" indicates a determined person who grasps at opportunity.

In another language *climb* might be conceived of solely as an animate activity, so the equivalent of the word *float* might be used for the airplane rising. In our society, we often treat social structures metaphorically as if they were objects, so that we see corporations as ladders. Therefore, we go up or down them. Hence our metaphor for social or business climbing.[3] In another culture, one which conceives of power as being a hidden entity in the center of things instead of a metaphor for climbing up in the business world, the metaphor for success might be based upon an image of burrowing to the center of something.

Such prototypes help explain why semantic loads of words differ cross-linguistically and why there are often differences in metaphor in different languages.

Sociolinguistic Construction of Reality

For humans, reality is "filtered, apprehended, encoded, codified, and conveyed via some linguistic shape" (Smitherman 1991, 117). The words we use for concepts do help form our ideologies, attitudes, and behaviors. This doesn't mean, as Whorf thought, that we are prisoners of language. It does mean that language reflects cultural attitudes and that we unconsciously adopt those attitudes as we learn the language. Our consciousness can be raised. We can learn to recognize the biases in our language, and we can learn not to use sexist, racist, or otherwise prejudiced speech forms. Two areas in which this is very evident is in gender and race.

Sometimes positive attitudes are instilled because of our language. For instance, in Yiddish, there is a word *kvell*, which means 'to feel joy in someone else's good fortune or success.' German, on the other hand, has a word *Schadenfreude,* meaning 'to take joy in someone else's sorrow." I don't know what it does to one to grow up with *Schadenfreude*, but I do know that learning to *kvell* meant that even as a very young child, I knew I should be happy for others when they did well. Nobody explicitly ever taught me that moral lesson. I learned it from the language.

Unfortunately, the rest of this chapter will focus on the ways language can deprecate and teach poor attitudes.

Semantic Features

Words do not have holistic meaning. Rather, they are composed of features of meaning. For instance, *boy* is composed of features like [+human, +male, -power]. Features of one word can be transferred onto another, which is one important way we get meaning. Uriel Weinreich (1966) gave an apt example. *Pretty* has a feature of [+female]. If *pretty* is used with *boy*, the [+female] gets transferred so that *pretty boy* implies a feminine young male. In American culture, this often also implies a tinge of homosexuality. In the Eagles' song "Hotel California," it is sufficient to say that a woman is surrounded by "pretty, pretty boys" to indicate their sexual persuasion. *Handsome*, which has the feature [+male], when used with *woman* implies an older woman. This used to mean a woman who is past the prime of her sexual life. Nowadays, it can mean a young woman, but one who is a well-educated career woman, not one who is to be judged primarily on the basis of sexual attractiveness. This change in meaning coincides with the change in the expected roles of women.

Differences in meaning between two dialects or languages are often differences in the way features are attached to words. For example, in England, the features [+car, +top,+front] are attached to *bonnet*, but, in United States, to *hood*. Both of these words originally referred to head coverings. In the American South, the verb *favor* includes [-concrete, +appearance] the sense of 'looks like,' as in "she favors her mother." In the North, it is most likely to be interpreted as 'prefer.'

Even within the same dialect, choice of one word over another can subtly convey an attitude. If our side has to take a military action, we land on someone else's territory, but if our opponents do, they attack. The start of warfare against Iraq in 1991 was announced by our government as "Ladies and gentlemen, the *liberation* of Kuwait has begun." Similarly, in the 2003 invasion of Iraq, what has been stressed is that the United States is bringing freedom to that country. One country's liberation is another's invasion. One country's attack is another's bringing freedom. Our attitude toward a given activity is conveyed by the choice of synonym. If we don't wish to raise the specter of all-out war, then we "take military action," we don't "go to war." Furthermore, we call it an *operation* rather than a war, as in "Operation Iraqi Freedom." By utilizing synonyms this way, the media and the government and other institutions are able to influence public opinion without people's being aware of it.

Fairclough (1989, 50) gives the even more subtle example of how the media systematically build in the perspectives of dominant groups in society by their word choice. For instance, he says, that when industrial disputes are systematically referred to as *trouble* or *disruption* in the media, "that is systematically building the employer's perspective into industrial news coverage." The very term *labor troubles* implies that it is labor causing trouble to management, not the other way around.

Words take on the semantic features of [+good] or [+bad] according to how a particular culture feels about the item designated. If a word marked

CHAPTER 10

[+bad] denotes something that must be mentioned in the course of a daily routine, other words are substituted. The substitutes, called euphemisms, are close in meaning but do not quite mean the "bad" thing. Instead of having the feature [+bad], they are neutral or even pleasant. Think of little girls who *tinkle* instead of pee. That's a euphemism.

The feature [+bad] is firmly attached to *fat* nowadays in America. It is no longer desirable on meat, much less on people. This poses a problem for clothing stores that wish to sell specially cut garments for the obese. These certainly can't be called what they are: clothes for fat folk. Rather, for girls there are *chubbette* or *pretty plus*; for boys, *husky* or *husky plus*; for men, *portly, big*; and for women, *women's sizes* (as opposed to *misses* or *junior*) or, my favorite, *woman's petite* for short, fat women, as opposed to just *petite* for short, thin ones. So taken in are some women by labels that mean 'small' that I have had females who are very plump proudly tell me that they take petite sizes, even though these "petites" are size 18. (Clothes sizes for women range from 0 to 18 and up. An 18 is a very, very large size.) There are also *queen size, full sizes, half-sizes*, and *hard-to-fit. Stout* used to be euphemism, as in *stylish stouts*, but when it ceased being used in the general language in its original senses of 'healthy' and 'brave,' it came too directly to mean 'fat.' One hardly, if ever, sees the term in clothing departments anymore. Similarly, the male *portly* has been replaced by *big* on labels.

Some of the euphemisms for *fat* used to be words meaning 'strong' and 'tough' such as *stout* and *husky. Portly* used to mean 'imposing, dignified.' The euphemistic character of *pretty plu*s is obvious, as is reference to *half-sizes* instead of the true 'size and a half.'

Even in casual conversation, referring to a person's bulk, people skirt around the word *fat*. Instead they say, "Well, he certainly is big" or "It's hard for a big woman to find clothes." *Plump*, an older, favorable term for *fat*, is today pretty much reserved for chickens or pillows. Students in my classes, when asked to rate words for *fat*, typically consider *plump* archaic and humorous. The only word associated with obesity that can be positively evaluated is *jolly*. Even so, this is restricted to Santa Claus, the Jolly Green Giant, and babies, who are still allowed to be fat in our society.

Cultures that do—or did—not find fat repugnant treat it differently in their word stock. In both Italian and Yiddish, for instance, the same word can be used for both *fat* and *healthy*. Occasionally, in English, *fat* and *healthy* can be used synonymously, as in *fat profit* and *healthy profit*. The choice of one over the other depends on our feeling about the profit in question: *fat* if we disapprove of or are gloating over the profit, *healthy* if we approve. For instance, a stockbroker would tell you that an investment gives a *healthy* profit, but a reporter in a story about a shady businessman might call it a *fat* one.

As part of what Geneva Smitherman calls the semantic inversion of AAVE, an inversion which explained why earlier AAVE introduced *bad* to mean 'good,' *fat* (spelled phat) has been inverted to mean 'good' rather than something negative. Whites have adopted this usage.

Euphemism

When a culture frowns upon an activity or situation, typically it creates **euphemisms** to refer to it. Euphemisms usually occur in sets of several words, none meaning exactly the thing being referred to. When one euphemism becomes too directly associated with the disvalued meaning, it is replaced by other euphemisms. This is clearly seen in the euphemisms for the places where Americans urinate and defecate. Even with the supposed lifting of taboos in modern times, American prudishness about voiding remains in full force. Taboos about swearing, sex, and nudity have all weakened, but the bathroom functions still disgust us. One consequence of this is the dearth of public restrooms in United States. In England, as one enters a town, there is usually a welcome sign proclaiming *Toilets*, with an arrow pointing the way. When Sigmund Freud visited the United States, he was appalled at the lack of facilities. Fortunately, if one travels on a highway today, there are roadside rests advertising food courts, which, it is understood, have facilities.

The discomfort Americans have in mentioning elimination is well illustrated by the preceding paragraph. Except for the erudite Latinate *defecate* and *urinate*, there is not one direct polite term for the process under discussion. Nor is there even one direct term for the room where the body functions are performed. *Bathroom* actually means 'the place where one takes a bath.' In England it still means that since, unlike Americans, the British do not keep the tub and the "hopper" in the same room. *Toilet* originally meant 'getting dressed,' as in the archaic, "She made her toilet," and in the survival *toilet water*. It must have been assumed that part of the process of getting dressed was *going*.

Of course *restrooms*, another designation of the place to *go* are not for resting. Since we all know that the only place to rest when away from home is a hotel room, we hear *restroom* as a euphemism for the place in which we rest (stop) briefly for unmentionable purposes. How unmentionable these purposes are is seen by the general terms like *facilities* for the place, and *going* for the acts. In many languages use of very general, virtually empty terms, indicates a taboo. In English the word *facilities* usually has to be followed by *for X* as in *the facilities for cooking*. When it occurs alone, as in "I have to use the facilities," it usually means the "loo," to use the British slang for it. Similarly, *going* is normally followed by an adverb of place or manner as in "going to New York" or "going by plane." By itself, it means one is voiding. Compare this with the general *doing it* used without reference to a previously stated act, which means 'fornicating,' another Latinate substitute.

The sheer number of euphemisms for voiding indicates the degree of discomfort Americans have about bodily waste: *powder room, comfort station, head, lav(atory), John, little girls' room, little boys' room, lavette, half-bath, commode*. In a restaurant, one often has to guess if the right room has been found, especially if a coy picture is used on the door. Usually, there are two signs indicating male and female gender: *buoys* and *gulls*; *knights* and *damsels*; *his, hers*; *signor, signorina*.

In contrast, there is only one word in English for the place where food is prepared: kitchen. Clearly that is not taboo, which, when you think of it, is odd in a society which disvalues fat.

Propaganda is a kind of euphemism, calling unpleasantness by another name. The difference is that propaganda is euphemism used by governments and other political organizations. The term *ethnic cleansing* was intended as propaganda. It really meant 'genocide: massacring a group of people with a shared identity.' The seemingly innocuous word *apartheid*, literally 'apart-hood,' 'the state of keeping something apart,' really meant 'keeping blacks in South Africa in poverty and servitude.' The only 'apart' for them was being herded into special, poverty-ridden townships apart from the white folks.

In the United States, all one need to do to justify almost any action is to speak of "freedom" and "rights." The NRA has successfully kept gun-control laws to a minimum on the grounds that they would violate our "freedom" and our "rights," despite the fact that every other free society in the world has strict gun controls, and far fewer murders from shooting. The kicker is that the "rights" are "constitutional," another potent word in American politics. The word itself is used as a justification.

Sometimes propaganda and common euphemisms coincide. A case in point is death, another phenomenon with which our culture is uneasy and which governments have to discuss. Again, we can tell that English speakers are uncomfortable with death by the number of euphemisms for it. People do not die, they "pass away," "pass on," "go to sleep," "go to the other side," "meet their Maker," "go to rest," "go to their final reward," "croak," "kick the bucket," "buy the farm," "buy it," and become "traffic fatalities," not corpses. Also, we "lose" our relatives, as in "I recently lost my favorite aunt." Our pets are "put to sleep," "put away," or "put down," not killed (except by a cruel outside party). Gangsters "deep-six," "waste," or "off" their victims rather than "murder" them.

Our uneasiness about mentioning death conflicts with the military's need to talk about it. The military is in an exceptionally difficult position, for if we cannot talk directly of natural death, how can we talk of unnatural death? Yet soldiers must deal with both killing and being killed. Death must be mentioned in their training, but if it were mentioned too directly, soldiers would be too often reminded of their mortality and of the true awfulness of what they are supposed to do.

Robert Sellman, a ROTC student, examined military euphemisms for death in a field manual, *The Combat Training of the Individual Soldier and Patrolling*. He showed that the manual is written in a highly impersonal, distant style which is "designed to negate the psychological impact of killing and destroying." One way this is done throughout is to use the modal auxiliary *may*, as in "A nuclear explosion may cause heavy casualties among your leaders" and "may even completely destroy your unit's chain of command." Nuclear explosions will cause these disasters. There is no "may" about it. By using *may*, the field manual makes it much less certain, much less frightening. Also, referring to "heavy casualties" as a cover term, rather than elucidating with direct words like *the dead, the burned, the wounded*, or *radiation sickness* glosses over the true horror. The stress on the leaders' being destroyed is especially interesting. Nuclear bombs are not selective. Anyone around gets dead. By overtly citing "leaders" and "chain of command" but not actually mentioning enlisted persons or peers, the potential deaths of the ordinary soldiers are backgrounded. It is not so much that the manual lies; it just mentions part of the truth.

Sellman focused on two other terms: *fire for effect* and *engage the enemy*. The first is the command to the artillery to destroy an area with its explosives. Sellman points out that the emptiness of *for effect* matches that in the euphemism *do it*. He feels that this emptiness minimizes the personal involvement of the artillery observer who has to give the command. The second term also does not mean what it says. It means 'fight, shoot, kill.' It says "take part in an activity with the enemy." The soldier has no difficulty extrapolating the meaning, but the meaning is never explicitly given. The reason is simple. If the field manuals were explicit, if they directly reminded soldiers what they were training for, to kill and to be killed, getting soldiers on the battlefield could become more difficult.

Both of these terms illustrate a common factor in euphemism: **circumlocution**, which means spreading meaning over several words rather than using a single one. This weakens meaning and is one way to avoid confronting an unpleasant issue head-on. *Kill* is not only more semantically direct than *fire for effect*, it is more powerful because meaning is concentrated on one word. In the same way, *engage the enemy* is weaker than *fight*. A beautiful example of the semantic weakening by circumlocuting is the U. S. Army's statement of intent, "the management and application of controlled violence." In other words, *war*.

Sellman also examines the slang terms that soldiers use for death. He notes that these allow soldiers to discuss the unpleasant aspects of their job while still keeping their courage and morale up so that they can function as soldiers. The euphemisms for death are unusually explicit, but they keep soldiers at a remove from the true horror by denying the humanity of the corpse. For instance, *die* is "get iced" or "get waxed." Dead fish are usually put on ice, and mannequins are made of wax. "Dog tags" are really death tags, used to identify dead soldiers, but who would put them on if they were constantly being reminded of that? Sellman suggests that "[M]aking the dead seem inhuman allows the individual to say it can't happen to him. This is the attitude that the soldier must have in order to throw himself in front of bullets."

Euphemism is also accomplished by **understatement**, using words which have combined semantic features that do not add up to the meaning intended. Saying that children are "nutritionally deficient" when you mean 'starving' is an example. Sellman also gives one from soldier slang: *zap* rather than *kill*. *Zap* can also mean 'strike a blow' that is not fatal.

There are more overtly damning ways of doing propaganda as well. For instance, the November 6, 1987, edition of a South Florida newspaper, *The Sun-Sentinel*, featured a story with an accompanying picture of a hand-some, young, tall, slender rabbi wearing a prayer shawl who was leading a group in prayer. The headline read, "Rabbi planning to **peddle** Judaism over the airways" (boldface mine). The choice of the word *peddle* not only shows the author's contempt for Jews and their religion, but also gave the implication that the rabbi's religious program was for his personal material profit,[4] not for the spiritual well-being of listeners. Since the article also stressed that the rabbi didn't look like one because he was tall, young, and handsome, the negative message was doubly reinforced. This, too, is how to sway opinion and reinforce stereotypes by manipulating word choice.

Metaphor and Idiom

The preceding section claims that things people are uncomfortable with have many euphemistic names and phrases. These all mean roughly the same thing, although typically they do not mean quite what they say. **Metaphors** and **idioms** are very common as euphemisms, perhaps because they are the embodiment of circumlocution, of not calling a spade a spade.

A metaphor is a word used so that its central meaning cannot be taken. Rather, one must extend its meaning. For instance, *that old bag* in the right context means 'the old, unpleasant, unattractive woman.' The extension of *bag* to mean 'woman' is a metaphor.

Idioms are different from metaphors in that a mere extension of meaning of the words used will not give the intended meaning. Frequently, idioms consist of whole parts of sentences, typically a complete predicate. The meaning of the idiom is not garnered by an examination of its parts. Rather, the entire group of words has a meaning as if it were one word (Chafe 1968). For instance:

Idiom	*Literal Word*
put X's foot in X's mouth	blunder
shake a leg	hurry
pull X's leg	deceive
chew the fat	talk
shoot the breeze	talk
kick the bucket	die
roll in the hay	fornicate
shake the dew off the lily	urinate

Because the actual meaning of idioms is so removed from the meaning of the sum of their parts, idioms are the epitome of beautifully indirect reference. It follows, then, that one way to uncover the attitudes of a people is to examine their idioms and other euphemisms.

At the beginning of this chapter, it was mentioned that a culture has multiple terms denoting items or activities that are important to it. There is a difference between these multiple terms and euphemisms. In euphemism, all the terms mean the same thing. In contrast, multiple terms for culturally important referents all refer to slightly different aspects of the same activity, object, or concepts. Consider the synonyms of *talk*:

chatter, gab, prattle, gossip, jabber, nag, babble, clack, yakkety-yak, yada-yada-yada, jaw, jibber-jabber, B.S., shoot the breeze, shoot the shit

All of these refer to idle talk or ordinary sociable talking with no intellectual or business purpose. People who talk a lot are:

talkative, gabby, wordy, glib, bigmouthed, fatmouthed, full of hot air

or are:

gossips, nags, shrews, chatterboxes, windbags

Although there is no noun that specifically means 'a person who does not talk a great deal,' there are a number of adjectives to describe such a person:

quiet, laconic, reticent, taciturn, reserved, closemouthed

Recall how many words exist for idle talk. Just about all have the connotation of 'not desirable' and 'stupid.' Some, like *prattle, babble*, and *chatter*, also carry the connotation of 'childish' and 'feminine.' Besides the feminine *gossip* and *nag* with their connotations of 'nastiness' and 'triviality,' the only phrases for idle talk that do not carry bad overtones are those that refer to the casual speech of men, *chew the fat* and *shoot the breeze*. In other words, all words for talking which have semantic features of [-good, -important] also have one of [+female]. Likewise, the adjectives listed above denoting people who talk a lot are not only demeaning but feminine. From the semantic features on these words, it certainly seems that the speech of men is more valued in our society than that of women. Notice that there are few common words to describe someone who does not talk very much and those that do are somewhat literary. In contrast with the words for talking too much, none of these is exclusively feminine.

Two things bear special mention. Both *gossip* and *nag* are considered feminine activities (or types of women). However, men do both things and do them all the time. For instance, male "shop talk" is gossip. It involves talking about people who are not present and making judgments of their behavior or business tactics. What else is that except gossip? Since I have remodeled three old houses, I am very used to having crews of workmen around all day. Whether they be plumbers, carpenters, plasterers, painters, or electricians, they talk nonstop while they work. What do they talk about besides sports? And that often involves the private lives of athletes. They gossip about who's just bought an expensive car which he couldn't possibly afford, who's cheating on his wife, who's gambling, and so on. Such talk has been common no matter what crew I've hired and who's on it, just so long as they're male. As for nagging, certainly men harp on someone's behavior, ordering them or exhorting them to stop it, and they do so over long periods of time. Is this not nagging? I've heard men nag their wives about losing weight, not spending money, their poor cooking, and even their inept housecleaning. At least the women I know have the good grace not to do this publicly. The point is, if women do it, it is nagging. If men do it, it is not.

In any event, talking per se is not a highly valued activity in the general American culture. There is no term in English that is the equivalent of the Yiddish *shmuesen* 'social talking for the purpose of enjoying each other's company,' a word applied equally to adults of both sexes and which has very pleasant connotations.

GENDER AND LANGUAGE

The very fact that so many words for unpleasant talk have a semantic feature of [+female] on them tells us a good deal about how women are valued in this society. Gender is so pervasive and so important a part of society that when we find clear attitudinal differences in references to it, we are constrained to look into the matter. We cannot overlook the amount and quality of important research that has been done into these differences. Gender-biased language affects everyone, both males and females. Women and their treatment are an inextricable part of society. There is no way to investigate human and cultural behavior without considering women. Nor can we ignore attitudes toward men. When we examined speech activities in Chapter 6, virtually all of those discussed were male. The reason is simple. Studying speech and other social behavior has been largely a study of male activities. Yet, all-male-centered accounts of society are woefully incomplete and inaccurate. Speech about and by women is a superb example of how language behavior mirrors social attitudes and facts.

Attitudes toward women are clearly revealed in English vocabulary and confirmed by differences in male/female speaking practices. It is also confirmed by what is implied but never stated. By now, it seems that everyone has been made aware of the fact that *man* includes *woman*, and that *he* can refer to *she*, but the opposite can't occur. In Old English, the word for a male was *wer* and *man* meant 'human.' In time, the word for human, then, became the word for a male, but there was no corresponding change for *woman*, originally *wifmann*. Many people, even women, defend the practice of using *man* to stand for women nowadays because of its historical origin. However, that such usage makes women invisible can be shown by usages of other terms for human beings. Eckert and McConnell-Ginet (2003, 243–46) quote an anthropologist as saying something like:

When we woke in the morning, we found that the villagers had all left by canoe, leaving us alone with the women and children.

The women and children were also villagers. The insidious thing is that this implies that women (and children) are not full members of this human category, that of being villagers. Eckert and McConnell-Ginet also cite an NPR broadcast on January 14, 2000: "Over a hundred Muslim citizens were killed, and many women and children." This implies that Muslim citizens don't include women and children. In both instances, and these are hardly rare examples, males are taken as the default people, not females.

These authors add that it's not only male humans who are the default category of humans, but heterosexual males, as when a linguist urged:

> language as it is used in everyday life by members of the social
> order, that vehicle of communication in which they argue with
> their wives. (Eckert and McConnell-Ginet, 244)

So, "members of the social order" are gendered. They are heterosexual
males only. Women aren't part of the social order? Homosexuals aren't?
Hearing and reading this kind of gendered generics makes one unthinkingly think only of males as significant human beings. Think also of
phrases like "the settlers and their wives . . . " or "three Brazilians and a
woman. . . ." The context revealed the latter to be a Brazilian female.

It is not that women are never considered the gendered generic. I have
heard women say, "Back then, people stopped working when they got married." If one knows social history at all, one knows that men didn't stop
working when they got married. Only women did, and privileged ones at
that. Women of working and lower classes and many women of color
never had that option, so such a comment creates a generic that indicates
'only middle-class white women.'

The insidious thing about such usages is that it keeps those who aren't
part of the generic group of humanity below the consciousness of those
who are. Their concerns, their problems, their desires are very likely to be
ignored, as happened for centuries with African Americans, and, yes,
women, both those of the privileged classes and those who were not. One
wonders if the Holocaust would have happened had people not considered
only Christians as generic human beings. Would the United States have
closed its portals to Christians who were targets of genocide as they did to
European Jews? Language use is not a trivial matter. It impinges directly
on behavior.

Women's Talk

It has already been demonstrated that English vocabulary reflects a
disvaluing of talk for its own sake. Moreover, it was shown that most
words that mean 'idle talk' in SE are also marked [+female] and/or
[+trivial -good]. A person who is *gabby, talkative,* and *gossipy, a nag, a
shrew,* or *a chatterbox* must be a woman.

What are the male equivalents? There are none. A woman is a nag
when she asks for something too often. What is a man? Persistent. A man
who is aggressive and ambitious is aggressive and ambitious. He is also a
success. A woman who is aggressive and ambitious is a "power bitch." If
a woman bests a man in an argument, she is said to castrate him, or to be "a
castrating bitch." A man who bests another man or a woman is just being
forceful. A woman who complains or criticizes is a "shrew" or "bitch."

What are men called who do the same? There is no single word for it. Women gossip. But men? They "shoot the breeze," a far more pleasant and potent activity. Notice there is no favorable term for a woman who is strong, dominant, and intelligent. Such qualities earn women derogatory labels. Our language tells us that women are supposed to be submissive. This is as true in 2007 as it was when I first wrote this fourteen years ago.

An important difference between words marked [+female] and those marked [+male] is, in fact, potency. All the words that refer to women's talk mean 'talk that is inconsequential.' It is not talk of important, valuable issues, or indeed, of issues at all. The equation between women's talk and baby talk is seen in words like *babbling, chattering,* and *gabbing*, all essentially mindless, aimless, speech production. Furthermore, note who babbles: babies, women, the insane, and brooks.

Men may be glib, but this implies expertise in using language persuasively. Glibness does have a negative connotation, but it is still positive in that it denotes a speech trait leading to success and, unlike those ascribed to women, one applied to goals. I can refer to men as "bigmouthed" or "fatmouthed" although many of my students find even these apply to women. "Loudmouthed" seems to describe both genders. Words like these that do refer at least sometimes to men are more potent than those reserved exclusively to women. Someone who is "full of hot air" is not a quiet, retiring type; hence, men may also be so described.

The term *eloquent* is one of the rare ones in SE for one who talks both well and at length. Ostensibly, both men and women can be eloquent, but the *Oxford English Dictionary* (OED) gives as examples of usage recorded over the centuries (hence the unusual spelling and capitalization):

1. Eloquent speakers are enclined to Ambition.
2. Her dark eyes—how eloquent.

And the quality of being eloquent is illustrated by:

3. His eloquence was irresistibly impressive.
4. Her tears were her only eloquence.
5. A Scantling of Jack's great eloquence.

When the female is specified, it is only tears and eyes that give eloquence, not her speech. Under the entry for *nagging*, only feminine nouns and pronouns are given as examples.

To complete the picture, the words for male idle talk are all idioms with at least one word that indicates [+power,+activity]: *bullshit, shoot the breeze, chew the fat.* Not one word for idle trivial talk in English refers exclusively to men, although several refer exclusively to females—and babies, fools, and the mentally ill. Words for idle talk that are masculine at all are marked for potency and activity. Those that are exclusively feminine have no sense of potency or activity. Clearly, not only is the mainstream attitude toward talk revealed by vocabulary but also very different cultural attitudes toward the talk of men and women.

Our Lopsided Language. This lopsidedness when referring to males as opposed to females pervades the entire vocabulary. In what has since become a widely known and quoted book, Robin Lakoff (1975) pointed out that words that were once ostensibly equivalent terms for males and females have often diverged in meaning over time. Consider the following, for instance:

Master/Mistress

These were once counterparts of each other, as shown in the children's rhyme, "Mistress Mary, quite contrary, how does your garden grow?" The modern *Mrs.* was originally an abbreviation of *Mistress*, although today they can seldom, if ever, be interchanged. It should be noted, however, that originally a woman could become a mistress only by marrying a master, but a man was born a master. Rare survivals of the original meaning of *mistress* do occur, as in:

1. The walls are full of pictures of famous people, all of them autographed to the mistress of the house, former movie star Shirley Temple Black. (DuBois and Crouch 1975)

Note that this quotation expands on the word *mistress* so that the wrong meaning is not derived. Moreover, the mistress here is that paragon of sweetness and virtue, Shirley Temple. Therefore, the older, nonsexual meaning of *mistress* is forced. The first meaning of *mistress* today—that is, the more common usage—is 'woman kept by a man for sexual purposes.' One can't say "She is a mistress of her trade" as one can say "He is a master of his trade" unless one means she is a prostitute. It is probably not without significance that the surviving pronunciation for the abbreviated spelling, *Mrs.*, hides the original derivation from *mistress*.

Sir/Madam

The same fate has befallen *madam*: it too has taken on a sexual meaning. Its older use as a form of address signifying respect does survive, at least in impersonal situations, as when sales clerks address female customers. Even here, it is usually replaced by its short form, *ma'am*. Despite its survival as a politeness marker, "May I help you ma'am?" its primary meaning is 'keeper and procurer of women for men to use for sexual purposes.' In other words a madam is a mistress of a house of ill repute.

Some might object that, after all, *madam* and *ma'am* still do survive as polite forms beside *sir*, and ask what difference it makes that *madam* has also taken on another sexual meaning. The difference is that, over time, terms for females in authority have taken on sexual meanings, but those for men have remained the same. Worse, these terms originally denoting high female position have been demeaned to refer to women with the least admirable feminine sexual behavior. The lofty *mistress* and *madam* have been lowered to provide elevated terms for those held in contempt: whores and procurers. A mistress is one better than the prostitute on the streets or in the houses that are not homes, but still, she is a whore. The madam? Well, we do not call a pimp a "sir." Elevated terms for men do not suffer such a fate.

King/Queen

This is also evident in the words for the highest ranking of all in the English-speaking world. A *king* is either a crowned head or a top dog. A woman may be the former and, in her home, the latter. Elsewhere, if she acts like a queen, she is likely to be considered a bitch rather than a top dog.

But *queen* has two other meanings as well, both unfavorable, both sexual. The first, most common today, at least in the United States, is 'male homosexual who acts like a woman.' A female homosexual who acts like a man is not called a king, however. Rather, she becomes a "butch," an older nickname for a tough, lower-class boy. An outcast male who acts like woman is called a queen, the highest ranking for a woman. A woman who acts like a man becomes a lower-class boy, not even a man, much less a king.

The second use of *queen*, occasionally still found among older working-class men in Eastern New England[5] is for the woman other than his wife with whom he has regular sexual relations. This may come from older *quean*, as the <ea> used to be pronounced differently from <ee>. The *Oxford English Dictionary*'s definition of *quean* tells it all:

A woman, a female, **hence** in disparagement: a bold or ill-behaved woman; a jade; a harlot, strumpet (es. 16–17 c.)

The notation in parentheses means that this usage was most common in the sixteenth and seventeenth centuries. In this definition, note especially the logical connector *hence*. It follows for the writers of that venerable dictionary that a woman who is bold is sexually promiscuous. It also seemed to follow for them that a term for a woman would be demeaned as a matter of course.

The latter sense of *quean* eventually won out, so when *quean* began to be pronounced just like *queen* (just as *meat* came to sound like *meet*) then *quean* pretty much died out. Some historians of the language think that this is because of its scurrilous meaning, which conflicted with the fact that England does have a queen. In context, *queen* as a homosexual male causes no confusion.

Another derogatory usage of *queen* is seen in the putdown *drama queen*, as in "Oh, she is such a drama queen." I know of no parallels with *king*.

Gentleman/Lady

This pair shows a curious disparity. *Gentleman* seems to be dying out. It survives in the stock salutation "Ladies and gentlemen." In a fancy restaurant or store one might hear, "This gentleman wishes to order." And once in a while one sees it on restroom doors. It has been replaced for the most part by *men's* as a designation for clothing departments, stores, and toilets. If not used as gender specification, its meaning seems limited today to 'very polite and honorable,' as in "He's a real gentleman."

The feminine counterpart, "She's a real lady" also survives. Beyond that, some strange things have happened to *lady*. Robin Lakoff (1975) pointed out that, unlike the many terms for females that have taken on a sexual connotation, *lady* can connote sexlessness. It also connotes triviality. She gives as examples:

2a. She's my woman, so don't mess with her.
2b. *She's my lady, so don't mess with her.[6]

A perhaps more telling contrast is:

3a. Girl, you're a woman now.
3b. *Girl, you're a lady now.

The first instance refers to the girl's being sexually mature now. The second, if said at all, simply implies that she is now polite.

The song from the movie *Saturday Night Fever*, "She's More than a Woman to Me," also shows that *woman* in and of itself implies sexuality. The force of Bob Dylan's song "Lay, Lady, Lay" ("upon my big brass bed") is that ladies are not usually objects of seduction. *Lady* seems to have become a desexed term for *woman*. This, in itself, is noteworthy.

Why do we need such a word for women? There isn't one for men. If *gentleman* ever was a candidate, it certainly is not now, as its usage is becoming more and more restricted.

The expression *lady of the evening* shows that *lady* did start on the path of sexual derogation. Also, the term *foxy lady* indicates a sexually attractive young woman. In Providence, there is a club for "exotic dancers" by that name. However, these are the exceptions to the notion of *lady* as a polite female who is not a sex object. Such a notion is necessary only in a social milieu in which women are primarily evaluated and valued for their sexual function.

Lady has had yet another fate. At the time of her writing, Lakoff pointed out that it was used in trivial contexts. It was "Women's Strike for Peace," but "Ladies' Garden and Browning Society." There is a "National Organization for Women," but what would you think of the "National Organization for Ladies"? Similarly, one doesn't usually speak of a "capable lady." That adjective is paired with *woman*, "capable woman." Several years ago a great-uncle of mine was complimenting me on my three sons, and admonished me, "Now don't go joining that ladies' lib." His choice of words gave me his opinion of it.

A third thing has happened to *lady*, this not at all unexpected in light of other once-elevated female terms. Women who clean houses as their jobs are called *cleaning ladies*, not *cleaning women*. Similarly, sales personnel are *salesladies*.

Although *lady* is still elevated, or at least genteel, in some contexts, it is insulting if used as an address form without a name. *Lady* followed by either first or last name is still an honorable title in England, as in "Lady Margaret" or "Lady Grey." However, "Look, lady" is a rude put-down. In contrast, "Look, sir," its counterpart, is very polite, even in anger. Its other counterpart, "*Look, lord," is not even said. Note also that the rude, equalizing "Hey!" does not co-occur with *sir*, although it does with *lady*, as in "Hey, lady, you dropped your wallet!" There is no equivalent "*Hey, sir, you dropped your wallet." However, men may be rudely addressed, as in "Hey mister. . . . "

Meier (1999) presents a change in progress in current usage of *lady*. Except for *cleaning lady*, she found that *woman* is the preferred term for females, and, as a designation for an occupation, *woman* is preferred in general usage. Yet, among the younger age groups that she surveyed, "associations of *lady* with decorum and conformity may be shifting to associations with spirit, with energy, with 'living on the edge' (67), and cites examples like *gutsy lady* and "Katherine Hepburn is one terrific lady." She cites a woman in her twenties as saying *lady* "conjures up an image of 'an intelligent woman of the '90's'" (61). This was in response to a survey done in the 1990's, but such usage isn't necessarily dead.

CHAPTER 10

Perhaps because, so often, strong, ambitious women have been termed as *bitches* or *tough cookies*, the need to name intelligent, spirited women in business, sports, and the professions has lead to an elevation of *lady* as an admirable label. I have recently heard women referred to as *one amazing lady* and *a real smart lady*. *Lady* is a good candidate for such usage because, unlike other terms for women, it never descended into being primarily a derogatory sexual term for women. "She's a real lady" always implied politeness, gentility, and propriety.

My own female students are about evenly divided about using *lady* to indicate a woman. One, for instance, said she finds *lady* in this context insulting because it implies that a lady isn't usually smart. Yet, she sees no disparity in calling a woman smart. It must be that, for her, the idea of a lady being weak takes precedence.

Almost unanimously, my female students dislike the practice of calling a woman's athletic team at our school *The Lady Friars*, although there have been ads for athletic shoes which refer to ladies and Meier says that:

> in speaking to one's athletic peers, however, "Hey Ladies" may sound 'sportier' than "Hey Women." Why this differential usage is found . . . may relate to two senses of *lady*: a sense of spirited determination, of feistiness, as well as an expression of solidarity. . . . (Meier, 61)

Whatever the outcome of this issue is, one thing is certain. As the position of women in society changes, so will the terminology referring to them.

None of this should be taken to mean that there are no derogatory terms for men. There certainly are. Deborah James (1998) found 343 male-referential derogatory terms, but only 206 female-referential ones. She made an extensive survey of such words, asking respondents which were male, which female, and which both. Interestingly, most derogatory words turned out to be gender-linked. Few are used equally of men and women.

However, upon reading her lists, I noted that my observations in Chaika (1994) still hold. The male terms are composed of words completely different from the titles used to signify respect for men. Terms for degraded men aren't degradations of elevated terms. Rather, they are completely different: *bum, thief, pimp, jerk, dope, drip, nerd, shlemiel*. Terms which we use to address men rudely are not debased versions of higher titles, either: *mac, bud, fellah,* and so on. Do *king, gentleman, lord,* or *sir* ever mean 'pimp' or 'stud' or 'cheat' or 'forger'? Yet, sirs, kings, lords, and supposed gentlemen can be all of those things as well.

Perhaps the most derogatory words for men are calling them women or homosexuals: *pussy, douchebag, fag, queer, girl, sissy* (derived from *sister*). To be a woman, or to be womanlike, apparently, even in this day and age is demeaning.

Derogatory words for men historically do not center on their sexual activity. Rather, they are terms indicating social ineptness. However, females now call some indiscriminately sexually active men *sluts*, and *dog* can mean a sexually nondiscriminating man, but, in AAVE, it also means 'male friend.' If a woman is a dog, however, she is so ugly that no man wants to have sex with her. There are terms for men whose sexual activity is disgusting and out-of-bounds, like *creep, lecher, womanizer,* and *sex freak*. James (1998) also lists *sleazeball* in this category, but my students classify this as more generally dishonest and unethical.

There is a clear disparity in terms for sexually active females and males. Those for men are admiring: *stud, player, Romeo, Don Juan*. Those for women are derogatory: *slut, whore, skank, skag, hootchie, tart, twat, piece of ass*.

There is also a curious disparity in equivalent terms for males and females. If he's easy, he's good-natured. If she's easy, she'll have sex with any man. If he's loose, he's relaxed. If she's loose, she'll have sex with any man. If he's a tramp, he's homeless. If she's a tramp, she'll have sex with any man. If she's a princess, she's a spoiled, nasty woman. If he's a prince, he's a wonderful guy.

There have been some changes in this sort of disparity. When I was growing up, "She's a professional" meant 'she's a whore," but "He's a professional" meant he was a professor, a doctor, or a lawyer. Now a female professional, like a male one, is a professor, a doctor, or a lawyer, but the expression "the oldest profession in the world" still refers to prostitution.

Note, most of the derogatory words for women refer to supposed excessive sexual activity, which is wrong for a woman, but admirable for a man. Few of the derogatory terms for women refer to their social ineptness as those for men do, although, as we shall see, there are terms for stupid women. Deborah James (1998, 403) says this is because "it is natural or inevitable that women should be weak in character compared to men." It also implies that a woman's main virtue is to be sexually selective, but that a man's virtue lies in his social competence.

Terms for women also indicate their stupidity, but many of these also refer to sexuality, such as *bimbo, barbie, dumb bunny*. Others just imply a very confused person who barely knows what time it is, like *ditz, ding-a-ling, fluff, bubblebrain, airhead,* and *space-cadet*. Terms for a stupid male like *dork, butt-head, boner, doofus,* and *shit-for-brains* seem to be semantically stronger than those for women. That is, the male terms go beyond someone who is just not with it.

James (402) also notes derogatory terms for females who don't buckle under to male authority: *ballbuster, battleaxe, bitch, biter, cunt, cow, shrew, tit, twat, witch*, among others. Interestingly, men who mistreat others are called such things as: *asshole, bastard, crook, dick, dickhead, jerk, motherfucker, prick, shithead, slimeball, scumbag*. None of these, of course, refer specifically to males who don't try to please females. Indeed, a man who does try to is called *pussywhipped* or *henpecked*, highly derisive terms.

The picture is clear. It is the duty of women to be sexually pleasing to men and to cater to them, but men who show the same consideration to women are objects of scorn. Some derogatory terms for males can be used admiringly, such as *bastard* or *motherfucker*. Derogatory terms for females usually can't. One exception is that younger females have co-opted the term *bitch*, as in *I'm his bitch, the bitch seat* (of a car). This is similar to African Americans addressing each other as "niggah" or homosexuals referring to themselves as "queers." Oppressed groups may neutralize derogatory reference terms by using them for themselves, even while decrying them when used by outsiders.

The persistence of multiple words which evaluate a woman's sexual attractiveness is also telling, words which aren't necessarily intended to be derogatory, such as *broad, piece, chick, filly, bird, fox, tigress, baby, poontang, sweet thang, ho, wench, honey* (as in "she's a fine honey"), *hottie, hoochie mama, hooch, babe*.[7] In old movies, we hear women being called *dish, tomato*, and *dame* (another originally elevated term), among other terms. There are also words which designate females who are not sexually attractive or who do not care to make themselves so, such as *prude, prune, beast, urchin, old bag, hag, busted, butterface*d, and *dog*.

Murnen (2000, 321) investigated whether men used more degrading terms for genitalia, especially female genitalia, and more aggressive words to indicate copulation than women do. She created lists of words for having sex, with violent terms being *ramming, banging, fucking*, and *screwing* and nonviolent ones like *making love, doing it, doing the nasty (dirty), boinking, getting it on*, or *hooking up*. She also used lists of degrading and nondegrading terms for genitalia for both sexes. Degrading terms for female genitalia included *pussy, cunt, snatch, twat*, and *gash* rather than less degrading terms like *vagina, down there, privates, clitoris, crotch, hairpie, muff, bush, hootchie*, and *inside*. Degrading terms for male genitalia were *prick, cock, meat*, which contrasted with *penis, dick, balls, privates, crotch, package, johnson, adam jr., down there*, and *thing* as nondegrading.

Both genders, 79 men and 88 women, were asked to indicate in writing which term they would use when speaking to different audiences. Men were more likely to report using aggressive terms to refer to copulation and use degrading terms for genitalia. This was especially pronounced among fraternity brothers, who presumably interact in all-male environments a great deal (322). It seems to me that this may be because men are encouraged to be more macho in all-male contexts, to exaggerate their masculinity.

The second part of Murnen's study had males and females judge if it was more acceptable for men to use degrading sexual language than women. She based this on the prediction that men would be "permitted" (her quotes) to use degrading sexual language more than women are. This is to be expected if performance expectations shape behavior. That is, if men are supposed to be tough, then they will act tough, and, presumably, will not be downgraded for doing so. Also, since men presumably have more power, they can display it by using more degrading and violent terms. Murnen also predicted that women who used more aggressive and degrading language would be downgraded more than men because they are weaker and not supposed to be threatening.

Murnen had subjects listen to audiotapes concerning two friends of the same gender who are having a conversation about "the night before" (323). What she found was that generally participants did not evaluate anybody favorably who used sexually degrading language. They were judged as less moral, less likable, and more aggressive. Women who used more aggressive language were judged the most aggressive, especially by other women. So, although men use such language more than women, they are not rated more favorably when they do it, contrary to Murnen's prediction.

What was a troubling finding is that the person described by the degrading language was also judged as less likable and less intelligent (326). What disturbs me is that, given that women are the ones most likely to be described this way regardless of their own morals or language use, this means that men have it in their means to degrade women simply by using degrading language about them. That is one way of keeping women in their place, and again it shows that language usage is not trivial. It has consequences. We will see this again in the situation of an infamous rape case.

The multiplicity of terms to denote the sexual attractiveness of women attests to the importance of sex as an evaluating feature of females. The early feminist cry that women were just sex objects seemed extreme, even laughable, when it was first stated. However, examination of the language for women, even today, does support such a claim, although, hopefully, more men have learned to regard women as full, intelligent human beings since the 1960's.

The language is curiously sparse when it comes to terms which denote sexual attractiveness for men, however. Apparently, a female's sexual attractiveness is still so important it merits a wide vocabulary, but a male's isn't. Oh, we can call him *handsome*, maybe even *pretty*, certainly *good-looking* and *attractive*, but we can use these terms for women, and, for them, we have all the others.

As further proof that this analysis of our vocabulary is on target, consider the sentences:

4. You know what SHE needs.
5. She needs a good you-know-what!

This last was once said to me by a Roman Catholic male professor about a nun! Everybody knows by such omissions that what the female "needs" is sex from a male. Notice these are empty sentences, equivalent to the empty phrases *do it* to refer to the sexual act, *go* for bathroom functions, or *fire for effect* for 'kill.' Both (4) and (5) above are empty in that the *she* in both might actually need anything from the universe of needs, but the answer to both is always 'sex.'

Institutionalizing Gender Bias. The very grammar of a language can attest to the sexism in language. Just as the generics noted above deny females personhood, so does grammar. Anne Bodine (1975) provides what is undoubtedly the clearest example of this view: the rules for pronoun agreement with indefinite pronouns such as *everyone* and *anybody*. Because English shows no gender marking in the plural, speakers and writers for literally centuries have used plural pronouns and verbs to refer to those indefinites:

Will **everyone** who wants pizza raise **their** hands?
Does **anybody** want **their** coffee black?

The purists are correct that, semantically, the *their* doesn't agree in number with *everyone* and *anybody*, but to use *his* instead doesn't agree in gender. The indefinite pronouns are not gender marked, so *his* is wrong in referring to them. Therefore, either solution, using a plural sex-indefinite pronoun like *their* or a singular masculine pronoun like *his*, is off by one feature. Why, then, has the solution been to make the agreeing pronoun one that is wrong in gender, rather than allowing the correctly gender-marked choice that happens to be wrong in number? Historically, *their* was always used to refer to indefinite pronouns. Author Henry Fielding wrote in *Tom Jones*, "Everybody were in their beds." Bodine shows that males in the British Parliament decreed the use of *his*, as they felt that the female is subsumed under the male.

British Parliament? British Parliament actually concerned itself with a matter of gender, one that would codify inequality of men and women? A history of scholarship, as well as of laws, shows that codification of social inequality has long been a prime mover of both scholarly and legal explanations. Truth is never pure and it is never simple, in scholarship or elsewhere. As Gilbert and Mulkay (1984) have so convincingly shown, the findings in even so apparently a value-free and objective area as biochemistry are slanted according to the views of the researchers.

Baron (1986) devotes considerable time to truly hilarious etymologies of words for women offered by reputable scholars, including such venerable names as Jespersen and Skeat. The latter, for instance, whose *Etymological History of the English Language* was long a classic, actually tried to prove that *wife* comes from *wib*,[8] 'tremble,' and Partridge as late as 1959 said that the German word for a woman thus means 'the vibrator' or 'the veiled one.' One scholar, Roger Westcott, actually decided that *wife* must come from a hypothetical Indo-European form *wey* which had seven different meanings: 'turn, twist' (wife as a weaver, hip-swiveler, fickle person); 'drip, flow' (menstruator); 'grow, sprout, gestator'; 'magic, sorcery' (witch); 'fault, defect' (weaker sex); 'strong, vigorous' (person of stamina); and 'wither, wrinkle' (one who both blooms and ages rapidly).

Reconstruction of words from proto-languages is an exacting science, and there is no way that *wey* in Indo-European could have become *wife* in English. In fact, the *Oxford English Dictionary*, which relies upon the most careful reconstructions of etymologies, says *wife* simply first meant 'woman' in the Germanic languages, not Indo-European. It may have come from the same root as *weave*. The first written usage of it in Old English was in 725, where it was used to translate Latin *femina* 'woman.'

Aside from the improbability of any one Indo-European root developing into so many contrary words in one language, one wonders why Westcott didn't see words like *wise* and *wonderful* as deriving from the hypothetical *wey*. Moreover, for Westcott or any other scholar to derive an origin from Indo-European[9] or any other ancient source, they would have to show regular sound changes that occurred in all words with the given sounds from their origin to today. Words do not change willy-nilly into other words. That is, such scholars would have to show that there was a word *wey* which miraculously grew sounds to produce *witch* and *wib*, and also somehow turned into all of the other words they claim. They would also have to show that English and other Germanic languages have words meaning 'drip, flow, strong, fickle, grow, sprout, magic, fault,' etc. and that these words today can be traced logically to an older *wey*.

Furthermore, they would have to show that some other Indo-European languages, such as the Slavic group, Hindi, or Celtic also had such a

CHAPTER 10

strange potpourri of words traceable to one root. These principles of reconstruction were well-known to scholars like Skeat and Westcott. Only when it came to figuring out the origin of *wife* did they seem to forget how to do so validly. Principles of reconstruction are the stuff of first-year linguistics. Strangely, etymologists have been far less fanciful as to the origins of *man*, and, where they have speculated, it is to suggest that *man* is derived from words meaning *mind* or *hand*. Thus scholarship itself through the ages has been in the service of keeping women in their place.

Even such a scientific endeavor as tracing the history of a language can be skewed to create and maintain superiority. The word *marry*, for instance, does come from Indo-European **mer* or **mor*, which clearly meant either sex, and which appears through the several Indo-European languages as a variety of words meaning 'young man' or 'young woman' (Baron 45). *Marry* came into English through French around 1325, and then, as since, it referred to both men and women. As we shall see, in Portuguese and Spanish, the same root did become specialized for men only, but in the sense of 'husband.' In any event, many commentators, all male, long after the fact, have tried to redefine *marry* so that it makes the woman a passive object and the man the agent. As one man said:

> Properly speaking, a man is not married to a woman . . . nor are a man and a woman married with each other. The woman is married to the man . . . we do not speak of tying a ship to a boat, but a boat to a ship. And so long as man is the larger, the stronger, the more individually important, . . . it is the woman who is married to the man." (quoted in Baron, 46)

As recently as 1973, the respected scholar Beveniste said that men do the marrying and women are just the objects of marriage. This, despite the fact that English has allowed both female and male subjects of *marry* since 1325. "Jane married" has been as grammatical as "John married" since then.

The Impact of Language

English is not the only language to suffer from sexism. Portuguese shows the same disparities. The most insidious thing about a sexist lexico-semantic system is that the attitudes are learned without anyone's ever teaching them overtly (Chaika 1984). This doesn't mean they can't be changed. They can. It's just that most people in the culture never notice the bias. If we examine Portuguese words for women and men, we find a situation much like in English, if not even more so. One is inevitably reminded of Fairclough's assertion that power is wielded by language because we respond to it subconsciously.

My informants, Dr. Gilbert Cavaco, Mr. Jose Antonio DaAscensao Battista and Ms. Maria Guerreiro, represent mainland, Island, and Brazilian Portuguese, respectively.

Since Portuguese still has gender marking on nouns and adjectives, it is especially easy to see disparities in words for men and women. The same lexical item takes on different connotations just by using the feminine -*a* instead of the masculine -*o*:

Feminine	Masculine
fodilhona 'wanton woman'	*fodilhão* 'stud'
porca 'slut'[10]	*porco* 'slob'
puta 'whore'	*puto* 'endearment for one's homosexual lover'
rapariga 'whore'	*rapaz* 'boy'
rainha 'snob, know-it-all, not chaste'	*rei* 'king'

Note the disparity in phrases as well; *ficar para titia* literally 'become an aunt' means 'old maid.' If a man becomes an uncle, his sibling had a baby. *Ela é feia mas é boa* is 'she's ugly but she is good in bed anyhow.' There's no masculine counterpart to this, either. A male's ugliness has no direct parallel to bedroom behavior. Mr. Battista told me that a man is desirable just because he is a man. His looks don't matter. It seems doubtful that this is so in practice, but that is the cultural attitude.

It gets worse. One male consultant told me that when he visited his mother in Portugal and asked her about his old friends, she commented about women only on their marital status and sexual behavior. She never mentioned male sexual behavior. Of women, she'd say *vergonhada* 'she has no shame.' *Shame* here refers only to sexual shame. There is no masculine counterpart.

Ela é boa means 'she is good,' which, naturally, can mean she's good you know where, but the masculine for this only means 'he's a good person.' As in English, only women gossip *fofogueira*. Rarely, if ever is a man *fofoqueiro*. Rather he is said to *bater papo* 'shoot the breeze.' In Brazil, a *chata* is a nag. *Chato*? He is a boor, so men don't nag although they can be rude.

An entry in a mainland Portuguese dictionary lists *sabio* as meaning 'wise man.' However, no feminine counterpart is given. The best a woman can be is *sabichona* 'a woman who presumes [dictionary's word] to know a lot.' This is closer to *sabichão*, 'he is crafty.' As in English, a woman who is smart is uppity. The gender disparity is evinced even further in *pensa em si misma* 'she thinks a lot of herself, is too aggressive.' But if he thinks a lot of himself, it means he is genuinely powerful.

Even in the matter of the respectably married, we see a disparity. The title *senhora* 'Mrs.' is as polite as *senhor* 'Mr.' but matters go swiftly downhill from there. A man refers to *minha mulher,* literally 'my woman: the woman I'm sleeping with or my wife.' A women does not refer to her husband as *meu homen 'my man.' She calls him *meu esposo* 'my spouse' or *meu marito* 'my husband.' A feminine version of the polite *marito* doesn't even exist.

This situation is paralleled in Spanish, in which *mujer* means either 'woman,' 'prostitute,' or 'my wife,' but *hombre* 'man' doesn't mean 'husband.' *Marido* does, and there is no feminine counterpart, although *esposa* can be used in formal situations. What is surprising in Spanish is that the generic term for 'woman,' *mujer*, also can mean 'prostitute,' despite the fact that it can occur with words meaning 'judge' or 'doctor' to indicate a woman in those roles.

What difference do such sexist vocabularies make? In southeastern New England with its large population of Portuguese speakers, several years ago a young woman having a beer alone in a bar was gang-raped by some Portuguese-American men. When they were arrested and indicted, surprisingly, the Portuguese population not only protested but actually held a march and candlelight vigil in support of the men. Why? Because the assumption was that if a woman was sitting alone in a bar, she was "asking for it." Therefore, the men shouldn't have been charged with a crime. There was no testimony showing that she was at all suggestive to the men, much less that she "asked for" anything. It seems not to have occurred to these people that she might have been sitting in a bar for reasons other than to be abused sexually, just as there are other reasons for men to be there.

Clearly, the cultural assumptions embodied in the language were enough for Portuguese-Americans to condone her rape. Both women and men participated in the demonstrations. It must be emphasized that this population is hard-working, decent, and religious. They are not wanton or considered tough or criminal. In discussing this event with my Language, Thought and Culture class, one of the students, the son of Portuguese immigrants, asked his father about it. In 2006, his father replied with words to the effect that she was, after all, a loose woman. The attitudes revealed in language use apparently haven't changed since the early 1980's.

Conversational Behavior of Men and Women

It is not enough to look at words. Do other conversational practices show an imbalance of power between the sexes? Some scholars are convinced that gender differences in talking are so pronounced that males and females can't even understand each other. Indeed, Deborah Tannen entitled one of her books *You Just Don't Understand*! This prompted women to assure me that men and women actually speak different languages. After all, respected researchers like Maltz and Borker (1982) had already claimed that males and females in the United States are products of different cultures, and Tannen seconded this conclusion.

Certainly, there may well be differences in how females and males carry out their roles via speaking practices, but does this mean there are separate male and female cultures? There are many possible roles in a complex, industrialized culture of millions of people, and each of them has some correlation with certain speaking practices. To say, then, that every difference in role behavior is an indication of cultural difference negates the meaning of culture. People learn to speak according to the roles they play within a given culture.

Female and male speaking practices may conflict at times. Women and men may well expect or want different kinds of conversation from the opposite gender, but this doesn't mean they don't understand each other. Anecdotal evidence of particular instances of misunderstanding may be fun to read about, but they don't prove that, in the larger scheme of things, males and females don't understand what the other is saying. Often, what the anecdotes really show is that they understand each other all too well, but don't wish to comply with the other one's wishes. When Freud famously asked, "What do women want?" (if he really did ask that), it is most likely that he knew very well what they wanted. He didn't want to be bothered talking to them, didn't respect what they had to say, or didn't care to be bound by their words. Wives often well understand that their husband's refusal to listen to their opinions stems from a disvaluing of what they have to say.

The man who tunes out his wife's discussion of the color of new drapes understands her all too well. However, our culture tells him he's not supposed to be interested in such things, so he refuses to attend to them, or to expand on her utterances. He may also understand very well that her discussion means she wants to buy those new drapes and he wants the money spent on a new widescreen TV before the Super Bowl game.

These are stereotypes, to be sure, but they are likely scenarios. Moreover, I am not presenting such an exchange as scientific evidence, only as hypothetically what is really going on when men and women don't seem to understand each other. The question now is, how much does other language behavior fit with the social image of women portrayed in English vocabulary?

CHAPTER 10

Women's Speech is Weak. Robin Lakoff (1975) asserted that women speak weakly and ineffectually. Without grounding her examples in systematic observations, she claimed that women use weak words like *charming* and *lovely*. They don't use swear words, substituting *fudge* and *shoot* for them. They further weaken their assertions by hedging, prefacing opinions with phrases like "This may sound silly, but . . ." or using modals like *should* before verbs, or adding adverbs like *maybe* and *perhaps*. She also claimed that women further weaken their assertions by using intensifiers like *so* or *awfully* before descriptors, as in "so-o nice." Perhaps most famously, she claimed that women unnecessarily use tags at the ends of statements, as in "Tastes good, doesn't it?" or "This is a nice car, isn't it?" She claimed that the combination of such behaviors prevents them from being taken seriously.

When I first read this, I was amazed that I had never noticed such hesitancy in women's speech, and even when it was pointed out, I heard little of it from my mother, my friends, or my colleagues. It has since occurred to me that I was raised in a working-class neighborhood with virtually no stay-at-home mothers, and as a teen, worked in a jewelry factory with many women. They certainly spoke directly and forcefully. I can hear their blunt assertions about life in my mind to this day. Also, I grew up in a neighborhood with a large population of African Americans, and those women didn't talk like shrinking violets, either. Recall Mitchell-Kernan's encounter in the park in Chapter 6. So, Lakoff's observations, if valid, were not necessarily valid for all classes or races of women in this country.

It also may be that women in different regions of the country speak differently. Many men have commented to me that a female southern accent is very appealing. When pressed, they mention its softness, the suggestion that the woman wants to please the man. Perhaps housewives from the Heartland spoke—or speak—less forcefully than East Coast women, for instance. I suspect, however, that the degree of weakness of a woman's speech is correlated with the degree of her economic dependence upon men. The notion of a woman's having to make a decision to work outside the home is pertinent only to middle- and upper middle-class women. Women from the working class traditionally had no such choice.

Researchers, stimulated by Lakoff's remarks, systematically investigated them and found that the feminine patterns Lakoff delineated are characteristic also of children and of men in subordinate positions (Crosby and Nyquist 1977; O'Barr 1982). Those of inferior status speak in certain ways. Such studies actually validated Lakoff's observations, for, insofar as they were valid, they were proof that women were socially inferior to men.

Reams of subsequent research have been inspired by Lakoff's assertions, some of it confirming, some disconfirming, and some, the most interesting to me, admitting she was right, but for the wrong reasons. Janet Holmes (1995) reinterpreted the very features Lakoff judged as weakness, showing that they were indicative of positive traits. In sum, Holmes saw female speech as cooperative, facilitative, and polite. In contrast, she characterized male speech as competitive, aggressive, and argumentative. This doesn't mean that women cannot express or exercise power by their speech. To the contrary, often a woman's cooperative, facilitative approach allows others to follow her suggestions, all the while mitigating the possibility of conflict and hard feelings, both very disruptive in attaining goals.

Eckert and McConnell-Ginet (167–73) point out that tags, which Lakoff specifically cited as being a sign of insecurity, are actually multifunctional. Those lower in the hierarchy use them to seek reassurance, but those higher use them to sum things up and even end the discussion (171). Overall, research has shown that women utter tags to be facilitative or mitigating, but men are more likely to use them to seek confirmation.

Tags also can be used as a way of opening the floor to other opinions. Eckert and McConnell-Ginet use an example of a question like, "The September 11th attacks . . . were frightening, weren't they?" They interpret this as initiating discussion of the war or suicide bombings rather than as a request for confirmation of the obvious. They also say that a tag not only invites another into an exchange, it also makes it difficult for the other not to respond, so that they actually can coerce. Tags can also be used to soften a remark so that it doesn't sound like an accusation, as in, "You weren't there last week, were you?"

Another signal of weakness is the use of hedges. Eakins and Eakins (1978) found that at academic meetings or conferences, there was a tendency for women to use more hedges or disclaimers than men, although they did not collect a significant number of such hedges in their sample. But, they were investigating academic women who are used to competing with men intellectually. Considering this, the fact that they found even a trend might be significant. Even these women preceded statements with disclaimers like, "I know this sounds silly but . . . ," "This may strike you as odd . . . ," "You're going to think this is stupid, but . . . ," and "Well, I'm not the expert, but. . . . "

Such data certainly support Lakoff's premise that women's speech habits weaken their assertions. However, I have found that male students, when called upon in class, are as likely to hedge this way as female ones are. I have asked students to count the gender of hedge-makers in their other classes, and they consistently find that, although women hedge more than men, the difference is slight.[11] This is an area that requires more careful observation of men and women in different situations. It would be interesting to find out if males who have female superiors hedge more than males who don't. Hedging may just be an artifact of one's place in a hierarchy, not of gender itself. If so, when Lakoff was writing, she may have been correct that women hedged more than men, but, as women have more and more assumed higher ranking in business and the professions, this may have changed.

Swearing. At the time of her writing, Lakoff was certainly correct that women didn't use swear words as frequently as men, if ever, and this seems to have been true of women who used otherwise forceful speech. All sources I have found agree on this, and, in my experience, certainly such words were never used by women, or, for that matter, in a woman's hearing by men until the 1970's. Once, while I was working in a store in an African American neighborhood, a man came in and, not seeing me, made a joke using the word *fucking*. As I stood up, he became very embarrassed and apologetic and left without making his purchase. That was in 1960.

As we saw in Chapter 6, African American men regularly used such words among themselves long before it became current among middle-class white men. So taboo were such words that one is hard put to find studies of their usage, for instance, even during World War II. We have the attestations from African American men only because sociologists collected the toasts and the dozens, which were littered with such words. Presumably, men used to have more leeway in using such words, especially in masculine company in informal situations.

By 1971, on the conservative college campus where I teach, in order to signal that they were liberated, many women deliberately uttered taboo words, especially when first meeting another woman.[12] It was a way of establishing that the speaker was a feminist. Often this was done only once at the beginning of an acquaintance. The taboo word functioned like an address form in that it made a statement about the speaker that was to be remembered throughout interactions with her. It also reminded me of people unsure of a new acquaintance's ethnicity, throwing out a word like Italian "Capiche?" This means 'understand?'

Since at least 1990, if not earlier, female students have increasingly used taboo words, often loudly enough to be heard from some distance away. They don't use them in class, but I certainly hear them in the hallways. Surveying expletive usage in the dorms in casual interactions, students consistently report that males talking to each other use more expletives than females do, but the females aren't far behind. Mixed-gender interactions seem to yield the least amount of swearing, but it is not absent even there.

Kottke and MacLeod (1989) examined the reactions to women therapists and their clients using profanity. One hundred sixty college students listened to tapes of female therapists interacting with both men and women clients. When the therapist herself used profanity, the students were less willing to say that they would go to her for therapy. However, when the client used profanity, the therapist was perceived as being more attractive and more trustworthy than when the client did not. Apparently, it was not all right for women to speak strongly, but it is a measure of their "niceness" if they let others do it. Despite their own use of expletives, still my students claim they would be offended by a professor's using them, and even more offended if a female professor did.

Eckert and McConnell-Ginet (70) found clear age-grading in acceptability of profanity. Predictably, retired persons found it more "ugly" in women than in men. Not so predictably, boys were more likely to hold the same position than were girls. Interestingly, although both women and men reported that their fathers swore more than their mothers, women's estimates of their mother's swearing were higher than men's. Could it be that mothers swear more in front of their daughters than in front of their sons? This wouldn't be surprising, considering the finding that "many men and some women still express discomfort at hearing tabooed words from women's mouths and in mixed company" (182). Eckert and McConnell-Ginet cite a law still on the books in Michigan under which a man was indicted in 1999 for using "foul" language in the presence of women and children.

So, the disparity in profanity is as much one of attitude as of reality. That is, women do use profanity, but it is perceived as improper even by young people who themselves certainly use it. Oftentimes it seems that *fucking* is their favorite modifier, and certainly in many movies today aimed at young males, it appears in almost every sentence!

Profanity is not just an American phenomenon. Stapleton (2003) and Bayard and Krishnaya (2001) show its prevalence in university communities in Ireland and New Zealand, respectively. Stapleton points out that its usage is part of a community of practice, and is done by both males and females as a way of bonding and being humorous, as well as a way of telling a good story. Swearing is a way for these university students to show that they belong to the community of practice. They also report its cathartic function, a release when they are stressed or angry. Although females employ a great deal of profanity within this community of practice, they recognize that it is not as acceptable as it is for males, and some mention that they wouldn't swear in front of people they didn't know well. The men, in contrast, swear in the larger community as well as within this group.

Another difference between the men and the women is that, for the latter, female genitalia are not considered appropriate, but, for the men, they are. Respondents in this study report that *cunt, fanny,* and *tits* are avoided, especially by the females. The men do not consider *tits* as obscene as the women do. Some women report "a degree of self-monitoring in their use of other terms (most commonly 'fuck,' 'screw,' and 'cock') while the men appear to use these more or less indiscriminately." So, even now among young people, there are more constraints on female's profanity than on male's. Bayard and Krishnaya's data show the same disparity among university students in New Zealand.

Why should there still be such disparity in profanity between males and females? It seems to me that profanity is a naked marker of power. It also signifies freedom from controls. As such, it may be seen by men as a usurpation of their dominance. This is especially threatening because men are in the uncomfortable position of trying to dominate other men. Women used to be a safe haven for them, but now, with women signaling their independence so overtly, men have lost that safe haven. Similarly, Eckert and McConnell-Ginet (182) explain:

> Anger is the emotion most expected and tolerated . . . from men. Raised voices and abusive insults are part of expressing anger: they can be frightening and thus function in social control. The power of anger, including the power of some swearing, probably arises from its capacity to produce fear, to intimidate . . . Women's increased use of obscene language in expressing anger can represent a repositioning that challenges male dominance and that claims authority.

To sum up, then, what was first taken to be weakness in women's language use has been shown, rather, to be nonconfrontational facilitation to effect goals. Although women have increased their use of strong language, they still have more constraints on it than men do. This is at least partially because of social expectations that nice women don't talk that way. It seems to me also that women prefer to wield power in a less confrontational manner than men.

Cooperation or Competition: The Gender Wars

It has become a truism that men are competitive in conversation and women are cooperative. That is implicit in much of what has already been said about gender differences in interactions.

Eckert and McConnell-Ginet (88) dispute such a notion, or at least the assumption that women aren't competitive and don't seek to form hierarchies. They say that the difference lies in the ways that women do this. We've already seen, for instance, that women use tags on statements for different purposes than men do. Whereas males, even young boys, establish clear hierarchies in each of their interactions, females do so by practicing elaborate systems of exclusion over a longer period of time. Boys compete over individual skills, but girls create more permanent systems of hierarchies and are more likely to exclude certain girls. We can think of the cliques formed by girls in high school and the cult of the popular girls. Not only do I recall such a social system from junior high school, but Hollywood movies such as *Clueless* and *Pretty in Pink* have immortalized it.

Women can be just as competitive as men, but they may use different strategies to compete. Eckert and McConnell-Ginet (125) point out that women don't use male tactics because "competition in the marketplace violates men's cultural prerogative." It seems to me that women are socialized to attain their goals differently from men and they're not necessarily buckling under to male prerogative when they use language differently. Women use language to control norms. Indeed, that has been known to be the function of feminine gossip in many societies, including nonindustrialized ones. Women's speech activities not only set up norms, but also create ties, rankings, and exclusions, and this activity starts in girlhood. They (Eckert and McConnell-Ginet, 125) quote Marjorie Harness Goodwin as showing that:

> Girls police and sanction one another's behavior . . . and they use clever insults as they shun undesirables. These girls are not constructing a tolerant egalitarian social order but one of peer-based social control in which some are "in" and others are "out."

It must be noted that these remarks are about young girls in school, not women in the workplace.

This may sound as if women insidiously control whereas men are more up front. That is one stereotype of female-male differences. However, as Janet Holmes and Maria Stubbs (2003, 82) show, women in high positions are capable of direct commands and give them. However, rather than imposing a solution on a team, a female manager, Leila, encouraged extensive discussion of an issue, explicitly seeking the views of participants. They also show that hedging and tag questions, far from being weak or indirect, are used to gain cooperation and superior performance from the other workers. Certainly this effects a more congenial work atmosphere, one in which employees are more willing to give it their all. The alternative, blunt criticisms and overt directives, build up resentments and damage face needs. Women's style, while maintaining power relations, is effective managerial practice, not a sign of buckling under masculine domination.

CHAPTER 10

I would note that women who don't make use of female style or don't make much use of it are subject to sanctions. Two examples come to mind. The first is Hilary Clinton, who was regularly lampooned by the press and in jokes that circulated widely, despite the intelligence of her proposals. As First Lady, she was seen as usurping her husband's Presidential powers, although any involvement in drafting proposals, such as the one for national health care, was at his behest. Her problem was that she was as direct as a man in presenting her plan. The other example is Martha Stewart who, because of her directness in the way she ran her business, has been portrayed in the media as being a super-bitch. I am not here speaking of her legal difficulties, but her managerial style. So far as I have been able to see, there is nothing she said or did that a man wouldn't, and that, apparently, was the problem. Had she been a man who ran her enterprises the same way, would she have been such an object of scorn? As Holmes and Stubbs show, it is possible for women to retain their speaking styles and still wield power effectively.

Deborah Tannen quips in her best seller *You Just Don't Understand* that men lecture (report), whereas women seek rapport. Women are cooperative in speech and men are dominant. Women seek to mend feelings and keep relationships viable. Men don't. She also claims that people who are subordinate in society are most interested in smoothing out personal relationships, keeping peace, and affirming personal bonds.

According to Tannen, people who are dominant aren't interested in such matters, but studies like Holmes and Stubbs show that this clearly isn't so. Unlike Tannen, they actually went into workplaces and recorded numerous hours of talking. An unfortunate amount of popular literature on male-female differences is anecdotal and unreliable. Before believing it, one must always ask, "What kind of data supports this conclusion? How were they gathered? How accurate is the analysis?"

How are children socialized into gendered language? Because they have been so influential and are so widely quoted, we must look at Maltz and Borker (1982). They claim that boys and girls learn to interact differently from early childhood. Girls do not play as competitively as boys. Girls see friendship as a matter of intimacy, not competition or power. This claim, as we saw above, has been weakened if not invalidated by Goodwin's findings of girls' clique formation. Maltz and Borker say that girls' relationships are horizontal rather than vertical. By the fifth grade, they have learned not to deal with disputes by quarreling. Rather, their friendships just break up. Maltz and Borker conclude that:

> Basically, girls learn to do three things with words: (1) to create
> and maintain relationships of closeness and equality, (2) to

criticize each other in acceptable ways, and (3) to interpret accurately the speech of other girls. (205)

Moreover, girls learn to form friendships through talk: through giving support, letting others speak, acknowledging what others say, and generally creating cooperation through speech. (206)

Boys, on the other hand, use speech to (1) assert [their] position of dominance, (2) attract and maintain an audience, and (3) to assert [themselves] when other speakers have the floor. (207)

Interestingly, the finding that boys use speech to gain dominance has been found to be independent of ethnic group or social class (213). These cultural differences determine only the forms of the verbal competition between boys, that is, whether or not they play the dozens, have boasting competitions, or show off erudite knowledge. Boys learn to gain an audience by becoming good storytellers, jokers, or narrative performers. Maltz and Borker claim that, in all social and ethnic groups, part of this skill resides in learning to deal with mockery, challenges, and side comments about their stories. Finally, boys have to learn to act as audience members, and this they do by asserting themselves and their opinions. Maltz and Borker see such behavior as a contrast to females, who form an appreciative, supportive audience.

Despite this, it must be noted that there certainly are low-key, soft-spoken men who do not overpower others in their speech. Many men aren't in dominant positions in their workplaces or within their social groups. The picture painted by Maltz and Borker does not accommodate those men who choose not to assert themselves all the time or who are not in a position to do so. Do they not, then, speak like men?

Thomson, Murachver, and Green (2001) ask "Where is the Gender in Gendered Language?" They do not deny that there are differences between male and female speech, but they show that people of both genders accommodate their speech to that of the other. That is, they match style, a phenomenon we saw in Chapter 3 (Coupland, Coupland, and Giles 1991). They claim that language is not just a set of features. It is a process formed in interactions. People's speech converges toward that of those they converse with. This doesn't mean that they actually mimic each other, but they modify a subset of the features of the other's speech. "Gender-preferential language is most pronounced within same-sex groups, and is diminished in mixed-sex groups" (171).

To test out the proposition that men and women accommodate their language to the opposite gender, Thomson, Murachver, and Green set up two studies designating netpals for participants. That is, the participant had to write e-mails to these unknown netpals over a two-week period. As Thomson, Murachver, and Green (2001) showed in the study described below, it is possible for people to predict gender accurately from electronic discourse. E-mail was chosen as the vehicle for language in Thomson, Murachver, and Green because "it allows us to examine the effects of language style in the absence of any other cues" (Thomson, Murachver, and Green, 171).

What they did was to use templates containing features of male or female language. Then the researchers, acting as netpals, wrote messages between 80 and 120 words long on subjects as varied as current events, exams, parties, and roommates. They also signed themselves with a female label like *Jane* or a male one like *Peter*. In actuality, the e-mails from the researchers weren't necessarily the same gender as their labels indicated, but the language features were congruent with the gender claimed. What happened was that a male, for instance, who received an e-mail supposedly from a female, began himself to use features of women's speech, and females who received e-mails from a male began to use features of masculine speech. Because the recipients did get labels that indicated gender and the style matched that gender, a second experiment was done to ensure that the style matching wasn't based upon the fact that the message ostensibly came from a woman or a man on the basis of the name provided. This one, too, allowed gender labels on the messages from the netpal, but the features of language did not necessarily match the gender of the label. Sarah, for instance, used masculine features in "her" messages. The results were that recipients' language was influenced by the gendered features of the messages more than by the gendered names. That is, even if a message supposedly came from Sarah, if "her" message used masculine features like stating opinions, a female recipient would also use some masculine features. If a message supposedly came from Jon, but "he" used feminine features like referring to emotions, then a masculine recipient also accommodated his style by doing the same. This doesn't mean that a recipient totally submerged his or her gender by using the netpal's supposed gender, but that he or she used more features of that gender than if he or she were responding to someone of the same sex.

What are the features of female speech? According to Thomson, Murachver, and Green (193), there are seventeen linguistic variables which can be used to classify gender with 87.5% accuracy. Women, for instance, are more likely to refer to emotions, use intensive adverbs like those identified by Lakoff, make compliments, use minimal responses, use modals (*could, might*, etc.), tag questions, personal pronouns, and subordinating conjunctions. They are also more likely to ask questions and use politeness forms.[13] Men are more likely to mention specific quantities, use non-standard forms or make grammatical errors, provide more opinions and justifiers, use more words and, in conversation, talk more often. These features are gender-preferential. It is not the case that women use all and only female features or men use all and only male features.

In addition, some members of a gender might use a different set of gender-preferential forms. For instance, some men tease and insult more frequently and others speak in longer utterance lengths (194). It must be remembered, however, that both men and women can use the same features. It is not an all-or-nothing situation. People change their speech style in different situations and to different people.

Thomson and Murachver (2001) also did a study that differed from Thomson, Murachver, and Green in that recipients of e-mail had to guess the gender of the sender. They were able to do so 91.4% of the time (199). What is interesting is that the messages were not overloaded with gendered features. In fact, there were few significant differences between female and male messages, but these few were sufficient to discriminate between genders. The females did make more mention of emotions, provide more personal information, use more modals, and more intensive adverbs. Females also showed a higher mean frequency of questions, self-derogatory comments, compliments, and apologies. Men were more likely to convey opinions, make insults, and write more. Again, the differences between the genders were small on all of these features, but they were defining. I must reiterate that all of the features marked as being more characteristic of one gender or the other were garnered from a large literature based on observations and analyses of actual linguistic productions. They were not anecdotally derived.

Talking and Interrupting

When the "old biddies" or "young chicks" start clucking at their "hen parties," a man is silenced. Right? Aside from the demeaning association of female speech with chickens, is it true that women talk more than men? When I first came across the studies which showed that men interrupt women frequently, every man I mentioned this to said, "If we didn't, we'd never get a word in edgewise." This from educated colleagues as well as husbands of friends, even my physician.

The actual evidence in interactions which involve both genders gives quite a different picture. As we already have noted, people are quite blind to the way they really behave as opposed to the way they think they behave. One of the most enduring myths of our society is that women talk more than men do. Virtually all actual investigations of the matter, those not confining themselves to anecdotal information, at least, have shown that men speak more than women in mixed-sex dyads (Mulac 1989; James and Drakich 1993; Thomson, Murachver, and Green 2001). Thomson, Murachver, and Green ascribe this to the fact that women facilitate in conversations and so elicit speech from men. If this is so, then one has to ask why women specifically elicit male's speech and men don't elicit women's speech? What Thomson, Murachver, and Green imply by such a statement is that women make it their business to keep men talking rather than making room for themselves to speak. If they are facilitators, why don't they facilitate the speech of other women as well as of men in mixed-gender groups?

There have been some exceptions to the finding that men outtalk women, however. O'Barr's (1982) study of legal proceedings found that women spoke more than men when women were in dominant positions. Aires (quoted in Lucas and Valli 1989) found that among white college students, women and men speak the same amount, or women may even speak more. Most recently, Nowell (1989) has shown that female ASL speakers produce more verbiage than males in informal conversation, but that males produce more than females in interview situations. His study doesn't distinguish between the topics of conversation, however. The raw question, "Who speaks more, men or women?" has little meaning in and of itself. There are obviously individual personality differences between the sexes. One has to ask who speaks more in what situations, what variables like ethnicity, social rank, and profession have on the relative amount of speech produced by each gender, and also whether we are speaking of mixed or same-sex dyads. All of these factors determine who speaks the most. When we look at these together, however, we find some interesting insights into the role of women.

Most studies have found that males dominate females in interactions between the sexes, especially in business settings, academia, formal committees, and the like. Unofficially, while a member of the Faculty Senate, I used to amuse myself by counting the number contributions by males and females, and also by timing the length of the contributions. On my campus, at least, men consistently talked more frequently and for longer periods. Also, I noted instances in which a female professor made a proposal which was ignored by the next speaker, but later presented by a male as if it were his own. I never observed the opposite happening. Although these may be dismissed as anecdotal, although careful and informed, observations and are intended to be taken as such, they do suggest an avenue of research that needs exploring.

Topic can also be expected to play a role in verbal production between genders. If the topic is nursery schools, for instance, women might speak more and longer than men. The questions then become: Do women speak of women's concerns in mixed company? Do men? In my own circles, intensive observations of East Coast high-involvement, professional couples sharing dinner show clearly that it is quite usual for men to talk about their business concerns and sports in front of women, but it is not usual for women to talk of fashion, housekeeping, or even their jobs in front of the men. Once, to see what would happen, I encouraged my female guests to persist in their topic. When the men couldn't change it, they left the table and went off to form their own discussion group.

My students who have examined these behaviors report the same phenomenon. One, from a Greek-American family, noted at Easter dinner that although men and women ate together, they did not otherwise interact all day. These occurrences again are presented only as observations which require formal study if they are to be accepted as usual behavior. However, there is research that suggests that these observations are on target.

Shibamoto (1985, 97–98) reports that the Japanese also subscribe to the belief that women outtalk men, but actual observation has shown that middle-class Japanese men speak more and longer than women. A recent study of Japanese conversation (Itakura and Tsui 2004) found that men dominated the conversations in eight mixed-gender dyads by storytelling and by claiming expertise. The authors ascribe this dominance to women! Their reasoning is that the women's other-oriented conversational style caused the men to hold forth.

Why do the women have such a style? Can it only be because they have been socialized not to speak themselves, but to encourage men to speak? Do women wish to be mere facilitators of male verbal displays? Do women wish not to have their ideas presented? Or are they forced into such a role by social conditioning, sexist social conditioning? The women in Itakura and Tsui's study apparently never claimed expertise and never engaged in storytelling. Are these researchers so naive that they suppose the women have nothing to say, so they encourage men to talk instead? Do the women in their study really want to hear only what the men want to talk about? Do the women not have topics that they want to air? The conclusion of this study is shocking sexism paraded as scholarship. It presents a lesson that must be learned. Scientific research is influenced by cultural beliefs. It is not objective or neutral.

Male control of topics, or rather, the interesting assertion that women are expected to listen to men's concerns but men are not expected to listen to women's, in and of itself helps explain disparity in amount of verbiage in mixed-sex interactions. Pamela Fishman (1978), for example, found that women raised as many as 62% of topics in ordinary household conversations with their husbands. If husbands did not respond to a topic, it was dropped. By contrast, 28 out of 29 topics raised by the husbands in this study got discussed. Even the remaining one was not dropped outright. Fishman claims that the content of the women's topics were indistinguishable from their husbands' but that men have the right to control what is being talked about. Fishman believes that women raise so many topics in an effort to increase their chance of success, because so much of what they say is ignored by men.

Okamoto and Smith-Lovin's (2001) carefully crafted study claimed that topic change is not a matter of gender per se, but of status. Higher-status individuals more successfully get the topics changed to what they want than do lower-status ones. They studied conversations of twenty-two mixed-gender six-person groups who were given a problem to solve in thirty minutes. In each group, those who initiated the most topics were higher status and were more likely to get their topics discussed and not have them lost as the conversation continued. Of course, the higher-status individuals are usually males. Not surprisingly, then, males are at less risk of getting their topics lost (869), but their topics were more likely to be changed collaboratively.

One reason that their topics weren't lost as much as females' is that men interrupted the females more (867), another common gender pattern. Males also introduced more topics, a sign of higher status, but this seemed to be because they talked more than females (865). Okamoto and Smith-Lovin conclude that successful topic change is more related to status than to gender, but since, in many situations, males have more status than females, the males are more successful in changing the subject.

However, the authors admit "that gender has a subtle effect: Men appear to discriminate and change the subject when it is being developed by a woman rather than other men" (871). It is interesting that Okamoto and Smith-Lovin don't ascribe gender as the factor in successful topic change, but, oddly, higher-status individuals: individuals who participate the most, who talk the most, who interrupt females, who are, in fact, men. So, why not just note that being male confers these advantages so that males end up reinforcing their higher status? Speaking practices indicate who those with higher status are.

Many well-known female speech tactics can be seen as ways of getting attention or getting some kind of control over conversation. Men do the same things as women when they want or need some attention and response. What is significant is that in ordinary male/female conversations, women resort to such tactics far more frequently than men do. For instance, women ask three times as many questions as men. Questions force hearers in a speech community to make a response and are therefore powerful controllers of interactions.

Women, like children, very frequently ask, "D'ya know what?" The response to this is "What?" This guarantees that the first speaker will be able to elaborate on his or her chosen topic. It is no surprise that those whose right to choose topics is curtailed, women and children, resort to this kind of opening question far more frequently than do men unless men are talking to male superiors. Women also introduce topics with comments like, "This is really interesting!" far more often than men do. Again, this seems to be a ploy to get attention. In some transcripts, it has been found that women use pause fillers like "you know" as much as ten times more than their male co-conversationalists. Women do this the most when men are giving the least response (Fishman 1978).

Interrupting as Dominance

Certainly another major reason that men have been found to talk more in mixed-gender interaction is, as noted above, that men feel free to interrupt women, but not vice versa (Zimmerman and West 1975). Since those who interrupt are signaling power, I would have thought that, with the advances of women in the past thirty years, males' interruptions of women would have lessened. As we have just seen, however, Okamoto and Smith-Lovin's 2001 study still noted it.

In 2006, two of my students did their term papers on interruption and both found women still being interrupted by males. To discuss such a matter intelligently, we have to consider what an interruption is, how we count something as an interruption rather than a mere overlap, or an accidental stumble into someone else's sentence. The interruptions cited by Meredith Lobsitz and Angela May qualify as true interruptions. By true interruptions, I mean that, as a female was talking, a male broke in so that she couldn't finish what she was saying.

Lobsitz observed groups of servers at a restaurant at which she works. The groups ranged from ten to fifteen servers with two managers and were observed at eight daily meetings held before shifts start. There was one male manager at six of these meetings, and, with him, was one of three female managers. A female manager opened the meeting, but before she could finish her sentence, the male interrupted and took over the discussion. After he broke in, he not only maintained the floor, but the female manager would remain silent or nod in agreement with his arguments or opinions.

The exception to this pattern occurred with a female manager who had been with the restaurant longer than the male. He interrupted her less, and, if he attempted to do so, she didn't yield the floor. Also, unlike the other female managers, she did not hedge or use tags. She spoke authoritatively. She also was the only female manager who interrupted the male, and she was successful at it. The most the other female managers did was interject short opinions without attempting to take control of the conversation. In those meetings that the male manager didn't attend, the female managers did interrupt each other, speaking almost simultaneously. In other words, the females felt free to interrupt each other, but not the male.

Angela May observed behaviors in the dorm for a month. Not only did she find the expected masculine interruptions of females, but she also found that, in an argument, the female tried to break in on the male after he interrupted her. When this happened, about as far as the female got was "I was trying to say . . . " and "You don't understand . . . " before the male disregarded her and continued to talk. As expected, she found that in female-female dyads, it was rare for the interrupter to take the floor. In an argument between two females, the females would allow the listener to speak when there was a pause, but then reverted back to what they were originally talking about by saying, "As I was saying before. . . ." Males, in contrast, would cut off the listener who attempted to break in during a pause by saying, "I'm not finished." Her most interesting finding, I thought, was that when males interrupted, they did so to boast! That is, they presented themselves as having expertise or as being powerful.

Interruptions can be counted in different ways. If one is using a model of interaction in which it is accepted that only one person speaks at a time, with regular strategies for turn-taking, there can be overlaps. These occur when two people speak at the same time, typically with one person chiming in close to the point where the first person will be giving up the floor. These can be a result of listener error. That is, the listener thinks the speaker is done, so he or she starts speaking. An interruption is a vocalization before the last word that could signal the end of a sentence. If the interruption prevents the speaker from finishing what she was going to say, or otherwise takes the floor from her, then it is an intrusion, a sign of dominance. Lower-status persons do not do this to higher-status ones. Not surprisingly, then, men are more likely to do this to women than women are to do it to men. The interruptions that Lobsitz reports from her male manager prevented the females from completing what they were going to say. So did those reported by May.

Zimmerman and West (1975), recording natural conversations in public places with a tape recorder hidden in a backpack, found that in same-sex dyads, interruptions and overlaps were equally distributed. They counted an utterance as an interruption if it occurred more than two syllables away from a possible turn transition place. If it occurred at a possible end of a sentence, it was counted as an overlap and attributed to the listener's error in determining that the speaker was finishing up.

In mixed male/female interactions, 96% of all interruptions and 100% of all overlaps were by men.[14] What is striking is that within same-sex conversations, only three out of twenty interruptions occurred. Women did not object when men butted in, although they did say, "One minute!" "Please let me finish," or "Wait till I'm done" if other women tried to interrupt. Zimmerman and West comment that the right of females to speak "appears to be casually infringed upon by males."

Eakins and Eakins (1978, 69) found that at university faculty meetings, men averaged a greater number of interruptions per meeting than women. Furthermore, males were interrupted far fewer times than females. The one female who did interrupt did so only to other females. The one female who got interrupted the most was also the only one without a Ph.D., so status is clearly involved in whether or not one is interrupted. Even so, females with Ph.D.s were interrupted more than males. Eakins and Eakins noted that one reason for males' interrupting so frequently is that they spoke more often. Their total number of turns exceeded those of women. What these data indicate is that both men and women subconsciously concede that men have the right to control conversation, that women may speak only if men wish them to.

In the thirty-odd years that have passed since this initial exploration, women have increasingly moved into higher-status positions. One would predict, then, that males would not interrupt females so casually anymore. Also the definition of what constitutes interruption has been refined, so that what earlier researchers counted as an interruption may not, in fact, be one.

First, our understanding of turn-taking in conversation has changed. The model of an orderly interaction has been disputed. In this model, one speaker holds the floor at a time and give cues when he or she is ready to let another talk. If such routines occur, they certainly do not in all situations, nor in all cultural groups. As we saw with High Involvement cultures, it is quite natural in many groups, regional or social, for more than one person to speak at a time.

Also, Deborah Tannen (1979) pointed out that certain kinds of overlaps and even interruptions don't serve the function of taking away the speaker's turn. Rather, they are words or sounds of encouragement like, "Really?" "Mmmhmm," and the like. These actually serve to encourage the speaker to continue talking and show that the listener is interested in what is being said. In fact, for many conversationalists, the lack of such backchannel cues, as they are called, makes it difficult for them to continue. It has been found that women are far more likely to provide such cues than men are.

Zimmerman and West found that males often allowed lapses of silence after women said something. They termed this "delayed listening responses," and explained that these, along with interruptions, subdued females. Female response to such male behavior is silence even when nobody else has yet started speaking.

CHAPTER 10

Typically men give women very little feedback during conversations. As men talk, women give little murmurs of encouragement, such as "mmhmm," "uh huh," "yeah," or "oh." Men do not reciprocate. "The promptly uttered minimal response, with its finely timed placement at various points within the current speaker's talk, is taken as a sign of active attention, encouragement to continue the turn, and support for the speaker's development of a topic" (Eakins and Eakins 1978, 71). It is very difficult to keep on talking if the other party does not make such sounds. Similarly, women look at men more when they are talking than men look at women. In effect, then, women encourage men to talk, but men do not encourage women to.

Furthermore, silences in conversations are not equally distributed between the sexes. Women are silent when men interrupt, and they remain silent longer after a man's interruption than a man does if he is cut off. Women are also silent if men give them a delayed minimal response. This is the dampening pause, as in:

Woman: [joyfully] Oh, boy! You'll never guess what happened to me today!

Man: [long, long pause] . . . What?

The man's delayed response is calculated to convey complete lack of interest. The impression is that the man responded at all only because of the woman's "You'll never guess . . . ," a powerful opener, equivalent to a question in eliciting the response, "What?"

The entire picture that emerges is one of men controlling male/female interaction in every way and not being overly concerned with what women wish to talk about. Women can, by special strategies, force their topics into the conversation, but men break in on them with impunity, or at least did in the late 1970's. These data made it very clear that women's business is to keep men talking while minimizing their own contributions and that men's speaking practices actively discourage women's speech. We have just seen that recent studies attribute male dominance in speaking to women's facilitation of men. So, this is still true today.

The studies on interrupting have inspired more research than just about any other subject on gender differences. Unfortunately, these studies have varied greatly in how data were collected, how interruptions were coded, what counted as an interruption, and its severity in a given instance. Even the gender of those judging the interruptions affected the conclusions. All these variables yield very different results. For instance, it has been found that females count more instances of interruptions than males do in the same interactions. It has been variously claimed that men do interrupt women more, that women interrupt men more, and that there is no difference between the genders in interrupting.

Anderson and Leaper (1998) did a meta-analysis of forty-three published studies of interruptions by men and women in conversations. Since individual studies have yielded contradictory results, some claiming no gender differences, some reporting male dominance, and some reporting female dominance, Anderson and Leaper considered several factors and applied statistical measures to them. They considered different kinds of interruption, having found that some studies lumped together the encouraging backchannel remarks typical of women with overt intrusions. They counted as most intrusive those remarks which resulted in the interrupter taking over the floor, what they termed as "successful interruption," as these are a sign of dominance (227). Because so many studies failed to count backchannel vocalizations separately from interruptions, Leaper and Anderson were not able to determine if women do make more encouraging sounds than men, or if men make them at all.

Factors that determined the number of interruptions included the subject of conversation, age, degree of intimacy, size of group, and type of interaction. They examined the effects of the year of publication of the studies, presuming that more recent ones would show less gender disparity, the gender of authors, the context of interactions, the topic of conversation, and the type of interaction. They posited, for instance, that naturally occurring data would yield more intrusive interruptions than those elicited in laboratory settings. People are more likely to act in socially approved ways when they are being scrutinized in an artificial setting.

The only measure that achieved a level of significance when all these studies were examined statistically is that men did make significantly more intrusive interruptions than women (237). However, they also found a slight decrease over time in such intrusions, so that studies published later showed fewer than the earlier ones did. An analog to this is the observation many of my students made in class, that when males interrupted females, they often apologized for doing it! Anderson and Leaper also found that female authors were more likely to report that men interrupted more than women, but male authors tended to report that women interrupted more! They also found more interruptions in unstructured activities than in specifically assigned tasks, and that gendered behaviors occurred more often with strangers than with familiars (242).

Okamoto, Rashotte, and Smith-Lovin (2002) took another tack in scientifically measuring interruptions. They asked if people perceived the same behavior as being interruptions. That is, do people within a conversation perceive interruptions the way a researcher does? This, of course, is crucial to any conclusions one can draw about interruptions. They noted that two kinds of measures have been used by various researchers. One is the Zimmerman and West model, in which one counts an interruption as a verbalization made more than two syllables away from a possible turn-transition, as opposed to an overlap when the speaker is nearer completion. The other measure is cultural, depending upon one's judgment of when it is appropriate for another speaker to take the floor (39). Citing Stephen Murray, they present three situations, beginning with the most severe:

- Cutting a speaker off before he or she had made his or her first point of the conversation.
- Cutting the speaker off before he or she had made the first point of a turn.
- Beginning to speak before a pause or other turn-ending signal.

Subcultures may view interruptions very differently. High Involvement speakers, for instance, expect more overlaps and interruptions than Low Involvement ones do. Also, men, having been socialized to talk more dominantly, to challenge, to direct, and to be less supportive, might have a more favorable view of interruptions (43). The aim of the research was to see if people using the Zimmerman and West criteria counted the same behavior as interruptions as did people who used their cultural expectations. The latter were termed "culture experts." Okamoto et al. point out that when conversants hear recordings of their own interactions, they cannot invariably identify whose turn was in progress (41). This indicates that more is going on in judging interruptions than mere counting of syllables or other formal syntactic measures.

They recruited 264 undergraduates, presenting them with videotaped statements of a convicted perpetrator and the victim of the crime (44). The subjects then participated in mock juries with one to three other students. The videotapes of the jury discussions were coded by a researcher using Zimmerman and West criteria. Then eight undergraduate coders independently judged where interruptions occurred based upon their own cultural knowledge. Interruptions were not defined for them. Both sets of coders identified about the same number of interruptions, but they didn't identify the same verbalizations as being interruptions!

The male and female culture experts identified interruptions so differently from each other, and so differently from the Zimmerman and West coder, that "the three conceptions of interruptions . . . capture different underlying constructs" (46). Moreover, they found that some culture experts were very sensitive to interruptions, coding them more frequently, and others were not. These corresponded with Tannen's (1984) High and Low Involvement groups (47). In other words, it was the perception of interruptions that became the issue rather than actual use of interruptions (47).

Okamoto et al. conclude that different types of coders view interruptions in significantly different ways (51). They found that men were more sensitive to interruptions than women were (51). They ascribe this to the fact that women pay more attention than men to the situational context, and are more influenced by factors like the speaker's power position, the total floor time of the speaker and interrupter, and the interrupter's intent. If I read them correctly, Okamoto et al. are implying that women expect powerful people to interrupt, so they don't notice it as much when they do. They sum up: "When determining speaker rights, however, men and women seem to attend to different aspects of the situation: women consider criteria other than Murray's severity principles" (52). In any event, both one's cultural style, High or Low Involvement and one's gender impinges upon one's noticing violations like interruptions.

Gender and Persuasiveness

It has been found that the gender of the speaker has a strong influence on persuasiveness, especially when coupled with the style apparently considered appropriate for that gender (Carli 1990). Carli observed both mixed- and same-sex dyads to see if there were gender differences in the ability to persuade others, using a topic on which they disagreed.

Women were more tentative, but only when speaking with men. This was not a disadvantage, as men found tentative women more influential than women who spoke more positively. Women, however, were less impressed by another woman who spoke tentatively. Considering that most women followed the practice of being more tentative with men than with women, apparently most women have learned their lessons well. Men were equally effective with both sexes whether or not their speech was tentative.

In a second study, Carli had 120 subjects listen to an audiotape of identical persuasive messages presented by either a man or a woman, half of each speaking tentatively. Again, tentative female speakers were more influential with men than with women, and again, assertiveness or lack of it made no difference upon male speakers' persuasiveness. The lesson is, one supposes, that women should not be assertive and direct around men if they wish to get their views adopted.

One is inevitably reminded of African Americans before advances in their civil rights when they spoke of "shucking" and "jiving" to the white man in order to be at all effective in their demands. That is, they had to dissemble and pretend to an exaggerated humility in order to hope to get any advantages from whites. One certainly hopes this is not still the case, although, considering the wrath that bluntly-speaking African Americans like Spike Lee call on themselves, one suspects that this such pretense is still as advantageous to African American males as it is to women.

More recently, it has been claimed that women do not use persuasive strategies as much as men do, that, in fact, women prefer to use narratives (Biber and Burges 2000, 21). This may be because women know they have less success using direct persuasive tactics, but that narratives that have as their aim persuading another are, for them, most effective. Then, again, I wonder what women were investigated to come to this conclusion. Clearly, they weren't the women who sell cosmetic creams at the department stores, convincing women to lay out $100 or more for a jar of something to rejuvenate their skins. Nor were they the women selling jewelry to men for Valentine's Day gifts.

LANGUAGE AS MIRROR

The vocabulary of a language indicates what is important to its speakers. It also reflects the attitudes of a culture: what is taboo, what is valued, and what is not. Speaking practices themselves tell us what position people have in their societies. So long as women's speech is chattering, nattering, babbling, and chit-chatting, we know their speech is not valued. So pervasive is our social attitude that women are inferior that even female scholars blame women for their own subjugation, saying that men are dominant because women encourage them to be so. This ignores the fact that society doesn't allow women not to be encouraging to men. Those who speak like a man are denigrated, even derided, as we saw with how the media treated women like Hilary Clinton and Martha Stewart, women who didn't soften their messages to be pleasing to men.

However, as Janet Holmes and Maria Stubbs (2003) have shown, women can be direct when their position needs them to be, but, more importantly, they can take the very forms of speech which have long signaled their weakness and use them to wield authority. They retain their power, but by their cooperative, facilitative, nonthreatening language allow corporations, teams, and committees to function smoothly with minimum damage to the face of coworkers. In fact, women's style may well be the style of the future: cooperation instead of raw competition.

Our language so shapes our consciousness that the gender disparity in language and interaction was not even noticed even as women began entering the business world and the professions. Part of Robin Lakoff's genius is that she noticed, thereby raising others' consciousness and stimulating a multitude of research.

Examination of a vocabulary can reveal a good deal about a culture. The lexicon of a language is a mirror of its speakers' attitudes and ideas. A mirror reflects. It does not determine; it does not hold prisoners. As Kay and Kempton (1984) point out, Whorf himself could not have thought that we can't break out of our cultural mode, since his works imply that we should do just that.

CHAPTER 10

Notes

[1] Lakoff and Johnson are not responsible for all of this analysis, however. I have added the feature of the motions and the metaphor for climbing in a job.

[2] That is, one uses first one leg then the other in a crawling motion.

[3] Lakoff and Johnson are not responsible for my analysis of how *climb* can be used to indicate rising socially or politically. They are, however, in delineating the underlying concepts inherent in English *climb*.

[4] Since Jews do not pass a collection plate around at a service, nor can a rabbi ask for personal donations, this implication is false.

[5] Perhaps elsewhere as well, but modern dialect studies don't seem to mention this.

[6] In linguistics, an asterisk (*) in front of a sentence means that native speakers would not be likely to say it because it is semantically or syntactically odd.

[7] This term has actually been in and out of usage since about 1915, according the *Random House Dictionary*, 2nd. ed.

[8] Actually, it has been accepted since the 19th century that if an Indo-European word had a *b* in it, that would turn into a *p* in the Germanic languages, so if there was a *wib*, it would have become *wip* not *wif*, the Old English term.

[9] English, like Latin, Greek, Hindi, Russian, Hittite, and most of the languages of Europe today came from one parent language which no longer exists, called Proto-Indo-European. The methods of tracing words back to parent languages have been rigorously formulated and tested out over the past 200 years. The earlier scholars who began this work developed the art of reconstruction so well that they were able to take modern Romance languages, for instance, and figure out what the Latin words must have been that gave birth to the different but related words in French, Spanish, Rumanian, Portuguese, and Italian. Then they could verify their reconstructions by going back to Latin texts. George Waterman's *Perspectives in Linguistic*, 2nd ed. is a good beginning treatment of how languages can be traced to ancestral ones.

[10] In Brazil, she, too, can be a slob.

[11] Admittedly, I have not done a statistical analysis of their responses, but the numbers are something like 5 females to 4 males.

[12] This coincided with the school's becoming coed. Formerly it was a males-only school. With the advent of female students, the college hired its first cohort of female professors. Since the male-run Catholic school had always been very conservative (and still is), women had to have a way of identifying themselves as conservative or not.

13 The authors cite the work of several researchers to validate that these features do distinguish female speech.

14 From my sporadic viewing of television talk shows with men and women arguing about some issue, it seems as if women are very willing to interrupt men and vice versa. Again, this points up the need to localize data and speak only about the situations which elicit the data. The same woman who casually infringes on a man's right to speak on Bill Maher's show might herself be infringed on by men at a party.

CHAPTER 10

Exercises

1. Examine how girls and boys are portrayed in children's books. Preferably select books for a certain age group and make a table of who does the talking in each, what kind of talking each does (advising, complaining, informing, comforting, rebelling, etc.). How much talking do men, women, girls, and boys do relative to each other? Does your research suggest that children are taught at an early age to value male speech more than female?

2. Collect examples of the kind of speech that Lakoff claimed indicated weakness. Try to find examples that are used in lieu of direct commands. How effective are they for such purposes? Do any of your examples signify a subordinate status as Lakoff claims?

3. Carefully observe and record the number of interruptions in male-male, female-female, and male-female dyads. Do your findings support those in this chapter? What tactics does each gender employ to deal with interruptions? Are there strong gender differences?

4. Ask a male and a female for directions on how to do something. What differences, if any, are there in the way they give those directions?

5. Write down all of the words you can find which refer to females either on television shows, movies, or just your own circles. Do your observations verify that women are still defined in terms of their sexuality and their submissiveness?

6. Make up a list of words like *intelligent, hungry,* and *athletic* which you think might be associated with males rather than females. Give a sample sentence for each word to five males and five females, but omit the subject. Have those tested supply an appropriate subject. Do they choose female or male subjects? What can you conclude about the semantic features on words associated with each gender?

7. Examine the front page of a newspaper. How many examples can you find of words being used to color one's attitude toward an issue or a person?

Chapter 11

Sociolinguistics and the Professions

Ignorance of linguistics and of what linguists do can harm innocent people in medicine, law, education, and psychiatry. Linguistics can even shed light on religious activities. Every facet of life is affected by language and how it is used. The contributions of linguists to the professions have been varied and wide-ranging. There are sociolinguists, psycholinguists, neurolinguists, forensic linguists, and just plain vanilla linguists, but they all have important input to analyzing issues that affect many people.

APPLICATIONS OF SOCIOLINGUISTICS

Robert Rodman (2002, 94) abstracts his article in *Forensic Linguistics* succinctly:

Ignorance of elementary linguistic concepts . . . [bears on] the conviction appeal of a Haitian-born American sentenced to twelve years for dealing cocaine . . . Although the drug dealer on the tape spoke a dialect of American Black English and the defendant speaks English with a Creole accent, the State persuaded the jury that the Haitian disguised his voice, by purposely dropping his accent. His ability to perform this feat was attributed . . . to the fact that he had been an interpreter . . . and was therefore a linguist, and therefore understood 'sound change' and therefore could . . . [be capable of] dropping his foreign accent . . . [T]he resulting miscarriage of justice . . . would not have occurred if the court knew that an interpreter is not necessarily a linguist, and that sound change refers to the historical development of languages.

Nor could it have occurred if the court knew that linguists specializing in bilingualism had been consulted about a nonnative speaker who had learned English when he was eighteen. The linguist, or even someone who has read this book, would have known that a person who learns a second language after puberty speaks with an accent over which he or she has no control. Often, as we saw in Chapter 8, the speaker doesn't even realize he or she has an accent. (Once, when speaking with a German acquaintance, I was asked, "Can you hear zat I haf un accent?" When I said, startled, "Yes," he responded, "Funny, I don't hear it.") In any event, an innocent man is serving a twelve-year sentence because of ignorance of linguistics.

Similarly, I have seen movies like *Mr. Holland's Opus* and dramas such as those on *Lifetime* network, but not confined to that one, about deaf babies. The movies always have a scene in which the desperate parents go to an expert who tells them never to respond to any signs the baby makes. Insist upon the baby's lip-reading or else he or she will never learn to speak. Well, anyone who has had an Intro to Linguistics course with a section on phonetics knows that the most one can get from lip-reading is 30% of the message. Looking in a mirror, try making an *m*, *p*, and *b* by saying "muh," "puh," and "buh." You will see that all three sounds look exactly alike. The lips are the same shape for all three. Then try *s*, *z*, *t*, *d*. Again, they are all made with the same tongue and lip movements.

Furthermore, one cannot lip-read unless one already knows the language! One certainly can't learn to speak that way. If a child is so profoundly deaf that he or she can't hear what sounds are emanating from someone's mouth, the only way that child can communicate is through signs. If you deny the child signs, you are denying him or her all communication. That is cruel! Imagine being a human who can't communicate with another and whose efforts to communicate are rebuffed by his or her own parents. Worse yet, there is a distinct possibility that if the child's language centers are not stimulated, the brain capacity to handle language will diminish. American Sign Language is a full language engaged by the same brain centers as oral language. Deaf children should be exposed to it as early as possible, just as hearing children are exposed to spoken language. Again, ignorance of linguistics can cause a grave injustice to the deaf.

The previous chapters have demonstrated the sensitivity with which language usage mirrors social realities. Studies of dialect reveal who individuals think they are, how a community or a country is stratified socially, where allegiances are, and what covert aspirations people may harbor, as shown by hypercorrection. Analysis of conversations show how to understand what people are really saying. Comparison of different styles of interaction sensitize professionals to what their clients and patients are signaling in their speech. Analyzing the relationship between speech activities and cultural conditions leads us not to condemn or belittle groups other than our own. Knowing about the variation in learning styles among cultures aids us in effectively educating everybody, not just the middle-class.

Institutional discourses are those with education, law, medicine, the mass media, religion, government, and corporate businesses. These are elite discourses because they are lodged in power centers and those who command these centers only allow access to those who can use their discourses. People who can't are penalized to one degree or another.

LANGUAGE AND MEDICINE

When we enter into each kind of institution, we are expected to enter into its specialized discourse patterns. For instance, if we go to a medical establishment in the United States, we are expected to address the physician by Dr. + Last Name and to have him or her address us by our first name, thus establishing his or her superiority. The physician's power is established in many ways, by use of TLN, as noted, but also by his or her right to ask the most questions, not to answer the questions of a patient, to interrupt, and to limit the length of the interview. Also, typically, the patient is not dressed when the physician enters the examining room, covered only by a jonny, which is more of a drape than an article of clothing. In contrast, the physician is dressed, sometimes in a special white coat denoting his or her status.

Patients are expected not to dispute the physician's analysis of their illness, the worth of the pills that are prescribed, or the value of any other diagnostic or treatment recommendations. The assumption is always that we will do what the doctor says, and if we don't, the doctor may become angry or refuse to treat us further. Although many doctors do allow patients to ask questions, these must be limited to the symptoms themselves and there is usually a short time limit in which to do the asking. Speech extraneous to the reason for the visit is severely limited. Almost everyone has had the experience of leaving the doctor's office and suddenly remembering that they forgot to ask at least one question about something that was bothering them.

The doctor is, of course, allowed to touch the patient, even to see the patient nude, but there is no reciprocity by the patient. These constraints on patients by the dominant medical personnel may be different from culture to culture, so that immigrants and those with limited command of English are at a great disadvantage in getting health care.

Although most physicians are committed to equal care for all who come to them, often disjunction in their speaking practices and those of their patients lead to real miscommunication. Moreover, unexamined social attitudes can have a strong effect on actual diagnosis and treatment.

First, the setting of the physician's office itself can be a real deterrent to effective communication. The patient is often very well aware of the physician's high status, which makes it difficult to speak up or criticize in any way. The physician, in turn, no matter how concerned, may not realize the difficulties caused by both the setting and relative social status of interactants in a medical setting. If we add to this the fact that many physicians are overworked, hence in a rush and not amenable to extended conversation, we have a situation rife with possibilities for resentment. Then, too, most physicians still are male (although this is changing), and their patients female. Since females have been socialized not to interrupt males and not to speak up forcefully, and since males have been socialized not to really listen to or encourage females, women are at a tremendous disadvantage in many medical settings.

Sue Fisher (1982) made a disquieting study which resulted in showing that a patient's social class was a prime determinant in the treatments administered when a Pap smear revealed precancerous cells. Using the techniques of sociolinguistic investigation, she blended verbatim linguistic data with ethnographic data and, as in other sociolinguistic investigations, found that neither practitioners nor patients overtly verbalized their reasons for decision making. For instance, staff would never say that certain women sounded uneducated or were poor, nor do they say:

> that a particular patient has all the children she needs because she is on welfare . . . They do not say that . . . asking too many questions, acting too passive or too aggressive, wanting children or not wanting children . . . contributes to the treatment recommended. (Fisher, 53)

The guidelines physicians are supposed to follow indicate clearly that hysterectomy, the removal of the uterus, rendering a patient sterile, is to be used only as a last resort, or if the patient wishes to be sterilized. What Fisher found, however, was that private patients never received hysterectomies, but seven out of thirteen patients at a community clinic did. Clearly, more was at stake here than decisions based upon the patient's incidence of abnormal cells.

One major difference between the two populations was that the private patients saw a gynecologist in his or her office[1] while they were fully clothed, and had an opportunity to discuss treatment in private. In contrast, the welfare patients were spoken to in the halls in the presence of other patients or in the examining rooms themselves, while sitting undressed. That the former situation allows more dignity goes without saying.

Still, this difference in circumstance was not the major reason for the disparity in treatment. What Fisher found, not surprisingly, was that physicians used different presentational strategies when talking to the private patients, discussing the many modes of treatment available. However, when speaking to the poor women in the clinic, they used persuasional strategies, designed to influence them to accept a hysterectomy. Moreover, it was clear that the more educated private patients were able to question the physicians more skillfully than the poorer women. A microanalysis of the medical interviews clearly showed the sociolinguistic influences on treatment decisions.

Ainsworth-Vaughn (1998), noting that questions are a way of doing power, claims that the person with the right to ask the questions can get to control the topic of conversation. This is especially evident in unequal power relations, such as doctor-patient interviews. Most research into doctor-patient discourse prior to hers has focused on the ways patients are institutionally silenced. One study found that patients asked only 9% of the questions (Ainsworth-Vaughn, 89). Ainsworth-Vaughn herself, perhaps because she studied oncology (cancer) patients who have a lot of questions about their condition and treatment options, found that physicians asked 61.3% questions and patients asked 38.7%. However, the ways that each asked questions were different.

Recall that questions don't have to be asked in canonical question form of the *do you think* or *what are the . . .* varieties. Questions can be **mitigated**, made less direct. For instance, the questioner could say, "I was wondering if. . . ." This is not a direct question. Ainsworth-Vaughn's central thesis is that questions themselves claim power on the part of the questioner, and she is correct, but, mitigated questions do not so directly claim power. Her data show that patients, like Ms. Hazen below, use mitigated questions:

> I know my *KIDS WAS WONDERING* if *you* thought I should be ah advised to have a . . . let me um stand for that . . . to uh have . . . get a whirlpool, hot tub or a whirlpool. (Ainsworth-Vaughn, 40)

This question is mitigated by attributing it to her children, by use of the *was wondering* form, by appealing to the doctor directly by *if you thought*, by hesitations like *um* and *uh*, by extraneous phrasing as in *let me stand for that* and repetition of *to have* and *(to) get a whirlpool* and, finally, weakening her request by offering an alternate, a *hot tub*. Added to all the mitigation in this request, she hesitates by pausing, making false starts to sentences that are never completed, and changing lexical choices like *have* to *get*. The persona she projects is of a very uncertain and powerless woman, thus erasing any implication that she is challenging her doctor or acting as if she knows more than he. Nevertheless, Ainsworth-Vaughn considers this as a way that the patient can claim power. In contrast, the doctor asks questions directly, such as "Did Dr. Marsh put a needle in that?" or "Did you lift a patient?" (36–37).

CHAPTER 11

The patient above was suggesting an alternate therapy for her pain as opposed to what the doctor recommended. That, of course, infringes on the doctor's authority, as he is supposed to be the arbiter of therapy. This explains the amount of mitigating the patient used, at least partially. Throughout the reported interaction, the doctor emphasizes his control by interrupting the patient as she is talking, finishing her sentences, delaying the answer to her question for nine turns. In fact, until the eighth turn, he doesn't even mention physical therapy and when he does mention the whirlpool in the ninth turn, it's to say "we'll see if . . ." His immediate response to the question was, "Take a deep breath," effectively ignoring it. Then he continues saying that "we," meaning himself, has to look at the whole picture, mentioning the possibility of more radiation treatment and reminding her that she had a big tumor. In short, he emphasizes his position as the oncologist, affirms that he is in charge, and he will consider her request only after he has decreed its worth.

Ainsworth-Vaughn's central thesis is that patients by asking mitigated questions are claiming power, even though the doctors maintain their power in the interaction. There is a gender component as well, which is not surprising since, as we have seen, issues of gender also involve power. Male physicians ask more questions than female physicians: 74.3% to females' 49.9%. She also found that patients directed about 26% of the questions to male doctors, but 50% to female ones (94).

As with Fisher's study, Ainsworth-Vaughn (90–93) did find that a patient's socioeconomic status and ethnicity, by which she actually means race, make a difference in a patient's opportunities for asking questions. She found, for instance, that a male upper-middle-class patient asked forty unambiguous questions. This male, a CPA, also claimed that his social position was equal to that of a physician, so he first-named them, an unheard of practice as a rule. His feelings of equality apparently derived from his being in a position of handling their money matters for them. Ainsworth-Vaughn also reports (93) that "nonwhites received less information and less positive talk than whites."

Ainsworth-Vaughn contends, "If power resides in making a decision about what will happen then both Dr. Miller and Ms. Hazen [above] exercised power" (42). Her point, and it is a good one, given the social circumstances, is that the patient's mitigated question allows negotiation, so that the patient has gained for herself a part of the power to make decisions. Had she spoken as authoritatively as the doctor, she would probably have been evaluated as threatening, hostile, and not willing to defer to the physician's superior knowledge. By speaking in a powerless manner, she is able to make her wishes known and acceded to. Although he doesn't answer her query about the whirlpool massage right away, further on in the interview Dr. Miller mentions it and agrees to have her evaluated for whirl-pool therapy.

Ainsworth-Vaughn sees Ms. Hazen's indirect, hesitant question as claiming power. On the one hand, Ms. Hazen's employment of linguistic features that indicate weakness reinforces the power differential in the medical situation. In fact, it specifically recognizes her subordinate role. On the other hand, it allows her to have her suggestion acted upon because she has in no way challenged the doctor. It is the doctor's place to recommend treatment, not the patient's. He has the skill and knowledge she doesn't, so her suggestion, poorly handled, could have been seen as encroaching on the doctor's turf. By mitigating her suggestion, then, she is assuring him that she still respects his opinion, and is not in any way hostile to his authority.

All of this is true, but, to me, the necessity for such a pretense is demeaning. Ainsworth-Vaughn is saying throughout her book that the way for patients to make requests of physicians is for the patients to figuratively bow and humble themselves, to assure the doctor they are not threatening his or her ego. Physicians are not gods empowered with incontrovertible diagnostic and treatment measures. It seems to me that patients should be able to engage them as equals, and that patient suggestions and questions should be answered directly.

The picture that emerges from studies of medical interviews is that physicians, especially male ones, pretty much determine what is going to be discussed. Medicine might be better served if patients had equal access to raising topics through questions, questions that are not so heavily mitigated they can be ignored or staved off. The very fact that a patient feels so insecure that she has to mitigate her request also indicates that she would not raise all the questions she might have. She would only raise the most pressing ones.

Having the physician control the topic by controlling question asking means that he or she may miss some important factor in diagnosis or treatment. There seems no need for a physician, when he or she does get around to responding, to reassert his or her power as part of the response. Ainsworth-Vaughn is probably correct that a patient's claim to power will go more smoothly if it is couched in the most servile manner possible, especially with male doctors. She does make it clear that studies have shown that female doctors are more approachable than male ones. Linguistic analyses of medical interviews can lead to important changes in the discourse of physicians and patients.

CHAPTER 11

PSYCHOTHERAPY

Psychotherapy, the talking cure, constitutes a social event organized around an exchange of information. As such, the ordinary rules of discourse come into play. For years, Freud and his followers interpreted the speech of clients in a highly idiosyncratic manner, treating the entire discourse as the linguistic unit, and fitting whatever the client said into a preconceived set of interpretive rules. An instance of this is the case of Carrie (Seeman and Cole 1977), which I have reported on extensively elsewhere (Chaika 1981, 1990, 283–86). One fragment of her speech and its interpretation illustrates:

1. You know what the experiment is geared to find is how vulnerable, I guess, and you know, if you get close to this person and how you feel about it and some pretty basic questions like it may have something to do with psychiatry, I don't. I'm beginning to think psychiatry is rather old-fashioned, you know there are young people on Yonge Street selling books about, I don't even know how to label them, but there are new ways for man coping with the environment and the people in it. And I haven't got into that but, I don't know I, I just, like you have your set ways of doing things and you're in control. You know and you're talking about yourself personally yesterday, you know, and I walked out of here yesterday and I didn't really have any feeling at all. It was kind of like a release. I like people to confide in me, but, like, where is it going? What, it must serve some purpose, I don't have any theories about it. All I know is that I do get involved with people and it usually ends the same way I, I become very angry and you know something, well not always, but I always get taken, I get sucked in, you know, and I, I was just immobilized last night I didn't accomplish anything and here again today. I, I haven't accomplished anything and I think it's your hang-up too, I, I really don't know. But I get involved in, with and when someone tells me I want to help out, and I want also to give something of myself like I'm older than you, like I would like to give you some of my own insights and I, I don't know if it's appropriate what are we talking about? We're just talking about relationships an they're different, you're a man and I'm a woman and I guess I identified a bit with your girlfriend because I've done that with my boyfriend.

Her psychiatrist interpreted this entire stretch of discourse as:

2. The whole segment can be taken to mean: Do you like me, and if you do, that puts me in an intolerable position. And if you don't, that's unbearable. There seems to be no solution.[2]

Carrie's discourse was produced during an experiment to show that the speech of schizophrenics disintegrates as the patient becomes more intimate with someone. To this end, her therapists had Carrie meet daily with a first-year medical student, a male, to discuss any neutral topics she wished. The medical student himself did not seem to contribute to the conversation. In light of what we now know about normal interactions, this experiment was faulty in several respects. First, it pitted, so to speak, a woman with a long history of schizophrenia against a male authority figure. Second, there was none of the usual give and take of ordinary conversation. Moreover, the experimenters at that time were unaware of the raggedy quality of most unplanned discourse, even in normals. Not only does Carrie's speech conform well to discourses reported in the linguistic literature, but it shows the kind of nervousness that anybody would have in such an unnatural situation. She seems to be rambling on, trying to fill up the silences in approved American/Canadian middle-class practices. These are exacerbated by the fact that women in American society are responsible for carrying the conversational ball until the man wishes to expound on a topic.

The medical student never seems to want to expound, leaving Carrie to prattle on. Moreover, she is quite clearly—using normal discourse analysis—telling this authority figure that she doubts that psychotherapy is effective and that this particular experiment is leading to any kind of beneficial outcome for her. Of course, she buries this criticism in a spate of verbiage, but note that she does mention the parallel with these experimental conversations and usual boy-girl relationships. All the maxims of conversations and the social situations that surround them come to bear on the analysis of discourse in a therapeutic situation. After all, that is a social circumstance, and all cultural and linguistic knowledge is not magically suspended during psychotherapy.

Anthony Wooton (1975, 70) gives an example from psychotherapy. Psychiatrists typically do not tell patients what to do. Rather, by asking questions, they try to lead the patient into understanding. The problem is that the questions asked and the answers they are supposed to evoke are different from those already learned as part of normal routines. As an example, Wooton gives:

3. *Patient*: I'm a nurse, but my husband won't let me work.
   Therapist: How old are you.

CHAPTER 11

> *Patient*:   Thirty-one this December.
> *Therapist*: What do you mean, he won't let you work?

Here, the patient answers the psychiatrist's first question as if it were bona fide, a real-world question. The psychiatrist was not really asking her age, however, as we can see by his next question. What he meant by that question was 'you are old enough to decide whether or not you wish to work.' His question was aimed at leading her to that conclusion.

The patient may have to learn new discourse routines in order to benefit the therapeutic situation. The therapist may use modes of questioning different from everyday discourse. This is not surprising, since the aim of psychotherapy is for the psychiatrist to lead the patient into self-discovery. Some patients become very annoyed by the questioning, feeling that the therapist is refusing to tell them anything.

In traditional psychoanalysis, it was accepted that there had to be a period during which the patient "fought" the analyst by refusing to dredge up the answers from the murky subconscious. It has occurred to me that this period may be caused by such a very unnatural situation. It is very hard to gain insights into oneself by sustained self-questioning, perhaps because questioning is rarely used that way outside the therapeutic situation.

Furthermore, repeated questioning is threatening. In many societies, including our own, it is associated with accusation of wrongdoing and ferreting out the truth of one's guilt. It is used as a technique for teaching, to be sure, but even then it is often done as a way of ferreting out the pupil's lapses in learning.

Many therapists now practice more relaxed conversational techniques, finding them far more fruitful. In that quest, a knowledge of speech act theory and other facets of discourse analysis can enhance the therapeutic process.

Gale (1991) convincingly discusses the efficacy of everyday conversational techniques in regards to family therapy. He calls the use of microanalytical ethnomethodology, as presented here in the chapters on pragmatics, orality, and speech communities, essential to discovering the practices through which interactants produce and interpret their own and others' behaviors. He points out that conversation analysis is not wedded to preconceived meanings, but, rather, is a "detailed examination of how the talk itself is a performative action that helps to both interpret and produce behaviors" (3), and also shows that context is produced as part of the conversation itself. A prime consideration in therapy is to create an environment in which the client can speak freely about matters which are painful or even shameful.

SOCIOLINGUISTICS AND THE PROFESSIONS

The following exchange was produced in a psychotherapeutic session between a clinically depressed patient and her psychiatrist:

4. *Patient*:   My brother used to wake me up in the middle of the night to make me type his college papers, and I had to practically rewrite them.

   Psychiatrist: [sarcastically] Oooh. And did we get good grades?

Although psychiatrists and psychoanalysts traditionally have been trained to be neutral and not judge what is told to them, this therapist clearly showed his disapproval. We know that interpretation of an utterance depends on our understanding of the intent of the speaker in making it. The patient in this instance held a doctorate and was an esteemed scholar, a situation which this psychiatrist, who was young, apparently found threatening. Furthermore, he surmised that her intent in telling him this was that she was bragging about her scholarly prowess as a young woman.

Quite another interpretation of her remarks accrues from a different consideration of her intent. The psychiatrist should have asked himself why she mentioned this occurrence, reminding himself that as a clinically depressed person, her self-esteem was low. Had he done this, instead of cutting off all further therapy and making the patient feel even worse, he might have seen that she was telling him about her low status in her family. Her brother was free to demand that she rouse and do his bidding. Since both parents were also in the house, apparently they saw nothing wrong in her having to be subservient.

Another application of linguistics is explicated by Lisa Capps and Elinor Ochs (1995) in their analysis of the personal narratives of a woman, Meg, afflicted with agoraphobia. They observe that people make sense of their lives by creating personal narratives. These narratives, told and retold, makes people fashion a persona for themselves. How often do you hear someone say, "The kind of person I am. . . ." Recall the discussion of ego-boosting in storytelling in Chapter 6? That is also an instance of narrative construction of self.

People see themselves as actors in the social scene. They also see themselves as coherent entitities, which they both create and reinforce by the stories they tell about themselves. They interpret and reinterpret memories, for instance. On the downside, such stories can reinforce an individual's irrational fears which cause debilitating mental illnesses like agoraphobia. Agoraphobia is an irrational fear of leaving the home, accompanied by persistent anxiety. Sufferers may spend most of their adult lives housebound. If they venture away from their home, some, but not all, have panic attacks.

CHAPTER 11

Capps and Ochs interviewed Meg over a period of two and half years, taping their sessions. Because they had the tapes to listen to repeatedly, they could analyze these narratives in greater detail than if they had been confined to simply taking notes in a therapeutic session. For instance, the tapings allowed them to see how Meg's personal use of grammar and word choice both revealed Meg's feelings, and also helped reinforce her agoraphobia, a concept also presented in Johnstone's (1996) research into the unique way we use the syntactic resources of our language. Their thorough linguistic analysis of Meg's narratives has shed light not only on the etiology of this mental disorder but also on how it became entrenched in Meg, and started to be passed on to her children.

Meg repeats her stories over and over, not only to Capps and Ochs but also to her children and family. Each experience encoded in her narratives remains alive and vivid with the constant retellings. They are suffused with adverbs that denote both the unexpected and the unaccountable (Capps and Ochs, 57) like "all of a sudden," "out of the blue," and "unaccountably." Such terminology pictures her as being a victim of forces beyond her control (Chaika 2000, 165). She emphasizes her terror and powerful feelings by repeating words like *agony* and describing herself as *helpless, trapped,* and *visibly shaking.* Such word choices highlight her "desperate, pleading rendition of her troubling thoughts" (Capps and Ochs, 63).

As one goes through the stories, however, one sees an interesting constancy in them. In all but one, Meg is doing some housewifely task, such as baking Christmas cookies. Her husband William then asks her to go visit relatives with him. She does not want to go, but does so anyway. Once on the freeway, however, she is gripped by panic and issues directives like:

> 5. I've got to get out *now.* I feel *terrible.*
> Can you please get *off* here.
> William, can we get *out* of here.

She further dramatizes the situation by:

> 6. I *begged* William, "*Don't* get on the freeway.
> I just *can't. Please* humor me. *Indulge* me.
> (Capps and Ochs, 108–09)

Only a heart of stone could resist such pleas, and William apparently hasn't got a heart of stone. Therefore, as Capps and Ochs themselves note, she effectively controls him and gets him to take her back home.

Capps and Ochs think that Meg suffers from a communicative disorder, such that she can't say "No" when first asked but defers her refusal until they have started their journey. They feel she has to learn to say "No" when she is first asked. It seems to me, rather, that two purposes are served by Meg's consenting to go or do what her husband wants and then having a panic attack while they're doing it. The first is that she controls her husband, although cultural models say a good wife is submissive, not controlling. The second is she does so without relinquishing her status as a dutiful wife (Chaika 2000, 166–67).

Charlotte Linde (1993) points out in her work *Life Stories: The Creation of Coherence* that people present themselves to others as conforming to society's dicta of their role. Meg presents herself as the good wife, baking, wrapping presents, cooking for her husband, and doing what he bids. Interestingly, one of her first panic attacks didn't involve going anywhere. It was brought on when she was advanced in pregnancy and cooked William a supper which he apparently told her he didn't like. She recounts her response in the present tense:

7. I'm so mad—I could just storm out of here in the car.

Capps and Ochs note that her use of the present tense for a long past event shows how real the event still is in her mind. In any event, she gives pregnancy as her reason for not leaving. Having been nine months pregnant three times, I can testify that doesn't prevent one from getting in the car and driving somewhere. Meg apparently didn't do that, however, because if she did, she wouldn't be the good little housewife.

There's another wrinkle to consider, however. When you're nine months pregnant, you have to have the baby, and, once you do, you're really tied down. It seems to me that Capps and Ochs present a woman who feels entrapped by her roles as a wife and mother. She also feels that she has no control. She displaces that entrapment onto other situations and does so in a way that allows her to control the situation, all the while protecting her identity as a model wife and mother.

Clearly, much can be learned from analyses of patient narratives by trained linguists. Capps and Ochs (174) say, "We encourage psychotherapists to explore linguistic perspectives . . . At the same time we encourage linguists to work with clinicians to develop more acute understandings of the interface between language and emotion." Ideally, a linguist trained in discourse analysis should be on the staff of mental health centers and even in group practices of psychiatrists and clinical psychologists. Linguists could render invaluable insights by objectively analyzing patients' narratives of their lives. The next step in treatment would have to be to teach people to re-author their experiences. Perhaps something as simple as showing Meg how her use of the present tense is keeping something vivid that should be allowed to fade. I'm sure that creative therapists could make good use of well-analyzed narratives.

My own research into schizophrenic speech illustrates well the importance of linguistics to any manifestation of language. My contribution, like Capps and Ochs' above, was simply to take samples of speech, in this instance, schizophrenic speech, some of which I elicited and some of which is in the literature. Then I analyzed its structure to find any deviance from normal utterances. I also looked at word choices, both deviant and not, and examined the degree to which they conformed to normal word choices.

When I first began researching schizophrenic speech, many psychiatrists thought that the patients produced gibberish deliberately, and some even posited that it masked coded messages designed to keep the psychiatrist from knowing what the patient was thinking. Some even overtly disapproved of it to a patient, reprimanding one who, for instance, confused *come* and *go*.[3] On one ward, I found a behavioral psychologist who had set up a system of rewarding schizophrenics who didn't lapse into glossolalia and taking away privileges for those who did. The theory was that patients deliberately spoke this way to avoid the therapeutic situation, so that they weren't cooperating.

My own research indicated that this was not true, that glossalia and other schizophrenic deviant speech were symptoms of an underlying malfunction in the executive portion of the brain. That is, the ability to choose correct words and syntax for what they wanted to say was impaired in these patients (Chaika 1982). This was later termed a *dysexecutive* problem (McKenna and Oh 2005, 132, 141, 145). Indeed, when I was eliciting speech on the ward, some patients apologized to me for their speech, or said after a bout that they knew what they wanted to say, but somehow it didn't come out right.

Nowadays, with the antipsychotic medications available, glossolalia is rarer in schizophrenics. In any event, it was always associated with the onset of psychosis and was not evident when the illness was in remission, showing that it was caused by the illness itself, not by deliberate misconduct and lack of cooperation.

My linguistic analyses of schizophrenic speech have radically altered how psychiatrists view the illness, and also how they treat it.[4] In fact, now many psychiatrists work with linguists in analyzing psychotic speech. Quite by accident, I happened to be the first linguist to tackle the issue of such speech and to subject it to objective linguistic analysis.

LANGUAGE AND THE LAW

We have already seen that location is very important in determining what speech activities can go on and what styles will be used. This is underscored greatly when we consider the law, for as soon as one crosses the threshold of a courtroom, one is suddenly in a world of *plaintiffs, negotiable instruments, demurrers, forthwith, torts, corpus delecti,* and *mens rea.*

The court may be called to order by a sheriff or bailiff who says, "Oyea, oyea, oyea" or "Hear ye, hear ye, hear ye," upon which everyone has to stand, as the sheriff continues, "All persons having any business before the honorable Superior Court come and draw near and you shall be heard." In Massachusetts, this is followed by "God save the Commonwealth and this honorable court. Mr. [or Miss/Mrs.] Justice X presiding. You may be seated." We are assailed with archaisms here, "Oyea," "Hear ye," and "God save." The address forms are suitably elevated, "Mr. Justice X" and "the honorable Superior Court."

One needn't enter a courtroom to hear all varieties of legalese. Go to a lawyer and ask him to write you a will. You wish to leave your jewelry to your cousin Tillie, so the lawyer writes: "I hereby grant, give, devise, bequeath, bequest all my jewelry including but not limited to my diamond and emerald earrings, silver and turquoise Indian bracelet, and any other items of adornment customarily worn and used as such which I may have in my possession, under my control, or for which I possess a power of appointment, express or implied to my dear and beloved cousin Tillie Smits if she survives me, or if not to her heirs."[5]

There are those who, uncharitably, blame lawyers for deliberately using obscure speech so people will have to go to them to straighten out the mess that the lawyers have created simply by using such language. Although sorely tempted, I will not pass such a summary judgment. The language of the law qualifies as a jargon. It serves to identify the lawyers (and judges) as being in the know. One of the ways we know a lawyer is a lawyer is the way he or she handles language pertaining to the legal system. Perhaps some lawyers deliberately do use the jargon to obfuscate and confuse. But it is a gross simplification to say that is a major reason for its existence.

As with other jargons, legalese uses specialized words with specific meaning. For instance, *of course* in lawtalk means 'as a matter of right,' *serve* means 'deliver legal papers,' and *contributory negligence* means 'legally defined specific acts or failure to act so as to injure another party.' All of these terms are used in nonlegal settings, but with different meanings. In instances such as these, the legal jargon is more precise than ordinary language. This can be seen as a positive adaptation of jargon. The repetition of words with the same meaning so often seen in legal documents as in "grant, give, devise, and bequeath" above is also an attempt to be precise. However, these violate the maxim of discourse of not saying more than one needs to in the context. Repeating synonyms is confusing, as the hearer or reader will assume that there is a special reason for mentioning them all so that he or she tries to figure out why each has been alluded to. What is intended as precision becomes nearly unintelligible.

Another function of legalese, one found also in other learned fields and in religious language, is that it separates the activities of the courtroom from everyday activities and does so by using high-flown language. In both religion and the law, archaic language is usual because it removes what is said from the ordinary here and now. The archaic legal "hear ye" has a counterpart in the religious use of *thou* when referring to God. Foreign language words are also typical of legal and religious languages. This, too, has the function of elevating language by making it more remote from the present and everyday activity. Legalese is loaded with lexical items from Latin such as *mens rea, nulla bona,* and *res judicata,* and French *voir dire, chose in action,* and *fee simple.* The last shows the French arrangement of putting the adjective after the noun.[6]

Excessive length of legal sentences, both spoken and written, also obfuscates understanding, but makes the language more serious. Long sentences are a mark of high-level literacy, hence a mark of education. Finegan (1982) discovered that sentences in wills averaged 39.8 words, those in government documents 25.5 words, and those in other kinds of writing only 19.3 words. In order to comprehend long, complex sentences loaded with difficult words, one has to be able to go back and forth, defining words and figuring out what goes with what in what relationship.

O'Barr (1982, 18), quoting Melinkoff (1963, 26), shows how a judge charges a jury orally using the rhetorical devices of high-flown writing. Although this makes his utterances clearly solemn and important, it also renders them incomprehensible. The jargon and overuse of synonyms make them virtually impossible to understand. It is difficult to decode even when written:

1. You are instructed that contributory negligence in its legal significance is such an act or omission on the part of the plaintiff amounting to a want of ordinary care and prudence as occurring or cooperating with some negligent act of the defendant, was the proximate cause of the collision which resulted in the injuries or damages complained of. It may be described as such negligence on the part of the plaintiff, if found to exist, as helped to produce injury or the damages complained of. It may be described as such negligence on the part of the plaintiff, if found to exist, as helped to produce injury or the damages complained of, and if you find from a preponderance of

all the evidence in either of these cases that plaintiff in such case was guilty of any negligence that helped proximately to bring about or produce the injuries of which plaintiff complains, then and in such place the plaintiff cannot recover.

In all fairness, prompted by the large body of research on legal proceedings, law journals have been presenting the case for making the language of the law comprehensible, and individual lawyers and judges have heeded the call, or are trying to, but a brief perusal of current transcripts of trials and written decisions by judges show that the battle is hardly won.

Because courtrooms are arenas for adversaries, it is extra essential that decorum is maintained, especially in the control of turns of who is going to speak at a given time. If people did not respect the proceedings or feel highly constrained against speaking out of turn or assaulting someone, then there would be too many physical confrontations. As we have seen, social routines often have the result of lessening the chance of direct confrontation. I suspect that much of the formality, high-flown language, and courtroom ritual proceeds from this need. As in religion, ritualized activities accompanied by unusual but high-flown language keep people in line, so to speak.

Juries are selected by a process called *voire dire* ('see say') by lawyers. As pompous as their language may be at other times, during the jury selection, lawyers frequently use colloquial, casual language. This is a way of putting the jurors at ease, in the hope that they will reveal their true selves instead of being on their guard. When questioning witnesses for the other side, lawyers may try to make nonstandard varieties of speech appear stupid. Conversely, when expert witnesses for the opposition are called, a lawyer may try to suggest that they are using big words to obscure relatively simple matters.

The outcome of cases is decided largely on the performances of witnesses. Although one would think this depended on what the witnesses have to say, it often results from how they say it. The trial manuals used by lawyers have an entire mythology about women, giving the lawyer such advice as "Be especially courteous to women," presumably because they are such delicate creatures that they can't be treated normally, like a man. Worse, we find that "women are contrary witnesses" and "they try to avoid the answers," and "like children, they are prone to exaggeration" and "given to fabrications" (Bailey and Rothblatt, quoted in O'Barr, 34). Needless to say, there is absolutely no evidence for such assertions.

O'Barr thinks that female speech styles contribute to this impression. Language may be **weak** (WL) or **powerful** (PL). As the previous chapter showed, Robin Lakoff (1975) speculated that women's speech is weak

CHAPTER 11

because women constantly hedge, qualify their statements, and generally give impressions of vagueness and weakness. Here is testimony from a woman talking about the death of a neighbor:

2. *Q*: State whether or not, Mrs. A, you were acquainted with or knew the late Mrs. X.
   A: Quite well.
   Q: What was the nature of your acquaintance with her?
   A: Well, we were, uh, very close friends. Uh, she was even sort of like a mother to me.
   (O'Barr, 66)

We see two characteristics of weak language here, the use of qualifiers and hedges like *sort of* and *quite*, and the fact that her answers are what O'Barr calls **fragmented** (F) style. That is, she doesn't completely answer the question, but has to have the lawyer pull it out of her. An appropriate answer to the first question would have been "Yes. We were close friends. She was like a mother to me." If she had answered fully like this, her testimony would be in **narrative** (N) style, which is a sign of strength and confidence. So is the omission of the hedge words.

However, O'Barr found that there are women who don't speak this way. For instance, from a female pathologist testifying in the same case we find a narrative style with no hedges:

3. *Q*: And the heart had not been functioning, in other words, had the heart been stopped, there would have been no blood to have come from the region.
   C: It may leak down, depending on the position of the body after death. But the presence of blood in the alveoli indicates that some active respiratory action had to take place.
   (O'Barr, 66)

From a man we see even weaker language than Mrs. A's:

4. *Q*: And you observed what?
   D: Well, after I heard—I can't really, I can't definitely state whether the brakes or the lights came first, but I rotated my head slightly to the right, and looked directly behind Mr. Y, and I saw the reflections of the lights, and uh, very, very, very instantaneously after that, I heard a very, very loud explosion—from my standpoint of view it would have been an implosion because everything was forced

outward like this, like a grenade thrown into a room. And, uh, it was terrifically loud.
(O'Barr, 68)

Not only do we see hedging here, but other signs of weakness such as using empty adjectives like *terrifically*, and repetitions of qualifiers as in *very, very, very*.

Hypercorrect forms also give messages of WL, but formal ones belong to PL. Examples of hypercorrect forms are *72 hours, rotated, implosion, not cognizant*. The formal variants of these terms are *three days, turned, explosion, not aware*.

O'Barr found that gender per se did not determine weak and strong styles, but social position did. Well-educated, professional, middle-class women showed few features of WL, whereas men who were unemployed or in subordinate lower-status jobs did show them. Examining further, O'Barr (69–70) discovered that upper- and middle-class educated witnesses of both sexes were more likely to use PL, although people who testify a good deal, such as police officers, also use PL.

To test how style affects the outcome of a trial, O'Barr created four versions of the same testimony, WL and PL by both sexes. He composed juries of undergraduates, law and psychology students who heard the testimony on tape, and evaluated the participants in the mock trial for competence and dynamism. He tested for the way both the lawyer and the witness was perceived. Although all of these jurors were educated and were in a university situation where they are accustomed to intellectual women, they still showed traditional sex biases (81).

Women who gave testimony in PL were believed more than women using WL, and the same was true for men. Clearly, using a powerful style leads to one's being believed. But there is a big "but" here: males were found overall to more convincing, truthful, and trustworthy. That is, there is a tendency to believe anyone more if they don't use WL, but men are, nevertheless, more believable than women (71–75).

There are interesting differences between the ratings of "jurors" in law school and the other "jurors" in O'Barr's study. Because women are supposed to be nonassertive, when they do talk in narrative style, the law-school jurors especially took this as evidence that the lawyer held a high evaluation of the witness, "as demonstrated by the fact that she is permitted to deliver narrative testimony" (81). That is, the lawyers didn't interrupt the females, which would have rendered their testimony fragmented. The other "jurors" rated the females the same in both styles. Female fragmented testimony seems to have been expected, so that wasn't downrated. Legally trained "jurors" were not taken aback by fragmented male style, probably because they expected lawyers to control the situation. However, the other "jurors," those not legally trained, gave particularly low ratings to a male who gave fragmented answers. O'Barr thinks that this was taken as "particularly indicative of the lawyer's negative evaluation of the witness" (81). It is assumed that if the lawyer doesn't allow a male his usual assertiveness, then that male is not to be trusted.

O'Barr also found that witnesses using hypercorrect style were downrated, but those using formal style were rated as more convincing, intelligent, competent, and qualified (86) than the hypercorrectors. The latter, apparently, are perceived to be phonies. Drawing upon research in social psychology, O'Barr speculates that the more listeners are like the speakers, as when both come from the working class, the more punitive the listener's evaluation is if the speaker hypercorrects (87). What this means is that if a working-class speaker says things like "dire need" or "rotated my head," he or she will be discredited by jurors who share his or her accent. Although O'Barr didn't tackle the question, I wonder if this would extend to someone who was trying to use upper-class pronunciations but didn't do so consistently, showing they weren't native to him or her.

O'Barr also edited his tapes to create four more experimental situations. In one, he edited out all overlappings of two speakers. In this tape, speakers talk only when the other has stopped. The remaining three contain simultaneous speech, but differ in who dominates: (1) lawyer and witness equally interrupt and persevere by not giving up the floor; (2) the lawyer interrupts and perseveres in three-fourths of the turns; and (3) the witness does the same in three-fourths of the turns. *Persevere* in this context means 'takes control of the floor, forcing the other to be silent.'

The first and most surprising result is that in all conditions of overlapping speech, the lawyer is perceived as losing control. The unsurprising corollary is that the witness is perceived as having control in those situations. That is, no matter who is interrupting more, the witness is perceived as being powerful and the lawyer weak.

However, this is not necessarily bad in the eyes of the juror. When the witness dominates by persevering more often, the jurors felt that he or she had a better opportunity to present his or her case. Similarly, the lawyer in this instance is felt to be more intelligent and more fair to the witness. The overall finding showed that the "jurors" prefer and evaluate most positively the situation in which there are no hostile exchanges. Hostility in real courtrooms is shown by lawyer and witness interrupting each other. Jurors don't like this, but, if the examining lawyer gives up the floor, he or she is rated more positively. O'Barr speculates that the lawyer who bullies a witness on the stand will do damage to him- or herself in the eyes of the jury (87–89).

SOCIOLINGUISTICS AND THE PROFESSIONS

As we saw in Chapter 3, people tend to match their style to that of the co-conversationalist. This has important consequences for the law. A lawyer can lead a witness into changing style just by speaking faster or slower, by pausing, by enunciating exceptionally clearly, and even by the varying the length of utterances, including questions. By using hypercorrect language, the lawyer can lead the witness into doing the same. Since, as we have seen, the style witnesses use colors the jury's evaluations, the lawyer can have quite an impact on the testimony.

Loftus and Palmer (1974) in a deservedly well-known set of experiments showed that the words used by a questioner had profound effects on what a viewer claims to have seen. They showed people films of auto accidents, then asked questions of the participants, changing the verb they used. For instance, "About how fast were the cars going when they *smashed* into each other?" elicited a faster supposed speed than if the verbs *collided, bumped,* or *hit* were used. Also asking, "Did you see *the* broken headlight?" elicited more "Yes" responses than if they were asked about *a* broken headlight, although there actually wasn't one. Similarly, during a trial the "object of an abortion" was referred to differently by the prosecution and the defense as a *fetus, person, male child,* or *baby boy* (O'Barr, 75). As O'Barr notes (29, 75), word choice wields enormous power, as do grammar choices and style, so that research into their effects has important implications for our entire legal system (66).

Anne Graffam Walker (1982) has shown yet more subtle biases inherent in the legal system, biases caused by factors that witnesses have little control over, as they are unaware of what it is that they are doing. As an experienced court stenographer, she was able to be present at depositions, a legal proceeding in which lawyers are allowed to ask questions of hostile witnesses before the trial.

She specifically investigated how lawyers evaluate **cospeech**, another word for overlapping and hesitations of witnesses. Cospeech can occur at different points in the speaker's turn and can have different meaning. It can take the form of a challenge, such as a lawyer's "I'll ask the questions here." This is termed disruptive as it is perceived as trying to take the floor away from the speaker. A more common type occurs when witnesses try to correct the lawyer's misinformation or they don't understand him or her. They are not trying to take the floor. They want to repair the situation.

Lawyers evaluate each kind of cospeech differently. One woman who had a great many overlaps even in the middle of a clause was regarded as "sweet." None of her cospeech was disruptive because she only answered questions. Her husband, termed "a good ole boy" (109) was not perceived as challenging. A third deponent interrupted counsel's turn 36% of time and the counsel didn't like it or him. Lawyers, on their part, were guilty of "overwhelmingly disruptive cospeech" (104) if the deponent gave an answer like "I don't know."

Walker maintains that in question and answer exchanges, silence is two-faced where issues of truth are important. One face is allied to someone's need to collect his or her thoughts, planning what to say next. The other is the hearer's need to attribute motives to a pause. That is, does a pause indicate that the speaker is being dishonest? Or that he or she is slow in formulating an answer? Actually, not all pauses are silent. Some are filled. By "filled," linguists mean those "uh," "hmm," "aah," and throat-clearing sounds, which both indicate planning what comes next and that the speaker doesn't want anyone to take the floor from them just because he or she has a glitch in encoding. Silent pausing before answering a question is interpreted as hesitancy (68).

Walker found that attorneys interpret those who used filled pauses before giving an answer to be straightforward and cooperative: wanting to answer questions, being responsive to questions, and speaking immediately at the end of every question. Those who used more silent pauses before answering were judged to be nervous and afraid, recalcitrant, not careful in answering, and not spontaneous. Judging this way is called **attribution**.

There was one exception to these judgments. The examining lawyer afterwards, having been asked to comment, said that one witness gave both "excess consideration to her answer" and "shot from the hip." Walker was puzzled because she found no evidence for either conclusion. What she did find was that the witness spoke faster than the lawyer, 5.3 S/S (syllables per second) to his 4.69 S/S, so actual speed couldn't have given the impression of slowness (the impression of "excess consideration"). However, the witness did not use a silent pause at all. That is, she never hesitated before answering. A full eleven of her answers came so fast they resulted in cospeech. Twenty-three were instantaneous, and only nine had pause fillers.

Walker considers two possible reasons for the lawyer's impression of this witness. One is that the nine filled pauses were so in contrast to the rest of her speech that they were specially remembered. The other is that she committed a cardinal sin early in the interview. She interrupted the lawyer. This resulted in her being viewed negatively. If you don't like people, you notice and remember the bad things. Walker's explanation for the attorney's belief that the witness shot from the hip rests on speed. Like the witness, Walker speaks rapidly. The lawyer, as indicated above, does not. Consequently, Walker got no feeling that the witness's responses were precipitous, but the lawyer, a slow speaker, did. Notice that the lawyer got two contrary impressions of the witness, both related to tempo.

Martha Komter (1998) has studied the dilemmas[7] inherent in defending oneself in a trial for a crime. If the defendant confesses, he or she is seen as cooperative. Additionally, a voluntary confession indicates that the defendant is, at bottom, a decent citizen despite the lapse into crime (25). Thus, a judge might give a more lenient sentence than if the confession were not forthcoming. The problem is, of course, if one confesses, one is admitting to the crime. Still, it is better, she claims, to confess if the evidence is overwhelming against one. However, there are ways of mitigating the crime. Once a defendant has established his honesty by his confession to some counts, he can then deny others, as his credibility has been established. This strategy is used by a large number of defendants who admit the more innocuous aspects of what they've done, but then deny the more serious ones (Komter, 26–27). Some do not admit their guilt, but say things like:

5. Look, if I had done it, I'd be the *last to say I have not done it. For I don't like abusing children.* (27–28)

Komter explains this strategy by noting that it is much more convincing to admit guilt. By combining a plea of innocence with an open recognition that a guilty plea might be more credible, one seems more credible. This is especially so when, combined with this recognition, one states that one dislikes the crime, thereby establishing that one adheres to community values.

When one can't claim innocence, one can still claim a lapse in memory. Since there is a gap in time between the crime and the trial, this is easy to assert. Also, in the heat of the moment, one may not be observant, so if a prosecutor asks if the defendant saw blood, the answer might be, "I can't remember" (45–46).

Another ploy is to weaken the prosecutor's assertion. For instance, in a manslaughter case, a defendant claimed he "**simply** wanted to show her [the clerk] that I was angry" (47). Another defendant corrected the judge's "you marched him out of the room" to "**simply** took his arm like this . . . he just **simply** stepped down the doorstep uh him<u>self</u>" (47–48). The use of *simply* in these testimonies is noteworthy, as it mitigates the action, making it seem less violent. Finally, another defensive strategy is to word something so that the defendant isn't overtly stated to be the agent of the action. For instance, one defendant, instead of saying, "I acted a little strange there," rephrased it to "Yes, things were a little strange yes" (49). Another defendant cast himself as a spectator:

6. Then I suddenly remembered my gun and I reached for it and then there were shots. (49)

First, note the use of *suddenly*. It's as if he didn't bring the gun along purposely to commit a crime. It just happened to be there. Then, although he admitted he reached for it, he phrases the shots so that they just happened. He doesn't present himself as the subject of the shooting. Another defendant, accused of violently attacking a girl while watching marathon runners, presents his story as:

> 7. I simply stood there b-b-by that road, and I was a little drunk, and I don't quite remember it any more, and I got pushed, and uh well I go angry and uh [pauses] all at once a complete swarm of people around me and uh then I was lying on the ground and uh with handcuffs on and so. . . . (57)

As Komter points out, "the suspect exhibits a whole repertoire of defensive strategies." He first presents himself as a passive bystander. Then he claims a lapse in memory, so he doesn't say what he did, only that he felt angry. He is also claiming diminished capacity by admitting he was drunk. He goes from feeling angry to his being on the ground with no mention of how he got there or what he did to have a swarm of people around him. Komter calls his usage of *all at once* a passivity marker. It indicates that something happened to him, but he didn't do anything. This reminds me of agoraphobic Meg's reiteration of adverbials like *out of the blue* to emphasize the capriciousness of what happens to her, which is also a way of denying responsibility for her actions.

The usefulness of linguistics for the law is evidenced also by the fact of there being a journal, *Forensic Linguistics*, dedicated to publishing research pertinent to all matters of legal justice and injustice.

DISCOURSE PRACTICES AND EDUCATION

In order to do well in American (and European) style schools, pupils must be willing to answer questions put to them and to otherwise speak out in the classrooms when the teacher wants them to. Philips (1970) showed that the Warm Springs Indians do not feel free to speak up in school because they are not socialized into the kinds of responses that most other Americans are. The Warm Springs Indians feel that to make mistakes publicly is very humiliating. When tribespeople have to learn something, they observe it until they think they know it. When they are ready, they ask others to come watch a demonstration. The idea of learning by humiliation, as in European-based societies, is repugnant to them. Scollon and Scollon (1981, 8) claim that Athabaskans feel that it is dangerous to the spiritual, mental, and psychological health of a child to make him[8] perform in public. They even feel that it is wrong to observe the child in any way that would intervene in his or her activities.

Erickson (1984, 88–90) explains a somewhat different state of affairs in the socialization of black children in Chicago. In the late 1940's and early 1950's, children were taught **controverting routines**.[9] These were ways of teaching a child to make a personal display in "the spotlight of public attention" (88). An adult would say something, such as, "Don't touch the refrigerator" to which the child answered "I gonna":

> and the subsequent interchanges escalating in intensity, with more and more drastic threats uttered by the adult. At the end of the routine an adult . . . would say admiringly, 'Oo:::h, he so ba:::d'[10]

Erickson says that such routines have been recorded among black migrant workers and New England Cape Verdean children as recently as 1979. Children socialized to "play argue" this way in the face of an adult command get into a great deal of trouble in school. Although Native American children don't learn to answer back that way, they get into equal amounts of trouble by their inappropriate silence.

Also, many non-middle-class children of color are not socialized to tell adults what they, the children, already know. Shirley Brice Heath (1983) documents this thoroughly in the Piedmont. One New York researcher asked an African American child where he lived. Since she had given him a ride from his house to the park where they were picnicking, he vaguely pointed 'over there.' Then her husband, who had not been in the car, asked the child. The boy answered with specific directions, complete with the requisite left and rights and numbers of streets to cross.

Stephen Boggs (1972) found that native Hawaiian children would not answer questions put to them directly by a teacher. They perceive questions directed at one child as threats. If the teacher asks questions of the group at large, however, pupils answer readily. Even if Hawaiian children today are socialized differently, the example serves to show the sorts of cultural differences one can encounter in the classroom and that teachers must be able to adapt to.

Researchers like Deutsch et al. (1967) and Bereiter and Engelmann (1966) claimed that black children were deficient in language skills. Labov (1972b) showed that the methodology these researchers used to test black language skills was guaranteed to produce defective language. Taking a child of color into a room with an adult white tester and then asking the child to identify something so obvious as a toy elicited silence or a scared "I don't know." The child suspected some kind of trap. Why else would this strange adult in this strange environment be asking such a stupid question? It has always seemed to me that when someone is summoned, especially in school or at work, the natural inference is that something is wrong. In any event, the threatening nature of this summons was especially strong for black inner-city children, as they are more used to interacting with peers than adults. Such children are used to questioning from adults only if the adult patently must know the answer.

Labov showed that one gets very skillful language from these same children by interviewing them in groups and setting up competition with each other. The same kind of children who mumbled and stumbled over Deutsch et al.'s and Bereiter and Engelmann's testing showed exceptional facility under Labov's, testing situation which was designed to duplicate the situations in which these children usually communicate.

In a world relying increasingly on the skills taught in school, it is frustrating not to know how to teach children who haven't been socialized into getting literacy skills. Middle-class black and white children are taught to tell adults all sorts of trivia, things that adults certainly know, such as "And what does the doggy say?" and "Where's your nose? And your tootsies?" But not all children receive this kind of training, and those who do not, do notoriously poorly in the typical public school. If children are not socialized this way, what do we do? Even providing preschooling for such children does not necessarily solve the problem, for, as the Scollons have shown, literacy skills actually begin in toddlerhood. It must be emphasized that even parents who are not middle-class are usually very anxious for their children to learn in school. In their frustration with the failures of the schools, they may accuse the system of deliberately making things tough for their children. However, we are just beginning to understand what a child needs to become literate, and we are far from knowing what to do for those who don't come from literate homes.

The persistent problem of low IQ scores in non-middle-class children may not be caused by culturally biased questions, but by culturally biased testing situations. Inner-city blacks are socialized into showing off their intellectual skills in oral displays and competition, not by sitting and marking answers with a pencil. Moreover, they are taught to be original in both their speech and their interpretations of others' speech. Robert Aronowitz (1984) demonstrates that such children fail at standardized reading tests because their answers are creative and perceptive, whereas the test makers prefer "maximally-redundant-minimally-informative . . . answers."

DIALECTS AND READING

We have already seen that dialects differ not only in pronunciation but also in syntax. Both circumstances can cause problems in teaching reading as well as affect a teacher's evaluation of certain pupils. In order to teach children successfully, it is essential to draw on linguistic knowledge about dialect differences, the divide between spoken and written language, and insights into cultural differences in interacting. We have seen this throughout this book.

The problem with dialectal differences is that schoolteachers typically speak one of the standard dialects. Even if they started out as non-SE, they usually think that nonstandard English of any variety is full of mistakes. As we saw in Chapter 7, and as could be illustrated many times over, this is not true.

It is not fair to isolate one form from a dialect and then compare it to a different dialect. It is such a practice that leads one to think that the other dialect contains errors. Teachers confronted with speakers of dialects different from their own should listen carefully and try to ascertain the ways the other dialect operates. Then they should try to analyze exactly how it differs from their own accustomed usage.

Everyone who reads well translates the printed sentence into his or her own dialect. For instance, recall the great differences between AAVE and SE in verb tenses. AAVE-speaking children are not likely to come across their own dialect's verb system in reading textbooks. Nor are NSE children of any other group. The teacher can point out to an AAVE-speaking child, for instance, "Oh, this 'I did sing' means 'I really DID do it' not 'I done sung'" or he or she can say, "'I will go' is the same as your 'agonna go.'" It is impossible to learn to read unless one knows how to relate the printed page to the speech one already has.

Some immediately object with horror, "But isn't that reinforcing undesirable speech habits?" Not really. In fact, the opposite effect is more likely. By nonjudgmentally pointing out to the child that others say things differently, one is helping the child notice the differences between his or her speech and that of others, including the standard. Also such equations give the child a handle on which forms to focus on.

PBS in 2005 aired a program *Do You Speak American?*, which showed a classroom in Los Angeles in which AAVE speakers were being taught SE as a competitive game with the class divided into teams. The teacher gave the AAVE sentence and the children had to change it into SE. Teams, not individuals, were the winners, so no one child was on the spot. The children were clearly enjoying the game. Recall that when we examined speech communities, we saw the factors that lead to a child's picking up new dialects. Humiliation because of one's native dialect is not one of them.

Similarly, understanding differences in pronunciation between dialects is essential to teaching reading and spelling. English orthography has a woefully poor fit to all varieties of English. No dialect of English is spoken the way it is spelled. We all had to learn how the written language corresponds to our spoken language. Some have to learn that the first vowels in *thorough, hurry,* and *her* are pronounced alike, as are the vowels in *talk* and *tock.* That is, they learn to ignore differences in vowel spelling. The *r*-less speakers learn that <ar> and <or> stand for two different vowels rather than a vowel and an <r>. For them <ar> is [a:] "ah" as opposed to the <a>, which is pronounced [æ], in *cat,* and <or> stands for one sound as well, [ɔ] "aw" as opposed to <o> in *cot.* Everyone has to learn that the <k> in *knee* is silent, as is the <gh> in *weigh.* We also all have to learn that the printed *have* in *they have gone* is really the *'ve* we are accustomed to hearing as "they've gone."

In order to learn to read, all speakers must learn the correspondences between his or her dialect and the written one (Labov 1967; Baratz and Shuy 1969). Early researchers like these did assume that AAVE and non-standard speaking students came to school with no clue about reading, but Heath's (1983, 190–235) study shows that such children do, although they don't use their preliteracy in ways that conform to traditional classrooms. It is up to the school, then, to relate reading to their pupils' dialects. Teachers should also be aware of the uses of literacy in their pupils' cultures, or if there are any uses for it at all. Without such knowledge, teaching can not be effective. With it, the teacher can capitalize on what pupils already know, leading them gently into the requirements of school.

We have already seen that people not only announce who they are by their speech variety but also by the positions they may take in society. It has been shown that people unhesitatingly assign others to a particular job category according to their taped speech alone. Bowlers, CB'ers, and other jargon users consider only other speakers of the jargon as really belonging, as being "in the know."

One implication of all this is that it is useful for those who wish to enter the professions or other jobs which call for SE to learn how to use it. This is not to say that the varieties of nonstandard speech are not useful. They certainly are, as we saw in Chapter 7. They announce one's feelings of identity with a certain group; they are perceived as natural, as macho, as real. There is certainly nothing wrong with being a construction worker, an electrician, a plumber, a painter, or a builder, to name but a few lucrative and respectable occupations that don't require SE. Personally, I feel that we gear too much of our public education system to the goal of getting into college. College and the jobs it prepares one for are not for everybody. I am a firm believer in vocational schooling for those who want it. Still, SE should be taught as a resource for children to draw upon if they ever need it.

Public schools traditionally and correctly felt that part of their duty is to introduce students to standard speech. They have done this by giving grammar lessons and having teachers correct pronunciation sporadically. None of this helps. In fact, it can be insulting to the students, telling them the way they and their families speak are not proper. Furthermore, not all people have a use for SE. A car mechanic or construction worker who spoke la-di-da would be ridiculed by his peers. As we have seen, children and adults speak like those with whom they identify. If they do not identify with the teacher and the middle class, nothing will make them talk that way, although they get the message about the inferiority of their native speech. They also become convinced that school is not for them.

Since they do not identify with the middle class, many students are not likely to identify with the values of school, that archetypal middle-class institution. Even those who do are often under peer pressure not to conform to the demands of school, including "proper" speech. When teachers correct their speech, many such children feel as if they themselves have been attacked. Considering the close connection between speech and identity, such feelings are justified.

Yet once they reach their twenties, some of these pupils will change their minds. They may start to see some value in middle-class ways and want to become better educated or to get higher-level jobs. Native Americans, by tribal custom, frequently do not start to prepare for adult roles until their late teens or early twenties (Ohanessian 1972). Black youths frequently make no attempt to adopt middle-class speech until their late teens or early twenties, either. In fact, this is true of many adolescent males. The biggest problem for education is that sometimes it is very difficult by that age to begin to use certain sounds and constructions with any consistency. The sounds hardest to change are just those the most implicated in social class marking, such as the "th" sounds.

There are ways out of this dilemma, ways that do not insult students or get their backs up so that they refuse to learn standard speech forms. Students can be asked to act out natural situations, such as being interviewed for a job, lodging complaints with authority, or impressing a schoolteacher. They should be directed to speak appropriately for the roles. Heath (1983, 317–320) stimulated children to become ethnographers, reporting on the kinds of speech used by different people and for different purposes. As part of a science unit, she had them interview people about farming techniques and then write a book about their discoveries. This, of course, enlarged the children's social networks and sensitized them to language differences.

Such techniques can be adapted to writing as well. Inner-city high school students with reading achievement scores as low as second grade proved able to write coherent newspaper articles for teachers in a college workshop that I guided (Chaika 1978). Students worked in groups, correcting one another's work, with the teacher floating from table to table to give help with mechanics. Teachers were pleased to find that such students show a hefty passive knowledge of standard speech and writing forms when these are not elicited punitively. Other tasks which allow students to practice standard speech include putting on plays in which the characters are middle-class, having students write and produce mock TV shows, pretending to be news announcers, and even asking them to instruct their classmates. Thus they can all practice educated speech, and, if they ever want to speak that way, the resource will be awaiting them. The school's aim should allow students to become functionally bidialectal.

APPLICATIONS TO BILINGUAL EDUCATION

Both bilingual education and ordinary foreign language classes share the same concern: to teach people how to communicate effectively in a new language. To this end, it is useful to examine how bilinguals themselves deal with their languages, how they use them, under what circumstances, and even how they have learned them, if not in a school situation.

There is still a great deal that we don't know about how bilinguals draw upon their separate languages, but it seems at least likely if not sure that they don't normally simply look for equivalents between their languages as they select one or the other for a given transaction. Yet, as noted previously, the traditional classroom focuses on translation.

Bilinguals often make mistakes in speaking their nondominant language (if both aren't equivalent for them). Very fluent bilinguals seem happily unaware that they do small violences to their second language in pronunciation, lexical choice, and syntax. Yet, the traditional classroom stops the student at every error. In the heat of conversation, bilinguals typically don't stop to repeat learned rules as they talk away. Yet, the traditional classroom belabors rules.

But the times are changing. As far back as 1967 when I attempted to dip my toes into Chinese at Brown University, Professors Jimmy Wrenn and David Lattimore taught by having us learn dialogues appropriate for myriad ordinary social interactions. Such an approach had the advantages of making us talk, but the disadvantage was that the dialogues were "canned." We had to memorize them. They weren't necessarily what we wanted to say. In those days, it was assumed that sheer memorization was the best way to learn a new language. There couldn't be too much drilling. This was before the research into language acquisition showed that language learning is an active, creative process.

More recently, the late Robert DiPietro (1987) applied his considerable sociolinguistic knowledge to language teaching. He set up scenarios, frames, then allowed his students to work out for themselves both what they wanted to say and how they wanted the scenarios to be resolved. For instance, one group of students might be told that they were having a heart attack, and another that they were the doctors. Students were given a chance to rehearse individually what they wanted to do. One "doctor" may wish to be indirect, and another might want to be blunt and even scold the "patient." Neither group knew how the other was going to behave, so that the students had to figure out the intentions of the other as they would in normal conversations. Each had to change tactics in response with the other.

As in real life, students were allowed to make errors, and to repair them. In short, they learned by doing, naturally. In dialogue-based instruction, students may even be allowed to make typical bilingual errors, sacrificing perfection for the sake of fluency and comfort in speaking the foreign language. To show that this method works, DiPietro recorded the students' conversations and edited out the errors. Then he had the students look over the corrected manuscripts, but not memorize them. Subsequently, when the students reenacted their scenes, they were far more fluent and made fewer errors the second time around, showing that they had actually learned.

LANGUAGE AND RELIGION

A major role of linguistics in studying religions is that of understanding the pitfalls of translation, as we saw in Chapters 8 and 9. That is a topic which would take another whole book to discuss. The awareness that linguistics brings as to the diversity of grammars and knowledge of the radical differences in the lineup of words to meaning across languages are core concerns of linguists. Linguists have been very involved with translating the Gospels into little-known languages and in developing translation theory. In fact, much of what we know of human language use today comes from linguists like Kenneth Pike and Eugene Nida, who applied linguistics to the task of teaching Christianity to people who spoke languages very different from the European ones. Both linguistics and religion have benefitted from their efforts.

We recall that formal uses of language increase the feeling of respect people have for others. This applies as well to religion. Everyday language is not usually suitable for religious purposes, as worshipers are supposed to pay special respect to the Deity and to their clergy. Consequently, many religions use now dead languages to increase their mystery, or, at the very least, archaic formal forms of their present speech. The former is illustrated by the Hebrew in a Jewish service, Classical Arabic in a Muslim one, and the King James' Bible for Christian English speakers.

CHAPTER 11

An unusual religious discourse activity is "speaking in tongues," known scientifically as **glossolalia**. This is unusual because the utterances aren't in a recognizable language if they were, then the activity wouldn't be "speaking in tongues." Nobody has ever been able to prove that the glossolalists are actually speaking another language. In fact, there is little proof that speakers make sounds not native to their own languages.

Indeed, one of the primary researchers in the field, William Samarin (1972, 1973a, 1973b, 1979), says that glossolalia bears no resemblance to any language, living or dead, although the speaker believes it does.[11] He points out that the intonation used in the speaker's "utterances" make them sound like real language, but they always lack the central feature of language: a semantic system tied to specific words and grammar.

In the 1940's and 1950's, Danny Kaye and Sid Caesar, two comedians, produced babbling which sounded like foreign languages in their routines, very successfully too, I might add. This is not said to disparage speaking in tongues, just to point out that there are parallels in that language-like sequences can be made, but, of course, for very different purposes. Even if the person who speaks in tongues is not speaking an actual language, for those who believe, it is a sign that they have the Spirit and have transcended into a higher spiritual state.

Although the speakers themselves do not or cannot explain what they have said, others in the church, either laypersons or ministers, interpret it. Laffal, Monahan, and Richman (1974) had a young minister speak in tongues in response to words they read him, and played the resulting tapes to different audiences. The audiences were willing to ascribe meaning to each portion, but the meaning they derived was not the same as that intended by the speaker.

Speaking in tongues proceeds from religious conviction. The New Testament is the authority for it, taking it to be proof of the Holy Spirit within the speaker. Samarin (1979) says that most think they are speaking a language: either direct speech of the Holy Spirit, or speech inspired by the Holy Spirit.

A great difference between glossolalia and ordinary speech is that the glossolalist can't repeat at will what he or she said, nor can he or she paraphrase it. Whereas ordinary speech is decodable by breaking it down into its components of recognized words built up from recognized sounds, glossolalic "speech" gives a meaning independent of such decoding procedures. Moreover, whereas ordinary speech can be decoded by most other speakers of the language, glossolalia typically can be decoded only by another at the meeting where it occurs.

Hamby (1980) says that glossolalia is a social phenomenon with a shared meaning. In other words, the fact of speaking in tongues gives its own meaning. One thing all agree upon, however, is that whatever meaning can be construed from glossolalic productions, it is not done by ordinary people using ordinary decoding means. Instead, another member interprets for the speaker.

One heated debate has pivoted on the question of whether speakers in tongues are in a state of altered consciousness. Felicitas Goodman (1972a, 1972b) is a firm proponent of the altered states theory. She investigated Apostolic congregations in Mexico, the Yucatan, and Indiana, finding that speaking in tongues is accompanied by a hyperaroused trance brought about by rhythmic clapping, music, singing, and praying. There are other physical manifestations, such as twitching, shaking, jumping, even a catatonic-like state. Those affected say they feel heat, floating, pressure and relief of tension. She was able to tape speech examples. She also claims that, in small congregations, a set of stock syllables develop. She claims that there is a striking agreement across congregations and across cultures in rhythmic patterns and intonation, even in speakers of different languages (Goodman 1969). She explains this surprising agreement as occurring because the glossolalic behaviors arise from speakers being in a trance.

Samarin (1972b, 1973b) vociferously denies this. Rather, he gives a sociolinguistic interpretation. He states that glossolalia is nonsense which is given the form of language by the speaker's intonation and pauses, but that it is not a trance which causes it but the belief in the Biblical authority for it. To its practitioners it is a symbol of faith and is another language in their religious repertoire. It is their beliefs, not a trance, which causes the phenomenon. He goes so far as to declare that all groups of Christians who indulge in such verbal behavior share theological beliefs and criteria for its use and even its form. He may well be correct, but this does not eliminate altered states as one cause of the glossolalia. It is entirely conceivable that people are able to achieve an altered state because of their belief that they can.

Samarin further claims that glossalia is a religious language, and that it can be explained by noting that it is simpler than natural language. It is caused by a general linguistic regression in which speech is produced unconsciously using rules of pronunciation acquired early, but modified somewhat according to the social and religious factors leading to glossolalia.

Usually, speaking in tongues utilizes a limited number of sounds, about twelve, and makes use of alliteration and reduplication.[12] Samarin compares glossolalia to other pseudo-languages, such as bebop talk, magical incantations, and jabberwocky, all of which have purely social functions apart from what we usually think of as communication of information.

In defense of Samarin's views, Spanos and Hewitt (1979) investigated Goodman's trance explanation, as well as speakers' susceptibility to hypnotism, and possible psychopathology of speakers. They found that speakers performed with their eyes open, and evinced none of the trembling, shaking, or disorientation that one would expect of those in trances. They also found no indication that the speakers were more easily hypnotized than anyone else, nor was there indication of psychosis. Rather, they shared religious beliefs and experiences with others.

Hamby (1980) describes how Catholic Charismatics learn to speak in tongues both from discussing it and by hearing others do it, as well as hearing others' interpretations. One of my friends who had been hospitalized for depression, told me that when she first went to a Charismatic meeting and people began to speak in tongues, she thought, "Oh, they're like the schizophrenic patients at Butler's."[13] However, she went on, "Then I got the spirit and began to do it myself."

Perhaps glossolalia is another way of elevating language, a way of creating a foreign language, so to speak. It is interesting that this phenomenon does not occur in Judaism, which uses archaic Hebrew for worship, nor, apparently, did it occur in Catholicism when masses were in Latin. For solemn functions, the vernacular just won't do for some people.

Spanos and Hewitt's studies support Samarin, but do not rule out the possibility of trance states such as Goodman posits. Both things can go on simultaneously at least for some speakers. My own research has been with schizophrenics, some of whom also produce glossolalia, but they do not do it in a particular social setting (Chaika 1974, 1982, 1990). For them it is linked to the severity of their illness, and is evidence that they are not "in their right minds." They don't look as if they are in a trance, nor do they twitch, or otherwise manifest an altered state. Anecdotally, I have heard stories of how someone locked in a back ward of a psychiatric hospital in the olden days learned to "speak schizophrenic" by listening to such patients, but I've never met such a person.

Religious and schizophrenic glossolalia are interesting in that they manifest themselves with the same kinds of strings of sounds, but apparently have very different underlying causes and mean very different things. Speech-disordered schizophrenics don't necessarily produce only glossolalia. They may also utter word salads, jumbles of recognizable words not in a grammatical frame, create strings of meaningless rhymes, or produce phrases that associated with each other, but are not subordinated to a topic, such as:

[in answer to a question of what color a chip was]
Looks like clay. Sounds like gray. Take you for a roll in the hay.
Hay day. May day. Help. I need help. (Cohen 1978)

A comparison is very much in order of the different glossolalic populations, such as the religious, the schizophrenic, the productions of comedians, of magicians and their incantations, of bebop singers in the 1940's, of Dr. Seuss and Lewis Carroll, and all who love their glossolalia. Even some of the rhyming heard in freestyle rapping verges on the glossolalic.

Besides the professions mentioned in this chapter, linguists have been involved in working on medical teams dealing with aphasics, people who have speech dysfunction because of injury or stroke. Linguists also began studying the language of the deaf, learning that sign languages are as complex and structured as oral ones are. They have applied knowledge of linguistics and language acquisition to bettering the ways oral language can be taught to the profoundly deaf. Linguists have studied the speech of congenitally aphasic children, the retarded, the autistic, and those with other speech pathologies.

As we have seen, linguists are in the vanguard of studying what it is to be human, because to be human is to talk.

CHAPTER 11

Notes

[1] My own experience with physicians as a private patient is that the physician conducts the examination and interview while I am covered only by a jonny in the examination room. Almost never am I told to get dressed and then meet the physician in his or her office. I presume this is to save the physician's time. Whether this is a regional difference in medical practice or whether it is that in the twenty-four years since Fisher's study doctors have become too busy for separate office discussions, I don't know.

[2] The psychiatrist, Dr. Mary Seeman, has long since written to me, telling me she realized that she agrees with interpreting Carrie's speech according to the rules of current discourse analysis. At the time she made her investigation of Carrie, she was using accepted psychoanalytic techniques of interpretation, and sociolinguistic discourse analysis was not yet widely developed or disseminated. This is being presented now only as an example of how to apply sociolinguistics to therapy.

[3] What was interesting here is that the psychiatrist clearly showed his anger by publishing what he said to the patient so afflicted. It was so taken for granted that patients could control their speech if they wanted to that such anger was considered both justified and professional.

[4] In fact, so well accepted has my work on schizophrenic speech and how to analyze it become that I was invited to speak to the X World Congress of Psychiatry: Symposium on Language and Psychosis, Madrid, Spain, August 26, 1996. I have also spoken before the Royal College of Psychiatrists at Leeds University in the UK, also as an invited speaker. This information is not being presented because I wish to brag, but to show how important linguistics is to any profession that relies on language use.

[5] Thanks to William Chaika, Esq. for providing this pseudo-will. It is, of course, a parody, but not far off the mark. He assures me that *he* would never word a will this way, but thousands of lawyers do.

[6] This is also true of names for officers of the government such as *surgeon general* and *attorney general*. These literally mean 'general surgeon' and 'general physician.' In other words, the surgeon and attorney for everybody. What has happened, however, is that English speakers have reinterpreted these to equate the *general* with army generals, meaning those of high rank.

[7] Actually, her book presents the dilemmas of both the defendant and of the judge, but since the Dutch judicial system is so different from the

American, here I only discuss the person on trial. In The Netherlands, for instance, the judge directly cross-examines the defendant and seems to be the sole arbiter of sentencing.

8 Pronoun choice theirs.

9 This may still be true; however, he gives those dates. Certainly, in the schoolyards, even in kindergarten, one hears African American children's clever wordplay today, suggesting that they have been socialized to engage in such routines.

10 The colons indicate long, drawn-out vowels.

11 One of my students told me he was positive he was speaking Hebrew, as he made many guttural sounds while speaking in tongues. He was, however, not able to reproduce his glossolalic state while talking to me, so I couldn't tell whether he did. However, he definitely was not able to imitate my renditions of Hebrew words.

12 Repetition of syllables produced consecutively as in "bye-bye," "bow-wow," and "higgly-piggly." It differs from rhyme in that (1) it can be a repetition of the entire syllable, and (2) rhyme has intervening words.

13 That is the name of the psychiatric hospital affiliated with Brown University.

CHAPTER 11

Exercises

1. Find several words with the spelling <ea>. How many pronunciations are there for this combination of letters? Do the same for the <gh> spelling and one other use of letters of your choice. Can speakers of any dialect pronounce English as it is written? On the basis of this mini-study, do you think it is possible to teach someone how to read who doesn't speak with a standard dialect or a strong regional one different from your own?

2. Find a contract or lease in your home. The statement of credit liability on a bill for a credit card is fine. What elements of legalese do you find on the document you chose?

3. Examine the language of a prayer of your choice. What archaic or unusual words or syntax can you find in it? Translate the prayer into everyday casual speech. What is the effect?

4. If you and a friend are studying the same foreign language, or if you have studied one that you know another friend has also studied, give yourself a topic of conversation and prepare what you want to say about it in the foreign language. Now try conversing with the friend. What difficulties do you find in expressing yourself?

5. Pretend that you are a physician and a friend is your patient. Try to talk as if you are his or her physician. What features of your speech behavior do you change? How does the friend's behavior to you change? Alternatively, poll people about how they talk with their doctors. How easily do they find they can ask questions, contradict his or her diagnoses or treatment, or tell him or her their problems? How much opening do they feel the doctor gives them in initiating topics?

6. For any of the topics covered in this chapter—or any other sphere of life—suggest other applications of sociolinguistics. For instance, consider the role of sociolinguistic investigation in discovering what kind of talk is persuasive, the best dialect to use, the kinds of kinesics, and how that might be applied to teaching effective pastoral counseling or selling used cars.

7. What stories did your roommate—or other friend—tell you about him- or herself to explain the kind of person he or she is? Alternatively,

write down the stories someone else has repeatedly told you. What kind of person do these stories present to you? What stories do you tell others about yourself? What persona are you projecting?

Appendix of Phonetic Symbols

What is the IPA?

This is the International Phonetic Alphabet. It uses one symbol for one sound. Each symbol stands for only one sound, and each sound is represented by one symbol. In other words, in IPA, homonyms; for instance, the homonyms *made* and *maid* are both [med]. Although in English orthography, *rapt* and *wrapped* are spelled differently, in IPA, they are both spelled [ræpt] as they are pronounced exactly alike. Note that the *-ed* is pronounced as [t], and the *a*, which in ordinary orthography may stand for different sounds in *can, cat, father, fate,* and *machine,* is represented by the symbol [æ] in IPA. There is a separate symbol for each of the vowels represented by the spelling <a> in the other words. Respectively, these are [ɨ], [æ], [a], [e], and [ə]. Letters in square brackets indicate the phonetic symbols and those in angle brackets indicate letters in ordinary spelling. So [get] is pronounced "gayt" but spelled <gate>.

Why Don't We Just Use Our Regular Alphabet to Depict Sounds?

First, as shown above, each letter in the English alphabet may stand for more than one sound. Second, some sounds are represented by more than one letter or combination of letters. Third, some single sounds are always spelled with combinations of letters. That is, English is missing symbols for certain sounds, all of them commonly used. Fourth, some letters are sometimes silent, not standing for any sounds at all in some words. Fifth, some spellings omit a sound which is pronounced even though English does have a letter which can indicate the sound.

How Widespread Are These Inconsistencies?

They are so widespread that we can only give a few examples here. Our entire orthographic system is riddled with them. It would take a long chapter or a short book to demonstrate them all. The book would be very long indeed if it also attempted to rectify the chaos in our orthography.

APPENDIX OF PHONETIC SYMBOLS

Inconsistencies:

The first is illustrated by the letters <c> and <x>.

The first may stand for an [s] sound, as in *city*, or a [k] as in *cat*. There is no separate sound represented by the letter *c*. It is either a [k] or an [s].

Similarly, the letter *x* doesn't stand for a unique sound. It represents a [z], as in the first sound of *Xerxes* or *xerox*. Otherwise, it stands for a combination of two sounds, but, even then, it's not for just one such combination. It may either be a *gz* as in *exact* or a *ks* as in *Max*. Note that in both *Xerxes* and *xerox*, the second *x* stands for [ks].

The shortening of the names *Alex* to *Alec* and *Max* to *Mac* is possible because *x* is really pronounced as [ks]. That is, in IPA, these names are [ælɛks] and [mæks]. Drop the final [s] and you get Alec and Mac. I do not know of any instances in which the [gz] pronunciation of *x* gets shortened to just [g], however. Perhaps this is because *x* is typically pronounced [ks] at the end of a word.

The second is illustrated by the [t] sound in *Tom* and *Thomas* or the many sounds indicated by the combination of <ea>.

Either a <t> or <th> indicates the sound [t]. Worse yet, <th> not only stands for the [t] in *Thomas*,[1] but for the first sounds in *thin* and *this*. In IPA, the first sound in *thin* is symbolized by [θ] and the first sound in *this* by [ð]. As you can see, the spelling <th> can represent three distinct sounds: the first sounds in *Thomas, thin*, and *this*.

The letters <ea> stand for different sounds in *meat, dead, great, heart, bear, ear,* and *create*. Thus, *read* may indicate either the present tense, like its homonym *reed*, or the past tense, pronounced like *red*. So, both the present and past of the verb *read* are spelled alike but are pronounced differently. The present tense of the verb *lead* rhymes with the present tense of *read*, but its past tense is spelled *led*. However, *lead* rhyming with *led* refers to the metal *lead*. Is your head swimming? Well, to sum this confusion up succinctly, *read* may be pronounced two ways, one for past and one for present tense. *Lead* is also pronounced two ways, one for the present tense of the verb and the other to indicate a metal. The past tense of *lead*, unlike the past of *read*, is spelled differently, as <led>, even though both of these verbs show the same alternation of vowel pronunciation in their present and past tenses.

The third is illustrated by single sounds always being represented by more than one letter, as with <th>, <ch>, <sh>, and <zh>.

We have already seen that <th> stands for two different single sounds, [θ] and [ð], as noted above. Similarly, <ch> stands for the single sound [ʧ] as in *chin*. There is no one letter for that sound. To make it worse, its phonetic relative the [ʃ][2] in *shin* is spelled <sh>, but in other words, the same sound is spelled <ch> as in *chute, Cheryl,* or *machine,* <ti> as in *nation,* <ssi> as in *mission,* or <su> as in *sugar* and *sure.*

The first sound in *Zhivago,* the second in *azure,* and the last in *rouge* are all pronounced alike. This sound may also be spelled <si>, as in *illusion* or <su> as in *pleasure.* In IPA, this sound is [ʒ].[3] English has no single letter to represent it, nor does it have any one combination of letters to stand for it. In ordinary orthography, it is spelled as <zh>, <zu>, <ge> (at end of words of French origin), <si>, and <su>. In phrases like "as you know," the <s> and <y> often become fused as [ž] as well.

In sum, there is no single letter in English orthography to represent any of the sounds [ð], [θ], [ʧ], [ʃ], and [ʒ]. All are written with two-letter combinations, known as digraphs. Each of the last three sounds are written with more than one digraph, such as <sh>, <ch>, <ti>, and <ssi>[4] all used for [š]. Some of the digraphs can stand for more than one sound, like <ch> representing both [č] and [š], and <su> representing both [š] and [ž].

The fourth is that of silent letters.

These are seen in the silent letters of *knee, night, made, scene, hour,* and *gnaw.* Looking at the IPA symbols for vowels below, you can see that these would be, respectively, [ni], [nait], [med], [sin], [aur], and [nɔ].

The fifth is that of missing letters.

We see this in *use, cute,* and *one.* The [y] sounds in *use* and *cute* are missing in their spelling. In IPA, they would be [yuz] and [kyut], respectively. Also note that the <s> in *use* is actually pronounced as a [z]. The [w] which starts the pronunciation of *one* is not represented in the spelling of the word, although it does appear in its homonym, *won.*

Bracketing Conventions Used in This Book.

Letters in square brackets indicate the actual sound made by a speaker. For instance, the IPA spelling [Iz] stands for the word *is.* Sometimes

APPENDIX OF PHONETIC SYMBOLS

speakers make a sound they are not aware of. For instance, put your finger in front of your lips and say "pit." Feel the puff of air as you say it. Now say "spit." You probably have no puff of air. The *p* in *pit* is **aspirated** and is written in IPA as [pʰ], but the *p* in *spit* is not aspirated, so it is written [p]. Chapter 1 explains when and why certain sounds are aspirated in English, although they may not be in other languages. Using square brackets around pʰ tells the reader that this is how an English speaker pronounces this sound. In contrast, [pɪt] represents the way a French speaker pronounces English *pit*. The English speaker hears the failure to aspirate as part of the French accent.

Letters between slanted lines, as with /p/, indicates that this is the sound English speakers think they are hearing when they hear either the [p] in *spit* or [pʰ] in *pit*. Chapter 1 explains this phenomenon, that of the phoneme. In the chapter on dialects, I often refer to /r/-full accents even though the [r] may actually be made somewhat differently by different American speakers. Using the slanted lines tells the reader that he or she will hear the different kinds of American *r*'s as /r/ despite phonetic differences between, for instance, an Eastern New England and a Minnesota pronunciation of /r/. Similarly, I may refer to an /a/[5] and note that some speakers actually pronounce this as [æ],[6] thinking they are making an /a/. As shown in the chapters on dialects and speech communities, people hear certain sounds as being different from what they actually say. This is because of differences in regional or social accents.

Letters between angled brackets indicate ordinary orthography, our regular spellings. Phonetic symbols are never put in these angled brackets. For instance, in English, [θ] is spelled as <th>. One would never write <θ> because it is not a letter in the English alphabet. Nor would one write [th] for that sound. Rather, [θ] is indicated by <th>.

To show how these are used in explaining actual speech, I could say that the <ea> in *dead* is pronounced as [dɛd] by many Americans, or [ded] by others, but all of them think of the word as /dɛd/ (see below for pronunciation of the vowel symbols).

Phonetic Symbols Used in This Book.

Here, the symbol in the square bracket stands for the sound pronounced by the letters in angle brackets, followed by examples of those letters as they are pronounced in the words used as examples. That is, [p] equals the spelling <p> in *spot*.

APPENDIX OF PHONETIC SYMBOLS

Consonants in American English:

[p]	<p>, <pp>[7] in *apple, spot, soap, repetition*
[pʰ]	<p> in *put, pretty, repeat*
[b]	<b>, <bb> in *but, abbey, nab*
[t]	<t> in *still, atlas, pot*
[tʰ]	<t> in *till, too*
[d]	<d> in *did, dog*
[ɾ]	<t>, <tt>, <d>, <dd> **in between vowels** as in *beauty, wetting, wedding, lady*[8]
[k]	<c> in *Mac, scuba*; <k> in *skill, maker, look*; <ch> in *Michael, Bacchus*; <ck> in *lock, rocky*; <qu> is [kw] as in *quit*
[kʰ]	<c> in *cut*; <k> in *kill*
[g]	<g> in *go, gate*, first sound in *garage*; <gh> as in *ghost, ghetto*
[ʤ]	<g> in *gem, rage*; <j> in *joy, jaded, jewel, major*
[m]	<m>, <mm> in *me, come, hammy*
[n]	<n>, <nn>, <kn> in *not, manger, nanny, knot*
[ŋ]	<n>, <ng> in *thank, sing* (the <g> in *sing* is silent)
[θ]	<th> in *thigh, mouth*
[ð]	<th> in *thy, mouthe, father*
[s]	<s>, <ss> in *so, mess*; <c> in *city, nice*
[z]	<s> in *is, busy, raise*; <z> in *zoo, raze*
[ʃ]	<sh> in *shore, mush;* <shi> in *fashion*; <ssi> in *mission*; <ch> in *machine*; <ti> in *nation*; <su> in *sure, sugar*; <ssu> in *pressure*
[ʒ]	<su> in *pleasure*; <si> in *fusion, Asian*; <ge> in *mirage, rouge*; <zh> in *Zhivago*; <zu> in *azure*
[ʧ]	<ch> in *church*; <ti> in *bastion*; <tu> in *fortune, feature*
[r]	<r>, <rr> in *rat, carry*; <ir>, <or>, <er>, <ur> in *girl, word, her, curl*; first <l> in *colonel*
[l]	<l>, <ll> in *lady, tally*
[ɫ]	<l>, <ll> in *pal, call*[9]
[w]	<w> in *won*; <wh> in *why*; <u> in *quilt*; and no letter in *one*
[y]	<y> in *you*; <u> in *use* (note: no <y> spelling)

Vowels:

Dialects differ primarily according to the vowel sounds in words. Consequently, it is often impossible to find words as examples that will reflect the vowels used by all speakers. For instance, some speakers pronounce the <o> in *coffee* and the <al> in *talk* alike. Some of those who do, rhyme *talk* with *tock* and use the vowel in those words for the <o> in *coffee*. Others use the vowel in *more* for the <al> in *talk* and the <o> in *coffee*, but use a different sound for the vowel in *tock*.

Vowels are produced by moving the tongue up and down, back, and forward, so we speak of high or raised vowels, low vowels, back, front and mid vowels. To feel this, pronounce the vowel in *beet*, and then make the vowels in *bit, bait, bet, bat*. You will feel your tongue moving progressively lower. Then, starting again with the vowel in *beet*, make the vowel in *boot* to feel your tongue move from front to back. Now make the vowels in *boot, bull, boat, bought, balm, bother*. The tongue is towards the back of the mouth all of these, but as you say the vowels, you will feel them move from high to low and, for *o*, you may feel it also move towards the middle. Now move from the vowel in *boat* to *but* and *ban*. Your tongue moved from the back to the middle of the mouth, and then it moved upward for *ban*, but not as far forward as the vowel in *beet* or as far back as the vowel in *boot*. Make the vowels in *beet, ban, boot* and you will feel the high front, central, and back vowels, respectively.

Symbols for Most Vowels and Diphthongs in American English:

[i]   <ee> in *meet*; <ea> in *meat*; <e_e> in *mete*

[I]   <i> in *mitt*; <u> in *busy*; <o> in *women*[10]

[e]   <a_e> in *mate*; <ea> in *great*; <ai> in *maid*; <ei> in *weight*

[ɛ]   <e> in *met*; <ea> in *head*

[æ]   <a> in *mat*[11]

[ɨ]   <a> in *man, Mary*[12]

[iə] <a> in *mat* and *man* for speakers primarily in the Great Lakes cities

[ə]   <a> in *about, sofa*; <er> in *player* (if <r> is dropped)

[ʌ]   <u> in *but, sun*; <o> in *son*

[a]   <a> in *father*; <al> in *calm*; <o> in *John, not*; <or> in *orange, horrible, Doris* in New York City, Rhode Island, other areas, and British English

[u]   <oo> in *boot, roof* (for some speakers)

[ʊ]   <oo> in *soot, hoof, roof* (for some speakers); <u> in *put*

[o]   <o_e> in *note*; <oa> in *boat*

[ɔ]   <ou>, <au> in *bought, caught* (if speakers don't rhyme them with *cot*); <or> in *orange, horrible* (for many Americans); <al> in *talk* as in New York City, Western New England, Rhode Island and educated British speakers; <o> in *dog, coffee* in many dialects, including New York City and Rhode Island, AAVE *dawg*

Diphthongs:

Diphthongs are formed when the tongue starts to make one vowel and then moves to another vowel position. The two vowels are considered one.

[ai]   <i> in *ride, time* (except for some Southern and AAVE accents)

[ʌi]   <i> in *right* (if speaker doesn't use same vowel as in *ride*)

[ei]   <ai> in *raid*; <ay> in *say*; <a_e> in *made*

[ɔi]   <oy> in *boy*

[au]   <ow> in *how*[13]

[ʌu]   <ou> in *out, louse* (if speaker doesn't use same vowel as in *how*— like Canadian *out* and *about*)

[æu]   <ow> in *how* (for many speakers)

[ow]   <ow> in *know*; <oa> in *road*

APPENDIX FOR PHONETIC SYMBOLS

Notes

[1]   Originally, *theatre, author,* and *Anthony* all were pronounced with just [t], but, because of the spelling, people began mistakenly to pronounce them as the <th> in *throw* and *math.* Sometimes one does see *Anthony* spelled *Antony* so that it will be pronounced as it originally was, and film buffs use the French *auteur* for the director of a film so that it is differentiated from *author*, although originally in English, it was also pronounced as [t].

[2]   Alternatively, the symbol [š] is used for this sound.

[3]   Alternatively, IPA has [ž] to represent this sound.

[4]   Technically, this is a trigraph, as it is composed of three letters for one sound.

[5]   The vowel in *not.*

[6]   The vowel many Americans use in *cat.*

[7]   In English, double consonants in spelling are pronounced just like single ones. That is, there is no difference in pronunciation of /p/ in *happy* or *hoping.* In some languages, like Italian, the double consonants are held longer than single ones.

[8]   In American English, a [t] and a [d] in between vowels are both pronounced by a quick flap of the tongue on the ridge above the upper front teeth. This sounds something like a *d*, but the tongue isn't held as firmly on the ridge as it would be for a [d] or [t]. Some British speakers use this sound for an /r/ between vowels as in *very* "veddy,' and Spanish speakers use it as an /r/ in *pero.* In American English, pairs like *latter* and *ladder, betting* and *bedding, seated* and *seeded* are pronounced alike. For instance, some Americans write that a problem is <deep seated> and others that it is <deep seeded>, meaning the same thing, and pronouncing the phrase alike.

[9]   Europeans who speak English as a second language with virtually no accent pronounce the /l/ in *milk* like the /l/ in *lady*, often the only indication that they are not native speakers. English speakers make the /l/ in the back of the mouth when it is at the end of a word or before /k/ or /g/.

[10]   Southern speakers also use this for the <e> in *pen* and the <a> in *many.* For them, the [ɛ] before a nasal sound like *n* and *m* raises to an [I].

[11]   Many Americans now make a higher vowel for this sound. Listen to a national newscaster to hear how he or she makes the short *a* sound in *bat, half, bad*, and the like. Chances are, they are making a true [æ] sound. New England and some Midwestern speakers make this sound

and it is the enunciation favored by broadcasters. Speakers in the Great Lakes cities often use a higher vowel in these words.

12   Most Americans use this sound for the <a> before a nasal and an [r]. Some use it for all short <a>'s. Try saying *bat, bad,* and *ban.* I use the same vowel in the first two words, but the higher one in the third. Some of you will use the lower one in *bat* and the higher one in *bad* and *ban.* Some will use the higher one in all three words, but use the [æ] for the <o> in *not.*

13   This is the sound that the elocution teacher uses in the movie *Singin' in the Rain* in the "how now brown cow" sequence.

Bibliography

Abbey, A., and C. Melby. "The Effects of Nonverbal Cues on Gender Differences in Perceptions of Sexual Intent." *Sex Roles* 15 (1986): 283–98.

Abbott, E.A. *A Shakespearian Grammar*. New York: Dover Publications, 1966. First published 1870.

Abercrombie, D. *Elements of General Phonetics*. Chicago: Aldine, 1967.

Abrahams, R.D. "Black Talking in the Streets." In *Explorations in the Ethnography of Speaking*, edited by R. Bauman and J. Sherzer, 240-62. New York: Cambridge University Press, 1974.

————. "The Training of the Man of Words in Talking Sweet." *Language in Society* 1 (1972): 15–30.

Agunis, H., and C. Henle. "Effects of Nonverbal Behavior on Perceptions of a Female Employee's Power Bases." *Journal of Social Psychology* 141, no. 4 (2001): 537–49.

Ainsworth-Vaughn, N. *Claiming Power in Doctor-Patient Talk*. New York: Oxford University Press, 1998.

Aitken, A.J. "The Good Old Scots Tongue: Does Scots Have an Identity." In *Minority Languages Today*, edited by E. Haugen, D. McClure, and D. Thomson, 72–90. Edinburgh: University of Edinburgh Press, 1981.

Allen, H. *The Linguistic Atlas of the Upper Midwest*. Minneapolis: University of Minnesota Press, 1973–76.

Allport, G.W., and H. Cantril. "Judging Personality from Voice." In *Communication in Face to Face Interaction*, edited by J. Laver and S. Hutcheson. Baltimore: Penguin, 1934.

Ambrose, J.E., and C.H. Williams. "On the Spatial Definition of 'Minority' Scale as Influence on the Geolinguistic Analysis of Welsh." In *Minority Languages Today*, edited by E. Haugen, D. McCLure, and D. Thomson, 53–71. Edinburgh: University of Edinburgh Press, 1981.

Anderson, K., and C. Leaper. "Meta-Analyses of Gender Effects on Conversational Interruptions: Who, What, When, Where, How." *Sex Roles* 39, no. 3/4 (1998): 225–52.

Anshen, F. *Statistics for Linguists*. Rowley, MA: Newbury House Publishers, 1978.

Arlotto, A. *Introduction to Historical Linguistics*. Boston: Houghton-Mifflin, 1972.

BIBLIOGRAPHY

Arminen, I. "Conversation Analysis: A Quest for Order in Social Interaction and Language Use." *Acta Sociologica* 42 (1999): 251–57.

Aronowitz, R. "Reading Tests as Texts." In *Coherence in Spoken and Written Discourse*, edited by D. Tannen, 245–64. Norwood, NJ: Ablex Publishing Corp., 1984.

Ascher, C. "Southeast Asian Adolescents: Identity and Adjustment." *Equity and Choice* 6, no. 2 (1990): 46–49.

Ash, S. "The North American Midland as a Dialect Area." In *Language Variation and Change in the American Midland*, edited by T. Murray and B.L. Simon, 33–56. Philadelphia: John Benjamins, 2006.

Austin, J.L. *How to Do Things with Words.* 2nd ed., edited by J.O. Urmson and M. Sbisà. Cambridge: Harvard University Press, 1975.

Avis, W.S. "The Contemporary Context of Canadian English." In *Dialect and Language Variation*, edited by H.B. Allen and M. Linn, 212–16. New York: Academic Press, 1986.

Ayer, G. "Language and Attitudes of Spanish-Speaking Youth of the Southwestern United States." In *Applications of Linguistics*, edited by G.E. Perren and J.M. Trim, 115–20. New York: Cambridge University Press, 1969.

Babad, Y.E., I.E. Alexander, and E.Y. Babad. *Returning the Smile of the Stranger: Developmental Patterns and Socialization Factors.* Monographs of the Society for Research in Child Development, 3–93, 1983.

Bailey, G., N. Maynor, and P. Cukor-Avila, eds. *The Emergence of Black English: Text and Commentary.* Amsterdam: John Benjamins, 1991.

Bales, R.F. "How People Interact in Conferences." *Scientific American*, March 1955, 3–7.

Baratz, J., and R. Shuy, eds. *Teaching Black Children to Read.* Washington, DC: Center for Applied Linguistics, 1969.

Baron, D. *Grammar and Gender.* New Haven: Yale University, 1986.

Baron, N. "The Acquisition of Indirect Reference: Functional Motivations for Continued Language Learning in Children." *Lingua* 42 (1977): 349–64.

Basso, K.H. *Portraits of "the Whiteman": Linguistic Play and Cultural Symbols Among the Western Apache.* Cambridge, UK: Cambridge University Press, 1989.

Bates, E., and L. Benigni. "Rules of Address in Italy: A Sociological Survey." *Language in Society* 4 (1975): 271–88.

Bateson, G. *Steps to an Ecology of Mind.* New York: Ballantine, 1972.

Bavelas, J.B., L. Coates, and T. Johnson. "Listener Responses as a Collaborative Process: The Role of Gaze." *Journal of Communication*, September 2002, 566–80.

Bayard, D., and S. Krishnaya. "Gender, Expletive Use, and Context: Male and Female Expletive Use in Structured and Unstructured Conversation Among New Zealand University Students." *Women and Language* 24, no. 1 (2001): 1–18, http://0=weblinks1. epnet.com.helin..84 (accessed November 12, 2003).

Befu, H. "Konnichiwa, an Essay Read at The Japan Society Luncheon, San Francisco." In *Questions and Politeness*, edited by E.N. Goody, 9. New York: Cambridge University Press, 1978.

Bellugi, U., and S. Fischer. "A Comparison of Sign Language and Spoken Language." *Cognition* 1 (1972): 173–200.

Ben-Zeev, S. "Mechanisms by Which Chilhood Bilingualism Affects Understanding of Language and Cognitive Structures." In *Bilingualism: Psychological, Social, and Educational Implications*, edited by P.A. Hornby, 29–55. New York: Academic Press, 1977.

Bereiter, C., and S. Engelmann. *Teaching Disadvantaged Children in the Preschool*. Englewood, NJ: Prentice Hall, 1966.

Berko, J. "The Child's Learning of English Morphology." *Word* 14 (1958): 150–77.

Bernstein, B. *Theoretical Studies Toward a Sociology of Language*. London: Routledge & Kegan Paul, 1971.

Bernstein, C. "Drawling Out the /ai/." In *Language Variation and Change in the American Midland*, edited by T. Murray and B.L. Simon, 209–21. Philadelphia: Johns Benjamin, 2006.

————. "A Variant of the 'Invariant' Be." *American Speech* 63, no. 2 (Summer 1988): 119–24.

Biber, D., and N. Burges. "Historical Change in the Language Use of Women and Men." *Journal of English Linguistics* 28, no. 1 (2000): 21–37.

Bickerton, D. *Roots of Language*. Ann Arbor, MI: Karoma Publishers, 1981.

Biever, C. "Language May Shape Human Thought." *New Scientist.com News Service*, 19 August 2004, http://newscientist.com/ article.ns?id= dn6303 (accessed July 22, 2005).

Birdwhistell, R.L. *Kinesics and Context*. Philadelphia: University of Pennsylvania Press, 1970.

Bloom, L. *Language Development: Form and Function in Emerging Grammars*. Cambridge: MIT Press, 1970.

Bloomer, R. "'You Shoulda Saw Me': On the Syntactic Participles in Spoken American English." *American Speech* 73, no. 2221–224 (1998).

Bloomfield, L. *Language*. New York: Holt, Rinehart, Winston, 1933.

BIBLIOGRAPHY

Blum-Kulka, S., and J. House. "Cross-Cultural and Situational Behavior in Requesting Behavior." In *Cross-Cultural Pragmatics: Requests and Apologies*, edited by S. Blum-Kulka, J. House, and G. Kasper. Norwood, NJ: Ablex Publishing Corp., 1989.

Boberg, C. "The Phonological Status of Western New England." *American Speech* 76, no. 1 (2001): 3–29.

Bodine, A. "Androcentrism in Prescriptive Grammar: Singular 'They'; Sex Indefinite 'He'; and 'He or She.'" *Language in Society* 4 (1975): 129–46.

Boggs, S. "The Meaning of Questions and Narratives to Hawaiian Children." In *Functions of Language in the Classroom*, edited by C. Cazden, V. John, and D. Hymes, 299–327. New York: Harcourt, Brace, Jovanovich, 1972.

Bowerman, M. "Beyond Communicative Adequacy: From Piecemeal Knowledge to an Integrated System in the Child's Acquisition of Language." In *Children's Language*, vol. 5, edited by K.E. Nelson. Hillsdale, NJ: Lawrence Erlbaum Associates, 1985.

Brady, M., and R. Eckhardt. *Black Girls at Play: Folkloric Perspectives on Child Development*. Austin, TX: Southwest Educational Development Corporation, 1975.

Brown, P., and G. Yule. *Discourse Analysis*. New York: Cambridge University Press, 1983.

Brown, P., and S. Levinson. "Universals in Language Usage: Politeness Phenomena." In *Questions and Politeness*, edited by E. Goody, 56–289. New York: Cambridge University Press, 1978.

Brown, R., and A. Gilman. "The Pronouns of Power and Solidarity." In *Style in Language*, edited by T. Sebeok, 253–76. Cambridge: MIT Press, 1960.

Brown, R., and M. Ford. "Address in American English." *Journal of Abnormal and Social Psychology* 62 (1961): 375–85.

Bucholtz, M. "'Why be Normal?': Language and Identity Practices in a Community of Nerd Girls." *Language in Society* 28 (1999): 203–23.

Bugental, D.E., J.W. Kaswan, and L.R. Love. "Perception of Contradictory Meanings Conveyed by Verbal and Nonverbal Channels." *Journal of Personality and Social Psychology* 16 (1970): 647–55.

Burgoon, J. "Nonverbal Violations of Expectations." In *Nonverbal Interaction*, edited by J.M. Wiemann and R.P. Harrison, 77–111. Beverly Hills, CA: Sage Publications, 1983.

Burt, M., and C. Kiparsky. *The Gooficon: A Repair Manual for English*. Rowley, MA: Newbury House Publishers, 1972.

Butler, C. *Statistics in Linguistics*. New York: Basil Blackwell, 1985.

Callary, E. "On the Use of Geographic Names to Inform Regional Language Studies." In *Language Variation and Change in the American Midland*, edited by T. Murray and B.L. Simon, 93–104. Philadelphia: John Benjamins, 2006.

Capps, L., and E. Ochs. *Constructing Panic: The Discourse of Agoraphobia*. Cambridge: Harvard University Press, 1995.

Carli, L.L. "Gender, Language, and Influence." *Journal of Personality and Social Psychology* 59, no. 5 (November 1990): 941–51.

Caro, M. "Caro's University of Poker," 2006, www.Poker1.Com/ absoluteig/mculib_videos.asp?categoryid=13.

Carranza, M.A., and E.B. Ryan. "Evaluative Reactions of Bilingual Anglo and Mexican American Adolescents Towards Speakers of English and Spanish." *International Journal of the Sociology of Language* 6 (1975): 83–104.

Carvalho, L. "Esperanto—the International Neutral Language." *CTJ Journal* 22 (December 1990): 47–50.

Carver, C. *American Regional Dialects*. Ann Arbor, MI: University of Michigan Press, 1987.

Cassidy, F.G., ed. *Dictionary of American Regional English*. Cambridge: Harvard University Press, 1985.

Chafe, W. "Idiomaticity as an Anomaly in the Chomskyan Paradigm." *Foundations of Language* 4 (1968): 109-27.

Chafe, W., ed. *The Pear Stories*. Norwood, NJ: Ablex Publishing Corp., 1980.

Chaika, E. "The Force of Linguistic Structures on Cultural Values: Some Distinctions as Exemplified by the Big Dan Rape Case." *Interfaces* 11 (1984): 68–74.

———. "Grammars and Teaching." *College English* 39 (1978): 770–83.

———. "Hi! How Are You?" Paper presented at *48th Annual Meeting Linguistic Society of America*, San Diego, California, 1973.

———. "How Shall a Discourse be Understood?" *Discourse Processes* 4 (1981): 71–87.

———. "Jargons and Language Change." *Anthropological Linguistics* 22 (1980): 77–96.

———. *Language: The Social Mirror*. 1st ed. Rowley, MA: Newbury House, 1982b.

———. *Language: The Social Mirror*. 3rd ed. Boston: Heinle & Heinle, 1994.

———. "A Linguist Looks at 'Schizophrenic' Language." *Brain and Language* 1 (1974): 257–76.

———. *Linguistics, Pragmatics, and Psychotherapy*. Philadelphia: Whurr, 2000.

BIBLIOGRAPHY

————. *Understanding Psychotic Speech: Beyond Freud and Chomsky.* Springfield, IL: Charles C. Thomas, 1990.

————. "A Unified Explanation for the Diverse Structural Deviations Reported for Adult Schizophrenics with Disrupted Speech." *Journal of Communication Disorders* 15 (1982): 167–89.

Chick, J.K. "Reflections on Language, Interaction, and Context: Micro and Macro Issues." In *The Interactional Accomplishment of Discrimination in South Africa*, edited by D. Carbaugh, 225–52. Hillsdale, NJ: Lawrence Erlbaum, 1990.

Ching, M.K. "How Fixed Is Fixin' to ?" *American Speech* 62, no. 4 (1987): 332–45.

Ching, M. "Marvin Ching Replies." *American Speech* 64, no. 2 (1989): 164–65.

Chomsky, N. *Aspects of the Theory of Syntax.* Cambridge: M.I.T. Press, 1965.

————. *Language and Mind.* New York: Harcourt Brace Jovanovich, 1972.

————. "Review of Skinner's Verbal Behavior." *Language* 35 (1959): 26–58.

Clarke, D., and M. Argyle. "Conversation Sequences." In *Advances in the Social Psychology of Language*, edited by C. Fraser and K.R. Scherer. New York: Cambridge University Press, 1982.

Cohen, B. "Referent Communication Disturbances in Schizophrenia." In *Language and Cognition in Schizophrenia*, edited by S. Schwartz. Hilldale, NJ: Lawrence Erlbaum Publishers, 1978.

Cook, G. "Debate Opens Anew on Language and Its Effect on Cognition." *Boston Globe*, 14 February 2002.

Cooper, R.L., and B. Spolsky. *The Influence of Language on Culture and Thought.* New York: Mouton de Gruyter, 1991.

Corsaro, W. "Sociological Approaches to Discourse Analysis." In *Handbook of Discourse Analysis*, edited by T.A. Van Dijk, 167–92. New York: Academic Press, 1985.

Coulmas, F. "Linguistic Etiquette in Japanese Society." In *Politeness in Language: Studies in Its History, Theory, and Practice*, edited by R.J. Watts, I. Sachiko, and K. Ehlich, 299–323. New York: Mouton de Gruyter, 1992.

Coupland, N., J. Coupland, and H. Giles. *Language, Society, and the Elderly.* Oxford: Blackwell, 1991.

Crosby, F., and L. Nyquist. "The Female Register: An Empirical Study of Lakoff's Hypotheses." *Language in Society* 6 (1977): 163–89.

Curtiss, S. *Genie: A Psycholinguistic Study of a Modern Day "Wild Child."* New York: Academic Press, 1977.

Cutler, C. "Yorkville Crossing: White Teens, Hip Hop, and African American English." *Journal of Sociolinguistics* 3/4 (1999): 428–42.

Dalby, D. "Black Through White: Patterns of Communication in Africa and the New World." In *Black-White Relationships*, edited by W. Wolfram and N.H. Clarke, 99–138, 1971.

Darwin, C. *The Expression of Emotions in Man and Animals*. Chicago: University of Chicago Press, 1965.

Davis, L.M. "American Social Dialectology: A Statistical Appraisal." *American Speech* 57 (1982): 83–94.

deBeaugrande, R., and W.U. Dressler. *Introduction to Text Linguistics*. New York: Longman, 1981.

Deutsch, M., et al. *The Disadvantaged Child*. New York: Basic Books, 1967.

deVilliers, J.G., and P. deVilliers, A. *Language Acquisition*. Cambridge: Harvard University Press, 1978.

Di Paolo, M. "Double Modals as Single Lexical Items." *American Speech* 64, no. 3 (Fall 1989): 195–224.

Dillard, J. *Black English: Its History and Usage in the United States*. New York: Random House, 1973.

DiPietro, R.J. "Got Your Ears On?" *Interfaces* 7 (1977): 1–3.

————. *Language Structures in Contrast*. Rowley, MA: Newbury House Publishers, 1971.

————. *Strategic Interaction: Learning Languages Through Scenarios*. New York: Cambridge University Press, 1987.

Dorian, N.C. "Defining the Speech Community to Include Its Working Margins." In *Sociolinguistic Variation in Speech Communities*, edited by S. Romaine, 25–33. London: Edward Arnold, 1982.

Douglas, K. "Lost for Words." *New Scientist* 189 (18–24 March 2006): 44–47.

Drew, P. "Precision and Exaggeration in Interaction." *American Sociological Review* 68 (2003): 917–38.

DuBois, B., and I. Crouch. "The Question of Tag Questions in Women's Speech: They Don't Really Use More of Them, Do They?" *Language in Society* 4 (1975): 289–94.

Dundes, A., J. Leach, and B. Ozkok. "The Strategy of Turkish Boy's Dueling Rhymes." In *Directions in Sociolinguistics*, edited by J. Gumperz and D. Hymes, 180–209. New York: Holt, Rinehart, and Winston, 1972.

Duranti, A., and E. Ochs. "Left Dislocation in Italian Conversation." In *Discourse and Syntax*, edited by T. Givon, 377–417. New York: Academic Press, 1979.

Dürscheid, C.. "Rechtschreibung in Elektronischen Texten." *Muttersprache* 1 (2000): 1952–61.

BIBLIOGRAPHY

Eakins, B.W., and R.G. Eakins. *Sex Differences in Human Communication.* Boston: Houghton-Mifflin, 1978.

Eckert, P., and S. McConnell-Ginet. *Language and Gender.* New York: Cambridge University Press, 2003.

Edwards, W., and L. Ash. "AAVE Features in the Lyrics of Tupac Shakur: The Notion of 'Realness'." *Word* 55, no. 2 (2004): 165–78.

Efron, D. *Gesture, Race, and Culture.* The Hague: Mouton, 1972.

Eibl-Eiblesfeldt, I. "Similarities and Differences Between Cultures in Expressive Movements." In *Nonverbal Communication: Readings with Commentary.* 2nd ed., edited by S. Weitz, 37–48. New York: Oxford University Press, 1979.

Ekman, O., and W. Frisen. "Measuring Facial Movement." In *Nonverbal Interaction.* 2nd ed., edited by S. Weitz, 64–76. New York: Oxford University Press, 1976.

Elgin, S.H. *The Gentle Art of Verbal Self Defense.* Englewood Cliffs, NJ: Prentice-Hall, Inc, 1980.

Erickson, F. "Rhetoric, Anecdote, and Rhapsody: Coherence Strategies in a Conversation Among Black American Adolescents." In *Coherence in Spoken and Written Discourse*, edited by D. Tannen, 81–154. Norwood, NJ: Ablex Publishing Corp., 1984.

Erickson, F., and J. Shultz. *The Counselor as Gatekeeper: Social Interaction in Interviews.* New York: Academic Press, 1982.

Ervin, S. "Imitation and Structural Change in Children's Language." In *New Directions in the Study of Language*, edited by E. Lenneberg, 163–89. Cambridge: MIT Press, 1964.

Ervin-Tripp, S. "An Issei Learns English." In *Language Acquisition and Communicative Choice: Essays by Susan Ervin-Tripp*, edited by A. Dil. Stanford: Stanford University Press, 1967.

Ervin-Tripp, S. "On Sociolinguistic Rules: Alternation and Co-Occurrence." In *Directions in Sociolinguistics*, edited by J. Gumperz and D. Hymes, 213–50. New York: Holt, Rinehart, and Winston, 1972.

Estabrook, C., and J. Morse. "Toward a Theory of Touch: The Touching Process and Acquiring a Touching Style." *Journal of Advanced Nursing* 17 (1992): 448–56.

Fairclough, N. *Language and Power.* New York: Longman, 1989.

Fasold, R.W. "The Relation Between Black and White Speech in the South." In *Dialect and Language Variation*, edited by H.B. Allen and M.D. Linn, 446–73. Orlando, FL: Academic Press, 1986.

Fennell, D. "Can a Shrinking Linguistic Minority be Saved? Lessons from the Irish Experience." In *Minority Languages Today*, edited by E. Haugen, D. McCLure, and D. Thomson, 33–39. Edinburgh: University of Edinburgh Press, 1981.

Ferguson, C. "Diglossia." In *Language Structure and Language Use: Essays by Charles Ferguson*, edited by A. Dil, 1–27. Stanford: Stanford University Press, 1959.

Fettes, M. *Europe's Babylon: Towards a Single European Language?* Esperanto Documents 41A. Rotterdam: Universal Esperanto Association, 1991.

Feyereisen, P. "Further Investigation on the Mnemonic Effect of Gestures: Their Meaning Matters." *European Journal of Cognitive Psychology* 18 (2006): 185–205.

Finegan, E. "Form and Function in Testament Language." In *Linguistics and the Professions*, edited by R. DiPietro, 113–20. Norwood, NJ: Ablex Publishing Corp., 1982.

Fischer, J.L. "Social Influences on the Choice of a Linguistic Variant." *Word* 14 (1958): 47–56.

Fisher, S. "The Decision Making Context: How Doctors and Patients Communicate." In *Linguistics and the Professions*, edited by R. DiPietro. Norwood, NJ: Ablex Publishing Corp., 1982.

Fishman, J. *Language Loyalty in the United States*. The Hague: Mouton, 1966.

————. *Sociolinguistics: A Brief Introduction*. Rowley, MA: Newbury House Publishers, 1970.

Fishman, P. "What Do Couples Talk About When They Are Alone?" In *Women's Language and Style*, edited by D. Butturf and E. Epstein. Akron, OH: University of Akron Press, 1978.

Fox Tree, J., and J. Schrock. "Discourse Markers in Spontaneous Speech: Oh What a Difference an Oh Makes." *Journal of Memory and Language* 40 (1999): 280–95.

Frake, C.O. "How to Ask for a Drink in Subanum." *American Anthropologist* 66 (1964): 127–32.

Frazer, T.C. "Sound Change and Social Structure in a Rural Community." *Language in Society* 12 (1983): 313–28.

Frazer, T., ed. *"Heartland" English: Variation and Transition in the American Midwest*. Tuscaloosa, AL: University of Alabama Press, 1993.

————. "Midland(s) Dialect Geography." In *Language Variation and Change in the American Midland*, edited by Thomas Murray and Beth Simon, 199–207. Philadelphia: John Benjamins, 2006.

Fromkin, V., and R. Rodman. *An Introduction to Language*. New York: Holt, Rinehart, and Winston, 1983.

Gaertner, S.L., and L. Bickman. "Effects of Race on the Elicitation of Helping Behaviour: The Wrong Number Technique." *Journal of Personality and Social Psychology* 20 (1971): 218–22.

Gale, J.E. *Conversation Analysis of Therapeutic Discourse: The Pursuit of a Therapeutic Agenda*. Norwood, NJ: Ablex Publishing Corp., 1991.

BIBLIOGRAPHY

Garcia, M. "Spanish-English Bilingualism in the Southwest." In *The Writing Needs of Linguistically Different Students*, edited by B. Cronnell. Los Alamitos, CA: SWRL Educational Research and Development, 1981.

Garfinkel, H. "Remarks on Ethnomethodology." In *Directions in Sociolinguistics: The Ethnography of Communnication*, edited by J. Gumperz and D. Hymes, 301–24. New York: Holt, Rinehart and Winston, 1972.

—————. *Studies in Ethnomethodology*. Englewood Cliffs, NJ: Prentice-Hall, 1967.

Gaudio, R. "Sounding Gay: Properties in the Speech of Gay and Straight Men." *American Speech* 69, no. 1 (1994): 30–57.

Gelb, I.J. *A Study of Writing: A Discussion of the General Principles Governing the Use and Evolution of Writing*. Chicago: University of Chicago Press, 1963.

Gilbert, G.N., and Mulkay, M. *Opening Pandora's Box: A Sociological Analysis of Scientists' Discourse*. New York: Cambridge University Press, 1984.

Giles, H., S. Baker, and G. Fielding. "Communication Length as a Behavioural Index of Accent Prejudice." *International Journal of the Sociology of Language* 6 (1975): 73–81.

Giles, H., and P. Powesland. *Speech Style and Social Evaluation*. New York: Academic Press, 1975.

Giles, H., D. Taylor, and R. Bourhis. "Towards a Theory of Interpersonal Accommodations Through Language: Some Canadian Data." *Language in Society* 2 (1973): 177–223.

Gleason, H.A., Jr. *An Introduction to Descriptive Linguistics*. New York: Holt, Rinehart, and Winston, 1961.

—————. *Workbook in Descriptive Linguistics*. New York: Holt, Rinehart, and Winston, 1955.

Gleitman, L. "Biological Dispositions to Learn Language." In *Language Learning and Concept Acquisition*, edited by W. Demopoulos and A. Marras, 3–28. Norwood, NJ: Ablex Publishing Corp., 1986.

Godard, D. "Same Setting, Different Norms: Phone Call Beginnings in France and the United States." *Language in Society* 6 (1977): 209–20.

Goffman, E. "On Face Work." *Psychiatry* 18 (1955): 213–31.

—————. *Behavior in Public Places*. New York: Free Press, 1963.

—————. *Frame Analysis: An Essay on the Organization of Experience*. Cambridge: Harvard University Press, 1974.

Goldman, M., and J. Fordyce. "Prosocial Behavior as Affected by Eye Contact, Touch, and Voice Expression." *Journal of Social Psychology* 121 (1983): 125–29.

Goodman, F. "Phonetic Analysis of Glossolalia in Four Cultural Settings." *Journal for the Scientific Study of Religion* 8 (1969): 227–39.

————. "Speaking in Tongues." *New Society* 22 (1972a): 565–66.

————. *Speaking in Tongues: A Cross-Cultural Study of Glossolalia.* Chicago: University of Chicago Press, 1972b.

Goody, E.N. *Questions and Politeness.* New York: Cambridge University Press, 1978.

Gordon, D., and G. Lakoff. "Conversational Postulates." In *Speech Acts,* edited by P. Cole and J.L. Morgan, 83–106. New York: Academic Press, 1975.

Gordon, M. "Tracking the Low Back Merger in Missouri." In *Language Variation and Change in the American Midland,* edited by T. Murray and B.L. Simon, 57–68. Philadelphia: John Benjamins, 2006.

Grice, H.P. "Logic and Conversation." In *Speech Acts,* edited by P. Cole and J.L. Morgan, 41–48. New York: Academic Press, 1975.

Grosjean, Jean. *Life with Two Languages.* Cambridge: Harvard University Press, 1982.

Grumet, G.W. "Eye Contact: The Core of Interpersonal Relatedness." *Psychiatry* 46 (1983): 172–79.

Gumperz, J., and E. Hernando-Chavez. "Bilingualism, Bidialectism, and Classroom Interaction." In *Functions of Language in the Classroom,* edited by C. Cazden, V.P. John, and D. Hymes. New York: Teacher's College Press, 1972.

Gumperz, J., H. Kaltman, and M.C. O'Connor. "Cohesion in Spoken and Written Discourse: Ethnic Style and the Transition to Literacy." In *Coherence in Spoken and Written Discourse,* edited by D. Tannen, 3–19. Norwood, NJ: Ablex Publishing Corp., 1984.

Gumperz, John. *Discourse Strategies.* New York: Cambridge University Press, 1982a.

————. "Fact and Inference in Courtroom Testimony." In *Language and Social Identity,* edited by J. Gumperz, 163–95. New York: Cambridge University Press, 1982b.

————. "Linguistic and Social Interaction in Two Communities." *American Anthropologist* 66 (1964): 137–53.

————. "Social Meanings in Linguistic Structures." In *Language in Social Groups: Essays by John Gumperz,* edited by A. Dil, 247–310. Stanford: Stanford University, 1971.

————. "Social Network and Language Shift." In *Discourse Strategies,* 38–58. New York: Cambridge University Press, 1982c.

Hakuta, K. *The Mirror of Language.* New York: Basic Books, 1986.

Hall, E. *The Silent Language.* Doubleday, 1959.

Hamby, W.C. "Glossolalia Among Catholic Charismatics: A Symbolic Interactionist Perspective." Mid-South Sociological Association, 1980.

Harvey, K. "Translating Camp Talk: Gay Identities and Cultural Transfer." *Translator* 4, no. 2 (1998): 295–320.

BIBLIOGRAPHY

Hazen, K. "The Final Days of Appalachian Heritage Language." In *Language Variation and Change in the American Midland*, edited by T. Murray and B.L. Simon, 129–50. Philadelphia: John Benjamins, 2006.

Heath, S.B. *Ways with Words*. New York: Cambridge University Press, 1983.

Henton, C.G, and R.A.W. Bladon. "Breathiness in Normal Female Speech: Inefficiency Versus Desirability." *Language and Communication* 5 (1986): 221–27.

Heslin, R., and T. Alper. "Touch: A Bonding Gesture." In *Nonverbal Interaction*, edited by J.M. Wiemann and R.F. Harrison. Beverly Hills, CA: Sage Publications, 1983.

Hoffman, L., J. Sable, J. Naum, and G. Dell. *Public, Elementary and Secondary Students, Staff, Schools, and School Districts: School Year 2002–03*. NCES 2005–314. National Center for Educational Statistics, 2005.

Holmes, J. *Women, Men, and Politeness*. New York: Longman, 1995.

Holmes, J, and M. Stubbs. *Power and Politeness in the Workplace*. New York: Longman, 2003.

House, J. "Politeness in English and German: The Functions of Please and Bitte." In *Cross-Cultural Pragmatics: Requests and Apologies*, edited by S. Blum-Kulka, J. House, and G. Kasper, 96–122. Norwood, NJ: Ablex Publishing Corp., 1989.

Huttenlocher, J., et al. "Early Vocabulary Growth: Relation to Language Input and Gender." *Developmental Psychology* 27, no. 2 (March 1992): 236–48.

Hymes, D. "Ways of Speaking." In *Explorations in the Ethnography of Speaking*, edited by R. Bauman and J. Sherzer, 433–51. New York: Cambridge University Press, 1974.

"In Maine a French Renaissance Emerges." *Providence Sunday Journal*, 2006.

Itakura, H., and A.B.M. Tsui. "Gender and Conversational Dominance in Japanese Conversation." *Language in Society* 33 (2004): 223–48.

Jackson, B. *Get Your Ass in the Water and Swim Like Me*. Cambridge: Harvard University Press, 1974.

James, D., and J. Drakich. "Understanding Gender Differences in Amount of Talk: A Critical Review of Research." In *Gender and Conversational Interaction*, edited by D. Tannen, 281–312. Oxford: Oxford University Press, 1993.

James, D. "Gender-Linked Derogatory Terms and Their Use by Women and Men." *American Speech* 73, no. 4 (1998): 399–420.

———. "Women, Men, and Prestige Speech Forms: A Critical Review." In *Rethinking Language, and Gender Research Theory and*

Practice, edited by V. Bergvall, J. Bing, and A. Freed, 98–125. New York: Addison Wesley Longman, 1996.

Janda, I.H. "English Hungarian and Hungarian English Interference in Chicago." In *Second LACUS Forum*, edited by P. Reich. Columbia, SC: Hornbeam Press, 1975.

Jarrett, D. "Pragmatic Coherence in an Oral Formulaic Tradition." In *Coherence in Spoken and Written Discourse*, edited by D. Tannen, 155–71. Norwood, NJ: Ablex Publishing Corp., 1984.

Jaworski, A. *The Power of Silence: Social and Pragmatic Perspectives*. Newbury Park, CA: Sage, 1993.

Johnstone, B. *The Linguistic Individual: Self-Expression in Language and Linguistics*. New York: Oxford University Press, 1996.

————. *Qualitative Methods in Sociolinguistics*. New York: Oxford University Press, 2000.

Jones, B.L. "Welsh: Linguistic Conservation and Shifting Bilingualism." In *Minority Languages Today*, edited by E. Haugen, D. McLure, and D. Thomson, 40–51. Edinburgh: University of Edinburgh Press, 1981.

Jones, S.E., and J.R. Aiello. "Proxemic Behavior of Black and White First-, Third-, and Fifth-Grade Children." *Journal of Personality and Social Psychology* 25 (1973): 21–27.

Kay, P., and E. Kempton. "What is the Sapir-Whorf Hypothesis?" *American Anthropologist* 86 (1984): 65–79.

Keating, C., et al. "Culture and the Perception of Social Dominance from Facial Expression." *Journal of Personality and Social Psychology* 40 (1981): 615–26.

Kendon, A. "Gesture and Speech: How They Interact." In *Nonverbal Interaction*, edited by J.M. Weimann and R.P. Harrison. Beverly Hills, CA: Sage Publications, 1983.

Keyser, S. "Wallace Stevens: Form and Meaning in Four Poems." *College English* 37 (1976): 578–98.

Kleinke, C.L. "Gaze and Eye Contact: A Research Review." *Psychological Bulletin* 100 (1986): 78–111.

Knapp, M. "Dyadic Relationship Development." In *Nonverbal Interaction*, edited by J.M. Wiemann and R.P. Harrison, 179–207. Beverly Hills, CA: Sage Publications, 1983.

Knapp, M., R. Hopper, and R.A. Bell. "Compliments: A Descriptive Taxonomy." *Journal of Communication* (Autumn 1984): 12–31.

Kökeritz, H. *Shakespeare's Pronunciation*. New Haven: Yale University Press, 1953.

Komter, M. *Dilemmas in the Courtroom:A Study of Violent Crime in the Netherlands*. Mahwah, NJ: Lawrence Erlbaum Associates, 1998.

Kottke, J.L., and C.D. MacLeod. "Use of Profanity in the Counseling Interview." *Psychological Reports* 65, no. 2 (October 1989): 627–34.

BIBLIOGRAPHY

Koyama, W. "The Linguistic Ideologies of Modern Japanese Honorifics and the Historic Reality of Modernity." *Language and Communication* 24 (2004): 413–35.

Kramer, E. "Judgment of Personal Characteristics and Emotions from Non-Verbal Properties of Speech." *Psychological Bulletin* 60 (1963): 408–20.

Krashen, S. *Principles and Practice in Second Language Acquisition.* New York: Pergamon Press, 1983.

Kuczaj, S.A. *Crib Speech and Language Play.* New York: Springer-Verlag, 1983.

————. *Language Development.* Hillsdale, NJ: Lawrence Erlbaum, 1982.

Kurath, H. *Handbook of the Linguistic Geography of New England.* Providence, RI: Brown University Press, 1939.

————. *A Word Geography of the Eastern United States.* Ann Arbor, MI: University of Michigan Press, 1966. First published 1949.

LaBarre, W. "The Cultural Basis of Emotions and Gestures." *Journal of Personality* 16 (1947): 49–68.

Labov, W., C. Robins, J. Lewis, and P. Cohen. *A Study of the English of Negro and Puerto Rican Speakers in New York City.* Philadelphia: U.S. Regional Survey, 1968.

Labov, W. "Contraction, Deletion, and Inherent Variability of the English Copula." *Language* 45 (1969): 715–62.

————. "The Linguistic Consequences of Being a Lame." In *Language in the Inner City*, 255–92. Philadelphia: University of Pennsylvania Press, 1972a.

————. "The Logic of Nonstandard English." In *Language in the Inner City*, 201–40. Philadelphia: University of Pennsylvania Press, 1972b.

————. "Negative Attraction and Negative Concord." In *Language in the Inner City*, 130–96. Philadelphia: University of Pennsylvania Press, 1972c.

————. "Rules for Ritual Insults." In *Language in the Inner City*, 297–353. Philadelphia: University of Pennsylvania Press, 1972d.

————. "The Social Motivation of a Sound Change." *Word* 19 (1963): 273–309.

————. *The Social Stratification of English in New York City.* Washington, DC: Center for Applied Linguistics, 1966.

————. "Some Sources of Reading Problems for Negro Speakers of Nonstandard English." In *New Directions in Elementary English*, edited by A. Frazier. Champaign, IL: NCTE, 1967.

————. "Stages in the Acquisition of Standard English." In *Readings in American Dialectology*, edited by H.B. Allen and B.N. Underwood, 491–93. New York: Appleton-Century-Crofts, 1964.

Labov, W., S. Ash, and C. Boberg. *The Atlas of North American English Phonetics, Phonology and Sound Change: A Multimedia Reference Tool.* New York: Mouton de Gruyter, 2006.

Labov, W., and D. Fanshel. *Therapeutic Discourse.* New York: Academic Press, 1977.

Laffal, J., J. Monahan, and P. Richman. "Communication of Meaning in Glossolalia." *Journal of Social Psychology* 92 (1974): 277–91.

Lakoff, G. *Women, Fire, and Dangerous Things: What Categories Reveal About the Mind.* Chicago: University of Chicago Press, 1987.

Lakoff, G., and M. Johnson. *Metaphors We Live By.* Chicago: University of Chicago Press, 1980.

Lakoff, R. *Language and Woman's Place.* New York: Harper and Row, 1975.

————. "Language in Context." *Language* 48 (1972): 907–27.

Lambert, W., and R. Gardner. *Attitudes and Motivation in Second Language Learning.* Rowley, MA: Newbury House, 1972.

Lambert, W., H. Giles, and D. Picard. "Language Attitudes in a French American Community." *International Journal of the Sociology of Language* 4 (1975): 127–52.

Lambert, W. "The Effects of Bilingualism on the Individual: Cognitive and Sociocultural Consequences." In *Bilingualism: Psychological, Social, and Educational Implications*, edited by P.A. Hornby, 15–27. New York: Academic Press, 1977.

————. "Psychological Aspects of Motivation in Language Learning." In *Language, Psychology, and Culture: Essays by Wallace Lambert*, edited by A. Dil. Stanford: Stanford University Press, 1969.

Lance, D. "The Codes of the Spanish-English Bilingual." In *The Language Education of Minority Children*, edited by B. Spolsky, 25–36. Rowley, MA: Newbury House, 1972.

Landau, B., and L. Gleitman. *Language and Experience.* Cambridge: Harvard University Press, 1985.

Laver, J. "Voice Quality and Indexical Information." *British Journal of Disorders of Communication* 3 (1968): 43–54.

Laver, J., and P. Trudgill. "Phonetic and Linguistic Markers in Speech." In *Social Markers in Speech*, edited by K.R. Scherer and H. Giles, 1–32. New York: Cambridge University Press, 1979.

Leap, W.L. "American Indian English and Its Implications for Bilingual Education." In *Linguistics for Teachers*, edited by L.M. Cleary and M.D. Linn, 207–19. New York: McGraw-Hill, 1993.

Lee, M.Y. "The Married Woman's Status and Role as Reflected in Japanese: An Exploratory Sociolinguistic Study." *Signs: Journal of Women in Culture and Society* 1, no. 4 (1976): 991–99.

BIBLIOGRAPHY

Lehrer, A. *The Semantics of Wine Tasting*. Bloomington, IN: Indiana University Press, 1983.

Linde, C. *Life Stories: The Creation of Coherence*. New York: Oxford University Press, 1993.

Loftus, E., and J. Palmer. "Reconstruction of Automobile Destruction: An Example of Interaction Between Language and Memory." *Journal of Verbal Learning and Verbal Behavior* 13 (1974): 585–89.

Lucas, C., and C. Valli. "Language Contact in the American Deaf Community." In *The Sociolinguistics of the Deaf Community*, edited by C. Lucas, 11–40. New York: Academic Press, Inc., 1989.

MacLaury, R. "Zapotec Body-Part Locatives: Prototypes and Metaphoric Extensions." *International Journal of American Linguistics* 55 (1989): 119–54.

Macnamara, J. "Successes and Failures in the Movement for the Restoration of Irish." In *Can Language be Planned?* edited by J. Rubin and B. Jernudd, 65–94. Honolulu, HI: University of Hawaii Press, 1971.

Malinowski, B. "Phatic Communication." In *The Meaning of Meaning (Supplement to)*, edited by C.K. Ogden and I.A. Richards. London: Routledge and Kegan-Paul, 1923.

Maltz, D. "The Significance of Noise in Pentecostal Worship." In *Perspectives on Silence*, edited by D. Tannen and M. Saville-Troike, 113–27. Norwood, NJ: Ablex Publishing Corp., 1985.

Maltz, D., and R. Borker. "A Cultural Approach to Male-Female Miscommunication." In *Language and Social Identity*, edited by J. Gumperz, 196–216. New York: Cambridge University Press, 1982.

Martin, J.R. "The Development of Register." In *Developmental Issues in Discourse*, edited by J. Fine and R. Freedle, 1–39. Norwood, NJ: Ablex Publishing Corp., 1983.

McDavid, R., I. Jr., and M.L. Davis. "The Dialects of Negro Americans." In *Studies in Honor of George L. Trager*, edited by M.E. Smite, 303–12. The Hague: Mouton, 1972.

McKenna, P., and T. Oh. *Schizophrenic Speech: Making Sense of Bathroots and Ponds That Fall in Doorways*. Cambridge: Cambridge University Press, 2005.

Mehrabian, A., and M. Wiener. "Decoding of Inconsistent Communications." *Journal of Personality and Social Psychology,* 6 (1967): 109–14.

Meier, A.J. "When is a Woman a Lady? A Change in Progress." *American Speech* 74, no. 1 (1999): 56–70.

Melinkoff, D. *The Language of the Law*. Boston: Little Brown, 1963.

Menyuk, P. *The Acquisition and Development of Language*. Englewood Cliffs, NJ: Prentice-Hall, 1971.

Michaels, S., and J. Collins. "Oral Discourse Styles: Classroom Interaction and the Acquisition of Literacy." In *Coherence in Spoken and Written Discourse*, edited by D. Tannen, 219–44. Norwood, NJ: Ablex Publishing Corp., 1984.

Millward, C. "Language of Colonial Rhode Island." *Rhode Island History* 34 (1975): 35–42.

Milroy, J. "Sociolinguistic Methodology and the Identification of Speakers' Voices in Legal Proceedings." In *Applied Sociolinguistics*, edited by P. Trudgill, 51–71. New York: Academic Press, 1984.

Milroy, L. *Language and Social Networks*. Baltimore: University Park Press, 1980.

Mitchell-Kernan, C. "Signifying and Marking: Two Afro-American Speech Acts." In *Directions in Sociolinguistics*, edited by J. Gumperz and D. Hymes, 161–79. New York: Holt, Rinehart, and Winston, 1972.

Montgomery, M. "It'll Kill Ye or Cure Ye, One: The History and Function of Alternative *One* Antecedents of the Midland." In *Language Variation and Change in the American Midland*, edited by T. Murray and B.L. Simon, 151–61. Philadelphia: John Benjamins, 2006.

Mufwene, S.S., and C. Gilman. "How African is Gullah and Why?" *American Speech* 62, no. 2 (Summer 1987): 120–39.

Mulac, A. "Men's and Women's Talk in Same-Gender and Mixed-Gender Dyads: Power or Polemic?" *Journal of Language and Social Psychology* 8 (1989): 249–70.

Murnen, S. "Gender and the Use of Sexually Degraded Language." *Psychology of Women Quarterly* 24 (2000): 319–27.

Murray, T. "A New Look at Address in American English: The Rules Have Changed." *Names* 50 (2002): 43–61.

Murray, T., T. Frazer, and B.L. Simon. "Need+Past Participle in American English." *American Speech* 71, no. 3 (1996): 255–71.

Murray, T., and B.L. Simon. *Language Variation and Change in the American Midland*. Philadelphia: John Benjamins, 2006a.

————. "What is Dialect? Revisiting the Midland." In *Language Variation and Change in the American Midland*, edited by T. Murray and B.L. Simon, 1–30. Philadelphia: John Benjamins, 2006b.

Myhill, J. "Postvocalic /r/ as an Index of Integration into the BEV Community." *American Speech* 63, no. 3 (Fall 1988): 203–13.

Newman, Edwin. *Strictly Speaking: Will America be the Death of English?* Indianapolis, IN: Bobbs Merrill, 1974.

Nichols, P. "Linguistic Options and Choices for Black Women in the Rural South." In *Language, Gender, and Society*, edited by B. Thorne, C. Kramarae, and N. Henley, 54–68. Rowley, MA: Newbury House, 1983.

BIBLIOGRAPHY

Nida, E. *Language Structure and Translation: Essays by Eugene Nida.* Edited by Anwar Dil. Stanford: Stanford University Press, 1975.

Nida, E., and W.E. Reyburn. *Meaning Across Cultures.* Maryknoll, NY: Orbis Books, 1981.

Nowell, E. "Conversational Features and Gender in ASL." In *The Sociolinguistics of the Deaf Community*, edited by C. Lucas, 273–88. Boston: Academic Press, 1989.

O'Barr, W.M. *Linguistic Evidence: Language, Power, and Strategy in the Courtroom.* New York: Academic Press, 1982.

Odlin, T. *Language Transfer: Cross-Linguistic Influence in Language Learning.* New York: Cambridge University Press, 1989.

Ohanessian, S. "The Language Problems of American Indian Children." In *The Language Education of Minority Children*, edited by B. Spolsky. Rowley, MA: Newbury House, 1972.

Okamoto, D., L. Rashotte, and L. Smith-Lovin. "Measuring Interruption: Syntactic and Contextual Methods of Coding Conversation." *Social Psychology Quarterly* 65 (2002): 38–55.

Okamoto, D., and L. Smith-Lovin. "Changing the Subject: Gender, Status, and the Dynamics of Topic Change." *American Sociological Review* 66, no. 6 (2001): 852–73.

Okamoto, S. "Situated Politeness: Manipulating Honorific and Non-Honorific Expressions in Japanese Conversations." *Pragmatics* 9, no. 1 (1999): 51–74.

Ong, W.J. *Orality and Literacy: The Technologizing of the Word.* New York: Methuen & Co, 1982.

Parker, F. "A Comment on Anymore." *American Speech* 3–4 (1985): 305–10.

Pelose, G.C. "The Functions of Behavioral Synchrony and Speech Rhythm in Conversation." In *Multichannel Communication Codes*, edited by S. Sigman. Edmonton, Canada: Boreal Scholarly Publishers, 1987.

Philips, S.U. "Acquisition of Rules for Appropriate Speech Usage." In *Bilingualism and Language: Anthropological, Linguistic, Psychological, and Sociological Aspects*, edited by J. Alatis. Washington, DC: Georgetown University Press, 1970.

———. "Some Sources of Cultural Variability in the Regulation of Talk." *Language in Society* 5 (1976): 81–95.

Pizziconi, B. "Re-Examining Politeness, Face and the Japanese Language." *Journal of Pragmatics* 35 (2003): 1471–506.

Pyles, T. "English Usage: The Views of the Literati." In *Contemporary English: Change and Variation*, edited by D. Shores, 160–69. New York: J.B. Lippincott, 1972.

Quick, V. "Does Anyone Here Speak Esperanto?" *Gifted Child Today* 12, no. 3 (May-June 1989): 15–16.

Remland, M., and T. Jones. "The Influence of Vocal Intensity and Touch on Compliance Gaining." *Journal of Social Psychology* 134, no. 1 (2001): 89–97.

Remland, M., T. Jones, and H. Brinkman. "Interpersonal Distance, Body Orientation, and Touch: Effects of Culture, Gender, and Age." *Journal of Social Psychology* 135, no. 3 (1995): 281–97.

Richardson, C. "Habitual Structures Among Blacks and Whites in the 1990's." *American Speech* 66, no. 3 (Fall 1991): 292–302.

Riecken, H. "The Effect of Talkativeness on Ability to Influence Group Solutions of Problems." In *The Psychosociology of Language*, edited by S. Muscovici, 308–21. Chicago: Markham Publishing Co., 1958.

Rodman, R. "Linguistics and the Law: How Knowledge of Elementary Linguistics May Affect the Dispensing of Justice." *Forensic Linguistics* 9, no. 1 (2002): 94–103.

Romaine, S. "What is a Speech Community?" In *Sociolinguistic Variation in Speech Communities*, edited by S. Romaine, 1–24. London: Edward Arnold, 1982.

Rommetveit, R. "Words, Contexts, and Verbal Message Transmission." In *Social Contexts of Messages*, edited by E.A. Carswell and R. Rommetveit, 13–26. New York: Academic Press, 1971.

Rubin, J. "Nonlanguage Factors Affecting Undergraduates' Judgments of Nonnative English-Speaking Assistants." *Journal of Higher Education* 33 (1992): 511–31.

———. "The Special Relation of Guarani and Spanish in Paraguay." In *Language of Inequality*, edited by N. Wolfson and J. Manes, 111–20. The Hague: Mouton, 1985.

Sacks, H. Discourse Analysis. Mimeo, 1970.

———. Lecture Notes. Mimeo, 1964–72.

Salami, L.O. "Diffusion and Focusing:Phonological Variation and Social Networks in Ile-Ife, Nigeria." *Language in Society* 20, no. 2 (June 1991): 217–45.

Samarin, W.J. "Glossolalia." *Psychology Today* 6 (1972): 48–50.

———. "Glossolalia as Regressive Speech." *Language and Speech* 16 (1973a): 77–89.

———. "Making Sense of Glossolalic Nonsense." *Social Research* 46 (1979): 88–105.

———. "Variation and Variables in Religious Glossolalia." *Language in Society* 2 (1973b): 121–30.

Sapir, E. "Speech as a Personality Trait." *American Journal of Sociology* 32 (1927): 892–905.

Saville-Troike, M. *The Ethnography of Communication: An Introduction.* Baltimore: University Park Press, 1982.

BIBLIOGRAPHY

Sawyer, J. "Social Aspects of Bilingualism in San Antonio, Texas." In *Readings in American Dialectology*, edited by H.B. Allen and G.N. Underwood, 375–81. New York: Appleton-Century-Croft, 1964.

Schatzman, L., and A. Strauss. "Social Class and Modes of Communication." In *The Psychosociology of Language*, edited by S. Muscovici, 206–21. Chicago: Markham, 1972.

Schegloff, E.A. "Sequencing in Conversational Openings." *American Anthropologist* 70 (1968): 1075–95.

Schegloff, E.A., G. Jefferson, and H. Sacks. "The Preference for Self-Correction in the Organization of Repair in Conversation." *Language* 53 (1977): 361–82.

Schenkein, J., ed. *Studies in the Organization of Conversation.* New York: Academic Press, 1978.

Scherer, K. "Acoustic Concomitants of Emotional Dimensions: Judging Affect from Synthesized Tone Sequences." In *Nonverbal Communication*. 2nd ed., edited by S. Weitz, 249–53. New York: Oxford University, 1973.

————. "Personality Markers in Speech." In *Social Markers in Speech*, edited by K. Scherer and H. Giles, 147–209. New York: Cambridge University Press, 1979.

Schlauch, M. *The English Language in Modern Times Since 1400.* Warsaw: Panstowe Wydaawnictwo Naukowe, 1959.

Scinto, L.F.M. *Written Language and Psychological Development.* New York: Academic Press, 1986.

Scollon, R., and S. Scollon. "Cooking It Up and Boiling It Down: Abstracts in Athabaskan Children's Story Retellings." In *Coherence in Spoken and Written Discourse*, edited by D. Tannen, 173–97. Norwood, NJ: Ablex Publishing Corp., 1984.

————. *Narrative Literacy and Face in Interethnic Communication.* Norwood, NJ: Ablex Publishing Corp., 1981.

Scovel, T. *A Time to Speak: A Psycholinguistic Inquiry Into the Critical Period for Human Speech.* Rowley, MA: Newbury House, 1988.

Scribner, S. "Modes of Thinking and Ways of Speaking: Culture and Logic Reconsidered." In *Thinking: Readings in Cognitive Science*, edited by P.N. Johnson-Laird and P.C. Wason, 483–500. New York: Cambridge University Press, 1977.

Scribner, S., and H. Cole. *The Psychology of Literacy.* Cambridge: Harvard University Press, 1981.

Searle, J.R. "Indirect Speech Acts." In *Speech Acts*, edited by P. Cole and J. Morgan. New York: Academic Press, 1975.

————. *Speech Acts: An Essay in the Philosophy of Language.* Cambridge: Cambridge University Press, 1969.

Sebba, M. "Spelling Rebellion." In *Discourse Constructions of Youth Identities*, edited by J.K. Androutsopoulos and A. Georgakopoulou, 151-172. Philadelphia: John Benjamins, 2003.

Seeman, M., and H. Cole. "The Effect of Increasing Personal Contact in Schizophrenia." *Comprehensive Psychiatry* 18 (1977): 283–92.

Sergestad, Y. "Use and Adaptation of Written Language to the Conditions of Computer-Mediated Communication." Ph.D. diss., Göteborgs Universitet, 2002. Abstract in *Dissertation Abstracts* 64, no. 3: 523.

Shaul, D., and N.L. Furbee. *Language and Culture*. Prospect Heights, IL: Waveland Press, 1998.

Sherzer, J. "Nonverbal and Verbal Deixis: The Pointed Lip Gesture Among the San Blas Cuna." *Language in Society* 2 (1973): 117–32.

Shibamoto, J. *Japanese Women's Language*. New York: Academic Press, 1985.

Shuy, R., W. Wolfram, and W. Riley. *Linguistic Correlates of Social Stratification in Detroit Speech*. Washington, DC: HEW, 1967.

Simon, John. *Paradigms Lost: Reflections on Literacy*. New York: Random House, 1988.

Slobin, D. *Psycholinguistics*. 2nd ed. Oakland, NJ: Scott-Foresman, 1979.

Smitherman, G. "Black Language as Power." In *Language and Power*, edited by C. Kramrae, M. Schulz, and W.M. O'Barr, 101–15. Beverly Hills, CA: Sage Publications, 1984.

———. *Black Talk: Words and Phrases from the Hood to the Amen Corner*. Boston: Houghton Mifflin, 1994.

———. *Talking That Talk: Language, Culture, and Education in African America*. London: Routledge, 2000.

———. "'What is Africa To Me?': Language Ideology and African American." *American Speech* 66, no. 2 (Summer 1991): 115–32.

Snow, C.E. "Conversations with Children." In *Language Acquisition*. 2nd ed., edited by P. Fletcher and M. Garman. Cambridge: Cambridge University Press, 1986.

Sommer, R. "Further Studies of Small-Group Ecology." *Sociometry* 28 (1965): 337–43.

Spanos, N.P., and E.C. Hewitt. "Glossolalia: A Test of the 'Trance' and Psychopathology Hypotheses." *Journal of Abnormal Psychology* 88 (1979): 427–34.

Spears, A.K. "Are Black and White Vernaculars Diverging, VI." *American Speech* 62, no. 1 (Spring 1987): 48–80.

Stapleton, K. "Gender and Swearing: A Community Practice." *Urbana* 26, no. 2 (2003): 1–14, http://0-proquest.umi.com.helin.uri .edu (accessed April 28, 2005).

BIBLIOGRAPHY

Stewart, E. "Talking Culture: Language in the Function of Communication." Paper presented at the First Delaware Symposium on Language Studies, Newark, Delaware, 1979.

Stewart, W. "Continuity and Change in American Negro Dialects." In *Readings in American Dialectology*, edited by H.B. Allen and G.N. Underwood, 454–67. New York: Appleton-Century-Crofts, 1968.

———. "Language and Communication Problems in Southern Appalachia." In *Contemporary English: Change and Variation*, edited by D. Shores, 107–22. New York: J.B. Lippincott, 1972.

———. "Sociolinguistic Factors in the History of American Negro Dialects." In *Readings in American Dialectology*, edited by H.B. Allen and G. Underwood, 444–53. New York: Appleton-Century-Crofts, 1967.

Stubbs, M. *Discourse Analysis: The Sociolinguistic Analysis of Natural Language*. Chicago: University of Chicago, 1983.

Sutcliffe, D. "Creole in the Ex-Slave Recordings." *Journal of Pidgin and Creole Languages* 14, no. 1 (1999): 137–42.

Tamura, E. "African American Vernacular English and Hawai'i Creole English: A Comparison of Two School Board Controversies." *Journal of Negro Education* 71, no. 1/2 (2002): 17–30.

Tannen, D. "A Comparative Analysis of Oral Narrative Strategies." In *The Pear Stories: Cognitive, cultural, and linguistics aspects of narrative production,* edited by W. Chafe, 51-87. Norwood, NJ: Ablex Publishing Corp., 1980.

———. *Conversational Style*. Norwood, N.J.: Ablex Publishing Corp., 1984.

———. "Indirection in Discourse: Ethnicity as Conversational Style." *Discourse Processes* 4 (1981): 221–38.

———. *Talking Voices: Repetition, Dialogue, and Imagery in Discourse*. New York: Cambridge University Press, 1989.

———. "What's in a Frame? Surface Evidence for Underlying Expectations." In *New Directions in Discourse Processing*, edited by R. Freedle, 137-181. Norwood, NJ: Ablex Publishing Corp., 1979a.

———. "When is an Overlap not an Interruption?" Talk given at First Delaware Symposium of Language Studies, 1979b.

Tanskanen, Sanna-Kaisa. "Discourse in Cyberspace: Studying Computer-Mediated Communication." *English Studies: Methods and Approaches* 16, no. 143–156 (1998).

Taylor, D. "Linguistic Change and Linguistic Challenge: Preserving a Native Language in a Foreign Environment: German in Bethlehem, Pennsylvania in the Mid-1700's and Chicago, Illinois in the Mid-1900's." In *Third LACUS Forum*, edited by R. DiPietro and E. Blansett. Columbia, SC: Hornbeam Press, 1976.

Terneus, S., and Y. Malone. "Proxemics and Kinesics of Adolescents in Dual-Gender Groups." *Guidance and Counseling* 19, no. 3 (2004): 1–

7, http://0-weblinks3.epnet.com.helin.uri.edu (accessed August 19, 2005).

Terrace, H. *Nim*. New York: Knopf, 1979.

Thomas, E. "Evidence from Ohio on the Evolution of /æ/." In *Language Variation and Change in the American Midland*, edited by T. Murray and B.L. Simon, 69–89. Philadelphia: John Benjamins, 2006.

Thompson, L., D. Driscoll, and L. Markson. "Memory for Visual-Spoken Language in Children and Adults." *Journal of Nonverbal Behavior* 22 (1998): 167–87.

Thomson, R., and T. Murachver. "Predicting Gender from Electronic Discourse." *British Journal of Social Psychology* 40 (2001): 193–208.

Thomson, R., T. Murachver, and J. Green. "Where is the Gender in Gendered Language?" *Psychological Science* 12, no. 2 (2001): 171–75.

Tiersma, P. "Linguistic Issues in the Law." *Language* 69, no. 1 (March 1993): 113–37.

Tran, T.V. "Language Acculturation Among Older Vietnamese Refugee Adults." *Gerontologist* 30, no. 1 (February 1990): 94–99.

Troike, R.C. "Fixin' To." *American Speech* 64, no. 2 (Summer 1989): 163–65.

Trudgill, P. "Acts of Conflicting Identity: The Sociolinguistics of British Pop-Song Pronunciation." In *On Dialect: Social and Geographic Perspectives*, 141–60. New York: New York University Press, 1983a.

———. "Sex, Covert Prestige, and Linguistic Change in the Urban British English of Norwich." *Language in Society* 1 (1972): 179–195.

———. "Sociolinguistics and Dialectolology: Geolinguistics and English Rural Dialects." In *On Dialect: Social and Geographical Perspectives*, 31–52. New York: New York University Press, 1983b.

Truss, L. *Talk to the Hand*. New York: Gotham Books, 2005.

Turner, L.D. "Problems Confronting the Investigator of Gullah." In *Black-White Speech Relationships*, edited by W. Wolfram and N.H. Clarke, 1–15. Washington, DC: Center for Applied Linguistics, 1971.

U.S. Census Bureau. *Statistical Abstract of the United States*. 125th edition. Washington, DC, 2006.

Van Riper, W. "General American: An Ambiguity." In *Dialect and Language Variation*, edited by Harold B. Allen and Michael D. Linn, 123–35. New York: Academic Press, 1986.

VanDijk, T. *Text and Context*. New York: Longman, 1977.

Walker, A.G. "Patterns and Implications of Cospeech in a Legal Setting." In *Linguistics and the Professions*, edited by R. DiPietro, 101–12. Norwood, NJ: Ablex Publishing Corp, 1982.

Weinreich, Uriel. "Explorations in Semantic Theory." In *Current Trends in Linguistics*, edited by T. Sebeok, 395–477. The Hague: Mouton, 1966.

———. *Languages in Contact*. The Hague: Mouton, 1968.

Weir, R. *Language in the Crib*. The Hague: Mouton, 1962.

BIBLIOGRAPHY

Weirzbicka, A. *Understanding Cultures Through Their Key Words: English, Russian, Polish, German, and Japanese.* New York: Oxford University Press, 1997.

Welger, H. "A Brief Introduction Into the Legal Constitution of the International Language." *Grundlagenstudien Aus Kybernetik und Geisteswissenschaft* 33, no. 1 (March 1992): 32–40.

Wells, J.C. *Accents of English.* New York: Cambridge University Press, 1982.

Werkhofer, K.T. "Traditional and Modern Views: The Social Consitution and the Power of Politeness." In *Politeness in Language: Studies in Its History, Theory and Practice*, edited by R.J. Watts, S. Ide, and K. Ehlich, 156–99. New York: Mouton de Gruyter, 1992.

Whorf, B.L. *Language, Thought, and Reality.* Cambridge: MIT Press, 1956.

Williams, C.H. "More Than Tongues Can Tell: Ethnic Separatism." In *Linguistic Minorities, Policies, and Pluralism*, edited by J. Edwards, 179–219. New York: Academic Press, 1984.

Williams, J. *Origins of the English Language.* New York: Free Press, 1975.

Wolfram, W., and R. Fasold. *The Study of Social Dialects in American English.* Englewood, NJ: Prentice-Hall, 1974.

Wolfram, W., E. Thomas, and E. Green. "The Regional Context of Earlier African American Speech: Evidence for Reconstructing the Development of AAVE." *Language in Society* 29 (2000): 315–55.

Wolfram, W.A. *A Sociolinguistic Description of Detroit Negro Speech.* Washington, DC: Center for Applied Linguistics, 1969.

Wong-Rieger, D., and D. Quintana. "Comparative Acculturation of Southeast Asian and Hispanic Immigrants and Sojourners." *Journal of Cross-Cultural Psychology* 18, no. 3 (September 1987): 345–62.

Wood, L.S., and R.O. Kroger. "Politeness and Forms of Address." *Language and Social Psychology* 10, no. 3 (1991): 145–68.

Woods, A., P. Fletcher, and A. Hughes. *Statistics in Language Studies.* New York: Cambridge University Press, 1986.

Wooton, A. *Dilemmas of Discourse: Controversies About the Sociological Interpretation of Language.* London: Allen and Unwin, 1975.

Yamamoto, M. "Birth Order, Gender Differences, and Language Development in Modern Japanese Pre-School Children." *Psychologia: An International Journal of Psychology in the Orient* 33, no. 3 (September 1990): 185–90.

Zimmerman, D. H., and C. West. "Sex Roles, Interruptions, and Silences in Conversation." In *Language and Sex: Difference and Dominance*, edited by B. Thorne and N. Henley, 105–29. Rowley, MA: Newbury House, 1975.

Author Index

AUTHOR INDEX

AUTHOR INDEX

AUTHOR INDEX

Subject Index

SUBJECT INDEX

SUBJECT INDEX

SUBJECT INDEX

SUBJECT INDEX

SUBJECT INDEX

Maoris, sign for 'yes', 118
marked vowel system, of English, 287
Marousis, Cynthia, 233
master/mistress, 438
matched guise technique, 39–40, 79, 259
Mathis, Johnny, 394
maxims
    flouting, 152–54
    guiding conversation, 152–55, 156–59
May, Angela, 465–66
McCartney, Paul, 396
mean (average) in statistics, 48
meaning(s)
    connotations and, 337–38
    indexical, 75–77
    in language, 3–5
    multiple, of words, 10
    social bonding and, 163
    social context and, 178
    translation and, 336–38
    of words, 426–34
media
    regionalisms and, 286–87
    word choice of, 427
medicine, language and, 479–83
mergers, losing distinction between vowels, 283–87
metaphor, 204, 229, 237, 425–26, 432, 474n1
Midland dialect, 275–81
    mergers of vowels in, 283–84
mimicking, inadequacy for language acquisition, 16, 18–19
mind
    bilingualism and, 329–31
    oral and literate mind, 204–7
Minelli, Liza, 323

minimal pairs, speech communities and, 378
mitigation
    of questions, 97–100, 454–54, 481–83
    of verbs, by Japanese, 96–97
modal auxiliaries, dialects and, 300–301
Monroe, Marilyn, 76
Moog synthesizer, 74
Morimuru, Mimi, 94, 102n12
morphemes, 9–10
multiplex networks, 388
Murray, Stephen, 470–71
Muslim
    black (in U.S.), vegetarianism, 209
    use of Classical Arabic in religion, 507
    each person's knowledge of prescribed prayers, 171
    gender bias in reporting about by NPR, 435
    individuals' knowledge of all prescribed prayers, 170, 171
    kinesics in Mosque, 171
    obligatory prayers five times daily, 171
    praying
        in sync with Imam, 170
        without Iman, 170
    prayer rug, 171
    required ablution before praying, 171
    silence during prayer, 171
Mussolini, Benito, 86

names, 93
    spelling of, 212–13
nicknames, 93

570

SUBJECT INDEX

SUBJECT INDEX

SUBJECT INDEX